TO: Brooklyn Wood

Allow God's Word to transform
you into a new person by
changing the way you think
(Rom. 12:2, NLT)!

Sheldon L. Malone

Changing *the* Way You Think

One-Year Devotional

Unlocking the Mind with the Word of God

Sheldon Malone

WESTBOW
PRESS®
A DIVISION OF THOMAS NELSON
& ZONDERVAN

WestBow Press books may be ordered through booksellers or by contacting:

Scripture taken from the *Amplified Bible*, copyright © 1954, 1958, 1962, 1964, 1965, 1987 by The Lockman Foundation. Used by permission.

Scripture taken from the Contemporary English Version © 1991, 1992, 1995 by American Bible Society, Used by Permission.

Scripture is taken from GOD'S WORD®, © 1995 God's Word to the Nations. Used by permission of Baker Publishing Group.

Scripture taken from the New King James Version. Copyright © 1979, 1980, 1982 by Thomas Nelson, Inc. Used by permission. All rights reserved.

Scripture taken from the King James Version of the Bible.

All Scripture quotations in this publications are from The Message. Copyright © by Eugene H. Peterson 1993, 1994, 1995, 1996, 2000, 2001, 2002. Used by permission of NavPress Publishing Group.

Scripture taken from the New Century Version. Copyright © 2005 by Thomas Nelson, Inc. Used by permission. All rights reserved.

Scripture quotations taken from the Holy Bible, New Living Translation, Copyright © 1996, 2004. Used by permission of Tyndale House Publishers, Inc., Wheaton, Illinois 60189. All rights reserved.

WestBow Press
A Division of Thomas Nelson & Zondervan
1663 Liberty Drive
Bloomington, IN 47403
www.westbowpress.com
1 (866) 928-1240

ISBN: 978-1-5127-2374-8 (sc)
ISBN: 978-1-5127-2373-1 (e)

Library of Congress Control Number: 2015920665

Print information available on the last page.

WestBow Press rev. date: 02/04/2016

Foreword

You may be wondering how this devotional book came to fruition, so please allow me to share my story. Being on active duty in the military has afforded me the opportunity to travel and visit many beautiful and exotic places around the world; however, with this travel also came separation from my wife and daughters, many times on isolated unaccompanied assignments overseas. It was in these long periods of separation that the most significant periods of my spiritual growth occurred with God positioning me to be free of routine distractions so that I could clearly hear His voice in order to learn what my assignment was.

During my last tour of duty on the small island of Bahrain in the Arabian Gulf, I finally quit running and answered the call of God that is upon my life and also stopped making excuses as to why I was not qualified to do what I knew I should be doing. "My friends, you must do all you can to show that God has really chosen and selected you. If you keep on doing this, you won't stumble and fall" (2 Pet. 1:10, Contemporary English Version).

Prior to arriving in Bahrain I was inspired to send daily e-mail devotionals written by a variety of different writers to an e-mail distribution list I accumulated over the years; I consistently did this for a period of three years at this point. While on this unaccompanied tour I continued to forward daily devotionals and also gave myself over to ministry through teaching weekly Friday School (a version of Sunday School) lessons through the chapel ministry at Naval Support Activity Bahrain. While there I was also fortunate to attend services at the National Evangelical Complex (NEC) with both Ethiopian and Indian Christian congregations in two separate worship services. God had placed me in a position to truly see the universality of the Church and ministry from a whole new perspective fellowshipping and worshipping with Christians from various locations around the world. I believe this opportunity to fellowship and worship with Christians of various races/ethnic groups and religious backgrounds gave me a broader view of the statement "Therefore go and make disciples of all nations" (Matt. 28:19, New Living Translation)," in that it applies to more than just the nation of the United States of America. We truly serve a universal God who is concerned for everyone on this earth; He is omniscient, omnipotent, and omnipresent.

As my military tour of duty in the Middle East came to a close, I was blessed with the opportunity to have dinner and fellowship with the Pastor and his wife (Pastor Cedrick and Karen Nazareth) and a couple of the leaders from the Good News Church of Manama, Bahrain (a congregation predominantly comprised of Christians from the country of India and a mixture of other nationalities). At the conclusion of dinner and fellowship, everyone prayed for my safe return home to the United States and for the plans God had in store for me and my family. Afterwards Pastor Karen received a vision and spoke a prophetic word to me stating that she kept seeing a pen (some type of ink pen) in my future; however, she was not sure what it meant at the time and that God would reveal it to me later.

I eventually returned to the United States and continued to forward the daily devotionals with the Nazareth's being recipients of the daily messages. One day Pastor Karen replied to a devotional I e-mailed saying (paraphrased) "the daily messages were nice, but she was looking forward to reading a devotional written by me". It was then the vision and word given months prior spoke directly to my future, because God intended for me to not just send devotionals written by others, but desired me to write devotionals inspired by Him through the Holy Spirit. Initially I thought, "I can't do this because I would not even know where to begin." However, one day I decided to give it a try asking the Holy Spirit to give me what to say, and I wrote the first devotional in January of 2009 and have been inspired to write over five hundred more since then.

In another place of isolation (during an Individual Augmentee (IA) tour to Baghdad, Iraq) I was again positioned to hear God more clearly and it was then that I was led to compile the devotionals written into a one-year devotional book designed to encourage readers to look at God's Word from a different perspective simply by changing the way he or she thought; because it was not until I changed my thinking that I truly began to see the transforming power of God manifested in my life in tangible ways. "And so, dear brothers and sisters, I plead with you to give your bodies to God because of all he has done for you. Let them be a living and holy sacrifice—the kind he will find acceptable. This is truly the way to worship him. Don't copy the behavior and customs of this world, but let God transform you into a new person by [CHANGING THE WAY YOU THINK]. Then you will learn to know God's will for you, which is good and pleasing and perfect" (Rom. 12:1-2, New Living Translation).

When I look back over the events that have transpired in my life, I can see it was God's hand guiding and directing my steps through both the good and bad times. "For God is working in you, giving you the desire and the power to do what pleases him" (Phil. 2:13, New Living Translation). However, it was not until I was able to separate myself from distractions and truly begin to hear the voice of God that I really connected to what my purpose was and I allowed God to use me despite what I thought my limitations were. God already knew the plan, He just needed me to follow through and then allow the Holy Spirit to do His part; faith without works is truly dead. "Anyone who doesn't breathe is dead, and faith that doesn't do anything is just as dead" (James 2:26, Contemporary English Version)!

There are no obstacles we cannot overcome or no deed we cannot accomplish in our personal lives, as well as for the Kingdom, when we remove the limitations from God. "There are some things that people cannot do, but God can do anything" (Mk. 10:27, Contemporary English Version). We have to allow God to expand our territory and horizon by allowing Him to change the way we think through His Word.

As you read each devotional, my prayer is that you will find strength and encouragement to allow God to propel you into higher heights and deeper depths in the things of the Kingdom as the Word of God gives you a different perspective and encourages you to change your thinking in order to achieve a new mindset.

Acknowledgements

I would like to thank:

God the Father through Jesus Christ and the Holy Spirit for giving me inspiration.

My father Elder Joe N. Malone, Pastor of Shady Grove II Primitive Baptist Church, Miccosukee, Florida and my mother Priscilla Robinson for giving me life and providing an example of what hard work and real service is all about, while also encouraging and supporting me over the years.

The spiritual shepherds and leaders placed in our lives over the past twenty plus years:

- The spiritual leader, father-figure, and mentor who did not simply introduced me to "church" but to Christ and a relationship while laying the solid foundation in my faith-walk, Bishop Vaughn M. McLaughlin and Lady Narlene McLaughlin, The Potter's House International Ministries, Jacksonville, Florida; thanks for being real and genuine, great role models, for your unique approach to proclaiming the Gospel message and ministry, and for providing the framework to what God would continue to build upon through various spirit-filled men and women over the years.
- Bishop B. Courtney McBath and Pastor Janeen McBath, Calvary Revival Church, Norfolk, Virginia; thank you for dynamic ministry, your great example as a married couple, and an introduction to and a deeper understanding of the power of the Holy Spirit. In His role the Holy Spirit brings power to change, and this empowerment forever changed my life.
- Dr. Sammie Holloway and First Lady Addie Holloway, Breath of Life Christian Center, Memphis, Tennessee; thank you for your example of integrity, practically teaching and living the Word, and a greater revelation and understanding of how to apply faith to daily life. Thank you for showing me it was not enough to just say I had faith but that I had to demonstrate my faith through action.
- Elder Darryl E. Holt and First Lady Evangelist Miriam Holt, Faith Life Church Church of God in Christ (formerly Saints Community Church of God in Christ), Chesapeake, Virginia; thanks for your mentorship and seeing in me what I didn't really see in myself. You challenged me to step out of my comfort zone into different areas of ministry. And thanks for providing a different perspective and a greater understanding of the Blessing and how it is to be applied to every area of life.
- Bishop Kim W. Brown and First Lady Elder Valerie K. Brown, The Mount (Mount Lebanon Missionary Baptist Church), Chesapeake, Virginia. Thank you for being real and godly examples. Your practical approach to preaching and teaching has immensely helped in expanding our thinking to know God "is able to do exceedingly abundantly above all that we ask or think, according to the power that works in us" and to see the principle of sowing and reaping being put into action to truly meet needs.

- Pastors Raymond Black III and Ceandrys Black, Living The Word Ministries, Honolulu, Hawaii. Thank you for stretching me outside of my comfort zone, challenging me to walk in my calling, encouraging me to view God's Word from a different perspective and for sending me forth on the course of ministry.
- To all the Chaplains I have been blessed to serve with: Chaplain Shelton Murphy, USN; Chaplain Otis Corbitt, USA; Chaplain Ryan Bareng, USN; Chaplain Ishmael Serrano, USA; Chaplain Jesus Wallace, USA; Chaplain Aaron Jefferson, USN; and although he was not a Chaplain but acting in the role of a Chaplain, Elder Ricardo "Rick" Pina (U.S. Army CW5 (Ret.)). Thank you for demonstrating true integrity and character, and for showing me it was still possible to be true to my faith even in a military setting.

Again, I would like to thank each of you for allowing my family and I to partner with your congregations and fellowships over the years, for your leadership, mentorship, guidance, direction, and most importantly for the spiritual seeds you deposited in us that continue to grow and bring forth fruit.

Pastor Karen Nazareth for being used as the voice of God in my life at that particular moment, it was your God-inspired words that encouraged me to write my first devotional. I am eternally grateful you were in tune with the voice of God and a willing vessel.

My beautiful daughters Denisha, Danika, Desiree, and Danielle for your love, patience, and support during my many absences away from home due to military duty and travels. Continue to follow the path God has laid out for you regardless of the obstacles you may face.

My beautiful and lovely wife Jasmine for always having my back and for providing encouragement while reminding me of who I am in Christ and not allowing me to just settle for less, but always pushing me to strive to be what God has called me to be. You are "bone of my bone and flesh of my flesh" and we are truly ONE!

Everyone I have met in my years of military service and travels, and to all who have forwarded an e-mail or ever spoken a word of correction, instruction, or encouragement to me; this often helped me remain focused by providing the fuel needed to keep pressing forward even when in the natural I was tempted to quit.

It is my prayer that each devotional will be a source of strength for every reader as he or she walks out his or her destiny journey and life's purpose. Once the mind has been renewed, the mind must then be constantly transformed with the Word of God.

January 1
A NEW BEGINNING AND FRESH START
Read: 1 Sam. 16:1-13

In the Old Testament book of 1 Sam. 8:6, we find the Israelites (Hebrew nation) making a demand for a king to lead them. The prophet and spiritual leader during the time was Samuel. Samuel was a righteous man; however, his sons did not walk according to his ways or the ways of the LORD.

At this time in the Bible saga Samuel was becoming old and only had a short time remaining on earth before dying. Fearing that his wicked sons would take the reins of leadership upon their father's death, the Israelites pleaded with Samuel and demanded that there be a judge or king appointed over them so that they could be like the surrounding nations having someone to rule and watch over them (1 Sam. 8:5).

Although the people's request displeased Samuel and was against God's desires, the LORD still obliged and gave the people exactly what they asked for even though it was against His will for them. Saul of the Tribe of Benjamin was then chosen to be the first king of Israel.

King Saul began his reign well following the ways of the LORD; however, over time he began to allow pride to set in, and started doing things his own way. And eventually envy and jealousy also began to consume this once upright king resulting in God's anointing being removed from Saul as the LORD sought out a new king.

The prophet Samuel was given the task of anointing a new king from the sons of Jesse the Bethlehemite. Jesse had a total of eight sons.

Samuel began his selection with the eldest son Eliab because of his stature and physical appearance, surely he must be the one. But the LORD said otherwise (1 Sam. 16:7).

Thoughts

1

Samuel systematically went down the line of Jesse's remaining sons until he reached the seventh son, yet none of them had been chosen by the LORD. But there was another son who was tending to his father's sheep; this son was none other than the youngest and eighth son of Jesse, David.

David had been overlooked in the process of selecting a king because of his stature and outward appearance. He did not have a tall or muscular build, or a domineering appearance, but was small with bright eyes, and was recorded in the Bible as being "good looking." In his father's eyes David was considered the least of his sons but not in the eyes of the LORD (our Heavenly Father).

Samuel told Jesse to send for the young man and bring him there; and when David arrived the LORD immediately said to Samuel, "Arise, anoint him; for this *is* the one" (1 Sam. 16:12)! From then on the LORD was with David. Just in case you did not notice, it was the eighth and last son that was chosen.

In the Bible, the number eight represents "new beginnings" and according to Matthew 20:16 "those who are last now will someday be first, and those who are first now will someday be last" (NCV). This is exactly what the LORD was signifying with the anointing of David as king, God was going to do a new thing through the last son, David and his seed.

Though you may feel unworthy, the least in your family, often overlooked and misunderstood or that your ministry may not be progressing as quickly as others; don't get discouraged because God sees you right where you are and has a plan for your life. Just as He chose David the least in his family to be king; God is looking to do a new thing in and through you.

January 2
ARE YOU ARMED AND DANGEROUS?
Read: Num. 32:20-22

Since the beginning of time and throughout the centuries there have been many conflicts and battles both fought and won. And even though one opponent ultimately leaves the battlefield in defeat, I personally don't believe that any of these groups, armies or military organizations went into battle with the mentality of "Boy, I'm sure glad we're going to lose today!"

Thoughts
_____
_____
_____
_____
_____
_____
_____

No, the objective for forces in any battle is to win. But in order to win, advance preparation is required and there are a few important principles that each soldier needs to know in order to stay alive and be effective, they: (1) have to know their weapons, (2) know how to use their weapons, and most importantly (3) know how to recognize the enemy. The same applies to Christians in the army of the LORD "so that satan will not outsmart us. For we [must be] familiar with his evil schemes" (2 Cor. 2:11, New Living Translation).

When we accept Jesus Christ into our hearts, we are adopted into His family by covenant, and then at the same time immediately drafted into the LORD's army whether we readily accept or acknowledge the enlistment or not. And as with any army, battles are inevitable; however, we are not to go into battle with a mentality of defeat because the Word declares that "overwhelming victory is ours through Christ, who loved us" (Rom. 8:37, New Living Translation).

The victory is already ours, but in order to win the battles we must change our thinking to align with what God's Word says about us, and at the same time we must also position ourselves as we continuously train and prepare for war. This is not so say that we go out and actively look for opportunities to fight, however, when the fight or struggle comes our way we must be prepared to not just sit by passively but ready to fight.

Check your spiritual armor today, many of us are armed for battle and dangerous to the enemy's camp and probably didn't even realize it. So let's begin to put our weapons to use and plan for victory today because just in case we didn't realize it, the battle is already won!

January 3
PUT IT DOWN, IT'S NOT YOURS!
Read: 1 Pet. 5:7

A mother visits a close friend bringing her two-year-old son along. The friend has a very exquisite home with fine art, sculptures, and figurines all within arm's reach; arm's reach that is, for a very busy and inquisitive two-year-old. And before the mother knows it, the son has an extremely large metal vase in his arms attempting to carry it across the room.

The mother immediately cries out, "Put it down, it's not yours!" I'm sure that in our younger days, many of us may have heard the same words from an older sibling, parent, or some other grown-up as we attempted to lift or carry something that was extremely massive or too large for us to handle, and to top it off it was also something that did not belong to us.

Thoughts

_____

_____

_____

_____

_____

For some of us the above phrase still echoes in our ears today, just in a different way and from a spiritual perspective.

_____

3

Many of us as believers are just as guilty as the rambunctious two-year-old, trying to lift and shoulder things that are too big for us to carry; things that do not belong to us. We carry around low-self esteem, anger, poor health, envy, bitterness, and financial burdens with this list having the potential to go on and on. However, this was never God's intent.

1 Pet. 5:7 states "Give all your worries and cares to God, for he cares about you" (New Living Translation). And in Lk. 12:25-26, Jesus Himself gave instructions concerning the proper response to the cares of this world as He spoke to His disciples, "Can all your worries add a single moment to your life? And if worry can't accomplish a little thing like that, what's the use of worrying over bigger things" (New Living Translation)?

This is why we must release all of our cares, burdens, concerns, and let them go because they were never intended or designed for us to carry; Put them down, because they are not yours!

January 4
LOST IDENTITY
Read: 2 Cor. 5:17

After an extended period of hard work and the hustle of everyday life, you are eventually convinced to take a break for the purpose of vacationing and spending time with the family. During a portion of the vacation you are fortunate to visit your hometown with hopes of seeing family and friends that you have not seen for years.

One day while out making a purchase at one of the local grocery stores you see someone that resembles the individual who was your best friend during high school. The both of you hung out after school almost every day, attended several classes together, were routinely paired together as lab partners, and each had aspirations of greatness and success upon graduating from school.

So, instinctively you begin to yell out his nickname yet he keeps walking. Since that did not work you then call out his full name but there is still no response. You chase him down and gently tap him on the shoulder saying, "Hey! It's me, your best friend from high school; how's it going? With a look of bewilderment and disconnection he looks you straight in the face and says "I don't know who you are."

Thoughts

_____
_____
_____
_____
_____
_____
_____

Your heart drops within and fills with disappointment because your friend does not recognize you even though you have not changed much at all since your time in school together. Although your friend was voted most likely to succeed and was once the high school all-American football star, now through years of drug abuse and self-neglect he not only loses the ability to recognize those who were once close to him but he himself no longer knows who he is as he roams and wanders the streets living in parks and under bridges.

The issue of identity is a major concern in society today with many individuals not being exactly sure of who they really are. Fathers have walk away from families and some mothers have even turned their backs on their children thereby creating disconnected families and broken individuals who don't know who they are and now attempt to find their identity in people, places and things. And to make matters worse, this is even a common trend among believers in Christ who through past or current circumstances lose focus on their true identity and what this identity can produce.

But there is great news, in Christ we are made new! Through the shed blood of Jesus Christ we all receive a new identity once we accept Him into our hearts as both Savior and Lord. "This means that anyone who belongs to Christ has become a new person. The old life is gone; a new life has begun" (2 Cor. 5:17, New Living Translation)!

Our identity as believers in Christ is not based on the external but rather is based on a life-changing transformation that begins internally and a renewing of the mind. In other words you have been accepted, now belong to God, and everything that is His is now yours by FAITH.

There is no mistaking this identity because God does not make any mistakes. Living in the blessing, abundance, and overflow is tied up in your identity. So, do you know who you are?

January 5
PLEASE, SQUEEZE THE ANOINTED!
Read: 2 Cor. 4:8-10

Many years ago there was a very popular television commercial aired that advertised the "Charmin" toilet paper brand. Customers would enter the grocery store, see the toilet paper and because of its softness would immediately begin squeezing the roll.

And almost without delay, the uptight grocery store manager Mr. Whipple would hastily jump out and say, "Please, don't squeeze the Charmin!"

It wasn't that the customers were really doing anything wrong; however, he did not want others to squeeze the Charmin simply because he wanted the enjoyment and satisfaction of

Thoughts

_____
_____
_____
_____
_____
_____
_____

feeling its softness all for himself. It was the quality of the product and what it was made of that prompted individuals to squeeze it.

Life sometimes has a way of pressing and squeezing us, sometimes in unique and uncomfortable ways. But in this pressing and squeezing, the goal is for God to get the satisfaction of seeing how we respond when the pressures come, to see if our response produces one that is evidence to others of a life filled with His Spirit. These pressures only squeeze out what's already on the inside.

An orange produces orange juice, and an apple produces apple juice.

Therefore, an orange cannot produce apple juice, and an apple cannot produce orange juice because each can only produce what is actually already on the inside, nothing more or nothing less. As Christians when you are squeezed, what comes out of you?

When a believer is squeezed just like the orange or apple previously described, it is also a given fact that what's naturally inside is bound to come out and to the surface. If the Word of God is in you, when the pressure comes the Word is going to come out. It is usually the ones with little to no Word within that respond through negativity, anger and/or fear.

Therefore, regardless of how bad you may feel at any given moment, the pressures of life do not come to destroy you, but are intended to strengthen, perfect and mature you. So, today when you are squeezed and pressed from all sides, continue to put the right things in, stand firm in faith and then you will be able to confidently say: "Please, squeeze the anointed" (2 Cor. 4:8-10)!

January 6
BEING PATIENT IN THE WAITING ROOM
Read: Rom. 4:16-25

Patience and the process of waiting is not an easy pill to swallow for many of us who profess faith in Jesus Christ, with many saying "Why do I have to wait to enjoy this, that or the other; I want it all right now. Why do I have to wait until I get to heaven to enjoy mine?

Thoughts

_____

_____

_____

_____

_____

_____

Yes, there are benefits of being Kingdom citizens that afford us the opportunity to enjoy the things that are ours by covenant and by right today (health, wholeness, and prosperity); however, receipt of these things often involve a process.

There are many examples in the Bible of individuals who patiently endured to receive what God had promised: Moses was called to deliver God's people from the clutches of Egyptian bondage; however, he spent 40 years in a desert to mature in faith and develop in a way that God could effectively use him (Exodus chapters 2 & 3). David was anointed king at the age of 17; however, he did not step into the office of kingship until he was over 30 years old (1 Sam. 16:13). Joseph had a dream of grandeur that was God-given and destined to become reality; however, Joseph endured being placed in a pit, sold into slavery, lied upon, and thrown into prison so that he could be in the right place at the right time to be a blessing to a multitude of people in the midst of a famine (Genesis chapters 37, 39-42).

Many times the process of patience and waiting is necessary to develop us, bring something to us and/or prune us to take some things out of us for the purpose of getting us to where God needs us to be.

A delay does not necessarily constitute a denial of the request or promise; but at the same time we also must learn to take our eyes off of what appears to be prosperity for the wicked, because their day of reckoning and a time of judgment will soon come.

As we each patiently wait on God's promises to be fulfilled in our lives and our individual breakthroughs to come to pass in the midst of seeing the wicked prospering, we should not be tempted to get frustrated or upset. It is in the "Waiting Room" that God works out His plan for our lives, as He monitors our use of the time, talents and resources that He has given.

Patience is truly a virtue, and a "wait" really won't hurt you.

January 7
MISPLACED TIME
Read: Ecc. 3:1, 9

In the popular children's story "Alice in Wonderland," there was a rabbit who always seemed to be in a hurry. He would pull out his waist-pocket watch, look at the time, and then scurry off saying, "I'm late, I'm late...for a very important date. No time to say hello, goodbye...I'm late, I'm late, I'm late."

But through all of his hurrying and lack of patience, he never seemed to go anywhere or ever get anything accomplished. Sadly, many of us suffer from this very same issue today as we waste the precious time that we have been given.

We live in a "microwave" society where everything has to be done "now" or in quick fashion, with no one desiring to wait. So what

Thoughts

_____
_____
_____
_____
_____
_____
_____
_____

do most of us to? You've guessed it, we just go along with the flow and in this instance it becomes very easy for us to get caught up in the hurried pace of daily living by placing our time, attention and focus on the wrong things.

To make this practical and something that most can relate to, this issue of misplaced time can be seen on highways all over the country with individuals driving along just trying to keep up with the pace of other commuters on the road, with speedometers reading sixty miles per hour or higher while driving in a fifty-five mile per hour zone. The usual justification and response to these excessive speeds is, "What's the problem? Everyone else is doing it, so it must be okay."

We often speed and hurry about, but still seem to go nowhere; so what's the big rush?

In general, the big rush usually centers on a society attempting to accommodate a multitude of activities, whether at work, home, or even in the church as we attempt to squeeze an elephant into a mini-van. Various meetings, conflicting schedules, and kids who seem to have more obligations and activities than we do that tend to take up and occupy a great deal of individual time. This usually causes one to become bogged down with excessive busyness.

Work and many of the activities we routinely do are very important; however, we must ensure that work and busy activity do not distract us from the needed time of rest in the presence of God and focus on what really matters.

None of us have the power to "turn back the hands of time;" therefore, we must make the best use of the time that we have now.

Time is the only resource that can never be regained once it is lost. This is why we must be careful to steward our time wisely, to not only make a difference in our own lives but also in the lives of those we encounter each day.

Do you have misplaced time (Eph. 5:11-17)?

Thoughts

_____
_____
_____
_____
_____
_____
_____

January 8
BETRAYED BY MY SPEECH
Read: Jn. 18:15-18, 25-27; Matt. 26:73

When I was stationed on a small island in the central Arabian Gulf in the Middle East I once heard the Crown Prince, who was a member of the royal family and the Minister of Defense (equivalent to the Secretary of Defense in the United States) for the country, give a speech.

I was amazed to hear a person born and raised in the Middle East and of Arab decent speak as if he were originally from the United States of America. The Crown Prince spoke with the eloquence of a Harvard scholar and was very articulate; and if one were to turn their back to him as he spoke, one would assume the prince was an intellectual or scholar of western decent, or to put is another way "his speech betrayed him."

As believers in the body of Christ, our lifestyle, character, and our speech should set us apart as citizens of the Kingdom of God; however, many times our speech may suggest otherwise. And just like the Crown Prince, our speech could paint the wrong picture of who we actually are.

As citizens of God's Kingdom we are to not become so influenced by the world's system that there is no clear distinction between a life lived for the world or a life lived in Christ.

Though we live in the world, we are not to be of the world or do the same things that are done in this system. "Don't be like the people of this world, but let God change the way you think. Then you will know how to do everything that is good and pleasing to him" (Rom. 12:2, Contemporary English Version).

This is important because if we are not careful, we can allow the influences of society affect how we live and what comes out of our mouths. And when we consistently connect ourselves to the wrong people and things, we will find ourselves subjected to the "Garbage in, Garbage out" syndrome.

As ambassadors of God's Kingdom and citizens of Heaven, we must stop attempting to just fit in and simply becoming members of the "In-crowd," but instead letting our true character and citizenship be made clearly evident and known. Have you been betrayed by your speech?

January 9
SOMEBODY GRAB IT, IT'S ON THE LOOSE AGAIN!
Read: James 3:7-8

Imagine being at the circus with your family and the show has been amazing with stunts and high-wire acrobatics, and then all of a sudden the unthinkable happens. An enraged elephant goes on the rampage and begins to charge towards the crowd of unsuspecting spectators, including hundreds of small children.

Thoughts

_____
_____
_____
_____
_____
_____
_____
_____

9

In this mayhem the elephant eventually tramples over one of the trainers, and then continues out into public streets literally damaging and/or destroying anything and everything in its path.

With no way to control the wild beast, authorities and animal control have no other alternative but to put the animal to rest (death). And with a couple of gunshots to the head, the wild beast is permanently halted in its tracks. This is actually from a true account.

Just like the uncontrollable elephant, many of us today have issues with trying to control one of the smallest, yet often the deadliest, member of our body—OUR TONGUE AND THE WORDS IT PRODUCES!

Although man has the ability to tame and control myriads of animals, it is very difficult for many to learn the art of controlling our tongues. The tongue is one of the smallest members of the human body, yet it can cause substantial damage if it is not brought under subjection and control (James 3:7-8).

Jobs have been lost, marriages destroyed, relationships broken, families separated, and churches have even split all because of careless and thoughtless words. According to Prov. 18:21, "The tongue can bring death or life; those who love to talk will reap the consequences" (New Living Translation). This means that whatever comes out of our mouths will either produce one of two things; either life or death, there's no in between.

"Those who control their tongue will have a long life; opening your mouth can ruin everything" (Prov. 13:3, (New Living Translation).

No matter how insignificant we may think they are, our words have meaning. Instead of speaking words of negativity, we must choose to speak words of life (Matt. 12:36-37).

"Watching what you say can save you a lot of trouble" (Prov. 21:23, Contemporary English Version).

Thoughts

_____
_____
_____
_____
_____
_____
_____

January 10
IT'S TIME TO SOAR!
Read: Deut. 32:11-12

Johnny's eighteenth birthday has arrived, and he is excited about the prospects of the future. High School graduation has come and gone, however, twelve months later he's still living at home with no job, or any clear direction. Then the familiar words of a mother, father, or guardian begin to ring in his ears, "You need to get up and do something with your life; you are old enough to now go out on your own."

Ouch! These words may seem insensitive, but the motive behind them has far-reaching ramifications when they are spoken in and with love. The parent or guardian just wants to see the young adult mature and succeed in life by learning how to step out in faith. Of course in this particular moment, the intent is more than likely not clearly evident to the now 19-year-old.

Throughout the Bible there are descriptions of one of the most popular and regal birds in the United States, which also just happens to be the national mascot of the country—the Bald Eagle. One Scripture concerning eagles that immediately comes to mind is from the book of Deuteronomy in the Old Testament (Deut. 32:11-12).

Eagles are very unique birds that have an heir of nobleness about them as if they already know their prowess, and that they are at the top of the food chain with none in their species having the ability to defeat them. This toughness can also be seen in the rearing of their young.

There comes a point in time when the young eaglets reach a stage of maturity, which is when the mother must demonstrate a kind of tough love. Although her first inclination is to nurture and to protect her young, the mother eagle loves them enough to push them from the place of comfort to purpose so they can learn how to fly and hunt for themselves.

Like young eaglet clinging to the nest, many believers often stay in their "comfort zones" due to fear, refusing to step out in faith

This is when God Himself, and not satan who we are often quick to blame negative things on, begins to stir the nest to make things uncomfortable with a purpose of getting us to move and step out in faith. Because when we are comfortable we tend to become motionless and choose to just remain right where we are with no forward progress. So God stirs the nest, not to harm us, but to develop our character and strengthen our faith thereby giving us the ability to soar in life as we rely and put our complete confidence in Him.

Therefore, as an eagle in the body of Christ today, allow God through the Holy Spirit to stir up the gifts that are within to bring you to a place of maturity so that you too can fly high. Get out of the nest, it's time to soar (Is. 40:29-31)!

Thoughts

_____

_____

_____

_____

_____

_____

_____

January 11
GET UP, IT AIN'T OVER YET
Read: 2 Cor. 4:8-9

In the "Rocky" movie series, the once under-rated and unknown boxer Rocky Balboa rose to fame, prominence and victory one fight at a time. In each movie there were formidable opponents that were designed to test Rocky's strength, courage, and endurance.

Each fight would go the distance, with Rocky advancing and then the opponent retaliating with a flurry of blows that normally knocked Rocky down to the canvas. But each time he was knocked down, he refused defeat and got back up because of his inner strength, drive and will to succeed and win.

At times, as we live in this world's system, we may occasionally feel the unwanted blows of opposition from all sides; with the pressures of daily living seeming to overwhelm us. In this instance if one is not careful, we could have the potential to revert back to our former way of thinking and doing things; a way that generally leads to agony and defeat. This often leads to feelings of anxiety because life has knocked us down.

However, there is hope, and though the world may knock us down, it is entirely up to us to remain down.

In Christ we already have the victory, and though we may get knocked down by the pressures of life; we don't have to stay there (2 Cor. 4:8-9). Therefore, when life delivers a flurry of blows and we get knocked down, we can either stay down in defeat, or get up and keep pressing forward. Refuse to stay down, and instead choose victory. GET UP, IT AIN'T OVER YET (Rom. 8:35, 37)!

January 12
IT'S COMING, JUST HOLD ON!
Read: Prov. 3:5-6

Has God made a promise to fulfill a pressing need in your life that has yet come to pass? God knows what you're going through. So, stand fast in the liberty in which Christ has set you free, and don't become entangled in the bondage of your former life and former way of thinking. Renew your mind because today is a new day, put the past behind you (Phil. 3:13).

What you're going through is just a test; it is only after you pass the test that your breakthrough will come. Jesus said that He would never leave

Thoughts

_____

_____

_____

_____

_____

_____

_____

you, nor forsake you (Heb. 13:5). He sent the Holy Spirit to comfort you and to be your guide (Jn. 16:13).

So, whether on the mountain top, or in lowest regions of the valley; He is there to lead, comfort, and help you in your time of need. Know that the same test or trial you face today, someone else is presently going through the same thing and another has come out victoriously; so you are not alone in the struggle. And always remember that God is faithful enough to bring you through it as well.

"No test or temptation that comes your way is beyond the course of what others have had to face. All you need to remember is that God will never let you down; he'll never let you be pushed past your limit; he'll always be there to help you come through it" (1 Cor. 10:13, The Message).

So, no matter the situation, test, or trial; refuse to lose sleep, become distraught or even upset-—your breakthrough is on the way! "Unrelenting disappointment leaves you heartsick, but a sudden good break can turn life around" (Prov. 13:12, The Message). Take your eyes off of what you can see; have faith and trust God. It's coming, just hold on!

"And we know that God causes everything to work together for the good of those who love God and are called according to his purpose for them" (Rom. 8:28, New Living Translation).

January 13
PLUG IT IN, PLUG IT IN
Read: Acts 1:8

Over the years there has been a number of memorable television commercials produced. For example, Oscar Meyer Bologna "Cause' Oscar Mayer has a way with B-O-L-O-G-N-A!"; Tootsie Roll Lollipops "How many licks does it take to get to the Tootsie Roll center of a Tootsie Pop?"; Kellogg's Tony The Tiger "They're Grrrrreat!"; Wendy's "Where's the beef?"; LifeCall's Medical Alarm System "I've fallen...and I can't get up!"; The Energizer Bunny "Just keeps going and going," just to name a few.

Well, in recent years the SC Johnson Company produced one such television ad/commercial also creating a popular slogan for one of its Glade air freshener products. But unlike other Glade products with the aroma being released simply by spraying it or by opening the container, this new product the "Glade Plug-In" required that the product actually be plugged into an electrical socket in order for the aroma

Thoughts

_____
_____
_____
_____
_____
_____
_____

13

and fragrance to get released into the air, with the slogan for this product being "Plug it in, plug it in."

This slogan contains a very memorable catch phrase that speaks towards the action required for the fresh aroma and scent of the plug-in to actually fill the air. No matter how pretty the plug-in maybe on the outside, our how much fragrance and aroma are stored within, until the device is actually plugged in nothing happens.

I had actually heard the Glade "Plug It In" slogan many times before, but on one particular day as I heard the words, I began to think about the relationship of believers in Christ to the Holy Spirit. Our spiritual life will not function efficiently nor effectively until we connect to and are empowered by the person of the Holy Spirit.

A candy apple red Lamborghini with a pristine exterior, custom interior, and mechanically enhanced/engineered engine without any gasoline in the tank may as well be put on display at some high-class museum. Because, without the fuel that is required to power the vehicle, it has no ability to move anywhere unless it is being pushed or towed by someone or something.

So it is with us as believers; no matter how good we think we look on the outside (being able to offer up vain repetitious prayers or quote a few Bible verses). It is what's on the inside, the heart that really matters and also what supplies our strength.

Until we each individually connect to the right source, we too like the Lamborghini with no gas will have no power to commit and/or effectively move while attempting to obey God's commands.

It is not until the believer is empowered by and with the Holy Spirit that we can truly become effective witnesses in our service for Christ (Acts 1:8).

Are you feeling powerless today? Does your service seem to be ineffective? Then what are you waiting for? Go ahead, I dare you; PLUG IT IN, PLUG IT IN!!!

Thoughts

_____
_____
_____
_____
_____
_____

January 14
FROM THE PIT TO THE PALACE, THE BLESSING DOES NOT CHANGE
Read: Gen. 39:21-22

The story of Joseph in the book of Genesis (Chapters 37, 39, 40, and 41) is very familiar to most of us. Joseph was the beloved son of Jacob (later named Israel by God), the son that received the coat of many colors above all of his other brothers. And not only was Joseph favored by his father, but at an early age he was also favored by God with the ability of dreams and visions.

It was his gift of dreams that eventually catapulted him through a roller coaster ride with a life of many ups and downs starting with his own brothers plotting to kill him. But instead of shedding his blood, his eldest brother Reuben convinced the other brothers to simply throw him into an empty pit that had no water and then lie to their father Jacob that Joseph was dead.

But instead of leaving Joseph in the pit, an opportunity presented itself which allowed them to sell their brother to a band of Ishmaelites traveling along the way, figuring that this was a more befitting way to rid themselves of their brother the dreamer. And so began Joseph's saga that would unfold over the next 13 years.

The Ishmaelites later brought Joseph to Egypt and sold him to Potiphar, a captain of the Egyptian guard and officer of Pharaoh (leader of Egypt). Even in Potiphar's house God was with Joseph. "The LORD was with Joseph, so he succeeded in everything he did as he served in the home of his Egyptian master. Potiphar noticed this and realized that the LORD was with Joseph, giving him success in everything he did" (Gen. 39:23, New Living Translation).

Although God's favor was upon Joseph, the tables were turned when he was falsely accused of making advances towards Potiphar's wife and later found himself in an Egyptian prison for remaining true to his God. But yet again, in another barren and empty place, Joseph found even more favor (Gen. 39:21-22).

Not only did Joseph find favor in prison, but it was this same favor that eventually caused him to be released and placed in the good graces of the ruler of Egypt; Joseph literally moved from the pit to the prison to the palace.

In each predicament he found himself in; Joseph did not complain, compromise his beliefs or waiver in his faith but chose to trust in the one True and Living God. It was because of his unswerving faithfulness and integrity that Joseph prospered.

God allowed adversity to occur in Joseph's life to position him for His plan and greater purpose. Though family may forsake you, jobs may come and go, the economy may be up one day and down the next there's one thing that you can be certain of, that fact is "THE BLESSING DOES NOT CHANGE!" Favor may not be fair, but it sure will get you there!

Thoughts

"When God approves of your life, even your enemies will end up shaking your hand" (Prov. 16:7, The Message).

_____

_____

_____

_____

_____

_____

15

January 15

HOW HUNGRY ARE YOU?
Read: Matt. 5:6

It's a few months into an expectant mother's pregnancy; the fetus inside is beginning to take form and is in the developmental stages. Suddenly out of nowhere and without warning, strange appetites and unusual cravings begin. Peanut butter and pickles, chocolate-covered bananas and potato chips, tuna and cheese, or lobster after midnight--the list of combinations can be staggering. Yet whatever the craving, the mother goes out of her way to see to it that these cravings or desires are satisfied by any means necessary.

The really amazing thing about this scenario is that the mother's cravings are usually not even of a personal nature or desire, but is actually directly related to the need and requirement to feed and nourish that which is growing on the inside of her. So, naturally and instinctively she eats; however, there are times when the fulfilled craving and that which is eaten has no benefit for the unborn child, because no real nutrients are gained from what is eaten.

I'm sure that you are well aware of this but, just in case you had a momentary lapse of memory, food is a vital component to our growth and development as human beings. The things we eat are intended to provide the protein, calcium and other important vitamins and nutrients required to promote growth, development and supply us with the strength needed to sustain us from day-to-day. Without food and the proper nutrients, strength in our body tends to dissipate fairly quickly leaving us drained and powerless.

Well, just as our physical body requires proper nourishment, so does the spirit man that resides within us.

As believers in Christ, we have the awesome privilege of carrying and transporting the Spirit of God (Holy Spirit) within us wherever we go because He comes to connect with our spirit. Unfortunately, our spirits often suffer from malnourishment simply because we have cravings for and invariably end up eating the wrong things.

Many of us are guilty of feeding the flesh while neglecting the Spirit that is designed to lead, guide, sustain us and provide us with the spiritual strength we need to overcome the seeds of temptation that come in our direction each day.

Thoughts

_____

_____

_____

_____

_____

_____

_____

In order to have the spiritual strength needed in our lives to overcome the temptations, our spirits have to be nourished and fed to ensure proper development so that we are able to walk in the power and authority that is rightfully ours (Lk. 10:19).

16

In order to accomplish this, we must crave and hunger after God's Word to receive the nourishment we need.

Like the expectant mother who goes out of her way to satisfy the cravings within no matter the time of day or night; we too must likewise satisfy the cravings of the One deep within us. So, allow your desires to align with the Spirit of God inside and you will never go hungry again! HOW HUNGRY ARE YOU?

"You're blessed when you've worked up a good appetite for God. He's food and drink in the best meal you'll ever eat" (Matt. 5:6, The Message).

January 16
HOOK-UPS FROM HEAVEN
Read: Job 36:11

Walking down a street in the metropolitan area of a city you come across an individual who appears to be in an under-privileged state, with a sign requesting some type of financial help or assistance. Not knowing if the need is valid or not, you look but continue to walk along. Then a voice pierces the air as the man yells out "Come on, can you hook a brotha up?" Being the kind-hearted Christian that you are, you pull out your wallet and oblige. Although this person was looking for a hand-out, what he really needed was grace and favor.

Before many of us came to Christ, we were in need of a "Spiritual Hook-up," because it was sin that literally left our spiritual accounts empty and us bankrupt. But through the shed blood of Jesus Christ, God's grace was bestowed upon us in our deepest hour of need.

"You were saved by faith in God, who treats us much better than we deserve. This is God's gift to you, and not anything you have done on your own. It isn't something you have earned, so there is nothing you can brag about (Eph. 2:8-9, Contemporary English Version). This is nothing more that the favor and grace of a Mighty and All-Powerful God.

Many are familiar with and use the acronym or acrostic G-R-A-C-E to represent: G - God's, R - Riches, A - At, C - Christ's, E – Expense; however, we can even take this a step further. Grace is God's unmerited (undeserved) favor; favor can also be defined as "God's unfair advantage" as others like to call it.

This type of grace cannot be bought, sold, or bargained for; it can only be received, because

Thoughts

_____
_____
_____
_____
_____
_____
_____

it is God's desire to bless and proper those who obey and serve Him. "If they listen and obey God, they will be blessed with prosperity throughout their lives. All their years will be pleasant" (Job 36:11, New Living Translation).

Are you in need of the favor of God? Are you in need of a "Hook-up From Heaven?" Receive God's grace today, it's totally free!

"And God will generously provide all you need. Then you will always have everything you need and plenty left over to share with others" (2 Cor. 9:8, New Living Translation).

January 17
BEHOLD THE DREAMER
Read: Gen. 37:1-11

There is nothing more encouraging for an individual to have than that of a dream and a vision focused on achieving something great. One such dreamer identified in the Old Testament of the Bible was Joseph, the seventeen year-old son of Jacob who was given a dream and a vision by God Himself.

In this dream Joseph would one day be exalted in status above his father, mother and all of his brothers in a place where he would exercise dominion, rule and authority over a great multitude of people. Already envied because of the favoritism shown to him by his father, Joseph's dream just made his brothers despise and hate him even more.

Think about it, Joseph was a teenager, and like the average obnoxious teenager he probably took this opportunity to rub the favor and blessing that was upon his life in the face of his brothers by saying "Look at what God has revealed, do you see what He's going to do for me? Obviously I'm special since He hasn't revealed anything to you." At any rate this vision or dream was God-given; therefore, the final outcome had to be "fulfillment" despite the opposition and the many haters inside the family and out that rose up against him.

As time went on Joseph was eventually thrown in a pit and then later sold into slavery by his brothers (Gen. 37:26-28), he was falsely accused of making sexual advances towards his Egyptian master's (Potiphar's) wife and later thrown into prison (Gen. 37:13-21). But in the pit and even in prison, God was with him as he continued to dream and receive favor. It was his ability as a dreamer that ultimately allowed him to correctly interpret a dream for the reigning Pharaoh which in turn resulted in Joseph's released from prison and being appointed second in command directly under this Egyptian ruler.

Thoughts

_____

_____

_____

_____

_____

_____

_____

18

In his new exalted and elevated position, Joseph was not only able to bring about peace and deliverance to his family, but to all of the inhabitants of the surrounding regions as well during a time of great famine and lack (Gen. 47:11-12). It was his ability to dream, keeping the dream alive and God's favor that made the difference.

"Hope deferred makes the heart sick, but a dream fulfilled is a tree of life" (Prov. 13:12, New Living Translation).

January 18
IS YOUR FIELD READY TO RECEIVE?
Read: Gal. 6:7-8

Several years ago I had the opportunity to live in the "Volunteer" state of Tennessee. My family and I lived just outside of Memphis, and every day as I drove to and from work a few miles down the road to the city of Millington, and as far as the eye could see on either side of the road was miles and miles of cotton fields that stretched all the way to the military base there.

Year after year it was truly amazing to watch the transition from what appeared to be fields of absolute nothingness to beautiful white-clouded oceans of cotton, and then afterwards the harvest began with some extremely large tractors.

Each year the same process would be repeated with these fields going from nothing, to flowing white fields of cotton, and then reaping the harvest.

Even though, for whatever reason, I actually never saw the most important component of this process happen during my commute to and from work, without it there would not have been any cotton to reap at the end of harvest. This step and process involved preparation of the ground through the sowing and planting of seeds, because without sowing there can never be a harvest.

This same principle also holds true in our lives today, reaping must be preceded by the process of first sowing.

There are many in the world today who are waiting on their big break, a financial miracle and/or a breakthrough. Sadly, many of these same individuals have not learned how or taken the time to ensure that their field has been properly prepared and ready to receive.

The process of sowing and reaping is a principle that works both in the natural and in the spiritual realm; that is when it is done correctly

Thoughts
_____
_____
_____
_____
_____
_____
_____

(Gen. 8:22). In order to reap a harvest, one must first sow; but more importantly we must sow the right thing.

Whatever the need may be in our lives today, the goal is to not allow the enemy to destroy our seed so that we can reap the right harvest. It is therefore essential that our seed is nurtured, protected and sowed in the right ground to ensure that we receive the correct harvest.

"God wants you to blossom right where you are planted," so make sure your field is ready to receive by first sowing the right thing (Gal. 6:7-8)!

January 19
HOW CLOSE ARE YOU?
Read: James 4:8

Driving is a skill in which one becomes better at over time and after some experience actually behind the wheel on the road. Therefore, riding with a novice driver, who also just happens to be an impatient person, can make for a very interesting commute on interstate or city roads. You know; that individual who brings a whole new meaning to the term "Tailgating." Who knows, maybe this type of driver actually describes you.

At any rate, individuals in this category really hate traffic and are extremely annoyed at slow drivers. So in order to prompt the car ahead of them to move, the individual normally follows the car so closely that they can literally count their own teeth in the other vehicle's rearview mirror. Talk about impatience.

Although this scenario may have been embellished a bit, I'm sure you get the point. These individuals are guilty of "following too close." Have you ever been guilty of this?

Now wouldn't it be a powerful witness for saints of God in our daily walk with Christ to be accused of following Jesus too closely? I really wonder how many Christians today; myself included, would be found guilty of this very act.

Though in the natural following too closely may result in an accident with an individual receiving a hefty fine and/or an inconvenient court appearance; in a spiritual sense, extreme closeness produces eternal rewards. And when we choose to draw closer to God and search for Him with our whole hearts, we will indeed find Him (Jer. 33:3).

Thoughts

_____

_____

_____

_____

_____

_____

So, take your foot off your spiritual brakes today and begin to follow the Master up close and personal. With that said there is only one question that remains to be asked: "How close are you?"

January 20
USING THE RIGHT TOOL
Read: 1 Jn. 4:7-8

Have you ever watched makeover or home improvement shows like "This Old House," or some of the more recent and popular shows aired on the Home and Garden Television (HGTV) or Do-It Yourself (DIY) Networks? What really amazes me, when I have the opportunity to view them, is watching how the very talented and skilled men and women on these shows take something that is mundane, ordinary and plain through a process of transformation that usually results in a beautiful work of art.

So, exactly how is this accomplished or done? Simple, they maximize the use of their resources: using who they know, what they know and above all else making the choice to employ the right tool(s).

The architects who design many of the homes showcased on these shows generally do not just pull out a piece of notebook paper and crayons to sketch and design these magnificent structures, although this could very well be done. Instead, the average architect today would more than likely employ the use of tape measures, laser levels, surveying equipment, and computer-aided graphics programs to create the best possible design.

Similarly, a skilled carpenter with any years of experience would not likely use the handle of a screwdriver to drive a nail through a piece of wood, or put a window in place utilizing Duct tape. No, he or she would undoubtedly use a hammer, or a pneumatic nail gun. There is nothing like employing the right tool for the right job, it just makes things a little easier.

This makes me wonder why so many in the body of Christ choose to either use the right tool for the wrong job, or just completely use the wrong tool altogether, that is when looking at this from a spiritual perspective?

As believers we not only have the Word of God and Truth at our disposal, but also have the tools of prayer, love, forgiveness, long-suffering, gentleness, kindness, meekness, and peace. Yet it is totally up to us to choose the right tool to employ for the job. So, ensure you are using the right tool while building on the foundation of truth in the spirit of love (1 Cor. 13:4-8)!

Thoughts

_____
_____
_____
_____
_____
_____
_____
_____

January 21
IT'S TIME TO CLEAN HOUSE
Read: 1 Cor. 6:19

Imagine that you've just received word that the President of the United States is coming to your home for a visit. He has heard about your outstanding volunteer efforts and the various activities you've instituted to better your community. And on this particular day, he wants to recognize your faithfulness and dedication to selfless service.

In addition to making trips to the mall to purchase something new to wear, what else do you think the average person in this situation would do? You've guessed it. There would more than likely be a mad dash to clean your house from top to bottom to ensure that every crack, crevice and corner was clean down to the smallest and most minute detail. The ultimate goal of these efforts, of course, is a home that is spotless, presentable, and ready for the reception of your special and honored guest.

Now just imagine taking this same analogy and approach, and then applying it to our spiritual lives and faith as believers in Christ, as we go to Scripture for guidance on how we are to maintain our temples (1 Cor. 6:19).

The "sacred place" described in the Scripture above is often rendered as the word "temple" in other Bible translations and versions, which is commonly used to represent and/or signify our physical body. In general, a temple is nothing more than a holy structure or place that accommodates a person or a group of people assembling for worship.

Another fact to consider here is that the common word used to denote a "temple" is translated as, or literally means "palace." A palace by definition is "the official residence of a king." This basically means that each one of us has been created to be temples or holy dwelling places for the Spirit of God.

Think about it for a moment, as God's temples we literally provide a habitation and spiritual place of residence for the King of Kings and the Spirit of the Living God that comes to dwell and abide within each of us when we first believe (Eph. 1:13). This alone should really make each of us more cognizant or aware of what we allow to enter our bodies and the residence of the King.

Thoughts

_____

_____

_____

_____

_____

_____

It is a natural principle that two objects cannot occupy the same space at the same time—one must give way to the other. Therefore, the spiritual truth is that when we are truly filled with God's Spirit, there should be no room for anything else. The King has very high standards of living and deserves nothing but our best.

So, simply stated: "It's time to clean house!" Outward transformation must first begin with inward change and renewal. We must be willing to receive the truth of the Word of God into pure hearts and also renew our minds if we truly desire transformation to take place from the inside, out (Eph. 5:26).

When was the last time you cleaned house? The spirit of the King is not just coming or on His way, but He is already here!

January 22
LOSING TO WIN
Read: Phil. 3:10-11

In our society today, there seems to be a constant and major focus placed on winning and achieving one's goals at the expense of everything else. Besides, when looking at the alternative, who in their right mind really wants to lose anyway?

If a group of young individuals were asked the question: Does it matter more to put forth your best effort, or should winning be the primary focus? The average person would most likely say "Win, Win, Win!"

Let's take a look at a world-class runner in a 200-yard dash. I'm sure someone in this category does not just lag behind saying to his or herself, "I'll just stay back here and let everyone cross the finish line ahead of me. Besides, winning really isn't all that important anyway." No! Most runners who have ever found themselves in this predicament instinctively press harder with the afterburners engaged in an all-out attempt to reach the finish line first. Because this is what world-class athletes do, they play to win!

Consequently, for many, second or third place is of little significance and is not an option, because winning is the primary and ultimate goal! This is why an individual who does not win may feel as if he or she did not accomplish anything at all; even though they did their best.

Even in the Body of Christ we hear phrases like: "More than a conqueror," "The head and not the tail," "Above only and not beneath," "Victorious in Christ." For those who truly profess faith in Christ, these phrases are all true and achievable; but, there is corresponding action required on our part. And though it may sound contradictory, part of this action is learning how to lose (Phil. 3:10-11; Phil. 1:21).

Thoughts

However, the very thing that appears to be a loss for us (in Christ) is really what brings us gain and causes us to win. In order to gain what Christ has for us we must be willing to die or

23

lose to ourselves, our desires, and aspirations that do not align with God's will for our life.

We accomplish this by crucifying, mortifying, and killing the fleshly nature, with its desires, that constantly attempts to rise up within; we must be willing to die to live (Rom. 6:6-7).

January 23
IN THE FIRE, BUT NOT CONSUMED
Read: Dan. 3:8-29

There are many examples in the Bible of how God's favor and anointing actually brought more challenges and literally placed individuals in the thick of the fire more than anything else. When David was anointed to be king over Israel, it wasn't until over twenty years later that he actually stepped into the office after being threatened and chased by the ousted King Saul. And after God revealed to him what his future would be, Joseph was thrown into a pit, sold into slavery and even imprisoned in a dungeon before he was elevated to a position of leadership.

And then there is the story of the three young Hebrew men: Hananiah, Mishael, and Azariah (also known as Shadrach, Meshach, and Abednego) who had the favor of God upon their lives, therefore, their hearts were set on worshipping the one True God and Him alone. As a result, they refused to bow to the golden image of the Babylonian king Nebuchadnezzar which resulted in them being placed in a fiery furnace (Dan. 3:4-6).

They were thrown into a fiery furnace not for anything bad they did, but for refusing to compromise their belief and trust in the One True Living God, the One who provides the anointing and favor.

Not only were the three thrown into the furnace filled with the normal heat and flames, but just for this particular occasion the flames were heated to temperatures seven times hotter than usual with the three being bound and thrown into the flames by the strongest men in the king's court. This was a true test of faith, but we serve an awesome God who is mighty to deliver.

Thoughts

_____
_____
_____
_____
_____
_____
_____

The king later went to the furnace to ensure the three got what he thought they deserved and was baffled at what he saw. I can imagine him coming before the furnace blinking his eyes, rubbing them, and then going back for a second glance, yet what he saw did not change. The three men had been preserved in the flames.

Can you imagine actually being thrown into the midst of a fiery furnace, having the door shut and the flames intensified, yet emerge without the faintest scent of smoke in your clothing or any evidence of burns?

The three were spared simply because they refused to compromise and God showed up on their behalf. As believers in Christ, we must also remember that the fiery furnaces of life are not designed to destroy us, but to perfect us (1 Pet. 4:12-14). This process occurs so the gifts that are inside can emerge pure, untainted, and ready for use because although we may be in the fire, we won't be consumed!

January 24
DON'T LET IT SETTLE, STIR IT UP
Read: 2 Tim. 1:6-7

I am really not one who cooks and definitely not a chef, because growing up my mother made sure that I had a hot meal every day of the week; so there wasn't a pressing need for me to really learn how to cook. And when my mom cooked, she really cooked and the food was good!

Each day the dish prepared was varied and the methods used to prepare the meal ranged from using a dish in the oven, a frying pan, or simply using pots and pans on top of the stove.

One of my favorite meals at the time was white rice covered with beef stew mixed with carrots, whole cornel corn, string beans and any other vegetable that added flavor and substance to the dish. Just recalling and thinking about my mom's beef stew is making me hungry right now.

To prepare the dish a pot was placed on the stove with the burner set for a specific temperature. The stew was then left to simmer to allow the flavor to soak into the beef and vegetables. However, the stew could not just be left to itself, but had to be constantly monitored and checked. If the stew was just left to itself with no attention, many of the denser and heavier ingredients would begin to settle on the bottom and inevitably begin to burn.

Therefore, to prevent the stew from burning or sticking to the bottom of the pot, my mother would occasionally tell me to go in the kitchen and stir it up. By doing so the stew would not settle, burn or then be unfit for use or consumption.

Just like the pot of stew left unchecked or unmonitored, a believer who has been filled

Thoughts

_____

_____

_____

_____

_____

_____

with God's Spirit and is full of the Word but chooses not to operate in his or her calling or chooses not to employ the gifts that have been so graciously given begins to let valuable substance settle inside, the gift then becomes of little use to anyone else.

Once we have received the knowledge of the Truth and are subsequently filled with God's Truth (His Holy Word) and His spirit, it is required that we each continually stir up the gifts that are resident inside of us so that we can affect change in the earth (Matt. 5:13).

Has the Lord laid His hands upon you? If so, don't let God's precious gifts settle inside, instead begin to stir them up so that His anointing may flow through lives that are poured out. So, DON'T LET IT SETTLE, STIR IT UP!

January 25
TIRED OF SITTING ON THE BENCH
Read: Jn. 14:16

A few years back there was a movie box office comedy called "The Benchwarmers" that featured three not so very popular middle-aged men. As adolescents the three were considered to be nerds and outcasts amongst their peers. Therefore, while growing up the three were constantly bullied because of their lack of the physical dexterity required to be effective at any sporting event. The focal sport in this movie was baseball, so in this particular case they were routinely benched and not allowed to play during the Little League baseball games at the time.

Years later another one of their nerdy friends, who just happened to also now be a billionaire, decided to put together a baseball team that consisted of the now mature nerdy trio in an attempt to show-up and upstage those who bully nerds and others who just don't seem to fit in. The trio initially started out poorly, but over time and with a little coaching, they began to get better and better to the point that they were eventually winning games.

A tournament was later setup where the trio, now as adults, played against teams of nine younger players. But as time progressed some issues from the past surfaced that disqualified the three which then prompted the billionaire to let his outcast son and other young benchwarmers to play in the final game.

Thoughts

_____
_____
_____
_____
_____
_____
_____

It was the ninth inning and the underdogs were down by forty-two points, and by some miracle the billionaire's son hit the ball and was able to score a point. But instead of the winning team storming the field, it was those considered nerds who were benchwarmers that stormed the field

26

celebrating the fact that they had not been shut out and that someone had given them a chance to make a difference.

Have you ever watched a sporting event in which the favored team had played their hearts out but consistently came up short being down by a large margin of points? But when the camera pans over to the sideline or bench the very best player of the team is seen sitting patiently waiting for the opportunity to jump in to aid in closing the huge point deficit. Of course everyone begins to wonder what's wrong with the coach and why has he not put the star player in the game.

Then with three minutes remaining a little hope begins to spark as the coach finally decides to bring the star player in. And once this player is engaged, instantly the tides of the game change resulting in a decisive victory. Just imagine what could have happened if the player had been brought in earlier; all the coach needed to do was bring the best player into the game to give him a chance to show what he's got.

There are many today who walk around living defeated lives when victory is not too far away. Yet each day many play the game of life without assistance from the One who sits alongside warming the bench waiting patiently for His opportunity to come to our aid.

This person is none other than the Holy Spirit, the One given to us to be our Helper and Guide (Jn. 14:16). However, the help we need only comes when we get Him off the bench and engage Him in the game.

January 26
WHEN THEY OPEN YOUR LETTER, WHAT WILL THEY READ?
Read: 2 Cor. 3:2-3

According to one source, there are well over 450,000 Christian churches in the United States. In many neighborhoods, there is literally a church on nearly every corner. But even with so many churches established and in place, this does not negate the fact that there is still a great portion of the U.S. population and in the world for that matter that will never step one foot inside of a church building.

What this means for the believer, Christian, and follower of Christ is that the only Bible that many people will ever see is the lifestyle that he or she portrays and lives based on his or her speech and actions.

Thoughts

Besides, just going to church is only a small portion of the commitment that we have to make according to God's Word (Heb. 10:25); however, beyond just going to church actually

27

being "the Church" should be our ultimate goal. Because it is our "being" that generally influences and controls our "doing."

A great example of "being" and "doing" can be witnessed through the tactics of a salesperson who travels door to door, or tries to attract our attention as we are walking through the mall or a retail store. They usually do not just have a general knowledge of the product they are trying to sell, but have an in-depth and detailed understanding and can break down the intricate details of the item in question.

Therefore, it is because of this in-depth knowledge they usually provide a very convincing and compelling presentation as to why their particular product will enhance our quality of life, and all we have to do is make three easy payments of $19.99 and we then purchase something that we don't even need.

Wouldn't it be amazing if we collectively as believers in Christ took the same zeal and approach as this salesperson but with a slightly different approach? Instead of trying to just sell Christ, our job would be to present Him through the very lives that we live. "You yourselves are our letter, written on our hearts, known and read by everyone. You show that you are a letter from Christ...This letter is not written with ink but with the Spirit of the living God. It is not written on stone tablets but on human hearts" (2 Cor. 3:2-3, New Living Translation).

As Christians and believers, we each are God's letters that are made alive through Christ, and through lifestyles of faithfulness, righteousness, and obedience. This means that the old nature must give way to the new, and what we use to do or use to be should no longer define us. Because when we are truly "In Christ" all things become new and He gives us a new heart.

But in order for the ink of the Spirit to truly be applied and remain on the pages of our heart, we must have a hunger and thirst for God's Word and then consistently "hide" His Word in our hearts.

Though your letter may not read exactly the same as mine or read the same as that of the next Christian for that matter, there should still be noticeable similarities in our books (our lives) if we truly have the same Author (Creator).

Thoughts

_____
_____
_____
_____
_____
_____

January 27
EAGER FOR MORE
Read: Ps. 103:7

We are living in an age where information and use of visual technology and/or visual stimuli prevail, with the use of this medium increasing more and more each day. This becomes very evident even when viewing routine television programming when many times there are actually more timeslots allotted for advertisements (ads) than there is for the regularly scheduled program.

Marketing experts know that we as human beings are stimulated more by what we see, as opposed to just hearing or reading about a particular product or subject.

This is exactly why the cost of one advertisement aired at half-time during the National Football League's (NFLs) Super Bowl can be so exorbitant. However, even though the cost may be high, this does not discourage companies, businesses, and corporations from paying outrageous prices because the goal is to get their product seen and then purchased by consumers.

This is why many experts have dubbed the current millennium as the "Visual Age," because of the enormous effects this medium is currently having and expected to continue having on society as a whole.

Although technology is great and many of the advances available today can also be used to further spread the Gospel message around the world while bring us all closer together as a people and society. At the same time if we as believers are not careful, we can be lulled into a false sense of security as we place more focus and value on what we see, instead of exercising faith in the unseen.

Technology is good, but faith is even better. As believers we must go beyond just the visual, as we learn the ways of the LORD and cling to the unseen. This requires that we not just depend on what we see in the natural, but rather eagerly seek more of God and that which is not seen each day (Heb. 11:1, 6)!

Seeing does not always result in believing, this is why faith goes beyond what the natural eye can see.

January 28
DRINK UP, IT'S FREE
Read: Jn. 4:14

Water is very valuable and a much needed commodity, especially for someone lost in a desert during high noon in the month of July. Water is also a very essential element for human life. Over seventy-five percent of the earth if covered by water and more than two-thirds of the human body is made up of the same; approximately eighty percent of the blood that flows through our arteries and veins is comprised of water.

Thoughts

_____
_____
_____
_____
_____
_____
_____
_____

These facts are clear indicators of the importance of water to life as we know. An individual can survive for weeks without food; however, our survival time greatly decreases to days and hours when the body is deprived of water.

A natural resource that once used to be free has now become another means for financial gain and corporate profit. All it takes is a visit to a local grocery store or market with the numerous brands and different types of bottled water stocked upon the shelves. Individuals can purchase carbonated or un-carbonated, flavored or unflavored, regular or spring; whatever the preference, there's a water to suit individual palatal needs.

Although regular water may satisfy our natural thirst, there is water that far exceeds the thirst-quenching qualities of anything currently on the market and it is totally free (Jn. 4:14).

The water Jesus spoke of in the preceding verse is none other than the Holy Spirit who comes to fill the believer upon accepting Jesus as both Lord and Savior. And just as we cannot drink natural water once and expect to be continually sustained, a one-time filling with God's Spirit is never enough to spiritually sustain and keep us as we go through life; we must continually be filled. "...But ever be filled and stimulated with the [Holy] Spirit" (Eph. 5:18, Amplified Bible).

If you are in a desert place and dying of spiritual dehydration, there is no time like the present to quench your thirst. Seek righteousness and be filled with the Holy Spirit today (Jn. 7:38). Go ahead, drink up—it's totally free!

"You are my God. I worship you. In my heart, I long for you, as I would long for a stream in a scorching desert" (Ps. 63:1, Contemporary English Version).

January 29
A READY VESSEL
Read: 2 Cor. 4:7

During my military career and service, I have made several deployments aboard U.S. Navy ships to various locations around the world. And with each deployment there was a specific mission or assignment. So, generally when a ship deploys it is normally filled with the essential components (supplies and personnel) needed for the mission at hand.

Thoughts

_____

_____

_____

_____

_____

_____

Well, I can recall one particular deployment that was a bit unusual. Supplies and various other components were on-loaded as usual; however, the ship departed without its complement of additional support personnel and equipment that it normally transported for their use. Why? In this particular instance the mission for this deployment was just a little bit different.

The ship (or vessel) departed almost completely empty, aside from the normal complement of the ship's crew that is normally assigned and already onboard. This time the ship's assignment was to go and retrieve support personnel and equipment that was already in place at a specified location; therefore, once the ship arrived on station, it remained in the general vicinity until the support personnel and equipment arrived. In other words the mission or assignment was for the ship to be a ready vessel, waiting to receive and get filled.

According to one dictionary definition, a vessel is nothing more than "an object used as a container." Well, in the Bible the human body is also often referred to as a vessel or container in a spiritual sense (2 Tim. 2:20-21).

Based on the preceding fact, the question I would pose is, "What type of vessel or container are you? What cargo do you routinely transport?"

As believers in Christ we have been equipped to carry and transport a very precious cargo; God's Holy Spirit! But before we can be filled with the instrument that God desires to lead and direct our lives with, we must first empty ourselves and then be willing to be filled and used. This emptying involves a state of spiritual brokenness that often comes through humility (Phil. 2:7).

Therefore, it is the Father's desire that we become "Ready Vessels" that are not just filled with our own preset destinations, but instead are vessels willing to adjust priorities and change our own missions to be filled with God's precious Holy Spirit so that we are fit for the Master's use. God longs to fill us with His Spirit; however, this requires that our vessels be ready, prepared, and cleaned ahead of time (1 Cor. 6:19-20).

Are you willing to be a vessel for God? Have you emptied and hallowed yourself out for the Precious Cargo that God longs to transport through you (2 Cor. 4:7)?

January 30
A CHOSEN VESSEL
Read: 1 Pet. 2:9-10

Thoughts

When airlines check-in passengers, one of the very first things accomplished is to determine how many bags are being carried on or checked, and what the weight of these bags are. This is important to know because excess weight could affect how high the plane flies because any extra

31

baggage has the potential to become a burden on fuel consumption with the jet fuel burning at a more rapid rate than normal.

To ensure that planes operate at optimum capability, only a certain amount of baggage and cargo is allowed to ensure that planes have the ability to fly as high as, as fast and as far as it should.

As believers in Christ, we each have been chosen to be vessels for God, and over time our vessels (or bodies) accumulate many things, some good and some bad. When the bad is brought to our attention we each individually have to make a conscious choice to get rid of those things that continue to weigh on us and slow us down in our Christian walk of faith.

Sadly, many of us are like planes that are weighted down with a lot of excess baggage, and are unable to soar as eagles the way that God intended (Is. 40:31). We often get weighted down by pride, lust, anger, bitterness, envy, unforgiveness and the like until we are grounded and no longer able to fly.

But thanks be to God for His mercy, forgiveness, grace, the ability to get things right and to release our excess baggage as He molds and shapes us according to His purpose for our lives. It's also great to know that He does not just discard us because He knows that we are just broken and in need of repair and restoration (Jer. 29:11).

Though you may feel as though you are broken today, don't be discouraged and don't despair. Stay on the Potter's wheel and allow God to mold and re-shape you. Don't allow the excess issues and weights in your life define who you are. You may be broken, but you are still usable and a prime candidate for repair because you are a chosen vessel!

January 31
BROKEN, BUT READY FOR REPAIR
Read: Jer. 18:2-6

Have you ever seen or known an individual who grew fond of a certain article or thing over a period of time? An item the individual just could not seem to live without? Now just imagine the day that this personal treasure just stops working with the individual attempting to figure out what's wrong, but to no avail.

Thoughts

_____

_____

_____

_____

_____

_____

Then in a last ditch effort he brings the item to someone who specializes in maintenance and repair of that particular item and comes to the realization that his prized possession is still usable and is only broken, but in need of repair.

Instead of discarding the item, he is convinced to allow an expert to complete the necessary repairs to restore it to its former use.

Many of us in the body of Christ are just like the above treasured item; though the world may want to discard us because of the things we may have done or what may be currently happening in our lives today, we may only be broken and simply in need of repair and restoration.

But our God is the Mender of the broken-hearted (Ps. 147:3); He is the only One who is capable of taking the broken pieces of our lives and putting them back together again. But even though He is the Master Potter, we must be willing to submit to and endure the process as we stay on the wheel until the needed repairs are complete.

It's a wonderful thing to know that just because of our issues and brokenness God does not just throw us away, but He chooses to take the time to mend and restore us so that we are fit for use again. "Whenever the pot the potter was working on turned out badly, as sometimes happens when you are working with clay, the potter would simply start over and use the same clay to make another pot" (Jer. 18:2-6, The Message).

Just as potter in the natural reuses the same clay to re-create a damaged vessel; so does our Heavenly Father, the Master Potter. When we are broken He does not just discard us, but instead just takes the broken pieces of our lives and uses them to reshape and rebuild us so that we may walk in our God-given authority here in the earth and remain fit for the Master's use.

Though you may feel as if you are broken today, don't get discouraged and don't despair. Stay on the wheel and allow Him to mold and re-shape you. You may be broken, but you're also ready for repair (2 Cor. 4:8-10)!

February 1
IT'S TIME TO GET OUT OF THE BOAT
Read: Matt. 14:22-33

In the Gospel of Matthew Chapter 14, Jesus sent His disciples on a journey to the other side of the Sea of Galilee on a boat ahead of Himself. During their journey to the other side, the disciples encountered a violent storm with winds that tossed the boat from side to side as all onboard were overcome with fear.

Thoughts

In the midst of the tumult as the boat is being tossed about, a figure begins to emerge out of the storm in the form of a man. It was Jesus, their Master and Savior, walking through the storm on top of the water.

The disciples began to question whether what they saw was real or not, and as Jesus continued to approach He reassured them that it was indeed He and not some unknown or unfamiliar spirit. He then comforted them with the words "Fear not" and in one translation it simply says "Stop being afraid!"

It has been stated that the phrase "Fear not," "Be not afraid," or some form of this phrase is recorded in the Bible 365 times, and there are 365 days in a year (except on Leap Year with 366 days). What this should signify is that God encourages us with daily reminders to overcome our fears with faith, because faith is what pleases Him (Heb. 11:6).

So as Jesus approaches, Peter being impulsive and quick to speak as he normally is, says to Jesus "if it's really you then allow me to walk out on the water with you." Jesus replies, "Come."

Peter then steps out of the boat and begins to walk on the white-capped waves of the water with his eyes fixed on Jesus. However, at some point and as the storm continued to rage around them, Peter began to notice the violence of the sea and the strength of the wind and as he took his eyes off of Jesus he immediately began to sink.

Afterwards Jesus lovingly rebuked Peter and rescued him from the water by getting him back into the boat. And as soon as both Jesus and Peter were safely inside the small vessel, the storm immediately ceased.

Though many consider this event to show a lack of faith on Peter's part as he began to lose focus and allowed what he saw in the natural to hinder him. In actuality this can also be viewed as a lesson in courage and what it takes to overcome fear and activate faith in our lives.

Although Peter's water-walking time was short, unlike the other disciples who were paralyzed with fear and chose not to move, at least Peter had enough courage to stand up and step out into the unknown. He made a choice to step out of a boat that was being violently tossed about and probably on the verge of sinking, simply upon hearing one word from the Master and then using Jesus as his point of reference and reassurance.

There are many in the body of Christ today who are like the disciples, they remain in the boat and never venture out, while Jesus is patiently bidding us all to "Come." He challenges us to come out of our comfort zones; therefore, like muscles in your body, faith only gets bigger the more it is exercised. With that said, it's time to get out of the boat!

"O you of little faith, why [do] you doubt" (Matt. 14:31, New King James Version)?

Thoughts

_____

_____

_____

_____

_____

_____

34

February 2
BIRDS OF A FEATHER FLOCK TOGETHER
Read: Matt. 24:27-28

Although as a child I grew up in the city, during the summer months I would often visit relatives in the rural or 'country' surrounding area. In the country one could see all manner of animals and critters from cows, bulls, horses and goats to creepy crawlers like centipedes, scorpions, and even rattlesnakes. And as it was described in the Disney animated movie "The Lion King," what was referred to as the "Circle of Life" happened routinely as some of these animals died and ceased to exist.

In these instances it was not uncommon to see a very large gathering of birds flying over one specific location in a circular pattern, this was usually an indication that something had died. And sure enough, I later learned these birds were actually vultures (sometime called buzzards), they were circling in preparation to dine on the carcass that lay lifeless below. The word "carcass," is just a noun or another word that identifies a "body."

Vultures are unusual creatures, and it is their nature to only prey on things that are already lifeless and dead. This is why large congregations of these birds of prey can often be seen together because they are like-minded and have a common agenda. They connect themselves to things that are not going anywhere, have no direction, and that have no life.

This brings to mind the very nature of our adversary the devil who has similar motives and a focus; that is "to kill, to steal, to destroy" and cause division by separating us from the Living Body that brings life (Jn. 10:10). He never gives life but only takes it away and is constantly seeking those who will allow selfishness to connect themselves with his agenda.

Yet this should never be the case for those who classify themselves as children of God, because these individuals are routinely described and characterized in the Bible in terms of another bird of prey, the "eagle."

Just as vultures are described by their nature, so is the eagle. First, the eagle has very keen eyesight and is able to spot small prey from miles away with superb vision. Secondly, the vulture only seeks out bodies that have no life and are already dead; however, eagles only prey on and congregate around that which is active and alive because they do not eat dead things. Thirdly, vultures are generally selfish and fight over their prey on the ground, while the eagle catches its prey and then flies high back to the nest to share it with the rest of the family. And lastly, eagles primarily associate and connect with other eagles, those who have the same vision and those who seek after that which is alive.

Thoughts

_____
_____
_____
_____
_____
_____
_____

35

In Christ we serve a Living God who gives us His Living Word (Heb. 4:12), with the Church often being referred to as the Body of Christ (1 Cor. 12:27). The significance of the body (or carcass) here is the fact that it is not designed to be dead or inactive, but a place of unity and life. So, wherever the eagles congregate, it is there that one should also find life because here they are to be like-minded, with one accord, and following the same vision with the ultimate goal of bringing life to others.

So, remove selfishness and selfish ambitions, adjust your sight and catch the vision, and come to the Body as likeminded members (Heb. 10:25). BIRDS OF A FEATHER FLOCK TOGETHER!

February 3
THE SIGNIFICANCE OF REMOVING AN ELEMENT
Read: 1 Thess. 5:19

Being on a military ship at sea requires the crew to basically become self-sustaining because when a casualty or mishap occurs, the ship can't just dial "911" and expect rescue assistance to pull alongside in the form of an ambulance or fire truck to render help. This is why crewmembers are taught valuable casualty and rescue principles and skills that can not only be applied to shipboard living, but applied to life in general.

One of the very first things taught to new personnel reporting to the ship is basic damage control, which is nothing more than implementing emergency control and response in the event of a catastrophe. The crew must know their role and exactly what to do and/or how to respond.

The primary area focused on during damage control training is that of basic firefighting and fire science. Since fires are the most common hazard aboard ships, the crew must demonstrate a basic knowledge of the elements of fire and the agents used to rapidly extinguish the various classes of fire.

A fire is made up of three basic components: "heat, fuel, and oxygen." This is commonly called "The Fire Triangle." Therefore, whenever any one of these elements is removed, the fire can no longer exist and will eventually go out. So, having these three key elements in place is essential for any fire to continue burning.

Thoughts

_____

_____

_____

_____

_____

_____

_____

Well, in our spiritual walk there are also three essential elements that we as believers must learn about and apply in our lives to live victoriously: the Father (our Source and Strength), the Son (the Word), and the Holy Spirit (Spiritual Power), also known as the "Trinity" (1 Jn. 5:7-8).

Many world religions today acknowledge God the Father, acknowledge the Son, and some even acknowledge the Holy Spirit; however, they do not recognize them as being "One" with vain attempts to weaken the awesome power this unified force has in the life of a believer in Christ.

The Trinity is foundational to our belief as Christians. If any one element (or person) of the Trinity is rejected or given lesser importance, the power of God will in turn begin to diminish in that individual's life, or in other words the spiritual fire begins to go out.

February 4
YOU HAVEN'T BEEN RELIEVED YET
Read: Ez. 33:7-8

For those who choose a life of service by way of joining the Armed Forces of the United States of America, Basic Training is generally the entry point.

"Basic Training – often called boot camp – prepares recruits for all elements of service: physical, mental and emotional. It gives service members the basic tools necessary to perform the roles that will be asked of them for the duration of their tour." No matter which branch of service an individual chooses, basic training is usually a very intense experience.

However, although each of the Services has its own training program, with a uniquely tailored curriculum to the specialized nature of its role in the national defense strategy, there is one thing common among the different branches of service.

A portion of the basic training curriculum focuses on teaching new recruits how to stand a proper watch as a sentry or guard on duty. Therefore, all U.S. military service members are required to learn a set of eleven orders known as "The General Orders."

Service members are required to commit these to memory, and be prepared to recite each one verbatim at a moment's notice.

One general order that readily comes to mind for me is general order #5, "To quit my post only when properly relieved." Although this general order is listed as #5, I believe that this is one of the most important aspects of standing a proper watch.

When on post or on watch, service members have the duty and obligation to remain in place and continue to be vigilant until properly relieved by someone else; an individual who is also qualified to fill the position. Even if the

Thoughts

_____
_____
_____
_____
_____
_____
_____
_____

next individual (on-coming watch) arrived over an hour late, it was the current service member's responsibility to remain in place until a relief showed up and a proper turnover was accomplished to ensure that which was been guarded remained protected and safe.

In chapter 33 of the book of Ezekiel, the prophet Ezekiel was commissioned to be and called a "watchman" for the people of Israel who were in Babylonian exile at the time. His charge was to serve the people by proclaiming the Word of the LORD in an effort to encourage repentance and restoration. As believers in Christ, we have a similar responsibility and obligation today (Ez. 33:7-8).

Believers are to proclaim God's Word of Truth to those who oppose themselves in a spirit of love; but, we are to leave the results up to God (1 Cor. 3:6-7). Our job is simply to remain on post and to stand an alert watch. (1 Pet. 5:8-11).

We each have to remain vigilant at all time. Your orders have been issued and passed down through God's Word the Bible "(B - Basic, I - Instructions, B - Before, L - Leaving, E - Earth)," so remain on watch until properly relieved; someone else is counting on you!

February 5
I CAME FOR THEM TOO
Read: James 2:1-4

According to author and theologian Dr. Homer Kent, "Discrimination is one of the great social tensions of our times. All sorts of people band together to exclude others from enjoying their special privileges. Discrimination can be based on race, color, religion, sex, age, wealth, or culture." Therefore, at its root discrimination is nothing more than reverse favoritism; that is showing special treatment to groups or individuals based on many of the distinguishing factors listed above.

In the Bible favoritism is defined as "partiality or respect of persons" (James 2:1, 9), and literally means "to receive a face." For many the face speaks of identity and worth; and when a person is shown favoritism they receive identity and worth in the eyes of some, while many others are excluded and literally have 'no face.'

Thoughts

_____

_____

_____

_____

_____

_____

_____

And as seen throughout history, this can be a great source of conflict. The use of favoritism not only causes division in the home and the work place, but can even become a great source of conflict in the church or assembly of God's people as well.

James addresses this issue when he discussed the reception of a rich man versus a poor man into a local assembly in chapter two of his epistle.

He shows how the rich man is preferred over the poor man because of external factors (appearance) and wealth, rather than looking much deeper.

Unfortunately this is still prevalent in many churches today, with individuals being placed in positions of authority and leadership not based on the spiritual attributes they bring, but on the size of the bank accounts, social status and/or influence.

Individuals are selected and placed in charge of choirs, as worship leaders, while others are elevated to positions as deacons and elders based on talent, great speaking ability, wealth and status, instead of the anointing. It is the anointing that destroys yokes of bondage; not talent, position, or status.

If left unchecked, this selective attitude can also begin to permeate the thinking of congregations of believers as many become judges and restrict who they share the gospel message with, based on the individual's physical appearance and/or social status. Individuals that have a form of godliness, but deny God's true power--"Having a form of godliness, but denying the power thereof: from such turn away" (2 Tim. 3:5, King James Version).

When we show favoritism, we in essence limit God's power to work in the lives of ALL who Christ came for as we focus our attention on a select few (Acts 10:38). The anointing came upon Jesus to bring liberty and freedom to "ALL" who were oppressed by the devil's power, not a select few. Even though Jesus was sent specifically to the Jews, He still demonstrated compassion for all because He had an anointing to LOVE!

Therefore, our treatment and reception of others should not to be based on personal preference, but centered on displaying godliness and LOVE to all of mankind, those who have been created in the image of God, as we are guided by the Holy Spirit and God's powerful Word. Love only sees the Blood, because Jesus came for them too!

"For God loved the world so much that he gave his one and only Son, so that [EVERYONE] who believes in him will not perish but have eternal life" (Jn. 3:16, New Living Translation).

February 6
UNCOVER IT
Read: James 5:16

Thoughts

Growing up there was an old saying: "Boys will be boys," simply meaning that boys are going to do what was considered boy things. And as a young boy, I can remember always wanting to go outside to play because I just hated being cooped up inside when there was so much I could do outside.

However, times have definitely changed with the youth of today, boys and young men in particular, who literally have to be told or forced to go outside or engage in any physical activity, as video games and other electronic devices keep them mesmerized and confined to primarily indoor activity.

When I was growing up being inside wasn't fun at all. For me there was no fun in being trapped inside when I could be riding my bike, climbing a tree, or playing an outside game with friends. And of course as "boys will be boys," injuries often occurred as a result of these outside activities.

Although there was some pain or discomfort associated with these injuries, i.e., scraping a knee, grass-burn to an elbow following a tackle or some other cut to another portion of the body, they were never really serious or life-threatening. And usually after an injury involving a cut or scrape the very first thing I did was run inside to get a Band-Aid or something else to cover up the wound. I don't know why, but even when the wound was small and not really noticeable at that age it just seemed popular to be covered with a few Band-Aids.

After walking around a couple of days full of Band-Aids like a wounded war veteran, my mom would remove the Band-Aid(s), cleanse the wounded area with some type of antiseptic designed to prevent bacteria and infection, and then apply a new Band-Aid, if needed.

The time eventually came that I was told to remove the Band-Aid, even though to me this did not make since. Yet it was absolutely necessary in the healing process to allow the wound to breathe and receive air. Sure enough after a couple of days with the Band-Aid removed, the wound began to rapidly heal.

Though I may not be able to articulate this process in medical terms, there is one thing that I do know; it was uncovering the wound and exposing it to air that accelerated the healing process. Although the Band-Aid offered protection for the wound, at the same time it slowed down the healing process.

There are many believers who have been wounded by sin and past hurts, while holding on to unforgiveness. We don't receive deliverance and healing simply because we refuse to uncover the wound(s) so that they can be exposed for God, the One who has the power to heal them.

Thoughts

_____

_____

_____

_____

_____

_____

_____

_____

If there are areas in your life in need of a touch from God, wounds that have lingered and festered for days, months, and even years; it's time to uncover it. I believe that Bishop T.D. Jakes said it best in his book *Naked and Not Ashamed* when he stated that "We've been afraid to reveal what God longs to heals." God already knows our issues; He's just waiting on us to uncover them and bring them to Him.

February 7

THE LAST OBSTACLE TO YOUR PROMISE
Read: Rom. 15:4

There are many promises in the Bible that are available to us as Christians or believers in Christ. To attain some of these promises there is nothing required of us just by virtue of the fact that we now follow Christ; however, attainment of others require some action on our part.

Many believers today are looking and expecting God to work a miracle on their behalf, whether the miracle is for physical healing, salvation for family members, and most commonly what seems to be that elusive financial blessing. Whatever the desire or need, there is a deep longing for God to move.

However, when days turn into months, and months turn into years without a manifestation of any change in the natural, the tendency for most of us is to complain. It is as this point that we must shift our focus from what we can see and begin to put our complete faith, confidence and trust in the unseen God (Heb. 11:6). Faith is the cornerstone of Christianity and our daily walk as believers in Christ. Let's look to the children of Israel for an example of what not to do when waiting and believing for our promise(s).

God's chosen people, the Israelites, wandered in the Judean wilderness for a period of 40 years for a journey that should have only taken them about 11 days. Can you imagine traveling on foot walking in circles for that long passing by the same waterhole and same landmarks over, and over, and over again?

I'm pretty sure many of us have experienced periods of being in very close proximity with family members over extended periods of time, this can be challenging with individuals getting annoyed with the other seeing the same person day after day. So, here was a great multitude of people seeing each other day after day in a close-knit community, and of course conflicts arose and complaining became the norm.

It was their complaining, in addition to disobedience and lack of faith and trust in God that kept them in a virtual holding pattern, with the promise so very near (Num. 14:2-3). But even in the midst of the unknown, God had a plan (Josh. 5:6).

Oftentimes journeys we are led to and through today are generally a component of God's larger plan and process of transformation; however, this process requires patience and endurance on our part (James 1:3-4). In other words, we must allow God to transform us while in our personal wilderness because even though it may not appear or feel good, it is all working out for our good (Rom. 8:28).

Thoughts

_____
_____
_____
_____
_____
_____
_____

So, re-evaluate your attitude, and more importantly check your gratitude while you are in the process of waiting on your miracle. "Be cheerful no matter what; pray all the time; thank God no matter what happens. This is the way God wants you who belong to Christ Jesus to live" (1 Thess. 5:16-18, The Message). Because the last obstacle to your promise may very well be YOU!

"Some trust in and boast of chariots and some of horses, but we will trust in and boast of the name of the [LORD] our God" (Ps. 20:7, Amplified Bible).

February 8
LITTLE BY LITTLE
Read: Ex. 23:30

There are many processes that occur with end results that appear grand and marvelous to the viewer, but at the same time these are usually occurrences that did not just happen overnight.

The Eiffel Tower, the Great Wall of China, and the Egyptian Pyramids are indeed great spectacles to see; however, these magnificent structures did not just appear overnight; on the contrary, they took multiple years to complete with focused and dedicated effort, and of course a lot of sacrifice.

Finances or money is something that most of us can easily relate to, whether we personally have a lot of it or a little. The amassing of wealth for the "average" person does not occur by happenstance overnight; it normally comes through discipline in finances, saving and investing, and making wise choices over a period of time. This too requires consistent focus and directed action over a period of time.

We can even take a look at a natural occurrence like the process of erosion to also glean a little insight through observing a single drop of rain repeatedly hitting the surface of an area of soil or ground as an example. One drop of rain generally does not cause much change or make a difference; however, several raindrops falling in the same spot over a period of time will cause a noticeable notch or dent in the soil. This happens "little by little" and through repetition.

Thoughts

_____
_____
_____
_____
_____
_____
_____

Similarly, as believers there is a spiritual process that we are to be mindful of in the context of things that generally don't just happening overnight, one in particular is the process of sanctification. Sanctification does not just consist of a bunch of "Do's" and "Don'ts"; for example, not wearing cosmetics or make-up, not going to see movies, the wearing of or not wearing of jewelry. These are all a matter of preference and have nothing to do with an individual's salvation.

To sanctify literally means "to set apart for special use or purpose" (1 Pet. 2:9-10). This is God's plan for every believer; but again, this does not just happen overnight because it is actually a continual process.

Therefore, we should not beat ourselves up just because our walk does not look like that of the next person, or because it may appear that someone else seems to be growing spiritually faster than us. Just as there are no package or group deals with salvation with each of us having to acknowledge our sin, confess our sin, turn away from sin and then receive the grace and forgiveness as we declare Jesus both as Savior and LORD in our lives; sanctification is also an individual process.

Even though there may be areas in our lives that continue to hold us back from being all that we can be in Christ; when we begin to turn these areas over to God while walking in obedience, and allow the transforming power of His Word to work in our lives, "little by little" we will see the things that once held us down like heavy weights and chains begin to erode and eventually disappear.

Therefore, if you are not where you think you should be in Christ today, don't rush the process. Through obedience to God's Word and actually living out what it says, "Little by Little," the old nature will begin to fade as you begin to possess everything that He has promised you!

February 9
NO RESERVATION REQUIRED
Read: 2 Sam. 9

Imagine receiving a phone call with an anonymous unofficial invitation to one of the most prestigious restaurants in town. The location of the restaurant is given to you along with directions, and a date and time for your expected arrival.

Not only is this restaurant known for its status, but it also just happens to be one of the most expensive places to eat in town. Additionally, it is customary for patrons to have and present their confirmed reservation as they enter the restaurant.

Because the voice during the phone call sounded so compelling and convincing, you decide to go ahead and get dressed; however, in the back of your mind the entire time you're preparing yourself, your thoughts keep going back to the

Thoughts

_____
_____
_____
_____
_____
_____
_____

potential cost of the meal, and how you don't even feel worthy enough to enter an establishment of this caliber.

The hour is at hand and you arrive at the restaurant and eventually find yourself at the front desk very fearful that you will be turned away because you still do not possess an official reservation. With a myriad of thoughts now running through your mind you muster up enough strength and courage to walk up to the front desk to state your name, why you are there and that unfortunately you do not have the right credentials for entrance.

After a long pause that seemed like an eternity the guest list is verified, your name is spotted and the receptionist replies, "No reservation required, you may order anything on the menu because your meal is paid in full. Your table is already prepared."

Similarly, there are many of us in the body of Christ today who miss out on God's best for us and the many blessings that He has bestowed simply because of fear as we choose to live beneath our privileges as Kingdom citizens when the door has been opened and the table already prepared.

In 2 Samuel chapter 9, Mephibosheth (the son of Jonathan and grandson of King Saul) was found living in place called Lodebar which literally means "without pasture," or a place of barrenness. Here was the son of royalty living in a barren state, like a beggar; living well beneath his privileges because he did not fully realize who he really was.

One day King David remembered the covenant he made with his dear friend Jonathan and restored Mephibosheth to his rightful place.

Even when we don't clearly understand our place in the Kingdom and/or who we really are; we can find comfort in the fact that the King knows exactly who we are and has gone to considerable effort to prepare a place for us. And what's even more amazing is the fact that our self-imposed limitations and other shortcomings no longer prevent us from entering in (Jn. 14:1-4).

Know who you are today and refuse to live beneath your privileges. The provision that you need can be found in the Father's house. What are you waiting for? Come on in, there's a seat reserved just for you!

Thoughts
_____
_____
_____
_____
_____
_____
_____

February 10
UGLINESS AND BEAUTY ALL IN ONE
Read: Rom. 5:8-10

During a child's early and formative years of school, recess and story time were probably the biggest highlights of the day. As a young child I can remember hearing, and then reading for myself stories that were called fairy tales, which were generally fictional accounts that had a deeper meaning. One story that particularly stood out for me was that of 'The Ugly Duckling.'

In this story a little duckling hatched; however, it did not look like any of its siblings or anyone else in the brood for that matter. As a result, the duckling was often ostracized, treated differently and pretty much considered to be an outcast among the rest of the barnyard animals because of its homely and unattractive appearance.

The duckling continued to make attempts to identify its place on the farm with the rest of the animals; but it was to no available because it just never seemed to fit in anywhere. Then over a period of time a unique transformation began to take place as the duckling began to mature and develop.

To everyone's dismay and unbelief, this once awkward and ugly duckling had developed into a beautiful swan full of grace. It had transitioning from an object of ugliness to something of immense beauty. This is similar to what the cross of Calvary was and also is to us.

Though Western society has often changed the way it is depicted, the cross of Calvary was in essence a symbol of ugliness. During biblical times, the Roman cross was one of the most painful and gruesome forms of punishment ever inflicted upon man; it was a sentence generally imposed upon and reserved for the worst of criminals. And even though He had done nothing wrong, this was the exact punishment levied against Christ, who was completely sinless.

However, as opposed to how we often see them depicted today, the cross of Christ was not overlaid with silver, gold, or precious stones or gems; on the contrary, it was an object of intense pain and suffering overlaid with the blood of the spotless, sinless and unblemished Lamb of God. Think about it, Christ endured shame, pain, and extreme suffering on the cross just for you and me. Now that's love!

Even though the cross of Calvary was full of ugliness; love is what makes it a thing of beauty (Rom. 5:8-10).

Even though the cross demonstrated the hatred and ugliness of man, it was the sacrifice of Christ and His love demonstrated on the cross that transformed it into an object of beauty.

Similarly, though we each may have been stained by the ugliness of sin in our past, and though many of us may even now feel unworthy because of the ugliness of sin in certain areas of our lives today. Through the cross of Calvary and the shed blood of Jesus Christ (a demonstrated act of love and compassion) we become objects of beauty and are now valuable to Him.

Thoughts

_____
_____
_____
_____
_____
_____
_____
_____

February 11
FOLLOW THE INSTRUCTIONS YOU ARE CLOSER THAN YOU THINK
Read: Josh. 6:1-20

There are many stories in the Bible where God's people faced seemingly grand and insurmountable obstacles. The Israelite encounter with the city of Jericho was one of these instances.

In Joshua chapter six despite what he and the people saw in the natural, Joshua (the leader of the tribes of Israel) received a word from the LORD that the city of Jericho was already theirs. "See! I have given Jericho into your hand, its king, and the mighty men of valor (Josh. 6:2, New King James Version).

Taking the city of Jericho appeared to be a formidable task for Joshua and the children of Israel, especially when they looked at the size of obstacle and what stood before them in the natural. In order to take the city, the walls were the first thing that would have to be overcome since the city was surrounded by a retaining wall (outer wall) and an inner wall.

Although the exact dimensions of the walls vary depending on the source, one commentary records that the outer walls of Jericho were approximately 12-15 feet high and the inner walls were approximately 25 feet high and 20 feet thick (wide enough for two chariots to navigate around on top side-by-side). How would the Israelites accomplish this enormous task?

In order to accomplish this mammoth undertaking and achieve guaranteed victory, Joshua and the Israelites had to follow very detailed and specific instructions. This would prove to be a huge test in humility and obedience because the instructions received were very unconventional and did not appear in the natural to be a sure route to victory.

Although the methods were unconventional, at the appointed time the Israelites flawlessly executed the instructions received from their leader Joshua to the letter and as a result the sound produced through the power of unity caused the walls of Jericho to fall flat as God's chosen people took the city! Humility and obedience were absolutely vital to the achievement of this victory.

Oftentimes when circumstances and situations appear to be tough or our obstacles seem insurmountable, God gives us specific instructions through His Word and that small still voice of the Holy Spirit. Yet many times we as believers often disregard these instructions with a deaf ear to God's voice and invariably choose an alternate plan.

Thoughts

_____

_____

_____

_____

_____

_____

_____

Don't allow the obstacles in your life to shift your focus from the victory that is already ahead; you must be strong, courageous, and keep your eyes on the Word and keep the Word inside of you (Heb. 12:2). When you humble yourself, and walk in obedience and do it God's way, the walls that are before you have no other choice but to fall down. Obedience leads to the place of blessing.

What obstacles are you facing? Think about any directions you may have previously received given, humble yourself, take your eyes off of the obstacle, and then follow the instructions no matter how unusual or unconventional they are because your victory and breakthrough is closer than you think!

February 12
USING THE RIGHT WORD
Read: Matt. 12:36-37

Words, words, words! Everywhere you go and all over television, radio, and print media, someone is talking or has an opinion about something—-whether what they are saying is right or wrong. According to one statistic the average person speaks enough words "to fill 20 single-spaced, typewritten pages every day," which is equivalent to producing about two 300-page books a month. But what exactly is being spoken? Every day words are often used without any thought as to what their use will produce.

Let's take the church and religious phrases for example. Over the years many have heard sayings like: "If you take one step, God will take two;" "Cleanliness is next to godliness;" or the all-time favorite "God helps those who help themselves." These all sound nice but are not biblical or found in Scripture, because in essence if we could help ourselves, there would be no real need to depend on God—this is just something to think about.

Phrases like the above and many others have given individuals a false sense of security, believing their words contained power to produce change when in actuality the words being spoken were powerless and truly ineffective. Everything that sounds nice may not necessarily be beneficial to the hearer.

As believers we must learn to speak (or confess) the right thing. I'm not just talking about mere positive confession, but speaking what God has already said about us in His Word and speaking those things that be not as though they already are (Rom. 4:17).

Thoughts

So, what exactly is a confession anyway? Well I'm glad you asked. The Greek word for confession is "Homologeo" which is broken down as follows: homo means "same" and logeo is derived from the word logos with means "to speak, as in a word." Homologeo literally means "to speak or say the same as the Word" or to

_____

_____

_____

_____

_____

_____

_____

47

speak the same as God. Therefore, when we speak (confess) God's Word, we essentially come into agreement with what He has already declared for us and about us.

Knowing the true power of confession and using our words wisely should make us all more "word" conscious. This is not so say that we should write down all of our sentences before we speak to critique the words we intend to use. But what this means is that we should become intimately aware of the principle of sowing and reaping, because the words we sow are exactly what we will reap (Matt. 12:36-37).

Instead of speaking in terms of defeat, fear, doubt, and unbelief, we are to say what God's Word already declares: "I can do everything through Christ, who gives me strength (Phil. 4:13);" "We are more than conquerors (Rom. 8:37);" "With his stripes we are healed (Is. 53:5);" and "No weapon turned against you will succeed. You will silence every voice raised up to accuse you. These benefits are enjoyed by the servants of the LORD; their vindication will come from me. I, the LORD, have spoken (Is. 54:17)!"

Begin to speak words of love, healing, deliverance, and most importantly of faith; then watch your situation turn for the better. Using the right word today can change your life!

February 13
SEED GUARANTEED TO SUCCEED
Read: Gal. 3:29

In a location where one has the opportunity to experience all four seasons of the year, the season of spring is generally one of the most beautiful times of seasonal change. In this season it becomes difficult, if not impossible, for an individual to overlook the wide variety of birds perched and singing, the colorful array of flowers blossoming, and a large majority of individuals putting forth the effort to present well-maintained gardens and lawns.

With weather neither to hot or too cold, spring has always been one of my favorite times of the year. And every time this season rolls around I am reminded of a television commercial that caught my attention and really intrigued me with the claim of the lawn care product being advertised.

Thoughts

_____
_____
_____
_____
_____
_____

The product advertised was for a particular brand of grass seed. This seed was alleged to be so potent the manufacturer promised that it would produce positive results whether the grass seed was used in the sun lighted or shaded locations.

This particular grass seed was endorsed to be so powerful that it was literally "Seed guaranteed

48

to succeed." Think about that for a moment, the manufacturers of this product were so confident in their product that their seed was guaranteed to produce regardless of its surroundings. Wow!

When it really comes down to their purpose, all seeds have an assignment, and that assignment is to produce according to its kind. When a tomato seed is planted, it would be ludicrous for someone to expect an apple, orange, or pear to grow. No! Based on the seed planted the expected product is a tomato seed. A seed will always produce based on its assignment and what it was created for.

So how can we now apply this principle to our lives as believers in Christ?

As believers we each have individual assignments in the body of Christ whether called as pastors, preachers, teachers, evangelists, prophets, missionaries, ministers, deacons, sowers (givers) and the list could go on. The point being made here is that we each have been called to do something for Christ as a part of His body (Rom. 12:4-6).

But even though we each may have different assignments, we all have the same purpose. That purpose being to restore God's glory in the earth by resetting "the Blessing" because of the seed that resides within us. "And if you are Christ's, then you are Abraham's seed, and heirs according to the promise" (Gal. 3:29, New King James Version). We are heirs to "the Blessing" and seeds of Abraham, and seeds are designed to be planted and produce.

Now the unique thing about a seed to be careful considered is the fact that a seed literally must die and be buried before it can produce anything. Therefore, in order for each of us to individually fulfill our assignments and purpose in the Body, we must die to our own will, wants and desires so that we can be fertile enough to accomplish God's greater plan thus bringing Him glory (Jn. 12:24).

In Christ no matter what your surrounding and/or surface may be, when you die to our own will, die to your own way and begin to sow in love, know that you in essence become seed that is guaranteed to succeed!

February 14
NO STRINGS ATTACHED
Read: Rom. 5:8

Thoughts

In our society today, sadly many relationships are based on what an individual can get out of it rather than what he or she has to offer and/or is willing put in. In these instances the love factor is often overlooked or completely forgotten.

So, instead many are motivated by "If you do this, then I'll do that;" you know the old "You scratch my back, then I'll scratch yours" quid pro quo "this for that" mentality. But when the desired response is not received or achieved, an all too familiar phrase readily comes to mind, "What's love got to do with it [anyway]?"

Although the lyrics of the a well-known song performed by a famous female pop singer were written many years ago; these words can still be heard in music, on television, in movies and in conversations about love today, "What's love got to do, Got to do with it?

So, exactly what is this notion of love? The world has its own opinion about love and how love should be expressed; however, this "worldly" view of love is often distorted and far from the Creator's intended purpose and plan.

There are a few Greek words that provide excellent definitions for the word "L-O-V-E":

First, there is "eros" which is passionate, or sensual love - the kind of love that should be expressed between a man and a woman only in the bond of marriage. However, according to the world, this type of love can be expressed by anyone and with anyone no matter the age, marital status, or gender.nSecond, there is "philia or phileo" which describes a general type of love—love expressed to family, friends, a neighbor, or in the community. This is considered to be a "brotherly love," which is where the city of Philadelphia derived its name "The City of Brotherly Love." Third, is "storge" which means "affection," and describes natural affection like that of a parent for their children, or a husband to a wife or vice versa.

All of these each have their respective place and have merit; however, none of them have the ability to truly last because they are all conditional and dependent on how the expressed love is given and/or received. And when any of these become distorted, the end result is a turn towards "unnatural affection," which is a major problem in the world today.

Yet there is a love that will last throughout all eternity, and this love comes with no strings attached—"agape" love. "Agape" literally means "I love you." This word can also be described as a "feeling of being content or holding one in high regard." This is the God kind of love; love that is unconditional and always available to those who are willing to receive it and then distribute the same.

Thoughts

_____
_____
_____
_____
_____
_____
_____

Though the world may ask the question, "What's love got to do with it?" For believers in Christ, love has everything to do with it (Rom. 5:8)!

Love is not a "second-hand" emotion but God's highest priority; love is demonstrated not just in word, but in action and deed (Matt. 22:37-39).

February 15
HIDE-AND-SEEK
Read: Ps. 91:1-2; 5-7

Standard news telecasts today can be very discouraging to watch for the average viewer. With all of the negativity and a people whose hearts have grown cold to righteousness, turning to violence and depravity; there appears to be absolutely nothing positive to highlight and report on. Murder, the loss of multiple lives of military service members, sickness, disease and an unstable world economy seem to pervade. This is definitely enough to make a person want to run away and hide from every problem. However, these events and occurrences should not faze those who have been redeemed by the Blood and have a personal relationship with Jesus Christ.

The childhood game of *Hide-and-Seek* is familiar to most and is "a variant of the game tag, in which a number of players conceal themselves in the environment, to be found by one or more "seekers"." This particular game reminded me of a small creature that I once read about called a rock badger. This animal is fairly small and usually makes his home in the cracks and crevices of rocks and cliffs; hence the name 'rock badger.' In its natural habitat, hiding in the rocky environment is designed as a defense mechanism that not only protects the badger from the elements (i.e., wind, rain, snow, excessive heat, etc.); but also shields it from predators or any potential enemy that may approach.

What a novel concept, the badger goes to the ROCK to hide and then seek protection. Can you imagine how liberating it would be for believers in Christ to grab a hold of this concept? Throughout the Bible Jesus is often referred to and called, "the ROCK" of our salvation. No matter what happens around us, when we find our home, refuge, and resting place in Him; we can be sure of His protection and sustainment.

Though we each individually may seem small in the midst of mass chaos and confusion, our God is Bigger!

Listen to what the Word has to say about this, "Those who live in the shelter of the Most High will find rest in the shadow of the Almighty. This I declare about the LORD: He alone is my refuge, my place of safety; he is my God, and I trust him...Do not be afraid of the terrors of the night, nor the arrow that flies in the day. Do not dread the disease that stalks in darkness, nor the disaster that strikes at midday. Though a thousand fall at your side, though ten thousand are dying around you, these evils will not touch you" (Ps. 91:1-2; 5-7, New Living Translation).

Thoughts

Though violence, pestilence, and disease may be raging around you, there is no need to fear. HIDE under the shadow of God's protection and SEEK Him today, it is then that you will find Him and the deliverance you need!

"When you come looking for me, you'll find me. "Yes, when you get serious about finding

51

me and want it more than anything else, I'll make sure you won't be disappointed" (Jer. 29:13, The Message).

February 16
SEMPER FI
Read: Lam. 3:22-23

If you have ever served in the military, or have been associated with the United States Armed Forces; at some point I'm sure you have heard the phrase "Semper Fi." Though I heard this phrase many times before, it was not until about halfway into my military career that I actually learned the true meaning.

"Semper Fi" is the motto of the United States Marine Corps, and is actually an abbreviated version of the Latin phrase "Semper Fidelis," which simply means "Always Faithful." I truly believe that this term rightly describes the attitude of each Marine as it pertains to their service and completing the mission.

Marines have a reputation for always being focused, determined and ready to get the job done; and I must say that throughout my years of my naval service and having had the benefit of working and serving directly with, and in support of Marines, the phrase "Semper Fi" accurately describes the majority of the Marines that I have encountered and personally known.

It is indeed a powerful testimony to be considered, "Always Faithful;" always being there ready, willing and able to do whatever it takes to get the job done and accomplish the mission. I believe, beyond a shadow of a doubt, that the above Latin phrase accurately describes the heart of a Marine and is something that is instilled during their basic training. They have the innate ability to maintain poise and composure, even in the most intense and demanding situations while remaining true to their code under great pressure.

But even though Marines are known for their single-mindedness towards getting the job done the majority of the time, there is One who can be counted on to get the job done ALL the time; He never waivers and He never fails. He is Jehovah, the LORD God Almighty!

Thoughts

_____
_____
_____
_____
_____
_____
_____

As believers in Christ, if we ever really sat down to think about it, we would truly have to admit that we serve an awesome and faithful God who is intimately aware of our every need. It is this same faithfulness that holds back the hands of the enemy, and keeps us from destruction even when we are unaware of impending danger; He does this by covering us with His mercy, compassion, and love (Lam. 3:22-23).

52

And because our God is so faithful, we do not have to fear the negative reports concerning things that may be going on around us or in the world, because He promises to keep and protect us (Heb. 13:5)!

Even though calamity and confusion may seem to surround you, and temptation may come at every turn; know that God is faithful and He is always there (1 Cor. 10:13).

Are you in an intense struggle or spiritual battle, seemingly with no support or anyway out? Are you tempted to believe the evil and/or negative reports that bombard your mind or constantly flow your way? Choose not to fear and don't lose heart, but instead maintain your poise and composure, and above all else remember that our God knows all, hears all, sees all and has everything under control. Like a Marine standing post, Our God is "SEMPER FI" because He is "ALWAYS FAITHFUL!"

February 17
DO YOU KNOW YOUR RIGHTS?
Read: Jn. 2:1-2

"You have the right to remain silent and refuse to answer questions. Anything you do say may be used against you in a court of law. You have the right to consult an attorney before speaking to the police and to have an attorney present during questioning now or in the future. If you cannot afford an attorney, one will be appointed for you before any questioning if you wish."

If you have ever watched a detective/police television show or movie, I'm sure that you've heard the above words read to those being taken into custody by law enforcement representatives; this is also better known as the "Miranda Rights." The Miranda warning ensures that individuals in police custody accused of allegedly breaking the law understand a couple of primary things concerning their civil rights as a citizen of the United States of America; (1) they do not have to speak to the police if they do not desire to, and (2) they have the right to have legal counsel available by way of the presence of an attorney.

Therefore, it is important that individuals have a clear understanding of what their rights are, because someone who does not know their civil and constitutional rights may inadvertently incriminate themselves by allowing law enforcement representatives to encourage or coerce them to waive their rights by getting them to divulge information that may be detrimental to their case and the charges levied against them.

Thoughts

_____

_____

_____

_____

_____

_____

_____

In these instances a coerced confessions may result in completely innocent people being falsely accused and charged simply because they did not know their rights. But when an attorney is requested or assigned, all of the evidence must first be presented and considered prior to judgment being passed.

In similar fashion and too often as believers in Christ, many times we may actually feel bound in custody to the accuser of the brethren, satan, (Rev. 12:10) who goes all out to get us to waive our rights so that he can falsely accuse us. However, just as we each have individual rights afforded to us as citizens of the United States of America, we also have Kingdom rights as children of the King and an Attorney (an Advocate) who consistently reviews the evidence and argues on our behalf, even when the charges have merit (Jn. 2:1-2).

And just to make it clear, I'm not calling the police or law enforcement representatives the enemy; this is just an analogy being used to establish a point. When a believer yields to the power of sin, the enemy immediately comes to speak condemnation (Matt. 13:19). And if not careful, we will begin to converse with the enemy, as we speak and say what he says about us thereby incriminating ourselves instead of saying what God says according to the rights given to us through His Word.

Knowing and understanding our Kingdom rights will ensure that we do not remain bound to sin and held captive to years of condemnation (Rom. 8:1-4).

As children of the King of Kings and citizens of God's kingdom, we have promises and rights afforded to us just by virtue of who and whose we are.

Whenever the enemy comes to you pointing an accusing finger, refuse to be intimidated and quit waiving your rights (Jn. 8:36).

February 18
THE SEASON BEFORE THE HARVEST
Read: Gen. 8:22

Fresh fruit has always been somewhat of a delicacy for me. If the opportunity presented itself and all I had was fruit available, I could literally enjoy just sitting around eating fresh fruit all day.

Thoughts

_____

_____

_____

_____

_____

_____

_____

And with all the various types of fruit in the world, I would have to say the apple is my favorite. Not just any apple but the green Granny Smith apples with the slightly bitter/ sweet taste. Of course, obtaining these apples come at a cost and at a price.

Therefore, one sure way to have this type of fruit every day would be to have a tree in the backyard with the ability to pick fresh apples right from its branches at leisure. However, for this to occur and for apple trees to grow in any specific location, a process must first take place. The Bible refers to this as "seedtime and harvest." In other words, we cannot expect apples to grow in a place that apple seeds were never planted (Gen. 8:22).

Until apple seeds are first planted, apple trees will not grow. This same principle applies to us as believers in Christ.

Sowing is required before a harvest can be expected. This principle is best known as the "Law of Reciprocity." And though sowing is a prerequisite for a harvest, beyond this we must still make it our purpose to sow the right things in the right way.

According to Ps. 24:1, "the earth is the LORD's, and everything in it. The world and all its people belong to him" (New Living Translation); and as His children everything that belongs to Him is now ours through the process of adoption. However, this does not mean that we should approach God as if He is a spiritual slot machine, whereby we put in a certain amount of money in the offering basket or do a specific deed just to get something in return—-this is sowing with the wrong motives.

The sowing of our finances, of our talents (our gifts), and of our time should be motivated out of love and a right relationship with the Father who desires to give His children the very best (Lk. 12:32).

Whenever a seed is sown, there should be an assignment attached with an expectation of receiving a return, because when seeds are planted in the ground there is an expectation for them to reproduce. But in order for the seed to reproduce, that seed must first die (Jn. 12:24-25).

So as we choose to give of our time, talents, and treasures (resources) for the benefit of others, we in essence become seeds that have died to our own needs, wants and desires; it is then that we are poised to be fruitful and to reproduce. Yet our motives must be pure, and we must also exercise patience as we wait for the manifestation of the harvest.

Always remember that the season before the harvest involves sowing because we are all blessed to be a blessing to others. Make a commitment today to sow in faith and in a spiritual sense choose to give yourself away. This is accomplished through selfless service for others that is motivated through "agape" love (Lk. 6:38).

Thoughts

_____
_____
_____
_____
_____
_____
_____

February 19
IT'S CLOSER THAN YOU THINK
Read: Prov. 13:12

One day while driving on the highway headed to the store to make a few essential purchases for home, you prepare to switch lanes to begin the approach to the exit. Being the cautious and conscientious driver that you are, instinctively you glance up at the rearview mirror and then the side mirror to ensure the path is clear.

Upon glancing into the mirror you observe a very large truck rapidly approaching, and before deciding to play the game of "Chicken" with the massive tonage of high-velocity metal on the move, you remember the words inscribed at the bottom of the mirror, "Objects in mirror are closer than they appear." Although the truck may have seemed to be far away, it was actually closer than it really appeared to be.

With this information in mind, you make the appropriate adjustments and prevent the creation of a potential highway disaster.

In this life we each experience hardships, difficulties, trials and tribulations. And no matter how spiritually mature we think we are, there will come a time that our faith will be challenged. Some of these challenges come as a result of making poor choices and bad decisions in the past like unwise financial investments, entering relationships that should have been avoided, or just living a life of disobedience completely separated from the presence, grace and mercy of God.

But the real kicker comes when we begin to experience challenges that come through no personal fault or actions of our own; things just seem to happen in rapid succession. It is in these times that we must all remember that these particular challenges are never designed to harm us but perfect us, strengthen us, and give us the ability to endure.

However, many times we abort what God is trying to accomplish in our life by attempting to circumvent or come out of a challenge or trial prematurely prior to Him finishing His divine work in us. In other words, we should stop running from the challenge and quit praying that God remove the situation or remove us from the situation so that His perfect work can be completed in us (Phil. 1:6).

"Consider it a sheer gift, friends, when tests and challenges come at you from all sides. You know that under pressure, your faith-life is forced into the open and shows its true colors. So don't try to get out of anything prematurely. Let it do its work so you become mature and well-developed, not deficient in any way" (James 1:2-4, The Message).

Thoughts

_____
_____
_____
_____
_____
_____
_____

With proper focus "We must keep our eyes on Jesus, who leads us and makes our faith complete" [Heb. 12:2, (Contemporary English

Version). Though our breakthrough may seem far away, we are not to get discouraged, but choose to stay the course, and don't make rash or hasty decisions based on our feelings or emotions. When we truly open our eyes, it is then that we realize our victory is really closer than we think!

February 20
ARE YOU LIVING OR SIMPLY EXISTING?
Read: Job 36:11

As believers in Christ, though we may be relegated to live in this world (or the world's system), we are not actually of this world. From the very beginning God had a greater plan for us. God created man in His image and likeness to have fellowship with him (Gen. 1:26-28).

Eden was the initial place for man to experience the uninterrupted presence of God and receipt of the command to be and live blessed. Eden is often depicted as a place of paradise, and was considered to be a place that represented supreme fertility and life. The Hebrew word for Eden is actually translated to mean "delight," which gives a clear understanding of how God initially intended for man to live, IN DELIGHT!

But as we have seen over the years, man has an uncanny knack to mess-up the most beautiful places and the simplest things due to selfishness and attempts to dominate one another instead of taking authority over the earth as commanded, going against God's original plan. It was also due to sin and selfishness that man forfeited everything that pertained to true prosperity for the seduction and lure of attaining knowledge over life in the Garden of Eden (Gen 3:1-7).

As the preceding Scripture demonstrates, satan is subtle and often encourages us to focus on self and getting what we want rather than focusing on what is right and obeying God.

Remember, man was created to be fruitful, multiply, replenish, subdue, and have dominion; but it was sin that aborted God's plan for all mankind; the sin of selfishness at that. So, as a result of disobedience, man was placed in a position of simply existing, rather than truly having life.

We all know the story and end result of the disobedient and selfish actions of the first man and woman; pain in child birth for the woman and the man having to work hard for the rest of his existence (Gen 3:16-19).

Yet there is a remedy. First knowing who we are or better yet knowing whose we are [in Christ]

Thoughts

57

and; secondly, walking in obedience. Christ was our perfect example who came to fulfill the will of the Father, He came to earth for the express purpose of giving.

It was through Jesus' selfless act of obedience that we were left an example to follow and emulate (Eph. 5:1). Jesus was blessed above all others because He gave His all in faithful obedience, and because of this "God elevated him to the place of highest honor and gave him the name above all other names" (Phil. 2:9, New Living Translation). Because of His giving Jesus was positioned to live in the very presence of His Heavenly Father to exist with Him forever throughout all eternity.

When we make it a purpose to really give of our time, talents, and resources to not just keep these to ourselves but to bless others, this is when we move to the place of spiritual prosperity. Refuse to simply exist and remove selfishness while putting your complete faith, confidence, and trust in the Father. Instead of simply existing, choose to give your all and truly live today!

February 21
STARVING WHILE SEATED AT THE TABLE
Read: Matt. 5:6

Imagine going to an extravagant feast with every appetizer, entrée, and dessert you can dream of, available and ready be consumed. However, you refuse to use the utensils designed to allow the meal to be eaten while staring at the food and literally starving. Uneaten food does little for the physical body because the nutrients in the right food are required to maintain a healthy lifestyle and promote continued growth.

This whole concept of starving with resources readily available brought the Greek mythology story of Narcissus to mind.

Narcissus was a very handsome young man, who soon came to realize just how handsome he was. One day while out hunting he came across a pool of water that was intended to be used for the purposes of quenching his thirst. But as he bent down for a drink he noticed his handsome facial features in the water, became enamored and immediately fell in love with his reflection.

Thoughts

_____
_____
_____
_____
_____
_____
_____

Not desiring to disturb the water or the handsome figure that was now seen in it, he eventually died of thirst while admiring his own reflection. The very thing needed to sustain his life and strengthen him for the journey ahead was already available; all he had to do was receive it.

There are many in the body of Christ who experience the "Narcissus syndrome," but on a spiritual level. Week after week church-goers flock into sanctuaries and buildings all over the United States, and around the world. They sit at the feet of anointed men and women who have the Word of God for them at that particular moment. Yet many of us often leave these settings where the power of God and the anointing is flowing, unchanged and unfulfilled.

Instead of receiving the gifts that are set before us and the anointing of the Father within these men and women of God; we tend to focus on ourselves: our problems, our hang-ups, our shortcomings, our sins and end up suffering from spiritual starvation while that which is needed to resolve our issues, satisfy our hunger, provide for our need and/or get us back on track is right before us (Eph. 4:11-12).

These gifts to the body of Christ prepare the table for us through various forms of ministry; however, it is up to us as individuals to look beyond ourselves and false perception, utilize the utensils given to us and then begin to eat.

Of course we have to be mindful of what we are being fed and who is feeding us, because there are many false prophets in the world. This is when we have to rely on the Holy Spirit to give us discernment so that we will have the ability to distinguish the real from the fake, and truth from error.

Have you been starving while seated at the Father's table? Refuse to leave God's presence empty and malnourished; arise, receive the gift, and eat!

"Blessed and fortunate and happy and spiritually prosperous (in that state in which the born-again child of God enjoys His favor and salvation) are those who hunger and thirst for righteousness (uprightness and right standing with God), for they shall be completely satisfied" (Matt. 5:6, Amplified Bible!

February 22
PUT IT TO THE TEST
Read: James 2:16

There's a local news station in the Hampton Roads area of Virginia that airs a weekly consumer awareness segment focused on proving the effectiveness of various products being advertised in the market. This news segment is called "Does It Work?"

Each week consumers have the opportunity to present a product to be actually used during the news segment to determine if the

Thoughts

_____
_____
_____
_____
_____
_____
_____

manufacturer's claim is actually true and if the product really works. Therefore, in order to prove whether or not a product was worthy of the manufacturer's claim, the product had to be tested.

Once a product was tried and tested during the news segment in front of thousands of viewers, there was no doubt in anyone's mind as to whether the manufacturer's claim was valid or not because everyone had the ability to see the product being tested for themselves.

This same principle can be applied to the believer and faith. In order for a believer to know whether or not the Word's (or the Manufacturer's) claim about faith really works, our faith has to be tested and challenged. Sometimes this challenge comes by way of doing or accomplishing things that are way beyond our natural ability or resources.

It's one thing to have faith for healing, but totally another to actually exercised faith with God's healing as the by-product, or to have faith for a financial breakthrough and then being placed in a position to where there is no other alternative but to depend on God to meet the need.

I once heard a friend say, "Untested faith is really not faith at all." In other words, it's real easy to believe God when everything is going well; however, the "rubber meets the road" when trials and circumstances beyond our natural ability and control arise. How we respond often provides a clear indication as to the level of our faith.

However, this is when true faith should begin to manifest because in these instances we have one of two choices either to trust and believe God, or don't--there's no in between. As believers in Christ, our faith must be both alive and active (James 2:26)!

In his first epistle, Peter also reminds us that we are not to be shocked about the tests and trials that come our way, they each have a purpose (1 Pet. 4:12-16)!

God gives us all a measure of faith (Rom. 12:3), but it is entirely up to each of us to individually exercise this faith. So, whenever the unexpected or unexplained happens do not be dismayed, instead put it to the test. Don't put God to the test but rather we must put our faith to the test, believe God, and then watch His awesome power manifest in our lives!

Has your faith been tested or tried lately? Have you been found worthy of the Manufacturer's claim? (Heb. 11:6, The Message)

Thoughts

_____

_____

_____

_____

_____

_____

February 23
DESIGNED ACCORDING TO SPECIFICATION
Read: Ps. 139:14

Engineers are individuals with a very unique and technical skill-set, and are those who usually possess an innate ability to be a visionary; that is being able to design or fabricate something exquisite and detailed out of raw material.

Many of these designs have made it possible for us to enjoy the simple things in life like the invention of the automobile, railroad travel between states, or travel by airplane or boat between continents. These unique designs and various modes of transportation were first seen in the mind of the visionary before actually coming to fruition.

According to one dictionary definition, a "design specification" is comprised of "characteristics of a structure or object that provide for a workable, sustainable, or pleasing creation...any functional thing made by human beings has certain specific details." In other words, every created thing is designed for a specific purpose.

For instance, an airplane is designed to soar through the sky to transport passengers, cargo, or both. If an individual were to connect a cable between the plane and the back of a fairly large truck dragging the plane down the highway or interstate, this would be a considerable abuse of the product based on the manufacturer's specific design and purpose. Similarly, placing a $4000 Bose Surround Sound System in a large pool of water would not only damage the product, but would also create a life-threatening environment for the user of this system.

There is nothing more annoying and frustrating to see than an object designed for a specific purpose being grossly mishandled. Theses misused and abused items never fully reach their intended potential because of the specific actions that contradict and totally disregard the manufacturer's intended design and purpose.

Sadly this is where many of us often find ourselves, using what God the Creator, Designer, and Master Engineer has designed for the wrong purpose. We each have been created with certain design specifications, and instead of following the Manufacturer's instructions for proper use and routine maintenance many of us continue to operate outside of the parameters of the intended design. This often leads to unnecessary suffering (Gen. 1:27-28).

From the very beginning man (mankind) was created and destined for greatness. However, disobedience and disregard to design specifications has caused many of us to live beneath the privileges of Kingdom citizens where we live off of God's economy (the Blessing and faith).

Thoughts

_____
_____
_____
_____
_____
_____
_____

No matter what color of our skin may be, our upbringing or pedigree, or socio-economic status; we each have been designed to prosper, reproduce, fill the earth, and take charge based on the Master's design. Man was created in God's image to exercise Kingdom authority in the earth; however, this requires that we first know what the standards are, that we utilize them, and that we obey.

Don't misuse God's divinely created product, which more specifically speaking is "YOU." So, instead pick-up the Manufacturer's Manual (The Bible) to determine the design specifications for your life today (Ps. 139:13-16)!

February 24
CHOOSE WISELY
Read: Deut. 11:26-28

Growing up as a young child I can remember spending summer days at my grandparent's home inside the city-limits of my hometown in Florida, along with two of my cousins who were fairly close in age to me and were almost like a sister and brother to me.

Every day we would go outside to play various games, sometimes just making up things to do. But around 11 AM, like clockwork, we would pause from our outside activities, sit in front of the television and watch the game show "The Price Is Right," a show that is very familiar to most living or that have lived in the United States with its host Bob Barker at the time.

On this show contestants were randomly selected from the studio audience with the potential to play in one of a variety of games, with the end result of winning a prize. Each game played on the show had one common theme that centered on individual "choice."

Each contestant was required had to make choices that would either cause them to win a prize, or stand the chance of leaving empty-handed. But making the right choice in these games always resulted in the contestant receiving a blessing.

In life there are many choices that we each as individuals have to make every day: should I buy this house, or that house? Should I invest in this stock or company? Should I buy it just because it's on sale or should I save? Should I get married, or remain single? Should I connect myself with this individual, or the next? Each choice comes with consequences that either produce life, or have the potential to create months or even years of unnecessary pain and suffering.

Thoughts
_____
_____
_____
_____
_____
_____
_____

Yet in all the choices that we make each day, the most important choice that anyone can make is the choice to serve, honor and obey God through a personal relationship with Jesus Christ. This choice not only affects the "here and now," but also has eternal effects as well.

Each day we have a choice to either receive life or death, a blessing or a curse according to our actions. This is why it is so important that we not be led by our emotions and our flesh, but that we allow the Holy Spirit to lead and direct us so that we remain on the correct path. When we allow Him to, He will direct us in our everyday choices—choices that lead to eternal rewards.

What choices will you make today? Will you choose the life behind curtain #1 or curtain #2? Choose the curtain that will not leave you empty-handed in this life. In everything that you do make it a purpose to choose wisely so that you can receive the blessing that waits, because making wrong choices can have dire consequences.

"I've brought you today to the crossroads of Blessing and Curse. The Blessing: if you listen obediently to the commandments of GOD, your God, which I command you today. The Curse: if you don't pay attention to the commandments of GOD, your God, but leave the road that I command you today, following other gods of which you know nothing" (Deut. 11:26-28, The Message).

February 25
RELIGION OR RELATIONSHIP
Read: Matthew 6:1-4

There are many individuals in the world today who claim to be spiritual, or attempt to find some connection to God or a god through a "religious" experience. Many even go as far as calling themselves "Christian," when in actuality they are far from it. No, we are not to judge others (Lk. 6:37); however, Jesus stated that we would also be able to identify or know a tree by the fruit it bears (Matt. 7:20).

To be a Christian is nothing more than being "Christ-like," that is demonstrating the very attributes, nature, and character of Jesus Christ Himself. Many movie stars, celebrities, politicians, and world-renown public figures profess spirituality based on religion having a form of godliness, but daily deny God's true power by living half-hearted lifestyles (2 Tim. 3:5). Sadly, this type of mentality has even permeated the church as we know it today.

Thoughts

_____

_____

_____

_____

_____

_____

_____

At its root, religion is nothing more than man's attempt through the flesh to connect with the Spirit of a Holy God. However, this is not what

God is seeking; His desire is simply to have genuine and authentic relationship with His creation mankind.

God is Holy and requires those who profess to be His followers to be holy as well. "For it is written, You shall be holy, for I am holy (1 Pet. 1:16)." Additionally, God is Spirit, which means that any interaction with Him must be done through our spirits to His Spirit and not through the flesh or man-made attempts (Jn. 6:63), "for God is Spirit, so those who worship him must worship in spirit and in truth (Jn. 4:24)."

Religion says "do," relationship says "be," and Christ says "done." In essence, what many call being a "Christian" is nothing more than a religious attempt in the flesh to "do" what appears to be spiritual things in an attempt to gain God's favor, rather than just "being" who God has called us to be because of what Christ has already "done."

What this means today is that we are not required to work to gain salvation (Eph. 2:8-10); however, once salvation is received, we then work as unto the LORD demonstrating our appreciation for what Christ has "done" (Phil. 2:12-13). In other words, we don't work to become or be saved but now work joyfully unto God because we "are" saved.

So, don't confuse religious activity with relationship; instead "be" who God created you to be through a personal relationship with Christ because of what He has already "done." Our motives should be to do good deeds for the purpose of pleasing God, not to gain the approval of man, but to live a life of true holiness. This begs us to examine ourselves and ask the question: "Lord, I am bound by religion or do I have true relationship?"

Take time today to check your motives and examine your heart—-there's no need to pretend because God already knows. Religion or relationship, the choice is entirely up to you (Ps. 139:23).

February 26
THE KEY TO ENJOYING RENEWED STRENGTH
Read: Neh. 8:10

Thoughts

_____

_____

_____

_____

_____

_____

_____

Over the last several years there have been a number of movie box office hits created based on the main character(s) and superheroes of classic comic book and cartoon like Captain America, Green Lantern, Spiderman, X-men, etc., which have brought back old childhood memories for me. Growing up I can remember the excitement and anticipation of waking up on the weekend to enjoy the multitude of Saturday morning cartoons aired each week, even though there were only three major television networks at the time as opposed to the hundreds of channels now available through cable and satellite television.

The cartoon classic *Popeye* was one of my Saturday morning favorites. In this particular cartoon the main character Popeye the sailor, a middle-aged, "one-eyed runt" with disproportionate muscular features and a way of speaking that could be classified as "sailor Ebonics", traveled to various locations as sailors are known to do. And in his travels he frequently engaged in conflicts with a variety of enemies and foes along the journey.

His primary enemy was Bluto who was about three times bigger in size than Popeye. It was this same Bluto that vied for and competed with Popeye over the love and affection of his sweetheart Olive Oyl.

As the struggle between Popeye and Bluto progressed, Popeye's strength would often begin to slowly dissipate. However, it was in this moment of depleted energy that he would open a can of spinach, eat the contents, and gain renewed strength as he overcame his enemy. With his strength and power rejuvenated, Popeye would then sing "I'm strong to the finish 'cause I eats me spinach, I'm Popeye the sailor man," followed by a toot of the corn pipe held snugly in his mouth.

Can you imagine having a Popeye remedy like this capable of renewing our strength when the attacks of the enemy and pressures of life seem to zap us dry? You know, something that would be classified as better than the best energy drink or 5-hour energy shot that are known to eventually wear-off often resulting in individuals coming down from an energy-high leading to the proverbial "crash and burn."

Well, just in case you didn't know it, there is a remedy that is readily available to believers in Christ who are willing to put forth the effort; this remedy involves "joy" and entering God's presence. According to Nehemiah 8:10, "the joy of the LORD is your strength," and according to Ps. 16:11 "in [God's] presence is fullness of joy; at [His] right hand there are pleasures for evermore."

Therefore, since it has been established in God's Word that the joy of the LORD is our strength and in God's presence is fullness of joy, this suggests that when the pressures of daily living seem to weigh us down and literally just drain us both physically and spiritually, our strength can be renewed simply by entering into God's presence the right way; not looking to get but looking to give God what He is rightfully due.

Thoughts

Whenever we begin to worship God the right way, the problems of life become insignificant and seem minute as He is brought to the forefront where He rightfully belongs and is magnified larger than and high above our circumstances and/or our enemies.

_____
_____
_____
_____
_____
_____
_____

February 27
MAYBE YOU NEED TO ADJUST YOUR VISION
Read: Jn. 8:12

If a poll were taken to ask individuals which one of the five senses they would give up if forced to do so, I'm sure for most vision or sight would be the last on their list. Individuals can generally function fairly well without the benefit of taste, smell, touch or hearing; however, when natural vision is taken away, things tend to become a little more difficult.

Many today do not suffer from complete blindness, yet others simply suffer from vision impairments called farsightedness or nearsightedness. Therefore, in order for the farsighted or nearsighted person to see clearly, adjustments to their vision are made either by surgery or through the use of contact lenses and/or by putting on optical lenses (also known as glasses).

Our visual acuity or accuracy is measured in terms of how much light is allowed to pass through the eye. When the correct amount of light is not allowed to enter, this is when our vision becomes impaired. It is clear to see (no pun intended) that light is very important as it pertains to our vision.

Jesus also reminded us of light's importance in Jn. 8:12, "Jesus spoke to the people once more and said, "I am the light of the world. If you follow me, you won't have to walk in darkness, because you will have the light that leads to life"" (New Living Translation).

When our vision is impaired, it would only seem logical for us to take the necessary steps to ensure this condition is corrected. Not only does corrected vision allow us to see more clearly close-up, but it also allows us to see with greater focus and clarity for what is to come ahead in the distance.

So it is with each of us in a spiritual sense, similar adjustments in vision become key and are often very crucial for those who profess faith in Jesus Christ who Himself declared that "He is the Light of the world;" because it is His light that allows us to see more clearly and gives us vision for the future that He has in store.

Thoughts

_____
_____
_____
_____
_____
_____
_____

February 28
WE OVERCOME
Read: Rom. 8:37

The ability to successfully navigate through any school or course of instruction usually requires a considerable amount of effort on the student's part, especially in unfamiliar subjects or curriculum. Therefore, instructors, teachers, and professors develop lesson plans with the purpose of getting students to an expected end beyond what the student can see or even imagine.

Throughout these lesson plans there are generally a number of smaller tests or quizzes administered randomly throughout the course that are designed to gauge the student's level of knowledge and also help reinforce that which was taught and hopefully learned during the process.

However, when an individual does not pay attention during the lessons or take the opportunity to study and read over the material outside of the classroom setting, failure of the test is usually the outcome. And of course, when a test is failed the individual is then required to retake the test until it is successfully passed.

Well, just in case you did not realize it, this same principle applies to believers in a spiritual sense. Many of us go through the same test day after day, week after week, and year after year, simply because we do not pay attention to the lessons taught through the Word of God beforehand.

Just as the tests in school do not come to harm us, the spiritual tests that come our way and that we have to endure are for the purpose of strengthening and building us up in our most holy faith. It is for this very reason that we should not attempt to hastily get out of the tests and trials that come our way, but allow God's work in us to be completed in and through the test, because it is then that a powerful testimony will come forth (James 1:2-4; 1 Pet. 1:6-7).

The preceding Scriptures simply lets us know that trials and tests that we each individually go through have a greater purpose if we could only look pass the temporary pain, aggravation, and suffering. But, this requires that we begin to see God's plan for us in and through the TEST and what it ultimately produces.

To get a better understanding of this, all it takes is simply taking a look at the word "testimony." The first four letters of the word: "TEST," and the fifth letter: "I." In order to get to the letter "I" in the word "testimony," you have to go through the letters "T - E - S - T."

So what does this mean and how can I make spiritual application? I'm glad you have asked; it is simple, in order to have a testimony "I" must first go through the "TEST."

As believers we overcome by our testimony; however, a testimony only comes to fruition only after we have successfully passed and completed the test (Rev. 12:11).

"In everything we have won more than a victory because of Christ who loves us" (Rom. 8:37, Contemporary English Version).

Thoughts

_____

_____

_____

_____

_____

_____

_____

February 29 (Leap Year)
BROKEN FOCUS
Read: James 5:16

My house, my car, my kids, my job, my cat, my dog; the list could go on and on. There are so many things that are potential distracters each day, and if we are not careful, devotional time can easily be replaced with alot of busy activity that does not produced any true spiritual growth.

Well, prayer and meditation are important elements needed for spiritual growth in our daily walk with the LORD. Setting aside quiet time is essential to bringing balance to the many demands that are placed upon us from day-to-day.

Even Jesus separated Himself from the crowds, setting aside time to pray alone to the Father during His earthly ministry. And we are to follow Jesus' example in our journey for Christ-likeness.

The Hebrew word for prayer "hxyX" literally means to "meditate, reflect, devote, or to voice." Prayer allows us to communicate with God - to adore Him, to confess to Him, to express our thanksgiving, and share our concerns and petitions. Prayer in its simplest form is nothing more than a conversation with God.

But when we pray, we should also be mindful of the fact that a conversation is designed to be a two-way exchange; God speaks and reveals more to those who are willing to go beyond just offering prayers and petitions, but are also ready to stop, listen and obey. What really amazes me is the fact that with the billions and billions of people in the world today; when we each individually pray, God is attentive and hears each petition and request that comes up before Him and is ready to respond (1 Pet. 3:12).

Now as it pertains to meditation; meditating for believers in Christ is not sitting on the floor with our legs crossed in a transcendental (or mystical) state. According to Vines Concise Dictionary of the Bible the word for meditate in the Hebrew is "hagah" which basically means to mutter, rehearse, or repeat the Word of God until it becomes real to us. "This word means to think about something in earnest, often with the focus on thinking about future plans and contingencies...speaking to God or oneself in low tones."

Thoughts

_____

_____

_____

_____

_____

_____

_____

It is very clear that prayer is essential to building our faith, because Scripture declares that "... faith cometh by hearing, and hearing by the word of God" (Rom. 10:17, New King James Version). As we consistently speak the Word of God and have it returned in our hearing, our faith is activated, strengthened and stimulated.

If we desire to see circumstances change in the world, in our families, in hour homes and in our individual lives, it must begin with prayer (James 5:16).

As that old saying goes, "Prayer is the key and faith unlocks the door." In other words, we can use our words (prayer), attached to faith to unlock the doors to God's Kingdom to receive everything that is already ours by the righteousness that we achieve through the shed blood of Jesus Christ.

Don't allow busyness to rob you of your Kingdom rights; begin to focus on what really matters.

March 1
ACCEPT NO SUBSTITUTE
Read: Acts 4:11-12

Generic or substitute products have increased in the marketplace over the years. Substitute products are basically considered consumer alternatives to other name-brand products. These products often give the consumer similar benefits from use, but at a reduced cost.

However, these substitutes are rarely perfect, and vary in quality depending on price and availability. Additionally, on occasion, some of these substitute products are linked to potential consumer health risks, as oppose to the benefit of using the real thing which comes at a greater price.

Many world religions accept a broad understanding of God; that is a god who is impersonal and one who does not routinely interact with mankind on any level. Therefore, whenever a personal relationship and commitment to our Heavenly Father through the Son Jesus Christ based on the elements of grace, forgiveness, and love is mentioned, the line of demarcation is instantly drawn.

Religion says it is fine to talk about God as long as there is no personal accountability. This type of thinking has even permeated many "Christian" churches today, and has caused many to substitute works and other religious activity for a personal commitment to Christ, which is the only thing that will truly last.

Thoughts

"For Jesus is the one referred to in the Scriptures, where it says, 'The stone that you builders rejected has now become the cornerstone.' There is salvation in no one else! God has given no other name under heaven by which we must be saved" (Acts 4:11-12, New Living Translation). This means that no one can come to God except through Christ; unfortunately, religion does not answer the mail because it is based on works instead of a relationship that is birth out of love.

Jesus is the anchor of our faith, and without the cross and His sacrifice; anything that an individual does in the name of "religion" is in vain. In our vertical relationship with God and our horizontal relationships with others, real love must be the motivating factor.

Sadly, many today substitute true devotion to God with busy "religious" activity that causes burnout, as they miss out on the blessings that await those who put their complete faith and trust in He who is real, through relationship and not religion. Burnout generally occurs when love is replaced with works in our lives, because love is the fuel that keeps us motivated and keeps us going.

Anything that is placed before the true and living God is considered to be an idol. So, don't be fooled and allow yourself to substitute religion for relationship or physical affection for true love.

Though many substitute or generic products, and pseudo loves may appear to be great and cost less, there is nothing like having the real thing. Jesus is real, and His love is true; so don't allow religious activity in the place of love hinder or separate you. Accept no substitute, instead seek after and pursue the real thing today (Rom. 8:37-39)!

March 2
THE MIRROR SIMPLY REMINDS YOU OF WHO YOU ARE
Read: James 1:22-25

I would venture to say that millions or even billions of people have an encounter with a mirror before leaving home or their place of residence every morning, and probably several more mirror encounters throughout the day.

In our society today with appearance often having high value, the average person would not dare leave home without first taking a look into the mirror to ensure his or her appearance was up to par. Having lived in a home with a wife and four daughters, I know this from experience. Mirrors in our home were an absolute must.

Thoughts

_____
_____
_____
_____
_____
_____
_____

When my daughters were younger the mirror was not really all that important or even a priority. However, as they matured and got older it was interesting to watch them compete for positions in front of the larger mirrors throughout the house to ensure their hair was in place, their clothes were properly adjusted, and that everything else was to their liking.

Some may be saying they don't have an issue with their appearance, so why is this important? I'm glad that you have asked.

Unless an individual is using a circus or carnival-type mirror that alters his or her appearance, mirrors generally provide an accurate representation or reflection of who we really are. Mirrors generally don't reflect your father, mother, sister, brother, aunt, uncle or some other relative or friend (unless you just happen to favor or resemble one of these individuals), instead it reflects that which is positioned directly in front of it—-it provides a reflection of you.

Well, just as we have a natural mirror to check the outer-man, there is another more important mirror that should be routinely gazed upon. This mirror far surpasses anything that the most skilled glass maker could ever craft, one that is designed to check the inner-man. This mirror is the Word of God.

Although this mirror is designed to reflect what is on the inside of us, its influence is so vital that it often affects and changes our outward appearance and actions. Yet sadly, many believers go from day to day, week to week, and even month to month without even gazing into the mirror of God's Word because they are unwilling to confront and/ or change what they see.

This mirror not only shows us who we truly are, but also gives us a glimpse or indication of where adjustments actually need to be made.

No person in their right mind (who had the proper resources available) would knowingly leave a mirror seeing himself or herself dirty, with filthy clothes on, and still choose not to make the necessary adjustments to correct their appearance. The same applies to the believer when it comes to looking into the mirror of God's Word; one generally does not leave a mirror the same way he or she came to it because what we see should prompt us to make a change.

Never forget who you are when seeing yourself in light of God's Word. Put the Word into action through faith that is both active and alive, and then make the necessary adjustments. Have you looked into the Mirror of God's Word today? If not, then don't delay because the Mirror simply reminds YOU
of who YOU really are (James 1:22-25).

Thoughts

_____
_____
_____
_____
_____
_____
_____

March 3

PASSING THE OPEN BOOK TEST

Read: James 1:2-4

For several years I diligently worked towards the completion of a degree that I was finally able to achieve some time ago. However, because of military assignments at sea and various other deployments and duties, this journey took a little longer than anticipated.

Yet even through all of the military demands and some personal setbacks, I continued to press forward and had the opportunity to take some truly amazing and life-changing courses along the way, and I could then actually see a little light at the end of the tunnel.

With most courses of instruction and no matter the program of study there will generally be tests administered by the instructor, teacher, or professor to determine and/or gauge the level of student knowledge that is attained throughout the process of instruction. This usually consists of several smaller quizzes throughout that culminate into a comprehensive test or examination later.

Over the years I've had a few instructors to administer open book tests/exams, meaning that any textbook for that particular course was authorized for used along with any other printed material, (i.e., PowerPoint presentations, articles, etc.) that were also discussed in the class. So I thought to myself, "Surely an open book test can't be all that difficult." Well, I was wrong!

As I took these tests what I began to notice and came to realize was the fact that open book tests actually seemed a bit harder than the standard test in which I was simply required to study for ahead of time, memorize a few concepts, and then respond to questions based on what I had previously read.

But based on this assumption, I must admit, there were a couple of occasions I did not really read or study the material ahead of time as I should have. My mentality at the time was that the books containing all of the answers I needed were right in front of me; therefore, I really did not need to study because I could wing it and just look up the answers quickly during the allotted time.

Well, I am a witness that this type of preparation does not have positive results, especially when strict time limits are imposed causing one to frantically flip through the pages of several course books looking for answers that might have been quickly revealed had I only properly prepared and read ahead of time.

Thoughts

_____

_____

_____

_____

_____

_____

_____

It was through this process of taking open book tests that I later discovered and learned a valuable lesson. With open book tests, as opposed to the standard test, "[individuals] are evaluated on UNDERSTANDING rather than recall and memorization" which is why a little advanced preparation is so essential.

Many today continue to fail the test(s) of life and have to repeat the same course of instruction over and over again simply because we do not seek God for revelation as the open book test is administered. So, use your Open Book (the Bible) the way that God intended because it is only then that you will be able to successfully pass the test; remember, your faith hangs in the balance! Are you preparing for your tests? (1 Pet. 4:12-13)

March 4
SHOW ME MORE THAN LEAVES
Read: Lk. 6:44

One day as Jesus departed a certain city returning to Jerusalem with his disciples, he became hungry from the physical toils of the journey. Along the traveled path He came across a fig tree. This tree was obviously adorned with beautiful green leaves that would invite one to partake of the fruit that should be present, otherwise Jesus and the disciples would not have stopped at this tree.

However, this was not the case for this particular tree. Upon further investigation, though the leaves were in full bloom there was no fruit to be found anywhere on the tree at all. Consequently, Jesus rebuked or cursed the tree because of its barrenness, and that fig tree never produced any fruit again.

"In the morning, as Jesus was returning to Jerusalem, he was hungry, and he noticed a fig tree beside the road. He went over to see if there were any figs, but there were only leaves. Then he said to it, "May you never bear fruit again!" And immediately the fig tree withered up" (Matt. 21:18-19, New Living Translation).

Just as the fig tree in this story was barren and fruitless, this is often an indictment on many of us who classify ourselves as "Christians" who like the fig tree appear to have it all together and are beautiful to the appearance, but when someone approaches to partake of our fruit there is none to be found.

According to Jesus' words in the Gospel of Luke, we will know a tree by the "fruit" it bears or displays, and not by the 'leaves' or outward appearance alone. "You can tell what a tree is like by the fruit it produces" (Lk. 6:44, Contemporary English Version). Each of us as believers in Christ have been challenged and encouraged to display God's Fruit (the Fruit of the Spirit) in our lives each and every day.

Thoughts

_____
_____
_____
_____
_____
_____
_____

Fruit on a tree is indicative of the process of growth and maturation. When a tree has gone through the stages required to reach maturity, real fruit is then manifested that becomes evident and visible to all.

As we begin to grow in the things of God through prayer, study of the Word, fasting, praise & worship, fellowship with other believers, we must also commit to dying to and beginning to release those things that continually weight us down (1 Pet. 5:7). This is when we begin to develop and go through the process of maturation, because it is this process that causes us to produce and bear fruit.

There are many in the world that are hungry for God (the True and Living God), who are looking for spiritual substance from something that is real. As believers we are God's physical representatives and ambassadors in the earth; therefore, it is our duty to display and bear His fruit which is designed to appeal to and attract others. A fruitless tree may be beautiful to the appearance and have the ability to provide shade and covering; however, a tree that is designed to be fruit-bearing that does not produce fruit will never come to the place of reaching its full potential.

When others come to your tree will they benefit from the abundant fruit that is displayed and readily available, or will they only find leaves? I can hear the Spirit of God saying today, "I've seen enough leaves, now it's time to bear real fruit!"

March 5
NO DEPOSIT, NO RETURN
Read: Gal. 6:7

Today, banks and financial institutions are numerous and available all over the world. And where there may not be an actual bank or financial institution readily available, we now have the convenience of Automatic Teller Machines (ATMs) providing the ability for patrons to deposit, withdraw, and complete electronic transfers of available funds at a moment's notice.

However, unless there is some huge mix-up with the "1's" and "0's" of a computer program, large sums of money do not usually just miraculously appear in an individual's account.

Thoughts
_____
_____
_____
_____
_____
_____
_____

In order for a bank customer or patron to make withdrawals or have the ability to transfer money from one account to the next, there must first have been some type of deposit made, whether by the Direct Deposit System (DDS) or the individual physically making the deposit.

This simply means that something first has to be put into an account before anything can be drawn out.

When nothing has been deposited and a withdrawal is attempted with no funds available in the account, the ATM generally spits out a little friendly reminder on a small piece of paper that usually reads "INSUFFICIENT FUNDS." In other words, with no deposits into the account there is absolutely nothing to draw from, no matter how many digits an individual punches into the ATM's key pad with hopes that something will just magically be dispensed.

In the above scenario, the ability to withdraw funds directly coincided with the account owner's prior deposits. Well, this same concept can be applied to our lives as believers in Christ and also to our commitment to the local and universal church.

If we fail to make it a purpose to spend time depositing spiritual things into our lives, when satan comes with the cares and pressures of this world to press us down there will be absolutely nothing in our spiritual bank account to draw from. These deposits begin with a seed and this seed is God's Word; the Word is what prompts us to obey.

A seed is representative of the beginning and the very source of life. Therefore, if we are in need of forgiveness, then begin to sow and deposit seeds of forgiveness; if in need of love begin to sow and deposit love; if in need of healing, begin to speak God's Word while confessing, sowing and depositing healing; if in need of a financial breakthrough and keeping the enemy's hands out of your finances, then honor God with your first according to His Word.

The principle of sowing and reaping can also be applied to many other areas in our lives; the prerequisite, of course, is simply to put forth the effort to sow consistently by making deposits and then apply of a little faith (Heb. 11:6).

It is a well-known fact that whatever we sow is what we will reap (or receive in return) (Gal. 6:7). Therefore, when we are spiritually and physically drained, unable to meet the need around us, and literally just hanging on by a string, it is then that we must ensure we have deposited something of substance to withdraw from in order to uphold and sustain us in the midst of trying times so that we can also be a blessing to others. Remember, with no deposit, there will be no return (Gen. 8:22)!

Thoughts

March 6

CHANGING YOUR DIRECTION
Read: Jn. 16:13

Today's modern technology makes it almost impossible for an individual to get lost while traveling from one location to another. Over

75

the years these new advances have allowed us to evolve from using and depending on a compass to provide relative direction through the use of magnetic poles, to satellite-based hand-held and might I add portable Global Positioning Systems (GPS) that provide precise and pinpoint direction.

Nowadays when an individual gets off course or may just happen to be going in the wrong direction, with the touch of a few buttons he or she can be back on track within a matter of minutes and sometimes even within seconds.

However, the significant thing to note here is the fact that getting back on track does not just happen by osmosis or mental ascent, but requires individual action (James 2:24-26).

The above Scripture simply says that "faith without works is dead." This does not imply that we have to work to receive God's grace and forgiveness when we recognize how far away we are from the truth and standards of His Word; however, it does mean that when we do get on the right path there should be evidence through our actions that His truth is now resident within.

In the United States Navy a ship's course is steered by a helmsman who maintains or controls the helm (also called the ship's wheel that is similar to a car steering wheel) in his or her hands. This individual receives course directions from an officer appointed over him or her; and when directions are given by the one who has been delegated authority to control the ship's movement and course, the helmsman then moves the helm (or wheel) which then signals the rudder of the ship to move to the left or right. But unless the helmsman turns the wheel, the ship will not change its course and will continue in the current direction, even if this direction is not the right way.

There are many in the world today who are going in the wrong direction and traveling along the wrong course, yet they don't even realize it; when all it takes is one turn in the right direction to get back on course.

God has provided each of us directions for the path that we are to follow through His Word (Ps. 119:133). However, when we choose to go in the opposite direction, we tend to come in direct conflict with God's will for our lives and thus get off course. He knows what is best for each of us and has the destination already mapped out (Jer. 29:11), our job is to simply follow His direction and orders (Ps. 37:23).

In other words, God is in charge and the Holy Spirit is our Helmsman who provides us with the instructions needed to remain on course; therefore we must follow the One that has been placed in authority and allow Him to provide the directions needed to not only get us back on track, but also keep us on track so that we can remain on a course with a true heading (Jn. 16:13).

Thoughts

_____
_____
_____
_____
_____
_____
_____

As believers, we have a System afforded to us that is far superior to GPS or any other direction finding system on the market, but we must be willing to use Him and allow Him to do His job. The Holy Spirit is ready to provide the direction we need if we would simply ask, receive and follow through.

March 7
LET IT RAIN
Read: Zech. 10:1

Being a native Floridian, I am very familiar with rainy weather. Growing up in Florida I can remember days of literal torrential downpours with streets being flooded, but then within a matter of minutes, after the rain ceased, the sun shined brightly again. In some instances, the rain would continue to pour even with the sun shining.

When my family and I moved to Hawaii, I was reacquainted with rainy weather again. It has almost been like déjà vu all over again.

Unfortunately for many, rain becomes a nuisance and/or hindrance to outdoor events and activities that are often planned weeks or even months in advance, especially when rain appears unannounced. In many cities rain even has the ability to cause a twenty-minute commute to become a one-hour plus drive home due to a commuter's inability to adjust to the wet road conditions. Though rain may become an obstacle or hindrance in many instances, it is an essential element to the delicate balance of life.

Rain is the primary source of fresh water for many regions of the world, especially in desert regions where water is scarce providing suitable conditions for life. Rain occurs when the atmosphere becomes saturated with water vapors and the temperature of the air changes at the same time. The end result, of course, is precipitation or most of us simply call rain.

To a farmer in a drought, rain is never a hindrance but a blessing beyond measure. Because in order for the seeds that were planted to grow thereby ensuring the success of the farmer's crop, water in the form of rain is needed and absolutely essential. This rain is produced and directly caused by climatic changes in the atmosphere.

As Believers in Christ we too have the unique ability to change and set the atmosphere around us. Therefore, it is important that we continue to set and adjust the atmosphere if we desire the rain of God's Spirit to fall in, over and through our lives. One way to accomplish this is through our words. The right word spoken at the right moment can change a situation for the better;

Thoughts

_____

_____

_____

_____

_____

_____

_____

conversely, the wrong word spoken at the wrong time can be the source of utter chaos and confusion (Prov. 18:21).

Whether we realize it or not, we each have the ability to adjust the atmosphere through our words because they can be the spark that ignites fire on an already volatile situation or the cooling water that puts out a raging fire of conflict while restoring peace.

When our words are rightly spoken we begin to plant seeds of righteousness that not only bring forth fruit and a harvest in our lives, but also in the lives of those we come in contact with on a daily basis. The bottom line is this—our words have an assignment to produce, whether the product is good or bad. Our goal should always be to produce the good. "Rain and snow fall from the sky. But they don't return without watering the earth that produces seeds to plant and grain to eat. That's how it is with my words. They don't return to me without doing everything I send them to do" (Is. 55:10-11, Contemporary English Version).

March 8
YOU ARE NOT EXEMPT
Read: 2 Tim. 3:12

Looking at the news on television, reading a newspaper or a magazine article, there seems to be an overwhelming number of people suffering all over the world who are going through and experiencing what could be classified as "trials and tribulations;" whether physically, psychologically, emotionally or financially, people just seem to be hurting everywhere regardless of title, background or socio-economic status.

But the thing that really may be surprising to most is that many of those in the "suffering" category are classified as "good people," and not those who commit murder, grand theft, or even steal from his or her neighbor. In many instances those in the "suffering" category are even those who profess faith in Jesus Christ.

And as a result of these situations and their unpleasant circumstances, many even begin to question God: Why do good people suffer, and the wicked prosper? Why do I give of my time and resources to the Kingdom of God, yet I don't seem to get ahead? Why did I lose my husband? Why did I lose my wife? Why did I lose my child? Why did I lose my job? Why? Why? Why?

Thoughts

_____
_____
_____
_____
_____
_____

Though the answer may seem a bit simplistic, it can be summed up with one three-letter word: S-I-N.

Even though an individual may not necessarily be actively engaged in a sinful life or lifestyle, the truth of the matter is that we live in a sinful world. Adam's disobedience in the Garden of Eden brought sin into the world, and whether we choose to accept or believe this fact, Adam's one act of rebellion continues to affect us all even today (Rom. 5:12).

And though we are freed from the power of sin in our personal lives by receiving new life through the shed blood of Jesus Christ, the fact remains that we all must continually deal with the after-effects of the original sin that was initiated thousands of years ago. In other words as long as we live, the opportunity to experience struggles is something that we must be mindful of, come to grips with and learn how to endure.

"Anyone who belongs to Christ Jesus and wants to live right will have trouble from others" (2 Tim. 3:12, Contemporary English Version). Yet even in this there is one important fact that we should all take confidence in; and that is the fact that even in our troubles there is hope!

In this life none of us are not exempt from persecution, trials, or tribulations; but when these afflictions do come our way, we should never faint or lose heart. Instead we are to remember that through Jesus Christ we have already overcome, and all we need to do is simply remain under the shelter of the Father's covering and protection because He promises to never leave nor forsake us. "For God has said, "I will never fail you. I will never abandon you" (Heb. 13:5, New Living Translation).

So, even in the midst of our testing, trials and tribulations we must remember to give the Father thanks, not for the trial or affliction but because He is always right there with us in the midst of it all. "Give thanks to the Lord, for he is good! His faithful love endures forever" (Ps. 118:1, New Living Translation).

March 9
KEEP THE FIRE BURNING
Read: Lev. 6:12-13

Based on Old Testament law, the priests during biblical times were the only individuals allowed to present the sacrifice on the altar. And though there were a few different offerings and sacrifices that could be presented, the priests were given specific instructions (according to the law, God's Word) concerning the Burnt Offering and how this particular sacrifice was to be presented.

Thoughts

With this sacrifice the priests were also charged with keeping the fire required for this offering burning at all times.

"Meanwhile, the fire on the altar must be kept burning; it must never go out. Each morning

79

the priest will add fresh wood to the fire and arrange the burnt offering on it. He will then burn the fat of the peace offerings on it. Remember, the fire must be kept burning on the altar at all times. It must never go out" (Lev. 6:12-13, New Living Translation).

Well, a fact that many of us often tend to overlook with regards to who we actually are in Christ is that according to 1 Peter 2:9 as believers we too are considered to be priests. "You are royal priests, a holy nation, God's very own possession. As a result, you can show others the goodness of God, for he called you out of the darkness into his wonderful light" (New Living Translation). Additionally, based on Romans 12:1 we each are also living sacrifices designed to be presented on God's altar each day, "I plead with you to give your bodies to God because of all he has done for you. Let them be a living and holy sacrifice—the kind he will find acceptable. This is truly the way to worship him" (New Living Translation).

Do you see it yet? As priest we each are instructed to keep the fire burning as we continually present ourselves as living sacrifices unto God as we live and walk out His Word every single day; this is one of the greatest forms of worship that any of us can ever present. As we offer and present ourselves to God through prayer, praise & worship, study & meditating in the Word, fasting, and fellowship with other believers in Christ, we keep the fire of the Holy Spirit burning within us; not just for our sake but also for the sake of others.

The Holy Spirit provides the encouragement and guidance that we need each day to endure and to continue strongly on this journey towards perfection (wholeness and completion), victory in Christ and God's Divine Glory (Heb. 10:36).

Remember, it is not the one who quits mid-journey that God uses to reveal Himself through, but "...everyone who endures to the end will be saved" (Matt. 10:22, New Living Translation). Though we may stumble or even fall, it is then that we must choose to draw from the strength that God provides within us to get back up and continue on in the race.

In this season no matter what struggles or challenges may come your way, remember that someone is looking for the character of Christ in you and are in need of your light (that fire burning deep inside). So, hold your torch up high, keep the fire burning, and refuse to let it go out (Matt. 5:14-16)!

Thoughts
_____
_____
_____
_____
_____
_____
_____

March 10
HAVING THE RIGHT CONNECTION
Read: Jn. 15:4-7

The invention of computers and creation of computer networks have forever changed the way many conduct business and has also changed the world in general, especially with the availability and ready access of the World-Wide Web and the Internet.

A basic computer network is nothing more than a group of interconnected computers with protocols (or languages) that allow each to communicate back and forth. Within any network there are various physical components such as hubs, switches, bridges, routers, etc., that also play important roles in providing the pathway for network connectivity.

Networks are defined by typologies which are basically classifications of the functional relationships that exist among the various components that make up a particular network; in other words the typology describes how components are connected.

One well-known and widely used typology is that of the Client-Server design or Star typology. "Client-server describes the relationship between two computer programs in which one program, the client program, makes a service request to another, the server program."

Although none of us are computers or machines, no matter how smart we are or think we are; we too as believers are to have a client-server relationship with our Heavenly Father with us of course being the "client" and God being the "Server" that contains all-knowledge. And whenever we need access to what has been promised to each of us in His Word, all we need to do is send a request (prayer) to the Father and then wait for Him to answer (Jn. 16:23-27).

However, in order to achieve this we must first have the right connection; but herein is the problem for many of us because too often we attempt to use the wrong protocol while making bad choices and improper connections. We connect ourselves with individuals who are going in a completely opposite direction than us and end up straying away from the path of righteousness that God intends for His family.

Rather than connecting to the Server, these individuals attempt to set themselves up as a stand-alone network completely separated from the True Source so that they can just do whatever they please. The Apostle Paul warns us about making the wrong connects in one of his epistles (2 Cor. 6:14-18).

So don't be among the many today that suffer needlessly simply because they attempt to establish a connection using the wrong protocol and password. To experience the benefits and obtain access to the blessings of God, we must sever bad connections while establishing and maintaining a connection to the one true Source. The protocol in our spiritual network is "Prayer" and the password is "J-E-S-U-S;" when this combination is used, it gives us direct

Thoughts

_____
_____
_____
_____
_____
_____
_____

81

access to the Server and everything we need, thus allowing us to establish and maintain the right connection (Jn. 15:4-7).

March 11
GIVING HONOR TO HIM
Read: Col. 2:14-15

Whether a person admits it or not, deep within everyone has a deep-seated desire to be recognized, celebrated and/or praised for their work or personal accomplishments. For many there is nothing more fulfilling than hearing their name announced or published for a "job well done."

These accolades often come by way of letters of appreciation or commendation; or in the military by the award of decorations and medals. Whatever the case, the individual's accomplishments are highlighted and brought to the forefront.

Now, the type of award or decoration presented to an individual is generally based on the merits of his or her actions; the more demanding, difficult, or heroic the action, the higher the recognition. So, let's take a look at this concept from the aspect of our praise and worship; more specifically our praise and worship towards our God.

The word "praise" comes from the Latin word pretium, which means "price," or "value," and is generally defined as an ascription of value or worth. The word "worship" comes from the old term "woerthschipe" or "worthship" which basically means to assign worth to someone based on their authority and worth.

When we praise someone we literally ascribe value to the individual by letting them know they are worth something and are worthy to be celebrated. Therefore, our praise to God should be our expression of His value and worth to us. One way to accomplish this is to praise by commending Him.

The word commend means "to entrust for care or preservation" or "to recommend as worthy of confidence or notice." When we praise God by commendation we acknowledge that we are willing to follow His lead and direction as given to us through His Word, and have entrusted ourselves to His care no matter what comes our way (Prov. 3:5-6).

Thoughts

_____
_____
_____
_____
_____
_____

This means that even though we don't always get the things we want in life, our God can still be relied upon to supply every one of our needs (Phil. 4:19).

God not only meets our daily need, He met our greatest need of all by sending His one and only unique Son to bring salvation to the world (Gal. 4:4-5). For this act alone God deserves our highest praise!

Just in case you did not know it, God does not need our praise or worship to be God; He simply deserves it just because He is worthy to receive it. And whether we choose to praise Him or not, He will eventually receive the praise that is due to Him (Lk. 19:40). Don't allow a rock to take your place, in offering a sacrifice of praise to God for yourself.

Though no earthly award or medal could truly compensate for what our Lord (Jesus Christ, God incarnate) has done, I believe He deserves a Purple Heart for being wounded for us (Is. 53:5), the Bronze Star for His valiant triumph over the devil (Col. 2:14-15), and most importantly He deserves the highest decoration of all, the Medal of Honor (Jn. 5:23), just for being God all by Himself. Because of His sacrifice He is worthy of all glory, all praise, and all HONOR!

March 12
SIGNED, SEALED, DELIVERED...HE'S YOURS
Read: Eph. 1:13

The United States Postal Service and many commercial delivery services ship and deliver packages all over the world, especially during the Christmas holiday period, to well-known locations as well as remote locations in places that many of us have never heard of or even seen on a map of the globe.

Today there are many delivery options available to the customer. Packages can reach their destination anywhere from three to five days and then there's even the option of overnight shipment and delivery of documents and packages, with a promise of guaranteed delivery and receipt on the distant end.

With only a signature and the right payment, overnight delivery, with confirmation of receipt, can be guaranteed; but this bonus comes with an added price.

When a person accepts Jesus Christ into his or her heart according to Romans 10:9-10, although this act of faith is free and guarantees salvation it still came with a price; that which was required and delivered to redeem mankind came at a price that far exceeded the cost of mere silver or gold; Jesus gave His very life (1 Pet. 1:18-19).

Thoughts

In other words our salvation was purchased, paid for and signed for with the very blood of Jesus Christ; therefore, we have been guaranteed the gift of the Holy Spirit and we are now sealed. "In whom ye also trusted, after that ye heard

83

the word of truth, the gospel of your salvation: in whom also after that ye believed, ye were sealed with that Holy Spirit of promise" (Eph. 1:13, New King James Version).

Yet because so many believers do not truly understand this fact, many tend to live beneath their privileges as sons and daughters of God the Father who is the Most High God and Owner of everything. The Holy Spirit comes to not only empower us for service, but also to show us who we truly are and what we now have the ability to possess (Jn. 14:26). In other words the Holy Spirit comes to remind us of who we are based upon what God has already declared about us in His Word (Deu. 28:9-14).

Again, God has already defined who we are to be in His Word; the Holy Spirit is simply given to gently remind us of who we are when we begin to doubt what is written in the Word (Prov. 30:5), are tempted to walk in fear instead of faith (2 Tim. 1:7), allow negative thoughts to take root in our minds instead of casting them down (2 Cor. 10:5), and/or start declaring the wrong things about ourselves instead of speaking life (Prov. 18:21). We have been created to rule and reign, not just here in the earth; but to rule and reign over our temples (bodies), through God's Spirit, in every area of our lives.

Once we are sealed, the blessing of Abraham now belongs to us, and everything that comes with it (Gal. 3:14); therefore, delivery confirmation is available to all who believe and receive by faith.

The gift and promise of the Holy Spirit has been signed, sealed, and delivered; therefore, the Blessing is yours. Refuse to live beneath your privileges, so get and begin to use your inheritance today!

March 13
THE GREAT EXCHANGE
Read: Is. 61:3

Over the years there have been an number of television game shows that have offered contestants an opportunity to win a variety of gifts and prizes. From appliances, to boats, cars, all-expense paid vacations, and even very large sums of money; whatever the prize, people went out of their way for an opportunity to win.

Thoughts

_____

_____

_____

_____

_____

_____

_____

Some of these game shows even offered contestants the opportunity to exchange current winnings to risk losing what they had already earned with hopes of being able to obtain even more by selecting what was under the next box or whatever was behind the next door or curtain. But, many times this gamble was just that, a gamble, and based on the individual's choice everything was lost.

In the big scheme of things, life itself came be view from the perspective of being a game. Because in life there are also many choices to make: where should I live, what house should I invest in, what car should I drive, should I go left or right? These choices all have consequences.

In the game of life there are also eternal choices that we each must make, choices that will have lasting effects on our future, what we are able to obtain, and the quality of life that we will have. Of course in any game the objective is to win.

And though in earthly games an exchange has the ability to cause us to lose, in Christ this is not the case because His exchange policy, even though we may have to lose some things (Phil. 3:8), results in a win-win situation. In other words, those who have been washed in the blood of Jesus Christ always come out on the winning side no matter how bad a situation may appear to be.

You see, at one point in time many of us were separated from the Grand prize by a veil or curtain in the Temple that kept us as individuals away from the presence of God. But when Christ came on the scene to offer Himself once and for all for our sins, the veil that once separated us from direct access to God was removed and we no longer had to wonder if we were making the right choice in selecting what was on the other side (Matt. 27:51).

We no longer have to guess what's behind curtain #1, because God has revealed Himself through the sacrifice of Christ and made access to the life that He now offers is available to all who are willing to receive it. However, it still comes down to a matter of choice.

When we make the right choices today not only do we have the ability to exchange death for eternal life, but we can also exchange sickness for health and wholeness, lack for prosperity and abundance, chaos and confusion for peace and rest in His presence, and exchange our sadness for His joy and strength (Is. 61:3).

No game show or department store has a better exchange policy than that offered to those who profess faith in Christ. So to make it more personal, you don't have to settle for sickness, lack, anxiety, poverty or despair in your life today when God has given you the opportunity to exchange your weakness for His strength as you give all of your burdens and cares over to Him.

Thoughts

March 14

RELEASE THE POWER!
Read: Acts 1:8

The United States Navy aircraft carrier is truly an awesome sight to see, especially when it has a full complement of various aircraft onboard.

Having been stationed on a couple of aircraft carriers before, the other thing that really amazed me was how all of this steel was able to float on water with even more steel resting on the flight deck and hangar bays.

Over the years I've had the opportunity to observe a number of aircraft during underway periods and have even seen a few fighter jets break the sound barrier. There's nothing like seeing the cloud that forms around the jet as it prepares to sound barrier and the thunderous after effects once the barrier has been broken.

Watching jets and airplanes soar through the sky is an amazing sight, especially when considering the mere weight of many of the larger planes as they seem to effortlessly stream through the air. One plane in particular is the B-52 Bomber.

Since the mid 1950's this aircraft has been used in many military engagements around the world. At a weight of approximately "265,000 pounds, length of over 159 ft. and a wingspan of 185 ft.," the B-52 is undoubtedly an awesome and menacing sight for the enemy to see coming their way.

And though the size of the B-52 may strike fear in the enemy's camp, it is the armament of the aircraft that actually makes it so powerful and causes it to literally leave an impact (no pun intended).

So, in actuality, it is not the plane's appearance but what it carries that makes it so powerful. Yet it is not until the power from the plane is actually released that the enemy begins to feel its full effect.

There are many believers who may be experiencing trials, troubles, and tribulations simply due to the fact they are a threat to the enemy (the devil) and didn't even realize it. However, we often tend to devalue our effectiveness by what we see on the outside and the external stimuli that comes up against us, when inside there is a lion trapped, poised, and ready to roar.

According to 2 Cor. 4:7, "We now have this light shining in our hearts, but we ourselves are like fragile clay jars containing this great treasure. This makes it clear that our great power is from God, not from ourselves (New Living Translation)."

The treasure that resides within each of us (these earthen vessels or jars of clay), those who are Blood-bought, Spirit-filled redeemed believers in Christ, is not only the authority of the Word but also the power of the Holy Spirit (Acts 1:8).

Thoughts

_____
_____
_____
_____
_____
_____
_____

It is the power of the Holy Spirit in the life of the believer that threatens the enemy and brings about change in the lives that we come in contact with each day. However, like the B-52 Bomber, no matter how powerful or even powerless we may appear to be on the outside, the power from within does not affect a change in anything around us until it is actually released.

March 15
WHY DID YOU TAKE IT?
Read: Jn. 5:6

Observing children (or siblings in particular) is an interesting sight. That is observing how they play, talk, and interact with one another. And of course, younger siblings are often known for going into the room of their older brother's and/or sister's to borrow items without obtaining prior permission. When the older sibling realizes an item is missing from his or her room; a search and recovery mission to reclaim the long-lost item begins.

When the younger sibling who borrowed the item realizes it is no longer in his or her possession with the older sibling reclaiming it, they generally have the nerve or audacity to ask the rightful owner, "Why did you take it?" The owner's (older sibling's) usual response is: "Because it's mine and it belongs to me!"

Many believers suffer at the hand of sickness, infirmities, and diseases because we take upon us that which rightfully belongs to someone else. We were never designed to carry these things around; however, due to the fall of Adam in the Garden, unfortunately the preceding came upon mankind.

In chapter five of the book of John, we find a man who had become comfortable in his lameness for over 38 years, daily laying on his bed of affliction because no one would help him get to the place where healing was available (Jn. 5:6).

But no matter how trapped we may think we are in our sickness, infirmity and/or sin, God has the power to deliver us, if we choose to apply a little faith and not make excuses for our condition and/or where we are at. This simply implies we have to stop making excuses when the answer for our issue is already found in God's Word.

In verse eight of John chapter five, Jesus told the lame man to pick-up his bed of affliction and start walking. The taking up of his bed was intended to be a clear indicator to everyone around he had been healed.

Thoughts

I believe Jesus gives each one of us the very same instructions. Simply stated, Jesus came to take from mankind that which did not rightfully belong to us anyway (Is. 53:5-6)!

_____
_____
_____
_____
_____
_____
_____

March 16
EXPECT HIM TO MOVE
Read: 1 Jn. 5:14-15

There's a story that I once read about a small Midwestern town that was in the midst of a very severe drought. The skies were clear and there had been no rain for months with none predicted in the foreseeable future.

Not knowing what to do and searching for solutions, as one community the residents decided to gather all of the clergy (spiritual leaders) in town together to pray and ask God for rain so that the terrible drought being experienced could be brought to an end. However, when all the residents assembled together with the clergy to pray, as they looked out over the crowd there was only one young girl who came with an umbrella.

Everyone looked at the innocent child but began to question why she would bring an umbrella when there was no rain in sight? For her the response was clear; not only did she believe that God would hear their collective prayers, but she also expected Him to respond.

This is a prime example of the confidence and type of faith that God expects us to have when we come to Him in prayer (Heb. 4:16). But first, we must be specific in our request. As Believers, we must learn to move away from generalities, and target our prayers to specific areas and things. This is one reason why many misdirected prayers often go unanswered; we must be specific in our request(s).

For a great example we have to look no further than the prophet Elijah in the Old Testament of the Bible. Not only did Elijah pray for God to shut up the skies to prevent rain from falling; but at the appointed time, he also prayed that God would once again open up the heavens to allow the water from above to pour down in abundance.

In each instance, Elijah's prayer was specific and God answered every time.

"The prayer of a person living right with God is something powerful to be reckoned with. Elijah, for instance, human just like us, prayed hard that it wouldn't rain, and it didn't-not a drop for three and a half years. Then he prayed that it would rain, and it did. The showers came and everything started growing again" (James 5:16, The Message). The New Living Translation of the Bible states it this way, "The earnest prayer of a righteous person has great power and produces wonderful results."

Thoughts

_____

_____

_____

_____

_____

_____

What prayer(s) are you believing God for? Be specific in your request, attach your faith, expect God to move, and the rain of blessings will come! Where's your umbrella?

"We are certain that God will hear our prayers when we ask for what pleases him. And if we know that God listens when we pray, we are sure that our prayers have already been answered" (1 Jn. 5:14-15, Contemporary English Version).

March 17
DEAD MEN DON'T FIGHT
Read: Gal. 2:20

The concept of "new birth," in a spiritual sense, may seem to be a paradox (something that is seemingly contradictory) for many; because in order to actually receive new life in Christ we must first die. For many this is a very tough pill to swallow; however, this is one of the prerequisites to the abundant living promised to those who profess the name of Christ and a life of service. Jesus said, "I came that they may have and enjoy life, and have it in abundance (to the full, till it overflows) (Jn. 10:10, Amplified Bible).

Yet there are many who continue to struggle day after day simply because we vainly attempt to accomplish in the flesh that which can only be completed in, through and with God's Spirit as we try to fight battles that were never intended for us to fight and then also (Gal. 3:3).

In all of my years of living, I have yet to see a boxing match featuring a heavyweight contender against a literal dead man. Why? Because based on natural law, a dead man does not have the ability to fight back or even move on his or her own.

Can you imagine what it would sound like for an announcer to introduce boxing contenders for a match of this type? "Good evening ladies and gentlemen, we have a great spectacle for you tonight; a match that you will soon not forget. Introducing to my right, hailing all the way from state of Illinois representing and representing the Southside of Chicago the boxing machine Windbreaker. And now to my left, a man who needs no introduction all the way from a place of no physical return dressed in all black representing what used to be; Sleepy Hallow."

A match of this type would be absolutely absurd, because dead men just don't fight. This is why our death as believers in Christ in a spiritual sense is so important. When we die we become just like the dead person described above; emptied, hallowed out and ready to be filled, not with human effort or things of the flesh but with God's Spirit that enables us to move the correct way.

Thoughts

The Apostle Paul understood this fact and summed it up best when he said, "Indeed, I have been crucified with Christ. My ego is no longer central. It is no longer important that I appear righteous before you or have your good opinion, and I am no longer driven to impress

89

God. Christ lives in me. The life you see me living is not "mine," but it is lived by faith in the Son of God, who loved me and gave himself for me. I am not going to go back on that" (Gal. 2:20, The Message).

In Christ we must first literally die in order to truly live and be positioned to serve. In other words, our life in the spirit is actually produced by our death to the flesh and our old nature. This means that we relinquish the reigns or controls in our lives and then allow the Holy Spirit to be our guide as He controls and moves us.

When we give our problems and issues over to the LORD and stop trying to work them out ourselves fighting in the flesh, this is when new light begins to shine and new life subsequently emerges in the situation. That is when we die to our flesh and then allow the Holy Spirit to bring about new life that also allows us to sacrificially serve.

March 18
A WHOLE LOT OF SHAKIN' GOING ON
Read: Heb. 12:27

As technology and ingenuity continues to advance, so has our convenience. In particular great strides have been made in the area of transportation. Early travel in the United States must have been an interesting experience, especially in the Midwest frontier.

With no cars or automobiles around, the primary method or mode of travel was either to walk, ride horse-back with a saddle, or use a horse-drawn carriage. Of course there were no neatly blackened asphalt or paved roads way back when with many if not most of the roadways being undeveloped. So I'm sure that travel along these uneven paths and roadways must have provided for a very uncomfortable and bumpy commute for the traveler, with a lot of ups & downs and shaking along the journey.

And though the carriage and travelers were often shaken and thrown about because of the uneven, bumpy and unpaved roads, the cart or carriage itself did not just break-up and fall apart because the spokes of the wheel provided a strength and stability that allowed everything to remain together.

Thoughts

_____

_____

_____

_____

_____

_____

_____

In chapter one of the book of Ezekiel, the prophet discusses and describes another wheel that provides great strength and stability in the midst of bumpy and trying times, "a wheel in the middle of a wheel"(Ez. 1:16, King James Version)." For those who have been purchased by the blood of Christ (Eph.1:7) and are heirs according to the promise (Gal. 3:29), God is our wheel and Jesus is the 'Wheel in the middle of the Wheel,' or the spokes that hold our lives together no matter how bumpy or rough the road of life may be.

Almost every day, fear is perpetuated by way of the news that attempts to shake us by amplifying the spread of another disease of epic proportion, the threat and constant focus on wars in various lands, natural disasters of all kind and the devastation left behind, and a constant reminder of an unstable economy. But those who look not to what is seen but unto the unseen (2 Cor. 4:18), putting their trust and faith in Christ will not be shaken. When chaos is all around and there seems to be no hope in sight, Jesus, the Wheel in the middle of the Wheel holds it all together.

When the storm clouds of life come and strong winds begin to blow, don't be afraid. And when the shaking comes we are not to be dismayed, because we have an Anchor in Jesus Christ, the Rock of our salvation who is unmovable.

As the wheels of life turn we can be confident in the fact that our God does not change (Heb. 13:8) and though shaking may come, He will not allow us to be destroyed but will provide a sure foundation of stability in the midst of it all. When the shaking is all said and done, will you still be able to stand (Heb. 12:25-27)?

March 19
IT'S BEEN FIXED
Read: 1 Cor. 15:57

A fight promoter is looking to promote one last grand event for an aging boxer. He looks for a worthy opponent, but at the same time an opponent willing to take it a little easy on the former champ to that his career can be closed in style. An opponent is selected, radio and television commercials are aired, and flyers are posted everywhere to announce this event. And with great anticipation, boxing fans all over the world eagerly await the match.

The night of the fight finally arrives, the bell rings, and the opponents meet at center-ring toe-to-toe with each giving a barrage of punches; uppercuts, jabs, left and right hooks, and the works. Blow-for-blow punches are exchanged; however, in a strange turn of events, the former champ begins to let his guard down thereby allowing the opponent to gain the upper-hand. The bell rings with both boxers complying and going to their respective corners. The fight promoter is bewildered; "How can this be happening? I've paid a high price to ensure that would be ours.

While seated in his corner, the former champ is approached and asked a very pointed question,

Thoughts

_____
_____
_____
_____
_____
_____
_____
_____

"How can you be losing a fight that has already been fixed?" All you have to do is make an effort to fight; you're guaranteed to win!

Hearing the words of the promoter sparks something on the inside of the champ as he begins to dig deep within for strength. The former champ actually starts believing that he can be victorious, takes the lead in the fight and actually wins. He just needed to do his part, and that part was to take a stand and fight.

Though many of us may not be in an actual physical fight like the champ; we all have a spiritual adversary who desires to defeat us through various devices, challenging our faith each and every day. This adversary does not play fair, and has no intentions of taking it easy on us. We are in a spiritual war and we must keep our guard up; however, there is some consolation – THE FIGHT HAS BEEN FIXED AND WE WIN!

God paid a very high price to ensure that we would be victorious by sending His only Son (Jesus the Christ—the Anointed One) to earth to win the battle in advance (1 Cor. 6:20; Col. 1:13-15).

Therefore, it is also important that we prepare for battle, not in our own strength and ability but in the Lord's power and might (Eph. 6:10). The Apostle Paul encourages us to "Fight the good fight for the true faith. Hold tightly to the eternal life to which God has called you, which you have confessed so well before many witnesses" (1 Tim. 6:12, New Living Translation). This simply means that we must keep faith in God and do our part. Just as a reminder, the fight has been fixed--WE WIN!

Are you feeling defeated as if the enemy has you trapped against the ropes? If this is you the Lord is asking one simple question today: How can you be losing a fight that's already fixed? When you get knocked down just get back up and keep pressing forward; we have the victory through our Lord and Savior Jesus Christ (1 Cor. 15:57)!

March 20
THE UNBEATEN PATH
Read: Matt. 7:14

Thoughts
_____
_____
_____
_____
_____
_____
_____

A youth group goes on a camping trip with some in the group deciding to explore the vast expanse of forest that awaited the young adventurers. As they traveled along over rugged terrain and through dense brush, some made mental notes of specific landmarks to ensure the journey back to camp could be found with ease.

On the return trip, some of nature's landmarks had shifted or were no longer present. As they circled around trying to find their bearing and remember from which direction they came, many began to get thirsty and hungry. But here's the irony, the campground was actually only a few hundred yards away.

Directly in front of them were two separate and distinct paths, one appeared to have been unused for months with rocks and a few obstacles along the way. The other path is one that had no obstructions with a visible trail that appeared to have been used by many.

Discussion began in the group with everyone asking, which path should we take? After a little discussion, the group decides to take the well-trodden and unobstructed path. However, to their surprise the journey back to camp took over five hours, an extremely longer journey than anticipated.

Upon returning to the campgrounds one of the adventurous youth asked a camp leader about the two different paths. The leader replied "if you would have taken the unbeaten path, though a bit more difficult to navigate, your trip back to camp would have taken less than twenty minutes. But because you decide to take the easy road, the time of your journey increased. The seemingly established path has been used over the years by many others who found themselves lost; they also experienced the same fate as yours. When in actuality the unbeaten path provided direct, ready access to the sustenance and provision that lost campers sought after."

Many times believers, like the lost campers, tend to join the crowd and take the easy road instead of utilizing the path that leads to true sustenance and life. "Sometimes what seems right is really a road to death" (Prov. 16:25, Contemporary English Version). When circumstances get tough we often choose the path of least resistance, when the promise is generally connected to our ability to endure. "Staying with it—that's what God requires. Stay with it to the end. You won't be sorry, and you'll be saved" (Matt. 24:13, The Message).

Though the easy road may not bring actual physical death, it often delays the blessings that God has in store for us. What appears to be a shortcut to blessings and life may actually be the total opposite.

"Don't look for shortcuts to God. The market is flooded with surefire, easygoing formulas for a successful life that can be practiced in your spare time. Don't fall for that stuff, even though crowds of people do.
The way to life-to God!-is vigorous and requires total attention" (Matt. 7:14, The Message).

Thoughts

The paths of life and death are set before us each day. "Which path will you take?" Though the journey at times may be rugged and require endurance, hold fast to faith and choose the path that leads to life (Matt. 7:14)!

_____

_____

_____

_____

_____

_____

_____

March 21

QUIT DRIVING ON EMPTY
Read: Eph. 5:18

Over the years and throughout the centuries modes of transportation have drastically changed. Whether travel was by foot, horse, horse and buggy, planes, trains or automobiles, getting from point A to point B and then back to point A has evolved in ways that has brought greater convenience to the traveler and a variety of ways to reach destinations.

Although there are various modes of transportation available today, nothing seems to be more affordable and convenient than having your own vehicle (or car), especially when the places you frequent are quite some distance from your residence or where you work.

And unless the particular car or vehicle of choice has the proper fuel, it becomes useless and is no longer fit to fulfill its intended purpose, which is to be an object in motion that provides transportation to and from.

Now I don't know why this happens, is a common occurrence, or maybe you have already experienced this or still experience this on a regular basis. But in the household there are certain individuals, who will remain nameless, that consistently drive vehicles but pay absolutely no attention to the gas gauge that seems to constantly point towards the far left on the gas gauge that is clearly marked "E."

Contrary to popular belief, this "E" does not represent an expectation for the gas to magically appear but means "empty." Yes there should be an expectation to place fuel in the vehicle, but this should not happen every time we prepare to drive especially when someone else just used the vehicle.

Anyway, now that I'm done venting, the point being made here is that it is no fun getting into a vehicle no matter how classic, clean, or exquisite it may appear to be on the outside that has no power to move because there's a lack of fuel.

Imagine that; no matter how good a vehicle may appear to be on the outside, without the proper fuel on the inside it will fail to meet its intended purpose every time. Yet there are many believers today who often walk around in similar conditions, powerless and not completely equipped to fulfill God's intended purpose for their lives.

Thoughts

_____

_____

_____

_____

_____

_____

_____

The power and fuel needed in the life of the believer comes by way of the Holy Ghost (or Holy Spirit); this is why it is not only important to receive the Holy Spirit but also accept the empowerment that He brings (Acts 1:8).

As Believers in Christ we are the vehicles for God's Spirit and at new birth are instantly indwelled with the Holy Spirit (Eph. 1:13). So, stop riding around on the former "E" (Empty) and begin to be filled by fuel that pushes your fuel gauge toward "F" representing (Fully Empowered). The Holy Spirit not only gives us the ability to serve, but He empowers us to serve with purpose and direction.

March 22
NO DUMPING ALLOWED
Read: 2 Cor. 10:5

When my family and I lived in Virginia several years ago, I generally took the same route or path to and from work each day unless there was massive traffic congestion along the way that prompted me to take an alternate route. During this commute along familiar roads I generally passed by the same locations and landmarks. And since the average one-way commute back then was on average forty-five minutes to one hour, there were a lot of landmarks to see along the way.

One landmark that stood out was an open area of land near an apartment building. It was a fairly large area of land adjacent to the roadside along the way. The nearby apartment building, on the other hand, had several units with a small community of homes nearby. Therefore, due to its location and large expanse, this open field just seemed to be the logical place for many to discard unwanted bulk items and personal possessions.

Over the years I observed old furniture, televisions, and various other items placed alongside the road in hopes that maybe someone would have a desire turn "trash into treasure" or that local sanitation workers would pick-up these discarded items to dispose of them even though this was not the proper place to dump them.

Well, I guess one day the owner of the land reached the point of having enough with people just discarding unwanted items on his property. Therefore, in an attempt to discourage illegal dumping, the landowner posted large signs along the road in the vicinity of the open field that "NO DUMPING ALLOWED!"

In essence the landowner made a declaration that his personal property was not the place for everybody to just dump whatever they wanted which in turn placed the responsibility for disposal of these items on him.

What a novel concept, not allowing illegal dumping to take place on one's personal property. Just imagine how much chaos and disorder we each could avoid if we each applied the same concept or principle to our daily lives by not allowing our minds to become dumping grounds for gossip, unwholesome speech/conversation and the negative things of this world.

Thoughts

_____
_____
_____
_____
_____
_____
_____

This is why it is imperative that we become conscious of whom we associate with on a regular basis, what we listen to, and what we watch on television, DVD/Blue-ray or via the Internet. Because if we are not careful and without even realizing it, we can become the dumping ground for our enemy satan as he uses subtle ways to encourage us to adopt and begin adapting to the ways that everyone else does things and the way the world thinks.

Once this worldly garbage is on the inside of us, there's no other recourse or option except for it to come out in some form or fashion. This often leads to incorrect speech (speech that is contrary to God's Word) and unhealthy changes in lifestyle.

So, don't allow your mind to become a dumping ground for the things of this world. Post a sign over your heart and mind declaring that there is "NO DUMPING ALLOWED" in your life today!

March 23
REALLY, I UNDERSTAND
Read: Heb. 4:15

In this life trials and tests are going to come our way, there is just no way around it. Jesus Christ Himself said, "In the world you have tribulation and trials and distress and frustration; but be of good cheer [take courage; be confident, certain, undaunted]! For I have overcome the world. [I have deprived it of power to harm you and have conquered it for you]" (Jn. 16:33, Amplified Bible).

This basically means that as long as we are alive and breathing, trouble is bound to come our way. It is our response to these outside and sometimes internal influences that make all the difference. Do we separate and isolate ourselves, or run toward our Heavenly Father and then surround ourselves with brothers and sisters in the faith who can strengthen and encourage us?

When these trials come we are often overcome with feelings of guilt and inadequacy and begin to say things like: "No one understands what I'm going through;" "No one can relate to my current situation;" "This pain is too much for me to bear;" "Nobody knows the trouble I've seen." The phrases we use to describe our feelings can go on and on.

Thoughts

_____

_____

_____

_____

_____

_____

_____

In some instances many individuals even go as far as spending countless hours, over multiple appointments to have therapists and counselors attempt to analyze their feelings and bring a sense of understanding to their current predicament. Yet when they depart the meeting, they feel no different than when they came.

We often feel helpless in our trials and tribulations, believing there's no possible way that anyone could truly understand how we feel, or understand what we're going through. Well, there is someone who does really understand and deeply cares; Jesus Christ.

"Jesus understands every weakness of ours, because he was tempted in every way that we are. But he did not sin" (Heb. 4:15, Contemporary English Version)! Though He was God incarnate (in the flesh), He was also completely human; it was through His humanity that He can now identify with every emotion, every pain and every hurt that we can or ever will experience or feel.

Since Jesus knows exactly how we feel; as a result we are now able to "...come boldly unto the throne of grace, that we may obtain mercy, and find grace to help in time of need" (Heb. 4:16, King James Version) because He understands our weaknesses and can truly identify with what we may be feeling. Jesus endured the awkward stares, people talking behind His back, gossip, betrayal, persecution, physical abuse and ultimately a horrific and gruesome death on the cross; He did it all without murmuring or complaining, and He did it all just for you and for me.

Whenever we attempt to isolate ourselves because of our current circumstances and situations, we must remember that there is nothing that we go through in life that someone else has not already experienced and/or overcome (1 Cor. 10:13) or that Jesus has not gone through Himself.

March 24
FAILURE IS NOT THE END
Read: Prov. 16:3

Life is full of wonderful surprises, and many times the way that things may appear may not be actually the way we perceive them to be. What may appear to be failure in our own eyes, may just be the very seed of victory and success if we would only change our perspective.

There are individuals throughout history, who by definition and their associated past work should have been labeled "failures."
However, they chose not to allow what others considered failure to stop them from achieving their goals.

Thoughts

_____
_____

Even though the following individuals are from different eras in time, they each have a lot in common and something that we each can take a lesson from.

_____
_____
_____
_____
_____

Thomas Edison is known for inventing the light bulb and the technology that we all use today to instantly transform darkened areas with light. However, what many may not know is that Edison actually made over 3,000 attempts to create the light bulb before he was successful. And when he was questioned about what others considered to be failure Edison simply replied "I didn't fail 3,000 times. I found 3,000 ways how not to create a light bulb."

Then there is Henry Ford, founder of the Ford Motor Company a leading force in the automotive industry even today. Ford suffered many failures and setbacks while attempting to manufacture an affordable gas-power automobile before finally designing the "Model T" (known as the first affordable American car) forever transforming personal transportation as we know it today.

And lastly there is Bill Gates who dropped out of one of the most prestigious colleges in the United States, Harvard, but now reigns atop the software and computer industry with a net worth in the billions and is consistently ranked as one of the wealthiest people in the world. He is the chairman and co-founder of the Microsoft Corporation with products that consistently in use every day on a world-wide basis meeting individual and corporate computer and software needs in every nation.

Though failure may have hindered the above mentioned individuals, each had an inner desire to succeed and chose not to give-up on their goals and dream. Because of their dedication and persistence, life as we know it has forever been changed by inventions and products that are not only conveniences for us, but have become essentials to everyday life. Their goals and dreams not only benefited and prospered them as individuals, but mankind as a whole.

Your dreams, aspirations and goals may not just be for you; but may be inspired from above, part of a larger plan and connected to someone else's assignment and destiny. This is why you must never allow failure to become your end.

Thomas Edison, Henry Ford and Bill Gates each provide excellent examples of what not giving up on your dreams can produce, no matter what obstacles may be in your way. According to Henry Ford, "Obstacles are those frightful things you see when you take your eyes off your goal," this is why you have to remain focused and not allow yourself to become distracted by what others are doing or what they say, and remain focused on your dreams (Prov. 16:3).

Thoughts
_____
_____
_____
_____
_____
_____
_____

March 25

YOU CAN ONLY SPEND IT ONCE
Read: Heb. 9:27

Honey bees are a rare and fascinating species. These bees generally operate in the vicinity of the beehive unless actively seeking out pollen or nectar. The honey bee is not really aggressive, that is unless there's a sense that the hive is in danger or it is roughly handled or feels that it is in danger.

The primary defense mechanism available for use in the honey bee is the stinger that is connected to its abdomen. This stinger is filled with a venom/toxin that can be very painful to the recipient.

An interesting fact is that when a honey bee stings an individual and the barbed stinger becomes lodged in the victim and separated from the bee, this is not only discomforting to the one receiving the sting but also becomes deadly for the bee. Once the stinger separates from the bee's body, the bee only has minutes to live.

Taking into account this fact, whenever a beehive or honey comb is under attack the honey bee has to make its defensive sting really count, because that will be its last opportunity to really affect a change.

In the day and age that we live in, Christians are routinely placed under the microscope of scrutiny as the body of Christ seems to be under constant attack. People are now looking to the church and the individuals comprising "The Church" to see if what we speak and preach about is true; and if Christ is truly real. They do this by observing our lifestyle.

"But you are our letter, and you are in our hearts for everyone to read and understand" (2 Corinthians 3:2, Contemporary English Version). As believers, our lives are open books and letters that are constantly being read by those around us; those who may never go to church. This is why it is so vitally important that we make our lives count.

As individuals we each only get one life to live, and how we spend it (using our time, talents, and treasures) is totally up to us; and then what comes next is judgment. "We die only once, and then we are judged" (Heb. 9:27, Contemporary English Version).

Listen to the words of the Psalmist as he contemplated the importance of his life, "You made my life short, so brief that the time means nothing to you. "Human life is but a breath" (Ps. 39:5, Contemporary English Version). And also the words of James in his epistle, "What do you know about tomorrow? How can you be so sure about your life? It is nothing more than

Thoughts

_____
_____
_____
_____
_____
_____
_____
_____

mist that appears for only a little while before it disappears" (James 4:14, Contemporary English Version).

Making the best use of our time should be our focus and goal. Human life here on earth is very short and we only get one chance to make it really count by treasuring the right things. "Be sensible and store up precious treasures--don't waste them like a fool" (Prov. 21:20, Contemporary English Version).

March 26
GOD DOES NOT HAVE IT TO GIVE
Read: 1 Jn. 4:16-17

After taking an initial glance at the title of this devotional, I hope that you do not just stop reading and/or prepare to cast your first stone declaring "heresy", but instead I pray that you please keep reading. Am I saying that the Creator of the Universe, the God of heaven and earth, the Omniscient, Omnipresent, and Omnipotent One is incapable of providing something to and for his people? Absolutely not; however, there is something that He just does not have to give because there is so much more.

Here is an illustration that may shed some light on the premise of this devotional's primary message. An individual discovers that a close relative and family member is experiencing kidney problems, and without a kidney transplant there's little hope for his survival unless he continues to receive life-giving aid through costly treatments and very expensive equipment.

Filled with compassion, not just for a fellow man but also for a close blood relative, a family member decides to be tested as a potential donor because among other things the blood types of the donor and recipient have to match; there's just something about the family blood that provides connection. Tests are completed and the potential donor has two good kidneys that are positive matches, so he decides to offer one of his kidneys to his ailing relative to help with extending his life.

The operation takes place and the kidney transplant is a success with the once ailing body readily receiving and integrating its new organ. The once bedridden relative is filled with joy and gratitude for the selfless act of compassion of a close relative who did not just throw money at the problem or try to find someone else to help, but chose to make a personal sacrifice and gave of himself.

Thoughts

_____
_____
_____
_____
_____
_____

In the above scenario, the kidney donor did not just give something that he had but actually gave of himself with no expectation of receiving a kidney or anything in return. This is a perfect example of the correlation between God and the believer as it pertains to love and then our subsequent response to other.

You see, when it comes to love God simply does not give of what He has, even though He really has a lot to offer. Instead He gives based on His nature and of the very essence of His being. Scripture does not say that "GOD HAS LOVE," it says that "GOD IS LOVE!"

And since we have been created in His image and likeness (Gen. 1:27), we too have been created by LOVE to not only love ourselves but are also commissioned to extend this love to others, especially to all who are in the household of faith (Gal. 6:10).

God loved mankind so much that He gave of Himself in the form of Jesus Christ incarnate (in the flesh) (Jn. 1:14; Rom. 5:6-8). If God loved us that much when we were sinners and outside the fellowship of believers, how can we possibly rationalize not loving others no matter who they are or what they may have done? (1 Jn. 4:16-17)

March 27
IT DOESN'T COME ANY OTHER WAY
Read: Rom. 10:17

Doctors, lawyers, judges, scientists/biologists all have very important and also lucrative jobs. Usually when these jobs are mentioned, for the average person the mind automatically starts to process dollar signs and imagine the lifestyle that this individual must be living and enjoying. But, each of these jobs required a bit of discipline beforehand, because one does not become a doctor or biologist simply by watching television shows like E.R. or C.S.I. (Crime Scene Investigation) every week; neither will just watching Judge Judy or Judge Joe Brown make an individual a lawyer.

Success in these fields and the personal benefits that come with each does not come by mental assent or just believing that a person is a doctor or lawyer; on the contrary, each profession requires a great degree of study, focus, and discipline to get to this point with an average of six or more years in undergraduate and graduate studies in college including rigorous certification testing and board approval before receiving a license to practice.

Unfortunately, many come into the body of Christ with this same microwave attitude and mindset; they see successful ministers and pastors on television and assume they can achieve the same status overnight. But what they fell to realize is the person they see on television has more than likely endured years of challenge that has developed faithfulness and commitment in them as they learned how

Thoughts

_____
_____
_____
_____
_____
_____
_____

101

to spend quality time with the Lord to get to their current position. Many want an individual's glory, without having full knowledge of their story.

Yes, according to Romans 12:3 everyone is given a certain degree or level of faith "... God has dealt to each one a measure of faith" (New King James Version);" however, it is totally up to each individual to allow God, through the Holy Spirit, faithfulness, dedication, and personal devotional time studying on God's Word to consistently develop and cultivate this faith.

It is presumptuous of an individual to walk around just repeating "I think I have faith, I think I have faith, I think I have faith," to really and truly believe that he or she has faith by virtue of simply repeating it over and over. Of course we are encouraged to speak those things that be not as though they are (Rom. 4:17); however, faith for the Believer comes by one primary method and that is through the Word of God. "So then faith comes by hearing, and hearing by the word of God" (Rom. 10:17, New King James Version). Faith is a prerequisite to speaking non-existent things into existence.

This simply means that many of us need to pick up those large Bibles that are so neatly displayed on living room tables, in the dashboard or rear window of cars fading in the sunlight, and dust off those that sit on nightstands in bedrooms collecting dust Monday through Saturday, and truly begin to study and mediate on the words written therein. It's fairly plain to see that we must open the Bible to develop our faith.

Though trials and circumstances may come to test our faith, it is the Word of God that increases and solidifies faith in the Believer. The ability to increase our faith comes by routinely hearing and meditating (rehearsing and repeating) God's Word, and then going one step further to actually doing what it says.

March 28
A FORMULA TO THE BLESSING
Read: Gal. 3:14-29

Whenever someone said that math is or was their favorite subject in school, I've always considered these individuals to be rather unique because having an affinity for and/or loving math takes a really special person.

Thoughts

_____

_____

_____

_____

_____

_____

_____

Personally, I was never really fond of math; however, words on the other hand always seemed to stimulate the synapses of my brain to bring about a creativity that lay dormant within. But for the mathematician, numbers and formulas are what bring about joy and fulfillment.

Just take a look at the following formulas: $a^2 + b^2 = c^2$ (Pythagorean Theorem); $E=IR$ (Ohm's Law); $2 * pi * radius$ (Circumference of a circle); and of course the popular $E = Mc^2$ (Relativity). For the non-mathematicians I pray that I did not resurrect any bad memories of high school and/or college math.

I previously stated or implied, math was definitely not one of my favorite subjects and it required me to apply myself a little more to be successful. An important part of learning math was the ability to understand and then master the formulas and equations.

Some time ago I was forwarded an e-mail that contained a very unique formula and one that I had never seen before; and though math does not peak my interest, I was compelled to see what the product or the solution was. Then one day while listening to the lyrics of Christian Hip-Hop song, I heard the very same formula as the foundation and basis of a rap song entitled "Salvation 101."

With that said, I took this as my cue from the Holy Spirit to write about this awesome formula which is simply this: 1 Cross + 3 Nails = 4-Given. Wow! I don't think that salvation can be explained any simpler than this.

And though no equation or formula can totally describe all that Christ did for mankind through his sacrifice on the cross, I believe this formula does an outstanding job in simplifying and summing up what He accomplished through His selfless act of love and compassion. It is because of 1 cross and 3 nails that we each have the ability to receive 4-giveness (forgiveness - a pardon or release from sins that we were actually guilty of) through Christ's shed blood (Jn. 3:16). God's love is truly amazing!

Not only do we receive salvation (being delivered from sin and darkness, and being redeemed or purchased back by God); but because of the sacrifice of Christ, we also now have the right to the "Blessing of Abraham" as heirs to the promise. An heir is simply someone who has been given the right to the property of another by law (Gal. 3:14-29).

Can you imagine receiving all of this because of one formula? "1 Cross + 3 Nails = 4-Given": apply it, live it and walk it out the in your life today!

March 29
MAKE HEALTHY CHOICES, YOU ARE
WHAT YOU EAT
Read: 1 Pet. 2:2

Thoughts

_____
_____
_____
_____
_____
_____
_____

Fitness crazes come and go with infomercials
detailing how you can lose weight in a matter
of days with use of a new piece of exercise
equipment, exercise routine, or a new diet fad.
One minute the talk of the town is exercise and

physical fitness, then over a period of time the excitement dies down with that tummy burning six-pack maker and hip shaper now neatly nestled under a bed or hidden in a closet collecting dust.

Physical fitness for each of us should be the norm and also should be an essential aspect of our daily life, with some type of physical activity and proper nutrition being the main focus. Now when it comes to the nutrition side there are many foods that are delicious, appealing to the eye, and are very filling; however, these often provide no nutritional value to the body at all.

Just imagine someone sitting at home all day eating banana splits with creamy vanilla ice cream covered with chocolate, chopped nuts, strawberries and a cherry on top. I can hear someone saying, "What's wrong with this, besides I'm getting dairy, protein, and fruit supplements with this one dessert." Although bananas, cherries, and nuts individually provide a certain degree of nutrition, with the addition of ice cream and chocolate the nutritional value drastically decreases. Eventually this individual not only denies him or herself the proper daily nutrients through malnourishment, but also stands the chance of adding unwanted and excess weight.

Malnourishment is the condition that results from "an unbalanced diet in which certain nutrients are lacking, in excess (too high an intake), or in the wrong proportions."

Today this same problem is evident in the Body of Christ with many experiencing malnutrition in a spiritual sense. Day after day many fill themselves with the things of this world that provide no spiritual nutrition for the inner man (the Spirit) through gossiping, surfing inappropriate Internet sites, hours upon hours in front of the television watching unproductive shows filled with tons of offensive language while promoting principles and ideas contrary sustaining a productive life, and the many other distractions we each face every day instead of placing focus on the one all-important dietary supplement that is designed to encourage us, strengthen us, and provide the daily nutrients needed to succeed in life—the Word of God.

Don't get me wrong, I'm not saying banana splits, conversation, the Internet, or television is the devil; however, all of these should be used properly and/or in moderation. Because what you feed your spirit is what will determine its growth or conversely its malnourishment; filling yourself with the wrong things may not only be harmful for bodily growth, but can be detrimental to your spiritual grow as well, thereby adversely affecting not only your body, but the Body of Christ as a whole (1 Cor. 12, 26-27).

Thoughts

_____

_____

_____

_____

_____

_____

_____

As Believers in Christ we each have a role to play in the Body, therefore we must choose to feed and focus on the right things (Phil. 4:8). Daily study of God's Word can be satisfying and oh so sweet (Ps. 34:8); so make healthy choices today, because you are what you eat (1 Pet. 2:2)!

March 30

IT'S NEVER TOO LATE TO SPEAK LIFE
Read: Jn. 11:44

Lazarus, the brother of Mary (the one who washed Jesus' feet with her hair) and Martha, and the beloved friend of Jesus was sick. Mary and Martha sent word to Jesus on behalf of Lazarus hoping He would come and heal their brother before his condition worsened.

Jesus agreed to make the journey, yet knowing that Lazarus was dying He and His disciples did not depart their current location for another two days. Then seemingly out of nowhere Jesus announced that Lazarus was dead, but nonetheless they all still prepared for the journey to now the tomb where Lazarus was buried instead of to his bedside.

Surely the disciples must have thought this would be a wasted journey; however, Jesus had bigger plans because He knew the power of God He possessed.

When Jesus finally arrived he greeted Mary and Martha, He reassured them that though Lazarus was dead he would in fact live again. Jesus said "I am the resurrection and the life. He who believes in Me, though he may die, he shall live. And whoever lives and believes in Me shall never die" (Jn. 11: 25-26, New Living Translation).

At this point Lazarus had been dead and in the grave for a few days with his body beginning to decompose as bodily fluids dried up with rigor mortis setting in. Yet this did not deter Jesus, the One who was and still is a Restorer and Giver of life.

After the stone had been rolled away Jesus used the power and authority of His Word to call out to his dear friend using three simple words: "Lazarus, come forth" (Jn. 11:43)!

There may be areas in your life today, whether finances, marriage, bad relationships, wayward children, employment, or just "stinking thinking" that may appear to be dead, has become a stench to you and those around you, or have you bound. Refuse to get discouraged, but instead begin to speak life to the situation(s) and watch God work.

Know today that Jesus (the Living Word) has the ability to resurrect that which is dead in your life. Though your current situation may appear to be dead, stinking, and hopeless, IT'S NEVER TOO LATE TO
SPEAK LIFE!

Thoughts

_____
_____
_____
_____
_____
_____
_____

March 31

A DIVIDED HOUSE
Read: Mk. 3:25

Awhile back I can recall watching a television show describing and documenting the tragedy of how an elderly woman literally lost everything she possessed, including 30 years of memories and items that could never be replaced, as she watched her entire house slowly destroyed right before her eyes.

This was a completely devastating event, not only for her but for her neighbors as well who feared that their homes may suffer the same fate.

It was later discovered that the woman's home had actually been built on two different foundations; one stable and the other a sinkhole. Sinkholes are generally formed when rocks below a surface are acted upon or shifted by external forces like underground streams or running water beneath the surface that over time deteriorate the once stable foundations.

Sadly, this is exactly what occurred in this particular case, the land/surface around the sink hole began to deteriorate and erode until it eventually reached the woman's house. Then one day without warning, the portion of the house built over the sink hole slowly began to collapse. And even though a portion of the house remained on solid ground, when the portion of the house built over the sinkhole gave way the entire house was affected because of the divided foundation.

According to 1 Cor. 3:9, "...[We] are God's field. [We] are God's building (New Living Translation);" therefore, since we are God's building (or house), it is imperative that we build on the right foundation to ensure that our house has a surface that will sustain us and enable us to stand no matter what external forces attempt to act upon us. In a spiritual sense this foundation is Christ, because "...no one can lay any foundation other than the one we already have-Jesus Christ" (1 Cor. 3:11, New Living Translation).

But, even though many have been convinced that Christ is a sure foundation, our "Solid Rock" and that a life in the spirit is the way, there are those who still attempt to build on this foundation with works, status, riches, manipulation and many other deeds and works of the flesh that do not enable us to stand; attempting to hold on to Christ and the world's system (or way of doing things) simultaneously resulting in a foundation that begins to crumble. Why? Because a house divided against itself cannot stand (Mk. 3:25, King James Version), one must give way to the other.

When our spiritual homes are not completely built on the foundation of the Rock (the Living Word of God), it will not stand. Then whenever the rains descend and the winds of trials and persecution come to eat away at our foundation,

Thoughts

_____
_____
_____
_____
_____
_____
_____

106

our house will have no other recourse but to fall. And just like the home that was partially built over a sinkhole; great will be the fall (Matt. 7:27, King James Version).

Make sure that your building is up to code and that your foundation is stable as you continue to build upon the Solid Rock, the Rock of our salvation today! Because a house divided against itself will never stand! Is your house built on the sure foundation (Eph. 2:19-21)?

April 1
ON THE ROAD AGAIN
Read: Prov. 16:17

One thing in life that I truly dislike is being stuck in traffic. When I lived in the Tidewater area of Virginia, this was often a common theme no matter which route I took.

Since the distance between my home and job required me to travel on highways and interstates, being stuck in traffic just became a part of my daily routine. My usual path was from Highway 58, I-664, I-264, to I-64; however, there were also a couple of different routes that I could have taken on any given day, but even this was often a gamble with me not really being able to determine the outcome.

You see, the primary consequence of my choice to pick a particular route on any given determined the amount of time it took to arrive at my destination. Therefore, if I chose the wrong route, my arrival stood the chance of being delayed.

Yet even among the many roads I have traveled throughout the years, there's another important highway that we should all strive to travel down each day, yet few venture to take this route. "You can enter God's Kingdom only through the narrow gate. The highway to hell is broad, and its gate is wide for the many who choose that way. But the gateway to life is very narrow and the road is difficult, and only a few ever find it" (Matt. 7:13-14, New Living Translation). The Message paraphrase Bible states it this way "Don't look for shortcuts to God. The market is flooded with surefire, easygoing formulas for a successful life that can be practiced in your spare time. Don't fall for that stuff, even though crowds of people do. The way to life—to God!—is vigorous and requires total attention" (Matt. 7:13-14, The Message).

Thoughts

This highway requires that we choose to be set apart, not to make ourselves better than anyone else, but for the purposes of being positioned to be used by God because He is Holy (1 Pet. 3:13-16).

_____
_____
_____
_____
_____
_____

Therefore, the highway being discussed here is none other than the "Highway of Holiness." "And a great road will go through that once deserted land. It will be named the Highway of Holiness. Evil-minded people will never travel on it. It will be only for those who walk in God's ways; fools will never walk there" [Is. 35:8, New Living Translation). Another term for this highway is "Route 66."

The Bible (The Word of God) is comprised of 39 Old Testament and 27 New Testament books: 39 OT + 27 NT = 66 Books of the Bible. With the number "6" representing the number of "man," 66 is a double encouragement for man to stay on the right path taking heed to God's Word. Therefore, it is not only essential that we hear the Word, but also receive it into our hearts, allow it to transform and renew our minds, and then put it into action while living it out each day.

As Believers in Christ when we choose to follow the correct path using Route 66, God will direct us by providing His light along the way; He knows our destination and our expected end and has our very best interest at heart. "For I know the thoughts that I think toward you, saith the LORD, thoughts of peace, and not of evil, to give you an expected end" (Jer. 29:11, King James Version).

April 2
I DON'T WANT IT, YOU CAN HAVE IT BACK!
Read: 1 Jn. 4:17-18

I can remember as a young boy exchanging toys with friends, in hopes of obtaining something better in return. Though this may give away my age, one toy in particular at the time were the miniature 'Hot Wheels' and 'Matchbox' brand cars/car sets which were very common. I always believed the Hot Wheels brand to be of better quality than the Matchbox. Hot Wheels were all metal; however, the Matchbox car was partially metal with a plastic bottom that was prone to easily being removed.

During a potential trade I would be prepared to release, in my mind, a high quality Hot Wheels car expecting a car of equal or better quality in return; but instead I was presented with a Matchbox car along with disappointment. Knowing my standard and the type of car I expected in return, the usual response in this scenario was "I don't want it, you can have it back!"

Thoughts

_____
_____
_____
_____
_____
_____
_____

Our enemy (the devil) uses a similar tactic and approach with each of us every day. He presents us with things that appear to be of high quality, but when we receive them and have the items in our possession, the end result is usually chaos and confusion, simply because we chose to settle. One area in particular that leads to this type of product is that of fear.

Many willingly accept fear from the enemy when the alternative, FAITH, yields a greater return. We listen to the enemy's voice telling us that we will never achieve our goals, we will always be sick, our wife, husband, children, relatives will never change, or you know you can't tithe because you have too many bills to pay. These are all tricks of the enemy that cause us to operate in fear. So, how do we counter this?

Although faith is a major component, we actually overcome fear with love (1 Jn. 4:18). When we begin to truly understand love and God's love for us, He lets us know that everything we stand in need of He will supply. This understanding of true love then turns our fear into faith.

"Can anything ever separate us from Christ's love? Does it mean he no longer loves us if we have trouble or calamity, or are persecuted, or hungry, or destitute, or in danger, or threatened with death?...No, despite all these things, overwhelming victory is ours through Christ, who loved us" (Rom. 8:35-37, New Living Translation).

Don't accept fear in your life. Begin to cast out fear with love as you learn how to turn fear into faith. When the enemy presents you with fear today, refuse to accept an inferior product and just say: "I DON'T WANT IT, YOU CAN HAVE IT BACK!"

"God is love. When we take up permanent residence in a life of love, we live in God and God lives in us. This way, love has the run of the house, becomes at home and mature in us, so that we're free of worry on Judgment Day—our standing in the world is identical with Christ's. There is no room in love for fear. Well-formed love banishes fear. Since fear is crippling, a fearful life—fear of death, fear of judgment—is one not yet fully formed in love" (1 Jn. 4:17-18, The Message).

April 3
THE POINT OF REFERENCE
Read: Josh. 4:22-24

With the myriad of interstates, highways, complex bridges, overpasses, and tunnels in the world today, vehicle commutes can become frustrating at times especially in major cities with five or more lanes on just one side of the highway. Therefore, when an individual does not really know where he or she is going, this only complicates things even more and often brings greater frustration.

Thoughts

For me, other than driving to and from work, to church, and a few other essential places; my travel and driving is somewhat limited. And since there are so many navigational aids like Global Positioning System (GPS), MapQuest and the standard hard copy (paper) maps

_____
_____
_____
_____
_____
_____
_____

readily available, when I travel on the road I tend not to really pay much attention to street signs and/or street names like the average person does.

However, whenever I am traveling in unfamiliar territory what I generally tend to do is look for specific landmarks (buildings, billboards, parks, statues, etc.) as my primary point of reference, because these landmarks become etched in my mind much quicker than any particular street name. And sometimes as I travel along the way I occasionally lose my bearing and/or sense of direction, therefore, it is during these instances that the selected point of reference generally gets me back on track leading me on the right path towards the ultimate destination.

In the Old Testament of Joshua, the children of Israel made a journey across the Jordan River into the Promised Land. Joshua, their leader at the time, commanded that twelve stones (representing the twelve tribes or nations of Israel) be removed from the riverbed and placed on land as a reminder to future generations of what the LORD had done for His people with the deliverance that had been achieved. Through a collective act of obedience and staying on the designated path, the Israelites were able to enter a place of prosperity and provision (Josh. 4:22-24).

The twelve stones were not only a point of reference for anyone who may have gotten off track or lost their direction in a natural sense, but also for those who may have forgotten all the LORD God Almighty had previously done for them from a spiritual standpoint. The stones were simple reminders to nudge and/or jog their memories and provide hope for whatever negative experience or situation they may have been going through at the time.

Well, we too have a point of reference today in the form of God's Holy Word (2 Tim. 3:16-17). God's Word was left for us as a standard and a point of reference to get us back on track whenever we deviate from the course that has already been prepared and laid out for us. This point of reference not only reminds us of what God has already done, but also provides a glimpse of what He is now capable of doing in the lives of His people today, those who choose the path of holiness and obedience. "God can do anything, you know—far more than you could ever imagine or guess or request in your wildest dreams! He does it not by pushing us around but by working within us, his Spirit deeply and gently within us (Eph. 3:20, The Message).

Whenever you get off course, what is your point of reference? Allow God's Word to be the landmark and guide that keeps you on the right path!

Thoughts

_____
_____
_____
_____
_____
_____
_____

April 4

IT'S TIME TO ENTER IN
Read: Heb. 10:19-22

Imagine that you've been invited to a friend's home for dinner and fellowship. Every time there is a gathering at this particular family's home, there is always a guarantee of enjoyable and fruitful time spent together.

Knowing that you will arrive soon, the front door is normally unlocked to allow immediate access upon arrival. But on this particular evening you arrive at the home, ring the doorbell and decide to wait; a voice from within says, "The door is open, you can come in." Yet still, instead of entering in for some odd reason you just stand at the entrance when what you came for (fellowship) is available just on the other side.

This too often happens in the lives of believers, as we experience unnecessary pain, hurt, suffering, sadness, etc., when what we are in need of and in search of is on the other side of the door.

During Old Testament times the temple was the designated place of worship and was divided into three distinct sections: the Outer Court, The Holy Place (The Inner Court), and the Holy of Holies. Before the finished work of Jesus Christ on the cross, individual entry into the Holy of Holies was only authorized for the High Priest once a year as he entered to offer a sacrifice for the atonement of everyone's sins. But now, through the shed blood of Jesus we each now have access to the most holy place; the Holy of Holies, the very place where God's presence dwells.

The curtain that once separated the Inner Court and the Holy of Holies has been removed once and for all. "My friends, the blood of Jesus gives us courage to enter the most holy place by a new way that leads to life! And this way takes us through the curtain that is Christ himself. We have a great high priest who is in charge of God's house. So let's come near God with pure hearts and a confidence that comes from having faith" (Heb. 10:19-22, Contemporary English Version).

With this curtain removed, we now have access to everything we need in this life (2 Pet. 1:3-4). Therefore, we each have the ability to move from the place of discouragement and frustration today because the door has been opened; so we can enter into God's presence to receive the joy and strength we need. In God's presence there is fullness of joy (Ps. 16:11) and this joy of the LORD is what provides our strength (Neh. 8:10); therefore, when we enter into God's presence we are then empowered to overcome the obstacles that we face every day.

Thoughts

God is looking for true worshippers, those who are not afraid to enter in. "But the time is coming-indeed it's here now-when true worshipers will worship the Father in spirit and in truth. The Father is looking for those who will worship him that way" (Jn. 4:23, New Living Translation).

Why remain outside when the door has been already been opened; Access to the fellowship and communion that you long for and desire is readily available. Go ahead, it's time to enter in!

"Let us therefore come boldly to the throne of grace, that we may obtain mercy and find grace to help in time of need" (Heb. 4:16, New King James Version).

April 5
IT'S ONLY AS BIG AS YOU ALLOW IT TO BE
Read: Matt. 17:20

Looking at objects through various visual instruments often provide different vantage points based on the device being used at the time. Although the moon may be millions of miles away from earth, when using the right telescope, it appears as if it were directly in front of us.

Likewise, one can look at a micro-organism through the lens of a microscope that cannot be seen with the naked eye. Though the organism may be smaller than a grain of sand, with the aid of a microscopic lens it appears to be much larger and can be easily seen.

This would suggest that the actual size of an object is really dependent on the type of lens used to view it.

Standing in front of Mount Everest, a mountain with one of the tallest peaks in the world, can be awe-inspiring just observing its sheer size elevating over 29,000 feet above sea level. However, if one were to take a flight on a commercial airliner, this same mountain would appear very minute and small based on this new vantage point. Therefore, it would be safe to say that how an individual sees an object or views various situations is based on vantage point and perspective.

Thoughts

_____
_____
_____
_____
_____
_____
_____

The same principle applies to the trials, tribulations, and obstacles that we each face from day to day. The size of any obstacle is actually based on our own vantage point and perspective. To put it another way, our circumstances are only as big as we allow them to be.

When one chooses to look at the mountain through natural eyes, the individual will generally continue to say, "I can't overcome this obstacle or challenge because it's too big for me to handle." But when he or she begins to look through eyes of faith, the mountain(s) begins to look smaller as God is enlarged in their vision.

By exercising faith and focusing our attention on God and His Holy Word instead of the mountain, we then have the ability to speak to our mountain or obstacle, and then watch it get removed. "I tell you the truth, if you had faith even as small as a mustard seed, you [can] say to this mountain, 'Move from here to there,' and it would move. Nothing [is] impossible" (Matt. 17:20, New Living Translation). Nothing is impossible when faith is applied.

As we look at the peak or very top of any mountain, we in essence lose sight of the large mass that sits below as we begin to place greater focus on the God of the heavens, the One who created the mountain, the one who has the ability to remain any mountain and the Source of our strength. Therefore, we must resolve to look up and change our vantage point.

Since it is God who created mountains, do you not think that He is capable of removing mountain-sized obstacles out of your way? Begin to look UP through eyes of faith and see your God as being BIGGER than any mountain you face today. YOUR MOUNTAIN IS ONLY AS BIG AS YOU ALLOW IT TO BE

(Ps. 121:1)!

April 6
DRESSED FOR THE OCCASION
Read: Is. 61:3

For many individuals, going to church has been relegated to nothing more than a huge fashion show. Too many believers come not to hear "Thus saith the LORD" or to experience the presence of God, but are more concerned with the label or brand name of the suit or dress he or she is wearing, or how big and stylish a person's hat is; when there are weightier matters and issues.

On the other hand there are churches that have a "Come as you are" approach for attendees and worshippers, where almost anything goes when it comes to the appropriate apparel for entering into God's house and His presence. Which is right? Though individuals should be allowed to come as they are based on the clothing they have in their possession at the time, we must ensure that when we come into the House of the LORD we are dressed appropriately and

Thoughts

_____
_____
_____
_____
_____
_____
_____

in a way that demonstrates reverence. There's nothing wrong with wearing expensive clothing and nice apparel; however, this should not be the primary focus of corporate worship.

Jesus condemned the religious leaders (the Pharisees) for this very thing: "Everything they do is just to show off in front of others. They even make a big show of wearing Scripture verses on their foreheads and arms, and they wear big tassels for everyone to see...You Pharisees and teachers are in for trouble! You're nothing but show-offs. You're like tombs that have been whitewashed. On the outside they are beautiful, but inside they are full of bones and filth" (Matt. 23:5, 27, Contemporary English Version).

However, there is another vital aspect we each should be mindful of, an aspect that is more important than the outward physical clothing we wear. That aspect being our spiritual adornment.

Each week believers come into God's House and enter His presence burdened down with the weights and cares of this world, preventing them from entering into true worship. According to 1 Pet. 5:7, "God cares for you, so turn all your worries over to him" (Contemporary English Version). Although the church should be a spiritual hospital for the sick, once we enter in we have the ability to cast our burdens and cares to God, and not leave the same way we entered.

When we come to God's House we should put on the right spiritual clothing. Our God gives us beauty for ashes, the oil of joy for mourning, THE GARMENT [CLOTHING] OF PRAISE for the spirit of heaviness...(Is. 61:3, Contemporary English Version). Therefore, it should not take a praise team to pump us up during a worship service. True worship begins as we learn to celebrate God at home or in the car prior to arriving at church. And then when everyone is with one accord, the worship experience is that much sweeter.

Therefore, as we enter God's House, we can just continue to release our praise, "Enter into His gates with thanksgiving, And into His courts with praise. Be thankful to Him, and bless His name" (Ps. 100:4, New King James Version). As you enter God's presence with the right attitude, your burdens and heaviness begin to fall away.

The next time you prepare for church or entering into worship, release your burdens and expect God to move; in other words, MAKE SURE YOU ARE PROPERLY DRESSED FOR THE OCCASION (Ps. 33:1)!

Thoughts

April 7

QUIT PLAYING, PICK A SIDE
Read: Josh. 24:15

When summertime comes to an end, this generally marks the official beginning of football season. Fans of all race, nationality, gender, and age then go out to purchase pennants, t-shirts, sweatshirts, mugs, and all other manner of football accessories to show allegiance and support for their favorite team. Whether the support is for a college or professional team, fans tend to emerge from all corners of the country and around the world.

And during the course of a season it is often not too difficult to identify those diehard fans, you know those having vehicles painted in their favorite team's colors, with magnetic logos affixed to the side, and window mounted flags of their favored team waving in the wind as the vehicle passes by. But, then there are the "bandwagon," or fair-weather fans.

These individuals only claim allegiance when a particular team is doing well; therefore, their commitment is very different from the diehard fan. A bandwagon fan may wear a specific jersey, but when that team's season starts to go south, the jersey is easily removed and replaced with that of another team.

For example, this type of attitude can be seen in a football game between two equally talented teams; you know, a game that goes the distance. As soon as one team marches down the field for a score, the opposing team returns the favor when the football is in their possession.

This intense action goes back and forth like a ball lobbed back and forth in a tennis match through all four quarters of the game; and when the game is really good, it requires overtime to determine a winner.

During a game like this it is also fascinating to observe individuals who claim allegiance to one particular team at the beginning of the game but quickly shift sides when their favored team appears to be losing; then all of a sudden they begin to cheer for the other team. But when the team the individual first favored begins to regain the lead, their allegiance then shifts back to the original team.

In these instances I can just imagine friends of this individual and everyone around him saying, "You need to make a choice, one team or the other; quit playing and pick a side!"

Sadly, this bandwagon type of mentality often prevails in the Church and is also common among believers in Christ. When things are going well it is a joy to serve God; however, when trials and tribulations come, it becomes

Thoughts

_____
_____
_____
_____
_____
_____
_____

easy for these individuals to revert back to their pre-Christ mannerisms engaging in the things of the little "g" god of this world and placing "I," or "self" back on the throne.

Are you straddling the fence in your faith and in your walk with Christ?

The choices before each of us today are the Kingdom of God, or the kingdom of darkness; simply put, we either choose life or death because there is no in between. Don't remain stagnant and in discomfort when peace and joy are readily available. QUIT PLAYING, IT'S TIME TO PICK A SIDE (James 1:8)!

April 8
PLAYING POSSUM
Read: Rom. 6:11

Our last home in Virginia was quite some distance away from the normal hustle and bustle of city life. In the area we lived in the local Super Walmart was one of the main shopping attractions; therefore, whenever we wanted to take a step up and actually enjoy the luxury of going to a mall, we had to jump in the car and drive a little ways to one of the other cities in the Tidewater area of Virginia that actually had a mall. In other words we literally lived in the country.

Country living also afforded us the opportunity to see a many different insects, and a variety of animals. You name it we probably saw it in the front or back yard, or off in the distance.

However, there was one animal that I found particularly interesting, that being the "Opossum" or "possum." These are rodent-like nocturnal creatures who generally sleep or rest during the day, and then come out at night to search for food.

In the evening, possums were often spotted in the neighborhood going through trash and garbage cans. And when these would-be thieves who were literally attempting to turn "trash to treasure" was caught in their search for food or approached by a predator, they employed a very unique self-defense mechanism which allows the possum to go into a comatose-like state, as if it was dead.

Thoughts
_____
_____
_____
_____
_____
_____
_____

Since most predators like the stimulating thrill of "the kill" and things that are fresh; an inactive possum does not bring excitement or satisfaction to the appetite and is often left alone. But as soon as danger no longer exists, the possum awakens and scurries on its way. This is where we get the very familiar phrase: "Playing possum."

Playing possum is nothing more than pretending to be unconscious or unaware of something in order to trick someone into believing that you are in a state that is totally opposite of where you actually are. This is often played out in our lives as believers in Christ.

The religious leaders, the Pharisees, of the Old Testament could be characterized as "playing possum." Jesus often rebuked the Pharisees and other pious religious leaders for their outward portrayal of religion with no inner change (Matt. 23:27-28). I believe this same attitude often characterizes some of us as believers today; we are simply playing possum and only pretending to be dead to our old nature. Many pretend to be alive to Christ by doing and saying the right things to make others believe we are in a particular state, but inwardly are separated from God.

In other words, during the day we do those things that make everyone think that we are fine, but then come out at night to rummage through the things and trash of this world and the temporary pleasures that this brings, the things that only produce death instead of the life that God intended for us. True life only comes in and through an intimate relationship with Jesus Christ, not just through outward actions.

Have you been playing possum with God?

April 9
CAN YOUR GOD STAND THE TEST?
Read: Matt. 6:21

Today there are more religions, denominations, cults and sects than ever before. And along with many of these religious groups, also come a plethora of different gods.

According to one dictionary definition a "god" is "any supernatural being worshipped as controlling some part of the world or some aspect of life or who is the personification of a force." In other words a god does not just speak of a deity, but can also be indicative of what an individual chooses to worship or allows to have dominion and/or control in his or her life.

In our individualistic and consumer-based society today; money, fame, status, sex, gambling, lying and even food are just a few of the gods that many are prone to worship. Simply put, whatever a person places more focus, attention, emphasis and value in has the potential to become that person's god or their treasure. "Wherever your treasure is, there the desires of your heart will also be" (Matt. 6:21, New Living Translation).

Thoughts

_____

_____

_____

_____

_____

_____

_____

_____

Though a treasure may seem valuable for the moment and may even provide temporary satisfaction; can it really stand the true test of authenticity when compared to the Living God? Can it bring true fulfillment, wholeness or real life? Sadly, these treasures often become the idols in our lives that draw our attention away from the only One deserving of our devotion and worship.

In the Old Testament book of First Samuel, the Ark of the Covenant representing the very presence of the True God--Jehovah was stolen and placed in the temple of the Philistine god Dagon. There is just something about the tangible presence of Jehovah that shifts the atmosphere when His presence is made known.

Each morning when the Philistines went to the temple to worship their little "g" god Dagon, the statue representing the Philistine god laid faced down before the Ark of God.

The Philistines would then pick-up their god and put him in his place again, only to find the statue prostrate before the Ark of the Covenant again, and in a worst condition than it was on previous days. That should have been a red flag to the Philistines in that any god that man has the ability to put back in his place is not truly worthy of god-status or deserving of our worship (1 Sam. 5:1-4).

When in the presence of the Ark of the Covenant that represented Israel's God Jehovah, Dagon had no other choice but to acknowledge the awesome presence and power of the only God and treasure that really matters. Likewise, anything that is placed before this same God in our lives will also have to bow.

No matter how big we may think the little "g" gods of our lives may be, they actually profit us very little, pale in comparison and eventually, at some point in time, will all have to bow down to the only True and Living God. We each must make the choice to denounce all false gods and idols in our lives today, no matter how important we think they may be. "...Be careful. Don't let your heart be deceived so that you turn away from the LORD and serve and worship others gods" (Deut. 11:16, New Living Translation).

Thoughts

_____
_____
_____
_____
_____
_____
_____

April 10
RELEASE IT AND LET IT GO!
Read: Mk. 11:25-26

In life there are a lot of things that come to weigh us down, yet we have a choice to either accept the weight or release it. So, picture this for a moment, a group of climbers all sign-up for a mountain/rock climbing contest where the grand prize awaits the one who can reach the top of the mountain first. The climbers all complete a little advance planning as they prepare the gear and accessories required for the journey towards the top.

However, in his finite (or limited) wisdom, one climber decided not only to bring gear essential for the climb but also decided to bring along some extra items that were not really needed but "just nice to have," adding extra weight to an already overloaded and heavy pack.

The day finally arrived as the climbers approached the starting line, the whistle sounded and the climbers began their ascent. Everyone appeared to move along with ease and at a nice steady pace; that is, all except the one climber with the extra gear and added weight. Every time he attempted to take a few steps upward and forward, the excess weight consistently pulled him back down.

The weighted down climber suddenly had an epiphany of grand proportion, "Why don't I just get rid of this unnecessary weight and all of the extra stuff that's not even required for the journey?" So he stopped, removed the excess baggage, release it, and let it go.

And almost instantly, the once weighed down contestant began to gain ground on the other climbers until he stood atop the mountain with a huge smile on his face for having achieved a victory thereby winning the grand prize.

If the climber had not released the superfluous gear inside his pack, along with the added burden the extra baggage and weight created, he would not have made it to the top in a timely fashion to receive the prize that awaited; but instead he would have continued to struggle in his attempts to progress onward and upward while actually going in the opposite direction and remaining stagnate because of the exhaustion the excess weight would have created.

This same situation and scenario often plays out in our lives as believers in Christ when we are unwilling to forgive for whatever reason. Unforgiveness has the power to hold us down like heavy weights limiting our ability to move.

Harboring a grudge and holding on to unforgiveness regarding current situations and/ or things from the past can become a stumbling block and very harmful to not only our Christian growth and development, but also towards our physical well-being. While the person(s) we are holding a grudge against and/ or unwilling to forgive are living and enjoying life, we often remain bitter and held down by the excess weight that unforgiveness brings.

Thoughts

_____
_____
_____
_____
_____
_____
_____
_____

Are you holding on to or harboring unforgiveness in your life today? Do you feel as though for some reason or another you just can't seem to move forward? If the answer to either of the preceding questions is "YES," then

I would encourage you to refuse to be burdened down any longer, RELEASE IT AND LET IT GO! FORGIVE! IT'S TIME TO GO HIGHER AND TIME TO MOVE FORWARD (Mk. 11:25-26)!

April 11
ALL IT TAKES IS ONE TOUCH
Read: Matt. 9:20-21

New advances in technology continue to astound consumers each year; from innovations in more fuel-efficient automobiles, voice activated electrical devices and personal handheld video teleconferencing capability via the use of the Internet, webcams, and smart phones. The technology viewed in science fiction television shows and movies years ago like Star Trek television seemed unachievable, unrealistic and light-years away, but today they are reality.

One technology that continues to amaze me is the field of biometrics. This particular technology uses the physical features and attributes of human traits to grant access to various systems and components via computers and networks. With the scan of a retina, facial recognition, or identification of a specific voice pattern, system access is granted. However, of all the biometric characteristics currently available and used, identification by hand print and/or fingerprint continues to be the most widely recognized and used.

Today there are keypads, iPhones, iPads and various other computer components that can be accessed with the single touch of a finger. Imagine that, with just one touch an individual can gain access to unlimited resources within a matter of seconds.

In the New Testament there is a story of a woman who was plagued with a physical infirmity for over twelve years. This woman suffered from her condition year after year until all of her resources were expended having gone from doctor to doctor seeking healing with no relief or help in sight.

One day Jesus came through her town on His way to perform another miracle. Having heard about the miraculous healing power of Jesus Christ, the woman made it up in her that if she could simply touch His clothing she would be made completely whole.

Thoughts

_____

_____

_____

_____

_____

_____

_____

With a goal in mind and a determination that could not be stopped, the woman pressed through the multitude of people that surrounded Jesus until she reached the Master. And simply with one touch to the hem of the clothing He wore, the woman was healed and made completely whole as His healing virtue flowed out and into her body (Matt. 9:20-21).

Well, just in case you didn't know it, this same healing power is still available to all today. Whether healing is needed in a relationship, marriage, finances or health in your body, the anointing and power of Jesus to heal is available right now by faith—all it takes is just one touch.

Are you in need of divine healing? With just one touch you too can have unlimited access to the anointed power of Jesus the Christ—the Divine Physician, Jehovah-Rapha, the Lord God our Healer today. By His stripes you WERE and ARE healed! "He personally bore our sins [our sickness and our disease] in His [own] body on the tree [as on an altar and offered Himself on it]...By His wounds you have been healed" (1 Pet. 2:24, Amplified Bible).

"...According to your faith and trust and reliance [on the power invested in Me] be it done to you" (Matt. 9:29, Amplified Bible).

April 12
GO AHEAD, TRY TO BREAK IT
Read: Ecc. 4:12

Unity is a very strong bond. And whenever a group of individuals unify, whether their purposes are for good or for evil, they become a force to be reckoned with.

This fact has been seen time and time again throughout history, for example, The Civil Rights Movement in America and the struggle for racial equality produced positive results for people of color as many (of all nationalities) unified and took a stand. And then there is an instance on a not so positive note involving a group within the Branch Davidian cult of Waco, Texas under the leadership of David Koresh in which all within the compound lost their lives in a long and intense stand-off with federal authorities as they stood defending false doctrine and what they believed to be right and true.

Again, the preceding demonstrates the awesome power of unity and what can be accomplished when two or more come together for one cause and one purpose.

Therefore, just as it is important for us to learn how to depend and rely on the guidance of the Holy Spirit, in a natural sense we must also learn how to trust and depend upon one another, our brothers and sisters in Christ and of God's family. "So let's not allow ourselves to get fatigued doing good. At the right time we will harvest a good crop if we don't give up, or quit. Right now, therefore, every time we get the chance, let us work for the benefit of all, starting with the people closest to us in the community of faith" (Gal. 6:9-10, The Message).

Thoughts

_____
_____
_____
_____
_____
_____
_____

The Apostle Paul also reminds us of this fact in Scripture (Eph. 4:2-6). Therefore, whether supporting a positive cause, on the job, in the home or in the church, unity is the main thing required to bring about progressive and effective change; we can't do it by ourselves. When internal focus, personal desires, and selfish ambitions are removed from the center, it is then through a unified front that we can accomplish great things.

As believers in Christ this is exactly what we must do if we expect to defeat the enemy and create an atmosphere of togetherness in the Body; we must depend on our brothers and sisters in Christ, as together we accomplish God's mission through selflessness, unity, and love (1 Cor. 12:12-14). Simply put, we each have a part to do; however, it takes us each individually doing our part together to bring about change.

When we are unified with one cause and for the right purpose we become an unbeatable force, a force that has a bond that is not easily broken!

"Two people are better off than one, for they can help each other succeed. If one person falls, the other can reach out and help. But someone who falls alone is in real trouble. Likewise, two people lying close together can keep each other warm. But how can one be warm alone? A person standing alone can be attacked and defeated, but two can stand back-to-back and conquer. Three are even better, for a triple-braided cord is not easily broken" (Ecc. 4:9-12, New Living Translation).

April 13
BOWING TO THE PRINCE IN THE PRESENCE OF THE KING
Read: Gen. 1:27-28

Governmental structures throughout the world are often as varied as the diversity of the people each government represents. Today the position of president is often utilized, which is a position similar to that of a king or queen but the way that government is executed is a little different. At any rate, these positions signify someone endowed with the highest power and authority.

And although the office of a king/queen in most countries is a position of the past, there are still a few countries like Europe, Africa, Asia, and the Middle East who utilize this form of government known as a monarchy. A perfect example of this can be seen in the news today with the recent birth of a son to England's Prince William and Catherine, Duchess of Cambridge. According to news media, with this birth there are actually now three living successors to the throne of England (Prince Charles, Prince William, and now the newborn son, the baby prince).

Thoughts

_____
_____
_____
_____
_____
_____
_____

In a monarchy, specific procedures are required to gain audience with the king/queen with one well-known protocol for entering the court of the king being to bow in his/her presence as a sign of reverence and respect. Imagine for a moment that Prince William is now the King of England, and he, Catherine, and their newborn son "the prince" are seated in a royal setting where protocol is expected. It would be a bit absurd for an individual to enter the court and presence of the king, but first bow to his son the prince instead—the one at this point who has little power and virtually no authority.

Yet many of us as Christians blindly find ourselves today doing the very same thing, but instead of bowing to an earthly prince or king, we bow to the prince of this world, satan, "the prince of the power of the air, the spirit who now works in the sons of disobedience" (Eph. 2:2, New King James Version) who is also referred to as the little "g" god of this world, because he actually only has the power and authority that we as believers in Christ give to him.

As believers we must acknowledge that Jesus has been given all authority in heaven and earth (Matt. 28:18), and not only does He have all authority, but He is even designated and often called the King of Kings (Rev. 17:14). Yet sadly, many who profess faith in the name of Christ routinely bow to the prince of this world instead, bowing to the one who has no power or authority.

Many bow to lust, envy, greed, sexual immorality, negative mindsets, and negative speech as we allow the dictates of this world's system to create our response thereby creating and perpetuating the wrong environment and atmosphere where the miraculous is hindered.

As believers, we must remember that we have the Greater One on the inside of us (1 Jn. 4:4). Therefore, although the prince may be in the world trying to establish his rule and reign, the KING has all dominion, power, and authority, and we are to live under His rule which is a theocratic monarchy or theocracy—ONE NATION UNDER GOD.

Are you bowing to the prince in the presence of the King? If so, then make it a purpose to follow the correct protocol since the KING is in authority, because just in case you didn't know it, the King's authority also now belongs to you (Gen. 1:27-28)!

April 14

HAVE YOU PREPARED FOR THE MEETING?
Read: Matt. 25:1-13

Throughout my years of military service I've noticed the further one progresses up through the ranks, the more prevalent meetings become. Meetings in the morning, meetings at noon,

Thoughts

_____
_____
_____
_____
_____
_____
_____
_____

meetings in the evening; meetings, meetings, meetings. It just seems as though the meetings never end. Yet meetings do serve a purpose when used constructively; however, when used unwisely a meeting can become counterproductive robbing individuals of one of life's most precious resources and commodities; TIME!

There is nothing worse than going to a meeting where there had been little to no preparation, and a waste of individual time. But when executed correctly, a meeting can be used for coordination, setup, and planning of future activities and events based on the information available at hand.

Today there are events and occurrences happening all over the world; entire cities being flooded, fires consuming acres upon acres of land, sickness and disease running rampant spreading at alarming rates, and senseless violence & destruction. Based on this information, what should one do? Simple, get ready and begin to prepare.

The majority of events happening today have already been predicted and prophesied in the Bible, "Famines and earthquakes will occur in various places. This is nothing compared to what is coming" (Matt. 24:6, The Message). The logical conclusion is that Jesus is soon to return, and return He will.

One day we will all meet the LORD, and He will return at a time that will be unplanned and unannounced. Therefore, it is our job as followers and believers in Christ to keep ourselves pure and be prepared for His return as the oil of His anointing continuously flows in and through our lives so that our light will continue to burn and prepare the way.

"With a loud command and with the shout of the chief angel and a blast of God's trumpet, the Lord will return from heaven. Then those who had faith in Christ before they died will be raised to life. Next, all of us who are still alive will be taken up into the clouds together with them to meet the Lord in the sky. From that time on we will all be with the Lord forever" (1 Thess. 4:16-17, Contemporary English Version).

Though we may not know the day or the hour, one thing is certain and that is the Lord is soon to return, and He expects us to be ready. It's up to each of us as individuals to make sure that we are prepared for His return; the preparation that we make is entirely up to us.

The signs of the time are all around us, if we would only hear with spiritual ears and see with spiritual eyes. Have you prepared for the meeting? This is not the time to straddle the fence or to be indecisive in your actions. Give your heart to Him completely today because out of it, life itself flows (Prov. 4:23). The TIME is now, for tomorrow is not promised!

Thoughts

_____

_____

_____

_____

_____

_____

"So stay alert. You have no idea when he might arrive" (Matt. 25:13, The Message).

April 15
WHEN A MAN LOSES VISION
Read: Judges 16

The role of the man in the family is very important, and although society and the media attempt to belittle and/or feminize who a man should actually be; this does not negate the fact that God has placed the man in the family as a symbol of strength and stability. Man was created to rule and reign, in a godly sense (Gen. 1:27:28).

Samson is a man who displayed the type of strength that is sorely needed in families today, and he is recorded as being one of the strongest men of biblical times. His exploits include tearing apart a lion with his bare hands, and killing 1,000 men from the enemy's camp with the jawbone of a donkey. Samson was not afraid to confront the things that sought to bring division or destruction, and chose to face all opposition head-on.

Samson's awesome strength had been given to him by God. Being a Nazarite by birth, his supernatural power and ability could be summoned at will as long as he did not cut his hair—one thing directly associated with the vow existing between he and God at birth that he was required to guard, maintain, and keep. So as long as his hair remained intact and uncut, unrestrained strength was available at a moment's notice.

However, Samson suffered from what many of us as men still fall prey to today, lust of the eyes and the fulfilling of fleshly desires. He was enticed by a beautiful woman named Delilah, to divulge the secret to his strength. Although it took Delilah a few attempts to pry the information out of Samson, her feminine charm overcame him as he eventually fell into the trap that caused him to literally "spill the beans" and reveal the secret to his strength and anointing.

As a result his hair was cut, he was immediately captured by his enemies, his eyes were gouged out, and he was then placed in shackles and chains becoming a servant and slave to his enemies. Samson literally lost sight of what was important and the main thing as he allowed seduction to lead him astray. He compromised his convictions, beliefs and vow to God for that which looked enticing and the thing that could only provide momentary satisfaction and pleasure.

Lust was Samson's fatal flaw and if we were honest with ourselves, this is often our fatal flaw as well, because everything that looks good may not necessarily be good for us. We may not necessarily lust after another person, but we can also lust after things we know we should not be doing and/or should not have. Succumbing to these things not only harms us, but also often detrimental to those who are connected to us as well; especially as men in the role as the head.

Thoughts

_____

_____

_____

_____

_____

_____

_____

No matter how strong we think we are or think we may be, when we allow the things of the world to seduce, entice and take our focus off of that which is really important (righteousness, peace and joy in the Holy Ghost (Rom. 14:17), suffering and heartache is usually the end result. Although having strength is good and is something we all need; strength and power without vision can lead to destruction (1 Cor. 10:12, The Message). When you lose sight (or vision), those in your sphere of influence who need your guidance, direction, and anointing suffer as a result (Prov. 29:18).

April 16
GIVE-AND-TAKE
Read: Gen. 2:24

By definition, "relationship" is generally thought of in terms of "connecting or binding participants, and kinship [family]." I believe the primary and most important word in any definition of the word relationship is "connection."

The notion of relationship was established by God in the very beginning with the first man and woman (Adam and Eve). This has also been the focus of Scripture from Genesis to Revelation, God restoring man to his proper place of relationship with Him; restoring the right connection.

Experts contend that "in a healthy relationship, there [needs to] be an equal amount of give and take...Unfortunately, it's very common to encounter a person who is at [one extreme of give and take, with no balance]." Those who are currently in a relationship or have ever been in a relationship will probably agree, that for the most part, the preceding statement is fairly accurate and on point.

Relationships (the right kind of relationships that is) can be a beautiful and fulfilling experience; however, they require time and effort by both parties and must be established in the proper context (based on God's Word).

Having been married now for more than a few years, I've learned from first-hand experience that an unbalanced relationship, either on the giving or receiving end can be detrimental to maintaining the oneness that is to be achieved after uniting as husband and wife. This requires considerable effort both from the husband and the wife.

Thoughts

_____
_____
_____
_____
_____
_____

"That's why a man will leave his own father and mother. He marries a woman, and the two of them become like one person" (Gen. 2:24, Contemporary English Version).

However, true oneness only comes when each individual (the man and the woman) find completeness and wholeness in Christ first, spend quality time together, have an understanding of one another's goals & ambitions, likes & dislikes; this requires quality time, communication, commitment, and a dying to SELF. However, "the most important part of any healthy relationship between two people is being able to talk and listen to one another;" in other words, relationships involve a connection with a two-way exchange.

When communication is lost in a relationship, the connection naturally begins to disintegrate; this is when the problems begin.

The same concept applies in a spiritual sense. In order to truly understand God the Father and know His ways, we have to develop a relationship or connection with Him to maintain proper balance; this is only achieved by spending quality time with Him in prayer and meditating on His Word.

"If you live in Me [abide vitally united to Me] and My words remain in you and continue to live in your hearts, ask whatever you will, and it shall be done for you" (Jn. 15:7, Amplified Bible).

April 17
JUST PASSING THROUGH
Read: 1 Pet. 2:11

When writing devotionals I tend to draw from my military travels abroad because having been in the Navy for more than half my life, this has been my experience. With that said, serving on active duty in the world's finest Navy has afforded me the opportunity to visit many countries around the world: Greece, Turkey, France, Singapore, Italy, Denmark, Korea, Africa, England, Portugal, and various countries in the Middle East just to name a few.

Visiting the majority of these countries was very enlightening from a cultural perspective, along with being able to physically see and actually visit what many only have the opportunity to just read about or see in history or humanities books. Therefore, my military travels have allowed me to see historical artifacts and structures up close and personal. Yet at the end of the day, that country's cultural experience is not my experience since my citizenship resides elsewhere.

Thoughts

So whenever I get back on the plane or naval vessel that provided me travel to a specific location, my citizenship or affiliation with that country does not remain (that is unless I chose to apply for dual-citizenship there); however, I continue to be a citizen of my home country or nation the United States of America. Countries abroad are nice for short visits; but when compared to the governmental structure of the United States (U.S.) and the make-up of our country, these other nations cannot compare with the liberty and freedom that we are afforded in day no matter how bad things may appear to be at times.

But in order to visit these various countries and nations, a passport was required to enter and depart the right way. This passport identified who I was and the nation I was connected to. Therefore, when traveling all it takes is a simple display of a passport and other supporting documentation to grant me access to various countries around the world, all while retaining my identity and remaining a citizen of the United States.

As Believers in Christ, we are granted similar privileges. At new birth or conversion we receive a passport from death to life, and become citizens of the Kingdom of God (1 Pet. 1:23). Though we may physically live here on earth, we must remember that this is not our home because we have a new home in heaven waiting on us; God's Word tells us so (Jn. 14:2-3).

However, in order to get to our final destination there are some things that we must first do, the primary requirement is that we remain on the right path. Therefore, staying on the right path requires us to live right and walk in obedience to God's Word in every way and every day (Is. 26:7-10).

Righteousness and holiness is what allows us to reach our final destination as we pass through (Prov. 8:20).

According to author, leadership expert, and motivational speaker Dr. Stephen R. Covey, "We are not human beings on a spiritual journey; we are spiritual beings on a human journey." This is why we should not conform our thinking and actions to the ways of the world (Rom. 12:2). In other words, we are not earthly beings having a spiritual experience, but rather are spiritual beings having an earthly experience. This is why we must constantly remind ourselves as believers in Christ that earth is not our home and we are only visiting.

Thoughts

_____

_____

_____

_____

_____

_____

_____

April 18
THE MASTER KEY
Read: Matt. 7:8

A college student returns to her dorm room after a long and trying day of classes. She walks a hallway that seems to never end, and then finally reaches her room door. She opens her purse to retrieve the key; however, her keys are nowhere to be found.

A frantic search ensues, she begins to retrace her steps of that particular morning prior to departing the room; suddenly she realizes that she had left her key ring on the night stand. Unfortunately her roommate is at work, and there is no spare key hidden above the door frame or under the doormat.

She has a ton of homework to do, with the resources needed to complete these assignments locked away inside her room, what is she to do? Dorm student advisor to the rescue!

The anxious student remembers that the student advisor is equipped for situations like this. The dorm advisor arrives within a matter of minutes with a key ring and a master key, the door is opened in an instant. The exhausted student was then able to receive the much needed rest she so desperately longed for before diving into hours of homework; all it took was one key.

Just as there are natural keys that have the ability to open locked doors, there are also spiritual keys that work utilizing the same principle. One of these keys is prayer (Matt. 7:7-11).

It is clearly evident that prayer is an essential component to opening the locked doors in the various areas of our lives.

Over the years I've heard a familiar phrase concerning prayer stated over and over again; it basically says that "Prayer is the key, and faith unlocks the door." In other words, prayer changes things and opens up unlimited opportunity to those who believe in faith; nothing is impossible to those who pray and believe (Heb. 11:6).

Sadly, many times we allow seemingly locked doors to prevent us from obtaining the rest and peace we search for and seek after, when the key is already in our possession.

Doors generally remain locked until it is opened with the right key. Do you have any locked doors in your life today that are keeping you from resting in the fullness of God's presence?

Just in case you didn't know it, you have the Master Key (prayer) readily available and at your disposal, and it is absolutely free of charge; but it's up to you to open the door(s) by spending quality time with God and seeking His face.

Don't let locked doors keep you from the rest and peace you long for. God desires to refresh you, so pull out your spiritual key ring and begin using your Master Key (Phil. 4:6-7)!

Thoughts

_____
_____
_____
_____
_____
_____
_____

April 19
REMOVE AND REPLACE
Read: Matt. 12:43-45

In the day and age we live in, with the population increasing and growing more and more each day; land and property has become a hot commodity especially for developers and real estate experts who look to capitalize on meeting the immediate need. However, land development and cultivation, and preparing it for commercial and personal use is no easy task, and is something that takes considerable time, resources, and requires a focused effort.

Well, one day a property owner decided to remove several large trees from the five acres of land he owned. So he employed a local tree removing business that specialized in extracting trees; not just cutting them down but actually removing them from the root. The workers arrived to begin the process, and with a lot of great equipment and even more manpower, one by one each tree was removed.

But even though the trees had been removed, there were now several fairly large holes spread out across the property. As a precautionary measure (to prevent injury to personnel from falling into these massive openings) and to beautify the area, landscape experts advised the property owner of the need to fill in the holes to avoid any potential problems in the future.

A few days had passed and then a couple of weeks had gone by without this issue being addressed. During this time there was a shift in the weather in which an over-abundance of rain was predicted in the forecast and had actually fallen as if buckets of water were literally being dumped from the sky.

Because the property owner chose not to take advantage of the opportunity to fill the holes when it was appropriate and more convenient, there were now several small ponds on the land attracting not just one single insect but masses of potentially disease-carrying mosquitoes posing a health risk to all who stepped foot on the land.

As believers in Christ, when we receive knowledge of the Truth (Jn. 14:6), we too must begin to remove some things. We must begin to use our time, resources, and focused our efforts to uproot and remove sin, idols and unforgiveness from our hearts and our lives. But beyond that we must then take immediate action to fill in these gaps and voids with something else—-the Word of God.

Thoughts

_____
_____
_____
_____
_____
_____
_____

It's good to identify and confess sin and unforgiveness in our lives, and it's even better to address these areas and actually begin to remove those things that continue to weigh us down. But it is critical that when sin and unforgiveness is removed, that we immediately fill the void with the right thing. This is absolutely essential to ensuring our enemy the devil has no room to setup camp in our hearts through the cracks and crevices we allow to remain, which in many instances place us in a worse state or condition than when we began (Matt. 12:43-45).

Don't give the enemy a place to take up residence in your heart; once sin and unforgiveness is identified take immediate action to deal with the root cause and then begin to REMOVE AND REPLACE!

"Leave no [such] room or foothold for the devil [give no opportunity to him]" (Eph. 4:27, Amplified Bible).

April 20

STOP TRYING TO FOOL GOD, HE ALREADY KNOWS
Read: 2 Tim. 2:19

There are a select group of individuals who make their living pretending to be someone they are not; "impersonators for hire." According to one dictionary definition an impersonator is "someone who imitates or copies the behavior or actions of another." With a little makeup, change in hairstyle, and the right clothing; these impersonators can look so much like their subject, that fans and associates may find it difficult to tell the difference believing the impersonator to be the real thing.

But when these individuals come in contact with close relatives, those with an intimate knowledge of the individual; the impersonator can be immediately identified and weeded out. The same applies to Christ, believers, and the non-believers. An individual may pretend to be Christian and get away with it for awhile, but when they come in contact with true believers, those with an intimate relationship with God the Father and understanding of His Holy Word; the truth comes out.

In the parable of the wheat and tares (Matt. 13:24-30) from the time the seeds were sown, both the wheat (the real) and the tares (the fake) grew side-by-side; both looked identical even up to the time that each were full-grown. However, on the day of harvest when it was time for the sower to reap or collect his crop, he could immediately differentiate the real from the fake. He then brought in the wheat, but discarded the tares because they had no real substance.

Though the wheat and tares may grow together, the one with an intimate knowledge of what He has sown will be able to make a distinction between the two.

There are many who profess to be "Christians," that really are not. They know how to talk the talk, and attempt to walk the walk; but they have no real substance (or true relationship). I've

Thoughts

_____
_____
_____
_____
_____
_____
_____

131

heard it said, that "sleeping in a garage will not make you a car, just as going to church will not instantly make you a Christian;" it's about a personal relationship with God the Father through the Son Jesus Christ.

Conversely, there are also Christians who try to fit into the mold of the world's system. Doing what the world does, saying what the world says, and living according to fleshly desires; when they actually belong to another system, or better yet Kingdom. But like Peter in the New Testament who continually tried to deny Christ, our speech (or lifestyle) will betray us as well (Matt. 26:73). When we truly belong to God although we may be able to run for a while, we can't hide for long because that which is resident on the inside will eventually manifest itself on the outside.

In both scenarios above we see individuals putting up a front and pretending to be something they are not; so there is no need to slip and slide while trying to hide or fake it until we make it. God already knows who really belongs to Him.

Are you confused about your identity, or who you really are? Well, God isn't and He knows who truly belong to Him. So, stop trying to fool God because He already knows!

April 21
DON'T PICK IT UP AGAIN
Read: 1 Pet. 5:7

Among the more common every day, non-life threatening ailments; back problems and issues with joints probably top the list for patient complaints to doctors. Imagine someone going to see a chiropractor for reoccurring back pain; the physician completes a routine examination and comes to the conclusion that the individual has pulled several muscles in his lower back.

The physician then begins to make inquiries as to what activities could have caused such a strain. The individual's reply to the physician is, "In a test of testosterone, I was challenged by someone to pick-up a weight that I already knew was too heavy for me to carry. But not wanting to appear weak, I attempted to lift the object anyway."

Thoughts

_____

_____

_____

_____

_____

_____

_____

With a raised brow and inquisitive look the physician replies, "Why would you attempt to lift something that you already knew was too heavy for you to bear? My advice, that is if you truly desire to rid yourself of this pain and want to prevent further injury, is to not pick it up again."

Common sense should have prevailed in this scenario, yet it didn't. The individual knowing that an object was too heavy for him to carry decided to pick it up anyway, relying upon his own strength and ability; however, the end result was unnecessary stress and pain. He allowed his pride to push him towards a place that would only cause more discomfort and suffering.

Although many of us may not go as far as the above individual to pick-up an object that is too heavy for us to bear; in a spiritual sense we try to carry the weight, cares and burdens of this world that were never designed for us to pick-up and definitely things that were never designed for us to ever carry.

Ps. 55:22 admonishes us as believers to "Pile your troubles on GOD's shoulders—he'll carry your load, he'll help you out. He'll never let good people topple into ruin" (The Message).

Oftentimes we recognize our dilemma, cry out to God for help and a breakthrough springs forth while receiving our deliverance as we release the weight of burdens that hold us down. But like a hamster on a wheel we go right back to repeating the same cycle again by picking up the very issues, problems and sin that had just been laid down as if we have the ability or strength within us to change them. This of course invariably brings pain and suffering back to ourselves while the remedy is right in front of us in the Word.

It is amazing to see how quick we are to receive and accept a diagnosis and the subsequent advice of an earthly physician, but are often reluctant to receive and follow the instructions of the One who created us, and has healing in His Word and in His hands.

Jesus Christ is the Divine Physician (Jer. 8:22), and He knows what is best for us. He never encourages us to carry anything that is too heavy for us to bear; instead He gently reminds us to give it all over to Him so that He can bear the load for us. "Give all your worries and cares to God, for he cares about you" (1 Pet. 5:7, New Living Translation).

Don't allow the enemy to challenge you through pride to pick-up or carry burdens and weights you were never designed to bear. What are you carrying that you need to put down today? What have you put down and then picked up again? Quit trying to shoulder burdens and cares that were never intended for you to carry; release it, let it go, and DON'T PICK IT UP AGAIN!

Thoughts

_____
_____
_____
_____
_____
_____
_____

April 22

IT REALLY IS ABOUT YOU
Read: Lk. 19:10

There was a popular gospel song released a few years ago with lyrics that mentioned the fact that "It's Not About Us;" and went on to say that it's all about Jesus. The preceding is in fact an accurate statement, but I would suggest there is more.

This particular song is very nice and I personally enjoy listening to it; however, not to take anything away from the song or its intended message I would submit that if it is not about us, then why would God send His "only" Son Jesus Christ to earth in the first place?

It was because of the fall of man in the Garden of Eden, the place where sin initially came into the world, and of course the only remedy for sin was and still is a sacrifice, however, not just any sacrifice, but a perfect offering. Jesus (the only Unique One) was the only begotten of the Father and only one qualified for this task because he was without sin and knew no sin. Therefore, His sacrifice for our sin on the cross was not about Himself or solely for Himself, but was about you and me.

Jesus did not come to save Himself, although it was completely in His power and ability to do so by calling on the assistance of a legion of angels to remove Him from the cross. He knew that He had a purpose to fulfill, a purpose that involved coming to save you, me, and the rest of mankind. "For the Son of Man came to seek and to save that which was lost" (Lk. 19:10, Amplified Bible), God sent His Son to die a sinner's death because of His unfailing love for us all.

"For God so greatly loved and dearly prized the world that He [even] gave up His only begotten (unique) Son, so that whoever believes in (trusts in, clings to, relies on) Him shall not perish (come to destruction, be lost) but have eternal (everlasting) life" (Jn. 3:16, Amplified Bible);" "whosoever" encompasses and includes you as well.

As a result of God's love, you and I no longer have to live defeated lives because there is victory in Christ through the cross. "But thanks be to God, Who gives us the victory [making us conquerors] through our Lord Jesus Christ" (1 Cor. 15:57, Amplified Bible).

Although it is not about us in that "It's not about money; it's not about fame; it's not about titles;" I would suggest that it is about us being one with God and complete in Christ acknowledging Him for what He has done. And He did it all for you and for me.

Thoughts

_____
_____
_____
_____
_____
_____
_____

Since Jesus laid down His life for us, we are to do the same for others. "This is how we've come to understand and experience love: Christ sacrificed his life for us. This is why we ought to live sacrificially for our fellow believers, and not just be out for ourselves" (1 Jn. 3:16, The Message).

Know today that the cross is about you, and as such you have an obligation to display, reciprocate, and extend the same sacrificial love of God that has been so freely given to you out to others. It's not just about us as individuals, but about each of us as individuals being complete in Christ thereby adding and supplying to the overall strength and unity of the body of Christ as a whole!

April 23
BETWEEN A ROCK AND A HARD PLACE
Read: Phil. 2:8-10

Situations in life often place us in positions of uncertainty with no physical map or navigation system to provide direction. And as we travel down unfamiliar roads or the unknown paths of life approaching the literal forks in the road, at that point we are then challenged with the decision to either go left or right.

Decisions, decisions, decisions; should we make a particular purchase now just because the item is on sale and suffer the consequences of bad stewardship later or would it be wiser to just wait until a more appropriate time? Should I connect myself to this man or woman based on external qualities and physical attraction, or allow holiness and commitment be the central focus in the relationship?

Life is all about choices, and these choices often determine our destiny and future. And sometimes making the right choice requires a sacrifice.

I am reminded of a story of a father who set out for a recreational trip at sea in a small boat with his son and son's best friend. Initially the weather was nice, everyone was enjoying themselves, and everything was going well, and then all of a sudden out of nowhere a fierce storm erupted causing the two young men to be thrown overboard.

As the boat was tossed about to and fro by the ravenous ocean like a small tree branch amidst the mighty waves, the distance between the boat and the two young men continued to increase. The father now faced a very difficult issue in that he could only save one individual with the single life ring that was available. So what was the father to do, save his son or save his son's friend?

The father had a very tough decision to make; however, he knew that his son's friend was not a Christian and that if he died he would spend an eternity in Hell. But his son, on the other

Thoughts

_____
_____
_____
_____
_____
_____
_____
_____

hand, had accepted Christ at an early age so he knew that if he died he would see him in Heaven again someday, yet at the same time he deeply loved his son and wanted to spare his life.

With a dreadful decision to make and anguish on his face, the father yelled out to his son that he loved him and then threw the life ring to his son's best friend. By the time the friend was pulled to safety and was now safely situated in the boat, the father's son had been swallowed by the raging sea. The father chose to sacrifice his own son's life to save another, giving up that which was very precious and dear to him.

As the story goes and as time went on, not only did the son's best friend eventually accept Jesus Christ as his personal Lord and Savior, he also went on to become a well-known pastor who led many others to Christ.

Sometimes we each are called to make tough and unpopular decisions; however, when we look beyond self, there is often great reward in the end. Jesus chose to make the tough decision to purchase our salvation by sacrificing His own life so that many could live, and for this God the Father rewarded His faithfulness and obedience(Lk. 22:42). Are you between a rock and a hard place today? Then seek to do the Father's will.

April 24
JUST WHEN YOU THOUGHT IT WAS OVER
Read: Jn. 19:30

I've never really been a big fan of theatrical plays; however, I do recall attending my first play several years back. I never thought a live drama production could be so long, sitting for what appeared to be an eternity when in actuality the time spent was just a few hours.

Don't get me wrong it was a very good production; it just seemed a bit too long for me. And as with any good movie or television show, throughout the play there were shifts in the plot with various twists and turns that helped keep my attention.

At one point a large curtain began to descend and the once dim lights were slowly illuminated. With excitement I thought to myself, "Surely this must be the end."

Thoughts

_____
_____
_____
_____
_____
_____
_____

It was then that I realized this was merely an intermission and there were actually a few more acts with another two hours remaining; just when I thought it was over.

Theatrical/drama productions are usually divided into acts (which are nothing more than divisions of drama) ranging anywhere from one to as many as five. And between every act, the curtain would descend giving the appearance or impression the end had come; however, the show was not over because there was always much more!

Well, one of the greatest books ever written, a book that tops the bestseller's list year after year (the Bible) is filled with wonderful stories of history, humor, practical application and drama. One of the best dramas written therein is Jesus' journey to and the events associated with Calvary. A story filled with deception, betrayal, and ultimate victory.

When Jesus cried out "It is finished" (Jn. 19:30) as He hung on the cross, Satan thought he had achieved certain victory. Surely this would put an end to the prospect of a Messiah, a Savior and new King coming to rescue the Jews (God's chosen people) from their oppressors; redemption of mankind from sin; and the bringing of salvation into the world. But contrary to what the enemy thought, these words came to signify so much more and actually produced new life.

Just when you thought it was over, everything you have need of today is wrapped up in the three powerful words "IT IS FINISHED!"

April 25
BE NOT AFRAID, ONLY BELIEVE
Read: Mk. 5:35-43

In Mark chapter 5 of the New Testament, Jesus had just delivered a demon-possessed man who was filled with multiple evil spirits and had also healed a woman who battled with an issue of blood for over twelve long years. I'm sure Jesus wanted to get away from the people to enjoy some well-deserved and much needed rest, but as He made His way through the crowds He overheard a conversation concerning the death of a 12-year old girl. And because of His nature and being who He is, His compassion compelled Him to move on her behalf.

The girl's father, who was a religious leader in the synagogue, came to the crowd with the sole purpose of seeking out Jesus to perform a miracle of healing for his daughter, but unfortunately the young girl died while the father searched for the only One who could heal. And as it is today, when we are believing God to do the miraculous by bringing rivers of water out of a desert and making a way where there seems to be no outlet; it is then that the nay-sayers, doubters, and haters attempt to discourage us.

Thoughts

_____
_____
_____
_____
_____
_____
_____

137

As the father approached Jesus for help, the crowd that was also filled with other religious leaders told him not to bother Jesus with his issue and that it was too late because the girl was already dead. But isn't it great to know that we have a God of faith who speaks faith to us through His Word. "Words kill, words give life; they're either poison or fruit—you choose" (Prov. 18:21, The Message).

As the story goes, the father eventually finds Jesus who accompanies him on the journey to his home with a few of Jesus' disciples. When Jesus heard the unbelief and faithless words coming from the crowd of people that gathered to mourn the death of the young girl He simply said "the girl was only sleeping." But upon hearing Jesus' words the crowd mocked and laughed at Him.

At this point Jesus did not allow His emotions to overwhelm Him like many today who are quick to pull out a gun or go to their purse for that blade thereby making a bad situation worse, instead He simply dismissed everyone from the room except those who were like-minded, those who believed and had faith. He only wanted those present who could believe for the miraculous while standing in the midst of the horrendous.

Jesus then said to the dead girl's father, "Do not be afraid; only believe" (Mk. 5:36, New King James Version). Jesus took the young girl by the hand and said "Talitha koum," which means, "Little girl, get up." At that, she was up and walking around! This girl was twelve years of age" (Mk. 5:41-42, The Message).

Many times as Christians we allow the world's opinion and popular thought to strike fear in our hearts as we are often mocked for our uncommon beliefs, rather than listening to and believing what it says in God's Word. We are encouraged to not be afraid but believe the Word of God and the promises contained therein. This is exactly what we must do if we expect to see the miraculous happen, simply have FAITH and BELIEVE!

Fear is nothing more than the opposite of and an absence of faith. Does your current situation appear to be hopeless and/or dead? "Don't be afraid, only believe;" turn your fear into faith and then watch God move (Rom. 4:17-18)!

Thoughts

_____
_____
_____
_____
_____
_____
_____

April 26

A CAPTIVITY THAT PROMOTES FREEDOM
Read: 2 Cor. 10:3-5

Over the years there have been a number of movie box office hits that were based on the premise of the captor/hostage scenario. In these movies a hostage is usually taken by a captor for the purpose of obtaining something of value in return/exchange for the captured individual, or unsuspecting bank patrons are held for ransom in order to meet the outlandish demands of power-thirsty and money-hungry thieves.

In these scenarios individual control is forfeited and literally thrown out the window in what becomes a state of captivity because the hostage must yield to and comply with the captor's demands. A hostage is defined as "one that is involuntarily controlled by an outside influence;" therefore, in a hostage situation, the captured individual basically gives up all rights to do what he or she wants or pleases to do.

Well we too have an adversary, a captor if you will, who is well aware of this tactic and often uses it against us and to his advantage while literally keeping us in bondage to our past by negatively influencing our minds and thought processes.

He does this by placing unfair demands on us that often restrict our individual preference and/or control through thoughts of inferiority, low self-esteem, poor self-image, the acceptance of the notion that "this is how it will always be," doubt, fear, and unbelief. Our minds are held captive as he wields and manipulates control.

But this should not be so, because our God always has a better plan and it is high time for us as believers in Christ to "flip the script" as we begin to exercise the authority that He has given to us as we wage war in the battlefield of our minds.

"We do live in the world, but we do not fight in the same way the world fights. We fight with weapons that are different from those the world uses. Our weapons have power from God that can destroy the enemy's strong places. We destroy people's arguments and every proud thing that raises itself against the knowledge of God. We capture every thought and make it give up and obey Christ" (2 Cor. 10:3-5, New Century Version).

Every negative, self-defeating thought the enemy attempts to plant in our minds must be brought into the captivity and obedience of Christ the Living Word (Jn. 1:14), because if we allow the enemy's negative seeds to be planted they will eventually grow and reproduce after their kind. This is why our thoughts must literally become hostage to the Word Himself since only He has the power to shatter any shackle or chain that tries to keep our minds in bondage.

However, He (the Word) must be employed and put to use in our lives if we desire victory in the battlefield of our minds because faith alone is not enough, there must also be corresponding action that is solidified with obedience (Heb. 4:12). The enemy does everything in his power to constantly remind us of who we "WERE," while God continues to encourage us and already has determined who we "ARE" and "WILL BECOME."

Thoughts

_____
_____
_____
_____
_____
_____
_____

Is your mind being held captive to the enemy's influence and hindering forward progress? Then take authority over this precious commodity by flipping the script and bringing your thoughts under the obedience of God's Word (Jn. 8:36).

April 27
STOP TRYING TO COVER IT
Read: Gen. 3:8-10

Oftentimes as believers in Christ, when there are areas in our lives that we know are not pleasing to God we attempt to hide or cover them from those around us, and also from God as if that were really possible. We put up a façade to give everyone the impression that we are in a better position than we actually are. We talk the religious talk with the ability to quote Scripture at will but all the while putting up a good spiritual front and a mask to cover where we really are. But deep down inside our soul is crying out "HELP!"

In this instance we attempt to hide our issues or better yet our sins from others and even God as if He doesn't already know.

When sin begins to creep into our lives and then cleverly makes its way into our hearts, it does not travel alone but also brings its best friend "fear" along with it. The first man and woman (Adam and Eve) in the Garden of Eden are a perfect example of this. It was because of their disobedience and subsequent attempt to cover what they had done that sin and fear entered the world.

Adam and Eve were placed in the Garden of Eden (a fertile place, a place of delight) to enjoy God's presence. However, they allowed temptation and sin to separate them from God's presence which caused Adam (the man) to abdicate and forfeit the authority that had been granted to him to have dominion.

Just as the first man and woman were created to have communion and fellowship with God, we as 21st century believers have been created to do the same. Yet many consistently choose to disobey God's commands while following our own desires and end up on the path of unrighteousness which is the total opposite of "right standing" with God; as a result our sin begins to separate us from His presence (that fertile and prosperous place) as fear takes the reins and begins to control our actions, our motives, and desires.

Thoughts

_____
_____
_____
_____
_____
_____
_____

Once Adam and Eve both yielded temptation, it was at this point that their understanding was enlightened and their minds opened as they attempted to hide from God (the One who created them, sustained them and desired communion with them). Since they now knew

140

exactly what they were doing, instead of desiring, seeking and enjoying the normal fellowship in His presence they were normally accustomed to they instead chose to cover-up the wrong they had done. Sin and fear was the separator and common denominator (Gen. 3:8-10).

Imagine that. Here were the only two human beings on the face of the earth attempting to hide from the Creator of all things, the Omni-Present One who is everywhere at the same time. And even though there are billions of people on the earth today, God still knows each of us individually by name (Ex. 33:17) and knows exactly where we are, both physically and spiritually.

Instead of trying to hide what is already obvious to God, we must allow the light of His Holy Word to shine into the dark recesses of our lives if we truly seek and desire real transformation.

Sin prompts us to cover it and hide, while confession and repentance through Christ allows us to be transparent and gives us the ability to be prosperous and thrive. So, stop trying to cover it because He already knows!

April 28

DON'T ALLOW YOUR EXCESS TO BECOME WASTE
Read: 1 Pet. 4:10

Christmas morning finally arrived; for weeks the kids anxiously anticipated the arrival of this day hoping to receive the gift they longed for all year. And even though the sun was barely up, the excitement of what was in store caused the children to awaken from their sleep and run downstairs to a tree filled with unopened gifts and presents underneath.

All of the commotion in the house caused the remainder of the family that was sleeping to get up and since they were now up, the parents decided to get up and head towards the tree as well, of course with camera in hand to capture the expression on each child's face as gifts were unwrapped.

But in an unusual turn of events the atmosphere immediately shifted and the excitement began to dissipate. Instead of opening their gifts, each child just sat near the tree staring aimlessly at the unopened presents. And within minutes, a time that was envisioned to be a joyous occasion and exciting moment suddenly turned into a solemn and somber event.

Thoughts

_____

_____

_____

_____

_____

_____

_____

The presents or gifts were designed to bring excitement and joy; however, the corresponding action needed to bring about this joy required the gifts to be actually opened and used. A gift given to someone is useless unless the gift is opened and then used.

For instances, what good would it be to have a 3-carat platinum diamond ring neatly wrapped in a box sitting on a shelf somewhere if the box were never opened, with the ring never being put on and/or displayed? For ladies possessing a ring of this magnitude is something they would want everyone to see.

Yet in the above instance, thousands of dollars would literally just sit on a shelf somewhere collecting dust, with no one able to gaze upon its beauty. This is just one example of excessive waste.

As believers in Christ, we often demonstrate this pattern of excessive waste on a regular basis, in a spiritual sense. Week after week, many of us sit in God's house receiving His Word for at that moment in what can be described as "Obtaining our spiritual fix for the day so that we can get full with the Word."

We often go to church with a selfish mentality expecting the LORD to just meet our needs, to bless us, and make us feel good. And when we receive our fill for the week, what do we ordinarily do? We do absolutely nothing with it as the excitement of what was received begins to go to waste.

Sadly, the customary thing for many of us to do after eating a good meal is fall asleep and then wake-up asking for more when we are already stuffed as it is. As we apply this to our lives as Christians, God does not just fill us with His love, His mercy, His compassion, and His Word for us to keep it to ourselves. We are designed to be dispensers of His blessings and the gifts He has freely given.

We each have specific assignments and gifts that are designed to be used in the building of God's Kingdom. According to Eph. 4:7 "Christ has generously divided out his gifts to us" (CEV); however, it is entirely up to each of us to unwrap these gifts and begin using and employing them.

So, don't keep the gift that God has placed inside of you wrapped up, release it so that His blessings may continue to flow. And above all else, don't allow your excess to become waste (1 Pet. 4:10)!

Thoughts

_____
_____
_____
_____
_____
_____
_____

April 29
RELEASE YOUR TREASURE
Read: 2 Cor. 4:7

In the New Testament book of Matthew, there was a group of men known as "wise men" who made a journey to the east after being prompted to seek out and follow the star that would ultimately lead them to the new king of the Jews who was prophesied to be born, a Messiah who would deliver His people. This Messiah was none other than Jesus the Christ.

After a fairly long journey traveling through desert plains, up, over and around mountains; these men eventually reached their final destination and found themselves in the presence of the One they sought out. And when they arrived, these men did not come empty-handed; instead each was prepared to present a gift.

Knowing the importance of the moment and to whom they were honoring, they did not present trinkets or re-gifted items that were previously received. Instead they presented their very best, gifts that were precious and of significant value: gold, frankincense, myrrh. Even though they might not have realized it at the time, these gifts were in essence treasures being released in sincere acts of worship.

And though each of these gentlemen were obviously prominent, well-established and wealthy individuals who could have sent messengers or servants to deliver these gifts on their behalf, each chose to get up from their place of comfort and go in order to release and present their individual gifts from their treasure chests themselves (Matt. 2:1-2, 11).

Each of these men went out of his way to release their individual treasure in wonderful acts of worship to this newborn King, with no concern about the toils of the journey or even how much expense or cost involved. Well, we each have the ability to do the very same.

The Bible clearly indicates that we too, as believers, have a treasure, "But we have this treasure in earthen vessels, that the excellency of the power may be of God, and not of us" (2 Cor. 4:7, King James Version). Although it is inside of us, this treasure is not just for our benefit. But just like the wise men, our treasure is released when we begin to worship in and through our service to and for others.

As long as we focus on how tough the journey may be, as we consistently think about the cost and its effect on our present level of comfort, our treasure chests will remain closed and of little benefit to anyone else. It is when we make a conscious decision to get up and move out of our comfort zones to release the seed of the treasure that we have abiding deep within that change begins to happen. This comes through wisdom.

Thoughts

_____

_____

_____

_____

_____

_____

_____

Attaining true wisdom and understanding of who we are and what we possess inside of us is a precursor to rendering acceptable worship to the Father. He does not just want us to present the rest, but desires that each of us present our very best.

Someone is in need of the spiritual gifts that are locked up and stored within you. Choose to release your treasure in acts of true worship today!

April 30
NO LONGER CONDEMNED
Read: Rom. 8:1-2

A beautiful home sits along the shoreline of one of the most popular vacation resort areas in the country. Travelers from locations all around the world migrate to this locale each year for rest, relaxation, and some well-deserved fun. The owner already has several other homes and can only use one at a time, so he decides to rent this vacation get-away to visitors providing a comfortable home away from home filled with every amenity possible.

But unexpectedly with the ever-changing effects and unpredictability of the weather, out of nowhere a terrible storm strikes the area leaving a path of destruction behind with anything that stood in its way. Although this vacation home is directly hit by the storm, it managed to survive and was not completely destroyed. However, because of its now weakened condition, the city had no choice but to place a "CONDEMNED" notice on the severely damaged structure.

Due to unforeseen circumstances and issues with insurance, the homeowner was not able to affect the necessary repairs in a timely manner as the condition of the home continued to worsen. But then, just like the storm, out of nowhere an unknown philanthropist came to the rescue.

Having enjoyed the comfort of this vacation home in the past, a wealthy businessman stepped in to provide the resources required to restore the home not only to its previous state, but also with added features and even more amenities than the home had before. In place of the city's sign of condemnation the homeowner then proudly displayed a sign that read "NO LONGER CONDEMNED, AVAILABLE FOR USE."

Thoughts

_____

_____

_____

_____

_____

_____

_____

As believers our pre-Christ state was very similar to the vacation home after the storm. It was because of our sin nature and the storms faced as we walked in disobedience that we were once condemned. But thanks be to God for sending His one and only unique son Jesus the Christ! Through the cross at Calvary and His shed blood, Jesus provided the means for our restoration by giving His very best to us all.

Like the wealthy businessman, Christ paid the price so that we would no longer be condemned, but fit for the Master's use (Jn. 3:18).

Restoration through Christ has made our end-state better than when we began; through a renewed life, the Master Builder has made us better than we were before as new creations in Him. If you have truly been restored through Christ, then don't allow the enemy to bring condemnation from past deeds to the forefront. The price has been paid and you are no longer condemned!

"THEREFORE, [there is] now no condemnation (no adjudging guilty of wrong) for those who are in Christ Jesus, who live [and] walk not after the dictates of the flesh, but after the dictates of the Spirit. For the law of the Spirit of life [which is] in Christ Jesus [the law of our new being] has freed me from the law of sin and of death" (Rom. 8:1-2, Amplified Bible).

May 1
MOVING ON WHAT YOU HEAR
Read: Rom. 10:17

Years ago and way before my time, movies were made without sound, having captions of the words associated with a particular scene displayed at the bottom—thank God for advances in technology. So no matter how good the movie may have been, the full effect of what was taking place on the screen could not really be felt until sound was connected to what was actually happening.

So it is with our faith. We can look at or read Scripture all day, but there is just something about hearing the Word coming through our ears that begins to move us.

According to Rom. 10:17 "faith comes by hearing [what is told], and what is heard comes by the preaching [of the message that came from the lips] of Christ (the Messiah Himself);" and based on Rom. 12:3 "God has dealt to each one a measure of faith." In other words, God has given each and every one of us a certain degree of faith, and this faith can be either increased and diminished not by what we see, but is significantly affected by what we hear and/or choose to listen to. This is why we must constantly be on guard and always mindful of what we allow to come into our ear gates.

Thoughts

_____
_____
_____
_____
_____
_____
_____

The responses to what we hear can be seen in just turning on regular television today. Unless an individual is looking at a Christian-based network (although even in this we have to be careful and mindful of what we hear), there is rarely anything positive being depicted or spoken. Instead of receiving the Good News that is designed to get us to a place of spiritual wholeness, spiritual prosperity, and increased faith we are often bombarded with highlights of bad news by way of social injustice, destruction, devastation, war and famine from almost every region of the world.

The "Breaking News" on the average network channel is rarely anything positive or uplifting, and as a result we have been programmed and conditioned to expect something negative even before the broadcast journalist begins to speak. Needless to say, in this instance we are rarely disappointed because we generally receive news of death, destruction, chaos, fear, and lack. And what makes the matter even worst, many of us actually begin to move on the information we hear, which is generally information that usually causes us to make bad or incorrect decisions.

But when we hear and listen to the right thing(s), our faith is built up and strengthened to the point that we believe God and begin to receive the blessings associated with everything He already has in store for us (2 Pet. 1:3). The blessing comes not only in hearing the right thing, but then acting or moving on what we hear.

What have you been listening to lately? What are you allowing to feed your faith and spirit? The amount of faith you have today is directly proportional to what you hear and what you have been listening to. Close your ears to the negative and ensure you are listening to and hearing the right things so that your faith will not falter or fail. Because "...the just shall live by his faith" (Hab. 2:4, New King James Version).

May 2
NO MIDDLE GROUND
Read: Josh. 24:15

As Christians there are often many challenges and struggles we must endure and have to face, on a personal level, a corporate level and even on a family level. Wars surface and battles begin with the potential to stir-up all manner of emotions, having the ability to cause division and bring separation.

Thoughts

_____

_____

_____

_____

_____

_____

_____

In any war or battle there are generally two or more opposing groups with each side attempting to establish themselves as the dominant force or authority. And when no mutual agreement between these groups can be achieved, the battles begin and intensify with each side launching offensive attacks in hopes of causing their opponents to surrender.

On occasion and when a battle becomes too intense with one side prevailing, soldiers or individuals from one camp cross the line of demarcation to join the opponent's side; but even in this action a conscious choice is made to choose one side over the other.

Every day, as believers in Christ, we are engaged in a war with battles waging all around us. The enemy launches attacks in our minds, while at the same time attempting and doing his best to bring division within the church and in the home through opposing ideologies, pride, selfishness, and a general lack of love and compassion.

However, a fact that we should always remember and be cognizant of is that our war is never a physical one, but is spiritual (2 Cor. 10:3-4). This is why must ensure we are equipped for battle and above all else must make a decision to pick a side.

When we accept Jesus into our hearts we are, for all intents and purposes, then enlisted into the LORD's Army and become spiritual soldiers in the body of Christ. And in His army there are no inactive or ready reserves, we are each called to active duty and must be engaged in battle on a daily basis because we are always on watch praying for ourselves, our church, and family (1 Pet. 5:8-11).

So even in all of this, there is good news because the fact of the matter is the outcome of our battle has already been determined. Though at times it may appear the enemy has the upper hand, when we read and then internalize what it says in God's Word; through the finished work of Jesus Christ on the cross at Calvary, WE ULTIMATELY WIN!

"But thanks be to God, Who gives us the victory [making us conquerors] through our Lord Jesus Christ" (1 Cor. 15:57, Amplified Bible).

We must remember that in true warfare there is no middle ground. Therefore, we must be willing to engage in the fight for stability in our minds while also endeavoring to maintain unity in the church and in the home. We each are either on one side or the next (the kingdom of darkness and destruction, or the Kingdom of God that brings prosperity and life)—-there is no in between. We are either on the LORD's side or enemy's camp, but the choice is up to us.

As the battle wages all around, which force will you allow to dominate and control your life? Make sure that you choose the right side because there are no double agents in the Kingdom of God, and there is no middle ground (Josh. 24:15)!

Thoughts

_____

_____

_____

_____

_____

_____

_____

May 3
THE PROMISE IS FOR YOU
Read: Gal. 3:14

Throughout Old Testament Scripture, God provided reassurance to His chosen people that He would always be with them through a series of promises in the form of covenants. Below are a few of the major covenants between God and man:

Abrahamic Covenant: to make of Abraham a great nation and to bless those who bless him and curse those who curse him and all peoples on earth would be blessed through Abraham.

Covenant with Jacob: to give him and his descendants the land on which he stood, and (Israel) that his descendants would be like the dust of the earth.

Mosaic Covenant: to make the Children of Israel His special possession among all people if they obeyed God and kept His covenant; to make the Children of Israel a kingdom of priests and a holy nation

Davidic Covenant: establishes David and his descendants as the rightful kings of Judah until the Messiah, the rightful King comes to rule and reign. The Davidic covenant is an important element of Jesus' claim to be the Messiah.

There are many more promises by way of covenant throughout the Bible in the Old and New Testaments. A covenant is defined as an "a written agreement or promise usually under seal between two or more parties especially for the performance of some action." Therefore, a covenant is nothing more than a promise. The word promise is defined as "a declaration that one will do or refrain from doing something specified."

Now the word "promise" is derived from the English word "promittere" with an etymology of pro = forth + mittere = to send, which basically means to send forth. What this means for us as Christians and believers in Christ is that God sent forth His Word (His Promise) in the form of Jesus Christ so that we could lay hold to every one of God's promises as given to us in His Holy Word. "When the fulness of the time was come, God sent forth his Son" (Gal. 4:4, King James Version). This "Son" was no other than Jesus the Christ, God's Anointed One and one Unique Son.

Thoughts

_____

_____

_____

_____

_____

_____

_____

Jesus was and still is the promise that was manifested in the flesh for all to receive even today, not only to escape the fiery pits of Hell just for a free ticket to Heaven; but also giving us the ability to live the abundant life in the here and now. He even told us why He came to earth as recorded in Jn. 10:10, "I came that they may have and enjoy life, and have it in abundance (to the full, till it overflows)" (Amplified Bible); the "they" referred to in this Scripture encompasses both "you" and "me."

Has God made a promise of things to come for you? Well, a covenant is a two-sided agreement that requires action by both parties. God has done His part by sending His Son, now it's up to us to do ours. His Promise is His Covenant with you, so honor Him by positioning yourself to receive through obedience. Obedience is truly better than sacrifice (Job 36:11).

May 4
REMAIN ON THE ALTAR AND LET HIM FINISH!
Read: Romans 12:1-2

What exactly is worship? Based on Rom. 12:1-2, God has given each believer very clear and concise guidance on how we are to live in service to the Kingdom. We are to present our bodies as living sacrifices on God's holy altar. Of course the altar represents the place of sacrifice, obedience, blessing and worship.

The Old Testament book of Leviticus provides a little more insight into the holiness of God and what was required of God's chosen people by way of holy living and sacrifice. This particular book also provides detailed instructions on how the priests were to present offerings of sacrifice to the minute detail. God demands absolute obedience of His people, and this obedience often involves sacrifice.

According to 1 Pet. 2:9, we are a "royal priesthood;" in other words, as believers in Christ we each are in essence New Testament priests. Therefore, as priests we now have the obligation to present our sacrifices to God in the correct way. In a nutshell, this involves laying our entire lives out before the LORD on the altar, presenting our all and giving Him complete control.

And though we are commanded to present our bodies (our very lives) as "living sacrifices", and some of us actually follow through; the common problem with a living sacrifice that often plagues us is the fact that we still have the ability to get up from the altar before God completes His work in and through us.

This is why we must each learn how to remain on the altar if we are to become that true sacrifice, the kind that is acceptable to God. When we sacrifice ourselves completely, our lives then become pleasing and come up before Him as a sweet aroma and a fragrance that brings grace to His nostrils (Lev. 1:9). In turn, this allows us to become faithful servants and blessings to the Kingdom and to the world.

Thoughts

_____
_____
_____
_____
_____
_____
_____
_____

This simple act of sacrifice or worship is what God expects from us each day. In the Old Testament, the Burnt offering had a little more significance than some of the other offerings. Why? Unlike the other offerings, i.e., Peace Offering, Grain Offering, Trespass Offering, etc., where only a portion of the sacrifice was often presented, when the priests presented the burnt offering the entire sacrifice was placed on the altar and completely consumed.

Wherever our individual altars of sacrifice may be, as living sacrifices we should be mindful of our innate ability to routinely jump up from this sacred place before allowing God to complete His work in us. Instead, we are to remain on the altar until we have been completely consumed by the fire of God's presence; "For our God is a consuming fire" (Heb. 12:29, New King James Version). His fire comes to purify us, thereby allowing us to be holy and presentable in service to Him.

Your worship is based on the presentation of your sacrifice. So, remain on the altar and allow Him to finish the good work in you.

"And I am convinced and sure of this very thing, that He Who began a good work in you will continue until the day of Jesus Christ [right up to the time of His return], developing [that good work] and perfecting and bringing it to full completion in you" (Phil. 1:6, Amplified Bible).

May 5
STAY IN THE FIGHT, YOU ARE NOT ALONE
Read: Ex. 17:8-16

In Exodus Chapter 17 we find God's people in the midst of a battle with the Amalekites. Moses had positioned himself atop a hill in plain view of the Israelite army holding up the rod of God as a point of reference to provide strength and encouragement to the soldiers engaged in battle. And as long as Moses' hands were raised, Israel would advance and prevail; however, whenever his hands began to lower, Amalek would begin to win.

As the tides of battle went back and forth Moses began to tire and as his hands began to drop lower and lower, the Israelites began to get overtaken by the Amalekites. Thankfully Moses was not alone and had the support of other leaders. So, what was his support team to do?

Thoughts

_____
_____
_____
_____
_____
_____
_____

Recognizing his tiredness, they placed a stone on the ground under Moses for him to sit on, and then his trusted companions Aaron and Hur positioned themselves on either side of Moses to hold up his hands to increase Israel's odds for victory. With new found support and hands uplifted, Moses obtained the support he needed and Israel was able to defeat the Amalekites in a decisive victory as they looked to their leader for strength and encouragement.

As believers in Christ although we may not physically see our enemy, we too are at war every single day. And if we are not careful, just like Moses we may find ourselves wearied from the battles of life we often endure. However, there's one thing we must always remember; we are not in this battle alone and there are other believers who are also in the same fight; therefore, we must learn to draw support, help and strength from one another.

In other words, there is strength in unity (Ecc. 4:12). This is why fellowship is so vital in our Christian walk because we draw strength from one another as we come together in His name. "For where two or three are gathered together in my name, there am I in the midst of them" (Matt. 18:20, King James Version).

And even in the moments were there may be no one physically around us, we are still never alone because "goodness and mercy shall follow [us] All the days of [our] life" (Ps. 23:6, New King James Version), and God promises that He "will not leave us or desert us" (Heb. 13:5, New Living Translation). Therefore, we are actually never alone.

Moses found stability and drew strength as he sat upon the stone or rock. We too can find stability and strength as we stand upon the solid rock of God's Living Word who is none other than Jesus the Christ Himself. "Even our enemies know that only our God is a Mighty Rock" (Deu. 31:6, Contemporary English Version). His Word also reminds us that the battle is not ours (2 Chron. 20:15), we are not in this fight alone, and that God is always right there. The key is learning to accept His help and draw from His strength, as well as learning to trust and rely on one another.

"Be strong. Take courage. Don't be intimidated. Don't give them a second thought because God, your God, is striding ahead of you. He's right there with you. He won't let you down; he won't leave you" (Deut. 31:6, The Message).

When you are tempted to just give-up and throw in the towel, refuse to quit and stay in the fight because you are never alone. VICTORY IS YOURS IN JESUS' NAME!

May 6

Thoughts

IT AIN'T OVER
Read: Judg. 16:23-31

The judges were put in place to help rule and guide the Israelites during that particular time of Bible history. "The Israelites often fell away from God and into the hands of oppressors.

God sent "judges" to lead and deliver them." Samson was the twelfth Old Testament judge.

Although Samson was a judge, like many believers today, he started out strong but allowed temptation to lure him away from the path of righteousness that ultimately led him into bondage and literally being chained.

Samson allowed his emotions and feelings to cloud his judgment as Delilah, a beautiful woman from the Philistine territory of Sorek who was used by Samson's enemies to entrap him, captivated him with her outward appearance and charm. For years the enemy conspired to find the secret of his strength, but to no avail. This is when Delilah, the Philistine secret weapon, was employed.

In actuality Delilah really didn't have to do much to entice Samson, because he was already mesmerized by his own lust (James 1:13-15). Delilah simply used the powers of the female persuasion and her feminine wiles to seduce Samson into revealing the true nature and secret of his God-given strength, with the precise intent of setting a trap for the enemy, who promised to pay her a specific price, to ensnare him.

It was because of fleshly desires that Samson revealed his secret ultimately resulting in his hair being cut, God's anointing being removed, his eyes gouged out, and then being bound and forced into hard manual labor. It was his own lustful desires that literally caused him to lose his sight and the power of the anointing from over his life.

After being freed from his chains Samson was led to the meeting place of the Philistine nobility to be made mockery of, but just so happened to be positioned between the two foundational pillars of the building. And even while still powerless, blind and bound; Samson knew enough to call out to God in his time of trouble and need (Ps. 55:16).

Samson asked God to give him the strength to strike one last deadly blow to the enemy (Jdg. 16:28). God heard Samson's plea, obliged and allowed him to complete this one last mighty act under the anointing. Mustering up all the strength that was afforded to him through the anointing, he pushed down the two pillars thus completely destroying key leadership of the enemy, which would undoubtedly thwart any future Philistine attacks against Israel.

Though Samson appeared to be defeated, he was still able to achieve one last victory because he had enough intestinal fortitude and the wherewithal to call out to God for help. In this one selfless act, he achieved a greater victory over the enemy than he had with the use of his eyes.

We too can achieve a similar victory. Just because we get knocked down due to a momentary lapse in judgment when we give in to temptation, this

Thoughts

_____

_____

_____

_____

_____

_____

_____

does not mean the fight is over. Many boxing matches have been won with one good punch in the last round.

So, whenever you get knocked down; just get back up, because IT AIN'T OVER!

May 7
IT'S NEVER TOO LATE
Read: Jn. 11:1-44

Lazarus, the brother of Mary (the one who washed Jesus' feet with her hair) and Martha, and the beloved friend of Jesus was sick. Mary and Martha sent word to Jesus on behalf of Lazarus hoping He would come and heal their brother before his condition worsened.

Jesus agreed to make the journey, yet knowing that Lazarus was dying He and His disciples did not depart their current location for another two days. Then seemingly out of nowhere Jesus announced that Lazarus was dead, but nonetheless they all still prepared for the journey to now the tomb where Lazarus was buried instead of to his bedside.

Surely the disciples must have thought this would be a wasted journey; however, Jesus had bigger plans because He knew the power of God He possessed.

When Jesus finally arrived he greeted Mary and Martha, He reassured them that though Lazarus was dead he would in fact live again. Jesus said "I am the resurrection and the life. He who believes in Me, though he may die, he shall live. And whoever lives and believes in Me shall never die" (Jn. 11: 25-26, New Living Translation).

At this point Lazarus had been dead and in the grave for a few days with his body beginning to decompose as bodily fluids dried up with rigor mortis setting in. Yet this did not deter Jesus, the One who was and still is a Restorer and Giver of life.

After the stone had been rolled away Jesus used the power and authority of His Word to call out to his dear friend using three simple words: "Lazarus, come forth" (Jn. 11:43)!

There may be areas in your life today, whether finances, marriage, bad relationships, wayward children, employment, or just "stinking thinking" that may appear to be dead, has become a stench to you and those around you, or have you bound. Refuse to get discouraged, but instead begin to speak life to the situation(s) and watch God work.

Thoughts

_____

_____

_____

_____

_____

_____

_____

Know today that Jesus (the Living Word) has the ability to resurrect that which is dead in your life. Though your current situation may appear to be dead, stinking, and hopeless, IT'S NEVER TOO LATE TO SPEAK LIFE!

May 8
ARE YOU DRESSED FOR THE OCCASION?
Read: Eph. 6:10-20

A mother prepares her young children for a couple of events for the day including a family outing. So to save time, the children were dressed and prepared in advance of each event. Their clothes were pressed and ironed to ensure that everything was wrinkle-free. The right shoes were placed together with their outfits ensuring everything matched; their hair was combed and styled, with bows and ribbons strategically placed to accentuate their ensembles.

Everyone was finally dressed and ready for the planned activities; however, although the father left work early, he was delayed by traffic during his commute home which placed them behind schedule.

A few minutes passed, 30 minutes passed, and then before they knew it an hour and a half had elapsed. With the kids now growing restless the mother advised them to play lightly; however, they were not to do anything that would mess-up their hair or clothing.

How many parents know that there is always that one child that just has to defy the standard? In an effort to exert her right to free will, one child decided to remove the clothes prepared by her mother to put on something else more comfortable that would allow her to play more freely. Under the circumstances this probably seemed to be a logical choice or the correct thing to do right? Well, from the mother's vantage point this was not the case.

A few minutes later the father pulled into the driveway, after having been in traffic for almost two hours due to an accident; he then blew the horn to signify he was ready to depart because they were now pressed for time. If the family did not make the first engagement on time, the entire deposit would be forfeited and the family would incur a loss.

Thoughts

_____
_____
_____
_____
_____
_____

The mother heard the horn and called out, "Your father is home, so come on its time to go." All of the kids promptly came downstairs dressed and ready, all that is except for one. The mother went upstairs to determine the delay.

154

When she reached the daughter's bedroom she discovered the child had not only removed the clothing prepared for her to wear, but had also loosened her hair which was now a complete mess. Naturally the mother was upset and exclaimed, "I only said you could play lightly until your father arrived, but who told you to get completely undressed?"

Because the child had to get completely dressed again, to include having her hair combed and styled, the family missed the first engagement and forfeited a considerable amount of money. In a spiritual sense, when we as believers get undressed, we have the potential to forfeit so much more.

As Christians and believers we receive specific instructions through God's Word in the book of Ephesians chapter six as to what we are to wear for the engagements that we bound to face on a daily basis; not just another cute outfit, pretty dress and heels, or a stylish suit, but the "Armor of God."

This armor is designed to support us as we engage in spiritual warfare with our enemy the devil as a means of defensive protection as well as provide an offensive weapon. Therefore, being unprepared and improperly dressed in the battle that we each have to face on a routine basis not only has the potential to adversely affect us financially, emotionally, or spiritually; but in extreme cases and if we are not watchful, it could cost us our very lives. We must be ready at all times. Are you properly equipped and DRESSED FOR THE OCCASION?

May 9
LEARNING TO LET GO
Read: Mk. 11:25

Holding on to things in life has the potential to leave us paralyzed and immobilized when we refuse to let go. This is exactly what happened in the story of "The Rope."

In this particular story a mountain climber decided to scale the highest mountain he could find as an act of prowess to demonstrate his skills and capability. He spent many years of rigorous training in preparation for the journey to prove what he could do by himself, and because he wanted the glory and notoriety of reaching the mountaintop all for himself. As a result, he decided to make the journey alone without the company or support of others.

Thoughts

_____
_____
_____
_____
_____
_____
_____

The day finally came as the glory-seeker ventured towards the top of the mountain one step and one rock at a time, going into the long hours of night with no visibility and total

155

darkness at times. Despite not being able to literally see his hand in front of him, he continued to press forward making what he deemed to be remarkable progress.

But this is where the story began to take a turn for the worst. With only a few feet away from the top he lost his footing and grip on a side of the mountain that was now slick from the evening dew, and at an extremely rapid pace he began to fall.

As this individual who thought that he could make his difficult journey alone without the help or aid of anyone else plummeted like a 747 jet with no fuel, his entire life flashed before his eyes as death stared him in the face. Then suddenly he felt a firm tug around his waist as he dangled semi-conscious and limp at the end of the safety rope in mid-air and now freezing.

With no one around and no help in sight the climber pushed aside pride and called out to God for help.

Through the expanse of darkness that surrounded him a voice responded "What would you like for me to do?" The climber exclaimed, "Please save Me!" The climber was then dumbfounded and baffled at what he heard next as the voice replied, "If you believe that I can save you, then cut the rope and let go."

Being fearful of the unknown and unable to see what was below him, the climber chose not to heed the instructions of the voice.

The very next day a local news channel aired a story of a rescue team that discovered a climber found frozen and dead literally hanging from a rope only 7 feet away from the ground. What a way to go!

The climber could have survived if he had only listened to the voice (of God) and cut the rope as instructed. Instead he placed his confidence in the rope and holding on.

We each can receive a valuable lesson from the climber in the area of learning to let go. Many believers today are stagnant in their Christian walk simply because they refuse to let go of bitterness and unforgiveness from the past. And just like the mountain climber, we often become frozen, unable to move forward and dead in our faith. This in turn causes us to walk around with excess baggage that was never designed or intended for us to carry; burdens that we were never designed to bear. Release it any dead weight in your life and let it go!

Thoughts
_____
_____
_____
_____
_____
_____

May 10

THE BIGGER THEY ARE, THE HARDER THEY FALL
Read: 1 Sam. 17

The Bible account of David and Goliath is a very familiar story for most, and is one of the classic examples of the power of good overcoming evil. In this epic saga the children of Israel found themselves engaged in battle with the Philistine army. Although this army was similar to all of the other opponent nations previously faced by the Israelites, the Philistines had a secret weapon, a champion by the name of Goliath.

Each day Goliath came out to the opening of the valley that separated the opposing forces, sending out a challenge to the Israelite army requesting a warrior who was worthy to fight him. But no one could muster up enough strength and courage to face him because of his menacing appearance and the fact that he was literally a giant.

Goliath stood over 9-feet tall, wore bronze armor that weight approximately 125 pounds, carried a spear with a head or tip that weighed 15 pounds, and owned a shield so massive that a personal shield bearer was assigned to him for the sole purpose of carrying it. So, I can just imagine the type of fear this gargantuan struck in the hearts of the Israelites during the 40-day period as he presented the same challenge day after day. The Israelites were incapacitated by fear.

One day during a supply run and routine visit to check on his brothers who were soldiers in the Israelite army; David, the son of Jesse, a young shepherd boy heard the challenge of Goliath, and was appalled at what he heard and wanted to know what was going to be done about this atrocity. David did not just see Goliath's taunting as a challenge against the Israelites, but as a challenge against the armies of the Living God. To David the challenge had little to do with the Israelite army, it was the Most High God whose honor and reputation was at stake.

Although he was only 17-years old at the time and probably only weighed about as much as Goliath's armor, David accepted the challenge as he began to recall the faithfulness of God and each one of his own past victories. "I have been taking care of my father's sheep and goats," he said (1 Sam. 17:34-37)!" Instead of allowing his present fear to speak and encourage defeat, David pushed fear aside and began to speak to Goliath's (or his giant's) future end, facing fear head-on as he ran towards the enemy.

As the story goes David defeated Goliath with only a staff, a sling, five stones, and most importantly, the reassurance that God was with him and that victory was already his. When faith is in operation it has much more power than the greatest amount of fear in our lives and it causes our giants to fall.

Each day as believers in Christ we face various challenges that may appear to be giants standing

Thoughts

_____

_____

_____

_____

_____

_____

_____

in our way; and in these instances we can either face these giants with fear or faith. The actions of David provide a perfect example of how we are to respond: (1) He did not allow the voice of the enemy to hinder him from believing what he already knew to be true, victory was already his; (2) he did not see Goliath as a giant obstacle, but as an opportunity for God to receive the glory; (3) he did not run away from his giant, instead he ran toward Goliath to face him head-on; and lastly (4) David spoke the end result even before the fight began.

In life and in our Christian walk as we journey each day, we cannot allow the voice of the enemy to hinder us from attaining that which is rightfully ours; we are to activate our faith! What giants are you facing today? There is no need to fear or retreat. Face your giants with confidence because God is with you!

May 11

IT'S TIME TO BREATHE AGAIN
Read: Ez. 37

There are a number of elements that are essential to our life here on earth (i.e., air, water). However, even though water is an essential element to our very existence and life as human beings here on earth, it would be very remiss to overlook the importance of air to our survival. And though we may be able survive without water for a few days; in the absence of oxygen (air) our time of survival is significantly reduced to just minutes and seconds.

During creation after God created the heavens, the oceans, the moon and the stars, and other living creatures, He created His most prized masterpiece and possession. Man (mankind) was created from the dust of the earth on the sixth day; however, it was not until God breathed the breath of life into man that he began to actually live (Gen. 2:7).

This air (or wind) that God breathed into man is also symbolic of the Holy Spirit; this life giving breath is described in Hebrew as the word "naphach" which means "to inflate, blow hard, scatter, kindle." In other Words naphach speaks of God's power through the person of Holy Spirit to kindle, effect a change, and to reverse dead situations or the ability to revive that which was once dead and bring new life.

Thoughts
_____
_____
_____
_____
_____
_____
_____

Ezekiel chapter 37 details how the prophet Ezekiel is given a vision concerning the current state of the Israelites who once again found themselves in captivity due to their disobedience and were now not only in a physical wilderness, but also in a spiritually dry and dead state.

In this vision the prophet is led by the Spirit into a valley of very dry bones, which was representative of Israel's current state at the time. The LORD asked the prophet one simple question: "Son of man, can these bones live" (Ez. 37:3)?

Ezekiel was then instructed to prophesy, to speak, and breathe the Spirit into the valley of dry bones so that they might live again. And as the prophet spoke to the dead bones out of obedience, the bones came together with tissue, sinew, and skin beginning to appear. The once dry bones then stood up as an exceedingly great army.

The prophet Ezekiel was commanded to "prophesy" (Hebrew "naba" which means to "speak") to the dry bones and when he obeyed, the dead bones were revived and lived once again. Therefore, if we want to revive the dead situations and areas in our lives, we must do the same thing—SPEAK LIFE!

In Jn. 6:63 Jesus said, "The words that I speak to you are spirit, and *they* are life." As the prophet Ezekiel spoke, it was the Spirit that brought life. Well, when Jesus is made both Savior and Lord in our lives, He then begins to live on the inside of us. And since He now abides within, if the words that He speaks are spirit and life, then our words spoken with the right motives and in faith can also produce life and begin to revive anything that was previously dead.

Though we may be able to survive a little without food and an even shorter period without water; without air (the Spirit) we immediately cease to have power and cease to have true life. Therefore, whenever our past situations appear to place us in a dry and hopeless place, it is then that we must begin to speak God's Word and allow His Spirit to bring life to every dry area. We each have the power to initiate a fresh start in our lives today by speaking life. The Spirit of the LORD says prepare for a fresh wind because it's time to breathe again (Job 33:1-4)!

May 12
YOU CAN'T DO IT BY YOURSELF
Read: Is. 40:28-31

There is nothing like the refreshing feeling of a good night's sleep to start the day out right. This can often be determined by the type of surface that one sleeps on, that primarily being the mattress that one has on his or her bed.

Thoughts

In an effort to try and ensure that we get the best sleep that we possibly can, without going to purchase a brand new mattress every few months, my wife suggested that we flip our mattress ever so often to kind of even or balance things out. Well, on one particular occasion, being the man of the house, I was determined

_____
_____
_____
_____
_____
_____
_____

to accomplish this task by myself saying in my mind "I've got this!" So, for about 15 minutes my wife stood watching me struggle to flip this huge mattress, a king-sized mattress mind you, but to no avail.

After about 20 plus minutes into my solo he-man efforts with sweat running down my face as I gasped for air like I'd just run a marathon, I realized that I couldn't flip the mattress alone without damaging something else in the process. My wife then looked at me and simply said, "I've been standing here watching you struggle just waiting for you to ask me for help." If I had only asked for help ahead of time I could have finished the task within a matter of minutes and with a lot less effort. This would have also allowed me to enjoy rest much sooner, but pride held me back.

Sadly, this is where many of us in the body of Christ find ourselves each day, trying to sustain ourselves in this Christian walk alone while attempting to do things in our own strength and ability. This results in an ongoing and constant struggle in our efforts to do things apart from the presence of God's Spirit, the One who was sent to our aid.

When Jesus went away to be with the Father, He sent us a Helper (Jn. 14:16-18). This Helper, Comforter, or "Parakletos" (in the Greek) is none other than the person of the Holy Spirit, the One who comes along side to help, to lead, to guide and to direct us; our job is to simply let Him do just that.

Yet too often we struggle needlessly, when the rest we need is in His presence. Isaiah chapter 40 provides a great prescription for our struggle and the exhaustion that results when we try to do things alone and in our own strength (Is. 40:28-31).

As believers, we are to be like the eagle described by Isaiah. Eagles don't struggle to fly wasting valuable energy; instead they glide effortlessly while soaring upon the wind. The Greek word "pneuma" literally means "wind or air in motion;" this wind, of course is representative of the Holy Spirit. Eagles depend on the wind to carry them to where they need to go, thereby conserving their energy for those things that are really important.

When we truly realize the futility of our efforts in attempting to do things in our own strength and begin to rely on the power of the Spirit, we too can soar effortlessly and find the rest that we desperately long for. Choose today to stop struggling and begin relying on the Holy Spirit because He stands ready to help thereby allowing you to obtain the rest you so desperately need.

Thoughts

_____
_____
_____
_____
_____
_____
_____

Though there will be times that we may need the physical, emotional, and spiritual support of others around us; the help that is absolutely essential in our daily Christian walk is our reliance on the help of the Holy Spirit—-He will not steer or lead you astray.

May 13
BRING IT UNDER CONTROL
Read: Eph. 4:26

Growing up I was a big fan of Marvel comic books like Fantastic Four, Avengers, Spiderman, X-men, Kung-Fu Master, and the list could go on. And on occasion, these comic book super heroes would make it to television in the form of a weekly series.

Today, many of these comic book heroes have been transformed into movie box office hits. But one of my favorite superhero television series as a young child was the Incredible Hulk.

In this series a frail and fragile scientist, Dr. David Banner, conducted an experiment to determine how stress could potentially alter the body's chemical composition thereby increasing strength during intense moments of emotional anxiety. During the experiment he became the victim of a freak laboratory accident with him over-exposed to gamma radiation.

As a result the gamma radiation was now in his system, and whenever his adrenalin began to flow in moments of intense emotional distress, or when his anger was triggered he would transform into the massive seven-foot tall, 300 plus pound green creature "The Hulk," possessing potentially destructive strength.

Throughout the remainder of the series Dr. Banner conducted research with the intent of reversing this process in an attempt to overcome his anger, thereby taming the beast within. Like the Incredible Hulk, anger out of control in our lives can cause senseless destruction.

Although Dr. Banner was actually meek, mild and a good person at heart; his entire disposition changed whenever the anger of the beast within was aroused. And in each instance, some form of destruction was often the end-state.

Many people today let anger control their lives, as they allow themselves to become slaves to their emotions. Prisons and jails are filled with ordinary people and individuals who were categorized as "good" people, but in a moment of intensity and anger, committed one act that resulted in devastating consequences.

No matter how good we think we are, when anger consumes us the dormant beast within is then released.

Thoughts

Anger is a natural emotion (Matt. 21:12-13); however, as it is with any other emotion, anger must also be brought under control and given a proper outlet. As believers we must place our emotions under the blood of Christ, give them over to Him, and allow the Holy Spirit to guide

_____

_____

_____

_____

_____

_____

_____

our actions, our responses and then control our anger. Anger only has the ability to consume us if we allow it (Eph. 4:26-27).

Don't allow your emotions, especially anger, to consume and/or control you because if it is not checked or addressed early, anger can destroy you and others in the process if you permit it. It's time to bring it under control and allow the Holy Spirit to assume His role as the water of the Spirit begins to quench and saturate the fiery flames of anger (Col. 3:8).

May 14
EXPOSURE TO THE "SON"
Read: 1 Jn. 4:9

There is nothing a family trip to the beach bringing a picnic basket, a beach umbrella, spreading out a large blanket and enjoying time together under the bright rays of the sun. During summer months, people from various locations and of different nationalities flock to various beaches in the world to enjoy sun, surf and fun near the ocean.

Although time spent on the beach may be exhilarating and fun, one must always be mindful of what overexposure to sunlight can do. Ultraviolet radiation can cause severe damage when individuals expose themselves to direct sunlight for extensive periods of time. And in very severe cases, skin cancer has been the end result.

And even though one person's skin pigmentation may be a little darker than another, this should not preclude him or her from taking precautionary measures by using sunscreen to protect against the damage of ultraviolet rays in order to prevent sunburn. When protection is not used, one should expect some discomfort and pain.

You may be asking, "So, what does all of this have to do with my Christian walk and life in Christ?" I'm glad you asked.

God sent His only Son into the world to provide a sacrifice and atonement so that we (mankind) would not have to experience discomfort and pain from a different type of burning; He came to save us from literally burning in hell and eternal damnation (1 Jn. 4:9).

Thoughts

_____
_____
_____
_____
_____
_____
_____

Jesus sacrificed His life on the cross to purchase our freedom and liberty; He defeated the power of death over and in our lives. *"O Death, where is your sting? O Hades, where is your victory?"* The sting of death *is* sin, and the strength of sin *is* the law. But thanks *be* to God, who gives us the victory through our Lord Jesus Christ" (1 Cor. 15:55-57, New King James Version). We now have access to total victory because of Jesus' sacrifice, the cross and His blood, our job is to simply receive it and apply it.

Total commitment to Christ is what allows us to come under His protection and the covering of His shed blood or "SON-screen" as I like to call it, this type of body exposure is always beneficial to our health and well-being. As we immerse ourselves in His blood, it is then that the glory of God's SON can shine brightly in every area of our lives.

Hell is hot and eternity long; exposure to the SON is the only thing that will prevent you from burning forever. Have you truly applied SON-screen to your life today? Even though His blood may have been shed thousands of years ago, there is still more than enough available for all of us to apply today.

May 15
IT'S ALL ABOUT PERSPECTIVE
Read: Num. 13:30-35; 14:6-9

In chapter 13 of the book of Numbers the Israelites led by Moses crossed the Red Sea and wandered in the Judean wilderness for a number of years; they were finally preparing to cross over into the promised land of Canaan.

But before crossing over into an unknown region as a nation, spies were sent ahead to conduct a little covert reconnaissance to assess the land and its current inhabitants. Twelve spies went in and the initial assessment was completed. Surprisingly the majority of the group had absolutely nothing positive to say, and were quick to provide a negative report which immediately incited fear amongst the people.

"We are not able to go up against the people, for they *are* stronger than we...The land through which we have gone as spies *is* a land that devours its inhabitants, and all the people whom we saw in it *are* men of *great* stature. There we saw the giants; and we were like grasshoppers in our own sight, and so we were in their sight" (Num. 13:30-35, New King James Version).

Do you know anyone like this? No matter what the situation is or the environment, he or she always seem to have a negative report. These individuals continue to see the glass half-empty instead of being half-full. Thank God for a remnant that sees beyond the natural and believes God at His Word. The majority saw the task of occupying the land as being impossible; however, there were two that were ready to proceed and take over.

Thoughts

_____
_____
_____
_____
_____
_____
_____

Joshua and Caleb were two among the initial recon group that saw the same land and same inhabitants; yet they refused to be moved by what they could see. This is exactly why their report was given from a different perspective (Num. 14:7-9).

The twelve spies all saw the same land, same conditions, and the same inhabitants, yet only two believed the collective Israelite goal could be achieved. So, why did their reports differ? Simple, it was all about perspective.

The word perspective is derived from an English word that means "to look through, or see clearly." The difference in the two reports was all about how they saw themselves in and through their circumstance while not relying on their own strength and ability; in other words the two with the positive report knew exactly whose they were—children of the Most High God!

Several spies returned with negative reports seeing the land, its inhabitants and themselves through eyes of fear, doubt and unbelief. With their own mouths and in their own words they declared themselves to be just like tiny insignificant grasshoppers able to be crushed in an instant and with little effort. This was not based on what the giants saw, but was based on how they saw themselves.

When you face challenges and obstacles, how do you see yourself? Do you see yourself defeated or victorious? What mental picture do you have of yourself? In this situation you must watch your words to ensure that you are speaking the right things, things that are in line with God's Word and what He says about you; seeing yourself victorious through eyes of faith. Even though your words have the power to set your destiny in motion, it is faith that gives substance to the things you hope for but yet cannot see (2 Cor. 4:16-18).

May 16
UNINVITED GUEST
Read: 1 Cor. 6:19-20

Have you ever experienced individuals just showing up at your house without any prior notice or invitation? And when they arrive, a comment like "We were just in the neighborhood" can usually be heard even though they live 30 miles away.

Thoughts

_____

_____

_____

_____

_____

_____

_____

_____

These individuals usually show up at inopportune times. You know, when you are in the middle of a project at home, working on the car, cutting the grass, cleaning the house, or just enjoying a relaxing day with the family. You do the Christian thing of greeting them and welcoming them in; however, at the same time you try to find a polite way to let them know they have disrupted your plans. The childhood story of Goldilocks and the Three Bears highlights a scenario where an unwelcomed guest made herself at home.

As believers in Christ, whether we acknowledge the fact or not, our bodies or temples actually belong to God (1 Cor. 6:19-20). Therefore, we should not allow just any and everything to take up residence within a place that has been specifically set apart for God Himself. The devil knows this and does his very best to break the lease so that he can enter in; and when he enters he tries to break our connection with God and our good relationships with others.

Like the uninvited guest and story of Goldilocks, our enemy often shows up at the most inopportune times as he attempts to plant negative thoughts and sow seeds of doubt in our minds that often contradict God's Word. And if we are not careful, we can begin to dwell on these thoughts allowing them to take up root and residence within us; this in turn causes many of us to live powerless, defeated lives as we deny the true authority and power that we have been endowed with.

According to Matthew 28:18 Jesus said, "All authority (all power of rule) in heaven and on earth has been given to Me" (Amplified Bible). And as Christians, based on 1 John 4:4, Jesus, Greater One now lives on the inside of us; "He [Jesus] Who lives in you is greater (mightier) than he who is in the world" (Amplified Bible). If all authority and power has been given to Jesus, and He lives inside of you and me, this means that we now have the same authority and power that He exercised when He walked the earth.

Just as Goldilocks strolled through the forest eventually becoming an uninvited guest, our enemy the devil walks around seeking those whom he may destroy (1 Pet. 5:8). This is why we each have to be keenly aware of who and what we connect ourselves to and what we allow in our temples and begin to cast down every negative thought (2 Cor. 10:5].

Don't give any place to the enemy. Check the rooms of your temple today to see if there are any ways or thoughts that contradict God's Word; who knows, you just may have an uninvited guest.

"Surrender to God! Resist the devil, and he will run from you" (James 4:7, Contemporary English Version).

Thoughts

_____
_____
_____
_____
_____
_____
_____

May 17
WALKING THROUGH YOUR OBSTACLE TO THE PROMISE
Read: Josh. 3:9-17

In life there are going to be obstacles and challenges to face, there is no way around it. But the thing that is really important to be mindful of in these situations is how we choose to respond to the challenges that come to oppose and/or hinder us.

Throughout the Bible the Israelites faced many challenges. Some challenges overtook them, while other seemingly insurmountable obstacles were easily overcome, that is when the situation was approached from the right perspective. The following is an example of the latter.

The time had finally come for the children of Israel to cross over into the land that God had promised to them; however, there was a huge obstacle that literally stood in the way--the mighty Jordan River.

After crossing the Red Sea, the children of Israel wandered in the Judean wilderness for a period of forty years. This journey was required to bring God's people to a place of putting complete faith and total trust in Him by allowing all who had the old mindset of just doing enough to get by to die off so that the new generation could go in and possess the land. It's never a good thing to enter a place of promise with a carnal and unrenewed mind, because instinctively these individuals habitually return to doing what they know to do.

So here we have the Israelites who for forty long years walked along the same paths, and the same dusty and rocky roads while seeing the same landmarks over and over again. You would think that in their multi-year journey, passing by the same river should have allowed them to observe the characteristics of this great body of water; especially the effects on water levels as the seasons changed.

Just to put things in perspective and give an idea as to exactly what the Israelites faced, the Jordan River was approximately 156-200 miles long, 90-100 feet wide, and 3-10 feet deep. Here were the Israelites now being challenged to cross this massive body of water without any earthly idea as to how this would be accomplished.

To make matters worse, at a certain times of the year during the harvest season, the banks of the Jordan River would rise substantially higher than normal thus making any crossing that much more difficult. You would think that after wandering in the wilderness for forty years that the Israelites would have observed the levels of the river based on the seasonal changes, and crossed over at a more opportune time when the levels were lower. Instead they were directed to cross the river when it was actually at its highest levels. It was not at a time of their choosing, but at a time chosen by God simply because He said so.

Thoughts

_____
_____
_____
_____
_____
_____
_____
_____

This type of "blind" faith is exactly what God desires and requires from each of us. We are to follow His direction and guidance without question so that we can fulfill His purpose and plan according to His timing—without hesitation. Yet too often many of us allow our circumstances to dictate the path we take when God knows what's best. Joshua chose to follow God!

The Jordan River here not only represented an obstacle to the people of God, but it was also a pathway to the place of promise and blessing. What obstacle(s) are you facing today? Is it your boss, a co-worker, bills, a demanding work schedule, a challenging spouse, unruly children, sickness and/or disease? Don't fret because God has a greater plan.

May 18
EVERYTHING MUST GO
Read: Num. 33:50-56

I was recently reminded of a movie from the mid-80's called "Brewster's Millions," in which the main character Brewster, a minor league baseball player, received a $300 million inheritance from an unknown distant relative. However, there was a catch; to test his stewardship a stipulation was added to the will and the prerequisite to receiving the inheritance was that Brewster dispose of $30 million in a 30-day period.

He was to do this without wasting any of the money, or having any assets at the end. And if he were successful, he would inherit the entire $300 million. Can you imagine attempting to spend $30 million in 30-days without wasting one cent or having any assets to show in the end?

Well, this is similar to what we are asked to do when we come to Christ. We are to literally become spiritually bankrupt, ridding ourselves of the things from our former life until we have nothing left. This allows Christ to fill us anew so that there is less of us and more of Him.

This is exactly what the Israelites were commanded to do when they entered Canaan, the land of promise. They were told to drive out all the inhabitants, destroy all idols and pagan places of worship. Why? Because anything that was not driven out would become an irritant and/or future source of discomfort if it was not dealt with quickly and decisively (Num. 33:50-56).

Thoughts

Today, many of us needlessly suffer from various issues simply because we refuse to let certain things go. We often allow negative thoughts to fester that invariably begin to affect our hearts as we then begin to act out on what we perceive to be right in our own eyes thereby creating our own idols of hatred and confusion (Gal. 5:19-21).

_____
_____
_____
_____
_____
_____
_____

When we accept Christ, we must not only receive Him as Savior but must also be willing to submit to Him as LORD. This means that we must drive out everything from our lives that separate us from His presence, causes division in the body of Christ and grieves the Holy Spirit.

This requires effort on our part to identify the areas in our lives that break the communion and fellowship that our Heavenly Father desires, as we begin to release those things that we hold near and dear to us (those dark areas in our hearts that we carry around like heavy baggage) in order to gain and then live the abundant life that God promises to those who walk in obedience to His Word (Jn. 10:10).

Knowing what is right and doing what is right are two entirely separate things. In other words, having faith and simply talking about obedience is never enough. We can't continue to hear God's Word but never do anything with it, especially as it applies to our personal faith-walk with Christ. We must be doers of God's Word in every sense. This is what the cost of real discipleship is all about.

Jesus Himself said, "Simply put, if you're not willing to take what is dearest to you, whether plans or people, and kiss it good-bye, you can't be my disciple" (Lk. 14:33, The Message). This means that every idol or sin that we continue to carry around like heavy bags must be let go of, if we truly desire to be disciples of Christ.

God is ready to do a new thing in your life, but first the old and former things in your life must go! This is when true transformation begins to take place and the gifts that may be dormant inside begin to flow!

May 19
LORD, PLEASE OPEN MY EYES
Read: 2 Kgs. 6:8-17

Have you ever gone through or maybe are currently going through a test or trial where you felt as though you were all alone? You may have felt or may even feel now as though no one else understands what you are really going through, and that no one can relate to your challenge. Well, this is never really the case (1 Cor. 10:13).

Thoughts

_____

_____

_____

_____

_____

_____

_____

There were many instances in the Bible in which God's people felt the exact same way: Samson, Gideon, Elijah, David, and even Jesus Himself as He took on the sins of the entire world and was separated from the Father. These individuals often experienced intense periods of isolation and loneliness, yet in each of their circumstances, God transformed what could have turned into an emotional pity party or what seemed to be abandonment into victory.

In chapter 6 of the Old Testament book of Second Kings we find the Israelites at war once again, this time against the Syrian army. And as this war progressed there was something that constantly troubled the King of Syria, it appeared that every time the Syrian king prepared to make a move or go a certain way, the Israelite army knew well in advance what the Syrian army was planning to do and were then poised to counter the offensive. The king probably thought there was a spy in the camp, but was later informed that the Israelites were simply being advised by a prophet.

Distraught over this situation, the king decided to send for the man of God, who just happened to be the prophet Elisha at the time, the successor of the prophet Elijah.

Elisha and his servant was lodging in a home in the city of Dotham, which was a considerable distance away from the Syrian king's current locale. But nonetheless, the king dispatched an entourage to seek out the man of God in an attempt to stop him from advising the Israelite army so that he could gain the upper hand.

The king's messengers and a great multitude of armed warriors arrived where the prophet was staying during the evening. The following day Elisha's servant arose early in the morning as he was accustomed to doing, but this time as he exited the house he saw a vast enemy army completely surrounding them comprised of horses, chariots, and fierce warriors, so the servant became fearful as he went to inform his master the prophet of what he saw and ask what they should do (2 Kgs. 6:15)?

Recognizing and knowing the authority that he had and Whom he represented, this did not move or faze the prophet in the least because he knew that help was already there. Then looking through eyes of faith at the unseen, Elisha boldly declared, "Do not fear, for those who *are* with us *are* more than those who *are* with them" (2 Kgs. 6:16, King James Version).

Elisha knew something the servant didn't know and could see beyond what the servant could see in the natural. The prophet then boldly petitioned the all-seeing God saying, "LORD, I pray, open his eyes that he may see" (2 Kgs. 6:17, King James Version). And immediately the LORD opened the servant's eyes allowing him to see a multitude of horses, chariots of fire, and warriors from the heavenly host surrounding Elisha with swords drawn and ready to fight.

So, whenever you feel surrounded by the enemy, and are tempted to believe that you are all alone with your emotions getting the best of you this is not the time to get discouraged or upset; because there are actually more with you than you can ever imagine. Simply ask God to open your eyes to clearly see.

Thoughts

_____
_____
_____
_____
_____
_____
_____

May 20
MY THINKING HAS CRIPPLED THE BLESSING
Read: 2 Sam. 4:4; 9:1-13

The news of King Saul and his son Jonathan's death made its way back to their home. Jonathan had a son, Mephibosheth, who was very young when his grandfather (King Saul) and father (Jonathan) were pronounced dead. When his nurse heard the news, fearing an imminent hostile enemy take over; she fled the palace to spare the child's life. But in her hasty retreat and attempt to get as far away from the palace as possible, the young Mephibosheth was dropped resulting in him being lame and crippled in his feet (2 Sam. 4:4).

The young child eventually ended up in a place called Lodebar, where he was reared and raised. This was a place that literally coincided with the natural meaning of its name. The word "Lodebar" actually means "without pasture" or a barren place. Barreness was an understatement to the deplorable conditions of this region; if there was a dictionary available at the time with the word "barren" defined therein, a picture of Lodebar would have been included with the caption.

Here was a son of royalty living in a barren place, crippled by his circumstances. It was his upbringing in this location and his physical condition that caused Mephibosheth to have an improper and negative image of who he was, even though he was an heir of royalty. He did not know who he really was.

Many of us give way to the same thinking, but in actuality in Christ we are royalty. Scripture declares that we are heirs to God's Kingdom with Christ (Rom. 8:15-17).

Too often we miss out on God's very best for our lives, as we live and exist beneath our privileges as Kingdom citizens simply because we have an improper view of ourselves not knowing who we truly are. Where we were raised or wherever our current location may presently be in life does not define us; it is what God says about us in His Word that makes all the differences.

The thing that we each should remember is the fact that when we accept Christ our souls are saved and our spirits are renewed as we become new creations; but unfortunately our thinking does not immediately change. This requires our constant attention and a conscious effort on our part to renew our minds through the Word of God each and every day. "Don't copy the behavior and customs of this world, but let God transform you into a new person by changing the way you think. Then you will learn to know God's will for you, which is good and pleasing and perfect" (Rom 12:2, New Living Translation).

Thoughts

_____
_____
_____
_____
_____
_____
_____

Mephibosheth was crippled living in a barren place based on the external and the perception that he had of himself. Many times we often allow our thinking to relegate us to a place of barrenness and lack when the blessings of God are already ours to receive because of our Kingdom status in Christ.

Mephibosheth eventually received a glimpse of who he really as he was restored to his rightful place and sat in the presence of the king. So, don't allow your old way of thinking to cripple the blessing and all that God has in store for you. You are already blessed and you are royalty, so alignment your thinking to the truth of God's Word as you begin to truly act and live like it! Don't allow your thinking to cripple the blessings that God has in store for you (Prov. 23:7)!

May 21
USE YOUR BACKSTAGE PASS
Read: Heb. 9

As a teenager in my before Christ days, music was a very big part of my life if not my life at the time. I listened to a variety of genres of music and a wide array of artists, but physically being at a concert was always better.

For me, seeing artists perform live was a great and unforgettable experience; but there was something that enhanced this excitement even more and could have been equated to the "icing on the cake" being afforded the opportunity have a backstage pass. Having this pass made the concert experience just that much sweeter, with the ability to meet the artist up-close and personal. From a spiritual standpoint, God provides us with this same opportunity today.

God has set the stage for each and every one of us, and even went above and beyond to ensure that we each had a backstage pass when He sent His Son, but it is entirely up to us individually to receive it and then use it.

Throughout the Bible and Scripture we can see the record and account of God compassionately attempting to get mankind back into His presence and into the environment that He designed for us as our Creator from the very beginning. The Old Testament Tabernacle and later the Temple provided great depictions of this.

The Tabernacle and Temple was divided into three sections: the Outer Court, The Holy Place (or the Inner Court), and the Holy of Holies. Each section had a specific purpose.

Inside each section there were different items that were symbolic or a type that pointed to Jesus Christ leading up to the Most Holy

Thoughts

_____
_____
_____
_____
_____
_____
_____

171

Place, the Holy of Holies. In the Holy of Holies was the Ark of the Covenant, which represented the very presence of God.

The general population was allowed to bring their offerings and sacrifices to be presented by the priests in the outer court; however, the priests were the only individuals allowed to go forward into the Most Holy Place, the Holy of Holies once a year to offer a corporate sacrifice for the people. But, even then the priest could only go so far.

The Holy Place (the inner court) and the Holy of Holies was separated by a veil, signifying that man because of sin was not fit to come into the presence of a Holy God. In an effort to restore the relationship shared with man in the Garden of Eden, God had a remedy; He sent His Son Jesus Christ to restore fellowship (Gal. 4:4-5, New Living Translation).

When Jesus died on the cross, the veil in the temple was split down the middle (Matt. 27:50-51) which signified that we now had direct access to the presence of God and every part of His dwelling place through Christ's shed blood. Since we now have the privilege of entering into the place that was once off-limits, I would encourage you to use your backstage pass!

"Let us therefore come boldly to the throne of grace, that we may obtain mercy and find grace to help in time of need" (Heb. 4:16, New King James Version).

May 22
DON'T ALLOW GOD'S SEED TO BE DESTROYED
Read: Jn. 10:10

Working in the communications field for the majority of my career has been an interesting journey and experience; observing how new technologies have brought about more efficient ways to communicate through cell phones, the Internet, and other innovative telecommunications systems has been extraordinary.

However, with all the new technological advances over the years, there is one area of communicating that has not changed and is an area that still requires due diligence to prevent any potential harm to the communications technician and/or operator. This hazard involves contact with Radio Frequency (RF) energy.

Thoughts

_____

_____

_____

_____

_____

_____

_____

RF energy is electromagnetic waves sent via communications antennas from a transmitter to a receiver. It has been documented that biological effects often result from direct exposure to this type of energy, and in some cases it has even caused individuals to become sterile, not being able to reproduce (children or seed).

In order to prevent exposure to RF radiation, markers and signs (generally in "RED", which should immediately caution those near it) are placed around the RF transmitting source to prevent possible exposure and to keep individuals away from the wrong environment.

Like the RF energy from a radiating antenna, our enemy the devil attempts to destroy the seed of God's Word that abides within by enticing us to operate in the wrong environment and in the wrong way with the ultimate aim of sterilizing us so that we will become powerless and unable to reproduce. Jn. 10:10 states it plainly, "The thief does not come except to steal, and to kill, and to destroy..." (New King James Version).

God gives us boundary markers through the principles of His Word and through the Holy Spirit. Yet many of us still choose to disregard these boundaries (His Word and His voice) and we often end up in an environment that causes us to be spiritually sterile when we were created and designed to reproduce.

This is why we must guard our hearts because that's where the seed of the Word is planted and where our very life flows from. "Guard your heart above all else, for it determines the course of your life" (Prov. 4:23, New Living Translation).

We cannot allow the enemy to lure us into the wrong environment as he attempts to sterilize our seed and make us ineffective. So, don't allow the enemy to destroy your seed!

May 23
WHEN THE THRILL IS GONE
Read: Ps. 22:3

When you think of summertime, what comes to mind for you? For me images of being out in the sun, beaches, vacation, and family reunions come to mind. This is also usually a time for family vacations, many of which include visits to amusement parks.

Raising four children in our home over the years, we've undoubtedly had our fair share of family trips and visits to amusement parks in various locations like Six Flags, Kings Dominion, Busch Gardens, Universal Studios, Island of Adventures, and Disney World, just to name a few.

Thoughts

For the kids, anticipation of arrival at the amusement park almost equaled or sometimes

173

exceeded the excitement felt once they actually arrived as they saw the rides and attractions from a distance. Once we arrived, a map of the park was acquired and then a brief discussion on the plan or strategy for visiting and riding each of the main attractions to maximize the best use of time.

Excitement was in the air as the family moved from one attraction to the next; however, of all the attractions in the park, it was usually the roller coaster that brought the most enjoyment and excitement. The Lochness Monster, The Big Bad Wolf, Anaconda, Space Mountain, The Kraken, The Incredible Hulk are just few of the amazing roller coaster rides we have been privileged to experience.

These rides generally twisted us, turned us in every direction, and even flip us upside down through multiple loops along the path. As a result, our heart rates increased and our adrenalin began to flow; but, within a matter of minutes the excitement of the ride was over and the thrill was gone.

Therefore, in order to experience this excitement and exhilaration again what does one normally do? You got it, we met at the ride's exit, turned around and then proceeded to the long line to wait another 30-45 minutes to experience the ride again.

For many believers this roller coaster ride is what we experience upon entering the sanctuary of God's house service after service and week after week. Many come in waiting for and expecting the praise team or choir to push them into God's presence until the power of His presence is felt as the anointing begins to flow. But as soon as individuals leave God's house, "the thrill is gone". They come to church for a spiritual high that only leads to a roller coaster experience, when there is so much more.

Praise and worship should not just be an emotional experience and we are not to wait for God's presence to show up before we start praising Him, because in actuality His presence is already there and it is up to us to invite Him in. Therefore, we each should come ready to praise Him and set the atmosphere for His glory to show up and dwell with us and in us. "But thou art holy, O thou that [inhabits] the praises of Israel" (Ps. 22:3, King James Version).

Worship is not about our "orders of service", the method in which it is done, or any of our other religious attempts to draw closer to God; true worship does not start until we begin to offer the sacrifice of praise that is due His name.

Thoughts

_____
_____
_____
_____
_____
_____
_____

This sacrifice is more than a once a week, Sunday-only experience; instead, this should be experienced every single day. When the thrill appears to be gone, don't let it go. Begin to praise and worship God, and set the atmosphere (Jn. 4:23-24).

May 24
SUPERSIZE IT
Read: Acts 1:4

According to statistics, "Each day, 1 in 4 Americans visits a fast food restaurant." Fast food restaurants are numerous, not only in the United States but all over the world; among them are Kentucky Fried Chicken (a.k.a., KFC), Popeye's, Subways, Burger King, and the most widely known of them all McDonald's.

These restaurants provide customers convenience with quickly prepared meals that are usually hot, tasty, and relatively cheap. However, many times customers are not satisfied with the proportion of the meal size, looking for a little more food for the price being paid, or as some like to say "A little more bang for the buck!"

To remedy this, in addition to providing a regular-sized meal, many fast food restaurants now offer the option to "Supersize" the meal. Therefore, for a nominal additional fee customers can obtain larger portions of their favorite value meal to satisfy the craving or hunger they may have with only a little added expense.

As believers in Christ we have a similar option in a spiritual sense. When we confess our sins, ask for forgiveness, and profess faith in the LORD Jesus Christ, we are filled with the Holy Spirit according to Scripture. "In Him you also trusted, after you heard the word of truth, the gospel of your salvation; in whom also, having believed, you were sealed with the Holy Spirit of promise" (Eph. 1:13, New King James Version).

At this point every believer is endowed with the presence of the person of the Holy Spirit to lead, guide, and direct us; yet there is more. And sadly, for many believers the simple assurance of salvation and access to heaven is enough because this is often all that many Christians aspire to as they wait to be raptured to meet Christ in the air (1 Thess. 4:17) and sit by doing nothing; but again there is more.

Prior to His ascension into heaven Jesus told His disciples, "Don't leave Jerusalem yet. Wait here for the Father to give you the Holy Spirit, just as I told you he has promised to do. John baptized with water, but in a few days you will be baptized with the Holy Spirit" (Acts 1:4, Contemporary English Version). This spiritual baptism provides the believer with added power, power needed to effectively go forward and do the work of ministry.

The word ministry in its simplest form means nothing more than "to serve, or act of serving." This is what a second helping of the Holy Spirit comes to do, empower Christians with the ability to serve on a deeper level (Acts 1:8). When the Holy Spirit comes upon us, He gives us the ability and power to be more effective witnesses for Christ.

Thoughts

_____
_____
_____
_____
_____
_____
_____

The power or empowerment described here is referred to as "dunamis" in the Greek, which is where the English word for "dynamite" is derived from. And of course we all know the effect that dynamite has when it is used; it has explosive power that immediately affects change in everything around it.

This is what the empowerment of the Holy Spirit does in the life of the believer; it gives us the ability and power to effect change in the lives of those we come in contact with, and the environment around us through Christ-centered service and/or ministry. Why settle for regular or ordinary when you can supersize the power and ability that God has made available to every believer at little to no additional cost; all you have to do is simply ask.

May 25

HE DESERVES YOUR BEST
Read: Gen. 4:1-7

The story of Cain and Abel is very familiar to most of us. Cain and Abel, of course, were the offspring of the first man and woman on earth, Adam and Eve. As the story goes, Cain tended the field and Abel the flock.

One day as Cain and Abel prepared to present the first recorded sacrifice offered by man in the Bible as a way to show gratitude for what God had done, Cain brought offerings of fruit from the ground to God since he was a tiller of the land (or basically a farmer). Abel on the other hand was a shepherd and keeper of sheep (or lamb). Scripture records that Abel "brought of the firstborn of his flock and of their fat" (Gen. 4:4, New King James Version). Abel offered a lamb as a sacrifice

God accepted Abel's offering, but did not accept Cain's offering. So, why was Abel's sacrifice better? Abel gave the best that he had, while Cain did not offer his best but simply that which was available to him at the time. What Cain offered had the ability to grow back at a later date, but what Abel offered required the supreme sacrifice of a life that could never be regained because in this instance death was final.

Abel's offering demonstrated that he was motivated by sincere faith and trust in God with an attitude that was pleasing, because he gave his first and best. Conversely, when Cain's offering was not accepted, he demonstrated the wrong attitude instead of trying to figure out what he needed to do to present an offering that would be acceptable. Cain's offering was rejected because he did not present his first and the offering did not come from a pure heart.

Thoughts

_____

_____

_____

_____

_____

_____

_____

Sacrifices and offerings in the Bible were usually presented as atonement for sin, to commemorate a time or place where God manifested His presence, or to invite God's presence to come, to dwell and abide. Whatever the case may have been in the story of Cain and Abel, Abel's sacrifice was more pleasing because he demonstrated his gratitude to God by giving Him his very best with the right attitude and motives.

There was are different ways of demonstrating our gratitude to God, but Cain chose demonstrate his gratitude based his preference and in his own way as he presented that which was acceptable in his own eyes as opposed to what God truly required—-sacrifice!

This still holds true today for us today, though we no longer have to bring a ram, sheep, or goat to church for presentation on the altar, God still desires and requires sacrificial offerings from us as well; sacrifices that come from pure hearts, with proper motives. One such sacrifice is our praise and worship.

In our praise we give God what He is rightfully due, but in our worship we have the opportunity to take it a step further to give Him above and beyond just the basics.

Through Christ we can now "continually offer the sacrifice of praise to God, that is, the fruit of our lips, giving thanks to His name" (Heb. 13:15, New King James Version). This sacrifice should not come out of duty or obligation, but out of our relationship with the Father through Christ and our subsequent love for Him. We are to praise God not just for what He has done or what He is going to do in our lives; but, we are to praise and worship Him simply for who He is! Don't just give God the rest, make it personal and give Him your very best (Rom. 12:1)!

May 26
WHO YOU REPPIN'?
Read: 2 Cor. 5:19-20

When I joined the Navy over twenty plus years ago, a couple of my primary goals were to utilize the educational benefits that were afforded to me and at the same time see the world. And though I'm still working towards the achievement of my educational goals there is one thing that I can say, and that is I have traveled extensively with the opportunity to see and visit many locations around the world, places I may have never seen if I had chosen a different career path or decided to remain in my hometown.

Thoughts

_____
_____
_____

Although there are shore duty assignments in the Navy, the primary mission of this branch of service is to put Sailors on ships and ships at sea. And as the Navy deploys to various regions of the globe, it is customary for naval vessels to

_____
_____
_____
_____
_____

visit ports of call for the purpose of providing the crew with a little rest and relaxation to break the monotony of the daily grind of being at sea for days, weeks and sometimes months at a time with no land in sight.

So when a ship prepares to enter port, the excitement and vision of some much needed liberty is felt throughout the crew as the atmosphere shifts. But even though the ship pulls pier side or anchors out in the harbor in preparation to release the crew, prior to anyone leaving the ship the Commanding Officer and the senior enlisted member onboard (Command Master Chief or Chief of the Boat) usually provide the crew with a port brief to discuss the "do's and don'ts" of liberty.

This port brief normally consists of an overview of attractions and/or locations to visit and see, identification of establishments and locations that are off-limits, and a simple reminder that as Sailors we are not only ambassadors for the United States Navy, but also ambassadors as citizens of our country the United States of America. Therefore, our conduct should be governed and reflected accordingly.

Whenever a negative incident occurred during a port visit, the local news headline did not just have a caption stating "Navy Sailor......," but generally had bold letters stating "AMERICAN." And unfortunately, many citizens of these visited locations based their entire perspective and view of America on the inappropriate actions of the few.

Well, the same thing often occurs in a spiritual sense. The reputation of Christians, more importantly the reputation of God the Father and Christ the Son, are often based on the actions of a few.

Whether we realize this fact or not, those who confess the name of Jesus Christ at conversion immediately become ambassadors for Christ and the Kingdom of God. An ambassador is defined as "an authorized representative or messenger;" therefore, as ambassadors for Christ when we go out into the world, our conduct should reflect favorably on the One we represent; the one whose message we carry (a message that may only be seen in our actions and not in what we speak).

In a natural sense the actions of a child are often a direct reflection of the father's actions. And in a spiritual sense the same applies to those who profess to be Christians or believers in Christ; our actions should be a direct reflection of our Heavenly Father as his ambassadors and direct representatives in the earth. In this world and in this life you will either represent Christ as His ambassador, or you will be an ambassador for the kingdom of darkness—-there is no middle ground. So, as the younger generation would say: WHO YOU REPPIN' (Prov. 13:17)?

Thoughts

_____

_____

_____

_____

_____

_____

May 27

DIVINELY FAVORED
Read: Dan. 1:1-21

Once again the children of Israel found themselves in Babylonian captivity, this time under the rule of King Nebuchadnezzar. One day the king requested that a few of the young men from Israel be brought to serve in the palace. Among the group of men identified were the Hebrew or Israelite men Daniel, Hananiah, Mishael, and Azariah.

But before these men would be considered fit for palace service they first had to undergo three years of specified training, to include maintaining a diet regimented by the king. However, there was one major drawback. The food that the king set before the Hebrews probably included items that were prohibited by Jewish customs, and were also things more than likely offered in idol worship.

Not desiring to be defiled by the king's delicacies; Daniel refused to eat the king's food and drink. He then requested that he and the other three Hebrew men be given an alternate diet consisting of only vegetables and water.

It was not customary for the young men in training to eat anything other than what the king placed before them. But God gave Daniel and the three Hebrew men favor. So the chief eunuch obliged and agreed to Daniel's terms and after ten days the he would compare Hebrew's outward features with the other young men who actually ate from the king's table.

There is nothing like God's favor (Dan. 1:9). As a result, the chief eunuch allowed them to eat the items established in Daniel's dietary plan, one designed to bring an inner purity and wholeness (Dan. 1:14-19).

Not only did the Hebrew men look healthier than the young men who ate from the king's table after the ten-day period, but they were also more knowledgeable about the things that pertained to life and were also endowed with God-given gifts.

This should make us all more conscious of not only what we eat physically, but what we allow into our spiritual temples. Because what we receive inside will eventually reflect outwardly and then what's truly on the inside of us will be seen by all (1 Cor. 6:19-20).

When the right things are going into our temples, in particular God's Word, then the right things are bound to come out for everyone to see. Therefore, we should not be quick to just eat and receive anything because individuals will either be cursed by what's produced from inside of our temple or blessed by the favor and hand of God in our life (Prov. 23:1-3). In other words, everything that looks good may not

Thoughts

_____

_____

_____

_____

_____

_____

_____

necessarily be good for you. When we don't defile God's temple, which we each are, we obtain God's favor.

According to one dictionary definition favor is "a special privilege or right granted; friendly regard shown toward another especially by a superior; or approving consideration or attention." Simply put for the believer in Christ, favor is nothing more than "God's unfair advantage."

Daniel was highly favored because he lived a life that was pleasing to God; he refused to allow his body (God's temple) to be defiled, even by the king. When the favor of God is upon your life, not even the enemy cannot thwart your God-given plans, and many times He will even use your enemies to bless you in the process.

Live a life that is pleasing to God and then watch His favor come to you and upon you. Favor comes through obedience. Are you divinely favored?

May 28

DIFFERENT PACKAGE, SAME DELIVERY
Read: Ecc. 1:9

The writer of Ecclesiastes, King Solomon, knew exactly what he was talking about when he wrote verse nine of chapter one, "Everything that happens has happened before; nothing is new, nothing under the sun" (Ecc. 1:9, Contemporary English Version). This statement was not only applicable back then, but is still true to this very day.

Economic problems, natural disasters, the spread of disease and sickness are not new; they have occurred before, but were just experienced on a different level by our ancestors and those that came before us. We can make this same association to our spiritual lives, there are no new temptations.

Though her legs may be longer, eyes more seductive, or his chest may be a little larger with biceps bulging; although the package may have changed, the method of delivery still remains the same. The temptations we each face and the stumbling blocks placed before us by our enemy (the devil), are not new; someone has already faced them, and also overcome (1 Pet. 5:9).

Thoughts

_____

_____

_____

_____

_____

_____

_____

But even though many of us suffer the same thing, this often stems from something that is already at work and resident within each of us—the lust of the flesh, lust of the eyes, and the pride of life (1 Jn. 2:16).

So, if the devil does not really have any new tricks, why do we as Christians continue to allow him to lure us into these traps? James in his New Testament epistle sums it up best as he describes how these yearnings and desires come from within. The devil knows exactly how to prey on this inherent weakness (James 1:13-14).

This is exactly why we each must constantly be on guard and don't allow the enemy to entice us because we have to recognize his schemes. He does not have anything new to throw our way so he just disguises the temptation in a different package. The Apostle Paul in his epistle to the Corinthian church warns us to not be ignorant of satan's devices or methods for attempting to trip us up (2 Cor. 2:9-11)!

The devil has one ultimate aim for each of us, his goal is to separate us from God's presence by keeping us bound by sin (1 Pet. 5:8-10). So, don't allow the devil to deceive you. He has nothing new to bring your way; be mindful of the package, because the delivery remains the same. But whenever we do give in, we can have confidence in the fact that God's grace is still available and sufficient.

"If we claim that we're free of sin, we're only fooling ourselves. A claim like that is errant nonsense. On the other hand, if we admit our sins—make a clean breast of them—he won't let us down; he'll be true to himself. He'll forgive our sins and purge us of all wrongdoing. If we claim that we've never sinned, we out-and-out contradict God—make a liar out of him. A claim like that only shows off our ignorance of God" (1 Jn. 1:8-10, The Message).

May 29
BE CAREFUL HOW YOU BUILD
Read: 1 Cor. 3:10-13

As we are currently being taught on how about the process of re-building the Temple at church, I was reminded of a story about a carpenter who was preparing for a change in life. He had been successful in building quality homes for many years, but was now looking forward to retirement.

The carpenter was one of the best in his region, one who had enjoyed a good reputation. Yet he knew that it was time for a change and that he needed to move on. So he informed his employer of his intentions to retire in the coming months. This transition would enable him to relax and truly enjoy spending time with his family with a more leisurely lifestyle, one that was less stressful and with few compressed deadlines. He knew that he would miss the steady pay, but at this stage in his life spending time with his family was more important.

Thoughts

_____
_____
_____
_____
_____
_____
_____
_____

When his employer heard the news, and although he was disappointed, he understood the carpenter's viewpoint and future goals. However, he was compelled to ask him to complete just one more thing. The carpenter was asked to build one last house as a personal favor to the employer.

Although he was somewhat reluctant, the carpenter eventually said yes and began the planning process for the building of this one last house with the designs provided by the architect. Yet, although he said "yes" to his boss, his heart was not truly in it.

So over the next couple of months, the carpenter went through the motions of constructing what appeared to be a dream home for a potential buyer—a seven bedroom, 3 ½ bath, 3-car garage and extremely spacious home on 5 acres of land with a private lake in the backyard. But again, because his heart was not in the work, he began to take shortcuts while also using substandard material accompanied by very poor workmanship. After years of exceptional work, this was not a befitting way for a carpenter of his caliber and reputation to end his career.

After weeks of a half-hearted effort, the home was finally complete with a home inspection immediately following. And although the work was a bit shoddy and not done to the carpenter's usual high standards, he did just enough to ensure that the home would still pass the basic inspection requirements.

Then after all was said and done, and in an unusual turn of events; the employer walked up to the carpenter, handed him the keys to the home and said "Congratulations, this home is actually yours!" To show the carpenter his appreciation for years of faithful service, the employer wanted to express his sincere gratitude by giving him the house and the land absolutely free of charge. Can you imagine the shock and the embarrassment the carpenter must have felt when he accepted the keys?

As believers in Christ we are considered to be God's temples, buildings, and the very dwelling place for His Spirit (1 Cor. 6:19); therefore, it is very essential that we are also mindful of how we build upon the foundation that God has already laid for us; because using inferior products and poor quality work will only result in a lot of unnecessary re-work over time. So, be careful how you build because the house you are building today is the place you may be required to stay (1 Cor. 3:10-13).

Thoughts
_____
_____
_____
_____
_____
_____
_____

May 30
OVERLOOKED BUT NOT FORGOTTEN
Read: 1 Sam. 16:1-13

In a blatant act of disobedience, King Saul was found guilty of usurping or unrightfully using the role and office of a priest through impatience by taking it upon himself to present an offering and sacrifice on behalf of the Israelite army in the absence of the prophet Samuel who was en route to perform the task (1 Sam. 13:8-14).

King Saul later demonstrated disobedience once again when he failed to completely obey the command of the LORD to kill King Agag, following a battle with the Amalekites as he was told to utterly or completely destroy the king and all of his possessions. But instead of obeying the LORD, Saul decided to destroy a few things and keep the best items from himself (1 Sam. 15:1-22). Saul initially started his reign the correct way; however, over time he began to allow disobedience to separate him further and further away from the will of God.

It was because of Saul's random acts of disobedience that the LORD sought a king who would honor and obey Him, "a man after His own heart." The prophet Samuel was then given the assignment locating and anointing the future king of Israel; therefore, he was sent to the house of Jesse a Bethlehemite.

Jesse had a total of eight sons, seven of which had the looks, stature, and qualities of what man would consider the makings of a future king; surely one of them would be chosen to lead God's people as the next king of Israel.

Jesse called for his sons, each having had the opportunity to prepare for this moment knowing of the prophet's arrival, to stand before Samuel. One by one each son was paraded before the prophet to see who would be chosen and anointed as the next king; however, even after the last son present there had been brought before Samuel, the LORD had yet to select the new king.

The prophet then asked Jesse, "Are all your sons here? [Jesse] said, there is yet the youngest; he is tending the sheep. Samuel said to Jesse, Send for him; for we will not sit down to eat until he is here" (1 Sam. 16:11, Amplified Bible). Jesse sent for his last son David who was young, good looking, small in stature, and had the job of tending his father's sheep; here was the son who was not initially brought before the prophet Samuel because he did not fit the bill, the standard, or image for what man considered to be kingly stock.

Jesse overlooked his son David based on what he saw on the outside in the natural, not knowing that there was a king waiting to break forth on the inside. And even though David did not have time to prepare for his screening with the prophet Samuel like his other brothers, who probably had the opportunity to change into clean garments, bathe, etc.; as soon as David arrived and stood before the prophet, the LORD said "Arise, anoint him; this is he" (1 Sam. 16:12, Amplified Bible).

Thoughts

_____

_____

_____

_____

The one who was kept in the background and overlooked by man, was the very one chosen and anointed by God to be king.

_____

_____

_____

There are many today who get overlooked for various reasons; however, the good thing about this is that God knows where each of us are and what we are capable of doing; and though we may often get overlooked by man, God has not forgotten us and stands ready to pour out His anointing that leads to His divine favor and blessings (1 Cor. 2:9).

May 31
THE "DAYS OF OUR LIVES"
Read: Col. 3:1-3

"As the World Turns," remember that you only have "One Life to Live" (Heb. 9:27). For those who are "The Young and the Restless," don't follow the pattern of this world or the "Passions" therein (Rom. 12:1-2); instead, let Christ be your "Guiding Light" (Jn.8:12) as He leads you to "Another World" (Jn. 18:36).

So, when you are feeling lonely and hurt at "Melrose Place," make your way to receive help at the "General Hospital;" remember, that by His stripes you are healed and through the shed blood of Christ you have already been made whole (Is. 53:5).

Long hair, short hair, straight hair or waves; the outer appearance is important, and there is also a focus in society on what everyone is getting paid. Therefore, in your "Search For Tomorrow" choose not to get caught-up in the world's system or opinion refusing to be swayed; knowing that in Christ you are "The Bold and the Beautiful" because you are fearfully and wonderfully made (Ps. 139:14).

When you are feeling lonely or depressed as if no one really cares, through Christ you are adopted into the family, and God says to "All My Children" I love you and I am always there (Gal. 3:26; Heb. 13:5).

You have been created in His image, to shine brightly for the entire world to see; as a king and priest you have been created to rule and reign with Christ in His "Dynasty" (Gen. 1:27; Matt. 5:14; 1 Pet. 2:9).

Who needs a Soap Opera when the "Days of Our Lives" are hid in God through Christ who gives us hope for a brighter future and tomorrow (Prov. 13:12). Rejoice today in the fact that God does not just give us life—He is our life.

Thoughts

_____

_____

_____

_____

_____

_____

"So if you're serious about living this new resurrection life with Christ, act like it. Pursue the things over which Christ presides. Don't shuffle along, eyes to the ground, absorbed with the things right in front of you. Look up, and be alert to what is going on around Christ—that's where the action is. See things from his perspective. Your old life is dead. Your new life, which is your real life—even though invisible to spectators—is with Christ in God. He is your life. When Christ (your real life, remember) shows up again on this earth, you'll show up, too—the real you, the glorious you" (Col. 3:1-3, The Message).

June 1

TRAVELING LIGHT
Read: Matt. 5:14

Preparations for traveling on a vacation or work-related business trip can be an interesting experience to say the least, especially when considering the mode of transportation to be utilized. The mode of transportation generally gives the traveler some indication as to how much he or she will be able to pack and bring along with them.

It is during these moments of travel that we are usually separated from the luxuries and/ or comforts of the daily items we generally have readily available at our finger tips when we are at home. So, in order to prepare for the journey we begin by packing essential items; things that we need or things that we think we may need.

We usually begin packing those things that are deemed essential for daily living into a limited amount of space. Things like toiletries, undergarments, shoes, socks or stockings (based on gender of course), clothing for each day, etc.

But once the essentials are out of the way, this is when the problem begins as we invariably start packing and adding extra items, you know those "what if" items for unexpected occasions or situations: that extra shirt, those extra pairs of pants, that extra dress, extra shoes, those extra purses (for the ladies) to accessorize with their outfits. And usually before we know it, we end up packing more than we actually needed or intended to.

This extra packing usually results in a lot of excess baggage; and when traveling by air, today this can become very costly. Any excess baggage now comes with an additional fee to the airline traveler, a fee that goes above and beyond the standard ticket price. The more extra weight there is, the higher the price.

Not only is the traveler penalized for carrying excessive weight, but he or she often ends up having the added burden of transporting and dragging this baggage around between connecting flights and various locations. So, to prevent added financial cost and the unneeded extra burden, wouldn't it just make better sense to travel light?

Thoughts

_____

_____

_____

_____

_____

_____

As believers we have been given the mandate and commission to go out into the world to proclaim the good news, the Blessing given to us by inheritance (Matt. 28:19-20). In other words, we have been commissioned to go and proclaim the great news about Christ.

However, this "go" may very well require and entail traveling; but as seen in the scenario above, it can become an extreme burden and turn into a very costly venture when we choose to travel with excess baggage. Therefore, before we attempt to "go," it is absolutely essential that we first release any excess cares and/or burdens that would prevent us from traveling light and being "light" as God has called us to be (Matt. 5:14-16).

Whatever our excess may be (our sins, anxieties, fears, doubts, or the burdens that we carry around like useless baggage and luggage) they must all be given over to God and released to Him. Giving all of our cares and burdens to God has been made easy because He is concerned about and deeply cares for each one of us (1 Pet. 5:7; Ps. 55:22).

If Christ is the light of the world (Jn. 12:46), and He is, and we are in Christ; then we too are light in the world. We become "traveling light" as we learn to travel light; pun intended! As we travel light, we are no longer encumbered by the weights and cares of this world and are then able to shine forth anywhere.

June 2
THE WILL OF CHRIST
Read: Heb. 9:16-22

Although many people are uncomfortable discussing death and making plans for when the inevitable happens; death is a reality and something we must all face regardless of who we are, our social status, or how much money we've accumulated.

According to Scripture "We die only once, and then we are judged" (Heb. 9:27, Contemporary English Version). This simply means at some point each one of us will die and then receive judgment for our actions during our limited and finite time here on earth (James 4:13-15).

Thoughts

_____
_____
_____
_____
_____
_____
_____

Based on the preceding Scripture, it would be prudent for each one of us to make preparations for that which will eventually come.

From a natural perspective many accomplish this by generating and leaving a document called a "will" behind for their family and loved ones. A will is nothing more than a legal document by "which a person determines the disposition of his or her property after death;" another name for a "will" is "testament." The will or testament when executed upon an individual's death usually provides the recipients with a better life and a new way of living.

But before a will or testament can go into effect, the testator (the person leaving a will or testament to be executed) must first die. In other words, the will has no legal backing as long as the individual is still alive. Death is a prerequisite for any will to become binding and legal.

This is where Jesus Christ stepped in on behalf of mankind with a New Covenant, or new Will and Testament. "Like a will that takes effect when someone dies, the new covenant was put into action at Jesus' death. His death marked the transition from the old plan to the new one, canceling the old obligations and accompanying sins, and summoning the heirs to receive the eternal inheritance that was promised them. He brought together God and his people in this new way" (Heb. 9:16-17, The Message).

Christ gave of Himself so that many would live (Heb. 10:12) because this was all a part of God's greater plan and a part of Christ's will. His will was not signed with a ballpoint or fancy fountain pen. No! The "Will of Christ" was signed with His very own blood through a perfect sacrifice.

As a result, we are all recipients of this will; however, in order for us to be true beneficiaries, we must first die to our own individual wills and then apply the Blood to our lives. Since we are already in the Will, why not enjoy all of the benefits.

"And since we are his children, we are his heirs. In fact, together with Christ we are heirs of God's glory. But if we are to share his glory, we must also share his suffering" (Rom. 8:17, New Living Translation).

Now if the prerequisite to being positioned to receive the benefits of a new life and a fresh start all began with the death of Christ, with Christ being our perfect example. Then in order for us as believers to effectively serve in God's Kingdom and also encourage change in the lives of those around us, a dying to self and our will is absolutely necessary. We must be willing to follow the example of our Leader, Christ the Head of the Church and God the Father of the family (Eph. 5:1).

Have you applied the Blood? The blood of Jesus Christ is what indicates your true connection to the Body (the church) and family of God. In the Will of Christ, death produces life and brings a blessing to the entire family.

Thoughts

_____
_____
_____
_____
_____
_____
_____

June 3

BE CAREFUL WHAT YOU PRAY FOR, YOUR DESIRES MAY LEAD YOU ASTRAY
Read: James 4:2-3

Prayer is a powerful tool, that is, when it is used in the correct way. Yet too often, many use prayer as just a means to obtain things and stuff while attempting to get God to agree with our wants and desires as opposed to praying "His will be done."

We pray for that new house, when we have not demonstrated the ability to be a good steward in maintaining the one that we have; we ask for a new car, yet fail to clean and ensure that routine maintenance occurs with the vehicle that we already possess; or we ask for a spouse or a "soul mate" without having established a good foundation in our own personal relationship with Christ, learning to be single and complete in Him first.

So, instead of praying "thy will be done" we often pray "thy will be done, as long as I get what I've prayed for" in attempts to literally twist God's Arm, if that were even possible, to get what we want even when the request has little to do with His plan for our lives. In doing so, we make God nothing more than a spiritual slot machine or some cosmic genie in the sky waiting to grant our wish based on wrong desires. As a result, our prayers are frequently offered without any thought and little regard to God's will and/or His perfect plan.

God says in His Word "I know what I'm doing. I have it all planned out—plans to take care of you, not abandon you, plans to give you the future you hope for" (Jer. 29:11, The Message). Yet even though God has the perfect plan mapped out, many of us still attempt to navigate through life based on human intellect and fulfilling the desires of our flesh.

In his New Testament epistle, James discussed the topic of inappropriate desires (James 4:2-3). Am I saying that we should not pray for ourselves and things that we need and desire; no, because Matt. 7:7-8 provides clear instructions pertaining to this, "Ask, and it will be given to you; seek, and you will find; knock, and it will be opened to you. For everyone who asks receives, and he who seeks finds, and to him who knocks it will be opened." However, our asking, knocking and seeking should be in line with God's will for our lives and not just based on selfish ambitions and personal self-gratification.

Although God may allow us to connect with that man or woman that we are pursuing, obtain that nice extravagant home that we've desired and longed for, or that better paying job with longer hours equating to more pay, there will be a price to pay in the long run when these do not align to His will. In other words, we must each take a moment to really count up the cost, because in the end there is usually a hefty price to pay (Lk. 14:28-30).

Thoughts

_____
_____
_____
_____
_____
_____
_____

No matter what the request or yearning may be, we must each begin to earnestly seek God first (Matt. 6:33) as we truly learn how to find our delight in Him because this is what moves Him to start giving us not only our need but also goes above and beyond to start granting the very desires of our heart (Ps. 37:4). This only happens when God, and not people or things becomes priority.

Make it a purpose to pray with the right motives as you seek God for His will concerning your request(s); be careful what you pray for, you just might get it!

June 4
WHEN IT'S TIME TO GET UP AND GO
Read: Gen. 12:1-9; 17:1-8

It is very easy to remain in a place to where all of our needs are met, a place where everything that we could ever think, wish or hope for is at our fingertips. Most of us like to enjoy comfort and the better things in life, but often find it very easy to remain within our comfort zones.

So, what happens when situations arise that cause us to reevaluate where we are currently at in a particular moment, challenging us to make drastic moves or changes? Well, this is exactly where we find Abram (who would later become Abraham the "father of faith") in Gen. 12.

Abram was living a good life with his family and all of his relatives in a place that was familiar to them, a place where everyone felt protected and a place that was comfortable to them. Not knowing where they were heading or what the final destination would be, Abram uprooted his entire family and all his relatives as he responded in faith and obedience to the voice of God (Gen. 12:1-3).

Though God may not be prompting us to physically uproot our families or move; that still small voice may be prompting us to step out in faith in a new area of ministry (service) or to a deeper commitment to the things of God. Don't be afraid of the challenge because obedience is crucial at this stage.

Whenever we are being led to get up and go, it is always wise to follow the prompting and direction of God through the person of the Holy Spirit. He will never lead us astray, and our blessing is usually just around the corner; but again, the blessing comes through obedience. "If you are willing and obedient, you shall eat the good of the land" (Is. 1:19, Amplified Bible).

Thoughts

_____
_____
_____
_____
_____
_____
_____

Although comfort is appealing and is often a nice place to be, many times the place of comfort for us may not necessarily be the place of blessing and/or destiny. Therefore, even when things are not comfortable we have to learn how to move in faith when prompted by the LORD to do so; He will equip us for the task and make provision for as we get up, go and begin to press and move forward.

We must never allow fear of the unknown to hinder us from clearly hearing, acknowledging, and responding to the voice of God. Instead, like the young child Samuel in 1 Sam. 3:10 we should respond and say, "Speak, [LORD], for Your servant is listening" (Amplified Bible). However, not only should we hear, but we should also be eager to respond and move.

Because of Abram's faithfulness and willingness to obey the voice of God without knowing what the end result would be, God changed his name from Abram ("exalted father") to Abraham ("father of a multitude") and said that He would make Abraham exceedingly fruitful, would make nations through him, and that kings would come from his seed or lineage (Gen. 17:3-8).

God is challenging many of us to come out of our comfort zones to expand His Kingdom and begin operating in unfamiliar areas of ministry. What is God challenging you to do today? When it's time to get up and go, how quick will you be to obey? Moving to a new place in God first requires that you get up and leave the old behind (James 2:21:24).

June 5
THERE'S GOT TO BE MORE
Read: Heb. 5:12

According to Rom. 10:9-10 we receive salvation when we confess, receive and believe; "that if you confess with your mouth the Lord Jesus and believe in your heart that God has raised Him from the dead, you will be saved. For with the heart one believes unto righteousness, and with the mouth confession is made unto salvation." Simple enough right?

Thoughts

_____

_____

_____

_____

_____

_____

_____

For many believers in Christ, the Romans 10 experience is the apex of their Christian journey and then there is a plateau with no movement beyond this point. Sadly, many are just content with having escaped hell and receiving the assurance of entry into heaven; but there has to be more. So what's next? What comes after faith you might ask?

The answer is simple, spiritual growth through application. In other words, we must move on from drinking milk to eating the meat of the solid substance of God's Word (Heb. 5:12).

What this means for the average Christian is that there is more to the "new life" experience than simply avoiding hell and remaining babes that must constantly be fed, never learning how to feed themselves. We must grow in grace and in the knowledge of the Lord Jesus Christ (2 Pet. 3:18) in order to affect change in those we come in contact with. In the natural, it is a rarity to see another infant feeding another infant.

God has already given us the tools needed to move from an infant, to adolescence and then on to maturity in Him; however it is totally up to us to remove these tools from our spiritual bags and begin to using them.

"We have everything we need to live a life that pleases God. It was all given to us by God's own power, when we learned that he had invited us to share in his wonderful goodness. God made great and marvelous promises, so that his nature would become part of us. Then we could escape our evil desires and the corrupt influences of this world. Do your best to improve your faith. You can do this by adding goodness, understanding, self-control, patience, devotion to God, concern for others, and love. If you keep growing in this way, it will show that what you know about our Lord Jesus Christ has made your lives useful and meaningful" (2 Pet. 1:3-8, Contemporary English Version).

Salvation is not the end of our journey, it's just the beginning. We must continue to add to our faith in order to grow and mature spiritually so that we are no longer going about as babes in immaturity; our growth in faith, our growth in knowledge and our growth in character is not just for our benefit, but is designed to be shared with others so that they may spiritually mature as well.

Retirement and stagnation for the Christian after salvation is not an option, we must continue to grow to fulfill God's eternal purposes. According to Kenneth Hagin, "In the Christian world, there is never room for retirement. We just refire! We need to get up, get moving, and extend some of that energy, that virtue, that's in us."

Although salvation is the beginning, true active faith in Christ is defined by so much more—-we must continually grow!

"Be very sure now, you who have been trained to a self-sufficient maturity, that you enter into a generous common life with those who have trained you, sharing all the good things that you have and experience" (Gal. 6:6, The Message).

Thoughts

_____
_____
_____
_____
_____
_____
_____

June 6
THE ONE THAT KEEPS GOING
Read: Heb. 12:1-2

In driving along the freeway or interstate in most cities, one is bound to see an occasional car or two on the side of the road out of commission. Now, seeing an old Ford Pinto, a Yugo or some other aged car on the side of the road would not be out of the ordinary or seem strange; however, seeing a newer model Mercedes, BMW, or Lexus in this same position would appear abnormal.

Seeing the above latter mentioned cars disabled on the side of the road would appear to be a strange occurrence since these newer, high-performance vehicles are generally expected to last longer and perform better than the rest because of their quality.

Now, in what may seem to be a paradox, I've actually seen many older model cars from the 70's and even as far back as the 50's seen moving along the roadways and highways with the rest of the pack having no mechanical issues while rolling pass one of those newer high-performance cars that had literally stopped in its tracks. So, what makes the difference?

In each case, it was more than likely a matter of regular maintenance with the vehicle. It does not matter how nice or pristine a car may appear to be on the outside if the engine is not functioning, appearance doesn't mean a whole lot in in this scenario.

Many believers often judge and/or are judged by what is seen on the outside, when this does not always portray a true picture. We often look at someone by what they wear, or where they live to determine their status, value, and/or anticipated quality of service when these external things do not accurately reflect who they are.

This is not the standard that God uses. "Looks aren't everything. Don't be impressed with his looks and stature. I've already eliminated him. GOD judges persons differently than humans do. Men and women look at the face; GOD looks into the heart" (1 Sam. 16:7, The Message). Therefore, we must be careful to not "judge a book by its cover."

I'm reminded of a story of a pastor/author who was on travel in California. He stopped at a local coffee shop in an upper-class neighborhood. And as he sat enjoying his cup of coffee and a donut while reading the newspaper he observed a very scruffy looking, unshaven man, with faded cutoff shorts coming into the coffee shop.

Thoughts

_____

_____

_____

_____

_____

_____

Although it was not his intent to pass judgment, the pastor's first thought was, "How dare this bum come into such a fine establishment in such a shabby condition and appearance." The unshaven gentleman walked up to the counter, order a gourmet cup of coffee with the works, paid for his purchase in cash, and then walked outside and got into his current year model Bentley Continental.

It appears that the gentleman was actually a successful businessman who just liked a relaxed, unkempt look on the weekends and was not concerned about how others perceived him, because he knew who he was.

The pastor was in awe, and asked God to forgive him for being quick to pass judgment. It is often very easy to focus on the outward appearance to determine value and worth, when true significance is actually determined by what's within.

An individual's usefulness for service is not determined by what can readily be seen on the outside, but is an internal issue because this is a matter of the heart.

June 7
THERE IS NOTHING WRONG WITH THE BODY
Read: 1 Cor. 12:26

A young child cries out, "Mom, I'm not feeling well!" So, the mother being the nurturer that she is, naturally and instinctively goes into action. "What's hurting you" she replies. The child responds, "I don't know, I just don't feel well." The mother completes a few routine checks, but finds nothing out of the ordinary.

But even though there seems to be nothing wrong, the complaints from the child increase. So, just to be on the safe side, the mother decides to setup a doctor's appointment to have her child properly examined.

At the doctor's office a full examination is completed with the results pointing to what the mother really knew in her heart all along, there was nothing physically wrong with the child. After completing a report of his findings the doctor called the mother in and shared the results of the numerous tests administered coming to the conclusion that "There is nothing physically wrong with the child's body, it appears to be all in his mind."

Sadly, this is where many of us in the body of Christ often find ourselves; the Body (or Church) itself is fine, but our individual minds collectively come together thereby causing it to appear dysfunctional. The mind is where feelings and emotions are generated, and these have a tendency to feed our souls the wrong substances which often leads to a malnourishment of our spirits.

Thoughts

_____
_____
_____
_____
_____
_____
_____

As believers, we all comprise the body of Christ, "That's how it is with us. There are many of us, but we each are part of the body of Christ, as well as part of one another" (Rom. 12:5, Contemporary English Version). This body is built on a firm foundation, which is the sound doctrine of God's Word.

However, this principle is often corrupted by our incorrect thinking, which in turn causes the entire body to suffer. "If one part of the body suffers, all the other parts suffer with it. Or if one part of our body is honored, all the other parts share its honor" (1 Cor. 12:26, New Century Version). In a natural sense when one part of our body is in pain or experiencing discomfort (no matter how small or insignificant we think it may be), the entire body seems to be out of whack. If you don't believe me, then hit your small toe on something and then watch how the entire body is affected.

When our mind is out of whack this can lead to a whole slew of problems, because the mind is associated with the head and the head determines which direction the body goes in. Therefore, when the head is confused, the body does not know where to go or what to do.

This is why we must allow God's Word to reveal, expose, and correct any incorrect thinking that we may have (Heb. 4:12-13). Our minds must be renewed, because when our minds are renewed our speaking will also change for the better!

According to Dr. Creflo Dollar, "If you can control your mind, you can control your destiny. But it will take a quality decision on your part to dedicate your life to changing the way you think." Renewing the mind through true application of God's Word is what it takes to dispel wrong thinking (Rom. 12:2). When we think right, we tend to speak right (Prov. 18:21); this in turn will cause us to begin living right. What a novel idea, Christians actually "Living the Word."

June 8
SELF IN NEED
Read: Rom. 3:23

Have you ever encountered a person who just seemed to be stuck on themselves? You know the type of person who is always broadcasting their accomplishments, their accolades, their educational status, how good they look (or think they look); boasting to the point of bordering on pride. They generally speak as if they have it all together, as if there's no fault in them.

Thoughts

_____

_____

_____

_____

_____

_____

There's nothing wrong with the pursuit of excellence, which we should all strive for;

however, our accomplishments, or even lack thereof, do not define us or make us any better or less than the next person in the big scheme of things.

When we really peel back the layers of the onion in our lives, the fact of the matter is that we all have a fundamental need; due to the fall of man in the Garden of Eden, mankind became separated from God because of sin. Sin, as I like to describe it, can be classified as S-self, I-in, N-need (Rom. 5:12-14).

As a result of mankind's sin nature and our propensity to sin, atonement (or compensation) for our sins was required back then and is still necessary and applicable today; the compensation that was required was too great for any of us to bear. Therefore, no matter how great we think we are or how grand our accomplishments may be, until we each settle the issue with sin, none of us can truly proclaim real success in this life.

When we choose to focus on the external successes and say that we have no sin, we are only deceiving ourselves. According to Rom. 3:23, "For everyone has sinned; we all fall short of God's glorious standard" (New Living Translation).

I can hear someone saying "I've never murdered anyone, I don't steal, I don't cheat on my taxes, I don't do drugs, I don't fornicate or I haven't committed adultery." In response I would simply point them to the Bible and James 4:17 which states "...to him who knows to do good and does not do *it*, to him it is sin" (New King James Version). Sin is not just doing something wrong, but it also encompasses not doing the right thing when it is required. This should be a constant reminder to us all, that we each are in need of God's forgiveness but we must first acknowledge the need and then receive it.

But in order to receive this forgiveness we must not allow pride to keep us in a state of denial and separated from the presence of God, because pride will cause us to remain stagnant and also in a position to continually fall (Prov. 16:18). No matter how good an individual thinks he or she may be, this goodness amounts to nothing when compared to God's righteousness that is only found in and through the blood of Christ (Is. 64:6).

In light of the above fact and in order to deal with our "self in need," God sent forth His Son Jesus Christ as a substitute to atone for each and every one of our sins (past, present and future)(Gal. 4:4).

This means that in order to truly be successful in this life and to receive all of its abundance, we must initially confess our sins to receive the gift of salvation, and then daily confess our sin to stay in right-standing (righteous) with God. We each, individually, are only made righteous through Christ—-no one is exempt (1 Jn. 1:8-10).

Thoughts

Don't rely solely on self because self has a need. Make it a purpose to admit your need and then choose to remain in right-standing with God each day.

June 9
THE MORE YOU FEED IT, THE MORE IT GROWS
Read: Gal. 5:16-18

Several years ago I was stationed overseas on an unaccompanied isolated duty tour without my family for a period of one year; the footprint or size of this particular military installation was fairly small. And since there was not enough space in the main building to accommodate everyone at the command I was assigned to at the time, trailers were positioned in the perimeter just outside the building inside the fence line to meet the overflow need.

Well, the team I was assigned to just happened to work in a couple of these not so great trailers, even though there were both advantages and disadvantages to being away from the main building.

Since we were literally outside and disconnected from the headquarters building and a little more exposed to the outside elements, there were a number of stray cats who would regularly congregate around the trailer area almost daily. One day an individual from an adjacent trailer began to feel sorry for one of the cats and decided to put a small saucer of cat food out.

I'm sure you can see where this is going. You got it! After receiving the initial meal, the cat began to return around the same time like clockwork every day expecting to have its desire fulfilled. The more the cat was fed, the more it wanted resulting in more frequent visits. And over time, the once emaciated and scrawny feline began to fill out and take shape as its cravings were being met and satisfied daily.

As it pertains to our Christian walk, this is also a fairly accurate depiction of the strength of the flesh in the life of the believer. Our flesh (our old sinful nature) attempts to dominate the Spirit (our new nature) within. It doesn't take rocket science to figure out that the one that gets fed the most typically has more power (Gal. 5:17). In other words, one is going to eventually overpower the other.

Thoughts

_____
_____
_____
_____
_____
_____
_____

When our flesh is in control, we can often be found doing things that we know are wrong and under normal circumstances would not even contemplate doing. Therefore, who we connect ourselves with as well as who or what we choose to listen to on a regular basis will significantly influence who has the greater power in our lives—-either the flesh or the Spirit.

This is why it is so important for us as believers to crucify the flesh, not just at conversion when we accept Christ, but every single day as we make it a purpose to walk in the Spirit (Rom. 8:13). Because as we walk in the Spirit we are less likely to fulfill any fleshly desire that comes to us—-desires that generally come from within (James 1:13-15).

And believe it or not, in this battle between the flesh and the Spirit another law is in action—-the law of seedtime and harvest (Gen. 8:22) or the principle of sowing and reaping (Gal. 6:7-8).

What could be simpler to understand than this? We each reap exactly what we sow. Therefore, if we want to reap the right things, then we must begin to sow accordingly and endeavor to feed the Spirit while simultaneously starving the flesh so that we can reap the benefits that include a life in the Spirit and connection with the Father as His sons and daughters.

The more you feed it, the more it grows; our life in Christ is not based on the flesh but rather a life in the Spirit, so feed the right thing!

June 10
DON'T TRIP, IT'S JUST A SETUP
Read: Dan. 6:1-28

Daniel was a righteous man who feared and reverenced God. He had been taken into captivity as a youth by the Babylonian king Nebuchadnezzar (also known as Belshazzar) along with many other Jews. But because of God's favor on his life, Daniel rose to prominence even in the midst of bondage.

Not only was Daniel a person of integrity, he was also one who made it a practice to do the right thing no matter the opposition or personal cost. It was this same devotion and faithfulness to God that caused other leaders in the king's court who served with him to become jealous, which led to unwarranted persecution.

In Daniel chapter 5, Daniel had just interpreted the king's dream, a dream that no one else in the entire kingdom could deduce, which resulted in promotion for himself and three of his closest Hebrew cohorts (Dan. 5:29).

Thoughts

Though Daniel was highly favored by God and the king, he was despised by his peers and with this promotion came persecution. In other words, we must remember that no matter how much good we do, there will always haters.

The governors and other leaders did everything in their power to find fault in Daniel or looked for a reason to bring charges against him, but they were unsuccessful. So instead, led by envy and jealousy, they devised a plot to use Daniel's consistent devotional time against him.

Knowing that Daniel had an excellent spirit, he was faithful to God, and a person of honor; the governors conspired together to establish a royal law or decree that prevented anyone from petitioning (praying to) any god or man for thirty days, except for the king. Anyone who disobeyed or disregarding the decree would be cast into a den of lions (Dan. 6:7). After being deceived by his trusted advisors and counselors concerning this decree, the king agreed and put the law into effect.

So, what does Daniel do? Knowing the penalty that awaited those who went against the king's decree; Daniel came home from work, took off his sandals, went upstairs, opened his windows and knelt down on his knees as he was accustomed to doing and began to pray in plain sight giving thanks to his God (Dan. 6:10). This is exactly what the haters anticipated and as a result Daniel was later thrown into a den of hungry lions.

The king was distressed because of what had transpired, however, he had to honor the decree as issued even though he respected Daniel. The king stayed up pacing the floor concerned for the fate of Daniel. However, the next morning Daniel emerged from the pit without even a scratch on him.

Even though his enemies tried to destroy him, their plan backfired causing Daniel to prosper even more than he did before simply because he made the first thing the first thing (Matt. 6:33) by consistently living a life of devotion, one that was pleasing in the sight of God.

Obstacles are often used to prepare us for the next level. Our job is to simply learn how to endure and overcome the obstacle or test because the blessing is usually just on the other side.

Therefore, what appeared to be a setback for Daniel resulted in his advancement and promotion to yet another level. So, don't worry or fret as haters plan and plot against you because their schemes will not prosper because many times what may appear to be setbacks in our lives are just setups for future success. So QUIT TRIPPIN', IT'S JUST A SETUP!

Thoughts

_____
_____
_____
_____
_____
_____

June 11

QUIT OPENING THE GATE, GUARD YOUR WALLS
Read: Prov. 25:28

During my years of military travel with various Navy port calls to many countries in Europe, I've had the opportunity to see, visit and tour several historical and famous structures like the Eiffel Tower, the Louvre Museum, and Arch of Triumph in France; the Leaning Tower of Pisa in Italy; Buckingham Palace and Big Ben in London; and the ruins of Greek temples in Greece, just to name a few.

Yet the structures that stood out the most to me were the castles situated in various locations in these European cities. If you have never personally seen one before castles are awesome sights to see from a distance, but even more awe-inspiring up close and from inside.

Castles originated in Europe and the Middle East during the Middle Ages during the time of knights wearing armor. And though they served a few purposes; castles, with their high and fortified walls, were primarily designed with protection and security in mind to keep the inhabitants (primarily the nobility) safe by keeping out intruders and/ or invaders. These structures were designed and built with both offense and defense in mind since they could serve as a base from which raids could be launched, or simply provide protection from an enemy attack.

As these castles were built, the size and strength of the walls had to be essential considerations by the architects to ensure that protection from any enemy attack could be achieved.

As believers in Christ, we are not only considered to be light in this world, but are also compared to cities that are set high upon a hill (Matt. 5:14). Can you imagine what would happen if the castles of the Middle Ages were built in valleys or low locations, with no external supporting walls? Or if a strong support structure was built around a castle, yet the main gate was constantly left open? You got it. It would provide direct and open access for the enemy to come in to do whatever he wanted to do.

This is exactly where many of us as believers often find ourselves; open and unprotected from the attacks of the enemy. We open the door through emotion al responses and reactions to external stimuli, providing the enemy direct and easy access in.

According to Prov. 25:28, "Whoever has no rule over his own spirit Is like a city broken down, without walls." In other words, when we have no rule over our emotions and are susceptible to losing self-control, we are as helpless as a city without walls of protection. When this occurs our adversary has open access and free reign to do with us as he sees fit.

Thoughts

_____
_____
_____
_____
_____
_____

Scripture reminds us that we must guard our hearts because this is where life itself flows from (Prov. 4:23).

What this means for us is that we must learn to remove emotions out of the equation when unexpected circumstances arise. Though emotions are a normal part of life and are to be experienced; they should not control what we say, neither should they control our actions or better yet our reaction.

Emotional responses are often just a cover-up for deeper rooted issues of insecurity, anxiety or fear. So don't allow your emotions to get the best of you; quit opening the gate and guard your walls because your heart, the center of your life is at stake! Allow God's peace to prevail!

June 12
WHAT ARE YOU BUILDING WITH?
Read: 1 Kgs. 6:1-37

In 1 Kings Chapter 6 we find King Solomon building the Temple for God. This was a task his father King David wanted to accomplish; but even though he was a man after God's own heart, he was also a man of war (1 Kings 5:3). God required a man of peace to build His Temple; therefore, God assigned this task to Solomon, David's son.

The name Solomon is actually adopted from the word "shalem" which is a derivative of the word "shalom" which means "peace" in Hebrew. Therefore, the name Solomon actually means "peace." So, the right man was selected for the job; and just as Moses followed the design specifications for building the Tabernacle in the wilderness, Solomon followed blueprints and designs provided by God for building His Temple to the letter. Every door, beam, wall, and chamber was built according to God's specifications.

According to Prov. 24:3, "Through wisdom a house is built, And by understanding it is established." Solomon was considered to be the wisest man in the Bible, not just because he judged wisely but also because he followed the specific instructions given by God in building the Temple, a place for God's Spirit to dwell.

Thoughts

_____
_____
_____
_____
_____
_____
_____

Solomon's actions and commitment prompted God to consistently act and respond on his behalf (1 Kgs. 6:12). God also stands ready to work on our behalf; however, we must follow the instructions and do our part. Well, just in case you didn't know it, as believers we too are considered to be God's temple (1 Cor. 6:19).

Therefore, as Moses had the responsibility to ensure the Tabernacle in the wilderness was properly setup, positioned, and established and Solomon having a similar responsibility with building the Temple; we too are to follow God's instructions on how to build our tabernacles, temples, or bodies that are representative of our very lives because how we choose to build not only has the ability to adversely affect us, but it can also affect those closest to us and those we are connected with. This is why location (where we position ourselves) and laying the right foundation is so vitally important.

The Tabernacle and the Temple were the central focus of life in the community of God's people during biblical times, which was clearly evident in the positioning of these structures. Although it was constantly disassembled, moved, and reassembled based on where the people were located at any given time, the Tabernacle was always at the center of the camp and setup according to the specifications given by God. Likewise, once the Temple was constructed it too was positioned exactly at the center of the holy city Jerusalem. The Tabernacle and the Temple represented the presence of God and the place of worship where His Spirit dwelled.

If we expect our lives to flourish and our families to prosper, God and worship must always be at the center of everything that we do. This also means that our lives must be constructed with material that has been uniquely designed and specifically approved by God Himself; this building material is His Holy Word which contains wisdom that promotes life.

What are you building your temple, your life, and/or your family with today? Building solely on your own intellect, the opinion of man, and that which is popular in society at that time will undoubtedly result in faulty construction. We must be built upon and have a foundation in the wisdom of God's Word (Josh. 1:8)!

June 13
JUST DO THE MATH
Read: Jn. 17:21-22; 1 Cor. 12:12-31

The field of mathematics has a wide variety of application. However, the type of math used by an individual largely depends on his or her career field, profession and/or occupation (i.e., algebra & trigonometry – scientists, physicists; geometry – builders, architects, etc.). And though many of us may not like math, it is an essential part of our everyday life. Therefore, a basic knowledge of math is essential to function effectively in our world today.

Although God's method of math may be a bit unconventional, the same theory applies in the body of Christ because when numbers come together, a product is always produced. For

Thoughts

———————————————
———————————————
———————————————
———————————————
———————————————
———————————————
———————————————

instance, look at Gen. 2:24 which states "Therefore a man shall leave his father and mother and be joined to his wife, and they shall become [ONE] flesh;" or, 1 Jn. 5:7, "For there are three that bear witness in heaven: the Father, the Word, and the Holy Spirit; and these three are [ONE]."

Based on the preceding verses of Scripture, it is clear to see that normal principles of math do not apply here. In Gen. 2:24, 1 + 1 = 1, and in 1 Jn. 5:7, 1 + 1 + 1 = 1; how can this be?

Simple, in Christ each individual member comes together to form one, this is representative of unity in the spirit and body (the Body of Christ—The Church). Though there may be many parts (individuals) in Christ, there is still just one Body (1 Cor. 12:12-14).

Unity within the body of Christ was and still is the goal; this desire could even be seen as Jesus prayed in John chapter seventeen. Jesus said, "I pray that they will all be one, just as you and I are one—as you are in me, Father, and I am in you" (Jn. 17:21-23, New Living Translation).

When the Body is functioning properly and is fitly joined together for one unified purpose, we (the Church) can do serious damage to the enemy and the kingdom of darkness.

Just as a basic knowledge of math in society is essential; a basic knowledge of Kingdom mathematics and principles is what it takes for us as believers to truly make a difference in the world today. UNITY PRODUCES VICTORY AND BRINGS GOD GLORY!

June 14
PUTTING FIRST THINGS FIRST
Read: Acts 16:16-40 and 2 Chron. 20:1-26

In Acts 16 we find Paul and Silas bond and imprisoned for casting a demon out of a slave girl. Can you even imagine or fathom that? Here we have two anointed men of God thrown into prison for doing a good deed by releasing this young lady from years of torment at the hands of oppressive demonic spirits. And not only were they thrown into prison, they were also beaten and then shackled to the point of not being able to move about freely.

Thoughts

_____

_____

_____

_____

_____

_____

_____

If you were in this literal predicament, what would your response be? Well, unfortunately for the average believer the immediate response would be to murmur, complain, and begin to question God as the flesh starts to rise up and trump the Spirit. But this was not the case for Paul and Silas.

In the face of adversity and after being beaten and bound, Paul and Silas began to pray and lift up their praises to God. "Around midnight Paul and Silas were praying and singing hymns to God, and the other prisoners were listening" (Acts 16:25, New Living Translation). And as they continued to offer a sacrifice of praise the foundations of the prison began to shake, all of the prison doors flew open as every chain and shackle that once held them captive fell off which then made every captive free. So, what happened? God's servants and anointed men set an atmosphere of praise that produced release!

In the next scenario (2 Chron. 20) the Israelites literally found themselves with their "backs against the wall" and the armies of three countries poised to attack. Based on what they saw in the natural, it was quite obvious that God's people would face a decisive defeat. So, what was King Jehoshaphat to do? Unlike many of us today, instead of turning to relatives, friends, or the world for advice first, the king turned to and petitioned God for help.

After seeking the LORD Jehoshaphat then proclaimed a fast, called the people together, and literally had a praise session in front of the Temple. And when the time came to prepare the people for battle, Jehoshaphat did something that was not customary or even rational for a leader with warriors who were skilled in combat with enemy armies approaching from all sides. With the people of Jerusalem and Judah standing by, he decided to send in the unarmed people of "Judah" first.

Something to note here is the meaning of the word "Judah." In Hebrew the word for Judah (Yehuwda'iy) literally means "celebrate" or praise, and in the Greek Judah is "loipon" which means "remaining." Therefore, instead of moving on what he saw, King Jehoshaphat moved on what he knew, remained steadfast in his trust in God, and then made the decision to send forth the singers and minstrels ahead of the group. In other words, he began a frontal assault against the enemy with the praises of the people and encouraged them to remain focused on God, the only One who could deliver them.

As Judah or praise went forth "first", the people began to repeatedly sing "Praise the LORD for His mercy endures forever" (2 Chron. 20:21, New King James Version), and then all of a sudden the enemy that surrounded them, the very group who was prepared to attack became confused and bewildered as God set ambushes against them. And in the midst of this confusion, the enemy of God's people literally began to destroy one another.

Thoughts

This should be a subtle reminder to us all that in any situation we face our praise must go forth first, and then we are to let God fight the battle in the spirit realm. The people of God did not have to lift one weapon or even fight in the battle (2 Chron. 20:17), because their praise opened the door to victory.

_____
_____
_____
_____
_____
_____
_____
_____

June 15

UNSTOPPABLE PLANS
Read: Num. 22 and 23

In today's Scripture text we find the children of Israel at the beginning of yet another move, this time into the plains of Moab in great droves. King Balak of Moab, knowing the reputation of the Israelites and their past victories, was disturbed by the possible threat of an Israelite takeover through the sheer large numbers of individuals that comprised this mighty nation of people.

So in response, King Balak dispatched messengers to Balaam (who was blessed with the gift of prophecy) to convince him to pronounce a curse over the Israelites that would basically prevent them from multiplying, and then eventually cause them to disperse from the region of Moab.

But when the messengers arrived, Balaam stated that he could only do what God commanded and that he could only say what God allowed him to say. After repeated requests and probably a few attempted bribes, eventually Balaam was convinced to make the journey to Moab to do the bidding of King Balak against God's will.

As Balaam traveled along the way, his journey to Moab was obstructed by an Angel of the LORD; but the presence of this angel had to be revealed to him in a very unique way.

Through a series of events and a discussion with a donkey, his eyes were eventually opened to the presence of the Angel, in response Balaam repented for having made the journey against the will of the LORD. Yet, even though Balaam had planned to go against God's command, he was still instructed by God to continue his journey anyway; however, he was only to speak what the LORD inspired him to speak (Num. 22:23-35).

When Balaam arrived in Moab, King Balak brought him up to one of the high places (places generally used for idol worship and sacrifices to pagan gods) in the region to look out over the people (the Israelites) for the pronouncement of a curse. Balaam replied, "How can I curse whom God hasn't cursed? How can I denounce whom God hasn't denounced" (Num. 23:8, Contemporary English Version)? Not giving up easily, the king persisted in his repeated requests and attempts to convince Balaam to curse the Israelites going through the same cycle two more times.

Thoughts

_____

_____

_____

_____

_____

_____

Three times a cursing was requested, but a blessing was pronounced instead. Just in case you didn't know it, the number "3" in the Bible represents "completion."

So how do we as believers in Christ make practical application of this Scripture text today? Though man may try to thwart or frustrate God's people and the planned destiny

204

for our lives; God's plans will never fail no matter what anyone else has to say about it. If God spoke it, it will come to pass.

This truth came be found in (Jer. 29:11). In other words, God has our very best interest at heart and He will cause His plans for us to succeed, when we choose to walk in holiness and obedience to Him.

When we align our dreams, goals, and ambitions with God's will for our lives; nothing can stop His plans. No matter how man, situations, or circumstances may attempt to hinder us; what God has blessed, no man can curse.

What dreams, goals, or plans has the LORD given you? When your plans are God-given and align with His will, they will remain UNSTOPPABLE (Job 42:2).

June 16
YOU CAN RUN, BUT YOU CAN'T HIDE
Read: Jonah (Chapters 1-4)

The instruction from a father to his son is, "Take out the trash before you go hang out with your friends. Make sure this is done before I return home." The father returns, the trash has not left the receptacle, and the son is nowhere to be found. The son returns home and the father issues punishment by grounding him from hanging out with his friends after school for an entire month for this disobedience.

Whether we choose to acknowledge and accept the fact or not; for every action there is a consequence.

This is where we find the focal character in today's scripture text, the prophet Jonah. The command of the LORD to Jonah was, "Arise, go to Nineveh, that great city, and cry out against it; for their wickedness has come up before Me (Jonah 1:1)." The prophet was given a simple task of going to proclaim God's Word to the disobedient people of Nineveh. So, what does Jonah do instead; he attempted to flee from the presence of the LORD as if God would not know the prophet's location or where he had planned to go. The proper response was to simply answer and correctly respond to the call of God.

Jonah then boarded a ship and went in the total opposite direction. Jonah was snugly nestled below decks catching up on a little sleep when a violent storm erupted. The sailors on the ship were afraid and started praying to their gods. Through the course of this ordeal, it is eventually revealed that the storm had been

Thoughts

_____
_____
_____
_____
_____
_____
_____

generated as a direct result of Jonah's disobedience as he attempted to flee from the presence of the LORD (the one and only True God).

With self-preservation in mind and their little "g" gods unable to help, the sailors decided to toss Jonah overboard. As soon as he touched the great expanse of tumultuous water, the sea ceased from its mighty rage.

Jonah undoubtedly struggled to initially keep himself afloat, thinking to himself the end was near. However, God had other plans. Just as Jonah was about to give-up while going down for the last time, a large fish appeared out of nowhere and swallowed him whole.

Although the fish had swallowed Jonah, he had not been consumed. Inside this huge fish Jonah remained alive, and for three days he had time to contemplate and really think about the actions that brought him to this outcome. After much reflection and careful consideration he eventually acknowledged his sin, repented, and began to thank the LORD for saving him from the perils of the sea.

As a volcano releasing hot lava from depths of its crater, the fish spewed out Jonah onto dry land in the direction he was initially instructed to go towards the city of Nineveh. With an powerful life lesson learned, this time the prophet answered the call, going to proclaim God's Word without hesitation. Not only did God change the prophet's direction, He also provided the transportation that would ultimately bring Jonah to the place of obedience and doing God's will.

There are many today who have the call of God on their lives who have been given specific instructions on what they are to do, where they are to go and what they are to accomplish; but instead attempt to run from the LORD's instructions and command to perform His will. Why delay the inevitable when God's purposes will eventually prevail. Answer the call today because though you may be able to run, no matter how far you try to go you can never truly hide.

Thoughts

_____

_____

_____

_____

_____

_____

_____

June 17

THE TASTER'S CHOICE

Read: Ps. 34:8

With America being the "Melting Pot" comprised of individuals from variety of cultures and backgrounds; along with the myriad of different cultures there is also wide variety of diverse foods for us to choose from each day. So food choices for many are nothing more than matters of preference.

Choices for me are usually fairly simple, if I don't like the way a particular entrée or dish looks I just won't eat it. Of course I'm often told, "If you don't try it, you'll never know how it tastes." I also apply this logic to desserts as well, with chocolate being one that I was really never fond of mainly because of the appearance.

Well, one day I was introduced to a dessert called "Death by Chocolate;" yeah, I know, the name doesn't sound to inviting or appetizing and it may also be identified by other names depending on which area of the United States or world you are in. This particular dessert is made from chocolate cake, chocolate pudding, whipped cream, and Nestle Crunch (or some other chocolate morsels) placed in multiple layers.

I can remember the first time my wife made this dessert and asked me if I was going to try it. And as she spoke, in the back of my mind I only heard "I hate chocolate, I hate chocolate, I hate chocolate."

But through the power of persuasion I was eventually convinced to try a sample putting aside what I thought to be a total hatred for chocolate. As I took a bite I can recall saying to myself, "How could something with a name like Death by Chocolate taste so good!" The light came on and then I understood the choice in name because the dessert was so good that it was literally "to die for"; needless to say, even though chocolate is still not one of my favorites, I've been hooked on this dessert ever since.

Just think about it for a moment, if I had never made a decision to taste it, I would have never known just how good this dessert actually was.

Well, this same analogy can be applied to our lives as believers in Christ. There are many today who accept Christ and His forgiveness just to receive their "fire insurance" and a ticket to Heaven, but never make Him Lord of their lives. You know, the individuals that do just enough to appear spiritual without fully committing and submitting every area of their lives to the Father; when in actuality all we have to do is try Him, or better yet just fully receive Him to see just how good He is.

"Open your mouth and taste, open your eyes and see — how good God is. Blessed are you who run to him (Ps. 34:8, The Message).

Believers who only receive salvation, but never partake of His Lordship often live in defeat because they only try Christ instead of actually receiving and tasting of all the benefits associated with a right relationship with Him, to include but not limited to: healing, health, wholeness, sound thinking, peace of mind, prosperity and abundant living. Jesus made this clear in (Jn. 10:10). Therefore, it's never

Thoughts

_____
_____
_____
_____
_____
_____
_____

enough to just know Him as Savior; we must go above and beyond to also make Him Lord of our lives.

Don't just take a small sampling of Jesus, instead make a decision to truly receive Him, put Him on, and taste of Him. When He becomes Lord, our flesh then submits to His authority; it is then and only then that we can truly enjoy the benefits of a complete relationship with Him (Rom. 13:14; Ps. 34:8)!

June 18
YOU KNOW YOU'RE SUPPOSED TO SHARE
Read: 1 Pet. 4:10

Have you ever had the experience of sitting down to enjoy a favorite meal, or favorite snack? You begin to eat and savor every morsel; you eventually get down to the last bite, or last item in the bag. And then out of nowhere comes your spouse, one of your kids or someone else asking if they can have some of what you're eating.

You look down and realize that there isn't enough for the both of you; and knowing just how good this item is, your first inclination is to say "No, you can't have any, don't you see I'm enjoying this. Why don't you go and get your own!"

As you begin to tightly grip the plate or bag with reluctance to let that savored thing go, all of a sudden you receive a spiritual tap on the shoulder and hear that still small a voice gently saying, "You know you're supposed to share."

Growing up as a small child, even though I was not raised in a Christian environment at the time, I can remember being taught to share and to help others. Yet for many, especially those who identify themselves as Christians, this is often hard and very difficult to do because there is a tendency to focus on self and our personal needs first.

The sharing being discussed here goes far beyond just what we share and give in the natural sense, but also applies to our spiritual lives. Let's look at the Old Testament book of First Samuel to see what insights we can glean from the example set by the priest/judge Eli and his sons as it pertains to keeping things to ourselves and not sharing.

Thoughts

_____

_____

_____

_____

_____

_____

Eli was the high priest in charge of caring for the tabernacle and was also a judge in Israel; however, his sons Hophni and Phinehas actually performed the day-to-day priestly functions. But Hophni and Phinehas did wickedly in the sight of the LORD, not only were they committing adultery with the women who served in the sanctuary; they were also taking the prime cuts or portions of meat from the sacrifices being presented by the people and keeping them for themselves. Though Eli knew of his son's behavior and chastised them, he did nothing to stop them thereby condoning their actions literally becoming a partner with his sons in their sins.

The LORD then sent a prophecy, by way of the young boy Samuel who would later become a prophet and the priest at Shiloh, to Eli and his house stating that they would be punished for their evil deeds, and that both of Eli's sons would die on the same day.

So it came to pass that during a battle with the Philistine army, both Hophni and Phinehas were killed, and the Ark of the Covenant was captured and taken away. With his eyes growing dim, and hearing the news of his sons and the fate of the Ark; "Eli fell off the seat backward by the side of the gate; and his neck was broken and he died, for the man was old and heavy" (1 Sam. 4:18, New King James Version).

Eli was heavy because he, like his sons, reaped the benefits of receiving the ill-gotten meat of the sacrifices that were to be presented for the people to God. What has been given to you that you know you're supposed to present, yet you continue to hold on to it?

Many of us often find ourselves in positions like Eli; we've become so heavy from the Word of God that we are receiving until we are spiritually unable to move when you know you are supposed to share (Lk. 6:38; 1 Pet. 4:10)!

June 19
THE LOVE OF THE FATHER RUNS DEEP
Read: Lk. 15:11-31

In the familiar story of the prodigal son, a land owner has two sons with one looking to get away and experience life in the world on his own. So, one day the younger son decides to ask the father for his share of the father's inheritance while the father was still yet alive. I'm sure the father did not agree with the son's request, but nevertheless, he eventually gave him his wish and heart's desire.

Now the older son, on the other hand, remained at home with the father helping to maintain their property and assisting wherever else he was needed. But with his new found wealth, the younger son departed to another city where he does any and everything that he yearned for; the Bible states that he "waste[d] his substance with riotous living" (Lk. 15:13).

Thoughts

_____
_____
_____

With no money and no place to stay, reality begins to kick in. He is now forced to take a job herding and caring for pigs, an animal that was considered to be unclean by the Jews. And

_____
_____
_____

although he had a job, the wages were not enough to meet his basic needs and he still suffered from starvation to the point that he even contemplated joining the pigs in eating the slop and leftovers that were usually given to them.

It was at this low point in his life that he came to his senses and began to recall the provision available in the Father's house when he said, "My father's workers have plenty to eat, and here I am, starving to death" (Lk. 15:17)! He then made it up in his mind to get up, run home to his father to beg his forgiveness and ask for the opportunity to just be one of the workers and servants there.

So, what does the father do when the son approaches? Does he turn the lights out and pretend there's no one home? Does he have the son arrested for trespassing? Does he curse the son out and tell him to never return? No, the father recognizing and seeing his lost son coming in the distance, runs to receive him with arms wide-open, places a robe on him, gives him a ring, and throws a grand "Welcome Home" celebration.

Even though the son went astray, and left the covering and protection of the father; the father's love for the son did not change.

This is the same love (agape) that our Heavenly Father has for each of us; through Christ we have been adopted into the family (Rom. 8:15). And though His grace is not a free license to continue in sin (Rom. 6:15), when we do sin he stands ready with open arms to receive us again and again (1 Jn 5:7). He sent His only son into the world to become sin for us that we would no longer be bound by sin's power.

He did this because He loves us (Rom. 5:8). The Father allowed His son Jesus to suffer and die that we would live. You see, no matter what we do or how far we stray away, when we come to our senses, repent and turn back to Him; God's love does not change because He does not change (Heb. 13:8).

So, no matter what we try to do and no matter how far we attempt to run away, nothing we do can separate us from the Father's love (Rom. 8:35). He sacrificed His very best so that we each would not only live, but that we each would "enjoy life, and have it in abundance (to the full, till it overflows)" (Jn. 10:10).

Remember, the Father (who is Love) does not keep record of our wrong and He is longsuffering because His love towards us runs deep.

Thoughts

_____
_____
_____
_____
_____
_____
_____

June 20

WHOSE YOUR DADDY?
Read: Rom. 8:15

At one point in time daytime television talk shows seemed to rule TV ratings and were sources of great attention. Back then shows like Phil Donahue, Sally Jesse Raphael, Geraldo Rivera, Ricki Lake, Montel Williams and Oprah Winfrey were common, well-known, and frequently watched by loyal fans.

And then tabloid talk shows came on the scene like the Jerry Springer and Maury Povich Show where conflict, profanity, and on-stage violence began to increase in popularity and acceptance. Men fighting men, women fighting women, men fighting women and vice-versa; whatever you can think of was probably acceptable as crowds cheered, which in turn encouraged even more chaos and confusion.

Although "Reality Television" has now hit the scene and become so big, a few of these talk shows are still aired even though their popularity and following have significantly decreased. I can remember when I was younger, that there was a time when one could not flip through the various television channels without coming across a talk show with individuals disputing about the paternity of a child and who the father was.

Arguments and accusations from the two individuals would go back and forth, as they often stood toe-to-toe defending what each thought to be right based on their own perspective and points of view. And then to silence the confusion and provide some finality, a paternity test funded by the hosting show host would be administered that usually consisted of obtaining and evaluating blood and/or DNA samples.

This was done because of the well-known fact that the bloodline of a child is determined, not by the mother although the child is physically connected and carried inside of her for nine months, but rather by the father. And no matter how much a father on one of these talk shows may have tried to deny or dispute it, the blood and DNA was the tell-all and provided the necessary evidence to close the case.

However, in many instances a blood or DNA test isn't even required, because with just one glance an individual can automatically tell who the child belongs to. I've often been told over and over again that I look just like my earthly father, and in addition to this we have the similar mannerisms, we have similar likes and dislikes, and even share the same favorite color. This of course primarily results from my father's blood and genetic make-up actually being a part of who I am.

Thoughts

_____
_____
_____
_____
_____
_____
_____

Well, in Christ it is through His shed blood that we each are adopted into the family of God and now have a new Father and Daddy. In other words, at the time of our conversion or new birth we also obtained a new bloodline; the bloodline of God the Father which now makes us His sons and daughters.

Therefore, we no longer have to search for our identity in others, or walk in fear and frustration because our loving Heavenly Father and Dad longs to care for us (Rom. 8:15). Do your motives and actions reflect the character of your Heavenly Father and that of the Son? Does the Father's divine genetics encompass who you are? If not make the necessary adjustments today (Eph. 5:1).

June 21
LIKE FATHER, LIKE SON
Read: 1 Kgs. 2:1-4

The role and example of parents in the lives of their children is extremely important, and even more so with the example of the father. I can remember a television commercial that aired on the Armed Forces Network (AFN) when I was deployed overseas a few years ago that demonstrated the profound influence a father had on his young son.

In the commercial the father started out going into the bathroom to complete his normal morning routine brushing his teeth and then shaving. As the father prepared to shave, he spread shaving cream on his face and began to go through the motions of removing the cream and hair beneath with the razor. In similar fashion the son spreads shaving cream on his face, but instead of using an actual razor he used the backside of a comb.

After getting dressed, the father then went outside to cut the grass; he fired up the lawnmower and began to walk back and forth mowing the lawn. Of course the son soon followed suit, only using a plastic mower as he mimicked the actions of the father from a distance.

Once the lawn work was completed, the father took a seat on the patio and grabbed the day's newspaper and began to relax after a hard day's work on the lawn – of course, the young son followed his father's example, grabbed his little chair, his Dr. Seuss book, and began to read.

Thoughts

_____
_____
_____
_____
_____
_____
_____

Being a person of habit, the father got up, walked away from the patio to light up a cigarette – and as you can now imagine, the son saws what the father was doing, thinking that it was OK; naturally wanted to be like his father, so he grabbed a cigarette from the pack left on the table and pretended he was doing what the father did; without the father's knowledge.

Although the story was embellished a little bit, I'm sure you get the point. Parents, but especially fathers or father figures play a vital role in shaping the futures of young impressionable minds; therefore, it is important that we as men exhibit the right qualities on a consistent basis.

As father's and as believers in general, we have a mandate to not only provide a godly example for our children but also for others to follow as well (Matt. 5:16).

Just as the young son in the commercial pretended to smoke a cigarette imitating his father, there are many watching our example each day; many who we may not know or ever see. I'm not saying that cigarettes will send anyone to hell, but just using this as one an example.

However, use of cigarettes does go against God's principles in keeping our temples (our bodies) pure and undefiled. Use of cigarettes are not a great witness for a child of God in the area of self-discipline; additionally continued use has the potential to shorten a person's lifespan and time here on earth before his or her God-given assignment has been completed and/or fulfilled. Anyway, this is just something to think about (Eph. 5:1). When we follow God through the example of His son Jesus Christ, we are sure to leave the right impression and a lasting example.

As believers, we are sons and daughters of God; therefore, we should emulate our Heavenly Father in order to leave a godly heritage for the next generation to follow—- LIKE FATHER, LIKE SON (1 Tim. 4:12)!

June 22
DO YOU HAVE FIRE INSURANCE?
Read: Acts 4:11-12

Having made several deployments on U.S. Navy ships to the Mediterranean Sea, I've had the opportunity to transit the Strait of Gibraltar near the southern tip of Spain multiple times. Just to the north of this location there's a huge rock that protrudes above the strait that is very familiar to most—this rock is called the Rock of Gibraltar.

Extending vertically about 1396 feet above the strait, the Rock of Gibraltar is an awesome sight to see. The popularity of the Rock of Gibraltar was further advanced when an American Insurance company, The Prudential Insurance Company of America, utilized the rock as the corporate symbol with the popular slogan, "Get a Piece of the Rock."

Life insurance was one of the company's largest sources of revenue. In its simplest form an

Thoughts

_____
_____
_____
_____
_____
_____
_____

213

insurance policy is designed to provide the beneficiary a sense of security and assurance. So, what better symbol and slogan could one find than obtaining a "a piece of the rock" since a rock is representative of stability and security.

Ps. 62 lets us know that [God] alone is our Rock and our Salvation; He is our defense; therefore, we will not be greatly moved. "God, the one and only—I'll wait as long as he says. Everything I need comes from him, so why not? He's solid rock under my feet, breathing room for my soul, An impregnable castle: I'm set for life" (Ps. 62:1-2, The Message).

According to 1 Jn. 5:7 "For there are three that bear witness in heaven: the Father, the Word, and the Holy Spirit; and these three are one" (New King James Version). This Scripture reminds us of the fact that God the Father, Jesus the Word (or Son) and the Holy Spirit are one and the same; therefore, Jesus is also the Rock (Ps. 95:1); Jesus alone provides our salvation (Acts 4:11-12).

This means that as believers and Christians we can find stability and security in the Rock when we put our complete faith, confidence, and trust in the finished work of Jesus Christ, and in what He accomplished on the cross at Calvary. It is now because of the contract that Jesus signed with His very own blood, that all who confess and profess faith in Him now have security and are snatched from the very fiery pits of hell because the keys to life and death now belong to Him (Rev.1:17-18).

There's no insurance policy that can provide better benefits and security than that which is offered through Christ (Is. 28:16).

Have you checked your policy lately? Do you have fire insurance, because Hell is hot and eternity is long? If not, don't just get "a piece of the rock," but instead put your complete faith and trust in the Rock of Ages. His benefits are literally out of this world, and they provide true "peace of mind" and an ever-present reassurance.

"Blessed is the man who trusts in the LORD, And whose hope is the LORD. For he shall be like a tree planted by the waters, Which spreads out its roots by the river, And will not fear when heat comes; But its leaf will be green, And will not be anxious in the year of drought, Nor will cease from yielding fruit" (Jer. 17:7-8, New King James Version).

Thoughts
_____
_____
_____
_____
_____
_____
_____

June 23

DON'T ALLOW THE FRUIT TO FOOL YOU
Read: Lk. 6:44

Have you ever met someone who appeared to be very spiritual; you know, they could quote a few of the more common Scripture verses, offer vain repetitious prayers that went no higher than the ceiling, and knew most of the religious clichés commonly used in church. But, when it came down to it they really had no power.

Don't get me wrong, I know that we are not to judge one another because this is not our job (Rom. 14:4) and none of us here on earth have a heaven or hell to place anyone in. However, I would submit that we can be "fruit inspectors." Jesus plainly stated that you would know a tree by the fruit it bears (Lk. 6:44).

Growing up as a city-boy in Florida, I can remember going into the country or rural area just outside of Tallahassee city limits while visiting relatives during the summer months. Florida is known for its sunshine and fruit; therefore, in the yard where I stayed there could be found apple trees, pear trees, plum trees, and various other trees bearing fruit often within arm's reach and ready for the picking. But, there was nothing more disappointing than picking a fruit, taking a bite, and then realizing that it was not ripe or ready for consumption.

When unripen fruit is consumed the end-result is usually an upset stomach followed by many trips to the bathroom being seated on the throne, the "porcelain throne" (the toilet) that is.

Similar to the trees displaying fruit that appeared to be good for consumption, there are individuals who attempt to be skilled in the Word with the appearance of bearing fruit, but have not given themselves enough time to develop. As a result, individuals that partake of this apparent fruit generally end up being caused more harm than good.

Yes, we are to seek after spiritual gifts; yes, we are to step out in faith and begin to operate in these gifts. But, at the same time, we must allow God to mature us through experience as we spend time meditating on the precepts, statutes, and principles of His Word.

A true teacher of Scripture generally has God's Word deep on the inside of them, and what's inside has no choice but to come out and be a blessing to the hearer (Jer. 20:9). But, when teaching is solely based on popular opinion and personal agenda, this has the potential to turn into fruit that is not ready for consumption and bound to upset the spiritual appetite.

Thoughts

_____
_____
_____
_____
_____

Those quick to be teachers and preachers of God's Word should beware. God's Word provides stern warning to all would-be teachers

_____
_____
_____

(James 3:1). In other words, these individuals will be held accountable for what they have spoken and taught, even that which is taught in "the name of Christ."

No matter how commanding a person's presence may be, or how great they are at public speaking; it's the content and substance of what is being spoken that really matters the most. This should make all teachers of God's Word more conscious of first being students of the Word to ensure that the right things are coming out, so that we do not become pawns of the "Garbage in, garbage out" syndrome that has the potential to cause another to stumble. What we take in is bound to come out whether it's good or bad.

Our words should be seasoned with truth and spoken in love (Eph. 4:15), because this is the type of fruit that has real substance. We can't allow the appearance of the fruit to fool us, but must give it time to develop. Ripened (or well-developed) fruit is generally better and more palatable (2 Cor. 13:5).

June 24
IT'S TIME TO GET FIT
Read: 1 Tim. 4:7-8

In order for an individual to achieve a certain level of physical fitness, there are specific areas that must be concentrated on in order to reach the desired end-state. This level of fitness requires focus, dedication, and even a bit of sacrifice.

However, anyone who is serious about getting into shape does not begin a fitness routine without first assessing and evaluating where they currently are physically. Because there may be health and/or physical limitations that could prevent a person from performing certain exercises; therefore, an evaluation is necessary to prevent further injury and/or bring about a more serious condition.

The same applies to anyone desiring a closer relationship and walk with God. Just as a basic exercise routine consists of a warm-up, aerobic conditioning, strength conditioning, and a cool down, the same applies to spiritual fitness. There are few key components that require focused attention to ensure we as believers are spiritually conditioned and remain connected to the Father: prayer, fasting, praise & worship, study of God's Word, fellowship, and witnessing.

Thoughts

_____

_____

_____

_____

_____

_____

PRAYER: Just as the warm-up prepares the muscles and the body for the demands of exercise to come. Prayer prepares us for any trial that may come our way; enabling us to endure and pass the test (Jude v.20).

FASTING: This allows us to bring our bodies under subjection as we deny our flesh and its desires (Ps. 35:13). Fasting also provides physical benefits as toxins and other contaminants are expelled from the body.

PRAISE & WORSHIP: As we draw near to God in praise and worship, He begins to deal with our hearts and increase our strength. His joy is our strength (Neh. 8:10b). And in His presence there is fullness of joy (Ps. 16:11). So, as we draw nearer to God in worship our strength is perfected and renewed.

STUDY OF GOD'S WORD: As we read the Word of God we exercise and strengthen our faith. As we study the Bible we get a deeper and clearer revelation of who God is and what our assignment is as it pertains to fulfilling our purpose in life. Reading the Word of God builds us up spiritually (2 Tim. 2:15).

FELLOWSHIP: There is strength in numbers. A three cord string is harder to break than a single string (Ecc. 4:12). As we assemble together, we can draw from one another (Heb. 10:25); obtaining encouragement and stirring up the gifts in each other. Though there are many members, there's only one body; therefore, we draw strength from the Body collectively, not as individuals (Rom. 12:4).

WITNESSING: Declaring the Good News of the Gospel of Jesus Christ to those around us, living a holy lifestyle. Witnessing allows the planting of seeds of faith that can one day be watered and cultivated (1 Cor. 3:6) thereby bringing another soul into the Body of Christ. We witness not only in word, but also through our conduct and our daily lifestyle. Therefore, God instructs us to be holy, because He is Holy" (1 Pet. 1:16).

Though physical exercise is important, our spiritual conditioning should become an even higher priority in our daily lives (1 Tim. 4:7-8).

Are you spiritually fit? If not, then give your spiritual muscles something to do by exercising your faith today!

June 25
DON'T OVERLOOK THE WOUNDED CLOSEST TO YOU
Read: Lk. 10:30-34

In today's Scripture text, Jesus tells the story of the Good Samaritan. As the story goes, a certain Jewish man traveled from Jerusalem to Jericho, and during his journey he was assaulted by a group of thieves. The man was stripped of his clothing, beaten, thrown into a ditch near the road, and was basically left for dead.

Thoughts

Priests and other religious leaders journeyed down the same road where this incident happened and where the wounded man lay, undoubtedly attempting to make their way to the temple for worship. However, when they saw the man in the ditch in his wounded condition and unable to help himself, they went to the other side of the road to avoid any involvement with assisting or having to deal with the man. This was a classic example of the "out of sight, out of mind" mentality with the religious leaders probably saying to themselves, "He is not my responsibility; besides, I'm trying to make it to the temple for worship God. This is more important."

Many other travelers probably journeyed down the same path seeing the man in his wounded condition, but did nothing to assist because they were too busy, concerned and focused on their own affairs. However, one Samaritan man came by, saw the need, had compassion, and rendered assistance. Not only did the Samaritan treat and bind up the man's wounds; he also made provision to ensure the man had lodging, providing a place for him to recover.

What really makes this story so amazing was the fact that the Jews and the Samaritans had no dealings with one another because the Jews despised the Samaritans. So, here was a Samaritan going out of his way, above and beyond the normal call of duty to assist someone who was a sworn enemy restoring a Jew and someone he did not personally know to a place of health and wholeness.

Sadly, there are many wounded and hurt people who sit next to us at work, in the church, and even at home that need our assistance or an act of compassion; yet we pass by them every day without lending a helping hand. This is often especially true within "the Church" where many times we are so focused in our efforts and aspirations to do great things for God (no matter how good our intentions may be), to travel all over the world, to minister to millions and to make a name for ourselves that we simply neglect to meet the need and begin to minister to the wounded that are nearest and closest to us.

We must learn to begin ministry in our own Jerusalem; whether that be on the job, at the gym, in the park, in the supermarket, or even at home. There are individuals who are near, dear and very close to us that are spiritually wounded and in need of a healing word from the Lord. "By the power of his own word, he healed you and saved you from destruction" (Ps. 107:20, Contemporary English Version). God's Word has power to heal; however, we must be willing to put aside our own agendas to see and then meet the immediate need of the wounded around us and begin to apply the healing balm just like the Good Samaritan.

Thoughts

_____
_____
_____
_____
_____
_____
_____

There are co-workers, friends, and even immediate family members who are in desperate need of the gift of God within us. However, if we are not careful, it can become commonplace to get so focused on going to worship God that we truly miss the opportunity to worship God through our actions! It is very easy to become so far-sighted with vision, desires for things to come and a better way of life that we can begin to overlook the wounded who are closet to us.

June 26
ASK FOR WHAT YOU NEED
Read: Lk. 11:11

Most fathers (good fathers that is) have their children's best interest at heart, and desire for them to be successful in life. Being a father of four daughters myself; I only want what's best for them, both naturally and spiritually. When one comes with a legitimate need, as long as it is within my power to grant and even if it requires me to go without something that I desire for myself, I will often go out of my way to see to it that the need is met.

So, if one of my daughters asked me for a glass of water, it would be illogical for me to give her a glass of motor oil; or if another asked for a piece of cake, it would be foolish to give her a pie filled with poison. Why? Because these things could not only bring about harm to them, but also has the potential to bring about death.

There are times as parents that our children ask for things that have the potential to harm them, and it is up to the father to exercise wisdom through prayer to discern between what is actually beneficial for the child and what is not, no matter how persistent they may be with their request. Even though I did not always get it right over the years, I did my best to not give my daughters that which could potentially harm them, and instead attempted to give them that which was needed and what was best. This is what our Heavenly Father does for each of us.

Many times God knows that what we are praying for is not beneficial to us or for us, and as a result He does not give us what we ask for no matter how long we stay on our knees, lay prostrate before Him or how long we pace the floor back and forth. It is not the length of our prayers and/or petitions that prompt God to move, it is our motives that determine His response.

Therefore, when we petition God and make requests, we must be direct (Lk. 11:11). Our loving Heavenly Father stands ready to meet our need; however, we must ask in faith and pray according to His will for our lives and not just based on fleshly wants and desires.

Thoughts

_____
_____
_____
_____

Sadly many have issues with this concept because they have never truly come to know God as their Father because of past experiences; instead they often just see Him as an All-knowing, All-powerful and distant God somewhere up there

_____
_____

219

who stands ready to rain down fire, brimstone and judgment at any moment. Although this is well within His ability to do, His greatest attribute and characteristic is that of love; "...for God is love" (1 Jn. 4:8, King James Version).

Love is not just something the Father has; it is who He is and is His very nature. It is the Father's love that compels Him to care for us as His very own.

Even though God is Love and He desires to bless His children, at the same time He is not a spiritual slot machine just waiting for us to pull the handle to get any and everything that we want. Our needs are met based on our relationship with Him; when true relationship is there then we can ask the Father for what we need. He desires to grant our requests when we ask in faith (Heb. 11:6), from pure hearts (Ps. 24:3-4), and with the right motives (James 4:2).

Just as a good father strives to give his children what is best for them out of love, our Heavenly Father loves each of us and knows exactly what we need; He's just waiting for us to ask.

Instead of coming to God with outlandish and/or unreasonable requests, just ask for what you need because the Father knows what's best (Matt. 7:7-8, 11)!

June 27
CHECK THE SOURCE
Read: James 3:11-12

When you stump your toe, bump your head, or accidentally slam your finger in a door; what comes out of your mouth? Is your response filled with a multitude of expletives or profanities that would require someone to blank out your words if the response was being recorded and aired over radio or television? Or would it be a cartoon with the caption above filled with various symbols representative of negative words?

Oftentimes when accidents like this occur and/or external pressures come upon us, our response generally provides a real indication of what truly resides in us. This is an area that we must bring before the Father in prayer so that it can be dealt with at its root.

Thoughts
_____
_____
_____
_____
_____
_____

Responding in anger and using the wrong words can't be blamed on the situation at hand, other individuals, or even the devil; I would suggest there is a much deeper issue that needs to be addressed.

If you have accepted Christ as Lord and Savior, His Holy Spirit should now take residence and abide within you. So, when the pressures of life come and begin to squeeze and press you like a vice-grip, what's inside (Holy Spirit and the anointing) should come out and begin to flow. However, in many circumstances and instances the total opposite happens with the wrong things proceeding out of our mouths. How can this be?

"Does a spring of water bubble out with both fresh water and bitter water? Does a fig tree produce olives, or a grapevine produce figs? No, and you can't draw fresh water from a salty spring" (James 3:11-12, New Living Translation). Since a spring filled with salty water does not produce fresh water, neither should a person filled with the Spirit of God release profanities and words that tear down rather than building others up. "Watch the way you talk. Let nothing foul or dirty come out of your mouth. Say only what helps, each word a gift [to the hearers]" (Eph. 4:29, The Message)."

Yes, we all have the innate ability slip and yield to sin; and yes, we can confess our sin and receive forgiveness (1 Jn. 1:9). However, grace is not a free license to continue in the same manner of our former lives just allowing anything and everything to freely flow and come out of our mouths (Rom. 6:1-3)!

Whenever an individual is just prone to saying any and everything out of his or her mouth, this may be a clear indicator that the root must be addressed because this is more than likely a matter of the heart. We must guard out hearts as instructed in Prov. 4:23; the heart must be guarded because this is where life itself flows from.

Jesus said "The Spirit can make life. Sheer muscle and willpower don't make anything happen. Every word I've spoken to you is a Spirit-word, and so it is life-making. But some of you are resisting, refusing to have any part in this" (Jn. 6:63, The Message).

If the wrong thing consistently comes out of your mouth, it is no accident; what comes out was produced by something already deep inside. You must find the source, deal with the root, and replace it with the right thing; God's Word!

The next time you stump your toe, accidentally bump your head, someone offends you, or cuts you off in traffic; instead of blurting out the first thing you think of or decide to give someone a piece of your mind, why not choose to give the thanks instead (1 Thess. 5:18). If you are consistently saying the wrong thing, then MAYBE YOU NEED TO CHECK THE SOURCE!

Thoughts

June 28

IT'S TIME TO CROSS OVER
Read: Deut. 11

Why are so many Christians set in their ways, and not willing to venture out into new areas of service and ministry in the body of Christ?

Many of us get comfortable in certain areas, trying to remain right where we are because there's nothing really challenging us.

Though comfort may be appropriate in other aspects of life, I've learned more and more each day that comfort when it comes to ministry (not just within the church, but in a broader sense) leads to stagnation. Remaining in our comfort zones can also be indicative of a lack of faith on our part.

From personal experience, for years I was comfortable serving God in the background not desiring to be in the spotlight or out front. In the churches that my family and I were blessed to partner with over the years I always volunteered for ministries that were not in the forefront.

I routinely found comfort serving in areas like the Media ministry operating audio/video equipment behind the scenes, when in my heart I knew that God was calling me for and to more. But I allowed fear of the unknown to hinder me, which in and of itself was a form of disobedience and sin because I knew what I should have been doing (James 4:17).

Several years ago a former pastor challenged me and gave me a word of knowledge as he said, "The Lord told me to tell you that it's time for you to come out of the background into the forefront." I immediately knew what he was saying and began to allow him to mentor me as he gave me assignments that pulled me completely out of my "comfort zone."

I then began to tread new water, like Peter, that required me to activate faith at a whole new level. I could no longer depend on my own ability or what I perceived to be a lack thereof, but truly had to depend on God (through the Holy Spirit) to lead, guide and direct me.

Many times we say that we trust God with our lips and our mouths, saying that we have faith; yet our actions, or lack thereof, often say the total opposite. However, it was when I made a decision to answer "the call" and crossed over from comfort to obedience that the blessings of God truly began to flow not only to myself, but for my family as well. There is nothing like the head (the head of the home, specifically the man) being in proper alignment. Because where the head goes, the body will naturally tend to follow.

Thoughts

_____

_____

_____

_____

_____

_____

_____

In Deuteronomy chapter 11, the children of Israel were coming to the close of their wilderness journey and travels; they were now in a position to go possess the land that God had promised them years before. But the land before them was unfamiliar territory, and I'm sure there was some apprehension about venturing out into the unknown.

Entrance into the land of promise required obedience and faith. Possessing this land "flowing with milk and honey" (representative of blessing and abundance) meant that the Israelites would have to cross over from the familiar and their comfort zones into new and unchartered territory. This is exactly what God is doing in many of our lives today, challenging us to cross over into new territory. However, it is totally up to each of us to individually accept the challenge and answer the call.

What has God called you to do today? Accept the challenge and don't let fear stop you, "for God has not given us a spirit of fear, but of power and of love and of a sound mind" (2 Tim. 1:7, New King James Version).

June 29
THE BENEFIT OF 20/20 VISION
Read: 2 Chron. 20:20

In 1 Kgs. 17:8-16, we find the prophet Elijah having spoken on behalf of the LORD God; in this declaration he proclaimed a drought in the land and later received instructions to make a journey to where provision had already been prepared and established for him. He was directed to travel towards the city of Zarephath where a widow had been commanded and set aside to provide for the prophet's need.

When the prophet arrived, there she was, a widow with no real source of income chosen to be the reservoir of blessing to the man of God. In the natural this would seem to be a poor or unlikely choice for provision, since the widow did not seem to have much to offer; however, God had a plan.

The widow was found gathering sticks to be used to kindle the fire for the meal she was about to prepare. So, the prophet asked her to bring him something to drink, then went further to ask for a morsel of bread to eat (1 Kgs. 17:12). With a drought wreaking havoc throughout the land and no hope in sight, the widow was preparing to fix the last meal for herself and her son, and then prepared to just sit around and wait to starve to death.

In an unusual and what seemed to be an almost selfish request, the prophet instructed her to continue with her plans, but first she was to make a small cake for him, then afterwards she could make provision for herself and her son. What would you have done in this situation? Here was the man of God, knowing the woman's plight, asking her to give of the little provision that she had remaining to him before taking care of her own needs.

Thoughts

_____
_____
_____
_____

Without hesitation the widow complied with the prophet's request. The Scripture states "the widow went home and DID EXACTLY what

_____
_____
_____

Elijah had told her" (1 Kgs. 17:15) utilizing the little resources that were available to her. And because the widow responded in faith to the prophet's request, the once bare bin of flour and depleted jar of oil were never empty again. The widow, her son, and the prophet Elijah had enough food to eat for many days to come.

Simply by catching the vision of the man of God as given to him through a Word from the LORD and by responding in faith, both the widow and her son were spared from impending death. A lack of vision has the potential to cause undesirable suffering, but clear vision brings with it much blessing. "Where there is no vision [no redemptive revelation of God], the people perish; but he who keeps the law [of God, which includes that of man]--blessed (happy, fortunate, and enviable) is he" (Prov. 29:18, Amplified Bible). This is why it is important to understand and catch the vision of our spiritual leaders; then follow their godly lead, instruction and example as they follow the example of Jesus Christ.

It would seem that having clear vision is very important; this is why for human eyesight a rating of "20/20" is used to measure the visual acuity or clearness that is considered the normal level for our vision. Therefore, from a spiritual perspective, it is catching the 20/20 vision of God-appointed spiritual overseers and leaders that allows us to see ahead clearly as the LORD makes our way and plans to prosper.

"Believe in the LORD your God, and you shall be established; believe His prophets, and you shall prosper" (2 Chron. 20:20, New King James Version).

June 30
IN HOT PURSUIT
Read: Hos. 1

Years ago there was a popular movie called "Smokey and the Bandit" that showcased a multi-state high-speed pursuit.

In this movie, the Bandit (Burt Reynolds) assisted his truck driver friend (Jerry Reed) in attempting to deliver a truckload of bootlegged liquor to a designated location for a large sum of money. He did all of this while trying to avoid a bloodhound-like sheriff (Sheriff Buford Justice a.k.a. "Smokey," played by Jackie Gleason) and his naïve son.

Thoughts

_____

_____

_____

_____

_____

_____

_____

In the midst of it all and along the way, Bandit picked up an unlikely hitchhiker (a professional dancer) named Carrie (Sally Field) who had recently runaway from marrying Sheriff Justices' son. So, not only was Smokey pursuing Bandit for the transport of illegal liquor, but to recover his son's fiancée.

224

Therefore, the majority of the movie was essentially one big high-speed pursuit. And despite leaving his legal jurisdiction; Sheriff Justice and his son continued to pursue Bandit, even as their squad car began to literally disintegrate around them due to the numerous accidents and mishaps that happened during their chase.

Throughout the movie Sheriff Justice could be heard saying, don't mess with me now "I'm in hot pursuit!" No matter what happened, the sheriff and his son refused give-up on their pursuit.

In the Scripture text for today's devotional we have another individual (the Prophet Hosea) who was in a pursuit of another kind. The prophet received what to anyone of us today would appear to have been a very unusual request from the LORD; he was instructed to marry a woman who was a known harlot or prostitute (Gomer).

Can you imagine the ridicule Hosea must have endured? Here was a prophet of God married to prostitute; and not only was he married and had children with Gomer, he was actually deeply in love with her as well. But no matter how much Hosea demonstrated love for his wife, she continued in her old ways consistently remaining unfaithful to the marriage vows.

After months of infidelity, Hosea's wife eventually came to her senses and returned to the love of a husband who never gave-up on her. Like the final scene of a play or a good movie, redemption and restoration came after Gomer remembered who she really was and made it a purpose to repent of her sins; Hosea was there to receive her with open arms.

The story of Hosea and Gomer paints the perfect picture of how God's love was and is still in hot pursuit of us even when we rebel and turn our backs to Him as we celebrate and revel in our sin (Rom. 5:8; 1 Jn. 4:9).

Even when we rebel and chase after the little "g" gods and idols of this world, the one true God stands ready to forgive and receive us back when we come to our senses, turn from our wicked ways and repent. Repenting is simply turning away from the old way of sin, leaving the past behind, looking ahead and then moving forward towards that which is new—life in Christ!

Though we may constantly attempt to speed away from His advances, God's love is always in hot pursuit (Ps. 139:7-12!

Thoughts

_____
_____
_____
_____
_____
_____
_____

July 1

THIEVES IN THE TEMPLE
Read: Jn. 2:12-16

After performing the miracle of turning water into wine at the wedding in Cana and just before the Passover festival; Jesus, His family, and disciples traveled to the city of Capernaum for a short visit. However, right before the Passover celebration Jesus decided to journey to Jerusalem.

While in the holy city of Jerusalem, Jesus visited the temple (the place designated and set apart for worship of the one true God—Jehovah) and was appalled at what He discovered there and what He saw.

Inside the temple he found individuals selling cattle, sheep, doves, and various other animals; He also found moneychangers with tables setup, exchanging Greek and Roman money for Jewish currency for a specific cost. So, what do you think that Jesus did? Did he just kneel and pray for them? Did he simply ask His Father to overlook this shameful activity? No, he grabbed some rope, braided them together to create a whip, and then began to drive everyone out of the temple who made a mockery of His Father's house.

As Jesus proceeded through the temple, He overturned the money tables with coins flying everywhere, and then chased the livestock out of the temple courtyard. This is probably shocking to some who just see Jesus as the little baby in the manger, or the meek Lamb of God; however, in this instance Jesus demonstrated a trait that is often overlooked in His character, the Lion of the Tribe of Judah.

Jesus did not tolerate nonsense then, and neither does He tolerate it today as He still addresses many of the same issues through His Word; He is still opposed to thieves in the temple.

Did you know there are thieves that sit in the temple (or church) with us week after week; people we would never consider or even imagine to be thieves? Who are these individuals you might ask, or maybe the thief is you? According to Scripture, a thief is anyone who does not honor the LORD with the tithe. In other words, when we take what belongs to God and begin to use it satisfy ourselves or for reasons contrary to its intended purpose, we in essence rob God.

Thoughts

_____

_____

_____

_____

_____

_____

A tithe is one-tenth or 10% of an individual's income and/or increase. Tithing is a form of "stewardship" that God requires of us as Christians and it is also considered to be an act of obedience that demonstrates our gratitude for all that God has done for us.

God really has no need of our money; it is more a matter of obedience and an indication of the state of the individual's heart. When God truly has our heart, money and giving will not be an issue. Besides, it all belongs to God anyway; He only asks for 10% with the tither retaining the 90%. So, why not just give God what belongs to Him –- giving of very our best (Mal. 3:8-11). Because when we do it God's way, His blessings are the result (2 Cor. 9:8).

So, don't be a thief sitting in the temple, honor the LORD with your first fruits (Prov. 3:9). It's not about giving our resources to a man or to a church, but it is about honoring God and ensuring that His storehouse is full to further advance His Kingdom. Remember, obedience opens the door to God's blessings.

July 2
STANDING BY A PILE OF ASHES
Read: Ps. 127:1

What is the relationship between works and salvation? Do we have to work to receive salvation? How is work related to my life as a believer after salvation? These are all relevant questions that are of utmost concern for many in the body of Christ today.

There are those who accept Jesus Christ by faith, but then choose to live their lives however they please because they now have the assurance of access to heaven. They pack their spiritual bags and wait for the Rapture and return of Jesus on the clouds, but really do nothing to benefit the kingdom of God or others. So for them grace is all they need, and their actions are of no consequence.

Then there are those who believe they must work to earn salvation. They give money, help the poor, and give of their time to aid charitable events and causes; but at the same time push faith to the side with no real relationship or connection with Christ since, according to their logic "good works" will grant them access to heaven.

According to Eph. 2:8-10, we are delivered from judgment by receiving God's unmerited favor (grace) through faith in Christ and our salvation comes through faith alone; therefore, we have been fashioned and/or recreated in Christ as a spiritual habitation (or dwelling place) to do good works (Eph. 2:22), and must ensure that this habitation is built on the right foundation. Yes, we should desire access to heaven and salvation that is eternal; and yes, we should also want to do good works. Yet these things need to be kept in proper perspective with the correct view of grace, faith and works.

Thoughts

We do not work to receive God's free gift of salvation; however, once we are saved it is our love and relationship with our Heavenly Father

227

that prompts us to share His gift of life with others through outward expressions of our faith (1 Pet. 4:10).

As believers in Christ we are "saved to serve," and our lives are to be built on the solid foundation of Christ and His perfect example as He came not to be served, but to serve others out of love (Mk 10:45); Jesus came to give. James also reminds us in chapter two of his epistle that faith with no works is of little benefit; in fact this type of faith is dead, fruitless and unproductive (James 2:26).

In other words, works apart from saving faith are just as fruitless as faith that has no corresponding action (James 2:24). Our lifestyle after having met Christ should provide evidence that we are truly His; therefore, our faith is to be demonstrated through the "good works" that we do.

There will come a day when we each individually will stand before the judgment seat of Christ to give an account for everything that we have done with the life that God has given us (2 Cor. 5:10).

Whenever it comes down to fully committing ourselves to doing what we know to be right, a popular statement is often made, "God knows my heart." This is a true statement, because we each will be judged based on the condition of our hearts and what we have done for the benefit of God's Kingdom and for others. Knowing is never enough, we have to do something with what we know (1 Cor. 3:13-15).

What are you building your life with? What foundation are you building on? Is it grace alone? Is it in works alone? Or is your life being built through faith that produces good works? Use your gift(s) wisely by putting faith into action that produces good works today (Phil. 2:12)!

July 3
REFUSE TO GIVE UP YOUR INHERITANCE
Read: 1 Kgs. 21:1-16

Thoughts

_____
_____
_____
_____
_____
_____
_____
_____

After the nation of Israel was divided into the Northern Kingdom (Israel) and the Southern Kingdom (Judah) due to civil unrest, there were a number of rulers crowned in both the Northern and Southern kingdoms. And as history records, none of the Kings of Israel judged wisely (that is, judging according to the leading of the LORD), and only eight judged well in Judah. Of the kings of Israel, one in particular stood out even more so for his evil ways; that being King Ahab who was considered to be one of the most evil kings to ever reign.

King Ahab and his wife Jezebel did despicable things and whatever it took to have their way. A prime example of this was Ahab's desire to obtain a certain vineyard that belonged to a Jezreelite named Naboth (the name Naboth means "fruits"). This vineyard was very well kept, and was directly adjacent to Ahab's palace. When Ahab saw the fruitfulness of this vineyard, he began to covet it desiring to make it his very own personal palace garden.

This vineyard belonged to Naboth's father, his grandfather, and others all the other relatives that came before them hundreds of years prior. And according to the law of the time, individuals were not allowed to sell their land but were required to pass it on as an inheritance from father to son. Even though this was the case, Ahab persisted with his request to obtain this fruitful vineyard.

Standing his ground Naboth refused to give in and said to Ahab, "The LORD forbid that I should give the inheritance of my fathers to you" (1 Kgs. 21:3, New King James Version)! Watching this saga unfold and becoming infuriated with Naboth's staunch resistance, Ahab's evil wife Jezebel devised a scheme to kill Naboth in order to obtain the vineyard because he was insistent and refused to willingly give up his inheritance.

To inherit means "to take possession of or receive something of value usually from an ancestor;" as believers in Christ, we too have an inheritance. And it is our responsibility, especially as parents, to pass on this inheritance to our children and on to the generations that are to come (Gal. 3:14). Everything that God promised to Abraham (his inheritance) is also now ours through Jesus Christ. Deut. 28:1-14 also provides a further glimpse into those things that are rightfully ours to possess NOW when we walk in obedience to God's way.

Many times as believers we give the devil too much credit for what we perceive him to be doing in our lives and/or the power that we think he has; when in actuality the trouble that we often experience originates from us giving him that which rightfully belongs to us by covenant in the first place (Gal. 3:29).

In a nutshell, we must refuse to give up our inheritance (the fruit of God's seed). The enemy desires that we give up our ability to produce in order to prevent future generations from being blessed. Though we may not have billions stored up in the bank like Donald Trump or Bill Gates, in Christ we are rich in the blessings that begin with the spiritual seeds we plant in our children.

The enemy would have us give our children over to the world allowing television, ungodly music, and other negative influences to speak into their lives at an early age, when it is our responsibility as parents to ensure that the right seeds are being planted. As these seeds are watered and nurtured with God's Word, they will continue to prosper and grow (1 Cor. 3:5-9).

Thoughts

_____

_____

_____

_____

_____

_____

_____

Whether you choose to acknowledge it or not, you have an inheritance in Christ. Refuse to give up your inheritance, begin sowing the right seeds today!

July 4
BOUND TO BE FREE
Read: Rom. 6:15-18

In America today, there are many who celebrate the many freedoms this great country has to offer those who come from various nations around the world where true liberty and freedom is only a dream. Although many come to America to seek a new way of life and actually receive this new found freedom, they often still remain prisoners and slaves to sin.

The Apostle Paul wrote many of his New Testament epistles (or letters) from a place of imprisonment where he was often shackled and bound having no mobility. Many of the spiritual truths that we as Christians cling and/or hold to today are products of the books of Ephesians, Colossians, Philippians, and Philemon that have been commonly called and labeled "Prison Epistles," since they were all written during a time of personal imprisonment for Paul.

But Paul's imprisonment did not come as a result of any malfeasance or personal wrongdoing on his part; he was repeatedly beaten and imprisoned for the defense of the Gospel as he stood boldly for the name of Christ and all that Christ stood for. Several times throughout the epistles, the Apostle Paul is recorded as saying that he is a "prisoner of Christ," this was his fuel and motivation.

Paul had made it up in his mind that he would purpose to live upright and accomplish the will of God at any and all cost, no matter what physical encumbrances came his way. And although he was often physically bound being placed in dungeons and prisons, he was still free in Christ to spread God's Word because no prison wall was able to stop the Good News of the Blessing from going forth. Even though he was physically bound, in Christ the Apostle Paul was actually free.

So, what then is true liberty and freedom? Is it the ability to walk freely unencumbered by chains and fetters, or does it go much deeper? I personally believe that the latter is true because there are many today who walk around physically absolutely free, but are still held prisoners to sin and the balls & chains in their minds.

Thoughts

_____
_____
_____
_____
_____
_____
_____

"The Lord and the Spirit are one and the same, and the Lord's Spirit sets us free" (2 Cor. 3:17, Contemporary English Version)."

It is a personal and authentic relationship with Christ that truly sets us free, so no matter what our physical state may be "...if the Son liberates you [makes you free men], then you are really and unquestionably free" (Jn. 8:36, Amplified Bible). Therefore, it is our connection and relationship to God through Christ and a willingness to faithfully serve that truly makes us free, so "as a prisoner of the Lord, I beg you to live in a way that is worthy of the people God has chosen to be his own" (Eph. 4:1, Contemporary English Version).

Do you have true liberty and freedom today? If so, then remember that this freedom came at a very high cost and at an extremely precious price, it was the very sacrifice of Christ and His shed blood that bought you real freedom. And although you are now spiritually free, it is your dependence on Him that really brings true liberty. Therefore, in Christ you are no longer held captive as a slave to sin because your "independence" is actually wrapped up in your "dependence" on Him. In Christ you are bound to be free (Rom. 6:15-18)!

July 5
YOUR MIRACLE IS IN YOUR MOUTH
Read: Matt. 8:5-10

There was a CNN article written by Elizabeth Landau a few years ago that discussed the effects of music on the brain entitled "Music: It's in your head, changing your brain." In the article Landau quoted an associate professor at John Hopkins University who had this to say about music, "It allows you to think in a way that you used to not think, and it also trains a lot of other cognitive facilities that have nothing to do with music."

The basic premise of the article is that it has been scientifically proven that music has a definite effect on the brain, especially concerning the area of memorization.

Upon reading this I was challenged to really consider what I listened to and then began to recall a popular gospel song released a few years back that was consistently played over the airways of gospel and Christian radio stations at the time. The song was "I Still Believe" by Bishop Harry Trotter and the Sweet Holy Spirit Combined Choirs.

The portion of the song that has really remained with me over the years was a small portion of the bishop's personal testimony detailing and comparing his trials and the things he endured to that of Job in the Old Testament. In the testimony he mentioned how Job lost everything he had, yet in all of his misfortune

Thoughts

_____
_____
_____
_____
_____
_____
_____

231

and calamity he refused to curse or say a negative thing against God for the bad things that were happening in his life.

The bishop then went on to say to God that no matter what happened "I still believe," and then towards the end of his testimony he offered a very powerful word of encouragement as he said "Your miracle is in your mouth!" This statement is both profound and also very true because the miracles we often seek are directly connected to what we both think (our beliefs) and say.

Too often as Christians we allow the wrong thing(s) to proceed out of our mouths during our tests, trials, and tribulations because we allow the wrong things to come in (Prov. 18:21). This simply suggests that many times the negative things that often happen in our lives are self-created and self-generated by the very things we say and allow to proceed out of our mouths.

Therefore, whenever the pressures of life seem to become too hard to bear, we must learn to take a step back, take an assessment of what is really happening and most importantly learn how to "develop an anointing to shut up and sit down" as I heard one pastor state it during a conference. This can go a long way in preventing us from saying and/or declaring the wrong thing and thereby bring about what we talk about.

When words are released they have an assignment to produce either good or bad, life or death because there is no neutral ground or in between; the resulting product is based on what we choose to say.

Having the faith for what we need is directly associated to what we say, but in order to say the right things we must first hear the right things (Rom. 10:17). What do you have need of today? The challenge before us all is to begin saying and declaring the right thing(s) by faith and in faith, because YOUR MIRACLE IS IN YOUR MOUTH!

July 6
JUST DO WHATEVER HE SAYS
Read: Jn. 2:1-11

Thoughts

_____
_____
_____
_____
_____
_____
_____

In today's Scripture text, Jesus' mother knew the importance of following the commands of her son Jesus because of the authority He possessed. It was here at the wedding in Cana that Jesus prepared to perform His very first recorded miracle after wine ran out.

Here Jesus gave the command to fill several water pots, not with grapes or anything that would produce wine, but with simple, plain water. I'm sure those in attendance began to question His command wondering how pots filled with water would provide that which was needed for the wedding guests. Again, knowing the power and authority Jesus had (and still has today), his mother simply said to the servants, "Do whatever he tells you" (Jn. 2:5).

Despite what seemed impractical and irrational, the servants obeyed. And it was because of the servants' obedience to the command of Jesus, the water in the pots miraculously turned into wine providing more than enough to satisfy all of the wedding guests. Not only did the water turn into wine, but the wine that produced from the water pots towards the end of the wedding feast was actually better than the wine served at the beginning.

When we follow the commands of Jesus, not only are miracles produced, but it causes our ending to be better than the beginning. What command has God given you to follow through with today? Don't just sit and think about it, or even try to rationalize it. God is not going to give you an impossible command to follow because He will also equip you with what you need to accomplish the assignment.

Our victory and blessing comes when we follow through and obey all of His command(s) as given to us through His Word. Whatever Jesus instructs us to do according to His Word; that is what He expects us to do.

So don't just sit around and wait, or even try to mull it over and/or contemplate; your breakthrough comes when you just "DO WHATEVER HE SAYS!"

July 7
IT'S TIME TO ADD SOME FLAVOR
Read: 2 Kgs. 2:19-22

Many times in life there are things that often appear difficult or burdensome to do, especially when we have a choice to do it or not. However, when we a placed in a position to where we have no other choice but to follow through, or either "put up or shut up" as I have often heard it said; this is when what we are truly made of and what we have learned is displayed and placed in the spotlight.

For years Elisha faithfully observed and followed the instructions of his mentor the prophet Elijah. But the time had come for Elijah to depart and Elisha to step up to the plate and prepare to run with everything that he had been taught over the years.

Thoughts

_____

_____

_____

_____

_____

At this point the prophet Elijah had been taken to heaven in a whirlwind leaving his apprentice,

_____

_____

233

Elisha, behind to pick up where he had left off. Not only was Elisha given the same abilities as his mentor, but God gave him "a double portion" of Elijah's spirit so that he would accomplish even greater works and greater miracles than his predecessor.

Once Elijah had been whisked away and was no longer in sight, Elisha grabbed the mantle or cloak that fell from Elijah as he was taken away by chariots of fire. He then struck the waters of the Jordan River with the mantle of Elijah and the waters divided to the right and left allowing him to cross over on dry ground. Although striking the waters was something that he learned from his mentor Elijah, this was representative or symbolic of Elisha leaving behind the former things, and then stepping across and over into the new. The very last miracle performed by Elijah just happens to be the very first miracle performed by his successor Elisha.

As he crossed over he proceeded to the city of Jericho. But even though the city was structurally sound, fortified, and well situated in its location; there was one major thing lacking, the water that flowed to the city was bad (filled with all types of impurities) which caused the land to be unproductive.

Hearing that a prophet was now near, the men of the city sought him out to address the city's water predicament. So, what does the prophet Elisha do to bring about change? He instructed the men of the city to bring him a container filled with salt. He then proceeded to the spring (the source of the water supply) and threw the salt in saying, "This is what the LORD says: 'I have healed this water. Never again will it cause death or make the land unproductive'" (2 Kgs. 2:21).

Imagine that! All it took to bring about change and transformation in the city and surrounding land from a state of barrenness to fruitfulness was to simply add a little salt.

As believers in Christ, we are often situated in places where there is barrenness that causes many all around us to be unproductive each day. And just like the prophet Elisha, it is up to us to add flavor to bring about change. According to Matt. 5:13, Scripture plainly reminds us of the fact that we, as faithful believers in Christ, are the salt of the earth (Matt. 5:13). We add salt by living consistent lifestyles of holiness as we are in the world, while not becoming a part of it (1 Pet. 1:16). Salt sitting on a shelf is of little use to anyone; therefore, it has to be poured out to begin effecting change. So what are you waiting for?

Thoughts

_____
_____
_____
_____
_____
_____

July 8
STANDING WHILE SITTING DOWN
Read: Prov. 16:18

Being blessed to raise children and watch them grow over the years is an amazing thing. Seeing their development from crawling babies, to stumbling toddlers, to adolescents trying to discover who they are, to teens who think they know it all is truly an interesting journey, but also a wonderful sight to see.

Watching how siblings interact with each other on a daily basis is also quite interesting, especially when the interaction is between younger and older siblings; with the older making a constant effort to assert his or her authority as the oldest child and more dominant sibling, while the younger does everything within his or her power to undermine the older sibling's authority through rebellion.

This rebellion is brought to the forefront even more as parents go out for dinner, a movie, etc., leaving the older sibling in charge. In this setting the younger sibling does everything to show the older sibling that he or she really has no authority to make demands, even though the request(s) may be valid.

When this occurs it is not uncommon to hear phrases like "You're not my mom!"; "You're not my dad!"; "You can't tell me what to do!"; and/or that all too common phrase "You're not the boss of me!"

Frustrated from repeated attempts to get the younger sibling to behave and to quit being a nuisance, the older sibling yells out, "That's it; I've had enough...just sit down and be quiet!"

The younger sibling, sensing the seriousness in the tone of the older sibling's voice, decides to take a seat in the family room but then says, "I may be sitting down on the outside, but inside I'm still standing." Though the younger sibling complied outwardly, inwardly pride was still in control and on the throne.

Many believers suffer this same syndrome today, but in our case instead of displaying outright rebellion we exhibit a false sense of humility, while inwardly pride is still seated on the throne. We do things out of obligation, when we should be responding out of love and compassion.

According to Prov. 16:18, "First pride, then the crash—-the bigger the ego, the harder the fall." Prov. 29:23 says, "Pride lands you flat on your face; humility prepares you for honors" (The Message). In other words, we must not allow pride and a false sense of humility bring us down.

If anyone had more reason to be full of pride, it would have been Christ Himself who had a name that was exalted above any other, and was given a seat at the right hand of the Father, God Himself. The right hand signifies the place of power and authority, all of which was given to Christ because of His selfless actions.

Thoughts

_____
_____
_____
_____
_____
_____
_____

So it was not pride that placed Jesus in this exalted position, but rather it was Christ's willingness to lower Himself that brought about promotion that caused Him to be glorified and lifted up. This required a total change of mindset; a mind that did not focus on personal ambition and/or gain, but a mind filled with humility, compassion and love. This is what we must also do.

July 9
HILLS AND VALLEYS
Read: 1 Kgs. 20:1-30

At this point in the book of First Kings, the Israelites faced a formidable foe in the Syrian Army who came against them with a great multitude of soldiers as compared to Israel's small army of seven thousand. Based on what was seen in the natural, surely Israel would face certain defeat.

But God had a different plan; though vastly outnumbered, the Israelites positioned themselves atop a hill and "slew the Syrians with a great slaughter" (1 Kgs.20:21).

Consequently, the Syrians attributed Israel's success to using the military tactic of "the higher ground" since fighting from an elevated position provided many benefits. Soldiers fighting uphill tired more quickly, they moved slower, rocks and javelins had less range when thrown upward, and they had a diminished field of view.

It was based on the above factors the Syrian servants said, "Their gods are gods of the hills; therefore they were stronger than we; but let us fight against them in the plain, and surely we shall be stronger than they" (1 Kgs. 20:23).

So, based on this assumption the Syrians planned to surprise the Israelites with another attack, this time in the plains on lower ground being confident of their sure victory since Israel's God would only cause them to prevail on hills, or so they thought. Additionally, as another precaution and to ensure their victory the Syrians increased the number of soldiers available to go into battle against the Israelites (1 Kgs. 20:28). Once again, against seemingly insurmountable odds, Israel prevailed, this time doing so while in the midst of the valley.

Thoughts

_____
_____
_____
_____
_____
_____
_____

The enemy thought that bringing the Israelites down low would surely bring defeat. However, this was not the case; they were victorious in the valley plains just as they had been in the hills. Our enemy (the devil) comes against us in a similar way; it is when we are at our lowest point that he attempts to bring defeat and tries to get us off-track.

We must remember that the same God who is with us on the mountaintop in victory is also the same God that causes us to have hope and press forward through the valley, even when we may be at our lowest point. The good news is that no matter where we may find ourselves, our God does not change (Heb. 13:8).

Scripture also reminds us that when we are at our weakest point, that is when God's strength shows up (2 Cor. 12:9-10). Although valley experiences are bound to come at some point in our lives, we should never accept defeat because we are already victorious in Christ, "But thanks be to God, who gives us the victory through our Lord Jesus Christ" (1 Cor. 15:57, New King James Version).

God is still God and is in complete control whether you are on the mountaintop, or deep in the valley allowing those unexpected things to come your way to develop your character and push you towards holiness (right living). So get ready because your hills and valleys are on the way!

July 10
WE NEED TO QUIT HAVING CHURCH
Read: Acts 4:31-34

In order to truly understand what the "church" is, one has to look at the terms temple, church and congregation.

First there is the "temple", which is the physical structure or building where individuals come to worship God. Secondly, the "church" is the people or believers that have been set apart for God. And lastly, there's the "congregation," which is nothing more than a gathering of the "church" or believers coming together to assemble in the temple. So, it is easy to see how the word "church" is often misused, and not always fully understood; yet is has a far deeper meaning and purpose.

According to Cooper P. Abrams III, "Today the word church has a wide variety of meanings from referring to a building to performing a religion service...It is essential that we understand its original meaning as it was used in New Testament times. In order to establish a New Testament church we must first know what the word "church" means in Scripture."

The modern day word for "church" was actually derived from the Greek word "ekklesia," which literally means a gathering of "called out ones," which is exactly what we as believers are (1 Pet. 2:9).

The early church was not "called out" to see who was the best dressed at the service, assemble

Thoughts

_____
_____
_____
_____
_____
_____
_____
_____

237

just to have bigger or better programs than the next, or to simply put a check in the box for having attended a worship service for the week; instead the original church came together to meet needs and to serve one another out of love; in other words they assembled to promote positive change.

In Acts chapter four, when believers assembled together and prayed the power of the Holy Spirit showed up as they "were of one heart and of one soul" (Acts 4:32); this is the power that brings about change, hearts that a working to achieve the same vision and mission.

When they (the church) were with one accord, it brought change that affected the lives of everyone assembled to the point there was no lack among them because the focus was on service and meeting every need.

It is essential for us as believers in Christ and as the 21st Century "Church" to remember that going to what we now call church is not about making a name for ourselves or trying to fulfill our own personal agendas; rather it should be about making the name of Jesus and our God great, seeing needs met, and desiring to see lives transformed and changed for the better.

When we come to God's house this is not just a place to have our feelings stimulated or receive an emotional high, and then leave out the door the same way we came in; instead we should consider it a spiritual hospital designed to bind of the wounds of the broken, open the blinded eyes that have been closed by religion, and to set the captive soul free.

So, don't get caught up in the hype of what many say church is all about; it's more than just a dance and more than just a shout. It's time to quit having church so that we can truly BE "the Church" (Acts 2:46-47).

July 11
DON'T GET MAD, YOU SAID IT
Read: 2 Kgs. 7

The Israelites had been overtaken in Samaria by the king of Syria, while simultaneously a great famine also spread throughout the land; this famine was so great that "...a donkey's head cost about two pounds of silver, and a small bowl of pigeon droppings cost about two ounces of silver" (2 Kgs. 6:5, Contemporary English Version). As a result of this lack of food and severe hardship, many even resorted to cannibalism eating their very own children.

Thoughts

_____
_____
_____
_____
_____
_____
_____

Prior to this point the king of Israel experienced much success in avoiding the enemy's plans by taking heed to the voice of the prophet; but now in an apparent attempt to play "the blame game," the king of Israel sought out the prophet Elisha to place the responsibility for the people's lack and misfortune upon him. It was the king's perception and belief that the nation's current plight was directly attributed to the hand of the LORD; therefore, the prophet, as God's direct representative, had to pay for this with his life.

In the midst of scarcity and lack, Elisha received a word from the LORD that provided a glimpse of hope and a promise for restoration and abundance throughout the famine-ravished land. But even upon hearing a word from on high, filled with doubt and unbelief, one of the king's chief officers said that abundance for Israel would not be possible even if the LORD Himself opened the windows of heaven and poured it out from the sky. In response to the negative confession of the king's officer, the prophet simply replied "You will see it happen, but you won't eat any of the food" (2 Kgs. 7:2, Contemporary English Version).

Eventually, just as the prophet had predicted, the tables began to turn in favor of the people as the LORD caused the enemy's army to flee their own camp leaving behind all of their possessions including horses, cattle, and food; abundance and prosperity had been instantly made available.

However, one person did not enjoy the fruit of faith, belief and speaking the right things. And just as Elisha prophesied, the king's officer who did not believe the Word of the LORD as spoken through the prophet but chose to speak out of fear, doubt, and unbelief, saw the abundance but was unable to partake thereof. The king's officer died in a state of lack while seeing the blessing right before him simply because he chose to say and believe the wrong thing.

According to renowned preacher and teacher Charles Capps, "As long as you say what you have, you will have what you say, then you again say what you have, and it will produce no more than what you say."

It is based on the authority that we have been given in the Word of God that we can literally have what we say, more specifically, we can have those things that align with God's will for our lives. This is not suggesting the "Name it, claim it, frame it" mentality, because when we are TRULY connected to God we will only ask for the things that help us to fulfill His will for us in the earth.

Thoughts

Sadly, many of us today continue to say what we based on what we see in the natural, then continue to suffer the consequences. This is the primary cause for much of the defeated and lack-based mentality experienced in the life of the believer each day when victory is just a word away. You have the power to set the course of

_____

_____

_____

_____

_____

_____

_____

your destiny in motion by the words that proceed out of your mouth each day. Don't die without having the benefit of enjoying the best that God has in store for you, according to His Word and yours (2 Cor. 4:13).

July 12
WE DON'T COME CHEAP
Read: 1 Cor. 6:20

There is an old saying that goes "Beauty is in the eye of the beholder;" meaning that the attribute of beauty is "subjective" and that each person can determine what beauty is or is not based upon their perceptions and opinions. Since beauty is often defined by the individual looking at a particular person or object, the question now before us then is how is true value really established?

If you have ever noticed, the finer things in life generally cost just a little bit more than those things considered average and/or mundane. For instance, a Cartier diamond is priced higher than a diamond sold at Wal-Mart; a Bentley Continental is a little more expensive than a Hyundai; or a 10-bedroom, 5-bath mansion in Beverly Hills costs more than a home of similar size in a different portion of Los Angeles. Why is it that similar products are separated by such wide margins in cost?

The difference-maker between the above listed examples and products are the quality and the manufacturer's design. For each of the higher-priced products the manufacturer undoubtedly went out of his or her way to ensure their product was not made with inferior material, but with the very best that life had to offer and that money could buy. And as it pertains to the example of the home and its value, value is not just based upon how the structure is built but location is also an important factor in determining real value and worth; the worse the neighborhood and surroundings, the lower the value.

Well, just as value and worth have been ascribed to things and inanimate objects, God has done the very same thing for those that He calls His own, but on a grander scale. Our value it determined by the quality of the Creator's design and also our current location.

Thoughts

_____

_____

_____

_____

_____

_____

_____

According to Gen. 1:27-28 we were created in God's image. Imagine that, we were created in the very image of the One who set the stars, moon, and sun in their place; the One who created both heaven and earth, and fashioned the intricate details of the entire universe. Yet in all of this, what was really powerful were the statements made by the Creator after He finished designing His long list of masterpieces, God said and "It was good." However, on the sixth day after He created His last work of art/ master design, and that which could have been dubbed or coined the "Mona Lisa or Sistine Chapel" of creation, MAN; it was then that God said "It was <u>VERY</u> good" [Gen 1:31].

Throughout the creation saga in Scripture, everything was created when "God said" or spoke things into existence. However, when it came to man, not only did God speak, but He took personal and intimate time to actually fashion and mold man from the dust of the earth with painstaking detail and then breathed life into him (Gen. 2:7).

Although man was created on the sixth day after everything had been brought into existence, I don't believe that we were an after-thought; No! On the contrary, I would submit to you that God saved the very best for last. God valued us so much that even when man strayed away because of sin, He sent his only begotten Son (Jesus the Christ) into the world to redeem (to purchase back) mankind in order to preserve His valued creation and possession (1 Pet. 1:18-19). In other words, WE DON'T COME CHEAP!

July 13
THE CONCLUSION OF THE MATTER
Read: Ecc. 12:13

There is nothing more exciting than reading a good book, or watching an action-packed movie. With each of the preceding there are main characters that go through a series of events that captivate the reader or viewer, encouraging him or her to continue following the story.

These stories often come with twists and turns in the plot that keep everyone's attention to the point that finding out the outcome of the book or movie is paramount.

And when the storyline is written well and the pinnacle arrives, everyone is usually in awe at the surprise ending. The person portrayed as being innocent was actually guilty, or the couple that everyone just knew would get married went their separate ways. Whatever the plot may have been, it was the conclusion that summed everything up.

Well there is a book that has topped the best-sellers list year after year; a book of exciting stories filled with twists, turns, and cliff-hangers designed to keep the reader's attention more ways than one, yet many fail to acknowledge its significance. This book is God's Holy Word, the Bible.

Every story imaginable can be found in the Bible; stories of action, romance, and of compassion. But more importantly, for the

Thoughts

_____
_____
_____
_____
_____
_____
_____

241

believer, the Bible is the source of practical guidance for our daily living and filled with many examples of how we are to simply serve.

According to Millard J. Erickson, "For a Christian believer living in today's fast-changing world, knowledge of the Bible is important. Knowing how to apply the Bible to present-day situations is equally important. This book will help the layperson experience what the Psalmist wrote: 'Your word is a lamp to my feet and a light to my path' (Ps. 119:105)." In other words, the Bible is not just another book to read, but is a guide given by God for us to follow.

And unlike the standard good book or movie, with the Bible we already know the end and this ending provides victory to the one who obeys what is written therein. King Solomon, who was recorded as being the wisest man to ever live, simply put it this way, "That's the whole story. Here now is my final conclusion: Fear God and obey his commands, for this is everyone's duty" (Ecc. 12:13, New Living Translation).

Although it is absolutely possible and within His power to do so, in our present day and age God does not usually speak to us through an audible voice; instead He chooses to speak to us through life's situations, other people, that still small voice (the Holy Spirit), and of course His Word.

Our job is to simply position ourselves to hear, and then obey what we hear and read according to the Word. One of the greatest attributes that those of us who consider ourselves to be children of God should seek to attain is the ability to follow the example of our Heavenly Father as we purpose to obey and serve out of love. Jesus Christ (God incarnate, in the flesh) is our perfect example of what true servanthood and faithful obedience is all about (Mk. 10:44-45; Eph. 5:1); so choose to imitate Him!

July 14
ARISE AND EAT
Read: 1 Kgs. 19

Throughout the Bible there are many stories that detail both victories and defeat for God's chosen people. And in each case, the event and its outcome was generally predicted beforehand by a prophet or someone who spoke as a direct representative of God, only declaring what God said. Elijah was one of these prophets.

Thoughts

_____

_____
_____
_____
_____
_____
_____
_____

At this point, the prophet Elijah had just performed one of the most amazing miracle and greatest victory in the name of the LORD that had ever been recorded in the Bible, he defeated and completely annihilated the prophets of Baal (idol worshippers) after calling fire down from above demonstrating the awesome power of his God (1 Kgs. 18:38-40)

When a victory is achieved the proper order of things is usually a celebration and then rest, correct? Well, this was not the case for Elijah.

Upon hearing the fate of the prophets of Baal, Jezebel the wife of the evil King Ahab who reigned at the time sought the life of Elijah seeking revenge for the loss of her prophets. Now, one would think that after having single-handedly slain over 400 evil prophets that Elijah would have no problem with confronting Jezebel since he had the ability to just call on the name of the LORD and achieve another victory. So what do you think Elijah did? Instead of standing strong, he ran and hid himself!

Making a near fatal mistake in his choice to run away, he demonstrated a confidence in his own strength and ability as opposed to maintaining confidence, trust, and reliance in the power of the God. He also appeared to have suffered from a type of mild spiritual amnesia in having quickly forgotten everything God had just done for him and through him until he was now physically, mentally, and spiritually depleted. He even began to believe that he was the only righteous person left, as he reached the point of wanting to die just to get away from his current misery.

But God had another plan for His prophet and sent an angel to Elijah with a simple but encouraging message saying, "Arise and Eat" (1 Kgs. 19:5, King James Version). Having been in a state of depression and malnourishment for days, the prophet finally decided to eat that which was provided by God's messenger and thereby received renewed strength for the journey ahead.

Many times as believers we also experience the Elijah-syndrome, we achieve tremendous victories in both a spiritual and natural sense through the power of the God, and then almost immediately the enemy comes to steal the seeds of faith that were sown by inserting fear and doubt into our hearts (Matt. 13:19) making us feel as though we are all alone and no one else understands what we are going through, when this is truly never the case.

The same problems and trials we each individually face are being experienced now and/or have been experienced by others before. In these troublesome times we must remember that God will never leave us alone (Heb. 13:5), He will be with us through the trial, and He will sustain us each day through His Word.

Thoughts

Are you feeling lonely, defeated, and/or powerless today? Well, you don't have to remain that way because you can rely on the strength that only God supplies; so ARISE AND EAT the best meal you can ever ask for and it is absolutely free (Jn. 6:35-38)!

July 15

DID YOU RECEIVE YOUR GIFT?
Read: Lk. 11:13

The date was set, the invitations delivered, and the celebration was fast approaching. The day finally arrived, and just a few hours prior to the event the room was decorated for the occasion—a birthday celebration. The guests begin to arrive; some from near and even a select few who traveled quite a distance for this special day. Everyone begins to mingle, then a few games are played in which the hostess/honoree gives away prizes.

Yes, you heard it right the first time, here was a birthday party in which the honoree and the one that everyone normally brings gifts to was instead handing out gifts and prizes to all who were in attendance.

So, as the party went on, everyone enjoyed a nice meal (not the typical hot dogs and hamburgers normally presented at the average birthday party); but rather roast, chicken, shrimp, etc. And to top it off, paper plates and plastic utensils were not used, instead the hostess brought out china plates, silver knives, forks, and spoons, napkins and the works.

It was the hostess' desire that everyone in attendance experience something different and unique. And although the focus and attention should have gone towards her, it was her wish that everyone departed feeling special by letting them know that they were worthy of the finer things because they themselves had value.

At the conclusion of the party prior to everyone leaving, the hostess personally greeted each guest and asked the following question: Did you receive your gift? Not only did she distribute prizes and gifts to those who participated and/or won the individual party games, but she also presented gifts to each individual just for their attendance. This is actually a true story and I had never seen a birthday party like this before. It was actually from one of my wife's birthday celebrations a few years back, who on her birthday wanted to make everyone else feel special by helping them recognize their value and worth.

Well, many years prior to my wife's birthday event, God acted in similar fashion and did the very same thing for each one of us by sending His only Son into the world, the greatest gift of all (Gal. 4:4-5). It was and still is Jesus the Christ, the One who laid down His own life so that many could experience the very best that God had and still has to offer.

Thoughts

_____

_____

_____

_____

_____

_____

And just before He departed the earth, Jesus literally placed the icing on the cake by leaving us with another gift in the form and person of the Holy Spirit (Jn. 16:7). It is for this very reason that "through Christ Jesus God has blessed the Gentiles (or non-Jews) with the same blessing that He promised to Abraham, so that we who are believers might receive the promised Holy Spirit through faith" (Gal. 3:14, New Living Translation) and then in turn use that gift to be a blessing to others.

Jesus left us all a free gift that we did not have to be conjure up, work for, or earn but only receive; and this gift is ours by promise. God spared no expense for us because He provided us with His very best through the sacrifice of His "One Unique" Son, and the added gift and power of the Holy Spirit. The empowerment of the Holy Spirit has been made available to all who will simply ask and receive. And the fruits of this gift are designed to be given away.

God spared no expense to give us His very best so that we could live eternally. Did you receive your gift? If not, what are you waiting for? Unlimited power is available, is yours for the receiving and is absolutely free (Lk. 11:13)!

July 16
RIDING IN STYLE
Read: 1 Cor. 6:19

Each year in the United States, high school students prepare for what is considered one of the premiere events of the year, The Prom. By definition a prom, "short for promenade, is a formal (black tie) dance, or gathering of high school students."

During this time teenagers and students can be found in malls, stores and boutiques looking for and purchasing that tuxedo, elegant evening gown, and accessories that will make this evening memorable while commemorating this special event with their classmates.

The prom is considered a very major event among high school students, and in many cases parents go all out in sparing no expense to ensure that the event leaves a joyous and memorable impression for their teenager by providing horse-drawn carriages and limousine service of all types with every car imaginable from extended Hummers, Chrysler 300s, to the traditional Lincoln luxury cars.

When this event occurs, parents not only want to ensure that their teenager looks his or her best, but also want to ensure that their precious cargo (their teenager) is also traveling and riding in style.

Thoughts

Well, as believers in Christ, we too have a precious cargo that comes to abide within when we accept Jesus Christ as our personal LORD and Savior; this precious cargo is none other than the person of the Holy Spirit, the third person of the Trinity (Father, Son, and Holy Spirit) (Eph. 1:13).

Scripture also goes on to let us know that we each are in essence temples or vessels for God. "You surely know that your body is a temple where the Holy Spirit lives. The Spirit is in you and is a gift from God. You are no longer your own" (1 Cor. 6:19, Contemporary English Version). And of course we know that a vessel is used to carry or transport cargo or things.

Can you imagine that? As believers we are not only temples or homes for God Himself, but we are also vessels that are used to transport His Spirit that abides within us from place to place wherever we go.

Although it is well within His power and ability to come down from heaven to go wherever he very well pleases; today God chooses to use willing vessels to accomplish His will in the earth. Yet many of us have a lackadaisical attitude when it comes to proper maintenance of the vessel that provides transportation for the Spirit of God. We fail to engage in self-evaluations, get regular check-ups, don't exercise enough, and pollute our bodies with the things that can cause us harm in the long run.

Many individuals take better care of their vehicles and their physical homes, as it is often seen on Sunday mornings, than they care for their own bodies. There are those who spend countless hours washing and detailing their cars, or cleaning and beautifying their homes; but take no time for regular physical body and spiritual maintenance.

Just as a vehicle has a regular maintenance schedule, we must ensure that we are scheduling routine maintenance for our physical and spiritual man as well. God has one physical body to us to give and we only get one life to live. This is why we must take care of our temples today; we have a precious cargo that deserves to travel and ride in style!

July 17
GETTING BEYOND WHAT WE FEEL
Read: Gen. 27

The scene of this story is set around the patriarch Isaac who was growing old in age, his sight failing as he approached the end of a prosperous life and now prepared to pronounce and pass his blessing on to the eldest son.

Thoughts

_____
_____
_____
_____
_____
_____
_____

Isaac had two twin sons; Esau was the first born, and then came Jacob. The custom of the time was to grant the blessing upon the eldest or firstborn son, so by tradition Esau was the rightful heir to the birthright blessing.

However, as he prepared to pass on the blessing Isaac had one last request of his eldest son Esau; he wanted Esau to prepare him a special meal (Gen. 27:2-4).

Esau was a skilled hunter and a rugged outdoorsman who was very hairy; Jacob on the other hand was more smooth-skinned and spent much of his spare time indoors with his mother Rebekah—it can be inferred here that Jacob was more than likely the proverbial "Momma's boy." Learning of Isaac's plan to pass on the birthright blessing to Esau, Rebekah assisted Jacob in devising a scheme to deceive Isaac into blessing him, the second-born son instead.

Rebekah instructed Jacob to go into the flock and find two choice goats for her to prepare a meal. Then Jacob used the goat skin to cover his smooth skin in a deceptive plot by giving the appearance of being hairy like his brother Esau.

The meal was eventually prepared and the scheme was set in motion. Jacob brought the meal prepared by his mother Rebekah to his father Isaac, all the while pretending that he had prepared food as if he were his brother Esau.

When Jacob entered the room Isaac summoned for his son to come closer (Gen. 27:22-23).

Isaac sensed that something was wrong when he heard the voice of Jacob attached to a body that appeared to be Esau. However, because Isaac was going blind and could only really identify Esau by touch and what he felt, the transplanted hair on Jacob resulted in Isaac giving him the blessing instead of the firstborn son Esau.

The lesson that we as believers in Christ can learn from this story is that our Christian walk with God is not based on feeling or emotion; but is based on relationship, and on hearing and obeying the voice of God through His Word that represents Truth (Jn. 10:25-27).

Isaac knew something was wrong when the voice his son did not match the one that should have been in his presence; yet he still chose to act on what he felt.

Many relationships today are damaged and some even destroyed simply because someone chose to act on feelings and emotion instead of the truth heard about faithfulness and commitment according to God's Word, and above all else LOVE.

Just because a husband or wife wakes up one day and may not feel like they are married because of something the other person did or said the night before does not negate the fact that a covenant was made that has more to do with commitment than it did with feelings and emotions. Truth causes us to look far beyond what we feel.

Thoughts

In order to receive the blessings that God places on covenant relationships, we must learn to get past how we feel! When we make decisions based on what we feel, the blessing that was designed for us could be missed and transferred to or obtained by another.

_____
_____
_____
_____
_____
_____
_____

July 18

SET THE ATMOSPHERE
Read: Ps. 100:1-4

Whether we realize it or not, our environment often plays a significant role in our interaction with others and also in our development as individuals. The events that transpire in a particular environment have the potential to set us up for success, or become a negative influence leading to our downfall and demise. Therefore, the right environment and atmosphere are generally advantageous for both personal and spiritual growth.

Now just imagine for a moment, or maybe this has already actually happened to you, that you have gone to visit someone you've considered to be a very close friend. But once you arrived and after going inside to take a seat, the host paid you no attention at all. There was no conversation, no queries for anything you may need (i.e., a drink of water, offer of a light snack, or offer to take your coat). Instead there was no hospitality shown at all.

The average person in this scenario would probably not feel welcomed and undoubtedly not have a desire to return. Because a good host would welcome you in, ask if there's anything they could get you, and even ask if the temperature in the room is to your liking. Granted, there may be things going on one day where a little hospitality may be inadvertently overlooked, with this not being the norm. The bottom line here is that a good host does what is necessary to set the atmosphere to ensure their guests are comfortable, establishing an environment that would cause them to have a desire to return.

This is why setting the physical atmosphere at home, at work, or even at church is important to providing an environment that will cause others to want to return. We all know that if we go to a restaurant where service is given with a bad attitude, there are long delays with getting basic necessities prior to the meal, and the food isn't all that great; we are not likely to return to that particular establishment or recommend it to anyone else.

Just as setting the physical atmosphere is important, setting the proper spiritual atmosphere is extremely essential, especially when we desire a move of God. Learning how to properly set the atmosphere for the presence of God and establishing an environment that creates a place for Him to abide and desire to return to pays big dividends.

Thoughts

_____

_____

_____

_____

_____

_____

_____

Sadly, many times we approach God in the wrong way with a huge list of requests (wants and desires, but rarely needs), praying for hours at a time, yet never see any results. We begin to feel as though God is distant, or somehow afar off; when this is never the case. God does not move, nor does He change; according to

248

Mal. 3:6 He is the LORD and He changes not. What He is looking for is the right atmosphere and environment to move and flow in.

The same words God spoke to the prophet Jeremiah are still applicable to each of us today, we have to seek Him the right way (Jer. 29:13). In his book "The Purpose and Power of Praise & Worship" Dr. Myles Monroe eloquently states it this way, "So often we go looking for God when we could be creating an environment that invites Him to come to us."

Therefore, like a good host, we must begin to set the atmosphere for God's presence through praise and worship; creating an environment for Him to feel welcomed, then ready to move on our behalf.

July 19
IT'S THE BLOOD THAT MAKES THE DIFFERENCE
Read: Heb. 9:22

It seems just like yesterday, even though it has almost been a number of years ago that I attended a community college in the city of Jacksonville, Florida. There was one particular course taken during my time there that I will never forget, the course was African-American History.

It was very interesting and exciting to learn the history of the African-American people, their accomplishments, and their many contributions to society that are often overlooked and not mentioned in standard history books.

But, over time I began to realize the instructor really portrayed everything from an afro-centric point of view no matter what the topic or discussion was, even in Biblical references. One lesson that stood out and that comes to mind was a lecture on names and their meaning. So I brought up Moses of the Old Testament mentioning that his name signified being "Drawn out of water", and how it spoke of his future assignment as a deliver to draw God's people out of Egyptian bondage.

The instructor immediately attempted to turn the discussion by saying Moses was of African descent, and then went even further to say that Jesus Christ was of the same descent, and that life as we know it originated in Africa. It's amazing how quickly everyone attempts to take focus away from the Word by placing emphasis elsewhere.

Thoughts

_____
_____
_____
_____

Although Moses was Hebrew, I do understand that Egypt where he grew up is in Africa. I also understand that the climate of the

_____
_____
_____

249

middle-eastern region where God's people lived during Biblical times would have caused the skin pigmentation to be a bit darker even in Jesus' case, especially since he was a carpenter who would have worked outside in the elements, specifically the heat and sun, which would have caused him to have a bronze complexion.

Even if the preceding is the case there is one all-important fact that remains, we were not redeemed by the shed skin of Jesus, even though His skin was ripped from His body through the intense beating He endured. No! We were redeemed (or purchased back) from the clutches of sin by His shed blood1 Pet. 1:18-19)!

I'm sure that if anyone were to visit the average hospital or medical facility and query the physicians and/or nursing staff about the color of any patient's blood, the answer would return with a resounding "Red". Whether a patient is Irish, Greek, Australian, Arabic, Indian, European, African-American, or of any other heritage for that matter; we all bleed the same and it is the blood flowing through our body that allows us to live.

Therefore, it is a biological fact that it is not skin that supplies life to the body, but the blood—-without the blood, there can be no life. Cultural knowledge and observance is great; however, know today that no matter what the color of your skin is or what your cultural background may be, it is "the Blood" that makes the difference!

"[In fact] under the Law almost everything is purified by means of blood, and without the shedding of blood there is neither release from sin and its guilt nor the remission of the due and merited punishment for sins" (Heb. 9:22, Amplified Bible).

July 20
FIRST ROUND DRAFT PICK
Read: Col. 3:17

The National Basketball Association (NBA) season was impressive to watch a few years ago, especially with expansion teams upsetting and defeating the long-standing powerhouse teams of the league. And being a Florida native, having the Miami Heat win the 2012 NBA Championship made this point even more evident and that much sweeter with the title being brought home to the "Sunshine State."

Thoughts

_____
_____
_____
_____
_____
_____
_____

During my Individual Augmentee (IA) tour to Iraq, I can remember having a conversation at the breakfast table with an Army Chief Warrant Officer (a.k.a. Chief), who is also a brother in Christ, about the NBA play-offs that were taking place at the time. The discussion focused on the fact that prior performance and statistics at the college level, etc. is what determines which round an individual is drafted in.

The smaller the draft number; the greater the player's value and worth—-first round of course being the best and most coveted. This factor also influences the terms of their contract and how much they are paid over a period of time. It is widely known that most professional sports icons are compensated very well for what they do on the court, field, arena, etc; their performance can also bring additional income by way of endorsements and commercials for various products and services.

During our discussion the Army Chief asked a profound question, "What if we in the military were paid similar to professional sports figures; do you think the performance and weekly output of service members would increase? If we were literally drafted by round like sports stars based on our performance, what round would we be drafted in? What kind of pay would our performance bring?" He then went on to say, "I would want to be a first round draft pick, and the best at what I do; better yet, I want to be a first round draft pick for Jesus."

Just imagine what the body of Christ would be like if we all adopted this attitude and said, "Lord, I want to be a first-round draft pick for you." Not in the sense that we flaunt our gifts and talents, but rather that we utilize what we have been endowed with in service to the Kingdom of God and to others (1 Pet. 4:10).

In the NBA, as well as with other professional sports teams, the goal of the coach and players is not only to win the championship game for themselves; but for the owner of the team, the city the team represents and the fans as well. Since we serve an excellent God who owns everything, He deserves excellent service from hearts that are fully committed to accomplishing His will through victorious living and faithful service while we are here on the earth.

Our assignment here is not to accomplish our own individual wills; however, our goal is to do the will of the Father; spreading the Good News of the Gospel and restoring God's blessing in the earth. This requires that we get off the sideline and get engaged!

Now the beauty of this is that we each accomplish this in different ways and in the ability that God has given us individually; in other words, everyone doesn't have to be a pastor, evangelist, prophet, teacher, preacher, priest, psalmist, deacon, elder, etc.; yet each of us is important because God uses the ability that He has given us individually (1 Cor. 12:4-6, 12-18).

Are you a first-round draft pick for Christ, or just a bench-warmer? Simply being on the winning team is not enough; we must all do our part!

Thoughts

_____
_____
_____
_____
_____
_____
_____

July 21
SOWING THE RIGHT THING
Read: Gal. 6:7

A few years ago during an overseas deployment, I had the opportunity to return home for a short two-week break. I was excited about seeing everyone and spending time with my family; however, in the back of my mind I was also thinking about all of the things I normally took care of at home that were probably not being done in my absence. One particular area of concern was the care of our lawn and garden.

I'm sure you can imagine the thoughts that must have gone through my mind with regards to the condition of the lawn since I had been away from home for over seven months, and prior to my departure the fall season had just begun with the grass already browning. In my absence, we normally arranged for someone to maintain lawn, primarily with just cutting the grass; but how many know that sometimes others just don't do things the way that you're accustomed to or based on a set standard.

My first day home I actually arrived late in the evening; therefore, I was not able to immediately see the yard. So, when I woke up the next morning I was eager to see what the outcome of the lawn's condition would be. Well, I must say that I was pleasantly surprised with what I saw.

There was a colorful array of flowers in the garden in the front yard, the grass was greener than I had ever seen it since moving into the home, and the fence line and edges along the side of the house were neatly trimmed and very well maintained. I thought to myself, "This must have taken a lot of time and was probably expensive." But this was not the case.

It appears that my wife had taken the time to plant flowers and vegetables of varying type in the small garden in the front of the house, and even personally aerated and seeded the lawn so that I wouldn't have to do any work during my break (with bruises and soreness that proved that she actually did the work).

This afforded me the opportunity to spend quality time with the family during my short stay at home before returning to complete the remainder of my deployment. Not having to concern myself with yard work and other outside chores resulted in me not consuming precious time. All I could say was "Wow! Thank God for my wife."

Thoughts

_____
_____
_____
_____
_____
_____

What a great example of service and looking towards the needs of another. I was able to enjoy my family during my short break, and also sit and look at the beautiful work that had been put into the lawn and garden.

However, in all of this there's something important to keep in mind, the yard did not get to its current state overnight, but was accomplished over a period of weeks with my wife sowing and planting seeds—not just any seed at anytime, but the right seed sown at the right time. Therefore, as believers in Christ, if we desire to benefit from an end product of a fruit-bearing life that inspires and draws others to Christ, it begins with our service and not only sowing the right seeds, but also allowing the right seeds to be sown into our lives (Gal. 6:7).

In order to achieve this, sometimes we have to look beyond ourselves with our wants and desires, to try meeting the needs of others. Sowing the right this is what determines the harvest.

July 22
SAYING THANK YOU IS JUST THE BEGINNING
Read: Lk. 17:11-19

Jesus always had a remarkable way of attracting those who were in need, but more specifically those in need of healing and deliverance because that's exactly what He was sent to earth to do (Acts 10:38). Wherever He went He could always be found helping those who had been rejected by society or had a particular need, thus fulfilling His purpose for coming in the world.

This was no different when He encountered ten lepers along His journey as documented in the New Testament Book of Luke. He was compelled to do what He was commissioned to do; and that was and still is to execute healing, deliverance and setting the captive free. And as Jesus entered this particular village near Samaria and Galilee, these lepers immediately recognized that deliverance was in their midst and said "Jesus, Master, have mercy on us" (Lk. 17:13)!

Although it was absolutely within His power and ability to do, Jesus did not just immediately heal them on the spot but gave them instructions (in their current condition) to go show themselves to the priests, and as they went on their journey healing would come. This required a great act of faith and corresponding action by demonstrating their belief in following the Master's command to "Go." And as the lepers went on their way, divine healing was manifested just as Jesus said.

With their newfound healing and no longer living as outcasts of society outside the village due to their previous unclean condition, gratitude to the Healer should have been the order of service and priority. I would have envisioned the ten having their own little praise party and then going to Jesus saying "Thank you Lord for my healing!" But even though there were a total of ten lepers healed that day, only one went above and beyond the norm to

Thoughts

_____
_____
_____
_____
_____
_____
_____

253

show appreciation or better yet gratefulness (Lk. 17:15-16). This one former leper made it a purpose to find his way back to Jesus to not only verbally declare but "demonstrate" his gratitude through his actions. Sometimes just saying thank you is not enough.

Each day our Heavenly Father manifests His love for us in miraculous ways through salvation, healing, deliverance, promotions, divine favor, and the works; and though we may verbally say thank you, many times our actions don't truly demonstrate the corresponding gratitude deserved with a life that is fully committed to Him. This is why it is time to move from simple "Thanksgiving" to the point that we begin to pursue "Thanks-living." We must go from just telling God thank you to demonstrating it with our whole being, presenting our very lives to Him as an offering.

Endeavor to make your life a praise and an offering unto God and stop giving Him lip service today, because saying thank you for what He has done is just the beginning.

"So here's what I want you to do, God helping you: Take your everyday, ordinary life—your sleeping, eating, going-to-work, and walking-around life—and place it before God as an offering. Embracing what God does for you is the best thing you can do for him. Don't become so well-adjusted to your culture that you fit into it without even thinking. Instead, fix your attention on God. You'll be changed from the inside out. Readily recognize what he wants from you, and quickly respond to it" (Rom. 12:1-2, The Message).

July 23
IT'S MORE THAN JUST A LUCKY CHARM
Read: Lk. 6:46-47

The night has arrived; celebrities, fans, and media have come from all over for the evenings presentations. Awards will be presented based on the performance of the various celebrities, with multiple categories covering a wide-range of genres. The host announces the nominees; however, of the five potential winners only one can be selected. An envelope is delivered to the host at the podium; the envelope is opened, and a drum-roll follows. The crowd then hears: "And the winner is..."

Thoughts

_____

_____

_____

_____

_____

_____

_____

A winner is announced who immediately proceeds to the stage with a large cross dangling from his neck; he accepts the award, greets the audience, and then proceeds to thank those instrumental in helping him to achieve such a prestigious honor. Then almost as if it had been programmed or scrolling across a teleprompter in front of him, he says "None of this would be possible without my Lord and Savior Jesus Christ."

Yet the award given just happens to be for a song filled with profanity, sexually suggestive lyrics; with the artist just recently being released from jail two weeks prior for alleged sexual assault and indecent exposure charges after a concert party. And then to top it off, he is later found being interviewed in a night club with a controlled substance in one hand and a strong alcoholic beverage in the other. And to think, just hours prior he was giving praise and thanks to Jesus, his Lord?

Although this story has been embellished a little to make a point, if this were a true story this is exactly the type of individual who would become a role model to youth not only in America but all over the world with his actions being the "cool" thing to do. Sadly, this individual does all of this while wearing a large cross dangling from a chain around his neck. What's wrong with this picture?

Today, more crosses can be found hanging from rear-view mirrors; dangling from gold, silver, and platinum chains; and tattooed over various body parts than there are in actual churches themselves. We as a society have relegated the cross of Calvary to become a symbol or charm, making Jesus Christ to be nothing more than a good luck charm.

Sadly, many cars and tattoos are better witnesses for Christ than the owners and/or individuals themselves, individuals who now use their "good luck charm" only when they are in a bind and in need of healing or a breakthrough.

Though none of us have the right to judge others and do not have a heaven or hell to place anyone in, Luke 6:44 lets us know that we will know a tree by the fruit it bears and James goes further to ask the question, "Can a fig tree produce olives or a grapevine produce figs? Does fresh water come from a well full of salt water?" (James 3:12, Contemporary English Version).

The preceding simply suggests that although we should not judge others, we can inspect their fruit. In other words, a person's actions should align with what he or she truly believes.

The cross is not simply a symbol of good luck and Jesus is definitely not our mascot; we must acknowledge Him for who He is and for what the cross truly symbolizes-- death, liberty, and love. Christ sacrificed all by giving up His own life, thereby bringing freedom and demonstrating His great love for all mankind (Jn. 15:13). Therefore, we must go from just carrying Christ to having Him dwell within us; because when He truly abides on the inside, those around will be able to see His Spirit that now lives within on the outside.

Thoughts

_____

_____

_____

_____

_____

_____

_____

July 24
WHO ARE YOU?
Read: Acts 19:11-20

Aside from Jesus Christ Himself, the Apostle Paul is one of the most influential ambassadors for the Gospel in the New Testament. And though he is accredited with having made several missionary journeys to Gentile nations and writing over two-thirds of the New Testament; he is also known for the mighty acts accomplished through him by way of the Holy Spirit—"Now God worked unusual miracles by the hands of Paul, so that even handkerchiefs or aprons were brought from his body to the sick, and the diseases left them and the evil spirits went out of them" (Acts 19:11).

We all know that whenever someone does something great, there's always someone around attempting to duplicate their works, etc., expecting the same and immediate results without knowing the full story and what it took for the individual to get where he or she currently is. There are many "mega-church" pastors/leaders who had very humble beginnings; with everyone seeing the prosperity, anointing, and power of God in their lives now, but don't know where they started (Zech. 4:10).

In Acts 19, seeing the mighty works and of Paul the seven sons of Sceva (a Jewish priest) took it upon themselves attempt casting out an evil spirit, while calling on the name of the Lord; they probably said, "Surely if Paul did it, we can do it as well." Yet nothing happened, so the evil spirit turned to them and said, "Jesus I know, and Paul I know; but who are you" (Acts 19:15)? Or in other words, by what authority are you using the name of the LORD?

Because they had no anointing or authority to do what they were attempting, the evil spirit jumped on the sons of Sceva, overpowered them, and caused them to run away naked and wounded. This is a great lesson and warning to believers. It's one thing to desire spiritual gifts (1 Cor. 14:1) allowing the LORD to develop them in us--because we should; but it's totally another thing to step out into the unknown trying to imitate another's calling or venture into areas without God's power or anointing.

The Apostle Paul was able to accomplish great acts for the Kingdom due to having an encounter with God on the road to Damascus; his life was never the same. Secondly, God had proven Himself to Paul over and over again demonstrating His power firsthand.

Thoughts

_____
_____
_____
_____
_____
_____
_____

If we desire to experience victory in our kingdom walk, we should not just attempt to imitate another's calling, gifts, and/or talents. According to Eph. 5:1 we are to be "imitators of God," not man; this begins with our own personal encounter with God (the Father) through Jesus (the Son) and the power of the Holy Spirit, as we operate in the areas that God has proven in us and anointed us to do.

256

The sons of Sceva tried their hardest to do something they were not anointed to accomplish; as a result they brought harm to themselves and could have caused even greater harm to others. We must know who we are in Christ and be what God has called us to be (2 Pet. 1:10) and to do; if we attempt to copy another's anointing the end result could not only lead to personal defeat, but also potentially bring harm to those connected to us.

Our power does not come from pretending to be something we are not; the anointing only comes from God Himself. It may be easy to copy actions and mannerisms, but we cannot copy the anointing. As I have heard it said, "We may be able to fool some people some of the time; however, we can't fool God."

July 25
YOUR BUSY SIGNAL DOES NOT STOP THE CALL
Read: 1 Sam. 3:1-11

Leading up to today's main Scripture passage, a young woman named Hannah endured the shameful taunting of those in the community because of her seeming inability to have children and bring forth seed. This prompted Hannah to enter the house of worship (the temple of the LORD) for prayer and supplication.

It was during this time of laying her all out on the altar before God that Hannah made a vow to the LORD that if He would open her womb and allow her to bear a child, that when the child was born she would give him back and present him to the God (1 Sam. 1:28). Hearing her prayers and sincere requests, God answered and she brought forth a son whom she named Samuel.

Being very conscious of the vow she made to God and now ready to honor her word, the young child Samuel was brought to the temple of the LORD and placed under the watchful care of Eli the priest in charge of the temple at the time. And as Samuel grew it became very evident the call of God was upon his life as he began to work diligently in the temple ministering to the LORD before Eli.

One night after a long day's work in the temple, Samuel lay down to sleep. And in the silence of night a voice began to call out him. Not recognizing the voice or call Samuel jumped up, ran to Eli and said "Here am I." Now awakened from his sleep, Eli let the young lad know that it was not he that had called for him, and then instructed the young Samuel to go lay down again. But as soon as Samuel lay down again, the same call came to him two more times and in each instance he instinctively jumped up, ran to Eli the priest and said "Here am I."

Thoughts

_____

_____

_____

_____

_____

_____

_____

By this point Eli was undoubtedly becoming frustrated with the many interruptions in the middle of the night that was causing him to lose much needed and precious sleep. In his semi-conscious state, Eli was now beginning to finally understand what was actually occurring; it was the LORD calling out to Samuel. So "Eli said unto Samuel, Go, lie down: and it shall be, if he call thee, that thou shalt say, Speak, LORD; for thy servant heareth" (1 Sam. 3:9, King James Version).

The LORD called out to Samuel again as He did three times prior; but this time Samuel responded, "Speak; for thy servant heareth" (1 Sam. 3:10, King James Version). It was when Samuel became still before the LORD from all of his busyness that the LORD began to reveal the great things He had in store not only for Samuel, but also for Israel as a nation.

Although the Word of the LORD had not truly been revealed to Samuel before his call, there are many believers today who've had God's Word revealed to them but still do not recognize God's voice and/or who are not willing to answer the call.

In today's fast-paced technological age everyone is constantly on the go, we have a tendency to replace moments of inactivity busyness. Unfortunately this 'busyness' often spills over into our spiritual lives. As believers it is very easy to replace devotion to God with a lot of 'spiritual' busy activities, while missing His true call in our lives simply because we do not take time to stop and listen.

Don't replace your devotion to God with busyness, because He patiently awaits your presence in the secret place. His voice is ringing out today (through the person of the Holy Spirit) so don't hesitate, go ahead and answer the call!

July 26
THE WILDERNESS IS ONLY TEMPORARY
Read: Deut. 8:2; Matt 4:1-11

The children of Israel wandered in a Judean wilderness for a period of forty years, but there is one all-important fact we should note, and that is the wilderness described in the Bible does not really compare to what we consider to be a wilderness in modern times.

Today when someone speaks of a wilderness we tend to immediately think of densely wooded areas near rivers, lakes, or streams; places filled with a wide variety of plants, vegetation and wildlife. In actuality, the wilderness referred to in the Bible is actually a desert place, a place of dryness and barrenness.

After their exodus from over 400 years of Egyptian bondage, the Israelite journey through

Thoughts

_____

_____

_____

_____

_____

_____

258

the wilderness was an essential part of their spiritual growth and development as a people. And though they saw the mighty acts of God which paved the way to their freedom through the plagues and ultimately the parting of the Red Sea; many still operated in fear, doubt, and unbelief on the other side.

In order to test his people God knew the wilderness--a desert, barren place--would be the perfect location to execute this lesson in faith and endurance (Please note the operative word here being "test" and not "tempt" (James 1:13).

God's chosen people wandered around in circles in a barren place for years being tested not even knowing where their next meal would come from, how they were going to quench the thirst of thousands of parched throats or where shelter would come from. Although the method may have been unconventional, the Israelites were learning to acknowledge God for who He truly was and trust in His ability to supply provision even when nothing could be seen in the natural.

Their wilderness journey continued until all who did not operate with faith eventually died so that only those who truly believed and trusted in God could cross over into the land of promise. One writer summed up the Israelite plight well when he said, "The Israelite people went through much turmoil and trouble, faced many unnecessary battles and conflicts, and went through many years of hardship and sorrow; all because they did not faithfully follow and obey the leadership of God."

Does this sound familiar? Well it should, because many of us as believers in Christ are still plagued with this same issue today. We have a guarantee of eternal life, we have the sixty-six books of the Bible as our roadmap and the precious Holy Spirit as our guide; yet we often fail to follow and obey God's leadership and direction as we endure trials in our own wilderness experiences.

According to James 1:3-4, we learn to ensure when our faith is tested; therefore, The wilderness allows us to toughen up, so that we can become rugged and strong in our faith in God. In Matthew chapter four, even Jesus Himself endured His own personal wilderness experience for a period of forty days, however, He refused to buckle and just give in.

So, what does all of this mean for us today? Simple, it means that we each will experience trials and/or testing at some point in our walk with Christ, and that we must endure and go through our own wilderness journeys (Jn. 16:33). Yet we can also find consolation in the fact that no matter the length or span of our wilderness experience, the journey is not permanent but only temporary and God promises to be with us through it all (Heb. 13:5).

Thoughts

_____

_____

_____

_____

_____

_____

_____

July 27

THE KING HAS SPOKEN
Read: Is. 14:24

When I was a young boy growing up in Florida, even though there were only a few network channels at the time, I can remember watching a variety of television shows. And each year like clockwork, there were a number of what I would classify as "old faithful" shows and movies that were guaranteed to be aired at least once during the year.

A few examples of these movies and shows are *The Wizard of Oz*, holiday specials like *A Charlie Brown Christmas* or *It's The Great Pumpkin*; *Frosty the Snowman*; *Rudolph the Red-Nosed Reindeer*; and *The Ten Commandments*. In addition to Saturday morning cartoons, these annual specials were something I really looked forward to each year.

Even though I did not grow up in church and I did not truly understand the spiritual overtones and the true meaning of various scenes in the movie *The Ten Commandments* at the time, it was still one of my favorites with main actors Charlton Heston as Moses and Yul Brynner as Pharaoh Rameses II (the king or ruler of Egypt).

Now that I am a Christian and have a better understanding of the Bible, the flow of the movie and various scenes all make sense and this production still tops my list of all-time favorite movies. And even after all of these years there is one statement or quote routinely made by Pharaoh during the movie that has remained with me, it was his declaration of "So let it be written, so let it be done."

There was just something about this statement that stood out to me because it was not just what he said, but how he said it that had the greatest effect. Because whenever he spoke, he did so with power and authority; that is with the power and authority of a king who could back up his words. Whatever Pharaoh declared or promised was carried out to the letter.

Well, just in case you did not know it God has given us His Word in the form of the sixty-six books of the Bible, and in the Bible there are promises made that belong to each of us as believers and saints of the Most High God, our Heavenly King (2 Peter 1:4); these promises now belong to us by right and through faith as sons and daughters of God; heirs to the kingdom of God and heirs to the promise (Heb. 6:17). In other words, God has made a promises that He intends to carry out.

Thoughts

_____
_____
_____
_____
_____
_____
_____

It is God's desire to fulfill every one of these promises in our lives; however, we must first have faith and believe that God is who He says He is (Heb. 11:6), and recognize that He has our very best interest at heart. We must also begin to view God not just as some supernatural cosmic being waiting to execute judgment; but also as a King that we are to reverence, as a Master we are willing to faithfully serve, and most importantly as a loving Heavenly Father because we each have been engrafted into the family by faith (Rom. 11:23-24).

What every "good" earthly father generally wants is to provide what's best for his family and children; so how much more do you think our Heavenly Father desires to give His very best for us (Matt. 7:11)?

Every one of God's promises is available to us today through His Word as we activate our faith. His Word is better than E.F. Hutton because not only does everyone listen when He speaks but there is always a guaranteed return on investment (2 Cor. 1:20). "If God said it, I believe it, and that settles it"—-the King has spoken!

July 28
YOU ALREADY HAVE THE
Read: Mk. 16:17-18

A father instructs his son to complete a few yard chores including picking up branches, cutting the grass, and removing any leaves that were present. The father being the handy man that he was had a garage stocked with every yard tool and motorized component available that one could think of.

And just prior to the father departing to complete a few errands he said to the son, "I don't care how you accomplish the task or what tool you use, just ensure that the yard is finished by the time I return." The son stands there for a minute in contemplation, "What is the easiest way for me to complete this task?"

In the garage the son finds electric shearers, a power blower, and a riding lawnmower along with every other tool imaginable. What do you think? Seems like a pretty simple task doesn't it? Well, that was not the case in this scenario.

Instead of using tools that were suited for each specific task, the son decides to do things a different way. He looks at the fairly new lawn equipment and makes the assumption that surely his father was not authorizing him to use such nice gear.

So, he pulls out a pair of hand-held shearers and begins to cut the grass on his knees, and then uses a rake to gather the small branches and leaves. He literally struggled through this simple chore for hours, and as he was close to wrapping up the last item he looked up, with sweat streaming down his face, to see his father returning.

Thoughts

_____
_____
_____
_____
_____
_____
_____
_____

The Father exclaimed, "Son, what are you doing! This simple task should have been completed hours ago. Either you were goofing off or you have made things much harder than need be. Every tool in the garage was at your disposal and you already had permission to use whatever you needed to complete the task."

Just as the son spent countless hours struggling to complete a task that could have been completed sooner and much easier; many of us as believers struggle for years through the problems that life throws our way and do not manifest the glory that God seeks to get out of our lives simply because we don't use the tools God has already given us permission to use (Eph. 4:8; Matt. 7:7-11).

When Jesus ascended into Heaven not only did He leave us gifts (including the Holy Spirit) that have been designed to be used to glorify the Father, but He also left us His name (Mk. 16:17-18). So why is it often so difficult for God to manifest Himself through our lives?

Here's one possible response to the preceding question: Since a lot of our problems are self-generated due to disobedience and a lack of faith, they really can't be blamed on the devil; however, when the enemy really does come up against us, many times we simply do not know or fail to realize that we have a weapon that is readily available and at our disposal for use at any time, and that weapon is Jesus' name.

But in order to tap into this power and use the authority that we have been given, we must first change the way we see ourselves, renew our minds, and tear down and cast aside any negative thought(s) that contradict God's Word (2 Cor. 10:3-6). There is power in the name of Jesus (Phil. 2:10-11). This means that we don't have to spend countless weeks, months, or even years fighting and struggling with the enemy or with the spiritual principalities of this world. You have already been given the Father's authority, so use it!

July 29
I'M SORRY, I FORGOT
Read: Heb. 8:12

The brain is an amazing organ with remarkable capabilities. However, in certain areas of our life it can be either a blessing or hindrance to us. For instance, a student prepares for a final exam by studying textbooks a few weeks ahead of schedule. Therefore, when the exam rolls around, the student looks at the questions and begins to answer them with ease. Why? Because the information committed to memory was readily available for recall and application.

Thoughts

_____

_____

_____

_____

_____

_____

On the other hand, someone may give an individual a certain task to do; for example, a wife requesting a husband to do something at home. The husband acknowledges the task while watching a sporting event on television but never quite gets around to doing anything the wife requested. When the wife later asks if the task was completed the all too familiar phrase is stated: "I'm sorry, I forgot."

The task was not forgotten because it was insignificant, but because it was not as important to the husband as the sporting event was at that particular time. How easy it is for us to forget those things that are not very important to us. In similar fashion, our past sins are no longer important to God; therefore, He does not bring them up again—-we do. Many of us are tormented by our long-term memories of past failures and sins that have caused us to stumble; this should not be the case.

According to Rom. 8:1, we are no longer condemned but instead we have renewed life through Christ Jesus. So, no matter how many times we may fall short, when we confess our sin God forgives us; "For a righteous man falls seven times and rises again (Prov. 24:16, Amplified Bible). We are not righteous because we keep falling, but righteous because we have a means to receive forgiveness and seek the only One who has forgiveness in His hands.

Therefore, a key point to remember in our struggle with sin is that we must learn to confess it, forsake it, and move on (Heb. 8:12). No matter how bad or unforgivable we think our sin may be, once we confess it God remembers it no more. If God does not remember or bring up our past sin again, then neither should we.

"When the devil tries to remind us of our past; we can remind him of his future!" God is not concerned about our past; He's more interested in our future.

"If we [freely] admit that we have sinned and confess our sins, He is faithful and just (true to His own nature and promises) and will forgive our sins [dismiss our lawlessness] and [continuously] cleanse us from all unrighteousness [everything not in conformity to His will in purpose, thought, and action]" (1 Jn. 1:9, Amplified Bible).

We must learn to stop beating ourselves up, recalling our past memories of failure; stop trying to resurrect the dead, LET THE PAST GO! The next time you bring your past to God don't be surprised when He says: "That's not important to Me; I'M SORRY, I FORGOT!"

Thoughts

July 30

I TOLD YOU IT DOESN'T MATTER
Read: Josh. 2

Instead of pulling out various novels to receive the adventure and excitement that many long for, we actually don't have to look any further than the Old Testament of the Bible which is filled with stories containing humor, action, adventure, suspense and love.

One such story surrounds Joshua (the newly appointed leader of the Israelites) and a woman of questionable character (Rahab, a prostitute who lived in the city of Jericho).

In a covert reconnaissance mission, Joshua (the successor to Moses upon his death, and now the new leader of the Israelites) sends two spies into the city of Jericho to determine what it would take to overthrow the city. Jericho was a well-fortified city with walls that were thick and wide enough to accommodate two chariots traveling side-by-side; therefore the mission of conquering the city would not be easy.

The spies were given instructions to lodge with a certain resident of the city. Now, one would think the spies would have lodged with someone with inside tactical knowledge, or maybe someone who could aid with solidifying their military strategy. But instead the spies were given instructions to lodge with the town harlot, a common prostitute (Rahab).

Well, eventually the ruler of Jericho discovered that the spies were in the city, at which time he instructed Rahab to bring the men to him that he might deal with them; in other words he wanted to dispose of or kill the current threat to his city. But instead of complying with the king's demand, placing herself in a precarious predicament endangering her own life, Rahab hid the spies which later enabled them to depart the city escaping the king's edict and judgment.

I'm sure that many have often wondered, out of the numerous people in the city of Jericho that could have aided the spies, why would God choose a prostitute, a person of immoral character to provide deliverance to His people?

I would submit that this is just a friendly reminder to us that God's ways are not always our ways (Is. 55:8)—-if left to us, we would have chosen a well–to-do merchant, a religious leader or an individual with military influence to assist the spies. But not God, "[No] for God selected (deliberately chose) what in the world is foolish to put the wise to shame, and what the world calls weak to put the strong to shame" (1 Cor. 1:2, Amplified Bible).

God knew exactly what He was doing, because it was in verses 9-11 of Joshua chapter two that Rahab declared her allegiance to the one True God. And it was because of her new found allegiance to God and aiding God's messengers that caused her and her family's lives to be spared once the city of Jericho was eventually destroyed.

Thoughts

_____

_____

_____

_____

_____

_____

_____

According to 2 Cor. 5:17, in Christ we become new creations, this simply means that God no longer sees us in our sin or how we used to be, but now only sees us through the Blood.

The lesson to be learned here is that our past no longer defines us; it is what we do today that really matters and has the most significance. And because of her actions, Rahab went from being a harlot to a heroine. Not only is Rahab listed in Heb. 11 "the Great Chapter of Faith" alongside the great figures of faith: Abraham, Isaac, Jacob, Moses, Joseph; but she is also now identified in the genealogy and lineage of Jesus Christ.

July 31
A WAIT THAT'S NOT TOO HEAVY
Read: Ps. 27:14

For those who frequent the gym; weight and resistance training takes considerable effort, that is, if the ultimate goal is to make some type of noticeable improvement with regards to increased strength and physical endurance.

The key for those seeking to increase body mass is to use heavier weights with fewer repetitions. But for those looking to decrease body mass and tone their muscles, the key is to use lighter weights with increased repetitions. So, when the focus is becoming leaner and getting rid of extra weight, the individual should use lighter weight; something that is a little easier to bear.

I was reminded of this concept a few years ago while attending a worship service and hearing the song *I Don't Mind Waiting* by Juanita Bynum ministered by the praise team. This song stuck with me throughout the evening until the following morning.

The song provided a vivid reminder of how a "wait" can actually help us endure the "weight" of our cares, because not only do we just wait on God, but we also have to learn how to wait in God.

When we are going through specific situations, circumstances or tests and trials; we often find it difficult to wait for God to answer our prayers. In these instances we expect an immediate response so the weight of our burdens can be lifted from us; and then want God to move on our timetable based on our desires and wants.

The aforementioned song reminds us that we have to be patient, wait on and in God, and let Him do that which He has promised to do for us in His Word. Our job is simply to give our burdens over to Him (1 Pet. 5:7). And when we release the weight of our burdens, we are no longer obligated to carry them.

Thoughts

_____

_____

_____

In a live recording of "I Don't Mind Waiting," the singer briefly ministered before singing by

_____

_____

_____

_____

quoting 2 Cor. 5:17, and then went on to say "I'm not just waiting on God, I'm waiting in God." What a powerful statement!

The key words here in the preceding Scripture are "in Christ" and in the singer's statement being "in God."

When we only wait "on" God there is a greater chance and potential that we will attempt to carry the weight of our troubles on our own. However, when we wait "in" God (in Christ), we give our cares and burdens to Him, He receives them and then begins to carry the load for us (Matt. 11:28-30). When we depend on God, He then begins to lighten our load. Our waiting is not designed to frustrate us, but produces an enduring patience; therefore (Heb. 10:36).

Are you tired of carrying a heavy load? If so, the perfect way to lighten your weight and trim down is to cast all of your burdens on God, learn how to patiently wait not only "on" but "in" Him, and then expect Him to move. Choose to wait "IN" God today (Ps. 27:14)!

August 1
WHEN ALL IS QUIET
Read: 2 Cor. 2:11

Watching the human growth process is an amazing thing and a great testament to God's creative power in how He intricately designed all of His creation, especially humans, to develop through various stages in life. However, I believe the early stages of human development are the most interesting, especially the stage of transitioning from infancy to toddler.

In this stage toddlers attempt to assert their independence as they venture out into the unknown; they begin to crawl, pull themselves up on objects, and even begin to stand. It is at this stage that "the child also learns a great deal about social roles, develops motor skills, and first starts to use language." And, inevitably there comes walking; when this occurs, peace and quiet is forever given a new perspective.

Thoughts

_____

_____

_____

_____

_____

_____

_____

It's normally by the age of two that toddlers begin to walk; and as they walk they begin to explore different areas in the home or environment, with the occasional crashing sound of something breaking as a result of the toddler's curiosity. Therefore, a parent is normally at ease as long as the toddler can be heard playing or roaming about the home; however, when it becomes quiet and there appears to be no activity, that is the time the parent should really be concerned the most.

It is during these times the toddler can usually be found in some type of mischief that will cause someone a little extra work that day. You know, finding the toddler under the kitchen table covered in peanut butter, ripped newspaper all over the living room, or the family pet covered in baby powder.

As long as there is noticeable activity and sound from the toddler, all is usually well; however, it's when everything goes quiet that the problems begin.

Similarly, in our walk with Christ, we should be on guard during those quiet times in our journey. Yes, we are to enjoy the abundant life that is promised to us in Jn. 10:10; yes, if we are obedient we can experience God's best (Is. 1:19); and yes, if we obey and serve God according to Job 36:11 we can live a life of pleasantness and prosperity; Yet at the same time Jesus also reminds us in Jn. 16:33 that we "will," not maybe or might, experience trials and/or trouble at some point (Jn. 16:33).

Based on the above Scripture, I would submit that any believer in Christ who never experiences any hardship in this life may want to check their relationship with the Father. I'm not saying that we should constantly experience trouble or consistently be in a trial; but at some point there will be opposition.

Just in case you didn't know it, we are at war——this war wages continually between the kingdom of darkness and the Kingdom of God. In this war there is no middle ground; we are either on God's side or not (1 Kgs. 18:21).

And when we do experience opposition, this may not necessarily come as a result of anything that we may have done, but for the simple fact of Who we have on the inside (1 Jn. 4:4); it's the Word he (the enemy) is after and Who we represent. The enemy attempts to destroy the seed of God's Word in us so that it cannot be sown into others to reproduce more. The devil knows that he is already defeated, so his campaign is to bring anyone who is a threat to his works here on earth down to his level.

Think about it, why would the enemy waste energy, effort, or even consider bothering someone who is not a threat to him or his mission? Therefore, when all is quiet, this is a good time to check your relationship with God.

August 2

GIVE HIM WHAT HE WANTS
Read: Gen. 17:1-6, 15-21; 21:2-3; 22:1-18

Thoughts

The name Abraham is repeated many times throughout the Bible, not only in the Old Testament but in the New Testament as well. Abraham was known for his love and faithfulness to God, and obeying God's commands without question.

267

When Abraham reached the very mature age of ninety-nine, the LORD told him a third time He would establish a covenant with him and multiply him (his seed) exceedingly, and it was in Gen. 17:1-6 Abraham was told that he would be the "father of many nations." Without an heir to carry on his name at the time, Abraham probably wondered exactly how this would all take place.

The LORD reassured Abraham that He would give him a son through his wife Sarah, who was also fairly mature in age being around ninety years old at the time. As time went on, Sarah still had yet to conceive or bear a son. So, in her own wisdom and trying to help God along in the fulfillment of His promise, Sarah devised a plan to give her handmaiden Hagar to Abraham in order to bring forth a son. Abraham agreed, Hagar conceived, and bore a son, Ishmael.

Although Abraham now had a son (who was legally the first born and heir to the birthright blessing), this was not the son the LORD promised.

Well, Sarah eventually conceived and brought forth Isaac, the one God actually promised. There was undoubtedly great joy in finally receiving the son of promise; but after some time had passed, the unthinkable happened. God decided to test Abraham's love and faithfulness in an unusual way, the LORD by requesting he sacrifice the promised son via the burnt offering (Gen. 22:2).

The burnt offering is significant here since, as opposed to the other offerings where only a portion of the sacrifice was presented; with this type of offering the entire sacrifice was completely consumed. This meant Isaac would have been offered in a way that there was no chance for survival or of being revived.

Can you imagine the emotions that must have gone through Abraham as he prepared for a journey knowing he would not return home with the son he loved? What would you do if you finally received the thing that God had promised you, the thing that was dear and precious to you, and then have the LORD ask for you to present it back to him as a sacrificial offering?

With hand in motion, an Angel of the LORD called out to Abraham and said "Do not lay your hand on the lad" (Gen. 22:12). Having demonstrated his faithfulness and love; the LORD provided a substitutionary sacrifice by way of a ram caught by its horns in nearby bushes. The LORD blessed Abraham because he did not hold back and was willing to give up the promised son.

Thoughts

_____
_____
_____
_____
_____
_____
_____

Many of us as believers in Christ try to hold on to the things that we consider precious to us (money, houses, cars, possessions, our gifts, etc.) while offering what we deem worthy; when the LORD is asking us to sacrifice those precious things through acts of love so that we might obtain something even greater.

God is asking many of us to present a sacrifice like Abraham,; to give up those things that we consider precious to us. True love is not just in word, but is demonstrated through action and deed. What are you holding on to today that God has told you to present to Him? Demonstrate your love for the Father today! "Give away your life; you'll find life given back, but not merely given back—given back with bonus and blessing. Giving, not getting, is the way" (Lk. 6:38, The Message).

August 3
YOU CAN'T GIVE WHAT YOU DON'T HAVE
Read: 1 Jn. 4:8

Giving is a beautiful and wonderful act of compassion, and is something that we as believers are instructed to do in God's Word with Lk. 6:38 being one of the more common Scriptures quoted regarding giving.

Although there are several dictionary definitions for the word "give;" there are a few that really stand out: "to put into the possession of another for his or her use," "to transfer from one's authority or custody," and "to deliver by some bodily action."

Based on the preceding definitions, the word "give" can be categorized as a verb; and based on everything many of us were taught in school at an early age, we recognize verbs to be associated with some sort of action. Therefore, when we give there should be some corresponding action based on what we have received.

In a grand marketing campaign to promote a new product, imagine an individual posting flyers all over town which stated that the first one hundred people to arrive at a specified location would be guaranteed receipt of a brand new washer and dryer absolutely free of charge. Many see the flyers and begin to make the way towards the location expecting to receive a free gift; however, when they arrive there are no washers or dryers anywhere to be found.

Embarrassed at his inability to deliver on his claim the individual then states, "I'm sorry that I don't have any washers or dryers to give, I never received my shipment." Through an individual administrative error and a total lack of experience in making bulk purchases and shipments, the items in question were somehow mis-routed to the wrong location and signed over to someone else.

Thoughts

Though his motives were in the right place, it was because of his inexperience that the free gift of the washers and dryers were unavailable to those with a need. Simply put, he was not able to give what he did not have.

_____

_____

_____

_____

_____

_____

_____

Similarly, but in a spiritual sense, many of us attempt to sow forgiveness, utilize our gifts and give love without the benefit of having experienced and/or received true love ourselves. In many instances, we attempt to emulate the poor examples of others based on what they learned from someone else or often learn through what we may have observed in our formative years all the while not knowing that true forgiveness and love only comes from God the Father Himself. "He who does not love does not know God, for God is love" (1 Jn. 4:8, New King James Version).

What this means for each of us individually is that in order to effectively use our gifts and give God's love, we must first experience and receive His love for ourselves based on the seed of His Word being planted within us.

It is an unfortunate thing to have individuals with "titles" as ministers, evangelists, preachers, etc. in the body of Christ who are dynamic speakers able to bring excitement to any worship service and able to do great works performing miracles; yet outside of the church setting these same individuals have no real evidence of God's love flowing through them, and neither is it manifested in the home or being transferred to the next generation.

Before a seed can be planted, it first must be in our possession. To truly give forgiveness, use our gifts and release God's love, we must first allow the seed of the Word to be deposited in our hearts because this is what allows us to share the same with others. You can't give what you don't have!

August 4
A WORD RIGHTLY SPOKEN
Read: Is. 55:11

Have you ever been in a supermarket, mall, or other public location where a parent is just shouting or screaming at their kid for something the child may have done? Granted, the child may have been absolutely guilty as charged; however, the verbal tirade that ensued was totally uncalled for—-followed by words and phrases like: Stupid! Idiot! You will never amount to anything! You are just like your (father or mother)! I wish you were never born!

Thoughts

_____
_____
_____
_____
_____
_____
_____

Many times this verbal bashing is accompanied by every four-letter expletive (or curse word) that one can imagine. And afterwards and almost instinctively, the child cringes, drops his/her head, and begins to withdraw.

Your heart goes out to the child because you immediately see the damaging affect that speaking the wrong word can have, especially on children in their formative years. The wrong word spoken at the wrong time or the right word spoken at the wrong time and in the wrong manner for that matter, can be the difference between future success and utter failure.

This is why the words that we speak are so very important—-words possess power, whether for good or bad. According to Heb. 4:12, "For the word of God is alive and powerful..." (New Living Translation) and Prov. 18:21 declares that "Words kill, words give life; they're either poison or fruit—you choose" (The Message).

Many wars and battles have begun simply because of harsh or wrong words spoken. "A gentle answer deflects anger, but harsh words make tempers flare" (Prov. 15:1, New Living Translation). It is for this reason and absolutely imperative as believers in Christ that we speak the right thing, using our words as seeds to bring life to those who hear them.

However, when God's Word is sown correctly it has no choice but to produce a harvest. "It is the same with my word. I send it out, and it always produces fruit. It will accomplish all I want it to, and it will prosper everywhere I send it" (Is. 55:11, New Living Translation). God's Word in our mouth produces the very same power as if God spoke it Himself, but our words must be spoken in faith and in love.

Instead of using harsh words, let's try speaking a word of encouragement to our father, mother, husband, wife, kids, neighbors, and those we routinely come in contact with; then over time watch the difference a kind word can make.

There are many instances recorded in history where the right word spoken at the right time made a world of difference. Therefore, we each individually have the ability to make a difference in the world every single day with our choice of words.

We all should make it our purpose to shift from using words of gossip, backbiting, and slander to utilizing words that edify, encourage, and empower others to achieve greatness. Words have unbelievable power, so let's use them to build others up instead of tearing them down. And though it may not happen overnight, eventually we'll be able to sit back and watch the positive results.

"Let no foul or polluting language, nor evil word nor unwholesome or worthless talk [ever] come out of your mouth, but only such [speech] as is good and beneficial to the spiritual progress of others, as is fitting to the need and the occasion, that it may be a blessing and give grace (God's favor) to those who hear it" (Eph. 4:29, Amplified Bible).

Thoughts

_____
_____
_____
_____
_____
_____
_____

August 5

IT'S TIME TO GO DEEPER
Read: Rom. 3:23

There was an individual some time ago who was experiencing serious problems with cable television reception at home. So, naturally the cable service provider was called to investigate the issue. A service technician arrived, verified both internal and external connections, checked all visible cables for any bends or splices, and then examined the digital cable box itself. However, nothing out of the ordinary could be found.

The technician then called back to his main office to request information on the cable run for that particular location to determine whether the line was situated above or below ground. Schematics were eventually located that identified the cable as being an underground run.

With this knowledge the technician began to trace the cable but at a certain point the cable began to travel underground, a little digging was required. The cable in question was located with the technician being in shock at what he found. Due to the proximity of the cable to a large oak tree; over time, the cable had become engrafted into the roots of the tree and had begun to deteriorate.

What was the technician to do? Dislodging the cable would not only make matters worse with the television reception, but would totally cut off the communication signal altogether. Doing what needed to be done; the technician removed the cable from the root, ran a new line above ground, and restored crystal-clear cable reception. Although there were a number of symptoms that appeared to cause the loss of reception, it wasn't until the root was addressed that the issue was resolved.

On a spiritual level, many of us as believers often experience similar symptoms. Our communication with our Heavenly Father is often cut-off, not because God is nowhere to be found--because the Word declares that He never leaves us nor changes (Heb. 13:5, 8); but because of the issues and sin in our lives that separate us from His presence. And usually when this sin begins to manifest itself, we attempt to place blame and focus on everyone except the true culprit—-OURSELVES, since the desires that cause us to sin usually come from within (James 1:14).

As a result, we are often guilty of allowing temptation to entice us to commit acts that are contrary to the Word of God even when we know better. This in turn causes us to lose proper focus and deviate from the path that God has already established.

Thoughts

_____

_____

_____

_____

_____

_____

_____

Many attempt to address a lot of surface issues (lying, cheating, slothfulness, lack of integrity and/or character, etc.); but never address the real issue. This is when we must go deeper; this is the time that requires us to deal with the root of the problem—SIN. When we yield to temptation, the end result is always sin.

Therefore, if your communication and connection with the Father has been severed, then quit dealing with the surface issues and get to the root of the matter. It's time to go deeper !

August 6

TRY CLEANING UP, YOU MIGHT FIND SOMETHING YOU NEED
Read: 2 Kgs. 22:3-20; 23:1-3

In the eighteenth year of his reign Josiah, one of the youngest and most righteous kings of Judah directed the priest to conduct repairs to the temple caused by years of neglect. In the process of completing the repairs and clean-up of the temple, the high priest finds the Book of the Law (2 Kgs. 22:8)—imagine that; finding God's Word in God's House where it rightfully should be.

After rediscovering God's Word, King Josiah then read the Book and upon realizing how far the people had strayed away from the commands of God he tore his clothes, demonstrating his sorrow and anguish.

Being the leader and man of God that he was, the king commanded all the people to assemble and he began to read the commandments of the Lord (2 Kgs. 23:1-3). When the people of Jerusalem heard the commandments of God in their ears, they all decided to take a stand to remember God's covenant. True worship of the one and only Living God was reestablished as a result of cleaning God's house and rediscovering His precious Word.

According to 1 Cor. 6:19, we each are considered to be a sanctuary, tabernacle and/ or temple to God, and just in case you didn't know it the words for "sanctuary" and "tabernacle" are actually derived from Hebrew words that mean "be holy" and "dwelling place". In other words, we each have been fashioned and designed to be holy dwelling places for God (1 Cor. 6:19-20).

Therefore, just as our spare rooms and garages in our natural homes occasionally get filled with junk and stuff that seem to accumulate quite rapidly, our spiritual temples often fall prey to the same thing when we allow the wrong things to be brought in. It is in these instances that we must make it up in our minds that we will begin to clean out anything that does not belong there; anything that hinders us from honoring God with and in His dwelling place, which we are.

As we clean, who knows, we just may find a word hidden in our hearts from some time ago; a word that was once precious to us that rekindles a spark and fans the fire from deep

Thoughts

_____
_____
_____
_____
_____
_____
_____
_____

273

within. And the more we continue to clean, the more of God's Word we begin to uncover that begins to show us our true condition, our options are then to either ignore it or choose to make the necessary change.

Let's make it a priority to begin cleaning our temples from the inside, out. You never know what precious thing of value you may find; however, it should never be a surprise to find God's Word in His temple. So try cleaning up, you just might find something you need!

"Create in me a clean heart, O God. Renew a loyal spirit within me. Do not banish me from your presence, and don't take your Holy Spirit from me. Restore to me the joy of your salvation, and make me willing to obey you" (Ps. 51:10-12, New Living Translation).

August 7
WAS IT REALLY WORTH IT?
Read: Gen. 25:19-34

None of us are impervious to temptation, because we are all human beings that have to contend with our emotions and feelings every day, because emotions and feelings have the potential to lead us astray. Whether we admit it to anyone or not, no matter how strong of a Christian we are or better yet think we are; we all are vulnerable to temptation.

The enemy (or the evil one) uses temptation with the primary goal of undermining God's will and plan for our lives, and to get us off track so that we begin to deviate from the path of righteousness and start to follow a path of our own choosing. The story of Esau and Jacob, the sons of Isaac, is a prime example of how yielding to temptation can easily and quickly get us off the established course.

Esau and Jacob were twins, with Esau being the firstborn (eldest) and Jacob the younger brother. Esau was very rugged and a skilled hunter; however, Jacob spent most of his time inside with his mother and was a bit more domesticated——today the common phrase to describe Jacob would be that he was "a momma's boy."

Thoughts

_____
_____
_____
_____
_____
_____
_____

I'm sure that there must have been a healthy competition between the two brothers to win the approval and affection of their father, with each attempting to outshine the other.

One day after a hard day's work in the field, Esau came in and was literally starving, famished, and desperately in need of something to eat. Of course being domesticated as he was and more of a home body, Jacob had been inside preparing the evening meal with his mother Rebekah, the meal was a pot of stew with its enticing aroma drifting in the air.

Smelling and then seeing the savory bowl of stew, Esau's flesh (his fleshly nature) began to speak as he said, "Please feed me with that same red *stew,* for I *am* weary" (Gen. 25:30). Paraphrasing Jacob's response, he probably said something along the lines of, "If you are really that hungry, then sell me your birthright and I'll give you all the stew you want."

As temptation knocked at the door of Esau's thoughts, he opened the door and replied, "Look, I *am* about to die; so what *is* this birthright to me" (Gen. 25:32)? We all know what happened next; Esau gave up his birthright, ate the stew to satisfy a temporary hunger, and then began to despise his brother Jacob when he finally realized what had transpired.

Many of us as believers in Christ often fall for very similar temptations; the enemy plants thoughts in our minds that lead us to seek temporary gratification instead of looking at the future consequence of our actions.

To satisfy a temporary hunger, Esau gave up a lifetime of blessings as he allowed his flesh to lead and guide him. However, the Apostle Paul clearly reminds us in Scripture of the correct course of action in these situations (Gal. 5:16).

Esau allowed temptation (the flesh, feelings, and emotions) to cloud his judgment and thinking as he sought the temporary over the eternal.

Temptation usually begins with a thought; therefore, when our thoughts are in alignment with God's Word, this lessens our urge to yield to our fleshly desires and the temptation that comes our way. So, don't make permanent decisions based on temporary circumstances because it is never really worth it in the end!

August 8
I TOLD YOU TO LEAVE ME ALONE
Read: Matt. 4:1-11

When I was younger I was often the smallest kid in the group with a very slim build (though not much has changed in this area today); I was also very shy and kept to myself. This combination of my thin size and quiet nature made me an easy target for bullies, surely someone of my stature and demeanor would just give in to their requests.

I can remember one individual during my middle school years who constantly attempted

Thoughts

_____
_____
_____
_____
_____
_____
_____
_____

to coerce me into bringing him a certain amount of money every day and then to top it off he would harass me while I was eating lunch begging for certain items of food on my tray. This activity went on for months with me simply trying to ignore this person, but he was really persistent.

It was another normal day in the cafeteria and he approached me as he normally did and began to repeatedly ask for items on my tray. Well, on this particular day I just got fed up and something inside rose up in me. So I stood up, kicked my chair back, and yelled "I told you to leave me alone!!!"

Since the location where I was seated was slightly elevated from the rest of the cafeteria, when the chair hit the floor it made a very loud sound and startled everyone near me, including the bully. I don't know what it was, maybe he thought I was crazy or something but from that point on he never bothered me again. I couldn't believe that all it took was my actions coupled with my words to make a difference in a situation that had plagued me for weeks.

Well, just in case you didn't know it, as Christians we too have a spiritual bully in the person of the "accuser of the brethren," satan or the devil who comes to harass and tempt us? You may be wondering "So how do I defend myself against a bully of this nature? I'm glad you've asked.

To confront the spiritual bullying of the devil, we can simply look to the perfect example provided by Jesus when He was tempted in the wilderness (Matt. chapter 4).

Satan attempted to ensnare Jesus using the same tricks he uses on many of us today by appealing to our fleshly nature, using what we see, and getting us to focus on self (1 Jn. 2:16). Whenever we yield to temptation, it can be traced back to the preceding verse.

It is vitally important as believers in Christ that we get God's Word deep down on the inside of us so that when the tempter comes and we go to draw water from the living well from within, we do not come up spiritually dry. But in order for God's Word to come out of us, it must first go in. "How shall a young man cleanse his way? By taking heed and keeping watch [on himself] according to Your word [conforming his life to it]. With my whole heart have I sought You, inquiring for and of You and yearning for You; Oh, let me not wander or step aside [either in ignorance or willfully] from Your commandments. Your word have I laid up in my heart, that I might not sin against You" (Ps. 119:9-11, Amplified Bible).

Thoughts

_____

_____

_____

_____

_____

_____

_____

Set aside time for daily study and mediation of God's Word. And when the tempter comes again, don't try to fight him in the natural but rather simply say "It is written...," and I TOLD YOU TO LEAVE ME ALONE!

August 9
IT JUST MAY NOT BE TIME
Read: Heb. 10:36

After months of attempts with her husband to become pregnant; the young mother finally conceives and is now excited at the prospect of carrying and bringing new life into the world. She begins to imagine all of the things she will experience in the years to come as this child grows and develops. However, at that she fantasizes about what can be, she is barely five months into the pregnancy.

One day she begins to experience pains and contractions to the point that she is almost convinced that it is time to begin pushing the infant inside of her, out. Doctors warn her against pushing because the infant has not sufficiently shaped into what he or she will be, since the normal term for a pregnancy is nine months.

If the baby were born now, not only would it be improperly developed but there would also be the potential that he or she could suffer serious health risks and future side effects. The young mother heeds the advice of the doctors, endures weeks of uncomfortable bed rest, and then delivers a healthy baby at the appointed time.

There are many believers in the body of Christ who are filled with purpose and destiny, who know that there is a calling of God on their life, and are pregnant with God's anointing that is ready to just burst forth; however, no matter how painful it may be to experience the labor pains without actually bringing anything forth, we must each learn how to hold on and patiently wait for the right time.

It may not be the appropriate time to deliver that which is on the inside yet; because if we give birth prematurely, it could not only adversely affect us, but have long-lasting side effects to those we come in contact with.

We must learn to wait on God and allow Him to develop us so that we can bring forth that which will be a blessing to others, and not a stumbling block.

Jesus Christ and King David are two prime examples of individuals who patiently awaited the promise. Jesus lived in the earth for thirty years before He was anointed and released for public ministry (Matt. 3:16-17). Imagine knowing that you are God in the flesh (Jn. 1:14), having all power and authority in your hand, but being unable to use this power because the timing was not right or had yet to be approved by God.

Thoughts

Then there was the little shepherd boy David and eighth son of Jesse. David was selected by God and anointed by the prophet Samuel to become the next king of Israel around the young age of seventeen; however, though he was anointed at an early age (1 Sam. 16:13), it

277

wasn't until some years later that he actually stepped into the office of king at around the age of 30 years old.

In the Bible, the number "30" is indicative of "Dedication." In both of the above instances there was a period of preparation required before Jesus and David were released for their assignments as they each dedicated themselves to completing the will of the Father and not their own will. It was because of their patient obedience that they were each richly rewarded.

We must learn to not get ahead of God, because the anointing upon us and in us is for the appointed time—-the time appointed by God, not us. God knows what is best (Jer. 29:11). Giving birth too early could not only be detrimental to you, but more importantly it could be harmful to others. We must learn to be patient and wait on God's timing.

August 10
HER BEAUTY SURPASSES THEM ALL
Read: Is. 33:6

If the average man were asked to describe qualities that he would like most in a woman, I'm sure that one of the first characteristics he would identify is beauty. Unfortunately, for the average man it is the outward appearance that often attracts him to one woman over the next, when there are other qualities that are far more important. This could even be seen in the choices of great men in the Bible who pursued women for outward beauty.

Now there were a number of women in the Bible who possessed true natural beauty; these were also women who either did great things for God or were instrumental in their influence on great men of faith: Sarah (Gen. 12:11-20), Rebekah (Gen. 24:15-25), Abigail (1 Sam. 25:1-3), Bathsheba (2 Sam. 11:1-5), Vashti (Esther 1:11-12), Esther (Esther 2:5-8), the daughters of Job (Job 42:15), just to name a few.

And then there was Rachel (Gen. 29:15-31), the wife whom Jacob loved so much that he worked 14 years of free hard labor just to win her hand in marriage. Scripture even raved of her attractiveness as it stated that "Rachel was beautiful and had a good figure (Gen. 29:17, Contemporary English Version). There are not too many instances in the Bible where a female is described in such terms. I'm sure that if the R & B group "The Commodores" from the 70's and 80's would have been around at the time they would have definitely called and classified Rachel as a "Brick House."

Thoughts

_____
_____
_____
_____
_____
_____
_____

Although the above women possessed astounding, head-turning beauty; there is still one who surpasses them all. Not only did she cause King Solomon to be recognized as one of the greatest men of the Bible; but she was also with God in the beginning as He established the foundations of the earth. Who is she you might ask? WISDOM!!! "For wisdom is better than rubies, And all the things one may desire cannot be compared with her" (Prov. 8:11).

According to Jer. 10:12, "[God] has made the earth by His power, He has established the world by His wisdom, And has stretched out the heavens at His discretion," and "Through wisdom a house is built, And by understanding it is established" (Prov. 24:3).

Relationships, friendships and our happiness should not be built on just the external-- because this does not or will not last. Happiness, joy and true fulfillment in relationships do not come from external things, but from that which is within (Prov. 3:13).

We must all go beyond being wooed by what we see externally, and learn to appreciate the truly valuable traits of those we connect and establish relationships with, with WISDOM being the principal trait. Not just an earthly wisdom, but a wisdom and internal beauty that only comes from God.

"Looks aren't everything. Don't be impressed with his [or her] looks and stature...GOD judges persons differently than humans do. Men and women look at the face; GOD looks into the heart" (1 Sam. 16:7, The Message).

It's time to go beyond looking without to looking within; choose true beauty—-with it comes long life and heavenly riches (Prov. 3:16); "Wisdom is the principal thing; Therefore get wisdom" (Prov. 4:7). Choose the only one with beauty that never fades, and build relationships and friendships on the right foundation today allowing wisdom to be your guide. This is real "Beauty by the BOOK," not based on worldly standards but established on God's standards looking not without, but instead looking within (Is. 33:6).

August 11
MAKE SURE YOU'RE PUTTING ON THE RIGHT THING
Read: Is. 61:3

Every morning that we awake, we have the ability to set in motion the course of our day. We can accomplish this by how our day is started.

We can either wake-up filled with ingratitude, complaining about the trials we may be experiencing or circumstances that have arisen;

Thoughts

or we can simply make the choice that no matter what may be happening, we are going to start the day with praise and thanksgiving. However, our praise to God should not just be contingent on what He has done or even for what He is going to do, but just for who He is.

For most, the usual morning routine may look something like this: we brush our teeth, take a shower (or bath), comb and/or style our hair, lay out or pick our clothing for the day, and then eventually get dressed. In most, but not in all instances, this is done without taking one second to give God thanks for the ability to live to see another day.

God gives us new mercies every single day; for that fact alone we should be thankful (Lam. 3:22-23).

Choosing to look at our lives and all the negative things that may be occurring around us and in the world in general, when we don't have the proper perspective and right attitude, has the potential to send us into a state of hopelessness, and in many cases depression. This in turn causes us to walk around frustrated, angry, and upset with our heads hung low, because we allow our issues and circumstances to be placed on our shoulders as we focus on the problem rather than on the Problem-Solver.

This is why we have to be willing to admit that we don't know everything and that there are just some things that are bigger than us. This requires us to humble ourselves and seek divine guidance from above.

Although God works on our behalf even when we don't praise Him (Matt. 5:45); it is our willingness to humble ourselves as we seek Him for clarity and direction, and our praise that begins to invite Him to move on our behalf even the more.

It is in this time He reveals to us that He is greater than we can ever imagine, He is much bigger than any problem we face and well-equipped to handle each issue. When we begin to lay aside our cares and burdens, and begin to magnify the LORD, every one of our problems and issues begin to seem miniscule and pale in comparison to the Majesty of our God (Ps. 34:3).

But in order to magnify the LORD, we have to approach Him with humble hearts as we place less emphasis on what we are going through, and a greater focus on how magnificent our God is.

Another important fact to note is that our praise may not change the situation or circumstance, but will often change us in the midst of our struggle until we recognize God for who He is and for what He is capable of doing (1 Cor. 2:9)!

Yet this requires action on our part, and that is by starting the day out with putting on the right things. This sets the atmosphere for the course of that day.

Thoughts

_____
_____
_____
_____
_____
_____
_____

So, make it your purpose to start the day off right. When you wake-up each morning instead of putting on frustration, heaviness, and grief; begin to properly clothe yourself, and make God bigger than anything that may be before you as you adorn yourself praise (Is. 61:3).

August 12
HOW DEEP IS YOUR LOVE?
Read: Gal. 5:13

A father is excited about the opportunity of spending an entire day with his young five-year old son. Between work and other obligations, the father had not been available at home much thus preventing him from spending any one-on-one quality time with the family and his only son.

One day, when job activity was expected to be a little slow, the father decided to bring his son with him to work to showing him exactly what his father did when he left for home each morning. The father was a draw bridge control station technician/operator; his particular station controlled a bridge that provided a path for a very long stretch of railroad.

It was a beautiful June summer day when the father and son duo arrived at the job site. Inside the control booth the father enthusiastically showed the son how to operate the various controls even allowing him to flip the switch and turn the control for a brief demonstration of bringing the bridge to the up position.

The father and son both went outside to see the bridge in its raised state; but all of a sudden a look of panic and alarm was displayed on the father's face as he heard the whistle of a fast-moving train approaching in the distance. So he grabs the son and immediately returns to the control tower to lower the bridge before the train approached.

The father then took his position in the control booth, and prepared to lower the bridge demonstrating the sequence of actions to the son. But when the father looked around, his son was nowhere in sight. Arrival of the train was imminent and the son had wandered off. The father then looked out of the control booth window only to see his son standing in the precise position that the draw bridge would land once it was lowered.

Thoughts

The father was faced with a dreadful decision, he could leave the bridge up causing the hundreds of people on the train to die, but spare his son's life; or he could lower the bridge killing his son in the process, but spare the lives of a multitude of people.

_____
_____
_____
_____
_____
_____
_____

The father stopped for a moment, said a quick prayer, cried out "Son, I love you," and then lowered the bridge. With only seconds to spare, the train crossed the bridge safely sparing the lives of all who were onboard. But sadly in the process, the loving father lost his only son. And though the father deeply loved his son, he knew the son's sacrifice was necessary to save and spare many.

This is what our Heavenly Father did for us; He sent His one and only unique son into the world so that many could be saved and spared from destruction (Jn. 3:16). And according to Eph. 5:1 we are to be imitators of God; therefore, as we imitate God, we too must learn how to demonstrate love the same way He does (1 Jn. 3:16).

God may not be asking us to physically lay down our lives for another person today, but He does require us to demonstrate His kind of sacrificial love to those closest to us and even to those we routinely come in contact with in an average day. True love is demonstrated in action, not just in word. Many times demonstrating this kind of love will cost us something; requiring a sacrifice of our resources, our talents, and most importantly our time. But it is truly worth it in the end (Gal. 5:13)!

August 13
YOU DON'T HAVE TO LOSE SLEEP ANYMORE
Read: Ps. 121:4

For some unknown reason, a young Christian couple began to experience trouble in their marriage. And then one day out of the blue the wife says to the husband, "I am not happy in this marriage." Of course an argument (oh, I mean discussion) began with both trying to get their points across; the bottom line being that the wife was not happy, feeling as though she had missed out on enjoying life because of having children at an early age.

As a result, the wife began to focus on her and her alone, with little regard to what was going on at home. She began to do all of the things that she thought would bring her happiness and satisfaction; going to parties, concerts, and staying out hanging with the wrong crowds to all hours of the night and early morning. The husband was left to care for the young children and all the affairs of the house; ensuring that everyone was dressed and ready for school and for church each week. He also remained faithful in doing the only thing he knew to do in the situation; to pray.

Thoughts

_____

_____

_____

_____

_____

_____

One night or early morning after an evening out on the town, the wife came home to find the husband sleeping soundly and peacefully. Feeling a bit bewildered, she awakened the husband to ask how could he possibly sleep not knowing where his wife was or what she was doing; surely he must not love her. The husband rolled over and replied, "Whatever is going on with you is out of my hands, so I've decided to pray and give it over to the LORD to let him work it out. The Scripture says that He does not sleep nor does He slumber; so I just figured there was no reason for both of us to be up."

If we believe that God is who He says He is, and we know that He is on the throne working things out on our behalf according to His will, then there really is no need for us to worry or to get upset. "He won't let you stumble, your Guardian God won't fall asleep. Not on your life! Israel's Guardian will never doze or sleep" (Ps. 121:4, The Message).

What a wonderful revelation, this is a truth we all as believers should cling to. The husband resolved not to waste precious sleep worrying about things he had no control over or things he could not change; he chose to rest in God, giving it all over to Him because our God is faithful.

It can become customary for us to consistently lose sleep over situations and circumstances we currently face that are beyond our power to change; we lay awake at night attempting to count sheep, cows, goats, lambs, or whatever we can think of in an attempt to get a good night's sleep. Many times we even go as far as to take pills designed to induce sleep, believing that this will bring the rest and peace we so desperately long and are searching for; when actuality all we really need to do is cast our cares and burdens upon God (1 Pet. 5:7) and allow Him to bear them (Matt. 11:28; Phil. 4:6-7).

August 14
FREE MEDICINE WITH UNLIMITED REFILLS
Read: Prov. 17:22

When my children were younger, as kids often do, they would occasionally get sick or require the attention of a doctor. I can remember visits to the naval hospital/clinic in the area, or to a Tricare healthcare provider to have their symptoms evaluated. Upon completion of the evaluation the physician would provide us with his or her diagnosis, which was usually accompanied with a prescription for the acute symptoms or condition.

Thoughts

With the prescribed quantity and periodicity of dosage, the medicine was taken until it was nearly depleted, especially when antibiotics were given. At this point, if the condition still persisted, we would call the phone number

283

listed on the bottle to request a refill. And within a day or so a fresh supply of medicine was readily available.

Well for the believer, in addition to God's Word, there is a medicine that is also absolutely free and readily available; this medicine is laughter.

According to Prov. 17:22, "A cheerful heart is good medicine, but a broken spirit saps a person's strength" (New Living Translation). The "cheerful" described in the preceding Scripture is indicative of laughter, and just in case you were not aware it has been scientifically proven that laughter actually has real medicinal value. Let's take a look.

Although laughter can be a great source of relief to the believer or individual in general, I'm not advocating that anyone stop taking any prescribed medicine, because there is nothing wrong with taking medicine. Yes, as believers we are healed by Jesus' stripes (Is. 53:5) and are to operate in faith, but it is also God that gives physicians the wisdom needed to make proper diagnoses and prescription of the right medicine (Prov. 2:6).

Therefore, when an individual has a persistent condition that requires medicine, it would be wise to continue taking the medicine while simultaneously confessing healing and exercising faith. Again, whether to take medicine or not is a matter of individual preference, between the individual and God.

So, whenever you begin to feel down, discouraged, or under the weather; bring your condition to the LORD and try taking a healthy dose of God's Word and laughter. This medicine will boost your spirit and encourage your soul, and the best part of all is that this medicine is absolutely free and has unlimited refills.

"He will once again fill your mouth with laughter and your lips with shouts of joy" (Job 8:21)," because "the joy of the LORD is your strength" (Neh. 8:10)."

August 15
MORE THAN A FATHER
Read: Matt. 7:9-11

Thoughts
_____
_____
_____
_____
_____
_____
_____

Good relationships are key components to life in God's kingdom. From the very beginning it was God's desire to have relationship with His creation mankind above all other created beings; it was God's desire to create a family. God is more than just an omnipotent (all-powerful), omniscient (all-knowing), omnipresent (everywhere at once) being sitting on heaven's throne waiting to execute judgment; He is our loving Father.

The fact of the matter is that God wants relationship with the crown of His creation, man. When he created everything prior to man, and was finished the Scripture records that "It was good." However, when God created man, His very own prized possession, the scripture said that when God saw what He had made "It was VERY good" (Gen. 1:31). Everything that God has put in place and established for man is centered on His desire for fellowship and relationship.

Our fellowship was broken by sin in the Garden of Eden (Gen. 3:6); therefore, God sent His son into the world to restore fellowship so that He could once again have His family back. And as our Father, God wants us to have and experience what is best for us (Matt. 7:9-11).

There are many today who were not fortunate to have a father around growing up, had a father who was physically there but emotionally detached, or have fathers who are no longer here and have passed on. Whatever the case may be, we can find consolation in the fact that through the shed blood Jesus Christ we are now adopted into the family of God and have a Heavenly Father, and a new Daddy. Another important fact to remember is that in the legal process of adoption, the adopted child has the same rights to a father's inheritance as those who are naturally born to him.

Being a father of four daughters I only want what is best for my children, and when they have a need or request, as long as it is within my power to do I will see to it that the need is met. And for me, many times I can tell how important the request is by how my daughters address me. When they have a request and address me as father, to me it sounds a little official and somewhat impersonal; but when they say "dad or daddy," I know the request is important or is something they really need. This usually determines how I respond.

When we approach God not just as a distant Father but as our loving Dad, I can imagine this also prompts Him to move on our behalf even the more; but this begins first with finding joy and fulfillment simply in who He is and not just what He can do for us (Ps. 37:4).

So, begin to see God not just as your Heavenly Father, but also as a loving Dad who delights in not only meeting your need, but granting the deepest desires of your heart (that align with His will for your life) because He's more than just a Father!

"This resurrection life you received from God is not a timid, grave-tending life. It's adventurously expectant, greeting God with a childlike "What's next, Papa [Daddy]?" God's Spirit touches our spirits and confirms who we really are. We know who he is, and we know who we are: Father and children. And we know we are going to get what's coming to us—an unbelievable inheritance" (Rom. 8:15-16, The Message)!

Thoughts

_____

_____

_____

_____

_____

_____

_____

August 16

I'VE FALLEN, BUT I CAN GET UP!
Read: Prov. 24:16

In the late 1980s and early 1990s there was a popular television commercial in the United States for a medical alarm and protection company called "LifeCall." This company provided a system designed primarily to aid senior citizens.

Users of the system would receive a pendant (with a self-contained microphone) that when activated would enable the user to verbally call out and speak directly to a dispatch service without the need to physically reach a telephone—assistance or emergency services would then be available in minutes.

Again, this service primarily targeted senior citizens who lived alone, those who might one day require emergency medical assistance when no one else was around to provide help; and though they may not have been able to reach a phone, the activated pendant summoned the help they needed. The catchphrase for the commercial was "I've fallen and I can't get up!"

As believers in Christ, we all at some point in time experience hardship, persecution, test, trials (Jn. 16:33), or may even give in to temptation that leads to sin (James 1:14). We fall and just like the senior citizen who is alone with no one around to provide assistance, we give in to the assumption that we can't get back up; but, in actuality the help we need is already there.

Exactly what is a person to do when he or she finds themselves in the predicament of yielding to sin (whatever that sin may be) as feelings of guilty creep up with the enemy constantly attempting to bring up the past by highlighting former deeds and/ or sinful acts? Should this individual just stay down wallowing in self-pity, shame, and condemnation? No! When we fall we each have the ability to get back up and re-engage again as we remember that we are no longer condemned (Rom. 8:1).

According to Prov. 24:16, "For a righteous man falls seven times and rises again;" this means that no matter how many times we slip-up, no matter how many times we give in to temptation; when we confess our sin and get it right with God, we can get back up again (1 Jn. 1:9).

Thoughts

_____

_____

_____

_____

_____

_____

_____

However, though we are freely given God's grace when we do fall, we must never use this grace as a "blank check" to continue in sin; "Well then, since God's grace has set us free from the law, does that mean we can go on sinning? Of course not" (Rom. 6:15, New Living Translation)! But, when we do fall, we can call on One who is much better and provides a quicker response time than "LifeCall;" we can call out to say: "Jesus! I've fallen and I need your help to get back up!"

Even though you may fall down, you don't have to remain there—when family and friends are nowhere to be found, activate your "ChristCall", and then He will come to your rescue because He is already there (Heb. 13:5). It is never too late to get back up and continue moving forward; because God knows your potential and still has a plan for your life (Jer. 29:11).

August 17
SPEAK NOW OR FOREVER HOLD YOUR PEACE
Read: Lk. 19:37-40

All of the wedding guest had arrived and were seated; and as they looked around, everyone was in awe with the great extent of detail and designing that had been put into making the ceremony a memorable day for the bride, the wedding coordinator received rave reviews from all who were in attendance.

The hour was now at hand for the bride to make her grand entrance from the outer foyer area into the main sanctuary. The guest all stood to their feet in anticipation as the processional song began to play.

The bride was elegantly arrayed in a white diamond-studded gown with a train that seemed to flow for miles behind her; holding on to the arm of her father, she proceeded down the aisle to the bridegroom who waited patiently to receive his bride. The journey short journey came to an end and she now stood before the man that she had prayed and longed for. The minister said a prayer and the wedding ceremony began.

Both the bride and the bridegroom exchanged their vows, and then the minister said, "If any of you has reasons why these two should not be married, speak now or forever hold your peace." The bride and the bridegroom each took a deep breath and inwardly said a quick prayer hoping no one would object to their union.

With nothing heard there was a quick sigh of relief from the two. The minister then said "By the power (or authority) vested in me, I now pronounce you husband and wife." The union was complete and the celebration began.

When a man and woman are married, there is usually a connection and both individuals generally have things in common.

In the Bible the "Church" (its people—the saints of God) are often referred to as the bride of Christ, with Christ Himself being the bridegroom (Is. 61:10). The picture being presented here is that of the Church standing

Thoughts

_____
_____
_____
_____
_____
_____
_____

by ready as a bride waiting at the altar for the coming (or return in this case) of the Bridegroom (Christ).

When the Bridegroom returns there will be rejoicing and praising by some, or sadness and sorrow at the prospect of eternal damnation for others. The choice is totally up to each of us individually to either accept or reject Christ; but nevertheless, the choice will have to be made (2 Cor. 15:10).

Lk. 19 provides a foreshadowing of Christ's triumphal return to claim His bride; the Scripture describes Jesus as He prepared to enter Jerusalem before His crucifixion. Along the road there were many of His disciples (followers of Christ) who rejoiced and praised at His coming. However, the Pharisees began to rebuke the disciples for making such a scene for the Master. Jesus then replied, "I tell you that if these should keep silent, the stones would immediately cry out" (Lk. 19:40).

In other words, if the disciples or no one else praised the LORD at His coming, the very rocks and stones they were standing on would come to life and given Him praise because He is worthy of all praise (2 Sam. 22:4).

Are you prepared to receive the LORD with rejoicing and praise at His coming? Does your lifestyle reflect one that is worthy of similar praise? Then prepare for the union and make a choice to effectively serve today. Your actions speak much louder than words, so "Speak now or forever hold your peace."

August 18
ACTIONS SPEAK LOUDER THAN WORDS
Read: Acts 3:1-10

A certain man crippled since birth was carried daily to a gate at the Temple entrance. He was positioned there for the purpose of begging for money as devout Jews and Gentiles entered and exited the house of the LORD.

Having been in this condition and placed before the Temple entrance for many years, many of the Pharisees, Sadducees, and other religious leaders obviously looked at this man everyday seeing his need, but did nothing to render assistance—-since they were focused on what they were going to do, primarily focused on getting to the temple to worship God without realizing that they were actually missing an opportunity to worship God in a practical way.

Thoughts

_____
_____
_____
_____
_____
_____

Day after day, week after week, month after month, and year after year, this man sat at the gate called Beautiful begging, seeking assistance, or just looking for that glimmer of hope that surely someone would provide a helping hand.

Then finally one day as Peter and John, disciples of Jesus Christ, prepared to enter the Temple during the afternoon hour of prayer, they stopped to focus their attention on this beggar. I can imagine seeing the lame man grabbing at their cloaks as they attempted to pass by with him repeatedly saying, "Do you have anything that you can give a crippled man like myself? I have no family or any source of income, and I'm begging you to please help me?"

Peter and John stopped, then Peter said, "Look at us;" (Acts 3:4) I don't have anything monetarily to give you, but I do have something that is so much greater. Peter then took the man's hand and said, "In the name of Jesus Christ of Nazareth, rise up and walk" (Acts 3:6)!

Scripture records that immediately the bones in beggar's ankles and feet received new strength. Money or handouts were not what the man needed; what he required was the life-changing power that only comes through the power and authority of Jesus Christ, the Word and the Spirit all operating together. Peter and John demonstrated true worship in a practical way by stopping to meet a real need.

This same power is resident in each of us as believers today (1 Jn. 4:4); however, it requires that we activate our faith to initiate this Source from within. We do this by demonstrating our love for our neighbor (Phil. 2:12); a neighbor is not just someone who lives next door to us, but is considered to be anyone we encounter who may be in need or have a need (Lk. 10:27).

If at the close of a worship service you observe an individual who did not come forward when the invitation was given but still seemed somewhat distressed in need of some form of ministry, but your stomach was empty and you are looking forward to eating a well-deserved meal and beating the crowd out of the parking lot—would you be sensitive to the need at hand or make filling your stomach the priority?

It is very easy for each of us to get so focused on our personal wants, desires, and agendas that we sometimes miss the bigger picture of helping others. We enjoy going to worship services to learn about God so that we can become more like Jesus, yet many rarely put into practice anything learned inside the four walls of the church. What good is learning about love and compassion if we never begin to demonstrate it? True ministry begins when we exit the doors of the church; the world is our mission field (Matt. 28:19). ACTIONS REALLY DO SPEAK LOUDER THAN WORDS!

Thoughts

_____

_____

_____

_____

_____

_____

_____

August 19

THE JOY OF PAIN
Read: Heb. 12:1-4

Today, there are more exercise programs and new weight loss methods than ever before. Whether one is a novice or an avid fitness enthusiast, there's something available for anyone who is willing to put forth the effort.

And when summer months approach gyms all across the United States and around the world begin to fill at a rapid pace with patrons making preparations for their annual pilgrimage to various beaches. Many go to the gym attempting to lose weight, some go just to maintain a basic level of fitness and remain tone, and then there are those who go for the express purpose of obtaining the proverbial wash-board abs. Whatever the motive or goal maybe, statics prove that gym membership and general use during certain times of the year increases drastically.

Yet, there are many who do not agree with this focus on the gym and exercise; that is those in this instance could labeled here as "Super Saints" who feel that exercise is not all that important while using Scripture as their basis quoting 1 Tim. 4:8, "For bodily exercise profiteth little: but godliness is profitable unto all things…"

Their belief is that our entire focus should solely be on the spiritual aspects of godliness, with no regard to our physical well-being, which I would submit is only partially correct. Taking and using this particular verse literally and in this manner would be to take the Scripture out of context.

1 Tim. 4:8 does not say that exercise profits "nothing," but says that bodily exercise profits a "little," meaning that although the focus should not just be on physical fitness, there is benefit in exercise.

Research indicates that "Being physically fit not only helps people live healthy lives, it also helps people live longer…doing some kind of physical activity or exercise on a regular basis helps to increase strength and flexibility, improve endurance, control weight, increase bone mass, and improve self-esteem, as well as reduce stress, anxiety, depression, and the risk of developing high blood pressure." However, achievement of these milestones will require some work and sacrifice on the part of the individual.

Thoughts

_____
_____
_____
_____
_____
_____
_____

Obtaining a specific level of fitness may require a sacrifice of time, a sacrifice and laying aside of those favorite and tasty high-calorie dishes or desserts, and lastly, this may even require the body to experience a little pain to accomplish the ultimate goal. But when the end result is achieved, joy is produced.

Jesus Christ provides another example of joy that was achieved through pain in His sacrifice on the cross. Although His body was beaten, battered, and bruised for our sin, the end result of His pain and sacrifice produced great joy (Heb. 12:1-4).

Jesus' pain, suffering, and sacrifice not only brought joy to the Father, but also now brings joy to all who call upon His name, in faith. He demonstrated what it truly means to humble ourselves and endure a little suffering in service that ultimately brings others joy through our sacrifice. Service in God's Kingdom requires a degree of commitment and sacrifice. Therefore, just as our sacrifice for the sake of physical fitness while enduring temporary pain can benefit our overall well-being; a sacrifice of our service and temporary discomfort for the sake of others produces and yields great results for God's Kingdom (Rom. 12:1).

August 20
ALL DOUBTERS AND HATERS MUST GO
Read: Matt. 9:18-20, 23-26, 32-35

As Jesus went about doing what the Father sent Him to earth to do, "teaching in their synagogues, preaching the gospel of the kingdom, and healing every sickness and every disease among the people" (Matt. 9:35); a ruler came to Him who was in much need of divine intervention, his daughter had just died so he came worshipping Jesus looking for a miracle.

The ruler said, "My daughter has just died, but come and lay Your hand on her and she will live" (Matt. 9: 18). That in and of itself is a powerful statement of faith; beyond what he saw in the natural, he knew Jesus had the power to resurrect his daughter with just one touch and with His words. So, Jesus and His disciples journeyed to the ruler's home.

When they arrived, the normal commotion of the crowd of wailers was present as they went through their ritual of mourning. Jesus entered the home then said, "the girl is not dead, but sleeping" (Matt. 9:24). Immediately the crowd began to laugh and ridicule Him; in essence they doubted His ability to perform this miracle. It was due to this collective unbelief and lack of faith that Jesus commanded the crowd to be removed from the home to ensure the right atmosphere was present, an atmosphere that was conducive for a miracle.

After all the doubters and those of little faith were dismissed, Jesus went inside and took the young girl by the hand; she immediately stood on her feet leaving her death bed behind.

Although Jesus had the power to perform the miraculous; the right atmosphere had to be present for God's power to manifest and move.

Thoughts

_____
_____
_____
_____
_____
_____
_____

This could also be seen when Jesus returned to His own country of Nazareth, He was not able to perform many great works because those who knew Him as a child growing up doubted who He claimed to be, and the power & authority that He now claimed to possess (Matt. 13:58).

Jesus stands ready to perform miracles in our lives today; however, fear, doubt and unbelief often hold Him at bay because of what is nothing more than a lack of faith on our part.

Many times our lack of faith results from our associations and who we allow to speak into our lives, to include close friends and relatives. As that old saying goes, "Bad company corrupts good morals." In other words, those who we routinely associate with or listen to could be filling our hearts and minds with everything that is opposite of faith and contrary to the truth written in God's Word.

A great reminder of the above fact can be found in 2 Cor. 6:14 and is something that we should all take heed to. Yes, we should have interaction with doubters, haters and those who oppose themselves for the purpose of winning them to Christ (Matt. 9:13), but at the same time we should never allow them to influence us in our behavior with their fear, doubt, and unbelief but rather influence them for the sake of righteousness.

It takes faith and belief in the information (the promises) and truth we receive through God's Word that allows us to see the miraculous come to pass; remember, it also takes faith to please our God. Our Heavenly Father stands ready to perform miracles for you today; however, all doubters, haters and blessing-blockers must first go (Heb. 11:6)!

August 21
DIRECT CONTACT
Read: Jn. 8:36

Summer in the Middle East can be a very interesting time. In addition to the extremely hot temperatures and unpredictable dust/sand storms, one has to also get accustomed to the beaming rays of the sun directly touching the eyes.

Thoughts

_____
_____
_____
_____
_____
_____
_____

During my last tour there I arrived in the region at the beginning of fall, so I thought that I was good to go with regards to having enough protection from the sun with my prescription *Transitions* eye glasses. But when the even hotter summer months arrived, I soon realized this was insufficient for the sun's brightness that seemed to intensify as the months progressed.

This became a reality for me one day while walking to the dining facility on post. As a walked along the road, I literally had to squint the entire way due to the beaming rays of the sunlight. Then I thought to myself, there's a problem with this picture, I paid a decent amount of money for lenses that are supposed to transition based on the sunlight or lighting conditions.

With *Transitions* lenses, as lighting diminishes the lenses clear up and as the intensity of the light increases, the lenses are designed to automatically become darker. I had seen this process occur in the past, so it was now a mystery to me why there was no transitioning was taking place.

All of a sudden it dawned on me exactly what was happening. When in uniform (which was the majority of the time when assigned there) I was required to wear a cover (which is headgear or a hat to the layman). What this meant was that even though I may have been outside in direct exposure to sunlight, my cover prevented the sunrays from reaching the lenses to start the transition process. The lenses required direct contact with the rays of the sun for the change to occur.

On that particular day as I began to walk, it was as if the Holy Spirit spoke saying that this is how we all were in our pre-Christ condition. Before accepting Christ the darkness or covering of sin prevented the "Son" from coming in to bring about the change we so desperately needed (Gal. 4:4). The Son came to remove our darkness, to bring light and give us freedom.

Once we accept and receive Him according to Rom. 10:9-10 we then become new creations (2 Cor. 5:17)! Just as *Transition* lenses require direct exposure to sunlight before transformation takes place, it is our direct contact with the light of the "Son" that brings transformation in our lives each day.

Though we receive and have liberty in Christ at new birth, our continued liberty requires contact with the "Son" each and every day (Jn. 15:1-8). When we make direct contact, we then have the ability to begin seeing our transition and transformation take place right before our very eyes.

Whenever the enemy tries to keep you under the cover of trials, testing and temptations; refuse to allow sorrow, frustration and shame to overshadow you. Instead receive direct access and exposure to the "Son," because when "...the Son makes you free, you shall be free indeed (Jn. 8:36, New King James Version).

Thoughts

_____
_____
_____
_____
_____
_____
_____

August 22

MORE THAN A ONE NIGHT STAND
Read: Gen. 4:1-2

Today's scripture text provides a little insight on the first man and woman created on earth, Adam and Eve. The name Adam in Hebrew means "man or mankind" and Eve means "living one or life," in other words the mother of the living or life. In Gen. 4:1 it states that "Adam knew his wife; and she conceived;" therefore, "to know" in the biblical sense speaks of sexual intercourse that produces offspring or seed. In this case, it speaks of the natural intimacy that is to be experienced between a man and a woman in the bond of marriage.

This is intimacy that is demonstrated in total love knowing "all" about each other; this intimacy goes beyond the proverbial "one-night stand," but is birth out of relationship and commitment that is developed over time. To be intimate literally means to be "familiar," and to be familiar means to be "well acquainted with something [or someone]."

This should be the goal of every Christian in our natural relationships, but even more so from a spiritual perspective; we should desire to not just know about God, but have a deep, intimate, and personal relationship with Him that we may be truly acquainted with Him.

It's never enough to just believe in God, James reminds us of this fact in his epistle "You surely believe there is only one God. That's fine. Even demons believe this, and it makes them shake with fear" (James 2:19, Contemporary English Version).

Therefore, it is not just our believing that produces intimacy with God, there has to be more because even the devil and all of his demons believe there is a God as well. Our intimacy or knowing God is birth out of focused relationship with Him as we demonstrate our love and commitment by spending time studying His Word, meditating on His Word, communing with Him in prayer (where there is a two-way exchange petition & supplication and then being still long enough to hear what He has to say), and fasting as we learn to deny the flesh in order to place our concentration completely on Him.

We cannot just believe Him to be the God of our wife, husband, mother, father, brother, sister, grandmother, grandfather, etc. And yes, even though He is the God of Abraham, Isaac, and Jacob, at some point in our life He has to become our personal God too.

Thoughts

_____

_____

_____

_____

_____

_____

_____

It takes more than just knowing about God; we must each personally know Him for ourselves (Ps. 46:10). It also goes beyond mental ascent (mere head knowledge) and/or just speaking about God (Matt. 15:8), it requires a total change of the heart (Jer. 17:10).

Our goal should be to embrace the attitude of the Apostle Paul, as he chose to disconnect himself from anything that would hinder his personal relationship with Christ. Who are you connected to that may be blocking the blessings and love of God from flowing to you and then through you?

We each must make it our purpose to know God in a real way and not just have a "one-night stand;" we must know Him every day and in every way. When we truly know Him we connect ourselves to the Living, and His life is then conceived on the inside thereby producing the seed of His Word and the love on the outside, the type of love that is required to truly reach others. Do you really know Him, or did you just have a one-night stand?

August 23

IT'S TIME TO COME OUT OF THE CLOSET
Read: 1 Sam. 10:1-23

The Israelites, wanting to be like all the other nations, demanded a king to judge and rule over them (1 Sam. 8:6). God was disappointed in this request, but nonetheless granted the people's desire.

Saul, from the tribe of Benjamin, son of Kish was chosen to be the first king of Israel. Subsequent to being chosen, he was anointed by the prophet Samuel to solidify the fact that he had been appointed and approved by God for this position.

Scripture records that when the anointing came upon Saul, he began to prophesy and literally became a different person (1 Sam. 10:6-7). Saul began to prophesy with such authority that the people started asking "is this really the son of Kish?" Therefore, with the anointing comes power.

Now the hour had come for the prophet Samuel to publicly announce Saul as the new king of Israel. All the people were gathered eagerly anticipating the introduction of one who would judge and rule over them as they had requested. However, when Saul was sought out, he was nowhere to be found. The prophet Samuel then inquired of the LORD concerning Saul's location, and the LORD replied, "There he is, hidden among the baggage [or stuff]" (1 Sam. 10:22, New King James Version). So, a group went to retrieve Saul, removed him from the baggage, and stood him before the people in his rightful place.

Here was the recently anointed king of Israel hiding in a closet with baggage; he was obviously hiding among the stuff because of his uncertainties concerning the anointing that

Thoughts

_____

_____

_____

_____

_____

_____

_____

was now upon him. He obviously questioned whether or not he would be able to carry out the task at hand.

It literally took someone going into the closet to bring Saul out for him to come to the realization of who he really was, and the power and authority that he now had as a result of the anointing. The anointing represents God's Spirit and His power which is given to destroy the works of the devil and bring about positive and lasting change.

There are many believers who have God's anointing on their lives; yet instead of doing what's needed to allow this anointing to flow, they choose to fit in or blend in with the people and things of this world by putting their lights under bushels and deciding to just remain in the closet where it appears to be safe.

Today we have individuals that have the power to lay hands on the sick and watch them recover, the ability to cast out demons and all manner of evil spirits (Mk. 16:18) and even the capacity to do even greater works than Jesus Himself (Jn. 14:12) remaining in the closet because they know that with this anointing there is a hefty price to pay and sacrifice to be made.

Therefore, if we ever truly expect to operate in the power and anointing like the example of God incarnate, Jesus Christ when He walked the earth, it requires that we come out of the closet as we leave all of our old baggage there, separate ourselves from the cares and negative influences of the world, and then let our lights shine (Matt. 5:16) as we live and walk out God's Word through obedience. This is when God's anointing truly begins to flow to us and then through us (Acts 10:38).

Have you been running from God because of the anointing and the commitment that this power brings? Well, today it's time for you to come out of the closet and begin to exercise the authority that you now have in the earth.

August 24
I'M JUST SAYING…
Read: 1 Sam. 15:1-23

Thoughts
_____
_____
_____
_____
_____
_____
_____

In today's illustration we have a young couple preparing for a long awaited vacation. Months of planning had gone into preparing for a vacation to a remote Pacific island; an island known for its beautiful white sanded beaches, comfortable temperatures, and beautiful sunsets.

The secluded island was owned by a wealthy Australian land developer who spared no expense to ensure that visitors and guests had a memorable experience. So, each month the young couple began to put away money in their savings and also purchased items that they might need during the vacation over a period of time, and even booked their flights and resort reservations months in advance.

The day of departure finally arrived and the couple was excited about the adventure that waited; they were dropped off at the airport by a close friend, obtain their boarding passes, cleared security, and then later prepared to board the plane for the 12-hour flight. During the flight the couple flipped through brochures for the resort with eager anticipation of enjoying each amenity that this home away from home had to offer.

Although the flight was twelve hours long, it actually felt like days to the young couple; but eventually the plane reached its final destination. The couple gathered their carry-on luggage, picked-up their checked luggage after a 45-minute wait, and then proceeded to Customs.

With Customs cleared there was only one last obstacle between a long tedious flight and much needed rest and relaxation, this obstacle was passport and visa verification. The couple approached the station and presented their passports; the clerk then stated, "Your passports are good, but where are your visas?" The young wife looked at the husband and said, "I thought you took care of this when we applied for our passports a few months back? There were forms and specific instructions for the visas included; did you complete them?"

The husband looked at the wife and said, "I thought having the passport was sufficient, so I didn't complete the other forms. Since we've paid so much for this vacation, I'm sure they won't turn us away." The clerk then said, "I'm sorry, but we cannot grant you access. In most countries a visa can be purchased on the spot, but due to increased security restrictions imposed by the island's owner, without the visa you cannot enter." So, after months of preparation and hours of flying, the couple had to book a return flight home much earlier than desired, missing out on the blessing of fun and relaxation that awaited due to one not following the instructions.

Although the above story may be a little far-fetched, just imagine how many times we as believers in Christ experience similar scenarios in which God's choicest blessings awaited and were ready for us to receive; however, we missed out on them because we did not follow His simple instructions.

God provides us with instructions each day through His Word, by the still small voice of the Holy Spirit, and through other people, yet we often fail to listen. I'm just saying, we could be our very own blessing-blockers; because when we follow the instructions given there is a greater chance for God's blessing to flow.

We must learn to follow the instructions (as given), because true blessing comes through

Thoughts

_____
_____
_____
_____
_____
_____
_____

297

obedience. I'm just saying, because in actuality partial obedience is the very same as complete disobedience. To obey or not to obey; the choice is completely up to you (1 Sam. 15:22).

August 25
NOW IT'S TIME TO PUSH
Read: Lk. 1:44

The young expectant mother was having premature labor pains with only five months into the pregnancy, and although she was ready for the child to come forth, she had also been warned against attempting to push because the baby had not yet properly developed and would more than likely come out prematurely with a potential to suffer serious birth defects and long lasting illnesses in his or her lifetime. Though she was anxious for the baby to come, she listened to the doctor's advice and heeded the instructions.

But now a few more months had passed, and it was actually time to deliver. The nine-month gestation period had finally elapsed and the life that had been developing for months on the inside was ready to come out. But even though this was the time the mother had longed for and anxiously awaited, she was now somewhat hesitant about doing what was necessary to bring this baby and new life into the world, especially when the reality of true labor pains manifested and she was required to push.

Between contractions and screams, in her mind she thought, "What was I thinking when I got pregnant? Is all of this pain really worth it?" Of course the answer was "Yes!" Meanwhile, her husband and father of the unborn child was there throughout the entire birth process coaching her while also providing encouragement saying, "Come on just one more push, you can do it! The baby is almost here."

After what seemed to be an eternity for the mother, the baby that had been nurtured and developed on the inside of her had now entered the world—-healthy, whole, and full of life.

Like the young mother there are many today who have been filled with purpose and destiny, with the calling of God on their life, and who have been pregnant with God's anointing and a praise that has been ready to break forth for months and even years. But when the labor pains of bringing forth the seed that had been planted and conceived by our Heavenly Father begins, there is often hesitancy on our part because we are too focused on ourselves and our discomfort; not realizing what is inside has the ability to reshape the atmosphere and transform lives. Our praise changes things!

Thoughts

_____
_____
_____
_____
_____
_____
_____

So when the labor pains begin, there is no need to fret; though bringing forth this new life may seem painful initially, when this praise breaks forth it will not only change the deliverer's life but also forever change the lives of those around for the better and has the potential to become a source of joy for all. "They that sow in tears shall reap in joy (Ps. 126:5)," because the joy of the LORD is what produces our strength [Neh. 8:10] and God's strength in our lives is manifested through our worship and praise.

In the delivery room with a full-term baby on the inside is not the time to hold back; now it's time to push. Push so that the seed the Father has planted inside of us can spring forth. God says, "I'm about to do something brand-new. It's bursting out! Don't you see it? There it is! I'm making a road through the desert, rivers in the badlands" (Is. 43:19, The Message). What you have on the inside will pave the way and provide access to life-giving water to those who are in dry places, but you have to push. You must push pass the hurt, pass the pain, and pass any doubts or fears. Don't hold back, NOW IT'S TIME TO PUSH!"

August 26
AND YOU WONDER WHY YOU'RE TIRED...
Read: Is. 40:29-31

I can remember some time ago hearing a message in which the man of God encouraged the congregation to not simply look to ourselves as a source of knowledge and information when the various situations of life come upon us, but rather we are to put our confidence and complete trust in God, and God alone knowing that He is Omni-potent (all-powerful), Omni-present (everywhere at once), Omniscient (all-knowing), and Sovereign (has complete control). Therefore, as believers in Christ this should make placing our dependence on God a simple task, right?—-Not! So, why is this often not the case?

Many of us have issues with putting trust in God because we have grown accustomed to putting our confidence in a man or a woman ("the arm of the flesh"), who by their very human nature are already flawed at best. And when these individuals let us down, there is usually great heartache and anguish.

So, when the time comes and we are now asked to put our confidence and trust in God, we remember the outcome of placing confidence in man and naturally tend to believe that God will respond the same way. This in turn causes us to struggle, as we attempt to do things in our own strength and ability since we can no longer depend on anyone but ourselves.

Others may find it hard to trust God because of their riches or having it all together, so they may think; individuals can often be heard saying,

Thoughts

_____
_____
_____
_____
_____
_____
_____

"I have wealth, riches, and everything I need; so, why do I need God?" Sadly, these individuals place confidence in a job, a car, a house, the stock market or a large bank account at the expense of their souls. But when all of the preceding is gone, what then? Instead of turning to God, the alternative is often man-made schemes to amass wealth again relying on our own ability so that we can boast of "Pulling ourselves up by our own bootstraps;" again this amounts to nothing more than human effort.

There are a number of other scenarios that can be looked to; however, the bottom line in all of them is that our reliance on God is often hindered due to our own human effort in some form or fashion. The Apostle Paul clearly reminds us in Phil. 3:3 that we are to "have no confidence in the flesh" since due to our sin nature, nothing good dwells in our flesh (Rom. 7:18). As a result, when a problem arises or an unforeseen situation presents itself, the natural inclination for most of us is to attempt to fix the problem ourselves, often at the expense of not engaging God for resolution first.

Frantic phone calls are made, we work and toil for hours, days, months, and even years trying to find answers or fix the issue 99.9% of the time to no avail. At that point and when all of our options are no longer available, what do we normally do? We then turn to God when He should have been our first option (Prov. 3:5-6).

The prophet Isaiah also provides a perfect example of what we are to do when it comes to trusting God in the above and similar scenarios; we are to "Wait on the LORD" (Is. 40:31). This "waiting" is placing our confidence and trust in God, and not our natural thinking or human ability.

If you've ever wondered why you were so tired and had no explanation, maybe it's because your human effort alone is getting you nowhere. So stop overexerting yourself and working in the flesh, and instead spread your wings and begin to soar and allow God's Spirit to bring you REST (Matt. 11:28-30)!

August 27
GOOD TO THE LAST DROP
Read: Ps. 34:8

Thoughts

_____
_____
_____
_____
_____
_____

Most of us have a favorite beverage, dish or dessert that causes us to go out of our way to obtain. You know the one thing that just the thought of makes your taste buds begin to dance in your mouth.

For many it may be the taste of delectable dark chocolate; an ice cream sundae with bananas, strawberries, whipped cream, and a cherry on top; a seafood platter of King crab legs, lobster, and shrimp; that down home southern dish of catfish, fried chicken, macaroni & cheese with the works; or that tall glass of sun-brewed ice tea.

I'm sure that as you read this, you can picture your specific item in your mind and you are probably formulating a plan on how you can obtain it (smile). Whatever the favored beverage, dish or dessert may be, once we have obtained the item, every morsel is savored and every drop of the beverage is enjoyed; because it is just that good. Eating a particular dish or drinking the specific beverage just seems to bring a sense of euphoria, freedom, and satisfaction.

This reminded me of the longtime slogan of the Kraft Foods Corporation for the "Maxwell House" brand of coffee. The company's claim is that their brand of coffee is so good that the drinker would not be able to put it down until it was all gone and the cup was empty, in other words it was "Good to the last drop," as its slogan suggested. This is indeed a powerful claim.

As believers we have something that far surpasses our favorite dish and/or beverage; He also has the ability to bring even greater joy, satisfaction, and delight than any food or drink we could ever imagine. He is the Bread of Life (Jn. 6:35) and water for the thirsty soul (Jn. 7:37); His name is J-E-S-U-S.

"O taste and see that the [LORD] [our God] is good! Blessed (happy, fortunate, to be envied) is the man who trusts and takes refuge in Him" (Ps. 34:8, Amplified Bible). Because of Christ's sacrifice on the cross and the blood that He shed, all who accept Him now have liberty and freedom in Him. "Therefore if the Son makes you free, you shall be free indeed" (Jn. 8:36, New King James Version). It is the Blood of Christ that not only sets us free, but perpetually makes us free!

What this means for the believer is that there is a guaranteed fountain that continues to flow with the precious, spotless blood of the Living Christ. And though His blood was shed over 2000 years ago; the forgiving, cleansing power of the Blood is still available to all of us today.

Sadly, although many of us walk around free from physical chains and shackles, we often remain in bondage as slaves to sin because of the poor choice we make on a daily basis. Christ died and rose again so that each one of us could live and experience true liberty, freedom, and enjoy good relationships (2 Pet. 3:9).

At some point in time, we each must make our own individual 'Declarations of Independence;' declaring our independence and separation from sin, the deeds of the flesh and the ways of the world, and announcing our allegiance to God the Father through Jesus Christ the Son.

In Christ true liberty and freedom is available to all because His blood continues to flow even

Thoughts

_____

_____

_____

_____

_____

_____

_____

301

today. Are you in need of a blood transfusion? The Blood of Christ is J-positive, available and compatible to all and is "Good to the last drop!"

August 28
ARE YOU WILLING TO WORK FOR LOVE?
Read: Gen. 29:1-30

In this portion of the Old Testament of the Bible, Jacob had just deceived his brother Esau by tricking him out of the birthright blessing and was now on the run for fear of losing his life. He eventually found himself in the land of the people of the east.

And after a long journey through the rugged, dry Middle Eastern terrain, he was obviously thirsty as he searched for a well to refresh himself with water. He then noticed a well in the distance with sheep gathered around, so he made his way there as his strength began to dissipate. He finally reached the well and as he refreshed himself he looked up and saw what he thought to be the most beautiful thing in the world approaching him, it was Rachel the daughter of Laban.

Scripture records that "Rachel was beautiful of form and appearance" (Gen. 29:17), and if the R&B group "The Commodores" would have been around back then they would have proclaimed that she was definitely a "Brick House."

Rachel was so beautiful that she literally had Jacob's nose wide open. Jacob fell head over heels in love with Rachel from the very first moment that he saw her and was willing to do whatever it took to win her affection and hand in marriage. He loved Rachel so much that he entered an agreement with her father Laban to work seven years for her, absolutely free of charge—for no wages in return.

Can you imagine working seven years without receiving one single paycheck or seeing any fruit of your labor? Well, this is exactly what Jacob did and he did it all in the name of love. However, the type of love that Jacob had for Rachel was probably not the correct love needed at the time, but could better be classified through the use of the Greek word "eros", which is a fleshly and erotic type of love that is usually hormone-driven.

Thoughts

_____

_____

_____

_____

_____

_____

The seven years of labor had finally come to an end and it was time for Jacob to claim his new wife; however, Laban had other plans. Since Rachel was not the firstborn daughter, Laban chose to trick Jacob instead by giving him his oldest daughter Leah, who was probably less attractive and obviously not Jacob's first choice.

Jacob was undeniably upset about the deception that had taken place, "What is this you have done to me? Was it not for Rachel that I served you? Why then have you deceived me" (Gen. 29:25)? Yet his heart still yearned and longed for Rachel. So, what did Jacob do? He agreed to work for Laban an additional seven years free of charge for the sole purpose of marrying Rachel. I can imagine the second seven-year iteration passed by in a flash for Jacob as he focused not on the work at hand, but on the prize that he would receive in the end.

At the conclusion of fourteen years of free manual labor, Jacob finally received the woman of his dreams, the woman whom he adored and loved so dearly. Not only did he work the fourteen years for Rachel, it is inferred in Scripture that he also worked an additional seven years after receiving her hand in marriage (Gen. 29:30)—now that's love! Love is a very powerful thing, especially when it is channeled the right way.

Similar to Jacob, we are to pursue love and make it the object of our desire; that is AGAPE love, the God-kind of love. Showing kindness and doing good for others does not take a sign from heaven above, but requires a heart of mercy and compassion, while demonstrating the Father's love—love requires action!

August 29
IT'S NOT ABOUT THEM
Read: Matt. 13:24-30, 26-43

Have you, as a believer in Christ, ever just sat back while taking a look around and wondered if maybe you were doing something wrong? You were trying to live a life pleasing to God honoring His covenant as a consistent tither, regularly attending and participating in worship services and Bible studies, and made it a purpose to demonstrate love to your neighbors in the way that Jesus modeled for us to follow in the Word throughout His earthly ministry. Yet, more and more, those who were living according to the world's system and making sin a lifestyle just seemed to prosper and appeared to be getting ahead.

You find yourself constantly struggling in different areas, but still vow to do your best to live holy; while those who have a "form of godliness," with no lifestyle of commitment and integrity seem to walk around footloose and carefree. Even the Psalmist David was troubled by this issue in the Bible (Ps. 7:2-3).

It is often very easy for us to focus on the prosperity of the wicked to the point that we become judgmental, and then we begin to ask God the question, WHY? However, it is during these times that we must learn to keep proper focus, learn to respond in God's love and recall the wisdom of King Solomon when he said, "To

Thoughts

_____
_____
_____
_____
_____
_____
_____

everything *there is* a season, A time for every purpose under heaven" (Ecc. 3:1, King James Version).

The above Scripture still remains true for all of us today. We are not to become anxious or overly concerned with what appears to be prosperity for the wicked; because Scripture also declares that a day of reckoning and a time of judgment will come. Although we have the ability to inspect their fruit, it is not our job to judge in this instance (Rom. 14:10-12).

Scripture goes even further to remind us in 2 Cor. 5:10 that we all someday will give an account for what we have done (individually) before the judgment seat of Christ, whether our deeds were good or bad. Therefore, we must not focus on others, but give attention to ourselves in this regard. In other words, we must continue to honor God's Word, purpose to do good and live holy no matter what others are doing around us.

According to Hab. 2:4 "the just shall live by HIS faith;" notice the emphasis on the word "HIS," because our faith has nothing to do with another person's faith and/or lifestyle. We each are called to individual accountability.

The Christian lifestyle and access to heaven is not based on group packages, but is based on individual accountability to God through the person of Jesus Christ. So, don't agonize, worry, or lose sleep because of those not living right in your eyes and seeming to prosper around you; God knows who they are, and their day of accountability and reckoning will come. Our job is to just let them live as we continue to be beacons of hope and light; in the end the truth will be revealed and there will be a separation between the real and the fake, the righteous and unrighteous (Matt. 13:30).

Never let the actions of others or even your own perceptions become the standard used to judge between what is right and what is wrong. We must each look into the true standard and mirror of God's Word for ourselves, and make adjustments accordingly (James 1:25).

It's not about them, but more about us as individuals doing what we know to be right so that we can live holy and set apart lifestyles, with a purity of heart that pleases and honors God (Rom. 14:4).

Thoughts

_____

_____

_____

_____

_____

_____

_____

August 30
ALL IT TAKES IS A LITTLE
Read: Matt. 13:31-32

During both high school and early college years, I had a fascination for the subjects of Biology, Chemistry, and Science in general. But of the three subjects, I would have to say that biology (the study of life) has always been my favorite.

It amazes me to see how human growth and development occurs, how the exposure of the inside of an apple to air initiates an enzyme reaction thereby altering its color, or how mixing two completely different elements come together to form a specific substance.

And although I really do not watch a lot of television, shows like CSI, Lost Without a Trace, and Cold Case intrigue me since many elements of the above mentioned subjects are used to solve cases during episodes.

However, for years there have been numerous and ongoing debates between proponents of science and those who champion Christianity; with many scientists focusing on physical evidence and fact, with the Christian on the other hand focusing on the unseen or faith.

But the fact of the matter is that science exists, as well as faith and when you really look at it God created both (Col. 1:16). So, it is simply up to each of us to look at and approach the relationship between science and faith from a proper perspective—God created it all.

With all that said, I can distinctly remember a simple science experiment that I once completed in school that could actually be used in attempted explanations of faith; this experiment involved the use of a perfectly clear glass of water and an eye-dropper filled with a colored dye.

In this experiment one drop of dye was placed into a fairly large glass of water and almost immediately the entire composition of the water inside the glass changed from being crystal clear to the opaque color of the dye that was used. It only took one single drop of dye to change the entire appearance of the water. Well, this is exactly how sin creeps in to contaminate us as believer; it clouds our judgment and begins to severe right relationships and connections.

When an individual generally gets off course, it usually does not happen by way of any major or drastic changes all at once, but occurs little by little with subtle things occurring over time. Instead of going to church every week there is a change to going every other week; instead of reading and studying the Bible every day the change goes from once a week, to once every month, then virtually none at all; or the individual might say "I prayed to God two weeks ago, I'm sure He still honors that time spent together, right?"

Then there is an area that many choose not to address because they don't see any harm with its use, that being television. Television in and of

Thoughts

_____

_____

_____

_____

_____

_____

_____

_____

itself is not the issue; however, the issues arise when we begin to watch shows, movies, etc. that may be inappropriate as we enjoy off-colored, profane, or derogatory jokes, and/or are enamored and infatuated with relationships that totally contradict the Word of God, all in the name of "entertainment."

And before we know it, all of these little things begin to snowball into something bigger that eventually gets us completely off-track and out of God's will, again little by little.

Our relationship with God is not based on chance or random drive-by meetings; real transformation in our lives can be accomplished when we actually begin to apply God's Word as we also activate our faith. All it takes is a little (Matt. 17:20).

August 31
IT ONLY APPEARS TO BE DEAD
Read: Jn. 12:24

In John chapter eleven Lazarus the brother of Mary and Martha, and also a close friend to Jesus died. Jesus was summoned to his dear friend's home with hope that a miracle could be performed that would restore Lazarus to health once again. However, by the time Jesus actually arrived on the scene Lazarus had been in the grave for four days (the point at which medical science says is no returning from as rigor mortis sets in and tissue decay begins).

Yet, in spite of what the physical facts stated, Jesus still insisted that the stone be moved away from the entrance to the grave. One of Lazarus' sisters, Martha, then exclaimed "Master, by this time there's a stench. He's been dead four days" (Jn. 11:38, The Message)! This did not faze Jesus because He knew the power and authority that was within Him and He knew what He possessed.

Once the stone had been rolled away Jesus "...cried with a loud voice, Lazarus, come forth" (Jn. 11:43)! Immediately Lazarus arose and came forth out of the grave completely bound from head to toe; so they removed his grave clothes, loosed him and let him go. Lazarus was raised from the dead by the power and authority of the Word. In Jn. 6:63 Jesus said, "The words that I speak unto you, they are spirit, and they are life."

Thoughts

_____
_____
_____
_____
_____
_____
_____

With just a quick glance at the external, a seed appears to be inanimate and dead; but when that same seed goes into the ground and is nurtured, it has the ability and begins to produce much fruit. Knowing this fact, we too can begin to sow the seed of God's Word into any lifeless situation and watch His fruit manifest in whatever the dead situation or circumstance may appear to be.

Jesus said, "I am the resurrection and the life" (Jn. 14:6);" additionally Jn. 1:1, 14 states that "In the beginning was the Word, and the Word was with God, and the Word was God...And the Word became flesh and dwelt among us." Since the Word and Jesus are synonymous, and Jesus brings life; this would suggest that the Word also brings life.

As believers in Christ we now have the same authority that Christ used to raise Lazarus from the dead available to us today. Because Jesus also said that we would do even greater works than He did. "I tell you for certain that if you have faith in me, you will do the same things that I am doing. You will do even greater things, now that I am going back to the Father" (Jn. 14:12, Contemporary English Version). What this means is that we must begin to exercise the authority that we now have as heirs to the promise while we are here in the earth.

Though marriages, relationships, and the prospect of salvation or restoration for wayward children and relatives may appear to be dead; or even when the healing that has been sought for family, friends, or even for yourself appears to be an object that is unattainable, this is not the end. Speak life!

We must begin to take authority over broken relationships, sickness, disease, poverty, and also claim salvation according to God's Word. There is power in the spoken Word of God (Heb. 4:12). However, this Word must be confessed or spoken in faith, believing that God will do exactly what He has promised.

Everything required for a seed to bring life is already resident and inside of the seed; in other words life itself is in the seed. Therefore, instead of complaining, getting frustrated, or giving up on what may appear to be a dead situation in the natural, instead choose and begin to speak life by sowing seeds of faith according to God's Word. Though that marriage or relationship may appear to be dead, know that the seed of life is only one word away (Prov. 18:21).

September 1
SOMETIMES YOU JUST HAVE TO LET IT DIE
Read: Rom. 8:1

Have you ever encountered individuals that just seemed to be stuck in the past? Many times their clothing and/or hairstyle may even suggest they have never truly let the past go. And whenever these individuals come around, the conversation just seems to naturally go back to the lifestyle you were once a slave to, yet is a lifestyle they are is still bound by.

Thoughts

You have moved on and now have a new nature, a new outlook on life, and a renewed mind. Yet the only thing these individual seem to do is constantly bring up our past and what we used to be, what we used to do, and what we used to do together with them. These types of individuals could very well be business associates, co-workers, old hometown friends, family members and sadly to say even those who claim to be believers in Christ who "knew us when..." and the type of person we used to be.

Invariably, just when we begin to move forward in Christ forgetting the former things (Phil. 3:13-14), these individuals consistently bring up the past causing us to remember the bad deeds from long ago making us feel condemned and unworthy of God's call on our lives.

Well, the fact of the matter is none of us are worthy in and of ourselves; the Prophet Isaiah reminds us of this fact (Is. 64:6). Therefore, any righteousness we obtain only comes by way of the blood of Jesus Christ (2 Cor. 5:21).

The Apostle Paul also highlights the above fact in Rom. 5. This simply suggests that our justification or right-standing only comes by faith through the finished work of Christ at Calvary, that place where He accomplished everything the Father sent Him to do—-bringing restoration and reconciliation between God and man back into the earth.

So, when someone brings up our past, we can just remind them we are no longer condemned and that we have an expected end. God knows the plans He has for us (Jer. 29:11).

This is why it is so important that we become cognizant of whom we connect ourselves with and allow to speak into our lives; whether they are a Christian or not. Influence is a very powerful thing, and whoever/whatever has the most influence in our lives has the potential to direct the course of our future.

Some time ago I remember reading a quote that spoke volumes of wisdom concerning the area of influence and connections: "God brings people into your life for either a REASON, a SEASON, or a LIFETIME. The hardest part is knowing which category an individual belongs in. How many times have you put Lifetime energy into a Seasonal person?" The preceding is a question we must all ask ourselves about our current relationships and connections, because whoever we connect ourselves to today can significantly impact our tomorrow, for the good or bad.

Thoughts

_____

_____

_____

_____

_____

_____

_____

Though we are to be witnesses for Christ to all we come in contact with and are to demonstrate His love, there comes a point in time that we have to sever counter-productive relationships that literally drain the life from us, and then leave the results up to God (2 Cor. 6:14-15). So, instead of connecting ourselves with individuals who constantly bring us down and only point out the worst in us, we should endeavor to connect ourselves to those who speak the truth in love and point us towards the only true source of life as we abide in God's Word (Jn. 15:4); because when we make the right connection, we get the right results—-PEACE and RECONCILIATION in God!

September 2

SOMEONE IS READY FOR YOUR SERMON
Read: 2 Cor. 3:2

There is nothing more encouraging than attending a worship service that is filled with powerful prayer, anointed praise & worship, and a power-packed, spirit-filled word from on high. Not just the average word intended to provoke or bring about excitement and simply stir emotions, but a word from God that is spoken directly to the heart designed to prompt action and change in the individual hearer.

According to Rom. 10:17 "faith *comes* by hearing, and hearing by the word of God (KJV)," and based on James 1:22 we are to "be doers of the Word [obey the message], and not merely listeners to it, betraying yourselves [into deception by reasoning contrary to the Truth] (Amplified Bible)." What these two Scriptures basically suggest is that our faith is increased as we not only hear God's Word but truly begin to act on what we hear because this is how we transform hearing into belief and belief into action.

Many times the Word of God comes to us in the form of a preached/teached message or sermon. By definition a sermon is "a religious discourse delivered in public usually by a clergyman as a part of a worship service; a speech on conduct or duty." 2 Cor. 3:2 reminds us that we are epistles or letters that are open to be read by all.

Well, in Christ and according to the Word we are now considered to be part of a royal priesthood (1 Pet. 2:9). Therefore, since we are priests (or clergy in a since), and our lives are open books to be read by all, it is our job to deliver a public discourse through our daily conduct and lifestyle that is pleasing to God—-in other words our lifestyles should preach a sermon.

Our very lives are designed to be messages preached (or lived) in public with the ultimate goal of bring others to a saving knowledge of God's power to transform.

In everything that we do, we should strive to demonstrate and live by an excellent example that will bring glory and honor to our Heavenly Father through our actions. Does this mean that we have to be perfect? No! However, our goal should be to strive for perfection (completeness and wholeness) in Christ through holy living by letting our lights shine in a dark world.

Thoughts

_____
_____
_____
_____
_____
_____
_____
_____

"Let your light so shine before men that they may see your moral excellence and your praiseworthy, noble, and good deeds and recognize and honor and praise and glorify your Father Who is in heaven" (Matt. 5:16, Amplified Bible).

If your life were a sermon, how would it preach? Would it bring about lasting transformation and change; or would it only engender temporary excitement and emotion? And most importantly, would your sermon point others to Christ?

Just in case you did not know it, as a Christian and believer in Christ your life may be the only Bible or sermon a person will ever hear or see; so make sure that you are "preaching" the right message. The pulpit of the world is standing by for you today, so you better go ahead and preach! Someone is ready for your sermon!

"Above all else, you must live in a way that brings honor to the good news about Christ" (Phil. 1:27, Contemporary English Version).

September 3
GO AHEAD, JUMP IN
Read: Ez. 22:30

In the field of communications, there has been a lot of change in technology and new capabilities over the years. For instance, when I joined the military some twenty-plus years ago, there were only a few satellites providing the primary communications source for Navy ships at sea. These satellites were strategically placed to ensure appropriate signal coverage was available no matter where ships were required to deploy; to the layman this signal coverage is known as the satellite footprint.

However, since there were only a few military satellites in orbit back then designated for military use, there were still areas where the coverage or footprint did not always overlap to provide uninterrupted connectivity.

To address this issue another satellite was developed and deployed to provide the necessary coverage for these open areas or gaps; this satellite was called "Gapfiller." What a befitting name for a satellite that literally described its function. With these satellites in position, ships could theoretically deploy with the assurance that satellite coverage would be available when required.

Thoughts

_____

_____

_____

_____

_____

_____

_____

As believers we have the ability to provide coverage for our co-workers, friends, loved ones, and family in the spiritual sense through the avenue of intercessory prayer as we build a spiritual wall to keep the enemy out and also provide the requisite coverage.

Many times we allow circumstances to get out of control, or we wait until the situation is almost at the 12th hour with current time being 11:59, before we go to the Father in prayer when this should be the very first course of action. Instead of using prayer as a defensive weapon (when or after the enemy attacks), we must also learn to employ it offensively before trouble starts.

In the book of Ezekiel, the LORD was grieved by the oppression of his people and the mistreatment of the poor and needy, and looked for someone who would stand in the gap to intercede for them and establish a hedge that would hold and keep the enemy at bay; but he could not find on (Ez. 22:30).

According to 2 Chron. 16:9, "The eyes of the LORD run to and fro throughout the whole earth to show Himself strong in behalf of those whose hearts are blameless toward Him;" in other words, He is looking for those that will lay aside their own issues, problems, and desires to stand in the gap for those who may not know how or who are unable to even pray for themselves. There is power in prayer!

Prayer in its simplest form is communicating with God by way of petition, supplication, thanksgiving, or praise & worship usually for individual needs or requests. However, intercessory prayer takes this one step further as individuals communicate with God on the behalf of and for the needs of others. An intercessor is simply someone who takes the place of another or pleads another's case. This does not require a degree in divinity or years of seminary training, just a heart for people and a desire to see God's will fulfilled in the lives of others.

So go ahead and jump in, there are still gaps in many lives that need covering through our prayers; when we do our part, we each have the power and ability to help build or rebuild this spiritual wall of protection. When the LORD looks for someone to show Himself "mighty on the behalf of," can He count on you? Become a "Gap-filler" today and begin to intercede for others; the rewards are great (James 5:16).

September 4
DON'T EVEN THINK ABOUT IT
Read: 2 Cor. 4:8-12

Christianity is often merely viewed as a group of religious fanatics gathering together or a social club for individuals to make business and other connections for personal means; however, there is frequently no connection with the suffering also associated with belief in the one the religion represents; Jesus Christ. As a result, many are inclined to believe that once we make a commitment to turn away from sin

Thoughts

———————————————
———————————————
———————————————
———————————————
———————————————
———————————————
———————————————
———————————————

and the things of this world, as we give our lives over to the Lordship of Jesus Christ that everything from that point on will just be a flowery bed of roses or life on easy street, when this is not the true.

So when trouble, failure, or disappointment comes, we begin to think something is wrong or that we may have done something wrong; however, this may be the case. The fact of the matter is that when we give our lives to Christ, we effectively switch from the enemy's (satan's) camp over to the Kingdom of God. And of course, the enemy is not pleased with this decision; therefore, we immediately become targets for his attacks.

Now as soldiers in the LORD's army we are direct threats to satan's kingdom; the little "g" god of this world (the world's system and way of doing things). He attempts to blind us so that we cannot see the True Light (2 Cor. 4:4).

1 Peter 5:8 warns us that we are to "Be on your guard and stay awake. Your enemy, the devil, is like a roaring lion, sneaking around to find someone to attack (Contemporary English Version)." Notice that the scripture says "like" a roaring lion, meaning that he is basically like a lion that has a loud roar but is toothless and with no bite; in other words he has no power. Jesus made an open show of him on the cross forever removing the sting of death (1 Cor. 15:55-57); and because of this we now have power over all the power of the enemy (Lk. 10:19).

Throughout the Bible there are many stories of believers who were challenged in their faith and eventually triumphed through their suffering. Therefore, when the pressures of life seem to be too much to bear, we should turn to the many witnesses of faith in the Bible who endured and did not give up with Jesus being our prime example (Heb. 12:1-2).

This also suggests that compared to what Jesus endured to purchase our redemption and salvation, the things we go through are truly just "light afflictions;" however, these afflictions are usually designed to prepare us for even greater things; our job is simply to endure (2 Cor. 4:17-18).

Therefore, when life begins to press from all sides with failure, disappointment and/or discouragement, this is not the time to give up or give in; so DON'T EVEN THINK ABOUT IT! Stand firm in faith, endure like a good soldier, and fix your eyes on Jesus!

Thoughts

_____

_____

_____

_____

_____

_____

"We've been surrounded and battered by troubles, but we're not demoralized; we're not sure what to do, but we know that God knows what to do; we've been spiritually terrorized, but God hasn't left our side; we've been thrown down, but we haven't broken. What they did to Jesus, they do to us—trial and torture, mockery and murder; what Jesus did among them, he does in us—he lives! Our lives are at constant risk for Jesus' sake, which makes Jesus' life all the more evident in us. While we're going through the worst, you're getting in on the best" (2 Cor. 4:8-12, The Message)!

September 5
TAKE THIS JOB AND LOVE IT
Read: Eph. 6:7

Each year, job dissatisfaction seems to continue to be on rise. And with the recent turn of events with the economy, many are not satisfied with what they do during the course of a normal work week. "Research shows that about one-quarter of the workforce reports that they are just "showing up to collect a paycheck. [Research also indicates that] only about half of all Americans report being satisfied with their jobs. Of this 50 percent only 14 percent report being "very satisfied."

Years ago a popular song was written by David Allan Coe, but made popular by the country music singer Johnny Paycheck summed up this job dissatisfaction sentiment, the song is entitled "Take This Job and Shove It."

For many employees in the workforce, this song became their anthem and is still the anthem for many on the job today with the first line of the chorus starting with "Take this job and shove it / I ain't workin' here no more." Overall job satisfaction is described by how content an individual is with his or her job, and can be based on a wide variety of factors to include leadership management style, office favoritism, or lack of empowerment to do a job.

Although causes for job dissatisfaction may be legitimate, we as believers in Christ are to take a different approach in our response. According to 1 Tim. 6:6, "godliness with contentment is great gain." In other words we are to be content with where God has placed us, and work as though we are working for the Lord and not man until God gives direction to move or not (Eph. 6:7).

Many times as believers, we look to receive a job or assignment where there is nothing but other believers in the office. But, what good is there in placing a light in a room already filled with light? Light is needed in places where there is darkness because, like Jesus, we are lights in this world (Matt. 5:14).
As such, we are each strategically placed in the workforce as God sees fit; we must remember who we are truly working for.

Thoughts

So, don't adapt to the world's way of saying "Take This Job and Shove It;" instead be encouraged, labor and work as unto to the Lord, and then "Take Your Job and Love It."

_____
_____
_____
_____
_____
_____
_____

"So, my dear brothers and sisters, be strong and immovable. Always work enthusiastically for the Lord, for you know that nothing you do for the Lord is ever useless" (1 Cor. 15:58, New Living Translation).

September 6
GET TO STEPPIN'
Read: Josh. 6:1-21

After becoming the new leader for the Israelites in the wilderness, Joshua was given a command, instructions and a promise from the LORD to lead the Israelites into the land of promise (Josh. 1:3). And all Joshua and the Israelites had to do was follow the instructions of the LORD and believe that what He said would actually come to pass.

As one can imagine, every time we make it up in our hearts and minds to do what the Word of God says, opposition and challenges will come prior to the fulfillment of the promise. During their wilderness journey the Israelites encountered a challenge by way of the city of Jericho that would prove to be a great test of their collective faith and ability to follow instructions.

Jericho was a well-fortified and secure city; it would take more than human effort to overcome the city. But the LORD reassured Joshua that the city would be given to him (the city, the king, and all of its inhabitants). All Joshua had to do was get the people to follow the instructions as given by the LORD to bring their victory to fruition.

The instructions were for the people to march around the city once for six days without talking or making a sound, with the priests out front holding ram's horns and carrying the Ark of the Covenant. However, on the seventh day everyone had to march around the city seven times and at the command of Joshua, the priest were to all blow the trumpets, and then the everyone was to shout with a loud voice. I'm sure that the people probably thought to themselves, "Although these sound like fairly simple instructions, how will this give us access to the city and bring about victory without a fight?"

Can you imagine walking around a certain city in circles not saying a word for six days while having the city's inhabitants hurl insults saying you looked like idiots and that your efforts would be futile? Nevertheless, all of the people from the youngest to the eldest followed the instructions of Joshua as they had been given to him by the LORD.

Thoughts

_____
_____
_____
_____
_____
_____
_____

And on the seventh day "the people shouted when the priests blew the trumpets. And it happened when the people heard the sound of the trumpet, and the people shouted with a great shout, that the wall fell down flat" [Josh.

6:20]. The number seven in the Bible represents "completeness;" therefore, it was on the seventh day that the people completed the instructions that brought about their ultimate victory.

Because of their collective obedience, as they followed the prompting and leading of God's Spirit, the very place the Israelites walked around in faith was given to them as promised.

What has the LORD promised you that the enemy says is impossible to attain? Is it promotion & increase, health & wholeness, peace in your marriage and/or family, salvation for loved ones & friends? Whatever the promise may be, we must lay hold to God's Word as we are obedient to the specific instructions as given and choose to be led by His Spirit.

Let's start walking around our own individual Jericho's as opposed to complaining about the circumstances we face to any and every one that we meet. Instead of talking about it, we need to start walking about it.

Take the first step and claim your victory as you follow and complete the instructions as given, and then begin walking in faith. IT'S TIME THAT WE ALL GET TO STEPPIN' (Acts 2:39)!

September 7
USE YOUR KEYS
Read: Matt. 16:19

Years ago as a young boy there were a number of television shows or SITCOMs (Situation Comedy) that I watched on a fairly regular basis; many of these shows I can still remember today.

There were a few of these old shows that also featured a handyman as one of the focal characters, and as I name a few I know that I'm giving away my age again. There were shows like "One Day at a Time" with Schneider, "Good Times" with Bookman, and the "Honeymooners" with Norton.

One of the main attributes of these handymen was their ability to fix household problems with ease; that is all except for Bookman if you've ever watched an episode of "Good Times." A handyman is typically a person skilled with the ability to complete a wide range and variety of repairs, or a "Jack of all trades" as some like to call them.

Thoughts

_____
_____
_____
_____
_____
_____
_____
_____

These individuals were also normally entrusted with a ring containing a key to every door in the building they provided service to. And as these individuals went about doing their daily tasks, their presence could often be recognized by the sound of jingling keys.

Now imagine a tenant in the building who is unable to entering his or her apartment because they are unable to find their key, with the handyman coming to the rescue. But when the handyman gets there he has a momentary lapse of memory and forgets all that he possesses, as he attempts to kick the door open with little success. He then takes a few steps back, gets a running start and tries to demonstrate his manhood by ramming the door with his shoulder—score: door (1), Handyman (0). In a last ditch effort, instead of using his body he decides to use a large object as a battering ram to open the door; however, the door still does not give way.

Standing there in disbelief and a little embarrassed, the handyman has an epiphany and remembers that he is wearing a key ring with master keys to every apartment in the building. He searches for the right key, pulls it out, and within a matter of minutes the door is opened. The handyman struggled wasting precious time attempting to resolve a problem with his own physical strength, when all he needed to do was use the right key.

As believers in Christ, we often fall as victims to the same trap as we attempt to resolve the problems and circumstances in our lives with our own intellect, strength and/or ability. As a result, the promises and blessings of God often remain locked behind the enemy's door.

According to Matt. 16:19, God has given us the master key ring (the Word of God with all of His promises), and with it we can take authority over everything that troubles us and that lead to many restless nights. This power is the ability to bind and loose the things that often come against us through our confession or declaration of God's Word as we speak to every obstacle, situation and circumstance that we face each day, but we must speak by faith.

To sum it up, there is no need to fight against locked doors when God has already given us what we need. So don't allow locked doors to keep you from receiving your blessing when you already have the Master Key. Locked doors easily open when you use the right key.

God's Word is the Master Key to the locked doors of your blessings—START USING YOUR KEYS (Matt. 16:19)!

Thoughts

_____
_____
_____
_____
_____
_____

September 8
WHAT ARE YOU WAITING FOR?
Read: Ps. 150:6

There is much activity going on in the world today and when we look at the current world state as depicted by televised news reports, magazines, and other printed media, it is very easy to fall into the trap of feeling gloom, doom, and despair accompanied by murmuring and complaining about the events and occurrences that have previously and are currently taking place. Because of the world economy, many are distraught that their homes have lost value, stocks and investments have plummeted, and the things that once brought security and stability are now shaky and unstable ground at best.

This simply suggests that when we look at things with the natural eye the logical response is to show dissatisfaction and begin to complain. However, this is never what God intended for those who are called by His name to do because He reminds us in Scripture that our words have power (Prov. 18:21).

Therefore, as we look at world events there is pestilence in various places, wars being fought all around the globe with thousands of lives being lost leaving many with the question, Where is hope in all of this? Yet when these things do occur, we as believers should not jump on the bandwagon with the rest of the world in complaining, but instead simply recognize it for what it is, that being the fulfilment of the Scripture (Matt. 24:6-8, 13).

God knew what would happen years before any of it actually occurred and also provided us with instructions on what we were commanded to do in the face of adversity and chaos all around us. James states it this way in his epistle "My friends, be glad, even if you have a lot of trouble. You know that you learn to endure by having your faith tested. But you must learn to endure everything, so that you will be completely mature and not lacking in anything" (James 1:2-4, Contemporary English Version). Verse 13 of Matthew chapter 24 also provides a little encouragement and hope, "But if you keep on being faithful right to the end, you will be saved" (Contemporary English Version).

You may be wondering, "So exactly what am I to do as I endure hard time while going through the valley of what appears to be adversity, confusion, and utter chaos? The answer is simple, Praise!

Our praise elevates our thinking and adjusts our focus as we begin to glorify and magnify God despite external circumstances. This takes the attention away from the problem and then places proper focus on the One who is the Problem-Solver. It is in this instance that our troubles become minute, insignificant, and pale in comparison to the glory and splendor of our Heavenly Father who is bigger than any problem or trial we face.

Thoughts

_____

_____

_____

_____

_____

_____

_____

Ps. 150:6 declares "Let everything that has breath praise the LORD. Praise the LORD!" This means that anything that is alive and breathing is commanded to praise God, no matter what condition he or she may be in, or what the current circumstances of life may be at any given moment. The word "breath" in the preceding Scripture is derived from the Hebrew word "neshamah" which means "vital breath; divinely inspired."

Everyday God gives us the power to live, move, and be who He created us to be [Acts 17:2]; for that alone we should give Him praise. In other words, we have been "divinely inspired" to express our love and adoration for Him for not only for what He has done or what He will do, but simply because of who He is. So, no matter how dark the situation and outlook may seem to be, what may be going on in the world around you or in your own personal life, God is still worthy of all the praise! So what are you waiting for? GO AHEAD AND PRAISE HIM TODAY (Ps. 33:1)!

September 9
A LIGHT IN THE DISTANCE
Read: Matt. 5:13-16

Imagine for a moment a ship has been at sea for several months as the crew prepares for their long anticipated journey and return home to their loved ones. There is excitement and anticipation in the air, with everyone chatting about their plans upon returning to include visiting family and friends, relaxing at the beach or that nice vacation to an exotic island or some other location. Whatever the case, knowing of the ship's return to homeport made the reality of each plan that much more attainable.

Then all of a sudden the unthinkable happens, all of the ship's electronic navigation and radar equipment unexpectedly went down simultaneously. And to make matters worse, the only technician proficient enough to repair these systems was recently flown home a few days early due to a family emergency. This made the job of each individual member of the bridge and navigation team that much more important, with the ship's Captain and Navigator now depending on the seaman's eye to ensure ship and crew safety. And to add salt to an already open and festering wound, an unexpected change in weather caused a thick, dense fog to roll in that significantly reduced visibility.

Thoughts

_____
_____
_____
_____
_____
_____
_____

Therefore, what was once a time of excitement and joy for a long-awaited return home, instantly transformed into a matter of finding a way to safely navigate the ship to the finally destination. So the Captain gives the order to reduce speed to prevent the ship from running aground or into another vessel afloat. Consequently, this reduction in speed would also significantly increase the time required for the return trip home.

318

With no navigational equipment or electronic aids available and a dense fog rolling in ahead, the ship's crew began to lose hope as morale began to dwindle at the thought of an extended journey to an expected celebratory return home.

Then from nowhere through the darkness of night and the thick layer of fog, a faint light was seen in the distance. Now with a glimmer of hope, the Navigator pulls out an old map that covered the approximate location of the ship which identified a lighthouse that should have been in the precise location of the faint light that was attempting to pierce its way through the darkness and dense fog.

Upon receiving this news, the Captain gives the order and command to steer the ship towards the light using it as a point of reference to keep the ship away from shallow waters and any other dangerous obstacle. So, by following the guiding light the ship was able to steer safely to its final destination preserving the lives of everyone onboard.

By definition, "lighthouses are used to mark dangerous coastlines, hazardous shoals and reefs and safe entries to harbors and can also assist in aerial navigation." And in a spiritual sense, this is exactly what we as Christians and believers are to represent in this world; we are to be lighthouses or "guiding lights" designed to point those in the thick of darkness to a place of safety and refuge.

In Jn. 8:12 Jesus said, "I am the light of the world. He who follows Me shall not walk in darkness, but have the light of life" (New King James Version). Therefore, since we are now in Christ and He is inside of us, we too are and can shine as lights in the midst of darkness. Because, as He was, so are we in the earth (1 Jn. 4:17, King James Version). Therefore, "As the World Turns" and many "Search for Tomorrow"; make it your purpose to be a "Guiding Light." Let your light shine in every way because you never know who may need it! Is your light shining today (Jn. 3:21)?

September 10
I ASKED YOU FOR IT A LONG TIME AGO
Read: 1 Pet. 5:7

Many of us have loved ones, friends, and close relatives that we are believing God for; those that we pray for hoping that one day they will give their lives to Christ. Then there are others who have dreams of getting free from debt, receiving a promotion on the job and increase, obtaining a new home or car, or enjoying that perfect vacation. These are all good marks on a target to aim for, yet these should not be pursued at the expense of losing proper focus while creating worry and anxiety in the process.

Thoughts

———————————
———————————
———————————
———————————
———————————
———————————
———————————

Therefore, as we bring our petitions and requests to the Father, we must not allow ourselves to become frustrated because we are not seeing results based on our timetable (2 Pet. 3:8). God's timetable is not our timetable, and what He really wants us to do is give every care, concern, and situation over to Him so He can do what He does best; turn things around for the good (Rom. 8:28).

There is a story of a woman who desperately wanted her husband to come to church with her and give his life to the Christ. She consistently prayed for him, but each Sunday he would remain at home lounging around watching television.

So, to help God along in the process she began to leave yellow Post-it notes with Scriptures written on them all over the house (on the bathroom mirror, the refrigerator, and on the living room table next to the television remotes) and would also leave a Bible open to passages focusing on salvation in hopes that her husband would read it, feel convicted, and then get an urge to attend church with her. However, this was all done to no avail.

Finally, after years of frustration with prayer, nagging (I mean consistently asking) her husband to come to church, and all of her other human activities that attempted to manipulate (I mean shame) him into coming to God's House with her, she simply said "LORD, I give up! I've tried everything that I know to encourage my husband to join me for church, and nothing seems to work. I surrender; I'm taking my hands off and giving this over completely to you."

In a loving fatherly voice God then replied, "I asked you for it a long time ago, but you didn't listen. How many times did I have to remind you to just release the situation and give it over to me? It was never yours to figure out or control anyway. Forgive him and let it go."

According to 1 Pet. 5:7 we are to cast all our burden and cares on God. This verse does not say cast some of our cares or hold on to the cares we think we are big and grown enough to handle, but says casting "ALL" our care upon God.

When something is cast it is literally thrown out and away like a fisherman casting his hook in the water with a fishing rod or reel. But unlike the fisherman, we are to cast with no lines or strings attached so we can't reel our problems back in to ensure we completely let them go so. This way God can have and handle every issue we have been carrying around like Samsonite luggage which is known to be tough and hard to destroy.

Sometimes it is not enough to just pray about certain situations, problems, or circumstances; we must also go a step further to actually release these concerns and give them completely to God. Because as long as we are holding on to them, we hinder the divine work and hand of God from bringing about the transformation

Thoughts

_____
_____
_____
_____
_____
_____
_____

we desire. What are you praying for and believing God to move on the behalf of? God says to each of us today, "I asked you for it a long time ago, it's time to release it and let it go (Phil. 4:6-7)!

September 11
HOW MUCH DID IT COST?
Read: 2 Sam. 24:24

In the materialistic society that we live in today, it is not uncommon to hear conversations that seem to focus more and more on material things, possessions, and status. Individuals talk about the type of car they drive, how big their home is, where the last vacation was spent, etc. often subconsciously boasting of what they have and/or possess.

In these conversations there is usually that one probing question that arises: How much did it cost? Don't get me wrong, there's nothing wrong with possessions and things as long as the things don't begin to possess the possessor and are also kept in proper perspective.

One person's purchase of a new car or new home may deplete their entire savings; however, for the next this purchase may be nothing more than another tax deduction that continues to build their capital and overall net worth. Although this notion of cost may continue to push us towards materialism and consumerism, at the same time we should never take the cost of things lightly; cost is very important because it often determines how much of a sacrifice one will have to make to obtain that which is desired.

Let's take a look at "cost" from a different perspective, that is from the perspective of worship, service and giving of time and resources by those claiming to be believers in Christ.

One story that immediately comes to mind is that of the widow and her mite. "Many of the rich were making large contributions. One poor widow came up and put in two small coins-a measly two cents. Jesus called his disciples over and said, "The truth is that this poor widow gave more to the collection than all the others put together. All the others gave what they'll never miss; she gave extravagantly what she couldn't afford-she gave her all" (Mk. 12:41-44, The Message).

During the LORD's time a "mite" was a coin equivalent to about one-fifth of a cent and was a coin of very low value. Here we have the story of a poor woman who literally had nothing but

Thoughts

_____
_____
_____
_____
_____
_____
_____
_____

currency that was equivalent to less than two cents left to her name; however, she pressed her way through the crowd of prominent and wealthy leaders who boasted of their large offerings and ability to give benevolently as she presented her small, but sacrificial gift and offering to the LORD.

So, what was the difference between the religious leaders and the widows giving? Simple, it was a matter of the heart. The rich gave just to be seen and recognized for how much they presented; however, the widow gave all she had sacrificially from a pure heart.

Therefore, as you go about your own agenda from day-to-day, week-to-week, or even month-to-month, ask yourself a couple of simple questions: How much does my sacrifice each day really cost? How much am I really willing to give-up or lay aside to present pure and holy worship to the Father? "Make sure you don't take things for granted and go slack in working for the common good; share what you have with others. God takes particular pleasure in acts of worship-a different kind of "sacrifice"-that take place in kitchen and workplace and on the streets" (Heb. 13:16, The Message).

September 12
WHEN YOU DON'T KNOW WHAT TO DO
Read: 2 Kgs. 6:8-17

The king of Syria was poised to launch an attack on Israel, and his army was now in position, surrounding the prophet Elisha and his servant. As far as the eye could see horses, chariots, and mighty men of war encircled the city. Unaware of their presence, Elisha's servant arose the next morning, went outside, and saw the multitude of warriors surrounding them ready to attack. With fear now in his heart, the servant franticly exclaimed, "Alas, my master! What shall we do" (v. 15)?.

The enemy had completely surrounded them with no foreseeable exit plan or strategy to overcome the multitude that would surely bring about defeat. What were they to do? The prophet Elisha then replied, "Do not fear, for those who *are* with us *are* more than those who *are* with them" (v. 16). I'm sure the servant must have thought his master had lost it, doubting his ability to come to grips with the reality of defeat. Then "Elisha prayed, and said, "LORD, I pray, open his eyes that he may see" (v. 17a)."

Thoughts

_____

_____

_____

_____

_____

_____

_____

And as LORD removed the blinders from the servant's eyes, he looked up and saw that "the mountain *was* full of horses and chariots of fire all around Elisha" (v. 17b). The LORD had been there all along with warring angels prepared to defend His servants; all they needed to do was look up.

So, when the enemy begins to surround us and there appears to be no hope in sight, this is not the time to hold our heads down in defeat or give in. Look Up! This is where our help comes from. "I will lift up my eyes to the hills—From whence comes my help? My help comes from the LORD, Who made heaven and earth. He will not allow your foot to be moved" (Ps. 121:1-4, New King James Version).

Though the enemy may attempt to bombard us with negative thoughts, pain in our bodies, or trouble on every side; the LORD always raises a standard. "When the enemy comes in like a flood, The Spirit of the LORD will lift up a standard against him" (Is. 59:19, New King James Version); this standard is His Holy Word.

Remember, no weapon fashioned or formed against us can ever succeed (Is. 54:17). However we must also note that the preceding Scripture says that every tongue that rises against us, "WE" will condemn. We begin to condemn the works of the enemy by lifting the standard (God's Word) by way our confession, declaring what the Word says about us--we are victorious, we are overcomers, we are the head and not the tail, above only and not beneath, we are more than conquerors.

When the enemy surrounds us and we don't what to do, we must LOOK UP! Our help comes from above.

"Lift up your heads, O you gates! And be lifted up, you everlasting doors! And the King of glory shall come in. Who *is* this King of glory? The LORD strong and mighty, The LORD mighty in battle" (Ps. 24:7-8, New King James Version).

September 13
NEW DESIGNER GENES
Read: Ps. 139:14

Although many fashions have come and gone over the years, denim jeans or blue jeans have been one of the most widely known and most frequently worn articles of clothing that I can remember, from the time that I was a child until today. Jeans were originally designed for the working class; however, "jeans are now a very popular form of casual dress around the world, and have been so for decades."

When I was young the jeans of choice were Toughskins, Wrangler, and of course the very popular Levi. These jeans were known for their durability and material that could withstand the rigorous activity and play of very active children. As a teenager the type of jeans worn shifted from durability to making a fashion statement with brands like Sasson, Jordache, Gloria Vanderbilt, Calvin Klein, Guess, and

Thoughts

_____
_____
_____
_____
_____
_____
_____

Sergio Valente; each jean with a specific design, logo, or insignia on the rear pockets to signify the brand.

Years later there came Sean John, Phat Farm, Akademiks, DKNY, True Religion and a host of others; but whatever the brand or the buyer's preference, wearing of the jeans seemed to give the individual a sense of importance and significance, in other words identity was achieved through the jeans or clothing being worn.

As believers in Christ instead of receiving the "jeans" of the world or even the "genes" of our natural parents to find identity, we receive "genes" that far surpass any designer jean on the market and our identity is found in them (2 Cor. 5:17; because in Christ we receive the genes of God our Heavenly Father. In Biology ("the study of life and living organisms"), genes are that portion of our DNA (heredity or physical makeup) that determines our outward features, traits, and characteristics.

According to Gen. 1:27 "God created man in His own image;" and in the beginning "...the LORD God formed man *of* the dust of the ground, and breathed into his nostrils the breath of life; and man became a living being" (Gen. 2:7, New King James Version).

Man (mankind) was fashioned and designed by the Almighty Hand of God. And a fact that is even more astounding and awesome about this creative process is that when we are born and brought into this world, we each are uniquely crafted, fashioned, and designed. There are no two individuals here on earth who are exactly the same; including identical twins who even have their differences. We are each unique and one-of-a-kind.

The Psalmist King David revels in this fact in (Ps. 139:14). Though we all are uniquely designed there is one common factor, our new 'genes'. These new genes should cause us to look like and behave outwardly like our new Father showing His features, character and traits (Eph. 5:1).

Our identity should not be wrapped up in the clothing we wear, how many college degrees we have, how large our home is, the size of our bank account or any other external factor. We receive our identity in God through the person of Jesus Christ and His finished work at Calvary, the righteous standards of the Word (the Bible), and God's precious Holy Spirit sent to lead, guide and direct us.

Thoughts

_____
_____
_____
_____
_____
_____

In Christ we receive new designer genes and are now perfect designs, and even though one size fits all they are still unique to the individual. Your Designer will determine the kind of life you live and the character being reflected from you to the world (Rom. 13:11-14).

September 14
PREPARING FOR THE FIGHT
Read: Eph. 6:10-13

Boxing matches do not seem to be as prevalent today as they were a couple of decades ago. There are probably great match-ups occurring; however, since I don't watch boxing as frequently as I did in my earlier years I really have not kept abreast of who the current contenders are.

In my earlier years I can remember many of those classic boxing bouts like Ali vs. Frazier, Ali vs. Foreman, Leonard vs. Hearns, Duran vs. Leonard, Hearns vs. Duran, Tyson vs. Holyfield. So, based on the preceding list of names, it is clearly evident I've been out of the boxing loop for a while.

However, there is another boxer that I would like to mention here even though he was only a movie character, Rocky Balboa who is another famous fighter that had several classic bouts during the long-standing and popular *Rocky* movie.

Even though boxing may not be as popular as football, basketball, or the beloved American pastime of baseball, boxing still seems to have a fairly large following. The average boxing match normally consists of a variation of rounds usually up to twelve at a length of just over two minutes each round. But even though there are only a few rounds with a very short duration for each, months and months of preparation usually take place for those who are serious about actually winning.

In reality, more energy and effort is often placed into the preparatory stages than is expended during the actual fight itself. Weeks, months, and even years of preparation often take place to ensure the fighter will have the strength, endurance, and stamina needed each time the bell rang.

During the *Rocky* series, Rocky Balboa was often seen running through the streets of Philadelphia, going into meat packing plants punching huge slabs of beef precariously hanging from large hooks, and then spending countless hours in the gym sparing, doing sit-ups, push-ups, pull-ups, and every other exercise imaginable that would physically prepare him for the challenge to come.

In other words, the above boxers did not just exercise for one day and then consider themselves ready to fight; on the contrary, it was their advance preparation that qualified and allowed them to endure the attack and barrage of punches from their opponents.

As believers in Christ, whether we acknowledge it or not, we are at war and in a daily fight with the little "g" god of this world and all of his principalities and powers of darkness. Yet many of us simply come to church on Sunday to hear

Thoughts

_____
_____
_____
_____
_____
_____
_____

a message from the man or woman of God receiving a little strength to carry on, but fail to capitalize on the message presented by spending personal time in the Word or in prayer throughout the remainder of the week, which are vital components needed to assist in building up our spiritual strength and faith.

Therefore, it is due to a lack of continued preparation on our part that we begin to develop spiritual atrophy as we become weaker with no strength to fight and thus allowing the defense of our protective wall to deteriorate as the enemy advances against us.

Being ready for the fight requires a little preparation on our part. Though others may be able to provide encouragement, no one can do this for us. The enemy constantly attempts to penetrate our spiritual walls of protection, so there is no time like the present to begin getting in shape, put on your armor, and to prepare for the fight (Eph. 6:10-13)!

September 15
IF YOU CAN'T STAND THE HEAT...
Read: 1 Pet. 4:12-13

During my time in the military, I've had the opportunity to serve in the Middle East on different occasions. Many of the assignments were during deployments on U.S. Navy ships; however, I also had the privilege of being assigned to shore-based stations there as well.

At certain times of year the atmospheric conditions in the Middle East just seem to skyrocket more so than usual, especially in the months of July and August with temperatures sometimes in excess of 130 degrees Fahrenheit of dry heat with no other factors like humidity, etc. affecting it. Shade in this type of environment only protects an individual from the direct rays of the sun; because even when the wind does just happens to blow, instead of feeling the nice sensation of a cooling breeze it feels as though a hair dryer set on high has been pointed directly at the skin.

Temperatures in this region have the ability to go so high it is quite easy for one to identify with a rotisserie chicken and the feeling of being slowly roasted inside the clothing being worn when walking from place to place.

Thoughts

_____

_____

_____

_____

_____

_____

In recent years not only have record-breaking temperatures been documented in the Middle East, but also around the world including certain regions in the United States. When outside temperatures are excessive, many search for new and innovative ways to remain cool while utility companies attempt to meet the increased demand for electricity as everyone cranks up the air conditioning. It is during these times as individuals go outside to brave the intense heat that a recurring phrase can often be heard: "Man is it hot!"

Many times as believers we often feel heat of a different type as we go through the flames of trials and tests in life. In John chapter thirteen, Jesus attempted to prepare one of His disciples, Simon Peter, for the fiery trials that would come his way when Peter made the rash statement that He would die for the LORD. But Jesus knew that when the real test came that Peter would deny knowing Him (Jn. 13:38).

Well, at various times in life we too will each have to take a stand for Christ and in doing so may begin to feel as though the heat is too intense to bear and there is no relief in sight. But having had personal experience in this area himself, Peter reminds us in God's Word that this is not an unusual occurrence and he then offers a word of encouragement (1 Pet. 4:12-13). In other words, the fiery trials we go through are not designed to consume us, but are intended to purify us, build us up, and prepare us to be who God created us to be.

Although being in the flames may feel uncomfortable at any given moment, this process is absolutely necessary to complete the work of God in us and through us. Everything that Peter went through eventually made him a better person, a better disciple, and a better witness for Christ.

Just as the increased temperature of boiling water removes impurities; the fiery trials we face are designed to purge, cleanse, and purify us as the heat intensifies (Mal. 3:2-3). Therefore, in the times we may feel the fiery trials are extremely intense or the temperature may appear to be too hot to bear; we must refuse to complain because there is a place that is a billion times hotter with eternal flames that will never burn out or end. But thanks be to God that through the shed blood of Jesus Christ, we now have eternal "Fire Insurance" and don't have to be concerned with the fiery flames of hell. Have you checked your policy lately? Be sure that you don't allow it to lapse, because hell is hot and eternity long so make sure that you have the right insurance today.

September 16
QUIT STANDING AROUND
Read: Matt. 20:1-16

Thoughts

"That's not my job"; "I don't get paid to do this"; "This is not in my contract or job description"; "Why should I help them? They never help me when I have a need"; or "I'm sure that someone else will take care of it"; unfortunately the preceding phrases are all too common in our society today. The guiding ideologies of the day seem to be selfishness and protecting one's own interest, with a greater focus on what the other person is doing rather than personal accountability.

As believers in Christ, we who profess Christian faith are held to a higher standard, that standard being one of L-O-V-E with Jesus being our perfect example. Jesus humbled Himself, allowed His body to be beaten, spat upon, battered and bruised in order to redeem mankind; now that's real love (Jn. 15:13). He did it all without murmuring or complaining, or worrying about what the next person was or was not doing (Phil. 2:5-8). He remained humble and accountable for His actions, and since He is our perfect example we should be doing the same.

In the "Parable of the Workers in the Vineyard" in Matthew chapter 20, a landowner went out early in the morning to look for laborers to work in his vineyard offering a standard flat-rate wage for work completed during that day. So, he went out several times at various hours of the day making the same offer to those passing by. Some workers accepted the offer and began to work early that morning, while others came towards the latter part of the evening. However, when the day was done and work completed, all workers received the same payment for their labor, no matter what time they entered the vineyard for that day.

Of course the workers that labored all day were angry because the individuals that came and only worked for an hour received the same wage as those who worked, sweated, and labored in the hot sun the entire day; however, the landowner reminded the laborers that his offer for a day's work was standard no matter what time the laborer actually began working.

Likewise, in the body of Christ there is much work to be done (Lk. 10:2) and Jesus is looking for laborers; and we should not be focused on what another person is or is not doing.

Each one of us will be rewarded for what we have done with our lives and our bodies, not that of the next person. And whether we started 20 years ago or we are just getting started today, when Jesus returns we will all receive the same wage (Matt. 20:16); our job is to just get started. We must quit standing around waiting for the next person to do this or that, when God is calling us all to service now.

We are all called to "personal" accountability in the body of Christ and must each do our part if the movement of the Body is to be effective; there is more than enough work for all of us to do. I've heard it said that "Our life is God's gift to us; what we do with our life is our gift to God." So, let's make it our purpose to quit standing around, because it's time to get to work!

Thoughts

_____

_____

_____

_____

_____

_____

"Don't excuse yourself by saying, "Look, we didn't know." For God understands all hearts, and he sees you. He who guards your soul knows you knew. He will repay all people as their actions deserve" (Prov. 24:12, Amplified Bible).

September 17
STOP BEING GREEDY, IT'S TIME TO SHARE
Read: James 2:18-20, 26

I'm sure that many of us can remember being told by a parent or guardian during those tender, young years that "You need to quit being selfish and learn how to share." The goal was to teach us to not be selfish as we placed focus and attention on ourselves. Whether it was a snack, a game, or that favorite toy; for many of us it was often very difficult to allow others to enjoy or share in the pleasure we received from this item, whatever it may have been at the time.

Well just in case you didn't know it, over the years various research and many clinical studies have even linked selfishness to being the root "cause of excessive anger and defiant behaviors in children and in teenagers." So, it would appear our parents or guardians knew what the effects of selfish behavior could produce if it was not addressed early and left unchecked.

When it is overlooked and the individual is allowed to cultivate this type of behavior, selfishness can lead to anger and frustration. Unfortunately this is where many who attend church find themselves today; frustrated and unfulfilled, especially when things don't go the way we would like them to go.

Selfishness and being an ambassador for Christ just don't mix (2 Cor. 5:20); an ambassador is defined as "an authorized representative or messenger." Therefore, on earth we are to be the "authorized representatives or messengers" for Christ, demonstrating His nature and character.

When Jesus walked the earth He did not focus on Himself and His needs, but on the needs of others demonstrating humility, compassion, and love.

There are many believers in the church or body of Christ who possess a "me, me, me" or "my, my, my" attitude. We come to worship services week after week looking for excitement and another "spiritual high;" now there is nothing wrong with this, because when we come to worship God we should expect Him to move and to do something not just to us, but in us—-yet there still needs to be more.

There are even those who take this to the extreme by not only seeking their "spiritual fix,"

Thoughts

_____

_____

_____

_____

_____

_____

_____

but also go from church to church, service to service just to hear a good word—which is also good to do because "faith comes by hearing" (Rom. 10:17); but sadly, there is rarely any practical application of what has been heard.

Going to worship service is not just about making us feel good or receiving spiritual goose bumps, but about spiritual application that leads to transformation; transformation not only in us individually, but also in those we come in contact with and encounter each day. What benefit is there in going to church week after week, month after month, year after year, and never release anything we have learned and/or received to help with the needs of others?

It is never enough to have faith alone; true faith requires corresponding action. Much of our frustration as believers in Christ will cease to exist when we learn to remove selfish motives as we look at the greater design of God's intended plan and purpose. Spiritual fulfillment comes by way of giving what we have received. The LORD says to each of us today, "Stop being greedy, because it's time to share!"

"Give away your life; you'll find life given back, but not merely given back—given back with bonus and blessing. Giving, not getting, is the way. Generosity begets generosity" (Lk. 6:38, The Message).

September 18
CHANGE COMES AFTER MIDNIGHT
Read: Acts 16:16-31

Several years ago I had the opportunity to visit the country of Iceland and I just so happened to be there in the heart of the winter months; I can truly say this country lived up to its name with freezing temperatures of the like that I had never experienced before, especially since I was born and raised in Florida.

My visit there was for official business and work-related, with an entire team of us traveling to the designated location. When we arrived we were greeted and then each given a large Parka overcoat to help mitigate the effects of the ice-piercing wind that made the outside temperature drop another few degrees. And to top it off, at this particular time of year there was 24-hours with no sunlight at all for periods of not just hours or days, but months. Thank God we were only there for a few days.

Thoughts

_____
_____
_____
_____
_____
_____
_____

Can you imagine living in complete darkness for months at a time? It truly amazed me to see the native Icelanders living in these conditions, but more so they were actually accustomed to this type of environment. Conversely, many of

330

the military personnel stationed there found it difficult to make the adjustment with a large number of personnel constantly battling with depression, irritability, and the sense of hopelessness brought about by the constant darkness. Of course this also produced other negative side effects like the inability for many to get a good night's sleep with rest patterns thrown out of sync with darkness being present when there should have been light outside.

But on a brighter note, during summer months the exact opposite occurred; daylight hours were extended providing 24-hour access to the sun and all the outside activities that are normally accomplished during the daytime. However, what is important to note here is the natural progression of things—first darkness and then the sun.

As believers in Christ we too experience seasons of darkness, seasons of discomfort and/ or seasons of pain. And though it may appear that midnight will never end this is not the time to give up hope, instead we are to keep holding on because the sun is coming. Jesus the S-O-N comes to bring us light!

In these times we must remember that our praise produces release and causes our seasons to change. When we remove the focus from ourselves, off of our circumstances, and begin to place proper focus on the LORD, it is then that we begin to realize He is much bigger than anything we face because He is now magnified and exalted. And even though darkness and weeping may try to consume us, we can be certain that better and brighter days are ahead.

Whenever your midnight seems like it will never end, remember that when the Son appears He comes to bring you light and joy. Your midnight season begins to change as you release your praise. Change comes after midnight!

"Weeping may last through the night, but joy comes with the morning" (Ps. 30:5, New Living Translation).

September 19
YOUR MIND IS A TERRIBLE THING TO WASTE
Read: Is. 26:3

When I was much, much younger, I can recall advertisements for a college fund campaign that could be heard on the radio as well as seen on television, and though it is often not promoted as much today, the campaign slogan is still readily recognized and still has merit in more ways than one, the slogan was: "A mind is a terrible thing to waste."

Thoughts

_____
_____
_____
_____
_____
_____
_____

The preceding slogan was used for the United Negro College Fund (UNCF) which was an initiative focused on providing underprivileged minority (African-American) high school graduates with aspirations of attending college the necessary resources to achieve this goal. The premise of the campaign was that, although they may often be stereotyped and looked upon negatively by society, many minorities had the ability to excel and accomplish great things if only given the chance and afforded the opportunity to receive a college education. This in turn benefits society by tapping into a large repository of unused potential.

Utilization of this unused potential not only required the generosity of caring citizens, but also required a change of thinking on the part of the potential college student. The student had to look beyond society's perceptions and stereotypes, and then see themselves as successful. They had to block out all words of negativity, fear, doubt, and unbelief, and then aspire to greatness.

In other words, they not only had to change the way they perceived themselves, but at the same time they had to literally change their thought process and start speaking the right way.

Well, this is not just true of those who have been granted UNCF scholarships, but it is also true for all of us as believers in Christ who are oftentimes the minority in today's society. Many of us settle for mediocrity in life based upon our thinking, the perception we have of ourselves, and the way we speak on a consistent basis, when in actuality we have been created and destined to rule and reign (Gen. 1:26-28).

However, our ability to rule and reign here in the earth is directly related to the way we think and our ability to exercise the measure of faith that we have been given (Rom. 12:3), yet many today give the devil control of their minds by meditating on thoughts that do not line up with the Word of God.

It is precisely at this point defeat begins to creep in for us as believers—-it all starts in the mind. This is why we must meditate on the right thing, primarily God's Word. The Word of God not only tells us who we are, but also has the ability to increase our faith by letting us know what we are capable of accomplishing (Phil. 4:13).

Therefore, we must constantly renew our minds (Eph. 4:23) and not allow the enemy to obtain a foothold in our lives through inconsistent and incorrect thinking. Our thinking is often contaminated by what we see and hear, so it is imperative that we look at and listen to the right things as we guard our eye and ear gates. Though we may not be able to control what we hear, we do have the ability to control what we listen to and how we respond to it.

Thoughts

_____
_____
_____
_____
_____
_____
_____

Our mouths often operate in conjunction with our minds, so if our thinking is wrong, our speech tends to be wrong as well. Don't allow your mind to become a dumping ground or wasteland for the enemy, but rather choose to simply renew it (Phil. 2:5) because YOUR MIND IS A TERRIBLE THING TO WASTE!

September 20
IN THE MIDST OF THE STORM
Read: Matt. 8:23-27

Although I generally don't have a lot of spare time to watch television, when I do have the opportunity I enjoy watching the Military Channel, National Geographic, Animal Planet, Discovery Channel, the Coolest Stuff on the Planet, nature shows, documentaries, and other shows of this nature. It amazes me to see how different species of animals survive and interact, and all of the other unique aspects of God's creation in general.

Having lived in Florida all of my life until joining the military, I am very familiar with the phenomenon of hurricanes and tornados based on first-hand experience from having endured a few, and I know of their destructive power. So, one evening while watching television, the show "Storm Chasers" caught my attention.

This particular show documented how, during the season of spring, a group of individuals load up their armor-plated and custom overhauled vehicles equipped with enhanced radar and camera equipment, including the advanced technology of Doppler radar. Their destination would be a section of the United States called the Great Plains but also known as "Tornado Alley" in search of the most deadliest and violent storms. The goal, of course, is the study of weather patterns in hopes of providing residence with increased early warning to create the opportunity for faster evacuations in an effort to further preserve lives.

These storm chasers go above and beyond by not just viewing these massive storms from afar, but often get up close and personal to the point of being pounded with golf ball-sized hail and ice, and almost being engulfed by the extreme force of the wind. But the surprising thing to see is the activity that occurs at the center (or "Eye") of the storm as recorded by the storm chaser's advanced equipment.

Generally in life, the center is usually the strongest point or provides the most stability and power for a thing. Therefore, when looking at a hurricane or tornado one would naturally think the "Eye of the Storm" or the center would cause the most damage, since technically this is where the most force should be generated from; but this is not the case.

Thoughts

_____

_____

_____

_____

_____

_____

_____

At the center of the storm there is actually very little activity. Can you imagine that? With destructive and powerful winds all around, the eye of the storm is characterized by "light winds and clear skies." Though the storm rages around it, the "eye" is the region where the weather is actually calm, tranquil, and peaceful.

Therefore, focusing on Jesus in our trials should bring consolation as we endure the storms of life we each face; both spiritually and in the natural. Though fierce and violent winds of struggle and turmoil often surround us, when Jesus is placed at the center we are guaranteed to have peace even in the midst of a violent storm. At the center of His will for our lives, the storms do not faze us because He brings peace, tranquility and stillness.

As the storms of life surround you today don't worry or fret. Make it a purpose to activate your faith, remain at the center, and let Jesus do what He does best; bring peace in the midst of the storm.

"Don't fret or worry. Instead of worrying, pray. Let petitions and praises shape your worries into prayers, letting God know your concerns. Before you know it, a sense of God's wholeness, everything coming together for good, will come and settle you down. It's wonderful what happens when Christ displaces worry at the center of your life" (Phil. 4:6-7, The Message).

September 21
JUSTIFIED
Read: Rom. 8:1

Several months ago I saw a newscast of a Texas man who had been released from prison after 27 years of confinement in a small cell because he had been wrongfully accused and convicted of a crime he never committed. Can you imagine that? For almost three decades this individual had been locked behind bars losing precious years from his life that he could never regain back, all for something he didn't even do. It was modern technology and DNA evidence that granted his newfound freedom. The DNA used to acquit him was found in the blood.

Thoughts

_____

_____

_____

_____

_____

_____

Here was a man that at age eighteen was wrongfully convicted, but 27 years later at the age of 45-years old he became a free man starting fresh with a clean slate, clean record, and a new life; just as if he had never been convicted.

This is exactly what Christ did for us on the cross; He made us free from the bondage and penalty of sin (Rom. 5:1,9,18. We are justified (treated as righteous and worthy of salvation) through the spotless unblemished blood of Christ.

Though we are now justified, unlike the innocent Texas man, we were all actually guilty as charged (Rom. 3:23). Unfortunately the preceding verse is where many believers stop, camp out, and setup tent as we remain under the cover of condemnation and the accusing finger of others.

Many times, although we have been freed from sin, we allow the past and the things we did in our B.C. (Before Christ) days make its way back to the forefront. And instead of walking in the liberty and freedom that comes through faith in Jesus Christ, we remain imprisoned by how we see ourselves and the opinion of others. This requires a total transformation of the mind and changing the way we think (Rom. 12:2).

We must also remember one all-important fact, the things we used to do no longer matter because they have been covered by and under the Blood; the places we used to go no longer matter, they have been covered under the Blood; and the things we used to say no longer matter, because they too have been covered under the Blood (2 Cor. 5:17). Did you catch that? The scripture says the "past is forgotten;" enough said!

If God has forgotten our past, then so should we. When God looks at us now, He sees us through the red lenses of the Blood; and though blood is actually red in color, He now sees us white as snow (Is. 1:18).

Therefore, know today that in Christ you are no longer condemned (Rom. 8:1). God loved us so much He allowed Jesus, His only begotten Son, to not only become our advocate (or attorney), but the propitiation (atonement) for our sins as well (Jn. 3:16). This means that not only did He receive the penalty for our sin nature, but He also provided the avenue that allows us to be forgiven for every sin we would ever commit (1 Jn. 1:9).

While hanging on the cross, I can picture Jesus entering heaven's courtroom in the spirit, saying, "Father, I know that [insert your name here] is guilty as charged, but I receive the punishment that [he or she] rightfully deserves simply because I love [him or her]." The Father replies, "Very well; the case is dropped, all charges are dismissed, and [he or she] gets a fresh start." Then Jesus simply cries out, "It is finished!"

As believers we must stop walking with our heads hung down when we fall to sin; instead the proper response should be to confess it, forsake it, and then move on walking in victory (1 Jn. 1:9; Jn. 8:36).

Thoughts

_____

_____

_____

_____

_____

_____

_____

September 22

LOVE DEMANDS A SACRIFICE
Read: Jn. 14:15

Love is a very powerful thing; however, it is sometimes misunderstood and very often abused. We say "I Love You" without really having a true understanding of what real love is, using it as a catch phrase to show a general affinity towards someone when true love actually goes so much more deeper.

As I heard one preacher say, "Love will make you stay up all night talking on the cell phone saying: No, you hang-up; No, you hang-up even when you have exceeded the minutes on your particular phone plan. Love will make you become a stalker," that is in a good sense, meaning that the object of desire is pursued until he or she is obtained.

When we truly love something or someone, our undivided attention is devoted to this object or individual; our thoughts gravitate towards them, and in some cases we even lose sleep because our minds are so consumed and totally focused on them.

There are many instances in the Bible where individuals sacrificed everything for the sake of love. Samson lost his eyesight and the power of the anointing for what he thought was love; Jacob pursued Rachel to the point of working 14 years for no pay or wages; and after sinning by numbering and counting the people, when David repented his love for God was so deep that he refused to offer a sacrifice that had just been given to him for free saying, "No, I insist on buying it, for I will not present burnt offerings to the LORD my God that have cost me nothing" (2 Sam. 24:24). The bottom line to all of this is that sometimes love comes with a cost and will involve sacrifice.

Concerning the area of love the Apostle Paul records a mouthful in (1 Cor. 13). In all of this the one common theme that continues to prevail is that real love does not place the focus on us, but rather on others.

As believers in Christ, everything we do must be centered and focused on love; whether we are giving of our time, talents, or resources, it should all be done in a spirit of love. A perfect example of this can be seen when taking a look at the "Fruit of the Spirit" listed in Gal. 5:22-23. "But the fruit of the Spirit is LOVE, joy, peace, longsuffering, kindness, goodness, faithfulness, gentleness, self-control." Just in case you didn't notice, the very first fruit listed is "LOVE." James also reminds us in his epistle, "Yes indeed, it is good when you obey the royal law as found in the Scriptures: "Love your neighbor as yourself" (James 2:8, New Living Translation). Love is the key.

Thoughts

_____

_____

_____

_____

_____

_____

_____

Love is considered to be a "royal law" because it has been given to us and decreed by the King of Kings Himself. And as followers of the King, we are now citizens of the Kingdom, and in this

336

case, heirs to the throne. Therefore, it is our obligation to obey the orders of the King as written and given.

In the natural, whenever an earthly king sent out a royal decree or order to his subjects after it had been signed, the scribe would take a candle and pour wax across the seal to make it. The king would then use his signet ring to make an impression in the wax to signify that this decree did in fact come directly from him and that it was official.

Well, our King has given us a royal decree to love and it has been signed and sealed with the precious, spotless blood of the Lamb of God, Jesus Christ Himself. Therefore, in everything we do, love must be paramount; love is not a suggestion, but a direct command from the King Himself. Real love, the God kind of AGAPE love requires us to not think more about ourselves, but place the focus on others as we learn to freely give of ourselves (Jn. 15:13).

September 23
JUST DO YOUR PART
Read: Neh. 4:6

As believers in Christ, we all have been commissioned to be ministers. Not necessarily as a minister standing behind a pulpit or standing before a group of people; but a minister in the broader sense. In simplistic terms a minister is equivalent to being a servant.

Therefore, when we freely receive the gift of salvation and eternal life by professing faith in the Lord Jesus Christ we are to share this precious gift with others (1 Pet. 4:10).

With this gift Jesus has given us the authority to represent Him as His ministers here on earth according to Matt. 28:19-20. And when we tell others about Jesus and minister according to His Word, we are following the direct command of the Master and are backed by His authority and power. But, we are to only do this in the ability that He gives us individually.

Yet within the body of Christ, too often we see believers attempting to duplicate another person's anointing, when God simply desires that we minister and serve in the ability that He has specifically given to us. As a result, we tend to become imitators of man instead of heeding the encouragement given by the Apostle Paul in Eph. 5:1 where the challenge is to imitate God.

Thoughts

_____
_____
_____
_____
_____

When we copy and emulate God's example, He empowers us to minister in the ability that He gives to each of us. Whether a bishop, pastor, evangelist, prophet, deacon, a prayer warrior, endowed with an anointing to give; or minister in jails & prisons, nursing homes, sing, or give of our time sacrificially out of love; we each have a function in the body that only we can supply. So, in our vain attempts to be like someone else, who is going to do our part (Rom. 12:4-6)? When each member simply does his or her part, the Body can accomplish great things.

In the Old Testament, the prophet Nehemiah had a challenging task before him; he assumed the responsibility for ensuring that the walls surrounding the city of Jerusalem were repaired. Of course there was opposition, but this did not deter him or the people from completing the task at hand. "So we built the wall, and the entire wall was joined together up to half its *height,* for the people had a mind to work" (Neh. 4:6, New King James Version).

In a unified effort, the walls were repaired within fifty-two days because everyone simply did their part (Neh. 6:15). In a nutshell, each family was assigned a section of the wall to complete. Half of the people stood guard and were poised to engage a potential attack of the enemy, while the other half worked diligently to repair the wall. Each family focused on the section of the wall directly before them; not on their neighbors section, or a section of the wall in front of the home of a brother or sister down the road—they specifically focused on the area they were assigned.

What gift has God given you? Where have you been assigned to employ this gift?

As believers in Christ we must learn to operate in the gifts and anointing that God has given and placed upon us individually, and recognize that our value to the Body only comes when we do our part and serve based upon God's instructions to us. Don't be concerned with what the next person is or is not doing, JUST DO YOUR PART! The blessing comes through YOUR obedience (1 Pet. 4:11)!

September 24
I'M STILL HERE
Read: Is. 55:6

In watching the news, reading a newspaper, magazine, or any other periodical; it is pretty evident that the signs of the time are upon us and we are living in the last days. Scriptures foretell that we will "...soon hear about wars and threats of wars, but don't be afraid. These things will have to happen first, but that isn't the end. Nations and kingdoms will go to war against each other. People will starve to death, and in some places there will be earthquakes. But this is just the beginning of troubles" (Matt. 24:6-8, Contemporary English Version).

Thoughts

_____

_____

_____

_____

_____

_____

_____

338

The preceding are the things that are expected to happen before the Lord returns, and many of these things are happening right before our eyes today; our job as believers, the Church, or the body of Christ is to be ready.

Our nation as a whole has even turned away from the very principles on which it was founded; in particular "In God We Trust." We have slowly turned away from the principles of the Bible through placing focus on secular humanism, postmodernism, and many of the other world religions that focus on human reasoning attempting to be all-inclusive or making everyone feel comfortable. This all occurs at the expense of the Truth being ridiculed while the very moral fabric of our society continues to unravel and decay.

As a result, the Bible and the principles of God have taken a backseat to modern thought and the opinions of man; when man is literally here today and gone tomorrow (James 4:14). But even in all of this, God patiently stands by saying, "I'm Still Here" because it is His Word and Truth that will last and stand forever (Ps. 119:89, Matt. 24:35).

In recent years there have also been movements to remove any reference to God from our society (from currency, federal & public buildings, etc.), as a continued push for an all-encompassing universal religion prevails. And if we as believers do not get God's Word on the inside of us and take a stand, we too could be deceived and be moved by the ebb and flow of society (Matt. 24:24-25). Therefore, if we are not watchful and on guard, the very elect of God can be deceived as well—-but, we have been fore-warned.

There will come a time when freedom of religion as we know it in America will be a thing of the past, and believers will no longer have Bibles readily available but will eventually have to hide their faith and also have to meet in secret places. Sadly, in many regions and nations around the world this is already a reality today. But God continues to say, "I'm Still Here."

Although these things must come to pass as prophesied, God has given us instructions on what we are to do in the interim. "Then if my people who are called by my name will humble themselves and pray and seek my face and turn from their wicked ways, I will hear from heaven and will forgive their sins and restore their land" (2 Chron. 7:14, New Living Translation). In other words, we must seek Him diligently!

The prophet Isaiah reminds us that we are to "Seek the LORD while He may be found, Call upon Him while He is near" (Is. 55:6, New King James Version). This simply suggests that we must pray to God while, study His Word, and seek Him with our whole heart and entire being while we still have a chance. What better time to seek Him than now?

All that has and is occurring in the world today is just confirmation that God's Word is true; therefore, turn to Him while there is still time.

Thoughts

_____

_____

_____

_____

_____

_____

No matter what may be happening around us today, God consistently says: "I'M STILL HERE (Jer. 33:2-3).

September 25
IT'S IN THE PAST
Read: Matt. 6:15

Harboring unforgiveness can be a very dangerous road to travel for those who make it a practice of holding on to grudges against others. Because traveling along this road generally leads to bitterness, hatred, physiological and health effects, and in extreme cases even violence and wrath; none of which come from the righteousness that a transformed life in Jesus Christ is designed to produce.

It is often in this broken condition that we come to God with prayers, requests, and petitions; praying earnestly believing that God will not only hear our cry but also grant our request. Yet many times there are no visible signs of change in the situation or circumstance at all.

There may even be times that we pray according to the Father's will (based on the Word) as we quote Scripture to remind God of His many promises towards us, and even go as far as attempting to activate our faith. But none of this matters when we continue to hold on to and nurse unforgiveness as we continue to feed it like a newborn baby.

And although we may have the ability to pray with the eloquence of Daniel (Dan. 9:21) or with the power of Elijah (James 5:17-18); in actuality many times our prayers often go unanswered and are hindered as if they are bouncing off a glass ceiling—this is a by-product of entertaining unforgiveness in the heart. Therefore, instead of being confident in releasing our requests trusting that they will be answered, instead they often return unanswered and thereby become an added burden and weight to carry around when all that is really required is of us is to release the hindrances that unforgiveness to the LORD (Ps. 55:22).

Jesus reminds us in Matt. 5:23-24 of what is required in this case. When we choose not to forgive, this directly contradicts God's "royal law," as James states it in his epistle, to love our neighbor as well as we love ourselves (James 2:8). Jesus also encourages us to love God with our entire being (Matt. 22:37-39).

Every time we don't forgive we transgress God's command to love and we literally sin according to James 4:17. And just in case you did not know this fact, it is our sin that separates us from God and hinders our prayers (Is. 59:2).

Thoughts

_____
_____
_____
_____
_____
_____

And when we really look at it, forgiveness has nothing to do with the other person that we are holding a grudge against but is more about us. There are many individuals today who are weighed down by the side effects of unforgiveness suffering both physically and mentally, while the person who may have unknowingly offended them is living a life that is full and carefree.

Whatever someone may have "done" (past tense) to us whether by word, action or deed, is just that; it is in the past. Learn to forgive quickly, because when we forgive others our Heavenly Father can then quickly forgive us of our sins and trespasses as we release all of the excess baggage and unneeded weight which in turn allows us to freely move forward as His love begins to flow in us and through us.

However, above and beyond learning how to forgive others, many times the biggest hindrance to our prayers being answered and being able to move forward in life simply boils down to learning how to forgive ourselves.

Refuse to hold on to unforgiveness in any form. Whatever the offense may have been, remember it is past tense; in other words it is in the past, so leave it there. Choose to release all excess weight as you not only learn to forgive (Matt. 6:14-15)!

September 26
HOW DEEP ARE YOUR ROOTS?
Read: Ps. 1

Many years back, author Alex Haley published "Roots: The Saga of an American Family" which was later made into a television mini-series. Haley traced his ancestry back to Gambia, Africa; then detailed the story and saga of their journey to and life in America during a period of slavery. He provided an in-depth look at the story of his family's transition and the struggles endured through each generation up to his current generation, tracing the roots of his family.

It is documented that "*Roots* received 36 Emmy Award nominations, winning nine; it also won a Golden Globe and a Peabody Award. It received unprecedented Nielsen ratings with the finale still standing as the third-highest rated U.S. television program ever." In the late 1970's when the mini-series aired, families all over the United States and around the world were literally glued to televisions watching the "Roots" saga unfold.

Thoughts

_____
_____
_____
_____
_____
_____

But in Christ there is an even better saga when we as believers in Christ trace our roots to see not only where we came from, but more importantly where we are going.

According to Gal. 4:4-5 "But when the fullness of the time had come, God sent forth His Son, born of a woman, born under the law, to redeem those who were under the law, that we might receive the adoption as sons" (New King James Version). This lets us know that we have been adopted into the family of God through the shed blood of Jesus Christ.

Now something that makes the process of adoption so significant is the fact that when a child is born to natural parents there isn't much choice on the sex, eye color, hair texture, height, etc. of the child; as a parent you basically get what you get.

However, with adoption individuals go through great lengths to seek out and choose a child according to the potential parent's preferences: age, height, nationality, etc. are all features that can be requested for in advance; and when the specific child is found he or she is then brought into the family. Not only is the adopted child a part of the family, but he or she now has equal standing with those who were born naturally to the parents having the same bloodline.

In similar fashion, God methodically sought us out and specifically picked each and every one of us. Scripture declares that He knows each of us by name (Jer. 1:5). Therefore, it is through the shed blood of Christ that we are now adopted into the family of God and are now in the lineage of our Heavenly Father. No matter whom our earthly father or mother may be or have been, in Christ it is now His blood that connects us to His body. And as members of our new family we have guaranteed rights because we are now heirs (Rom. 8:15-17).

In Christ our roots now run deep, this means our former nature and lineage no longer really matters; in Christ we are now like the tree planted by rivers of living water described in Psalm 1 with roots that go deep.

Just like a natural tree with roots that run deep into the ground, in Christ we find stability and nourishment through our connection; therefore, when the winds of trials, tribulation, and life in general blow, we may bend but we do have to worry about breaking because our foundation is sure. Therefore, when we remain tapped in and connected to our True power source, we provide the essential elements required to bring life to all who are around us. How deep are your roots?

Thoughts

_____

_____

_____

_____

_____

_____

_____

September 27
JUST TAKE A SEAT
Read: Lk. 10:38-42

As the years and centuries have progressed, it seems that more and more people find it quite difficult to pause, if even just for a brief moment. Today's fast-paced society places increased demands on us to be more efficient and more effective in everything that we do; with this has come many technological advances with systems and appliances that have made things that would have taken our parents or grandparents days or weeks to accomplish, now being able to be completed within a matter of minutes and seconds in some instances.

One would think that with all of this new technology, more of our time would be freed up so that we could actually slow down and take a moment to relax. Not!

So, instead of relaxing and using the free time this new technology affords us, we often fill these spare moments up with the use of even more technology; today everyone has Blackberry's, iPhones, iPads, portable Playstations, MP3s, laptops, PDAs, etc. Therefore, when we are placed in a position of having to patiently wait, instead of taking a moment to just inhale and relax, we pull out one of the aforementioned devices to fill in the empty timeslot.

Unfortunately, many of us become so busy that we often miss out on the more important things in life: assisting others, developing lasting relationships, spending quality time with a spouse and our families, and most importantly—SPENDING QUALITY TIME WITH GOD!

This is where we find Martha, the sister of Mary and Jesus' friend Lazarus. During a visit by Jesus to their home, Martha went about doing what she did best—serving and showing hospitality; while Mary on the other hand just sat at Jesus' feet and simply listened to Him speak.

I can picture Martha going back and forth to the kitchen providing drinks and food to the guests, washing the dishes, and picking up trash as everyone finished their meal, while getting more frustrated by the minute because her sister had not lifted a finger to assist her (Lk. 40-42).

Jesus was telling Martha that she was too concerned and worried about the small things when she should have been focusing on that which was more important—-spending time with the Master. In this instance, although she was serving, Martha was definitely not displaying the fruit of the spirit, "joy," (Gal. 5:22-23) in her service simply because she chose the mechanics of work over spending quality time with the One who gives us joy when we serve the right way.

We can find joy when we patiently wait in God's presence. "In thy presence is fullness of joy; at thy right hand there are pleasures for evermore" (Ps. 16:11, King James Version), and according to Neh. 8:10b "the joy of the LORD is your strength" (New King James Version). So, not only do we receive joy in the Lord's presence, but our strength is also renewed.

Thoughts

_____

_____

_____

_____

_____

_____

_____

343

As believers we are in fact called to serve, because that is exactly what Jesus came to earth to do (Mk. 10:45). However, our service is fortified when we set aside time for God's presence.

September 28
THERE'S NO TIME LIKE THE PRESENT [TO PUT ASIDE PRIDE]
Read: Acts 8:26-40

In Acts chapter 8, an Ethiopian eunuch who possessed great authority and a man of stature, was on his way to Jerusalem was on his way to worship. As the entourage traveled along, an angel or the Spirit of the LORD placed it upon Philip's heart to go and meet the eunuch as the Spirit said, "Go near and overtake this chariot" (Acts 8:29).

Philip was one of the seven men full of faith chosen to assist the apostles with meeting the daily needs of the people in the New Testament. He can be categorized as one of the first deacons recorded in the New Testament, and he was also considered to be an evangelist.

So, as the Ethiopian eunuch and his associates made their way towards Jerusalem, Philip made haste to catch up with them on foot. Philip was not a young man at this stage in his life; nevertheless, he obeyed the voice of the Spirit urging him to minister to the eunuch and then ran to catch the chariot as he was commanded.

As he approached the chariot Philip heard the eunuch reading the book of Isaiah aloud; obviously the eunuch was an educated man having the ability to read and was a person of wealth since he had his own personal copy of Isaiah. While still closing in on his targeted assignment, Philip eventually came alongside the chariot (while still running mind you), and then asked the eunuch if he really understood what he was reading. Although he was a man of power and obvious intelligence, the eunuch did not allow pride to determine his response but said, "How can I, unless someone guides me" (Acts 8:31)?

So Philip entered the chariot and began to explain the meaning of the Scripture and preached Jesus unto the eunuch. As they continued on the road they came near some water; the eunuch was so touched by the message of Jesus Christ he was ready to be baptized (Acts 8:36-37). After the eunuch's public confession Philip commanded the chariot to stop; then Philip and the eunuch entered the water for the purpose of performing the eunuch's baptism.

Not only did the eunuch make an immediate decision to follow Christ, but he also wanted to solidify and confirm his transformation by

Thoughts

_____
_____
_____
_____
_____
_____
_____

identifying with Christ's death, burial, and resurrection through water baptism (Mk. 16:16).

The eunuch was not concerned about his intellect, prowess, or socio-economic status; his primary focus was obeying the voice of Truth, by way of God's Word and the preached message of Jesus Christ. Likewise as believers, we are not to pretend as if we are so intelligent or just so wise that we know everything. Especially when we understand that only God is Omniscient and All-knowing.

Many times we faithfully come to worship services and have the Bible readily available, yet often read God's Word with little to no real understanding. This is why we need the Holy Spirit who comes to teach us what we don't know (Jn. 14:26).

No matter how intellectual we think we are, or what our status in society or the church may be; we must begin to lay aside pride and those things that block us from having true relationship with God. Well, there's NO TIME LIKE THE PRESENT to fully commit ourselves, come in humble submission to the Father, and then allow the Holy Spirit to teach us what we don't know (Jn. 16:13).

September 29
RAISING THE STANDARD
Read: Jn. 12:32

In Exodus chapter 17, we find the Israelites in the midst of yet another conflict. This time it was the Amalekites who set themselves against the host and army of Israel. At this particular time Moses was the leader of God's chosen people, with Joshua poised to lead the Israelite army into battle.

Moses told Joshua, "Choose us some men and go out, fight with Amalek. Tomorrow I will stand on the top of the hill with the rod of God in my hand" (Ex. 17:9). Joshua followed the instructions of his leader, selected men of war, and then went into battle. Moses then positioned himself atop a hill with his brother Aaron and their faithful friend Hur in plain view of the Israelite army. As long as the hands of Moses were raised the Israelites prevailed in battle; but whenever his hands began to lower and/or fall, the enemy would gain the upper hand.

Thoughts

Aaron and Hur eventually began to notice their leader's fatigue and then found a rock to place under Moses for him to sit on. And to ensure that their leader had the support he needed, Aaron and Hur each positioned themselves on either side of Moses to hold up his hands.

An amazing thing began to happen. When the people saw the rod that their leader Moses held in his hand lifted up, Joshua and the Israelite army found the encouragement and strength needed to allow them to defeat the Amalekites in a decisive victory.

The rod in the hand of Moses is representative of God's authority and the rock that he sat on is symbolic of none other than Jesus Christ, the "Rock" of our salvation (also known as the "Living Word"). Therefore, as believers in Christ, just as Israel prevailed while Moses' hands were lifted while holding his rod; we too can prevail when we begin to support our spiritual leaders, and also begin to lift up the Standard and Authority of God's Word.

In the present day and age that we live in, it is very easy to conform to the ideology of the status quo which, more times than not, invariably ends up in compromise and the lowering of our standards. Sadly, this type of behavior has already crept into many churches today where standards have been relaxed to the point of agreeing with the world's way of doing things, even when it directly contradicts the very Word of God.

Therefore, it is high time for Blood-bought believers in Christ to take a stand; standing on the authority of the God's Holy Word, the only True Standard. Our nation must return to the basics and the principles on which it was founded, "One Nation Under God" allowing U.S.A. to also represent "Under Sovereign Authority."

When we support true spiritual leaders and help them lift up the Standard of truth; every man, woman, boy, and girl (no matter the age) will be drawn to the Father as victory begins to reign. Jesus (the Word) said, "And I, if I am lifted up from the earth, will draw all *peoples* to Myself" (Jn. 12:32). In other words, we must lift up the standard of God's Word so that the world can see it; not just in our opinion, theory, or through popular thought, but as the infallible Word of the Most High God is lived out through the lives of believers.

Therefore, it is when we decide to take a stand and begin to lift up God's Standard that He also promises to lift up a standard on our behalf (Is. 59:19). Never allow the world's system to lure you into their ways or conform you through subtle compromise (Rom. 12:2). Instead choose to take a firm stand on the solid foundation of the Word, stay focused, are you willing to take a stand?

Thoughts

_____
_____
_____
_____
_____
_____
_____

September 30
VOICES AND CHOICES: WHO ARE YOU LISTENING TO?
Read: John 10:1-5, 11-15, 27

Whose voice is directing your life today? This is a very important question because the voice(s) that you listen to today have the potential to not only influence your life, but also shape and order your future and destiny. There are many messages and voices in the world today; and the one that you choose to listen to again will not only shape your life, but also determine the course and quality of your life experience.

In our society today everyone has a message, a revelation, an opinion, a theory, and/or a point. These often come by way of television, radio, music, newspapers & print media, and of course through the church. Whether we realize it or not, based upon what we expose ourselves to, there is the potential to hear literally hundreds of messages each day whether they are overt (evident) or subliminal (concealed).

The goal of each messenger is to attempt to get everyone to hear and receive their words while continuing to promote their message because they know one all important fact; whether it be one or one thousand, someone is going to listen.

Although there are many voices in the world, I would suggest that these generally come via three primary methods: the voice of the human spirit or the flesh, the voice of the devil (or the enemy) and the voice of God. However, it is entirely up to us to choose which voice we allow to direct our lives.

For many of us one of the greatest struggles or challenges in life is not what house to buy, what car to purchase, or even preparing for the future and retirement at some point. On the contrary, the greatest challenge that many of us face each day is determining which message or voice to listen to and/or follow.

Hearing and following the right voice is absolutely essential, because the voice(s) we listen to generally have the greater influence and control in our lives and over the direction of our thoughts and actions. It is for this reason that we must be mindful of the fact that we cannot trust everything we hear; sometimes this even applies in the area of church and the messages that come across some pulpits, television and/or other forms of media.

1 Jn. 4:1 provides us a stern warning; in other words, we must test the spirit of each message based on the standard of God's Word. When garbage goes in, garbage is bound to come out.

Therefore, we should never allow our minds and our hearts to become dumping ground for just any and everything that we hear, but instead we should make our hearts and minds fertile ground ready to receive life-giving instructions from God's Holy Word.

Thoughts

_____

_____

The goal of every believer in Christ should be to hear the voice of the Good Shepherd, the One who laid down His life for the sake of the sheep. He often speaks to us through His Word, through song, and even through other people.

_____

_____

_____

_____

_____

_____

However, we must position ourselves so that we can hear His voice clearly so that our lives can be led by Him. Because in order to be led by the Shepherd, we must first recognize His voice—-then we must listen and OBEY!

October 1

KEEP IT MOVIN'
Read: Ps. 23:4

In this illustration a young student is in a hurry to reach home after a long day of college classes with a primary focus of showering and putting on fresh clothing for an important meeting, a meeting that could determine his future at a prestigious law firm well-known throughout the entire state.

He jumps in his car and starts the commute home; but, for whatever reason, interstate traffic is backed up for miles as far as the eye can see. He attempts to contact the interviewer to explain the current situation and let him know there is a potential he might be a little late; however, he's unable to make contact.

Traffic on the other hand, continued to progress at a snail's pace literally moving a few feet every ten minutes. Getting frustrated, the young man began to contemplate just pulling his car off to the side, call the interviewer back to reschedule, and then just sit and wait for the traffic to clear.

Overriding his first inclination, he felt led to remain right where he was and continue with the flow of traffic, although turtles could have literally moved faster. He then began to wonder what could be causing such a halt to the normal flow of traffic.

After an hour and a half on a journey that normally took fifteen minutes, he approached two cars on the side of the road that had been involved in a minor fender-bender, with no personnel injuries. "OK" he thought, "The cars are not on the interstate blocking traffic, so what is the issue?"

Traffic had been backed up for miles because of the "rubbernecking" syndrome. Although the vehicles involved in the accident had been moved to the shoulder of the highway and no longer impeded traffic, commuters were repeatedly slowing down to be nosey as each attempted to get a closer glimpse of what was happening on the side of the road. Meanwhile one of the State Troopers responding to the scene stood directing and encouraging everyone to just "KEEP IT MOVIN'!"

Thoughts

_____
_____
_____
_____
_____
_____

The young man finally reached home somewhat discouraged about missing his interview, but as he entered the door he noticed a voice message on his answering machine. He listened to the message and it was the interviewer stating that the weirdest thing happened today, and then went on to explain how he had been stuck in traffic for the past two hours and to give him a call to reschedule the interview for later that evening.

Just think, had the student decided to follow his first impulse to pull off to the side, he would have still been in traffic and could have missed the second-chance opportunity for his interview. He finally met the interviewer and was determined to be the best qualified person for the position and hired on the spot.

Sometimes life has a way of seeming to halt our progress during our Christian journey of faith. Because although we may have many mountain-top experiences; the valleys of life are also common pit stops in our travels as well.

According to 2 Cor. 4:8-9 the Apostle Paul encourages us to not get discouraged, and simply reminds us that although from time to time we may have to walk through the valley, this is not a sign that we should stop or setup camp while murmuring and complaining, and expecting everyone to join our pity party; we have to KEEP IT MOVIN'!

Does life seem to have you stuck in a valley of despair? If so, I would encourage you to not get distracted but remain focused; your victory is on the other side!

October 2
IT'S TIME TO GET AWAY
Read: Mk. 6:31

As Jesus went throughout the land during His time, His popularity grew more and more each day as He fulfilled the will of the Father accomplishing the very things that He was sent to earth to do (Acts 10:38).

Everywhere that Jesus and His Disciples went, a crowd was not far behind because of the anointing of God on Jesus' life. Knowing that ministry was essential to meeting the needs of the people, Jesus consistently served and ministered often with no thought for His own physical needs. However, in Mark chapter six, Jesus began to recognize the price He and His Disciples were paying as they ministered all day without taking time to replenish with food and drink; He was reminded of the need to physically resupply in order to maintain the strength required to complete the ministry they were commissioned to do. Jesus then said to His Disciples, "Come

Thoughts

_____
_____
_____
_____
_____
_____
_____

349

with me by yourselves to a quiet place and get some rest" (Mk. 6:31, New International Version).

As believers in Christ going about our day-to-day activities at work, at home, in church, and in outreach to others, we must remember to set aside time to relax, refresh, and regenerate in the quietness of God's presence. Yes we are to serve; however, there also comes a time for rest to include both physical and spiritual maintenance (Ex. 31:17).

Case in point, even in our current fast-paced society the average person takes time to ensure their automobile receives regular oil changes, tire rotations, tune-ups, etc., which are all essential checks and balances required to ensure increased service life of the vehicle. How much more as spiritual beings do we need similar maintenance? Unfortunately, many of us fail to pull over for refueling and refilling with God's Holy Spirit and connection with our Heavenly Father in His presence to renew our strength (Ps. 16:11; Neh. 8:10; Eph. 5:18).

Jesus recognized the importance of those much needed moments of solitude and times of refreshing in God's presence away from chaos, confusion, the busyness of life, and all of the distracting noises.

Therefore, in order to fully function in the capacity of being effective on our jobs, in our families, or in ministry, we must learn how to separate ourselves for periods of rest to not only regenerate and rejuvenate our physical bodies, but more importantly refresh our spiritual being. We are not earthly beings having a spiritual experience, but rather spiritual beings having an earthly experience.

Jesus provided a great prescription for weariness and showing the need for rest in the Word (Matt. 11:28-29).

Are you feeling tired, over-worked, and over-burdened? Busyness does not equate to holiness. Jesus encourages us to come away with Him and find rest in His presence. So, make it a purpose to separate yourself and find rest in God's presence today, IT'S TIME TO GET AWAY!

"My Presence will go *with you,* and I will give you rest" (Ex. 33:14, New King James Version).

Thoughts
_____
_____
_____
_____
_____
_____
_____

October 3
I CAN'T COME DOWN
Read: Neh. 6:3

Distraught about the current condition of the walls of Jerusalem, Nehemiah (a Jew who was the cupbearer of the king of Persia) was authorized by the king to return to his home to oversee rebuilding the walls surrounding the city that now lay in ruins (Neh.2). Nehemiah was appointed governor of the region of Jerusalem and given the authority to do whatever it took to rebuild the city walls.

After receiving official release and the blessing of the king of Persia, Nehemiah journeyed to Jerusalem with letters from the king that authorized him to pass through each region unhindered until he ultimately reached his final destination. Upon arriving, Nehemiah was grieved at what he saw; he then took upon himself the task of ensuring that the walls of the city were rebuilt.

Jerusalem, or course, represented or was symbolic of the city of God, the place where God's Spirit dwelt, and was the focal point of life for God's people. The rebuilding of the walls was sort of symbolic of a return of God's strength to the community as a whole, and of His ability to provide protection for His people.

But, as with any effort to do the right thing and when we try to rebuild the areas of our lives that are in ruin, the enemy comes with opposition. This was also the case for Nehemiah with nay-sayers, mockers, and haters telling him that he was wasting his time and that he should just come down from the wall and just quit.

Nehemiah disregarded their comments and replied, "I *am* doing a great work, so that I cannot come down. Why should the work cease while I leave it and go down to you" (Neh. 6:3)? It was because Nehemiah did not listen to the wrong voice(s) that he was able to lead the people in completing the project of rebuilding the walls in record time; everyone was willing to simply do their part.

Just as Nehemiah refused to come down because of the great work he was accomplishing for God, there is One who completed an even greater work on a hill called Golgotha (Calvary).

Jesus Christ (God incarnate, in the flesh) was nailed to a rugged cross and raised up between two thieves to receive the punishment of crucifixion (one of the most gruesome forms of punishment at the time) for crimes that He did not commit. The walls of protection that once guarded mankind had been torn down by sin as man fell in the Garden of Eden being tricked and seduced by the devil. It was now up to Christ (the spotless, sinless Son of God) to rebuild our walls of protection by bringing salvation to man.

Even as he hung on the cross to fulfill the will of the Father, many continued to hurl insults and mock Him (Matt. 27:40-42), yet Jesus did not reply to their mockery, but simply said "Father forgive them."

Although it was very well within His power to call down the host of Heaven (angelic beings) to remove Him from the cross, He refused to come

Thoughts

_____
_____
_____
_____
_____
_____
_____
_____

down because He knew a greater work needed to be accomplished; not His will, but the will of the Father who sent Him to complete His assignment. As the sky darkened, symbolic of the sins of the world being placed upon Jesus, he cried out "It is finished... Father, into thy hands I commit my Spirit." His work was finally done.

Everything that God sent Jesus to perform was accomplished at Calvary because Jesus saw the bigger picture, and because of this we have all been blessed beyond measure.

October 4
FAITH THAT MOVES
Read: Jn. 20:1, 17-18

Jesus had been betrayed and given over to the chief priests for thirty pieces of silver; the crucifixion occurred next with Him accomplishing everything His Father sent Him to do as He took upon Himself the very sins of every person born and/or those who would ever be born into the world. His body was then laid in a borrowed tomb, one that had never been used before with a huge stone covering the entrance.

On the first day of the week (Sunday) following Jesus' crucifixion and burial, Mary Magdalene went to the tomb to complete a specific task; she traveled to the tomb of her Lord with oils and spices to anoint and properly care for the body of Jesus.

Yet there was an obstacle that would surely prevent this woman from accomplishing her mission; that obstacle of course being the huge stone covering the entrance to the tomb, a stone that undoubtedly took several men to put in place.

But this did not discourage Mary Magdalene from doing what she felt led to do, which was to "GO" fully expecting to accomplish her task. This woman did not go to the tomb with a hammer, chisel, or any other tool to force her way in, she simply went forward believing the obstacle that stood between here and her Lord would be moved out of the way.

What a great example and true testament to faith in action; believing in advance that the obstacle which hindered or impeded access to the blessing would be completely moved out of the way beforehand.

Thoughts

As believers in Christ we must have similar faith; we must have faith that allows us to believe that any obstacle we face has no other choice but to move out of our way. This is the type of faith that prompts us to speak to the mountain of problems in our lives and cause them to move (Mk. 11:23).

Therefore, whether you have to go around it, go over it, or go through it; speak to the mountains and obstacles in your life today in faith, then EXPECT them to move. It is then that you too will be able to clearly see the Lord!

October 5
LIAR, LIAR
Read: 1 Jn. 2:3

Growing up as a child, there were many old sayings and phrases that were popular back then. One that seems to remain in the recesses of my memory is the phrase "Liar, liar, pants on fire!"

For those of us who are a little more mature in age, I'm sure many remember hearing the preceding childhood phrase that was often used when one child believed the other was not being completely truthful and was more than likely telling a lie.

Lies were often told to avoid punishment, to manipulate others into doing what we want them to do, or even attempt to cover up something negative we may have done or planned to do. Yet at the end of the day and in all of this, deception was at the very root of each lie.

For many these lies are still very prevalent today. As I thought about this notion of "lies," I was reminded of the movie "Liar Liar" starring actor/comedian Jim Carrey.

In the movie, Carrey played a lawyer who was on the fast-track to becoming a partner with the law firm he worked for. He was very versed in law and the legal system, quick-witted, and could find a loop-hole in any case to free those who were actually guilty of a crime on minor technicalities; this was all done while bending the truth, or telling a "white lie" as some like to call it. However, he lied so well in his climb up the ladder of success, that it eventually began to affect his family and relationship with his son when he consistently made promises that he never kept.

One day while waiting for his father (Carrey) to arrive at his birthday party, the son made a wish that for one complete day his father would not be able to tell a lie; through a miraculous turn of events, the son's wish actually came true.

For the remainder of the movie every time Carrey attempted to tell a lie only the truth would come out. And eventually over a period of time he came to the realization that telling the truth actually felt better. As a result, he not only became a better person, but also restored his relationship with his son and reconciled his marriage.

Thoughts

_____
_____
_____
_____
_____
_____
_____

The world encourages us to get ahead by any way possible and by any means necessary; as a result many often cheat, steal, and lie their way up the ladder of success while destroying others, relationships, and their eternal state in the process.

As believers, lying is not an attribute for someone who claims to be a disciple or follower of Jesus Christ in any circumstance. And although the connotation that a "white lie" does not cause any harm whether it is black, red, purple, yellow or brown; a lie, is a lie, is a lie no matter how it's wrapped.

According to Jn. 8:44 those who lie are not of God, but are of their father (the little "g" god of this world) the devil. By definition, a "disciple" is basically one who follows the teaching of another; enough said. This means that those of us who have a deep, personal, and intimate relationship with God through Jesus Christ are to speak the truth, and are to speak the truth in love (Eph. 4:15).

So, don't allow the external factors of this world's system to dictate your response in any situation. When faced with telling the truth or compromising by telling a lie, remember that it is truth that makes us free (1 Jn. 2:3-4).

October 6
IT'S ALL ABOUT THE NAME
Read: Acts 4:11-12

Names are very important to us as individuals, because it is the name that often provides a distinction between one individual versus another. And although many may share the same common name; it is still our name that provides a sense of worth, value, and importance. "A name also [often] connotes attributes, characteristics, etc., connected with the individual."

For those who may feel that names are insignificant, just call some by another person's name and then watch their reaction.

Whenever individuals go to sit down, eat-in restaurants, etc. where reservations are required, the receptionist generally does not ask where you live, or what kind of car you're driving; no, it is the individual's name that is requested and is normally what the reservation is placed under. Therefore, when a reserved table for a specific group is ready for use, the receptionist/hostess does not usually say "Now calling the group driving the BMW's, your table is ready;" instead it is a specific name that is addressed and called upon.

Thoughts

_____
_____
_____
_____
_____
_____
_____

Whether making a business deal, requesting a recommendation for a particular college, or getting a resumé for a job into the right hands; having the right contact and using the right name can be very advantageous. Dropping or using the right name could be the difference between future success or failure.

The power of names and their use can even be seen in the military. When something of importance needs to be accomplished in a timely fashion and there may appear to be apathy or a lack of urgency concerning the matter, simply mention that resolution of the issue is being requested in the name of a certain general, admiral or flag officer, then sit back and watch not only how many jump, but how fast and high they jump. "Namedropping" usually gets the job done ninety-nine percent of the time; that is when the right name is used.

Over the years there have been many influential names that are known and recognized world-wide: Abraham Lincoln, Henry Ford, Dr. Martin Luther King Jr., Albert Einstein, Nelson Mandela, President Ronald Reagan, Elvis Presley, President Bill Clinton, Oprah Winfrey, Michael Jordan, Bill Gates, Michael Jackson, and many more. Without even consciously thinking about it, I'm sure that we can immediately associate a particular act or deed with each individual; and it's all based on "the name."

Therefore, when certain names are mentioned, they are often immediately recognized because the name has come to be associated with a particular profession, job, or act. In biblical times names and their meaning were very important. For example, Moses – "to draw out;" Abraham – "father of many;" Sarah – "princess;" Israel – "ruling with God;" Solomon – "peace;" and Judah – "praise;" just to name a few. These names not only provided identity but spoke of their future, signifying who they were to be and what they were destined to accomplish—in short, the name spoke of their purpose and destiny.

With all of the names used in the world today and the many variations, there is still one name that stands head and shoulders above the rest, and that is the name of Jesus Christ!

Jesus is derived from the Hebrew name "Joshua" which means "Jehovah is salvation." And contrary to popular belief, Christ is not Jesus' last name. Christ literally means "Messiah or the Anointed One," which spoke of Jesus' purpose for coming to earth-- Jesus was anointed by God to bring salvation to a dying world. And there is still power in this name (Phil. 2:9-12)!

Thoughts

_____
_____
_____
_____
_____
_____
_____

October 7
THE WITNESS PROTECTION PROGRAM
Read: Jn. 15:26

With the number of high-profile crimes occurring in the United States, witnesses are often called upon to testify in the cases that ensue. As result, witness protection is offered to those willing to testify.

Many individuals have witnessed horrific crimes and/or injustices, and now have evidence to put away the perpetrator. These witnesses are often kept in a safe place until afforded the opportunity to present their evidence and testimony before a court of law. As a result, the entire lives of these individuals undergo a radical transformation.

Not only are these witnesses relocated to undisclosed locations, but many times they are also forbidden to have any contact or communication with those from their former life including family and loved ones to ensure their safety. And to top it off, they are often given new names and identities until the perpetrator can be caught and brought to justice.

Similarly, in our Christian walk of faith, our enemy the devil does not want us to testify of the Good News of the Gospel or of the goodness of our loving and faithful God.

He attempts to do everything within his power to keep us silent, because he knows that once we start "spilling the beans" or declaring truth, salvation will begin to spread like a wildfire. This is why he attempts to keep us bound and entangled in our former lifestyles and so focused on self that we don't move forward with our testimonies and declarations of God's goodness and favor.

But there is no need to fret because we have a remedy. Through the shed blood of Jesus Christ we undergo a radical transformation of our own as we place our complete faith and trust in Him (2 Cor. 5:17)! And at this point we receive both a new nature and a new name; and the former things of our past lifestyles no longer matter because we effectively become witnesses for God through Christ.

As His witnesses, God provides us with His covering and protection by way of our advocate, comforter and protector—the Holy Spirit—-who empowers us to declare God's Word (Acts 1:8).

Thoughts

When truth takes the stand, no one can say anything against it. So, speak the truth and don't worry because you're in the Witness Protection Program; go ahead, it's time to testify!

356

October 8
BRING IT TO THE CLEANER
Read: Is. 64:6

Imagine for a moment you have been invited to a very special event, and because of those who will be present at the event you are determined to look your very best. As a result, you expend a lot of energy and go through considerable effort traveling from store to store, boutique to boutique, mall to mall to locate that perfect dress or suit at the last minute, of course with shoes and accessories to match.

After hours of shopping and searching, something finally catches your eye and meets your standards. And though the price is a bit high, you spare no expense to obtain this ensemble. With everything now in place, you prepare for the social event of the season. Many have come from both near and far to witness this monumental gathering and to just say that they were a part of the yearly festivities.

As you walk into the banquet all eyes are on you; with your stride and chosen ensemble giving you the air of royalty. The hostess leads you to your seat, and almost immediately the unthinkable happens. While on his way to deliver an entrée to an adjacent table, the waiter accidentally spills an entire platter of food on your new outfit--the outfit that took hours to locate and at a considerable cost. What was planned to be an evening of excitement and fun had been ruined in an instant.

Upset and frustrated, you then go home to attempt to remove the stains before they set into the fabric. Water, seltzer and various stain removers are all employed, but to no avail. So, the next morning you decide to bring the outfit to one of the local cleaners hoping the experts can remove the stains.

You arrive at the cleaners the following day excited about the potential of receiving the clothing back in its once pristine condition; but instead you are greeted with bad news stating that all attempts to remove the stains were unsuccessful. With the outfit now ruined, you decide to discard it and chalk it up as a loss.

As believers in Christ, many times our sin may appear to be like those unremovable stains on that perfect outfit. And no matter how good we think we may be, our perceived righteousness apart from God does not matter; because any residue from sin is going to leave a stain (Is. 64:6). Therefore, it is our sin that turns that which was once clean and pure into something vile and filthy.

However, we should find consolation in the fact that in the times we do become filthy with sin, that God does not just discard us and throw us away. Instead He supplied the remedy to remove each one of our stains through Christ (Rom. 5:17-18).

Thoughts

_____

_____

_____

_____

_____

_____

_____

Through the shed blood of Christ we now have the means to get it right (1 Jn. 1:9) and maintain our right standing with Him. But the really amazing thing in all of this is the fact that God can take something that is absolutely filthy (our sin), dip it in a red substance (the blood of Christ), and then have us come out white as snow, defying the laws of physics, chemistry and nature.

So, when your "Cheer" doesn't do the job; you've attempted to change the "Tide" but still can't "Wisk" it away; you have given your "All;" and you've exhausted all of your resources and can't even "Shout" it out; dip it in and put it under the blood of Jesus Christ and watch the stains of sin begin to simply fade away. In other words, just BRING IT TO THE CLEANER (Is. 1:18)!

October 9
A CHANGED THOUGHT COMES FROM A CHANGED MIND
Read: Rom. 12:2

Although the slogan "A mind is a terrible thing to waste" was geared towards providing under-privileged students the opportunity to achieve great things on an academic level; I believe there is also practical and spiritual application for believers in Christ in this phrase as well.

As earthly beings it is often stated that we are comprised of the spirit, mind (soul), and body——with these three components making up the total man. However, if there is no evidence of change or renewal in one specific area, it can and will invariably adversely affect the other two——that being the mind. A good majority of the struggles we are confronted with and/or face on a daily basis originate in or can generally be traced to a dysfunction of the mind.

The mind (soul) is composed of our emotions and will; this is the area that is always under constant attack by the enemy. If he can get us to begin making decisions based on our emotions and how we feel, the battle is almost guaranteed to be a victory in his favor. The end result is usually us doing something contrary to the will of God for our lives simply because of the battles and struggles we face in this one particular area. I believe Joyce Meyer was very accurate in her analysis of the mind being a battlefield, because this is where the enemy attempts to setup camp; however, it is our job to be on guard and not allow him to take up permanent residence (1 Pet. 5:8).

Thoughts

_____
_____
_____
_____
_____
_____
_____

So, how can we achieve victory in the area of the mind? Dr. Creflo Dollar states it this way, "To keep the devil from gaining a foothold in your life, you must develop a sound mind that is completely controlled and directed by the Holy

Spirit. In other words, you must renew your mind with the Word of God." A renewed mind only comes by way of studying and mediating on the Word of God and the things of God, and spending time fellowshipping and communing with the Father, and also being connected with other like-minded believers.

Even though the enemy attempts to plant seeds of fear, doubt, and unbelief, we can cast these negative and corrupt thoughts (seeds) down using the Word (2 Cor. 10:3-6).

Based on the preceding Scripture, whenever incorrect thoughts enter our mind we have the ability to cast them down by the authority of the Word of God. One of the greatest Reformation theologians of all time, Martin Luther, simply stated it this way: "You cannot keep birds from flying over your head but you can keep them from building a nest in your hair."

As believers in Christ, we may not be able to stop the enemy from attempting to plant negative thoughts in our minds, but the choice to either dwell on them or cast them down is entirely up us. We are often drawn away from the path of righteousness and get off-track when we dwell on these thoughts, contemplate in our mind ways to achieve them, and then when we act upon these negative seeds that is when they begin to grow and spread. So, make a choice to never play with negative thoughts, because the only true recourse should be to CAST NEGATIVE THOUGHTS DOWN!

Our victory comes as we truly begin to allow the Word of God to transform the very way we think. When we believe right, we think right; when we think right, we speak right, and when we speak right our faith then causes us to live right—-that is living in victory, power, and authority! God has many great things in store for us, but it requires a renewed mind and a changing of the way we think (Rom. 12:1-2).

October 10
IT'S JUST A BUILDING, THERE IS MORE!
Read: 2 Sam. 7:5-6

Being in the U.S. Navy has afforded me the opportunity to visit many overseas locations: Greece, Italy, Spain, France, Azores, Portugal, Denmark, Turkey, Crete, Singapore and many others. In each of these countries it was always interesting to see the landmarks and structures that provided insight into understanding the culture and history of each nation; having the ability to see in person structures read about in History and Humanities books in school.

Thoughts

_____

_____

_____

_____

_____

Of course many of the most magnificent and extravagant structures or buildings these

_____

_____

countries had to offer could be found in the churches that were built in each location. These structures were often comprised of exquisite stained glass windows, vaulted ceilings with astonishing paintings and designs, flying buttresses, arches, with detailed statues and artwork inside.

These places of worship were awesome sights to see; however, no matter how magnificent they were there was still something missing; the spirit and power of the church—-THE PEOPLE! It is the spirit of the people and not just the building that actually makes a church part of the bigger "Church." God does not just dwell within buildings made by hands, but in the hearts of His people (2 Sam. 7:5-6).

In the Old Testament the Tabernacle, which represented our modern day church at the time, was actually a tent setup and then disassembled as God's people moved from place to place and location to location. God is constantly on the move, this is why His people must also be ready to move. God sought to dwell within His people, not a permanent building or structure.

Now we should not take this to the extreme saying there is no need for a church or to place any thought into its structure, because we should want the house of God and the location of worship to be a place that brings glory and honor to the One we are worshipping and there should be a desire to fellowship with like-minded believers there (Heb. 10:25). However, we should not relegate ourselves to spending so much time inside these extravagant or uniquely designed churches attending services, conferences and meetings that we have no time to go out and actually "BE" the church as described in Acts 2:44-47. Souls were saved and added to the church as the needs of the people were met.

The walls and ceiling of any church are primarily designed to keep the elements (wind, rain, snow, etc.) out; not keep the people of God in. The term "church" is actually derived from the Greek word "ekklesia" which means a gathering of "called out ones." As a body of believers we have been called out not to remain in, but to go out of for the work of ministry as we demonstrate the Father's love.

Therefore, having service after service, and meeting after meeting are of no consequence, if lives are not being changed or transformed. It's not just enough to say that "I go to church;" it's time that we make it our purpose to actually BE THE CHURCH. This requires that we GO – "G" Get "O" Out; getting out of the walls of the church into the true mission field—-the WORLD (Jn. 3:16).

Thoughts

_____

_____

_____

_____

_____

_____

_____

God has now chosen us as believers in Christ to be His physical representation here on earth to "GO" outside of the four walls into the world. Remember, the physical church is only a building; there is really so much more (1 Pet. 2:9)!

October 11

USE WHAT YOU'VE GOT
Read: Mk. 12:41-44

One day Jesus sat next to the Temple treasury and watched as crowds of people placed random amounts of money into the treasury box (the offering container of that time). I'm sure the religious leaders, Pharisees and Sadducees, walked up with bells ringing so that everyone could observe them placing large sums of money into the treasury; these individuals were the rich in society at the time, giving out of their excess and abundance.

But then there came a widow with virtually no means of support or no source of regular income eagerly willing to present an offering even though she didn't have much to offer. She walked up to the treasury and pulled out two copper coins that would equate to about half of one cent today; however, this did not hinder her because she presented the very last and best she had to offer.

Jesus seeing this wonderful act of sacrifice then turned to His disciples and said to them "Truly and surely I tell you, this widow, [she who is] poverty-stricken, has put in more than all those contributing to the treasury. For they all threw in out of their abundance; but she, out of her deep poverty, has put in everything that she had--[even] all she had on which to live" (Mk. 12:43-44, Amplified Bible).

The widow found favor in the sight of the Lord because her faith allowed her to demonstrate sacrifice through giving the very best gift she had to offer, nothing more and nothing less.

Likewise, each of us in the body of Christ is given different gifts and talents designed to enhance the overall effectiveness of the Body (Rom. 12:3-8). Sadly, many of these gifts are often never employed or either misused.

Misuse and abuse of gifts often arise as individuals attempt to duplicate the gifts and talents of another. Many times individuals become frustrated and even jealous when they attempt to do things God has not gifted them for, equipped them to do, or has yet to develop in them. This then leads to feelings of condemnation, insecurity, and inadequacy with the individual now thinking he or she does not measure up based on another's talent when in actuality the task was not something they were designed or equipped to do.

We must each use the gifts and talents given to us by God to ensure the Body functions as designed. When we try to imitate another, we in essence become like a prosthetic limb designed to copy or simulator the original; it may look good, but in many instances it adds no real functionality to the body. Our gifts are given to us that we might serve God first and then

Thoughts

_____
_____
_____
_____
_____
_____
_____

serve others, as we become good stewards of what He has blessed us with. If we don't perform our specific part or function and give the right way, the entire Body suffers.

In Mark Chapter Twelve, the widow was not concerned with what the religious leaders and other individuals were placing in the treasury. She made it up in her mind she was going to offer the very best she had, giving her all. This is the attitude that God desires from us; we are not to focus on how much someone else has to offer, or on another's gifts or talents, but instead begin to use what God has given to us no matter how insignificant we think it may be. True discipleship and stewardship does not come from imitating another, but in giving our all for the sake of Kingdom building.

We are all given a measure of faith (Rom. 12:3); however, it is totally up to us to use what we've got in service to God and others while giving our all.

October 12
BLINDED BY THE BLESSING
Read: Dan. 4:28-36

During its era, Babylon was considered one of the most powerful kingdoms of biblical times. And though the Babylonian empire is often associated with the oppression of God's chosen people; this dynasty experienced much success by way of innovations and modernizations that are still used in society.

With this type of influence on society as a whole, any leader would be proud to rule a dynasty such as Babylon. This is where we find King Nebuchadnezzar, the reigning king of Babylon, who greatly benefited from the prosperity of his kingdom. One evening while resting and taking a nap, he had a disturbing dream. So, the king called Daniel to interpret his dream; Daniel was a Jew in Babylonian captivity who had been favored and elevated in position due to his uprightness and ability to interpret dreams.

When the interpretation of the dream was brought forward, it was not favorable and provided a stern warning to the king about being cautious of letting pride get in the way and literally blinding him to the true source of his prosperity. Daniel attempted to warn him (Dan. 4:27).

Thoughts

_____
_____
_____
_____
_____
_____
_____

So, what does the king do? Instead of heeding Daniel's warning, while walking about the palace one day he began to boast of his perceived greatness, "The king said, Is not this the great Babylon that I have built as the royal residence and seat of government by the might of my power and for the honor and glory of my majesty" (Dan. 4:30, New King James Version)? And almost immediately, the voice of

God pronounced judgment on the king resulting in him transforming into a strange beast that roamed in the wilderness for a period of seven years until he came to his senses (Dan. 4:34, 37).

1 John 2:16 warns us about pride and its origin. Therefore, as believers in Christ, if we are not careful to place things in proper perspective, we can fall into the same trap of thinking we had something to do with our prosperity and elevation as though we got there by our own merits. Promotion comes from God (Ps. 75:6-7), as well as anything else we possess (Ps. 24:1).

It was pride that transformed the king of Babylon into a beast and something he was never designed to be. Likewise, when we allow pride to rise up within us, we too become something we were never designed to be, as we become blinded and separated from the true Giver of all blessings. Operating in pride is the quickest way to be brought low and learn the true meaning of abasement. I would much rather choose to live in abasement rather than being forced to.

Like king Nebuchadnezzar, we must lay aside pride and begin to truly acknowledge where all of our blessings come from—they all come from the LORD. We should also endeavor to have the same attitude of the one in the group of ten lepers after being healed from years of an oppressive disease in Luke chapter 17. When he realized he was free of the leprosy that kept him bound and separated from society, he came back to Jesus just to say "THANK YOU."

When we receive that new home, car, promotion, increase, or that man or woman that God has specifically set apart for us; we should never think we received any of it in our own strength or ability, or place any of this before God. The blessings we each experience are based solely on God's unmerited favor, and we each are blessed to be a blessing to others. Don't allow pride to stop the blessing from continually flowing in your life.

"Pride lands you flat on your face; humility prepares you for honors" (Prov. 29:23, The Message).

October 13
WORSHIP COMES BEFORE SERVICE
Read: Matt. 3:16-17

Jesus Christ lived on earth for 30 years prior to being released for His three years of ministry. And from the time He was conceived of the Holy Spirit, Jesus was already perfect because He was and is God; He came already equipped to fulfill His purpose and assignment (Gal. 4:4-5).

Thoughts

Since Jesus was/is God, was sinless, and already had his marching orders from the Heavenly Commander-in-Chief at conception, there still seems to be a couple of questions that would seem logical to ask: Why did Jesus go to be baptized by John the Baptist in the Jordan River? Why would someone who was completely sinless and already perfect require the baptism unto repentance, when in actuality He didn't really need it?

I would submit that Jesus simply performed this act out of humility and obedience as He presented Himself completely to be used by the Father for service with this being a spiritual act of worship (Rom. 12:1).

In other words Jesus provided the perfect example for us to follow and emulate as He identified with man in every way, except He did not sin (Heb. 4:15). The illustration in Matthew chapter three simply lets us know that before we can effectively serve others, there must be a time of worship and connection with our Heavenly Father; the One who holds the Master plan and instructions for our lives.

Worship, therefore, is an essential precursor and component to our service in God's kingdom. It is difficult to operate in the anointing and power of God if we never spend time in His presence. Intimate time with the Father is the key that opens the door to receiving the instructions required to go out and do what He has commissioned us to accomplish, that primarily being to serve others—-we are saved to serve (1 Pet. 4:10).

Another by-product of worship is the ability to receive the strength needed to endure the many trials and tests that often come our way as we make it a purpose to present our bodies as living sacrifices each and every single day (Ps. 16:11, Neh. 8:10b). Our strength is renewed in God's presence.

To sum it up, our service in God's kingdom lacks true power unless it has been preceded with authentic worship. This type of worship centers on submitting ourselves to the power and authority of God, being covered and filled with the anointing of the Holy Spirit, and yielding ourselves in humble submission to the Father just like Jesus (Phil. 2:8; Jn. 4:23-24).

We worship God not just in a song, a dance, or merely with the words that proceed from our mouths. True worship involves giving ourselves completely to the object of our worship (God), as we deny worldly desires and the flesh, and begin to operate in the realm of the Spirit. It is at this point that our lives transform into objects of worship to God, as we give ourselves completely over to becoming "well pleasing" to Him.

Thoughts

_____
_____
_____
_____
_____
_____
_____

Serving in the Kingdom is great and is something that we should all aspire to; however, to truly become effective in whatever you do— your worship must come before your service.

"For it has been written, You shall WORSHIP the [LORD] your God, and Him alone shall you SERVE" (Matt. 4:10, Amplified Bible).

October 14

CONCENTRATED LIGHT
Read: Gen. 1:1-3

I recently read a book in which the author made an eye-opening statement concerning light and it was also something being studied at church at the time. The statement was: "Focused light has tremendous power. Diffused light has no power at all."

When you really think about it, this statement has great merit and is very true. For example, if an individual takes an ordinary flashlight (diffused light) and points it at a piece of paper, the wide beam of the light only illuminates the sheet of paper, but does nothing else. Now take that same sheet of paper with a concentrated beam of sunlight passed through a magnifying glass, not only is there illumination but the paper also ignites and catches on fire.

So, what made the difference? Light is just light, right? In this scenario it was the focused or concentrated light that sparked a reaction with the paper. This is just a practical illustration of how powerful light can be when it is harnessed for the right purpose with a proper focus. And no matter how small a light source is; when it is illuminated in a completely darkened room or area, the darkness has no choice but to give way.

The significance of light is also noted in the Old Testament book of Genesis with the description of creation. One of the very first things created by God was light (Gen. 1:1-3).

There are many forms of light used today: candles, incandescent light bulbs, fire, neon lights, and of course, natural light from the sun. Although each is a good source of light, there is one light source that has true power to provide illumination and bring about lasting change, and that is "SON"light. Jesus said He was the light of the world (Jn. 8:12). And He went on to say that as long has He was in the world that he would be the light of the world.

Since Jesus is no longer here on earth in a physical form, the baton of light-bearer has been passed to all who now profess faith in Christ and have Him, through the person of the Holy Spirit, living on the inside (Matt. 5:14-16).

Each of us have been commissioned to be light in a dark world; however, as a body of believers and as the family of God, we are to unify our lights for a focused cause and purpose.

Thoughts

_____

_____

_____

_____

_____

_____

_____

Therefore, it is our responsibility to let our lights shine through good works that are rooted and grounded in love. And though concentrated sunlight through the lens of a magnifying glass can generate fire; an even more focused beam of light in the form of a laser has the power to also through metal and many other solid objects. As lights in a dark world, we have the power to illuminate dark areas, ignite fires (representative of the Holy Spirit), and initiate transformation through focused action (love).

It is love that allows us to overcome fear, because we should never fear the light (2 Tim. 1:7). The great Greek philosopher Plato stated it this way, "We can easily forgive a child who is afraid of the dark; the real tragedy of life is when men are afraid of the light."

Will you be a diffused light scattered by the cares of this world just touching the surface of issues, or are you willing to unify with other light so that your collective focus can penetrate to the very core of matters and hardened hearts to bring about lasting change? Our lights must shine brightly and be unified if we expect to see positive change in the world today (Rom. 13:12).

October 15

NO LONGER OUTSIDE
Read: Matt. 27:50-51

It was a beautiful summer day with the sun shining brightly, birds flying overhead, and there was a gentle cool breeze. The deck and yard out back was set for a time of togetherness with fun and games. Everyone in the family put aside their personal agendas for an enjoyable time playing games and experiencing real fellowship with one another: volley ball, horseshoes, and board games--to include one of the most popular games of them all, "Monopoly." The laughter and joy emanating from this family could be heard throughout the neighborhood.

As the sun began to set and the evening progressed, the family prepared to enter their home bringing an end to all of the festivities. Then all of a sudden and out of nowhere the eldest child began to get upset after losing a game in which he normally prevailed against everyone in the family. He then allowed his anger to consume him and get the best of him as he flipped the board game with dice, game pieces, and game money flying in every direction.

Thoughts

_____
_____
_____
_____
_____
_____
_____

The parents chastised the child, instructed him to clean up the mess he created, and then told him to remain outside until he cooled off and got his attitude straight. An hour later after calming down, thoughtfully considering his behavior and complying with his parent's request; with a new attitude he entered the home and apologized for his actions thereby restoring his connection with his family. It was his attitude and actions that separated him from continued fellowship with the family.

In the Garden of Eden, because of Adam's disobedience sin entered the world and came upon all men (mankind) (Rom. 5:12). Therefore, when the Tabernacle and then later the Temple were instituted representing the place where God's presence dwelled (and also a type of Christ), there was now a distinct separation between God and man because of this sin.

The Tabernacle and Temple were divided into three major sections: the outer court, the inner court, and the most holy place (the Holy of Holies). Between the inner court and the Holy of Holies there was a curtain conspicuously placed that signified man's separation from God because of his attitude (or sin). Once a year, the high priest was allowed to enter the Holy of Holies to make an offering of atonement for the sins of the people by sprinkling blood from the sacrifice on the "mercy seat" of the Ark of the Covenant.

When Jesus sacrificed himself on the cross in an ultimate act of mercy, the veil that once separated man from God was torn down the middle signifying that we now had direct access to God (Matt. 27:50-51).

Because of this marvelous act of mercy we no longer have to bring bulls, rams, goats or turtledoves to church to make a sacrifice for our sins; nor do we have to sit in a confessional box hoping that a man can forgive us or absolve our sin. Through the shed blood of Christ we now have the ability to come boldly to the Father to receive the forgiveness we need and no longer have to remain outside (Heb. 4:16).

So, don't allow a negative attitude or sin to keep you out of God's presence and separated from His family. Christ paved the way and provided direct access the Father, it's now just up to each one of us individually to get is right. "He who covers his transgressions will not prosper, but whoever confesses and forsakes his sins will obtain mercy" (Prov. 28:13, Amplified Bible). The fellowship that you so long for and desire is readily available, and the family is waiting because you no longer have to remain outside (Rom. 5:18-19).

October 16
SEASONS CHANGE
Read: Ecc. 3:1-8

Thoughts

A few years ago while stationed in the Middle East, I made the comment, "You know you are in an extremely hot place when...the temperature drops to just above 100 degrees and everyone says it's getting cool, even in Iraq;"

367

but to receive cooler temperatures is a true blessing. For those that are currently in the Middle East or have had the opportunity to visit this region before, a well-known fact always remains before us—it is hot! However, even in a region that is known for dust storms and excessive heat, the temperature still changes with the seasons.

Though one may not be able to experience the full effects of seasons changing between spring, summer, fall, and winter; there are subtle changes in the Middle East as the temperature drops a few degrees here and there, and then receive "the icing on the cake"—a refreshing cool breeze! One of the greatest and most apparent indicators a seasonal change is about to take place, are changes in the weather and environment.

In life the average person, whether they acknowledge it or not, desires to experience and enjoy the comforts of a set routine and/or stability; you know, always being in good health, having your children behave and serve the LORD, having all financial needs met, receiving promotion and increase, or just having peace of mind. But even though we search for constants in life, there is only one constant we can truly count on: THINGS CHANGE. This is not only true in the natural or physical sense, but also in our lives as believers in Christ.

There are times when we have mountain-top experiences; when God is speaking to us through His Spirit, family life is good, work is great, and there are no financial issues or needs—this could be considered spring going into summer. Then there are times when it seems that nothing goes our way; we wait for promotion but are overlooked, there is discord in the family or marriage, and hearing God's voice seems to be a faint memory as we transition from fall to winter.

It's during our winter season of life that we often feel cold, isolated, and disconnected as if no one can identify with our feelings or what we are going through. In these times we begin to feel as if God has abandoned us to teach us some grand lesson, when this is not the case. Even in our season of winter, God is with us because He promises to never leave nor forsake us and that He would always be there (Heb. 13:5).

No matter how subtle it may be, we can find consolation in the fact that seasons change and we don't have to remain in winter. And though the seasons of our life may change as we experience a roll coaster of emotions in the process; we can also be confident that as we go through our ups and downs, God does not change (Heb. 13:8). Just as natural seasons are based on earth's revolution around the Sun; our spiritual seasons occur as we allow our lives to revolve around Jesus Christ the "SON" who never changes.

Thoughts

_____

_____

_____

_____

_____

_____

_____

Remember, no matter what season we may find ourselves in, God will not allow us to be pushed beyond what we are able to withstand and handle (1 Cor. 10:13). Don't worry about the season; instead place faith and confidence in the God of the season. He knows what we have need of and when.

Spiritual seasons often come to bring about a change in us. And though our seasons change, our God remains the same and continues to be faithful to us in the process and regardless of the season (Ps. 119:90).

October 17
WHAT'S HINDERING YOU FROM ENTERING IN?
Read: Heb. 10:19-25

Some time ago I shared a devotional entitled "No Longer Outside" from Matt. 27:50-51 discussing the veil in God's Temple being torn from top to bottom when Jesus gave up His spirit on the cross as He became the perfect sacrifice. And now because of this, mankind has been granted access to every area of the Temple and no longer has to remain in just the outer or inner courts. So, let's take a closer look at the symbolism and significance of this one supreme act.

In times past the high priest would enter the Temple, more specifically the Holy of Holies, once a year on the Day of Atonement to make an offering for the sins of the people. It was the responsibility of the high priest to ensure he was ceremonially clean and pure before entering the Temple; therefore, as a back-up measure bells were placed on the priest's robe and a rope tied around his waist.

As long as bells were heard during this process, everything was thought to be going according to plan; however, when the bells stopped ringing, this was a clear indication the priest had fallen dead while attempting to enter God's presence without completely purifying himself or in other words trying to enter in the wrong way. Consequently, the body would then be pulled out using the rope tied to the waist and another priest would then make an attempt to enter. Talk about having some big shoes to fill!

It was sin that separated man from God and required atonement in the first place (Is. 59:2). The veil which divided the Holy of Holies (the place where the Spirit of God dwelled) from the remainder of the Temple was symbolic of the separation that sin caused between God and man. Yet it was in His selfless, sacrificial death that Jesus literally became sin for all mankind to redeem us back to the Father while all together restoring the relationship and fellowship that was broken. Jesus did this all with His own blood.

What the blood of goats and rams could no longer atone for, the blood of the spotless Lamb of God was deemed a suitable and acceptable sacrifice to the Father who was well-pleased. It was the broken, beaten, and torn physical body of Christ that removed all barriers thereby granting direct access to the presence of God to all who confess Jesus as both Savior and Lord, those who now believe.

Thoughts

_____

_____

_____

_____

_____

_____

_____

As the physical body of Christ was ripped and torn in death, simultaneously the veil in the Temple was ripped from top to bottom allowing us to now freely enter into the Most Holy Place (Heb. 10:19-22).

Therefore, the veil in the Temple represented Jesus Christ Himself, our High Priest who went before God to make an offering for our sins once and for all; it was and still is a finished work. And since there was nothing left for Him to do to purchase our redemption, Jesus took a seat signifying that His work was complete (Heb. 10:12).

Jesus has opened the door to God's presence for us all, giving us the right to enter in whenever we desire; yet many continue to remain outside when God longs to spend time with us in sweet fellowship and communion. However, there is still a prerequisite that remains unchanged, and that is the fact that we must be pure.

We were created by God to be in His presence, created through worship for worship; however, entering His presence still requires that we have clean hands and a pure heart (Ps. 24:3-5).

The question before us all today is this: "What's hindering you from entering in?"

October 18
DIVIDE AND CONQUER
Read: Heb. 10:25

I have probably mentioned before that I am partial to documentaries and other shows of this type, especially those dealing with nature and wildlife. There is just something about seeing other species of animals in their natural habitat and gaining an understanding of how animals live that really intrigues me.

While I was deployed a few years back, I came across and was able to watch the Walt Disney Studio's first nature documentary feature-film simply entitled "Earth." The film takes viewers on a journey and tour of our planet with extraordinary pictures as never seen before; all narrated by the commanding voice of the renowned actor James Earl Jones.

Thoughts

_____
_____
_____
_____
_____
_____
_____

In this documentary viewers not only get to see amazing imagery of our planet, but are also afforded the opportunity to catch a glimpse of wildlife from around the planet living in their everyday environment from a perspective like never before. One segment of the documentary detailed the migration of gazelles across the African plain to a more fertile area, with literally thousands of these graceful creatures prancing across the dusty terrain; but then the challenge started.

Out of nowhere a pack of hungry lions began to lurk and prowl just outside the periphery of the gazelle herd. Although lions are powerful and naturally fast, their speed is no match for that of a full-grown and healthy gazelle.

So, in order for the lions to stand a chance of obtaining a meal for the day, they systematically employed the well-known tactic of "Divide and conquer". The lions started their chase from the outside and then moved inward with the ultimate goal of getting the gazelle herd to separate and split apart. And as the heard split the lions were then able to identify and target the weaker gazelles, the ones that could be chased down and overcome with ease—usually younger gazelles or those that may have been sick; the ones that could be easily separated from the rest of the herd.

As noted in the documentary, once divided from the safety and protection provided by the larger and more cohesive group, a lone gazelle was no match for the awesome power and brute strength of the lion.

This is nothing more than a military tactic that is often still used in warfare today and is also one of the major tricks of our spiritual adversary the devil, who attempts to separate us from fellowship with other believers and the security of the family. Heb. 10:25 reminds us of our need for togetherness as a body of believers.

Sadly, many believers choose to make the journey of faith alone, as a result they do not generally attend worship services or any Bible study during the course of the week. Yes, we can receive the Word of God via DVD, CD, television, or the Internet and never have to leave the confines of our homes; but there is nothing like obedience to the Word as we find fellowship and assembly with other like-minded believers who can provide encouragement and strength; this is where we find connection and a sense of belonging.

When we separate ourselves from the body of believers and the family, we not only cause "Dis-ease" by removing a needed part of the Body (1 Cor. 12:26-27), but we also often bring unnecessary pain and discomfort to ourselves. So don't allow the enemy to lure you into a false sense of security through isolation because he lurks as a lion on the prowl (1 Pet. 5:8). Instead choose to remain connected to the Body and family to ensure you receive the strength, comfort, and protection you need (Ecc. 4:12).

Thoughts

_____

_____

_____

_____

_____

_____

_____

October 19

NEVER ALONE
Read: Heb. 13:5

As I have stated in previous devotionals, being in the U.S. Navy has afforded me the opportunity to visit many countries around the world. And after being out to sea for any extended period of time, the crew looks forward to any and every port visit available. Of the locations I have visited, I would say the European ports during a Mediterranean deployment were really enjoyable (i.e., France, Greece, Turkey, Spain, Italy, Israel, Croatia); countries rich in both history and heritage.

I can remember one port visit in particular to a location in Greece; I was a junior enlisted Sailor at the time and had been a Christian for a few years. As usual, prior to arriving in port, a brief was given on the area to include a threat assessment to warn of any potential targeting of service members. And during this time the "Buddy system" was recommended to ensure Sailor safety and accountability. However, for a Christian on a Navy ship back then, it was often a difficult task to find someone like-minded, had a similar schedule, and was off at the same time as you.

It is sad to say the average Sailor only has two things in mind when departing the ship for a port visit (sex and alcohol); and neither was anything I could connect with. So, on this particular day I departed the ship solo to get a nice meal and enjoy the scenery taking a few pictures, since photography was one of my hobbies at the time. Well, while out walking around by myself, one of the military shore patrol (individuals on duty to maintain good order and discipline during our liberty call) stopped me and said "Where is you liberty buddy?" Of course I couldn't lie, so I said "I don't have a physical liberty buddy, but the Bible tells me that goodness and mercy follows me all the days of my life; therefore, I'm never alone."

I was expecting a scolding and then being told to return to the ship, but instead the shore patrol just instructed me to be careful. At this point my faith and confidence in God was at a point of truly believing He would honor His Word and protect me, as a result I did not have to fear harm no matter what the threat assessment or reports of man indicated. On the other hand, we must also exercise wisdom in every situation, because all scenarios are not the same. Back then the "Buddy system" was a suggestion; however, today it is mandatory during port visits; and of course I would now honor this policy.

Thoughts

_____
_____
_____
_____
_____
_____
_____

The point in all of this is that it doesn't matter what the media may report, or how man may attempt to stir up fear within us, we don't have to fear because God has our front, and the dynamic duo has our back—and this duo is not 'Batman and Robin'. When frontal attacks come, according to Is. 59:19 our God lifts up a standard against the enemy, and it is "goodness and mercy" that follows us all the days of our lives.

372

Therefore, I don't believe it is a coincidence that the sixth verse of Ps. 23 is stated as such. The number "6" in the Bible represents the number of man (i.e., man was created on the sixth day). I would submit that in this verse God is reassuring man that no matter where he is or what he may be going through, "goodness and mercy" will always be with us; therefore, we do not have to fear or be afraid of anything because we are in the safety and care of an All-powerful and loving God.

When we receive negative reports that are designed to incite fear causing us to be on edge; believers do not have to be afraid because we have confidence that our Heavenly Father loves us and He has our backs. It is His love that surrounds and keeps us (1 Jn. 4:18; Ps. 46:1).

October 20
PREPARE FOR THE DOWNPOUR, THE RAIN IS COMING
Read: Gen. 6:17-22

During the time of Noah, the wickedness of man on earth had become a stench to the very nostrils of God; and it grieved God that He had even created man (Gen. 6:5-6).

God then gave Noah specific insight into His plans to rid the earth of all who were of evil and wicked hearts to start fresh with those whose hearts were towards Him. However, since Noah was an upright man who found favor in God's sight; God devised a plan to spare Noah and his entire family.

The grand plan was brought forth with Noah being informed of a great flood to come; his job was to build an ark (a boat or ship) to house his family and two of every living creature on the face of the earth. Here was a man with his family in the middle of a desert place, not accustomed to even seeing rain or any other water in mass quantities, being instructed to build an ark that would somehow be moved by floodwaters that were only predicted to come.

Noah and his family took on this massive shipbuilding project, building something that apparently would have little use in the current environment. And though Noah and his family were ridiculed by the wicked inhabitants around him, he obeyed the instructions of God and constructed the ark according to the design specifications provided to him.

Thoughts

After years of hard labor, the ark was finally constructed. Noah's family and two of every living creature had been brought aboard the ark. As soon as everyone in Noah's family and every creature was onboard, the torrential down pour began. Those who ridiculed Noah and his family were no longer laughing but were now screaming to get inside the ark in attempts to spare their lives.

It rained for a period of 40 days and 40 nights until the entire surface of earth was covered with water (the number 40 represents "Trial, testing, closing in victory or judgment"). The element (water) that was a source of destruction for many was also the primary source of deliverance and blessing for Noah and his family. The rain not only washed away wickedness, but brought victory and preservation to the upright. Water, of course, is symbolic of the Holy Spirit, the One who comes to purify us.

Noah and his family were protected and thereby became recipients of God's blessing because they were obedient to God's instructions and took the appropriate steps to prepare for rain by building the ark according to the exact specifications given. God is trying to do the same for many of us as believers in Christ; He desires to rain down His blessings upon us, but it requires that we follow His instructions in building habitations that are pleasing to Him (Ps. 127:1). We are spiritual habitations or buildings of the LORD and transporters of the precious cargo of God's Holy Spirit (1 Cor. 3:16). Therefore, it is our responsibility to continue building our lives according to God's specific design and plan. He's trying to shower down His blessings upon us, all He requires from us is faith that works itself out through obedience. Remember, rain is what causes and promotes growth.

Are you in a dry place today? Refuse to remain in a dry and barren place because it is God's desire to shower you with His blessings; it just requires that you do your part because this is when the blessings come to overtake you. Through obedience ensure that you are building your life correctly and on the right foundation. It is then that you will be prepared for the downpour, because the rain is coming (Deut. 28:1-2; Zech. 10:1).

October 21
BEING IN THE WILL IS JUST THE BEGINNING
Read: Heb. 8:8-13

In Matt. 5:17-18 Jesus declares that He did not come to get rid of the Law of Moses but to fulfill it. It was on the cross of Calvary that Jesus executed every Old Testament prophecy concerning the purpose for His coming, and it was His blood that brought the fulfillment of a New Testament (or Covenant).

Thoughts

_____
_____
_____
_____
_____
_____
_____

"In everyday use a covenant describes an agreement between parties where there are benefits and responsibilities for the parties and penalties for non-compliance." Therefore, Jesus accomplished and honored His part of the agreement when He humbled Himself and allowed His body to be beaten, battered, spat upon, bruised, pierced, and broken for every sin that we would ever commit (past, present, and future). And because of this, through our confession and profession of faith (Rom. 10:9-10), we have the ability to receive the benefits that come along with now being God's sons and daughters (Eph. 1:3-5).

In our acceptance of Christ as Savior and Lord, we become beneficiaries of His Will— the New Covenant. A covenant can also be described in terms of a testament. Therefore, the New Covenant is in a sense Jesus' last "Will and Testament." By definition a will and testament "is a legal declaration by which a person, the testator, names one or more persons to manage his/her estate and provides for the transfer of his/her property at death." But there is one very important fact we must understand about a will; by law a will only becomes effective when the testator dies.

Well, just in case you didn't know it, Christ has already done His part through the use of three nails and a cross; our job is simply to reap the benefits of His actions and live the abundant life He has provided according to His Word (Jn. 10:10).

When we recognize our place in the will, we also begin to understand that we are now heirs of the promise and are to be recipients of every blessing He has pre-destined for us to have (2 Pet. 1:3).

On the flip side, although we are in the will it is totally up to us to acknowledge and then receive the benefits. Being the recipient of one million dollars will not benefit us or anyone else, for that matter, if we never actually accept and begin putting to use that which has been given to us. As believers in Christ we are already in the will as it pertains to the things that belong to God and what He has already prepared for us to have ahead of time; so let's start using the benefits.

And even though we are in His "general" will, this is never enough. We don't enter into what many call His "perfect will" until we not only begin to recognize the voice of the Testator (the Good Shepherd and Sacrificial Lamb), but also learn how to obey.

Truly being in God's will comes as a result of walking in OBEDIENCE, making our FAITH both ACTIVE and ALIVE through fruitful works, while learning how to use our benefits to bless others (1 Pet. 4:10). Obedience is always better than sacrifice (1 Sam. 15:22). Our obedience to the plan of God for our lives is essential to remaining in "the will" (Phil. 2:13).

Thoughts

_____

_____

_____

_____

_____

_____

_____

October 22
DOING THE RIGHT THING THE WRONG WAY
Read: 1 Chron. 13:1-14

The Ark of the Covenant (which represented the very presence of God) had been placed in safekeeping in Kirjath-Jearim in the house of Abinadab during the reign of King Saul; however, over a period of time the Ark had been neglected. David was now king and desired to bring the Ark back to its proper place in Jerusalem to receive the appropriate care and attention. Therefore, the Ark was prepared for travel.

The Ark was constructed with loops on each side that poles were designed to go through. Additionally, only the Levitical priests were authorized to carry the Ark. The proper way to carry the Ark was to place the poles through the loops on each side, with the poles then positioned on the shoulders of the Levites (the priests); the Ark was not to be touched by man.

In today's Scripture text, instead of transporting the Ark as commanded by God, the Ark was placed upon a cart and pulled by oxen. And at some point during the journey, the oxen began to stumble losing their footing, and the cart started to tip over with the Ark about to slide off and hit the ground. To protect the Ark from falling Uzza, who was assigned to help in the transport of the Ark, reaches out his hand and touches the Ark, and immediately falls dead before God.

I know you're probably thinking that this was cruel because his intentions were good; however, his actions were not in line with the proper order of things and guidance given concerning the Ark as prescribed by God. Not only was the presence of God being carried in an incorrect manner, it was also being transported by the wrong individuals.

The Bible is a book of laws, precepts and commandments, or better yet "principles." A principle can be defined as a law that is designed to protect and preserve a created thing, and to ensure its most efficient use and maximum performance.

In his book *The Power and Purpose of Praise & Worship*, Dr. Myles Munroe pointed out seven key facts about principles; "principles are permanent, work anywhere, protect the product, can never be broken, when violated produce destruction, and contain inherent judgment." Therefore, in 1 Chron. 13, even though Uzza attempted to do the right thing, he died because he violated one of God's principles in attempting to handle the presence of God (Spirit) in the flesh, the wrong way.

Thoughts

_____

_____

_____

_____

_____

_____

Many of us as believers are guilty of the same thing each week as it pertains to coming into God's house, and His presence; guilty of doing the right thing the wrong way.

By way of a practical example, just imagine a nail sticking out of a wall. To prevent anyone

376

from getting hurt you search for a tool to address the issue, but return with a screwdriver. You begin to pound the nail with the handle of the screwdriver and even make a little headway; but the screwdriver was not designed to be used as a hammer. A hammer is designed to be used as a hammer; and when the proper tool (the hammer) is used, the job is completed efficiently without causing you or anyone else harm.

Therefore, as it pertains to our praise and worship, we must learn to enter in the right way. Our praise and worship is all about God! When we come into God's presence with the right attitude, and with the right motivation; we then set the stage for Him to inhabit or dwell within our praises (Ps. 22:3). Our time spent in praise and worship is not designed to change God, because He does not change (Heb. 13:8); it is designed to change us as we enter in correctly.

October 23

THE BLESSING IS YOURS, IT HAS ALREADY BEEN SPOKEN
Read: Gen. 27:30-40

The story of Esau and Jacob is very familiar for most of us. In this saga, Esau the firstborn son is tricked out of the birthright blessing by his younger brother Jacob who, with the help of their mother Rebekah, deceived their father Isaac. During this time of Israelite history, the firstborn male child of the family was given the birthright blessing which signified the continued blessings of God upon his life and the receipt of an inheritance. Even if there were an older sister, by right and custom the blessing still belonged to the eldest or firstborn male child.

In Gen. 27, we find Esau distraught and Isaac somewhat confused after learning that the younger brother Jacob had received the blessing that was intended for the firstborn. Scripture records that when Isaac realized exactly what had transpired that he "started trembling" because of the deception (Gen. 27:33). What he said in the preceding Scripture is very key and significant; he basically told Esau that since he had already spoken the blessing over Jacob, it could not be reversed or taken back because it was sealed.

When Esau heard this, he despised his brother and at that point eagerly anticipated the death of his father Isaac for the sole purpose of having the ability to get even with Jacob intending to kill him for stealing his birthright blessing. Although Esau had a right to be upset one all-important fact remained, Jacob was now the rightful blessing heir because it had been spoken over him.

The key and significant fact here we should always remember is that there is true power in

Thoughts

----

the spoken word. This should be a reminder to each of us as believers of the importance of our words and the power of God's blessing. Let's take a look at two facts concerning God's Word in our lives that we should all consider.

First, once we speak and release our words, they now have an assignment to accomplish something. This is why we are to be so ever mindful and careful to truly think before we speak, and not let our emotions get the best of us. Another thing that is important to remember here is that once we confess and profess our faith, Christ then begins to reside on the inside of us—-Christ who is equal standing in the Trinity or "Godhead" (1 Jn. 5:7). What this means for us is that we also now possess the same power that God used to create the universe in our mouths. Therefore, we must use our words wisely because they will either produce death or life (Prov. 18:21); the choice is up to us because there is no in between.

Secondly, once the blessing of God has been pronounced or spoken over our lives; no man, no devil, no principality, or demon in hell can do anything to override this fact; as long as we continue to walk in obedience to God's Word (Is. 55:11). When we receive the blessing it is a done deal. When God says it, we are to believe it, and that should settle it. In other words we can "Take it to the bank," because God has the resources to back-up what He says.

We should all be thankful that we are no longer under the old laws and customs of our forefathers because it does not matter if we are the firstborn or the last; under the New Covenant, the blessing that God gave to the great patriarch and Father of faith Abraham is now ours by birthright since we have been adopted into the family of God according to the finished work at Calvary and through the shed blood of Jesus Christ (Gal. 3:14, 29).

If you are in Christ, then know today that God's blessing and Word has been spoken over your life; the blessing is yours by right, and no man can take it away (Eph. 1:13-14).

October 24
ALWAYS AT THE CENTER
Read: Acts 17:28

Thoughts

_____
_____
_____
_____
_____
_____

I am what most people consider an "early bird," and when I awake each morning it is usually still dark outside with the moon and stars still shining brightly. Several months ago there was a period in which I watched the moon's transition.

One morning there was only one-quarter of the moon illuminated and visible, two days later half of the moon was illuminated, and then before I knew it a full moon was on display for all to see. This caused me to pause in wonder and amazement at how awesome our God is, the Creator of the universe and how He made and fashioned all things for His purpose and by design (Col. 1:16).

Though the moon in transition is a fascinating sight to see; the moon is only a small portion of the glory God has placed in the expanse of space and the universe, with the sun being of major focus and importance in our solar system.

In our solar system there are nine planets that revolve around the sun: Mercury, Venus, "Earth," Mars, Jupiter, Saturn, Uranus, Neptune, and Pluto (just as a side note, Earth is the third planet and of course the number "3" in the Bible represents "completion; the signature of God"). God specifically fashioned the Earth for us, placing His distinct signature on it—the signature of life.

The sun is larger than any planet in our solar system and is roughly more than 100 times the diameter of earth, with extremely hot surface temperatures that are literally off the charts. Therefore, a planet's position in our solar system has a huge impact on its ability to provide and sustain life.

Planets that are farthest away from the sun are known for extremely low temperatures and poisonous gases which do not provide an atmosphere conducive for life. Now on the other hand, planets that are too close to the sun are prone to experience scorching surface heat and atmospheres that are not suitable for human life.

Then there is earth, the third planet from the sun which is close enough to enjoy the heat provided, but yet far enough away to sustain an atmosphere that produces the oxygen required for life.

God in His infinite wisdom placed the planets, moon, and stars in such a position that life as we know it would be dependent on our relative proximity to the "S-U-N." One statement concerning the importance of the sun simply says, "The Sun is the main source of energy for earth. It gives us heat and light and helps us to remove darkness and bring light all around the world." Sunlight also helps prevent the growth of bacteria, provides Vitamin D for our skin, allows plants to produce their food and oxygen, and is also a source of heat and produces light.

Do you see it yet? The relationship between us, earth and the sun has direct correlation to our relationship as believers with the Son of God, Jesus Christ Himself. To be a Christian is to be "Christ-like," therefore, the focus of everything we do should be centered on our relationship with the "S-O-N," and our relative proximity and closeness to Him.

Thoughts

_____
_____
_____
_____
_____
_____
_____

It is our closeness to the "Son" that prevents sin from growing in our lives, produces the very air that we breathe and need to sustain life (representative of the Holy Spirit), removes darkness from our world because He is the Light and provides God's vitamin D, "Destiny," for our lives.

Is the "S-O-N" at the center of your life (Jn. 8:12)?

October 25
IN THE RIGHT PLACE, BUT OUT OF POSITION
Read: 1 Sam. 13:1-15

A few years ago during a Sunday worship service, I was blessed to hear a powerful message as the man of God spoke about dealing with the real issues of sin, and not just what we see on the surface. The illustration used came from Jn. 5:1-14 with the lame man attempting to receive healing that could only be obtained by being first to enter the water of the pool at Bethesda, as the water was stirred by an angel at a certain time each year. But because the lame man was unable to get to the pool without the aid of others, he was always out of position and not able to receive his healing because someone else would always entering the pool ahead of him.

During this message the preacher made a very profound statement that really stuck with me; he said many believers are often "In the right place, but out of position." This is exactly where the lame man found himself, he was in the right place to receive healing and favor; however, constantly being out of position prevented him from truly becoming whole.

This immediately reminded me of King Saul and one of his many episodes of disobedience. In 1 Samuel chapter thirteen during his third year as king, Saul went to battle against the Philistines; however, a great multitude came against the Israelites to the point that the people became fearful (1 Sam 13:6).

While many in the Israelite army hid, Saul and a few others went to Gilgal to await the arrival of the prophet Samuel to offer the burnt offering and the peace offering at the appointed time in hopes that the tides of battle would then turn in Israel's favor. Prior to the army's departure, Samuel instructed Saul to wait for him to preside over the sacrifices that would then make Israel spiritually prepared for the battle at hand.

Thoughts

_____
_____
_____
_____
_____
_____
_____

Seven days had passed with the prophet nowhere in sight, subsequently the people were more frightened now than ever. So, what did Saul decide to do? He took it upon himself to usurp (or assume) the position of a priest and offer the sacrifice in the prophet's stead; but as soon as the burnt offering had been presented, the prophet Samuel arrived on the scene (1 Sam. 13:11-14). The end result of Saul being in the right place, but out of position was that his reign as king would be prematurely brought to an end.

You might be wondering exactly what did Saul do wrong? Presenting an offering is a good thing right? Although he ruled in power as a king, Saul's position did not give him the authority to present offerings in a priestly role. He blatantly disobeyed the established natural order of things and the command of God since priests were the only individuals authorized to officiate over sacrifices at that time. Again, Saul was in the right place, but out of position.

Many of us as believers in Christ often find ourselves in a similar place; we do things that, by nature, are considered to be "good;" however, these things may not be what God has called for us to do. We serve in positions out of necessity, instead of by assignment and calling. Needless to say, this generally causes us to waste a lot of time, energy and effort doing things in the flesh that were never designed or predestined for us to do, and we then wonder why God's hand is not in it or why His favor is not upon our lives.

This is when we should take time to pause and truly assess where we are because everything that appears good, or feels good to us may not necessarily be our place of destiny (Prov. 16:1). Obedience is truly better than sacrifice!

October 26
YOU DON'T HAVE TO STAY DOWN
Read: 2 Sam. 12:15b-20

Aside from Jesus and the Apostle Paul, there is probably no one else more readily recognized or known in the Bible than David. From the time he was a ruddy teenager, God's anointing and favor was on his life. David was a warrior with many mighty exploits, and this often caused others to be jealous of his accolades. And though he had a desire to rebuild the temple, he was not allowed due to his warrior status; he did the next best thing and purchased all the required material so that his son Solomon could complete the task.

David was also credited with writing over two-thirds of the book of Psalms, and he was even called "a man after God's own heart." However, even in all of this David had issues and faults just like many of us struggle with each and every day. One of David's greatest sins was in his adulterous affair with Bathsheba, the wife of Uriah (a soldier in David's Army). The result

Thoughts

_____
_____
_____
_____
_____
_____
_____

381

of this affair led to Bathsheba becoming pregnant, and in an attempt to cover up his sin, David devised a scheme to have Uriah sent out into the front lines of the deadliest location of battle so he would be killed.

After Uriah's death, David took Bathsheba to be his wife thinking he had gotten off with this act of premeditated murder; then God sent the prophet Nathan to pronounce judgment. The child conceived with Bathsheba would die, and David's household (his children would be in constant turmoil). David begged for forgiveness of his sin so that his relationship with God would be restored (Psalm 51 shows David's heart in this regard).

But even though David repented, the child born from his affair with Bathsheba became sick. As a result David refused to sleep, and then began to fast and pray seeking the LORD even more on behalf of the child (2 Sam. 12:16). But even though David pleaded and fasted, the child still died. The Bible clearly states "the wages of sin is death" (Rom. 6:23), meaning that when sin is committed something has to die.

So, what did David do in this instance? Did he remain on the ground, beating himself up for what he caused by way of his sin, or have a pity party? No, David got up, washed his face and went to the house of the LORD to worship (2 Sam. 12:20). David knew where his strength came from and who to turn to. Although David experienced many family issues and hardships throughout his life, he was still mightily used because of his heart and attitude towards God.

David provides a great example for us as believers to follow and emulate, not that we are to follow his pattern of sin, because God's grace is not a free license to sin (Rom. 6:15). But, when we do sin we can go and get it right with our heavenly Father (1 Jn. 1:9).

It's also comforting to know that even when we fall short or just completely mess up that God does not just discard us and throw us to the side; He continues to use "cracked pots" like those described by the LORD in an illustration given to the prophet Jeremiah concerning "the potter's house" (Jer. 18:3-6).

Sometimes we have to be broken before God can reshape and mold us. But even in all of this, we can rest and find assurance in the fact that even in a broken state we are still in His hands.

Thoughts

_____

_____

_____

_____

_____

_____

Therefore, when we fall we don't have remain broken and unusable; instead we can just get back on the Potter's wheel and allow Him to reshape and mold us according to His plan and purpose for our lives again. YOU DON'T HAVE TO STAY DOWN (Ps. 51:9-12)!

October 27

WHEN THE GIFTS BECOME A DISTRACTION
Read: 1 Cor. 13:11

While there are some in the body of Christ who may have issues with discovering and using their gifts, there are still many who take it to the other extreme.

It was Christmas morning and there had been excitement and anticipation of receiving that special toy for months preceding this day. The kids arose without stopping at the bathroom or even stopping at the kitchen to get anything to eat, running straight for the living room where a mountain of presents awaited.

In an instant and in a frenzy to discover what their gifts were, wrapping paper and fragments of cardboard become fast-moving projectiles as each gift was opened. The house was now filled with the sounds of every new toy, doll, or game on the market.

During this time, on the other hand, the grow-ups were in the kitchen laboring intensely to put together the meal for the day with the guests soon to arrive. As the kitchen activities continued, the children were in a world of their own laughing and enjoying the gifts that were specifically given to them.

But the time came to prepare the dining room table and make the house presentable for the guest and holiday festivities. The kids were then told to begin cleaning up and to get themselves ready; it was time to put away the toys.

The toys had to be removed to make room for the grown-ups and the mature crowd who were on the way. Though the children were reluctant, they eventually complied and removed the toys. Besides, everyone knows the excitement of Christmas morning is short-lived; the toys everyone just had to have normally ends up under a bed or in a closet within a matter of days, if not hours.

Like the children who were somewhat reluctant to put away their toys to take part in something that had greater significance, there are many grown-ups who also have issues with letting go of their toys and childish things as oppose to reaching for the mature things in life; and in some instances these individuals never really grow up. And though there is absolutely nothing wrong with playing video games like Playstation, XBox, Wii, etc.; whenever these toys take our focus and attention away from spouses, children, and more importantly our relationship with God, this has the potential to cause issues in the family/home and can also hinder our spiritual growth.

The Apostle Paul realized this fact as he stated in one of his epistles, "When I was a child, I spoke as a child, I understood as a child, I thought as a child; but when I became a man, I put away childish things" (1 Cor. 13:11, New

Thoughts

_____
_____
_____
_____
_____
_____
_____

King James Version). Many in the body of Christ succumb to the above issue, but from a spiritual standpoint with individuals placing more focus on receiving personal exaltation from the gifts that have been given than on their intended purpose, with misuse and abuse taking place.

Our spiritual gifts are not given to us just to be used as toys to be played with when we feel like it and lift us up, they are designed to edify and build up the body of Christ as a whole. Therefore, whenever our gifts become a distraction from their intended purpose, we must choose to put away the toys in order to first develop spiritual character and maturity.

"So it is with yourselves; since you are so eager and ambitious to possess spiritual endowments and manifestations of the [Holy] Spirit, [concentrate on] striving to excel and to abound [in them] in ways that will build up the church" (1 Cor. 14:12, Amplified Bible).

October 28
LET THE RIVERS FLOW
Read: Jn. 7:38

As I read and studied Scripture recently, I came across a very interesting fact about the Jordan River that flows through the nation of Israel. The Jordan River is actually connected to two bodies of water; on the northern end there is the Sea of Galilee and on the southern end there is the Dead Sea.

Since thirty-five percent of the water in the Dead Sea is comprised of dissolved salt minerals, there are no fish or any other normal marine life in or near this body of water because it is deadly to most living things; therefore, this body of water is only suitable to certain forms of bacteria and algae that have adapted to this harsh environment.

The shores of the Dead Sea are characterized and coated with layers of salt crystals. And even though salt has qualities that are beneficial to us, the primary point to remember here is that life is not sustainable in this environment because there is no outlet that allows water (or life) to also flow out.

Thoughts

_____

_____

_____

_____

_____

_____

When I read this I thought about our lives as believers, and how each one of us would characterize ourselves based on the above mentioned bodies of water. Do we receive God's Word and then allow the life-giving power of God given through the Holy Spirit to flow through us, or are we like the Dead Sea, holding everything in but never releasing anything out.

As believers in Christ, we are to be dispensers of the Blessing that we have freely received" (Matt. 10:8)!

In other words, the gifts, talents, and resources that God blesses us with are not designed to be heaped and just stored up for ourselves; but are to be used, shared, and released to bless others so that they too will become beneficiaries of this new flowing life. Releasing and giving is key.

Jesus said, "He who believes in Me [who cleaves to and trusts in and relies on Me] as the Scripture has said, From his innermost being shall flow [continuously] springs and rivers of living water" (Jn. 7:38, Amplified Bible).

When we release what we have, God continues to supply more (Lk. 6:38).

Remember, our faith must be moving, alive, and active; otherwise it is dead and of no use to anyone (Jas. 2:26). So, don't become stagnate; as you receive, let God's life-giving power flow from you each day.

October 29

MIS-DIRECTED WORSHIP
Read: Acts 10:25-26

In today's Scripture reading we find Peter journeying to Caesarea to meet with Cornelius following a vision from the Lord directing him to begin ministry of the Gospel to the Gentiles which was totally against Jewish custom and Peter's desires at the time (Acts 10:28). Yet Peter went anyway.

But when Peter came into the home of Cornelius Scripture records that, "Cornelius met him, and fell down at his feet, and worshipped him. But Peter took him up, saying, Stand up; I myself also am a man" (Acts 10:25-26, King James Version). Although God gave Peter the commission to bring the Good News to the Gentiles, Peter knew he was not the object of worship; just the vessel being used.

This is something many of us as believers should also become more conscious of. Too often we worship the man or woman of God, the messenger; instead of the One who gave the message. We place focus on the gift instead of the Giver of the gift. When Peter saw Cornelius' mis-directed worship, he told him to stand up because he was just a man like him.

Thoughts

_____
_____
_____
_____
_____
_____
_____

Yes, according to 1 Thess. 5:12-13 we are to recognize our spiritual leaders, and though we are to give these individuals honor and respect, nowhere does it say we are to worship them. Worship belongs to God, and to God alone.

The Apostle Paul also provided admonishment in the first chapter of Romans verses 24-32 to those whose mis-directed worship became a stumbling block to them, with God allowing them to continue in their folly and senseless ways. "So God let these people go their own way. They did what they wanted to do, and their filthy thoughts made them do shameful things with their bodies. They gave up the truth about God for a lie, and they worshiped God's creation instead of God" (Rom. 1:24-25, Contemporary English Version). This happened because the people worshiped the wrong thing the wrong way.

Even though God knows the end from the beginning, He gives us free-will and allows us to make the right choices; we can worship spiritual leaders, drugs, sex, alcohol, money, homes, cars, our jobs; or we can worship the God who created us in His image and to have dominion over all of these things (Gen. 1:26). Notice, in the preceding Scripture we were given dominion over everything except man; therefore, there should never be a man with "dominion" over us.

So, anything that has our attention and focus more than God has in essence become an idol and the object of our worship. We are to have no other gods before Him (Ex. 20:3). So, instead of worshipping created things, we have been designed to worship the Creator.

We were created by God for fellowship, relationship, and worship. Our fellowship was broken by Adam through sin in the garden, but because of the finished work of Jesus Christ on the cross at Calvary, we are now to worship God (not man) out of our newfound relationship with Him. However, this worship is not a one-time act to be performed only when we enter the sanctuary of God's house, but every single day (Heb. 13:15). WORSHIP IS A LIFESTYLE!

"Give to the Lord the glory he deserves! Bring your offering and come into his presence. Worship the Lord in all his holy splendor" (1 Chron. 16:29, New Living Translation).

Thoughts

_____
_____
_____
_____
_____
_____
_____

October 30
DON'T FORGET THE OIL
Read: Ex. 30:31

In today's society, oil has become one of the most relied upon natural resources, if not the number one. Oil, in some form or fashion, is used in virtually every area of life. Our economy and entire way of living can be changed in an instant when there is a lack of this resource and oil is in high demand.

It's amazing to see how a shortage of oil can cause so many ripple effects; for example, fewer sales in larger vehicles including the various models of the popular Sport Utility Vehicle (SUV), increased prices in airline and other mass transit fares, and even increases in the price for something as simple as a loaf of bread.

With its many uses, oil is very essential to everyday living. We are dependent on oil for heating and transportation, and also a long list of products many would never associate with oil, to include: plastics, synthetic rubber, fertilizers/pesticides, paint, photographic film, food additives, medicine, synthetic fibers, make-up, and dyes just to name a few.

This just gives an idea of how important oil is to everything we do. From the fuel needed to move automobiles, ships, and planes to the fertilizers and pesticides used by farmers, to the very clothes we wear; loss of this precious resource could be very detrimental to society and life as we know it.

Similarly, oil also has great significance to us as believers in Christ; with oil representing the anointing and is symbolic of the Holy Spirit. Throughout the Old Testament oil is referenced in terms of being used for holy purposes and consecration; oil was also used to keep the lamps burning inside the Tabernacle.

In Exodus chapter 30, the LORD gave specific instructions to Moses concerning the Tabernacle and what to do with the oil and how he was to anoint Aaron and his sons (Ex. 30:30). In this instance, anointing was symbolic of the Holy Spirit coming upon these men for service to God.

Today we don't have to wait for someone to pour oil or anoint us, we don't have to jump up and down, or flip upside down to receive the power of the Holy Spirit; all we have to do is believe, ASK, and receive (Lk. 11:13).

This reminded me of the American musical classic "The Wizard of Oz" featuring a young Kansas girl named Dorothy. In the story Dorothy sets out on a journey to the magical Land of Oz accompanied by a Scarecrow, a Tin Man and a Cowardly Lion all going to meet the Wizard for their specific need.

When Dorothy initially came upon the Tin Man, she found him standing completely immobile due to being exposed to the elements and rain, which caused his joints to rust. And as Dorothy approached, she could hear a faint murmur— "OIL;" the Tin Man continued murmuring "OIL" over and over again until Dorothy eventually saw the can of oil near his feet. Once the oil was applied not only could he speak, but he was able to move about freely.

Thoughts

_____
_____
_____
_____
_____
_____
_____
_____

This is exactly what the empowerment with the Holy Spirit does for the believer; He allows us to speak boldly and gives us the power to live effective lives as witnesses for Him (Acts 1:8).

Without the presence and power of the Holy Spirit in our churches and in our lives, like Tin Man we become powerless and ineffective. So, whatever you do, PLEASE DON'T FORGET THE OIL!

October 31
YOUR SEED DETERMINES THE HARVEST
Read: Gal. 6:7-8

Although I was not raised in the country, I had grandparents who lived in rural areas near farms I would visit during spring and summer break from school. As an adult I also had the opportunity to live near a rural area when I was stationed in the Memphis/ Millington, Tennessee area during a three-year military shore duty tour there.

Each year it was amazing to watch the process of how farmers worked the ground preparing it for the seeds that would soon be planted. They used large tractors with huge plows in tow to break-up the hard, sometimes stony, and untilled soil to ensure the seed had a suitable environment to be planted and to grow in. Once the ground was ready, the farmer would then sow the seeds.

Year after year I observed farmers planting cotton seeds since fluffy, white cotton balls were expected to be harvested at the appointed time. It would have been senseless and absolutely absurd for the farmers to plant apple, orange, or even peach seeds, and then expect to harvest cotton. It took the farmers sowing the right seeds to ensure the correct harvest was produced in the end.

Well, this same principle also applies to life in both a natural and spiritual sense; because whatever harvest we receive in life is usually directly connected to the seeds we have sown. The reference to seed here also goes beyond speaking of just money or in a financial sense, although this is one positive way to sow; however, this is referring to seeds in general.

"You cannot fool God, so don't make a fool of yourself! You will harvest what you plant. If you follow your selfish desires, you will harvest destruction, but if you follow the Spirit, you will harvest eternal life" (Gal. 6:7-8, Contemporary English Version).

In other words, every seed we sow is destined to grow and will eventually show, whether the seed is good or bad; this is why it is so crucial for us to sow the right thing.

Thoughts

_____
_____
_____
_____
_____
_____
_____

So, if someone desires to have and receive healing in his or her body it would be senseless to walk around saying "Woe is me! I'm never going to get any better. I may as well accept the fact that this is going to be a normal part of my life." Instead it would be better to say, "LORD, though I see the symptoms and feel the pain I thank You for my healing. Your Word declares that by Your stripes I am healed (Is. 53:5), so I stand on Your Word today."

Likewise, it would be ridiculous for someone expecting a financial breakthrough to walk around saying, "I guess I'm always going to be broke; my momma never had anything, my daddy never had anything, so I guess I'll never have anything." No. The correct response would be to say "Heavenly Father I thank You for calling me Your son/daughter, and since You own everything I know You will supply all of my need according to Your Word (Phil. 4:19); I am the head and not the tail, I am above and not beneath, and I am a lender not a borrower (Deut. 28:12-13)."

The principle of sowing and reaping is so elementary that we often over-think it, over-spiritualize it, and unfortunately end up missing out on the blessings associated with what this principle can produce. So instead of complaining, getting frustrated, or giving up on what may appear to be a dead situation—begin to speak life while sowing seeds of faith according to what God's Word says about the particular situation and then start expecting the right harvest (Gen. 8:22).

November 1
HE IS ALWAYS THERE
Read: 1 Sam. 17:33-37

In 1 Samuel chapter 17, the young shepherd boy David went to the front line of battle to check on his older brothers and bring provisions as requested of him by his father Jesse. And when he arrived he found the Philistine giant Goliath challenging the very armies of Israel, with every mighty warrior cringing in fear. David stood in wonder and amazement that no one had enough faith and courage to take Goliath up on his (1 Sam. 17:29, 31).

David did not view Goliath's challenge just as an insult to the armies of Israel, but also as a slap in the face of the God whom they represented. Therefore, David accepted the giant's challenge in order to defend the name and honor of the God who defended and protected him in the past. But when King Saul became skeptical and doubted David's abilities to stand toe-to-toe with the giant, David began to recount what God had done for him in the past (1 Sam. 17:34-37). David reminded himself God's faithfulness in every past victory.

Thoughts

So, with a sling and a smooth stone, David was able to conquer and defeat the giant that defied the entire armies of Israel, because he knew God was always with him. David's faith in God caused him to see and look at the giant from a different perspective, knowing that anyone or anything attempting to exalt itself against God would be brought low. David looked at Goliath through the eyes of faith with confidence knowing his God was there and able to deliver him.

This is a great lesson for us to recall whenever we face our own giants in life; we can be confident that God will always be with us because He loves us (Heb. 13:5). God does not just give us love, because He IS love and this love for His people has not and will not change!

November 2
THE WRITING IS ON THE WALL
Read: Dan. 5

In the Bible, over and over again, there are stories that illustrate how easy it is to allow success to go to an individual's head while easily forgetting the One who got them there. And in each instance, as the individual continued to prosper, more focus was placed on their human efforts and in the things accumulated more than giving thanks for the divine hand of God working behind the scenes and moving on their behalf. A prime example of this could be seen in Daniel chapter five with King Belshazzar.

By the way, this is also a classic example of an individual who did not learn from the example and fate of those that went before him, especially with what pride brought to his predecessor King Nebuchadnezzar. According to Rom. 15:4, former things were written for our learning so that we can find hope.

Belshazzar's father and predecessor, who was king of the Babylonian empire at the time, allowed pride to give him an exalted opinion of himself which resulted in God bringing him low. Belshazzar's father boast of literally building Babylon all by himself, therefore, according to him he deserved glory (Dan. 4:30)—Talk about pride

It was because of the above attitude that God's judgment was placed upon Nebuchadnezzar. One would naturally think his son (Belshazzar) would have taken note of what not to do based on his father's example and subsequent demise; however, I guess in this case the familiar saying was true: "Like father, like son."

Thoughts

_____

_____

_____

_____

_____

_____

_____

Belshazzar eventually fell into the same trap, following in his father's prideful footsteps. He commanded a great feast be given for the lords of his kingdom. Now the feast was not the issue, it was the king's command to use gold and silver vessels that had been procured and taken out of God's Temple in the holy city of

Jerusalem—-he was really pressing his luck. Then out of nowhere a large dismembered hand appeared and began writing on the wall; the festivities probably instantly turned from fun and revelry, to shock and awe.

The king was stunned and didn't know what to make of this occurrence (Dan. 5:6). With fear gripping his heart, he franticly searched for astrologers, magicians, and sorcerers to interpret the writing; but none were able to divulge the meaning.

Therefore, the king's advisors remembered Daniel a Jew who had God's favor on his life and the ability interpret dreams, etc. (Dan. 5:11-12).

Daniel then interpreted the writing that stated "MENE, MENE, TEKEL, UPHARSIN" which basically pronounced judgment on the king, in other words God had numbered the days of Belshazzar's kingdom that would soon be divided and come to an end; and that his human efforts had been weighed by God and found to be lacking. That very night the king was murdered (Dan. 5:30). Not only can pride bring us low, but it can also lead to our demise if we are not mindful of "I" (pr"I"de) in the middle instead of Christ.

This is why we are not to think more highly of ourselves than we should; but instead humble ourselves while acknowledging the true Source of all blessing (Rom. 12:3). As we choose to humble or lower ourselves, this is when God is then able to exalt and lift us up (Lk. 14:11). Humility in God's Kingdom is the key. "Humility is not thinking less of yourself, but thinking of yourself less." (Prov. 16:18, 1 Cor. 10:12).

November 3
STIRRED, BUT NOT SHAKEN
Read: 2 Cor. 4:8-9

One of my all-time favorite movie series is the popular James Bond 007 series created by Ian Fleming. The main character of this series is James Bond an officer of the British Secret Intelligence Service (MI6). In each episode the main character is placed in unusual circumstances and wherever Bond went, there was sure to be action and excitement nearby as he attempted to thwart the plans of world leaders, mad scientist, or the myriad of villains and criminals bent on world-domination.

Thoughts

James Bond is always depicted and portrayed as a suave, debonair character and a lady's man. In one scene from a movie a few years back, Bond stood at a bar not know he was speaking with a female double-agent from a sister agency. As he flirted with her he placed an order for his drink giving his preference saying to the bartender, "shaken, and not stirred." As I thought about it, it was actually the reverse of his statement that really described his character throughout each "007" movie. He would often be stirred by the evil plans of those seeking world-domination, often being held captive against his will. However, he never allowed opposition to shake him.

No matter what obstacle Bond faced even when battered, beaten, and bruised; he always came out victoriously and not shaken. No matter what the enemy threw his way, he was not moved. This is exactly how we as Christians and believers are to respond when attacks come with everything imaginable literally being thrown our way; we are not to be moved or shaken. And rest assured the attacks will come, we just have to be ready (1 Pet. 5:8).

When the enemy does attack, this should prompt us to begin stirring up the gifts God has placed deep on the inside of us, as we hold-on faithfully to the Word of God that we have heard, studied, and meditated on prior to the attack. But before we can begin to stir God's Word resident inside of us, we must first begin putting His Word in. Otherwise we will end up attempting to draw living water from an empty well that is barren and dry. It is therefore essential that we put the Word in, stir up our gifts, and not allow them to settle as it becomes powerless and ineffective to bring about transformation in our lives.

James Bond was effective in not being stirred by adverse circumstances and situations because he applied what he had been trained to do and did not let his training grow stagnant. When the enemy attacked, he was poised and ready for battle.

Another fact for consideration is that when the enemy attacks we should not automatically think something is wrong or strange (1 Pet. 4:12-13), or that we have done something wrong. On the contrary, these attacks are often a sign that we are on the right track, a path that is in-line with God's will for us.

The enemy is not going waste his time or attack someone who is not a threat to his objectives, which are to steal, kill, and to destroy (Jn. 10:10). Instead he attacks those who have the authority and power of the Almighty God resident on the inside of them, those who are able to overthrow his kingdom (1 Jn. 4:4).

Like James Bond, when the enemy advances against us and we get knocked down we don't have to remain down, but can just get back up again and again (2 Cor. 4:8-9).

Thoughts

_____
_____
_____
_____
_____
_____
_____

The trials and tests we often go through precede promotion with a goal that is designed to strengthen and perfect (or mature) us. Therefore, as the pressures of life begin to stir you, stand firm and resolve to not be shaken (1 Cor. 15:58)!

November 4
YOUR PRESCRIPTION IS READY
Read: Prov. 4:20-22

Visits to doctors/physicians can be very interesting and often require a lot of patience. Being told to get undressed and dressed again, moving from one waiting area to next and then having to patiently wait for the next set of instructions until receiving an evaluation by a physician for the condition that brought you there.

Although I enjoy exercise and do my best to maintain a certain level of health and fitness that generally keeps me from frequent visits to a doctor's office, there have been times when I experienced pain that was just unbearable requiring professional attention. I don't know what it is, but for whatever reason men just seem to hate visits to the doctor choosing to endure the pain, and often require a little prodding to get us there.

In these scenarios, after being told by my wife a few times I need to see a doctor even though I am somewhat reluctant, I eventually go.

At doctor's office there is the initial check-in where the condition is described by the patient and assessed for priority of service, next comes the reading and recording of vital signs—checking blood pressure, temperature, etc. Once this phase is complete, the usual wait ensues prior to actually being called back to be seen by a doctor. And even while seated on the examining table with a skimpy robe that provides little protection from frigid conditions in the examining room, there is yet more waiting.

The doctor arrives, completes the examination, and provides his/her assessment. In this particular instance the condition turned out to be something minor, but nonetheless required medication to be taken over a period of time. So, off to the pharmacy I went to endure another guaranteed period of waiting, and after 45 minutes to an hour seated patiently, I eventually hear my number or name called saying, "Your prescription is ready."

Since I am reluctant to go see a doctor, one can just imagine how I must feel about taking the prescribed medicine; I really hate taking medicine. There I was with the very thing needed to remove my pain and discomfort in hand, but refusing to take it but rather just placing it inside a drawer or medicine cabinet choosing not to take the prescribed dosage. As a result, my physical condition did not get better and the pain continued to plague my body, when in actuality the only thing I needed to do was just take my medicine, believe God for my healing and then allow the discomfort to go away.

Spiritual sickness in the body of Christ often happens in similar fashion and with the same mentality as described above. We wait and wait for God to do something and move on our behalf when He has already given us the

Thoughts

_____
_____
_____
_____
_____
_____
_____

prescription to deal with the very things that cause us anxiety, fear, pain, and discomfort by giving us His Word (Ps. 107:20).

King Solomon provides great advice in Prov. 4:20-22). Solomon knew how important the Word was and is to our daily living, and that everything we need to live healthy and prosperous lives is in the Word. Joshua also reminds us of the importance of God's Word in Josh. 1:8). Therefore, it's plain to see that God has already provided the prescription, but it's completely up to us to take our daily dosage.

Have you received your medicine (the Word) today? Don't worry about running out, your prescription comes with unlimited refills—so keep taking your dosage each day (3 Jn. 1:2)!

November 5
IF YOU QUIT FEEDING IT, THEN IT CAN'T GROW
Read: Matt. 5:6

The growth process for plants, human beings and animals in general all progress at differing rates and by various means. But one thing important to each, if not all, is the type of environment the growth process takes place in. For example, in order for a tomato to properly grow, it has a very high water requirement and must receive a lot of moisture. Therefore, constant water is essential to the growth of the tomato; while on the other hand, extended exposure to water by other plants would cause irreversible damage. Another important factor common with most plants is that exposure to sunlight is also essential for growth.

Similarly, a tadpole would never develop into a frog if it were in the wrong environment being fed the wrong things. A tadpole could not grow in a desert or sand environment, instead it has a requirement to grow and mature in the surroundings of water. And as the tadpole is properly nourished, it begins to grow, developing arms and legs as it transforms into a frog. Fully grown, the frog is now able to survive both in water and in an air environment.

Then there is the development of us as human beings. As an embryo in the mother's womb, connected by the umbilical cord surrounded by water; the umbilical cord provides the connection allowing the embryo to receive nutrients and also to get rid of any waste. And as the embryo is properly nourished and continues to grow, it develops into a baby that is birth into the world and life as we know begins in the natural. But in order for this baby to fully develop and grow, it has to be properly fed receiving the right combination of vitamins and nutrients to assist in this process.

Thoughts

_____
_____
_____
_____
_____
_____
_____

With all of the examples provided above, there are a couple of recurring themes; proper nutrition was a requirement, and there was a constant need for water. Humans can survive for extended periods without having food; however, the survival time is significantly reduced when there is no water received. Therefore, in order for each to properly grow and develop, they had to be properly fed and in the right environment.

This is also a crucial requirement for believers in Christ; we must be properly fed and remain in the right environment. Of course water is symbolic of the Holy Spirit who is essential to our environment in Christ. Therefore, although we have a fleshly body in the natural, if we desire spiritual growth we must feed our spirits. Because if we begin to feed our flesh more than our spirit, guess which one is going to grow? You got it, our flesh! This means we must feed on God's Word if we desire growth in our spiritual walk with Him (Matt. 5:6)

So, if we choose not to feed the flesh with its desires and remain in the right environment, the flesh cannot grow. The Apostle Paul reminds us of this in Rom. 6:16). In other words, we must feed the right thing; our spirit.

We are products that have been created and designed by God for the environment of His presence and in His Word that we might receive the spiritual nourishment needed for our daily growth in Him (Ps. 139:15).

Therefore, we must make it our purpose to not feed our flesh with everything that it desires, but rather nourish and build up our spirit; and remain in the right environment (Gal. 5:16). When we are in the right environment, we are more effective for God. Remember, when there is less of the flesh, we are bound to be blessed (2 Pet. 3:18)!

November 6
LONGING TO KNOW
Read: Phil. 3:10

Knowledge is a great thing. I can remember growing up watching television shows like *Sesame Street*, *Zoom*, *Electric Company*, and the *Schoolhouse Rock* segments where learning and knowledge were presented in a fun, easy, and understandable ways.

Thoughts

Much of this knowledge and information was presented in catchy tunes and songs that I still remember today. For example, "Conjunction Junction, what's your function;" "I'm just a bill. Yes, I'm only a bill. And I'm sitting here on Capitol Hill;" and "Lolly, Lolly, Lolly, get your adverbs here."

These segments were often accompanied by the recurring thought or phrase: "Knowledge is power." In other words, knowledge could unlock new doors when applied correctly.

Case in point, during the period of slavery in the United States of America, I'm sure that even after President Abraham Lincoln signed the Emancipation Proclamation (an Executive Order for the release of slaves) there were still many who remained in bondage as slaves even though by law they had been made free. However, when these individuals obtained knowledge of the freedom that was now rightfully theirs by law, decree, and Executive Order; they were able to shake off their bands and chains thus allowing them to walk in freedom and liberty.

Although freedom and liberty had already been declared and granted to those who were enslaved, it wasn't until these individuals came into the knowledge of what the Emancipation Proclamation actually meant that they were actually made free; it was their KNOWING that eventually released them from bondage.

Many today are seeking signs and wonders to connect with God, while others search and seek for some type of deep revelation in God to make themselves feel all the more wiser (1 Cor. 1:22). Yet in each instance, these in and of themselves don't allow the individual to truly know God in the right way—a way that brings true freedom. The Apostle Paul reminds us of this Phil. 3:10.

The word "know" in the Bible is used to describe intimacy. By definition the word "intimacy" means "a state of being familiar; something of a personal or private nature" (Gen. 4:1, 25). However, the intimacy discussed in the preceding verses goes beyond mere passion and sex, but involves communication, spending quality time together and developing a closer relationship.

This is exactly what's required of us as believers if we truly desire to know God and to better acquaint ourselves with Christ similar to the Apostle Paul. This first starts with not solely receiving Jesus Christ as our Savior, but going a step further to making Him LORD.

Having His Lordship simply means that He has complete control over every area of our lives; this becomes easier when we spend time in prayer communicating with Him, quality time studying His Word, and through learning how to listen to and for His voice, and then obey. Because when we know that He has our best interest in mind and at heart, it is that much easier to cast Him as the Director of our play called "Life".
This brings true freedom.

Thoughts
_____
_____
_____
_____
_____
_____
_____

When we intimately KNOW Christ, we no longer have to ask if we are free (Jn. 8:36); but can simply walk in the liberty that is already ours by right, a right that is produced out of a loving relationship with our LORD and Savior. Do you really know Him? If not, long to know Him today in the right way!

November 7

YESTERDAY IS A MEMORY, START LIVING FOR TODAY
Read: Is. 43:18

The children of Israel had seen the mighty hand of God work through the twelve plagues witnessed in Egypt, with the final blow to Pharaoh being the death of his first-born son. As a result, after over 400 years of Egyptian bondage with the people of God waiting on every beck and call of the Pharaoh, God's people received their release papers and were finally set free from years of persecution, abuse, and hard labor. And as they traveled they eventually reached the banks of the Red Sea with God yet performing another miracle by parting the waters and allowing the Israelite men, women, children, and livestock to cross over on dry land.

With the bondage of Egypt behind them and now under the leadership of Moses, the people moved out into the wilderness in search of the land that had been promised to them by God, a land "flowing with milk and honey"; however, many still longed for what they had in Egypt (Ex. 3:8; Ex. 16:1-3).

Here were a people that had been threatened, beaten, mistreated, and subjected to harsh labor for over four centuries, who were now completely free but still longing for the things they were accustomed to in their former years of bondage, and still living in the memory of the past. Sounds familiar doesn't it? This is exactly where many of us as believers in Christ find ourselves; freed from the bondage of sin, but still remembering the past and longing after and for our former lifestyles with the pleasures it used to bring.

Jesus released us from the power of past sins through shedding His blood on the cross, and because of this we are given a new outlook on life (2 Cor. 5:17). However, although we are now saved and our spirits have been renewed; our minds constantly take us on strolls down memory lane. This is why the renewal of our minds is so very important (Rom. 12:1).

God's Word is the key to unlocking and loosing us from past memories, hurts, and failures thereby renewing our minds. But even with knowledge of this fact, we often allow ourselves and others to bring condemnation upon us based on our past even though God has forgotten everything that was B.C. (Before Christ) and even a few things after. If God has forgotten, then so should we (Rom. 8:1; Jer. 31:34)!

The Apostle Paul is a perfect example of someone who had an imperfect past but still chose to have the right mindset (Phil. 3:13-14). In other words, leave the past in the past and choose to look and press forward to the favor, prosperity, and blessings that are ahead.

Yesterday is a memory, today is reality; but only God knows what tomorrow holds! So, start

Thoughts

_____
_____
_____
_____
_____
_____
_____

living today with anticipation and hope for a brighter tomorrow. God is simply saying, "Forget what happened long ago! Don't think about the past" (Is. 43:18, Contemporary English Version).

November 8
ALL IT TAKES IS ONE
Read: Rom. 5:12-21

Have you ever met an individual who was just self-righteous as if they could do no wrong, and as if they never did any wrong? You know, those who have experienced the liberating grace and power of God through forgiveness by the blood of Christ, but now look down their pious nose at others who may not be where they are spiritually.

And then there's the individual who says, "I don't sin. I don't steal, I don't lie, I haven't committed adultery, I haven't murdered anyone and I work hard to make an honest living." It really sounds good; but, this is still not enough.

Not doing the above things are all good; however, the fact of the matter remains that we are all born with a sin nature because of the fall of mankind in the Garden of Eden; it all links back to Adam's original disobedience and sin (Rom. 5:12). All it took was the disobedience of one man to bring condemnation upon many, and we are all living in the after effects of this one act to this very day. So, when an individual says they have no sin they are literally deceiving themselves (1 Jn. 1:8).

Even though we are no longer bound by the law and are now under grace; if an individual were to keep nine of the Ten Commandments but failed at one, they would be guilty of transgressing the entire law of God. It's good the individual doesn't steal, lie, covet, murder, commit adultery, etc.; but can the individual place nothing else before God (idolatry), honor father and mother, or simply love his neighbor? We can't just do some things, but leave the others undone.

At this point you may be wondering, how then do we deal with this issue of sin? Well, I'm glad you asked. Just as sin came into the world through one individual, righteousness and justification came through the finished work of Jesus Christ on the cross at Calvary (Rom. 5:18-20).

Thoughts

_____
_____
_____
_____
_____
_____
_____

So don't deceive yourself; we all have issues and areas in our lives we must constantly bring before the Father. As believers we no longer live a lifestyle of sin, however, at the same time by our very nature we are prone "to" sin.

All it takes is one drop of red dye to contaminate an entire gallon of water; likewise, all it takes is one sin to contaminate our lives. Sin of commission as well as sins of omission (James 4:17).

In other words, we all have the propensity to sin; but it is what we do after we sin that make the difference. We are not to condemn ourselves or let others condemn us; and we are not to have pity parties saying "Woe is me!" or "Nobody knows the trouble I've seen!" Instead, we are to get up, wash our face, confess it, forsake it, and move on (1 Jn. 1:9)!

Therefore, as it took was one to plunge us into sin and death; all it took was One to free us from the grips of death, hell, and the grave with life, liberty, sanctification and justification through Christ being the end result. Therefore, no matter what the sin may be, all it takes is one drop of Jesus' blood to cleanse us, make us whole and set us free!

November 9
FULLY PERSUADED
Read: Rom. 4:20-21

Most of us are familiar with the story of the faithfulness of the patriarch Abraham and the account of his preparation to offer his son Isaac as a sacrifice in Genesis chapter twenty-two. And because of what transpired during this account the Bible says the Abraham was considered to be righteous, or in right-standing with God. A question that might be considered here is this, "Was Abraham's faith inadequate before he offered Isaac?"

This saga and journey of faith began when God told Abram to get up and leave his country, family, and his father's house to go to a place that had yet to be disclosed to him (Gen. 12:1-3). So, what did Abram do? He didn't wait for a visible sign like Gideon and the fleece (Judg. 6:37-40), and neither did he call together a committee to vote on it. Although he brought a few individuals along that should not have gone on the journey with him, with nothing more than the command of God Abram still acted and went. God told Abram He would bless him and all of his descendants, and that his name would be great.

So, here was Abram and wife Sarai who were 99 years-old and 89 years-old respectively, and they had no children or descendants to fulfill the promise God had made to Abram. However, Abram continued to believe God, and in Genesis chapter seventeen his name was changed from Abram ("Exalted Father") to Abraham ("Father of a multitude"). And though Abraham and his wife Sarah (who also had a name change) were way beyond child-producing and child-bearing

Thoughts

_____
_____
_____
_____
_____
_____
_____

years; now at the age of 100 and 90 respectively, God fulfilled His promise to Abraham through the birth of Isaac the promised seed/son.

After waiting more than 25 years for an heir to fulfill God's promise of making Abraham's descendants like the stars in the sky and the sand along the seashore, Abraham's faithfulness and commitment would be tested by requiring him to offer the son of promise as a sacrifice in an obedient act of worship. Isaac was not one of ten, or one of twenty promised sons; Isaac was the one and only son promised to fulfill the covenant God made with Abraham, now God was asking Abraham to sacrifice this special son.

Abraham didn't know how it would be accomplished, perhaps God would resurrect Isaac even though resurrection had not occurred at this point in Bible history; however, Abraham was willing to go the distance and do exactly what God commanded, even if it required giving up that which was dear and precious to him—-the promised son (Gen. 18:9-10). Knowing exactly what the cost would be, Abraham's focus was still on completing his God-given assignment.

With knife in hand and hand in motion, an angel of the LORD stopped Abraham because God now knew that through this act of obedience, Abraham truly believed and trusted God. And though it is recorded that Abraham's faith was "perfected" or made "mature" or "complete" by this act; Abraham's faith was not at all inadequate before this time. He had already been declared righteous because of his previous acts of obedience and as a result, Abraham was called "the friend of God" and is listed among those in what is commonly called the "Hall of Faith" in Hebrews chapter eleven.

Abraham was fully persuaded and obeyed God out of his love and commitment to Him. Obedience is better than sacrifice (1 Sam. 15:22), and love sometimes does demand a sacrifice. We show God we love Him by keeping His commandments (Jn. 14:15) and being fully persuaded (Rom. 8:38-39)!

November 10
MAYBE EMPTY IS BETTER
Read: Phil. 2:5-8

Thoughts

_____
_____
_____
_____
_____
_____
_____

Life is filled with many ups and downs, joy and pain, with victories experienced, as well as defeat. With that said, there are often discussions that focus on looking at the situations occurring in our lives from two distinct points of view using the analogy of a glass of water.

For those who are considered optimists (having a positive point of view) when viewing a glass of

400

water that is not completely full, based on their outlook and vantage point they would be very likely to say the glass is "half-full." Now on the other hand, there are individuals who generally have a negative outlook on life (the pessimist) who sees the same glass of water but would consider the glass to be "half-empty." So, which point of view is right? In actuality there is really no difference, but rather it is all a matter of perspective.

Well, this same analogy of a glass of water can be used to illustrate the perspective we have as it pertains to being believers in Christ; but in this regards instead of our lives being full, the goal would be to have a glass (or life) that was empty in the end.

I can recall listening to a worship song in which the psalmist stated that when he gets to heaven he didn't want to arrive with a life on full, instead he wanted to live with a life poured out. What a profound concept, desiring to live a life poured out through giving and in service to others.

Today there are too many believers who have a different mindset and agenda, believing that they should "Can all they can get, and get all that they can." We receive the Word of God week after week, getting full with how to live blessed, how to live the abundant life, walk in God's Favor, and hear about the things that bring about transformation and a changed life.

Yet sadly, many of us never release anything we have received for the benefit of others. Instead we keep it to ourselves so that we can continue to prosper, get ahead in life, and continue to receive our weekly spiritual high.

The end result of this type of mindset will result in many arriving at heaven full of purpose, destiny, and lives that were designed to be poured out in service to others. But the goal we should strive to attain is arriving at Heaven's gates with a life that has a needle pointing to "empty" instead of "full."

The needle is not on "empty" because nothing was ever put in, but instead the life is empty because that which was received was poured out to benefit others. This is exactly what Jesus did for humanity, He gave until there was literally nothing left to give because He gave His very life—-He lived a life that was completely poured out and He is our perfect example (Phil. 2:5-8)!

Verse 7 of Philippians chapter two speaks directly to what was accomplished by Jesus on the cross as He humbled Himself. The Greek word used to describe this act is "kenosis" which means "to empty or self-emptying." Although He was completely man, Jesus was also completely God and He emptied Himself of His divinity and came down from Heaven to identify with and meet the need of frail humanity. Jesus literally emptied Himself as His body was broken and His blood poured out to redeem mankind.

Thoughts

_____

_____

_____

_____

_____

_____

_____

Jesus emptied Himself of His own wants, goals, and desires to obey the will of the Father and to meet the needs of others (Acts 10:38). Through the abiding presence of the Holy Spirit, God is with us as well; not just for us to fill ourselves up, but to also empty ourselves for the good of others. So, maybe, just maybe, empty really is better (1 Pet. 4:10).

November 11

ONE PERSON CAN MAKE A DIFFERENCE
Read: Jn. 15:13

Many of the liberties and freedom that we experience today came about because one person chose to make a difference. There are numerous stories of those in our armed forces over the years that have paid the ultimate price by willingly laying down their lives so that many could live.

One story that stands out involved a unit conducting a patrol in the vicinity of Baghdad, Iraq a several years ago. As the convoy traveled down the road, out of nowhere an Iraqi insurgent tossed a grenade inside one of the Humvees filled with young soldiers. And although he had direct access to a door and the opportunity to escape the vehicle; a 19 year-old Army soldier (Specialist Ross A. McGinnis) pinned the grenade between himself and the vehicle in order to save the rest of his team thereby sparing the lives of four individuals while sacrificing his own. You see, all it takes is one person to make a difference.

As we look to the unselfish act of Specialist McGinnis, to those who came before him and to all those who have come after him, we too should endeavor to follow these examples of personal sacrifice that go towards the accomplishment of the greater good. Although we may not be asked to physically lay down our lives, we are encouraged to make individual sacrifices for the benefit of others each day. And of course, Jesus Christ was our perfect example of selfless sacrifice.

Over two thousand years ago Jesus came into the earth for a specific mission and purpose; and from that point on the world as we know it has never been the same. He came with a purpose, mission, and assignment to complete that no one else could achieve but Him. And though He was completely human wrapped in flesh when He walked upon earth, He was also completely God and divine.

Thoughts

His presence on earth was so significant that even space and time were separated and defined by His very existence (B.C. – Before Christ and A.D. - "Anno Domini," which is Latin for "year of our Lord." Jesus was sent and anointed for a purpose, hence the name Christ which simply means "the Anointed One."

Many are of the belief that Jesus only came to redeem mankind by bringing salvation into the world; however, that was only a portion of the equation. According to Lk. 19:10 He came to seek and to save the that which was lost;" therefore, not only did He come to redeem (purchase back) a lost mankind from sin, but to redeem everything else man forfeited in the process (health and wholeness, peace of mind, and well-being, just to name a few) (Is. 53:4-5).

As Jesus was nailed to the cross, every one of our sins (past, present, and future) were nailed to the cross with Him; every sickness and disease known to man and those yet to be discovered were also nailed to the cross during this time. Therefore, Jesus did not come to die for the sole purpose of just bringing salvation to us, but He came to also bring liberty, freedom, and complete wholeness in every aspect of our bodies and our lives.

Jesus' accomplishment and selfless sacrifice on the cross is a finished work as evident in His words "It is finished" in Jn. 19:30. His words meant exactly that—IT WAS (AND IS) A DONE DEAL! It is now our job to simply believe, and then start acting and living like it through walking in our newfound freedom! One person can truly make a difference (Jn. 15:13)!

November 12
YOUR WORST ENEMY IS EVEN CLOSER THAN YOU THINK
Read: Prov. 16:7

There have been many movies and television shows with plots involving individuals who appeared to be very close friends. But as the movie or show progressed, and as the plot began to unfold; it became more apparent that certain individuals had ulterior motives.

Throughout the movie the individual presented himself or herself as one who could be trusted, one who would go the distance for their friend no matter the circumstance or situation; giving the appearance that they really had the other person's back. When in actuality they were in the relationship for selfish reasons, and really had improper motives.

Thoughts

_____
_____
_____

Imagine an individual attempting to target you; a person getting closer and closer, even befriending you until you trusted him or her with your most precious and prized possessions—-even to the point of trusting

_____
_____
_____
_____
_____

them with your very life. Then all of a sudden, when this individual has finally penetrated your inner-circle (the place where you have let your guard down), they began to show their true colors; and then the words of their mouth revealed that they were never really a true friend as they began to sow seeds of discord with a goal of attempting to destroy various areas of your life.

Sadly, many are still experiencing this same scenario in real life today even as this devotional was typed. As believers, we often continue to fall prey to this repeat offender because of how close to us they actually are. Yet in reality, the one that we thought was there to bless us was also the very one that brought about the seeds of a curse in our live with the intent of causing destruction.

The enemy being referred to is not only closer than we could ever imagine, but is actually a member and part of our own body—-the TONGUE and the words that proceed out of our mouths on a daily basis (James 3:8-10). Imagine that, here is something that small and is so close to us but is still powerful enough to cause a world of hurt and damage in our lives if it is not brought under control.

This is exactly why so many of us have been hindered and cannot move forward in life simply because we have been ensnared by our very own tongues and chosen to allow the wrong words to come out of our mouths (Prov. 18:21). As the old saying goes, "One day you'll eat your words."

The negative words we speak often become the very things we actually begin to eat as they exit our mouths, enter the ear gate and then planted deep within our spirits and souls to bring about spiritual death—-we unknowingly eat negative seeds that are sent on assignment to produce death. A seed only produces that which is on the inside of it—-what type of seeds are you sowing?

Rom. 10:17 says that faith comes by hearing. Therefore, just as faith comes by hearing life-giving words; saying and hearing the wrong thing has no alternative but to produce words that have no life in them at all. So, what are you consistently saying to yourself or about yourself, or even about others for that matter? Do you say you are healed, or do you wake up feeling pain saying I don't know how I will make it through the day? Do you say that God will supply all or your need, or do you say I'm always broke? Do you say that you'll never find that woman or man, or do you thank and bless God for the relationships that you do have?

Thoughts

_____

_____

_____

_____

_____

_____

_____

What we hear we often receive, and what we receive we eventually begin to believe. So begin to speak, hear, and receive the right things by faith. Never underestimate the power of the tongue and your words; and above all else be on guard because your worst enemy is closer than you think!

November 13
THE ADOPTION IS BINDING AND LEGAL
Read: Eph. 1:4-5

Establishing family was God's intent from the very beginning, so to be a part of a family is a beautiful thing because it was ordained by God Himself. When family comes to mind, many things begin to flow through the mind; however, what family is primarily intended to bring is a sense of belonging, togetherness, security, and most importantly love.

When I was younger, as I grew up in a single-parent home; therefore, I always knew that I wanted to have a complete family some day when I became a husband and father, and that I wanted to be there for my wife and kids. Although I primarily lived with my mother, my father was still in my life and always provided for me. However, there is nothing like having a father available and present in the home as that source of strength, stability, security, with the ability to impart and pass on things that only a father can.

Unfortunately, the traditional family with a man being the father and a woman being the mother seems to be a thing of the past according to the standards of society. As alternative lifestyles continue to increase, the structure of the family designed by God continues to erode more and more day-by-day with each drop of indifference. And on top of this there are those traditional parents who, for selfish reasons, just completely walk away abandoning his or her responsibility to the child or children (the gifts from God) they produced and brought into this world.

Today, not only is the institution of the church under attack but one of the key and foundational building blocks of the church, family, is also under serious attack. The statistics on divorce and its effect on the family are alarming, yet this is something that must be addressed. This is not to condemn anyone who has been divorced but is rather to point out and say this was never part of God's original plan.

God created man in His image and likeness for the purpose of establishing relationship; God's plan was to establish "FAMILY." It was sin in the garden that caused the divorce separating man from God; and from Genesis to Revelation God detailed His plan to reconnect man to the family he or she would need in order to survive and function effectively in life.

By design, men are given the role as heads of the home and family, not to be demanding or domineering but to be the initial source of security, protection, and love. Just as a physical body without a head ceases to function; a family without the proper head (father) in right position tends to be dysfunctional in some form or fashion as well. This is why the enemy attacks the family with a goal to divide and conquer (Jn. 10:10). A divided family cannot stand.

Thoughts

_____
_____
_____
_____
_____
_____
_____

This division brings with it many associated ripple effects. For instance, there are many issues prevalent among children and youth today that are directly associated to the absence of, not just a male, but a father-figure in the home. This is not to say those from single-parent homes are doomed to failure and can't succeed in life, but it does present challenges that will have to be addressed as issues arise requiring the wisdom and guidance of a father.

Many struggle today or have struggled at some point in life, even as adults, because there was never a real father-figure in the home. But there is good news! Know today that you have been specifically sought out and chosen by God, and now through Christ you are legally adopted into the family and have the legitimate right to every blessing associated with your new "sonship" (as sons and daughters of God). The adoption and connection with the Father is binding and legal, and you now also experience His awesome love! (Eph. 1:4-5).

November 14
TRY PUTTING ON SOMETHING NEW
Read: Rom. 13:14

Have you ever had a favorite shirt, T-shirt, shorts, sweatpants, pants, or some other article of clothing that was just comfortable; something you wore all the time no matter where you were or what the setting or environment may have been? You know, that item worn so much until thread in certain spots began to unravel, holes would begin to appear due to constant use, or the heel of the shoe become worn down so much you were literally walking on the side of your foot.

But instead of getting rid of the item for something new and in much better shape, what does one often do; you've guessed it, we pull out a needle and thread, sew it up or patch it up, and then put it back on, and in some cases we just wore it "as is," or just continue wearing the shoes until they can be worn no longer.

I can remember having articles of the above nature when I first got married; I would wear certain items of clothing over and over again because they felt good and were comfortable to me. Although they were clean, they needed much improvement in the area of appearance, but one day I was encouraged to try something new (Rom. 13:14). What this means for us as believers in Christ (in a spiritual sense) is that we must stop walking around with the same old raggedy clothes on day in and day out; but should opt for putting on something new, and then watch how God brings about a change on the inside of you that begins to reflect and manifest on the outside. So go ahead I dare you, WHEN YOUR OLD

Thoughts

_____
_____
_____
_____
_____
_____
_____

November 15

DON'T JUST STAND THERE, DO SOMETHING!
Read: Gal. 5:1

In this day and age, taking a stand for something, in my humble opinion is very important. Individuals are encouraged to stand up for their rights, stand in the gap for others, or take a stand for this cause or the next. But what does "to take a stand" really mean? There are actually several definitions for the word "stand:" "to support oneself on the feet in an erect position; to be in a position to gain or lose because of an action taken or a commitment made; to rest or remain upright on a base; to occupy a place or location; to remain stationary or inactive."

Sadly, many in society and even a pretty large majority in the church literally take the latter definition to heart as they remain stationary and inactive, when taking a stand should go far beyond this type of complacency.

When those who fought for and struggled to achieve racial equality during the Civil Rights Movement in America took a stand, they did not stand by idle doing nothing; instead they made their voices known and heard through sit-ins and protests demonstrating a unified front until equality was achieved.

And though many did not agree with the actions of the U.S. governmental administration that launched the war against the dictatorial regime of Saddam Hussein, the deposed leader of Iraq, in support of the Global War Against Terrorism; those in office did not just sit on their hands while innocent lives were being loss, whether the choice was wrong or right they opted for action.

Therefore, "taking a stand" goes beyond merely occupying space and doing nothing; it signifies corresponding action (James 2:26). This is also what the phrase should signify to us as believers in Christ.

In Gal. 5:1 the Apostle Paul admonished believers to "Stand fast" in the liberty of Christ that made us free). This "stand fast" does not mean we sit by doing absolutely nothing; however, we must do whatever it takes to not get caught up in the things that once held us in bondage and then begin to exercise the gifts we have so graciously been given to lift, edify and build up the body of Christ; because it is this freedom that now allows us to accomplish all that God has predestined for us to do.

Thoughts

_____
_____
_____
_____
_____
_____
_____
_____

In Lk. 19:13 Jesus spoke concerning the "Parable of the ten pounds" which detailed the faithfulness of ten servants. This parable speaks directly to those who consider themselves to be disciples (or followers) of Jesus Christ and the need for faithfulness and productivity; the servants were told to "Occupy till I come". The word occupy in this verse is not just referring to an individual taking up space and doing nothing, but rather this word is literally translated as "doing business."

This is exactly what God has given each one of us a commission to do, not just to take up space in church week after week doing nothing or solely being concerned with our own business; instead, the focus should be on Kingdom business. Therefore, as believers, once we come into a saving knowledge of Christ, we are not to just pack our spiritual bags as we sit by do nothing waiting on the Rapture and Jesus' return, or doing nothing in the church; as we are reminded in Lk. 19:13 we are to "occupy" and do the Father's business, Kingdom business until Jesus comes back for us again. We all have gifts and talents that are designed to be used for the up-building of God's Kingdom; so, DON'T JUST STAND THERE, DO SOMETHING (Phil. 1:27-30)!

November 16
AN ATTEMPTED REVERSAL OF ROLES
Read: Rom. 9:19-23

Today there are often instances where the younger (child) attempts to tell the elder (parent) what to do. Many of the younger generation have the mindset they know everything, and the opinion of the parent is of no consequence. Nowadays one can often hear comments like, "You just don't understand, things are different now than they were back then"; "You can't possibly know what I'm going through"; or "You lived your life, let me live mine and make my own mistakes." Therefore, the younger generation forsakes the wisdom of the elder generation because they now quote "Know it all."

This type of mindset is also prevalent in the military with a younger generation coming in thinking they know it all without any real experience to back up their supposition. One can often find a young recruit attempting to explain to a 20+ year veteran how things should be, and what the regulations are. In this instance the young recruit can often here the all too familiar phrase, "You need to just stay in your lane or in your paygrade."

Thoughts

_____
_____
_____
_____
_____
_____
_____

I have learned over the years that although methods may have changed with new technology with new methods of enticement; the end result is still the same and in actuality there is nothing new. King Solomon reminds us of this fact in the book of Ecclesiastes (Ecc. 1:9-10).

Unfortunately this attempted attitude of reversal of roles also spills over into the general life of mankind and of us as believers; in our finite thinking and limited ability, many question the very existence of God and His instructions to us as given through His Word. This leads to a creation who believes they actually know more than the One who created them and knows what is best.

Although this may seem elementary, imagine a toaster telling its inventor what it was created to do; for example, in a mock conversation the toaster says, "I was not designed to toast bread products, I was created to heat water." This reversal of roles would not only cause destruction to the toaster, but injury or even death to anyone who attempted to use it. The creator is the one who intimately knows the purpose of a thing. The same applies to God and His creation—mankind (Rom. 9:20-23).

Who better to direct the lifestyle of mankind than the Creator of mankind? And who are we to question an All-Powerful, All-Seeing, and All-Knowing God? We are provided the instruction we need to sustain the life that was predetermined for us by the Creator through His Instruction Manual (The Bible).

I have often heard a familiar acrostic or acronym routinely used to represent the word B-I-B-L-E: "Basic Instructions Before Leaving Earth;" this is exactly what God's Word should be for us; instructions and principles designed to protect and preserve us from harm. And anything that we don't know in our natural ability, God reveals to those who are in covenant relationship through the Holy Spirit (1 Cor. 2:11-12).

Refuse to bring destruction to yourself or to others; follow the instructions as given. Obedience through love provides a pathway to the blessings of God. Sometimes it truly is better that we just stay in our lanes.

November 17
IT DOESN'T MATTER HOW YOU START
Read: Phil. 3:4-7

At the time, Saul of Tarsus was one of the greatest opponents to the Church and the message of Jesus Christ that ever lived. He made it his goal and life's mission to persecute and destroy anyone and anything that represented the Gospel message and salvation through the person of Jesus Christ (Acts 8:3).

Thoughts

Saul's desire to see Christians killed was so intense he even went to the high priest to request letters giving him permission and authority to destroy any disciple of Christ as he journeyed along the way. But one day while on the road to Damascus, Saul had an encounter with the very

409

person he set out to persecute in attempts to discredit His name— he had a personal encounter with Jesus Christ Himself.

After Saul was blinded by the glorious light of the Savior and had a "close encounter of the first kind" with Jesus Christ, his life was no longer the same. His name was eventually changed from Saul to Paul, and the fervor and intensity he once had for persecuting the church was transformed and re-focused towards spreading the name of Christ and the Gospel message to all people and all regions of the earth at any cost.

The Apostle Paul is regarded as one of the most influential figures in the Bible having written over two-thirds of the New Testament; he also committed his life to the cause of Christ and became a messenger to the Gentiles (non-Jews). And although he started out the wrong way, it was actually how he finished that was more significant.

There are many today, non-believers and believers alike, who feel their past disqualifies them from receiving Christ, or even being found worthy to work towards the fulfillment of His mission for and in the church. Rom. 8:1 reminds us that nothing can disqualify us. In other words, we can leave the past exactly where it belongs--in the past.

Once we have an encounter with Christ our life is no longer the same, and in God's eyes our past is forgotten and our former lifestyle no longer matters (Heb. 8:12). This is exactly what Paul did as he forgot the past to reach for the prize of Christ that was ahead (Phil. 3:11-12). Besides, if Christ no longer brings up or remembers our past, then why should we?

Our Christian life is often compared to a race; a race that we must not only endure, but finish (Ecc. 9:11). The past or how fast we run is not important; it is our endurance and our ability to build a life that is pleasing to God until the end.

We must also remember that where ugliness and sin once abounded in our lives; the grace of our LORD and Savior Jesus Christ through our personal encounter with Him now much more abounds (Rom. 5:20).

It doesn't matter how you start; it's how you end that really matters, so make it a purpose to end strong! So, FORGET YOUR FORMER MESS, CHOOSE TO MOVE FORWARD AND BEGIN TO PRESS!

"Do you not know that in a race all the runners compete, but [only] one receives the prize? So run [your race] that you may lay hold [of the prize] and make it yours" (1 Cor. 9:24, Amplified Bible).

Thoughts
_____
_____
_____
_____
_____
_____
_____

November 18
WE'RE ALL IN THE SAME BOAT
Read: Mk. 4:35-39

After having just taught about the power of God's kingdom, Jesus and His disciples boarded a boat to journey across the Sea of Galilee to the other side. I'm sure that after teaching and performing miracles all day, Jesus must have been physically tired and spiritually drained releasing His virtue. This is probably why He went below decks to get some much needed rest.

And as the ship and its crew made the journey across the sea, a fierce storm arose with enough force and power to topple the boat throwing everyone aboard into the now violent and tumultuous waters. Undoubtedly, images of fear, dread and impending doom began to fill the minds of the crew.

Being in the Navy and having spent over half my career on sea duty aboard ships, I have my own "sea" stories and personal experiences of enduring some fairly severe storms; storms with enough intensity to cause waves of the ocean to literally rise above the flight deck of a massive aircraft carrier, with side to side motions that brought sea sickness to even the most experienced Sailors.

On another occasion I can remember going through a storm while on a Navy destroyer that was so powerful we were literally walking sideways on the bulkheads (walls) of the ship. Jesus and His disciples were probably in a ship or boat that was considerably smaller than any U.S. Navy vessel, so I can imagine the anxiety the crew must have felt and experienced.

So, as everyone frantically ran around trying to figure out what to do, Jesus was found below decks sleeping peacefully on a pillow. One of the disciples awoke Him and asked if He did not care about what was happening (Mk. 4:38-39).

Although the disciples and the rest of the crew responded in fear; with just the power and authority of His Words, Jesus calmed the violent storm. Jesus and the disciples were all in the same boat; so, why was His response to the storm different than that of the disciples? Jesus knew who He was and the authority He possessed; and knowing of His authority, He began to exercise this same by faith as He spoke directly to the thing that attempted to destroy them.

As believers, we are all in the same boat, and all face the same storms of trials, tests, and temptations. However, we should remember God has given each of us a measure of faith (Rom. 12:3), and we have to learn how to exercise that faith to help one another.

Even Jesus had to face temptations (Matt. 4), but instead of running from the trial or responding in fear, He used the authority of the Word that was within Him.

Thoughts

_____
_____
_____
_____
_____
_____
_____

Jesus experienced exactly the same things that we each eventually go through and have to endure (Heb. 4:15), and He is our perfect example of how to respond through humility and an attitude that was willing to serve and be available for others.

Likewise, we each face or experience similar tests, trials, and temptations; the only difference is how we choose to respond—either in fear or faith. A fear that causes us to focus on ourselves, or a faith that prompts us to move for the benefit of others (1 Pet. 5:9-10).

Therefore, we must learn how to put our faith into action and begin to exercise the authority we have in the earth in order to speak to our mountains, obstacles, and storms (1 Jn. 4:17). Jesus has given us His same power and authority, and He has also demonstrated how we are to humble ourselves and serve because we are all in the same boat (Rom. 12:9-13).

November 19
IT'S YOUR TURN NOW
Read: Eph. 1:3-6

With the plethora of technology readily available, nowadays it is often difficult to get the younger generation to go outside to engage in any type of physical activity. As a result, we now have youth and young adults who prefer to sit in front televisions with game controllers in hand playing X-Box, Nintendo, PlayStation, Wii, etc. as opposed to going outside to play or engage in any type of physical exercise. There is nothing wrong with playing these types of games; however, there should also be a little balance.

This gaming trend has influenced the increase in adolescent obesity, which has steadily climbed over the years resulting from a lack of physical activity among youth, when just a few decades ago it was almost the total opposite.

When I was younger playing outside was a must; however, parents provided instruction and direction to children to play as long as they wanted with one condition, "Make sure you are inside before the street lights come on." Back then kids could be found playing a multitude of outside activities and games like Simon Says, Red Light-Green Light, Hide and Seek, and of course sporting games like kickball, soccer, basketball, football, etc., activities that required physical movement other than fingers and thumbs manipulating a controller.

Thoughts

_____

_____

_____

_____

_____

_____

During my younger years I can remember gathering with friends to play a sport with two individuals being selected as captains for each team. Each captain would then go through the

412

group of kids to pick individuals for their team starting with those who would be more beneficial to winning the game, and then continue on with selections until all choices were exhausted.

There was no greater feeling than being chosen and selected for a team early, because this indicated you were not insignificant but had value and worth.

In similar fashion the Captain of our souls has selected and chosen each one of us, not based on our own merits and/or ability, but simply because He loved us (Eph. 1:3-6).

Before the world was ever formed God chose us to be his very own. And out of all creation, it was man that found a special place in His will and plan. This was very evident during the days of creation. After God created light, the heavens, water, earth, sun, moon, stars, sky, and other living creatures he said "It was good;" however, after He created man God said "It was VERY good" (Gen. 1:31). Why? Because man was the culmination of creation and God's very own prized possession (James 1:18).

However, even though God chose and adopted us ahead of time, He has also given each one of us free will to choose the correct path to take. We each have been created to worship, and one of the greatest forms of worship any of us can achieve is to humble ourselves and serve, not to benefit ourselves but to ensure we are doing our part on the team. This requires us to make the right choices.

The LORD has graciously chosen you, and you are valuable to the winning team; now it's your turn to make a choice to serve. Whatever the decision maybe, the choice is completely up to you. And since you've been chosen by God, it's your turn now. So, why not simply do your part—-because your worship determines your service (what you worship will determine how you serve).

"How long are you going to sit on the fence? If God is the real God, follow him; if it's Baal [the world's system], follow him. Make up your minds" (1 Kgs. 18:21, The Message)!"

November 20
HOW MUCH ARE YOU WILLING TO PAY?
Read: Prov. 23:23

There are many people today who are always in search of something rare, precious, or unique; something no one else has, or if more than one of these items exists then there is a very limited quantity.

These individuals search high and low, and go to great lengths to obtain these items—going

Thoughts

_____
_____
_____
_____
_____
_____
_____

from city to city, state to state, and even from country to country to find that rare precious stone, sculpture, painting, or other artifact to add to their collection. In these instances money is often not an object or concern, in other words no price is too high.

This can be seen at auctions, through online trading sites, and when individuals come into large sums of money where they are willing to pay exorbitant prices for seemingly insignificant things. For an example, the following items have been available for purchase and/or sold through a very popular online trading site: a Hot Wheels toy car collection being sold for $1,000,000; a grilled cheese sandwich that appeared to have the face of the Virgin Mary on it sold for $28,000; a Doritos chip shaped in the form of the hat worn by the Pope sold for $1209; and someone even attempted to sell the meaning of life; can you imagine that, for a set price the purchaser could receive answers to every question imaginable; NOT!!!

The above just goes to show people are willing to any amount for things that are either insignificant, and/or things that definitely will not last.

Well, King Solomon in the book of Proverbs has given us "insider tips" as to what we should really be purchasing and that which has real value; TRUTH (Prov. 23:23). This truth gives access to wisdom which allows us to make the right decisions in life. We obtain this truth through an intimate and personal relationship with Jesus Christ who is "the way, THE TRUTH, and the life" (Jn. 14:6); He is also the Living Word (Jn. 1:14).

Not only is wisdom obtained through our personal relationship with Christ, but also attainable through prayer, and not just reading, but through study and meditating in God's Word. However, this often requires sacrifice on our part, a sacrifice that may require us to relinquish things we believe are precious; it may also require a sacrifice of our resources, talents and also a sacrifice of our time.

Yet when we choose to sacrifice the things we deem important, there are a number of benefits that focusing on truth and wisdom bring (Prov. 13:13-18).

When we truly have the type of wisdom that comes only from God through the Word and the person of the Holy Spirit, we are less likely to be influenced by negative thoughts or evil forces that attempt to control our minds, and subsequently our mouths and bodies to do and say things that do not reflect the Glory of the One who abides within us (1 Jn. 4:4; Col. 1:27).

Thoughts

_____

_____

_____

_____

_____

_____

Therefore, the value of truth and wisdom far surpasses anything we can seek after or ever bargain for; but again, it will require us to give up certain things to obtain them (giving up our way of thinking, our way of doing things, and putting aside inappropriate feelings and emotions). How much are you willing to pay or sacrifice to lay hold to that which leads to real life?

A one-way ticket to heaven through Jesus Christ: GUARANTEED; walking in the authority of the Word: GOD'S WILL; obtaining wisdom and truth, and living out the blessing through faithfulness, obedience, sacrifice, and love: PRICELESS!

November 21

EXTRA! EXTRA! READ ALL ABOUT
Read: Prov. 25:25

All over the world each day, billions of newspapers, magazines, and periodicals are distributed with headlines and front page cover stories designed to attract and entice us to dig a little deeper to see what the real context is. But sadly and many times these headlines are usually connected to stories about the death of another serviceman on the frontlines of some foreign overseas battle, a missing person being searched for by federal agencies, the devastation and aftermath of the powerful forces of nature, or the ongoing saga of the break-up and divorce of a well-known Hollywood couple; yet there is rarely, if ever, any good news.

As a result, we as a society are now programmed to expect, see, hear, and receive bad news; because it is what many look forward to and in a morbid way have even grown accustomed to enjoy based on many reality television shows now airing. And even though good happens all around us in unsuspecting places like war zones and in the aftermath of deadly storms, this news hardly ever reaches the pages of printed periodicals or is rarely shown as a breaking story on any news telecast.

Many times the information presented and received is not even accurate; but out of habit and because we think we're getting the "inside scoop", we continue to read or listen as the "not so great news" being presented continues to unfold.

Well, there is actually good news out there; unfortunately it is often being cleverly hid (2 Cor. 4:3-5).

The good news referred to above is the Good News of the Gospel message of Jesus Christ, the one who came to deliver and set us free in the midst of bondage, sickness, chaos, and storm. In the greatest act of love, He freely gave Himself so that we could come out from under the authority of sin, sickness, and disease to live the abundant life that He promised (Jn. 10:10).

Thoughts

The message is simple: salvation (being saved from destruction) is only achieved for those who truly believe Christ died for our sins and rose again on the third day; and those who will call out to Him and acknowledge Him both as Savior and LORD.

415

So, don't allow the little "g" god of this world blind you with all of the negative reports; there is Good News available to all who will hear, believe, and receive it—-news of love, hope, peace, and prosperity (3 Jn. 1:2).

Once we have received this message, as believers in Christ, it is now our responsibility to present this Good News, the Truth of the Gospel to others (Matt. 28:19-20).

Though truth may not always come in pretty, nicely wrapped packages; it is still our responsibility to deliver it. Years ago, when newspapers were the primary source of information, whenever there was breaking news or something of significance to report, not only was the regular edition of the newspaper published, but an edition called an "Extra" would also be generated. "When an Extra came out, they would chant "Extra! Extra! read all about it" to call attention to the fact that something big has happened, and an Extra paper has been published."

Well, something big happened over two-thousand years ago with effects still ongoing today. There is enough devastation, gloom, doom, and despair in the world; therefore, we should never just keep this Good News to ourselves, but begin to declare: "Extra! Extra! Read All About It" with confidence and joy (Prov. 25:25).

November 22
IT REQUIRES MORE THAN GOOD INTENTIONS
Read: 2 Sam. 6:1-11; James 2:17-18

In 1 Sam. 4:10 the defeat of the Israelites resulted in the Ark of the Covenant ending up in the camp and hands of their conquerors, the Philistine army. But the next chapter of 1 Samuel went on to describe the heartache and anguish the Philistines experiences because they had wrongfully appropriated a power that was unfamiliar to them and one they had not submitted to, a power that rightfully belonged to and was only designated for the Israelites at the time—that power being God's presence as represented by the Ark.

After a string of bizarre encounters and a small taste of the power of God, the Philistines made a wise decision to have the Ark removed from their camp hoping things would go back to normal and business as usual. So, they built a cart for the Ark of the Covenant to have it removed; and not only did the Philistines make provision for returning the Ark, but they also provided a trespass-offering for having wrongfully taken it in the first place. Although the Ark was back in the hands of the Israelites, it was still not in its proper place (the City of David or Jerusalem).

Thoughts

_____
_____
_____
_____
_____
_____
_____

During the time of the Arks movement, David had been anointed as king of Israel and at the age of thirty-two he began to reign. As the new king, David was concerned about the Ark and wanted it moved to its proper place. So the king assigned men to the task of moving the Ark to where it needed to go; therefore, the men built a new cart in similar fashion to the one made by the Philistines; this was the first mistake. The Ark was then set upon the cart and pulled by a couple of oxen, when all of a sudden the cart became lodged in some rocks with the Ark about to fall to the ground.

One of the men in the group (Uzzah) decided to reach up to grab the Ark with his hand to keep it from falling; this was the second mistake. And as he touched it, he immediately fell to the ground dead. The first time I read this story I thought I had missed something. Here was someone trying to ensure the Ark of the Covenant (which represented God's presence) did not fall to the ground, yet he was punished for this act. His actions were supposed to be a good thing right? In this scenario everyone's intentions were good; however, what I learned after careful study of this story was that each approached the situation the wrong way.

First, based upon God's law there was a specific method for transporting the Ark, and it was to be transported only by designated individuals. Only Levitical priests (those who had been sanctified and set apart for the task) were authorized to carry the Ark, and when they carried it there was also specific guidance on how it was to be carried by placing poles through the loops on either side of the Ark, as the poles were then placed upon the shoulders of the priests and then carried (1 Chron. 15:2, King James Version).

Secondly, according to the law of the time no one was authorized to touch the Ark (Num. 4:15, King James Version), which is why Uzzah fell dead even though he attempted to do something good. Uzzah represents man attempting to handle God's presence through human effort, but Jn. 4:23-24 outlines true worship. In other words, we can't touch or feel God by any human effort or manmade ways; we enter His presence and begin to connect with Him through the spirit and the spirit alone.

When it comes to God's presence and drawing nearer to Him, we can't use worldly ways and expect to receive positive, godly results. We honor God not just by attempting to do the right thing, but by putting our faith into action through acts of obedience (James 2:17-18).

November 23

IS THERE ANYONE LEFT?
Read: 1 Kgs. 18:20-40

Prior to this point in history, many in the nation of Israel sat by in idle mode while year after year pagan worship practices began to prevail and threaten the very worship of the One and

Thoughts

_____
_____
_____
_____
_____
_____
_____

only True & Living God Jehovah. But on this particular day one prophet decided to take a stand, to not only challenge the Israelite nation to a higher standard, but to also overturn the pagan worship of Baal.

This is when the prophet Elijah posed the following question, "How much longer will you try to have things both ways? If the LORD is God, worship him! But if Baal is God, worship him!" The people did not say a word" (1 Kgs. 18:21, Contemporary English Version).

The prophet was encouraging the Israelites to make a choice, to either continue serving Baal with a little sprinkle of God on the side or to serve Jehovah completely. The prophet then commented, "I, I only, remain a prophet of the LORD, but Baal's prophets are 450 men" (1 Kgs. 18:22, King James Version).

Believing he was the only prophet left on the face of the earth (which was actually not the case), he took a stand and challenged the many prophets of Baal that stood against him and his God through a demonstration of power as consuming fire fell down from above enveloping the prepared sacrifice.

The prophets of Baal then prepared a sacrifice and began to call on their god expecting fire to fall down; however, after hours of crying out to Baal nothing happened and the sacrifice remained. Elijah then began to taunt the prophets of Baal (1 Kgs. 18:27). In all of this, nothing changed for the evil prophets.

It was now time to demonstrate to all the origin and source of true power, power that only comes from above. Elijah then repaired one of the altars of God that had been previously torn down using twelve stones and wood, and also dug a trench around the altar. He then placed the sacrifice on the altar, poured water on top of the sacrifice completely saturating it and also filled the trench that surrounded the altar with water.

Then at the appointed time for offering the sacrifice, Elijah called on the God of Abraham, Isaac, and Jacob; and immediately the fire of GOD fell and burned up everything on and around the altar (1 Kgs. 18:38-39)! Elijah then killed all 450 prophets of Baal.

Many times we may feel as if we are the only ones left; on our jobs, in school, and other places that we might frequent; but we are never alone. We may be the only Christian in our office, on the job, in our class, or in a particular setting at any given moment, and it is up to us, like Elijah, to begin to demonstrate not only the power, but the love of God doing our part to further and help build His kingdom. The question for the Church is simply this: Is there anyone left?

Thoughts

_____
_____
_____
_____
_____
_____

November 24

GO AHEAD, TELL HIM

Read: Lk. 17:11-19

In the day and time we live in, demonstrating gratitude and appreciation just seems to be a thing of the past. Many times it appears to be a task just for individuals passing by to even acknowledge one another and/or speak. Sadly, the focus is more on self with the prevailing attitude of "get what you can and can (or keep to yourself) what you can get."

Imagine it is a Saturday morning, a day normally set aside for family togetherness. You hear about a friend who is preparing to move into a new home and he's been soliciting help, with not too many takers. Being the person you are, you put aside your plans for the day, jump in the car and then drive nearly an hour out of your way to assist this individual move into a new home.

Upon arrival, you enter the home to discover room upon room filled with boxes that have yet to be packed and extremely heavy furniture located both upstairs and downstairs. So, for hours you all diligently labor packing, carrying, and then even assist with unpacking at the distant end until the job is done. Though intense heat prevailed and a few unforeseen obstacles surfaced during the process, everyone pulled together to make the move a success in almost record time. Your friend begins to feel a sigh of relief as he and his family are completely moved and beginning to settle into their new home.

But after all is said and done, you have given up an entire day to include a two-hour round trip commute to receive not so much as much as a pat on the back, a handshake, an offer of food and drink, some type of compensation or even words like "I really appreciate everyone's time", "I know you all had other things to do, but I'm glad everyone was here to assist", or simply those two famous words of gratitude "THANK YOU!"

For the average person there is nothing more demeaning than to be undervalued and unappreciated for hard work and effort that goes above and beyond the norm; because people, in general, love to feel appreciated and know that what they do truly matters.

Jesus faced a similar scenario when he encountered ten lepers on His way to Jerusalem in the New Testament Book of Luke. Here was the Messiah on His way, more than likely, with plans already formulated for what He was to accomplish once in the city, yet He chose to stop and render assistance to the ten outcasts without thinking of Himself or His scheduled plans for that particular day (Lk. 17:11-19); but out of the ten only one showed gratitude (Lk. 17:15-16).

Thoughts

_____

_____

_____

_____

Though it may not be widely advertised on television, radio, or through print-media, our Heavenly Father is still performing miracles,

_____

_____

_____

_____

419

dispensing blessings and continuing to work in each of our lives in unique ways today (Lk. 12:32; Rom. 14:17).

So, no matter what our current circumstances or situations may be in life, whether we are in the valley of despair or standing on the mountain top with joy, we must always remember to pause and seize the opportunity to show our gratitude. Whether times are good or bad, God is still worthy of our praise and we should always have a reason to demonstrate sincere gratitude. Our attitude determines our gratitude, have you told the Father "THANK YOU" lately (1 Thess. 5:18)?

November 25
IT JUST MAY BE A HEART ATTACK
Read: Prov. 4:23

There are many "natural killers" that threaten the lives of people all over the world (high blood pressure, diabetes, high cholesterol, etc.). But among these, heart attacks are considered to be a leading killer among both men and women in the United States. It is recorded that approximately 1.1 million people in the United States have heart attacks each year, with death being the end result for over half of these occurrences. Many of these attacks could have been prevented or immediately treated if the symptoms were recognized earlier.

The heart is a muscular organ that is responsible for pumping blood throughout the blood vessels in the body by "repeated, rhythmic contractions." The heart is not only responsible for supplying blood to the various parts of the body but it also supplies much needed oxygen to the brain. The heart is considered to be the single most important organ within the body; this is why any attack upon it can be detrimental and has the potential to lead to dead.

Heart attacks happen when any blood flow to the heart becomes blocked. However, prior to a heart attack there are a few common symptoms like shortness of breath and pain in the chest. So, the best way to counter these effects of a heart attack is simply to recognize the symptoms early and then seek immediate medical treatment and assistance. Statistics show that "treatment is most effective when started within 1 hour of the beginning of symptoms;" the individual or someone close by must call for help as soon as symptoms are noted.

Thoughts

_____
_____
_____
_____
_____
_____
_____

Just as the heart in the natural is the center of our physical life and existence, as believers in Christ the heart in a spiritual sense is also the center of our spiritual life. This is why you must guard it because life flows from here (Prov. 4:23). Since our spiritual life itself flows out from the heart, it is vital that we closely guard it and protect it by not allowing the wrong things to seep in.

As the natural heart is responsible for pumping blood to the entire body; our spiritual hearts are responsible for pumping the life-changing blood of Jesus Christ to every area of our body and life. The life of the body is in the blood.

And although the brain is also important and plays a major part in controlling bodily functions; our bodies can survive without any signs of brain activity for years. But when the heart no longer beats blood circulation is halted, its flow to the body is cut off and life as we know it ceases to exist.

We must learn to recognize the symptoms of the attack and begin to seek immediate help. If many of us would admit it, the same symptoms that one experiences during a natural heart attack are very similar to what we often experience when our hearts are attacked in a spiritual sense.

Although the enemy comes to take life, Jesus came to bring us life through His blood (Jn. 10:10).

Remember, the heart is always the heart of the matter, because whatever is in it is bound to come out. Therefore, when the spiritual attacks come we must learn to recognize the symptoms and seek immediate help, because time is of the essence.

Therefore, when the spiritual attacks come, instead of dialing 9-1-1 we are to call J-E-S-U-S the One who is always standing by ready, willing and more than able to respond when we call (Heb. 13:5).

"Take heed to yourselves, lest your [minds and] hearts be deceived and you turn aside and serve other gods and worship them" (Deu. 11:16, Amplified Bible).

November 26
SHOW ME YOUR SCARS
Read: Matt. 25:21

Over that years there have been a number of wars and battles fought for various causes and reasons. With each of these struggles, unfortunately, there have been casualties of war with those who were willing to sacrifice their lives for the sake of others and the greater good. Individuals who were rewarded for their strength, valor, and bravery resulting in them receiving the highest military decoration of

Thoughts

_____
_____
_____
_____
_____
_____
_____
_____

them all, the Medal of Honor. This particular award is not just given to those who show up, but rather to those who have been on the frontlines of battle in direct contact with the enemy.

Even though the majority of those assigned in any armed force generally show up and are actively engaged in battle. There are still those who are missing in action for the wrong reasons; those who choose not to engage or those who switch to the enemy's camp. As believers in Christ once we accept Jesus as our Savior, we are then enlisted or commissioned into the LORD's army. As such, we are to obey the commands of the General or Officer in Charge; we do this when we choose to make Him both Savior and Lord (Jn. 14:15, 21, 31)!

And though it cost Him His life, Jesus was obedient and actively engaged in the battle for our souls resulting in Him receiving the highest honor (Phil. 2:8-11).

We are to follow the example of Jesus as we remain in the battle willing to sacrifice and lay down our lives for others and for the sake of the Gospel (1 Tim. 6:12).

When the Lord returns, will you be considered missing in action or receive the highest honor? Though the battle is not ours, we are still required to show up and report for duty; then allow God to do the rest. According to Elbert Hubbard, "God will not look you over for medals, degrees, or diplomas, but for scars." Have you been actively engaged in the battle? Will you hear: "Depart from me" or "Well done."

"His master said to him, Well done, you upright (honorable, admirable) and faithful servant! You have been faithful and trustworthy over a little; I will put you in charge of much. Enter into and share the joy (the delight, the blessedness) which your master enjoys" (Matt. 25:21, Amplified Bible).

November 27
WHO ARE YOU CONNECTED TO?
Read: Jn. 15:4-5

A while ago we were given a very nice computer printer that came neatly packaged in the manufacturer's box complete with new unopened ink cartridges, software, USB cables, operator's manuals, etc; however, there was one very important thing missing, the power supply and power cable. As a result, I set out on a journey to find a compatible power supply that would bring this printer to life starting with a bag of old connectors and power cords I had accumulated over the years.

Thoughts

_____

_____

_____

_____

_____

_____

_____

I was eventually able to locate cords that appeared to be a perfect fit; however, upon closer investigation I noticed the voltage was incorrect and therefore could not be safely used.

I then went to electronics specialty stores in search of the correct power supply, but with no success. After a few trips to various stores eventually spoke with a sales representative in the computer section of one store explaining my current dilemma and how I had been unsuccessful in attempting to find a suitable power supply for the printer model in question.

Almost instantly the sales representative knew the answer and solution, and simply replied, "Printer power supplies are normally designed to be unique for a specific printer; the power cord would have to be ordered from the manufacturer." Even if I had located a power supply that would connect and appear to work, it still could have created an improper connection with the potential to cause even greater harm and/or damage to the printer.

In life it is also easy for us as individuals to make the wrong connections. Too often we tend to connect ourselves with people and things of the world that were never designed for us to attach with; things that do not bring us power, and things that do not lead to life.

On a routine basis, many believers often enter bad relationships marrying the wrong man or woman just because it feels right and the external, or enter business partnerships that are not based in honesty and integrity while only focusing on the potential of financial gain. These connections can have long lasting repercussions and cause a lot of unnecessary pain.

Scripture reminds us to not love the world or worldly things (1 Jn. 2:15). In other words we must disconnect ourselves from the wrong source and then make every effort to consistently connect ourselves to the right people (or right source) to receive the correct input; and when the input is correct, this allows us to produce the proper output (2 Cor. 6:14-17).

Connecting ourselves to what may appear to be good may very well be detrimental to the right spiritual link that we should endeavor to maintain with our Heavenly Father, the One who manufactured and created us. It is our connection with Him that brings us to real life itself (Jn. 15:5).

Whenever we can't seem to find the right connection for the power we really need, we can't accept any substitutes but instead we must go directly to the Manufacturer—the one who "fearfully and wonderfully" made us (Ps. 139:14), and He will give us power from on high (Acts 1:8). When we connect to the right

Thoughts

_____
_____
_____
_____
_____
_____
_____

source He gives us power to not only be effective witnesses, but also gives us power to live.

Who or what are you connected to? The wrong connections have the potential to cause great harm and damage. Right connections produce the right results!

November 28
DON'T GIVE UP
Read: Matt. 14:28

Throughout Old Testament Scripture there are many stories that demonstrate how failure is not always the end, and that good things often come out of seemingly bad situations. Our job is to look for the good in every circumstance. In the Bible there are stories of conflict and war; love won and love lost; victory and defeat. However, in each instance and no matter the end result, there was always meaning and a purpose behind it all.

I can personally look back over my military career, marriage, and just life in general at the times I completely blew it, didn't pass the shipboard evaluation/assessment, marriage was on the rocks, or when bad financial decisions were made. But in each instance I learned what not to do to prevent future failure so that success would be the outcome. And if I had not tried, I may not have ever failed and if I had not failed I might have missed a very important and valuable lesson designed to move me forward and elevate me to a different level.

A good example of what many see as failure can be found in the New Testament book of Matthew Chapter Fourteen when Peter attempted to walk on stormy water towards Jesus as the Master came towards the boat filled with His disciples. As Peter stepped out of the boat he actually began to walk on water, that is until He took His eyes off Jesus and started looking at the roaring wind and waves that surrounded them, which was a costly mistake causing him to begin sinking.

Seeing Peter beginning to doubt his ability to continue walking towards Him, Jesus then said, "O you of little faith, why did you doubt" (Matt. 14:31, New King James Version)?

Thoughts

_____

_____

_____

_____

_____

_____

_____

When this Bible account is read, many often view and associate this as a failure on Peter's part; however, even though Peter had a momentary lapse of faith, in actuality this was somewhat of a small victory. Just in case you didn't notice, there were eleven disciples who chose to remain in the boat; only Peter had enough courage and faith to move. And though he lost sight of what should have been his focus, at least he stepped out and tried.

It is often said that "He who fails to plan, plans to fail." However, many times even when we make preparation for the things we know are coming while developing the most elaborate plan, failure may still be the by-product.

But even when this occurs, this is not the time to fret or give up; instead we must do exactly like many of our predecessors have done over the years—learn from our mistakes and keep moving forward. Many of the problems we bring upon ourselves could be avoided, if we would simply take heed of the examples of those who have come before us (Rom. 15:4).

Everything in the Bible, whether success or seeming failure, is all there for a reason; it is there for us to learn something so that we don't have to endure many of the struggles our forefathers, parents or relatives went through. This is not to say we will never have struggle or go through hard times (Jn. 16:33); it just means that when we do experience struggle, we have examples to cling to that give us hope for a brighter tomorrow. Everything happens for a reason (Rom. 8:28), because it is during these times that God is working out His plan for our lives (Phil. 2:13). So, don't be afraid to fail, because the only true failure is the one not try willing to tryl (Prov. 16:3, Amplified Bible).

November 29
DON'T JUST TAKE MY WORD, SEE FOR YOURSELF
Read: Jn. 4:13-14

In chapter four of the Book of John, Jesus encounters a Samaritan woman at a well preparing to draw water; a conversation then develops with Jesus comparing the water He had to offer to that of the water in the well (Jn. 4:13-14).

Upon hearing this, the Samaritan woman became excited about the prospect of receiving the water Jesus had to offer; however, she made the mistake of thinking she would no longer have to come to the physical well again and her life would be that much easier. This is where many of us as Christians often get off-track thinking that when we come to Jesus that our lives will just become a flowery bed of roses, when this is clearly not the case.

Thoughts

This is why many individuals today often associate their salvation to the Christian experiences of other relatives and people; and since they are connected to these relatives and/ or individuals, in their mind, this means they too must be in right-standing as well when this

_____

_____

_____

_____

_____

_____

is far from the truth. And rather than allowing the challenges of the Christian walk to mature and develop them, they prefer to live vicariously through another.

What great grandmother, grandfather, father, mother, auntie, uncle, etc. did may have been good for them and kept them in the grace of God at that particular time; yet this does not equate to salvation or abundant living for another individual. In other words, an individual can't live the Christian life based solely on someone else's experience; we must each have a personal encounter with the Savior for ourselves.

Therefore, in order to grow and mature, we must individually receive a daily helping of God's spiritual food for ourselves (1 Pet. 2:2). However, we must move from just receiving milk to the meat of the Word as we develop in our faith. Daily spiritual nourishment can be received through the Word (Jesus Christ).

The Samaritan woman had a personal encounter with Jesus Christ that forever changed her; she then had spiritual food and drink that would last an eternity. And once she was changed from the inside out, she encouraged others to not just take her word, but challenged them to come see the Giver of unending spiritual food and water for themselves (Jn. 4:29)!

We each need a personal encounter with Christ; however, don't just take my word, "TASTE AND SEE" FOR YOURSELF!

November 30
PURPOSE OR APPEARANCE
Read: Ps. 139:13-17

New technological advances have caused the cosmetic surgery industry to grow and continue to boom each year. From liposuction, to breast augmentation, laser hair removal, eyelid surgery, chin and cheek implants, facial rejuvenation, and other innovative enhancement procedures; many make attempts to fit into society's picture of how we as individuals are to look in order to achieve success. Therefore, these new technologies have made procedures once only available to the wealthy, famous, and elite open and affordable to the average citizen. Millions of dollars are spent each year altering and changing features that will not last, and are only temporary (James 4:14).

Thoughts

_____
_____
_____
_____
_____
_____
_____

God created man in His own image and likeness (Gen 1:26), and from the very beginning it was His desire that man (mankind) walk in dominion and authority. We were created differently than any other creature, because we had and still have a specific purpose.

While we were yet in our mother's womb, God formed and fashioned us for greatness (Jer. 1:5). Through intricate details and loving care, we were all uniquely created for a specific purpose, and individual assignment; this purpose and assignment has nothing to do with the outward appearance.

Yes we should watch what we eat, yes we should maintain a certain level of fitness, and yes we should have a desire to take care of our body in general as a whole; however, we should not focus on our physical appearance to the point that it detracts from us fulfilling our purpose; that purpose is restoring God's blessing in the earth; restoring the Garden experience of true fellowship between God and man.

No matter what your skin pigmentation may be, your eye color, the length of your hair, or the physical dimensions of your body; know today that you were "fearfully and wonderfully made" (Ps. 139:14). And though your outward appearance may please or displease man; God looks at your heart. "GOD judges persons differently than humans do. Men and women look at the face; GOD looks into the heart" (1 Sam. 16:7, The Message).

Your appearance has nothing to do with true success, and even less to do with fulfilling your purpose and assignment. Learn to be content with who you are in Christ.

December 1
DISCOVERING THE KING IN YOU
Read: 1 Pet. 2:9

One of my all-time favorite Walt Disney feature animation movies is "The Lion King." The story focuses on a young lion cub (Simba) in Africa who loses his father and leader of the pride (King Mufasa). Throughout the movie the young cub struggles with trying to identify what and who he is.

Mufasa's death was a scheme conjured up and orchestrated by his evil and power-hungry brother (Scar) who had personal desires to become king, this was the impetus of Simba's journey. However, young Simba was tricked into believing he was the cause of his father's untimely death. So, he was later convinced to live in exile and encouraged to run away from the safety and protection of the "Pride Land" in an attempt to hide from the potential repercussions of his alleged act leading to the death of his father.

Thoughts

_____

_____

_____

_____

_____

_____

The young lion cub ran off into the African desert with no direction. And without water and nourishment to sustain him, he began to succumb to scorching desert heat that brought about in both hunger and dehydration. But, just as the vultures and birds of prey began to circle, he was rescued by a meerkat (Timon) and a wharthog (Pumbaa). And because Simba did not know who he really was, he began to live like, behave like and even ate the same way that Timon and Pumbaa were accustomed to.

Here was a lion known to be the "King of the Jungle" eating worms, grubs and other insects when he could have eaten real food like the other lions. Simba was now a king in the making living extremely below his privileges and rights.

As the movie went on, one day while out looking for food Simba who is now an adult encountered a childhood friend and female lion (Nala), who just happened to be doing the same thing, realized who he was and reminded him of his responsibility to return home to assume his role as the new king since the conditions of the Pride Land had only worsened under the tyrannical leadership of Scar. But being comfortable where he was, Simba chose to remain in the jungle with no worries or responsibility saying and singing "hakuna mata" which is Swahili phrase literally meaning "There are no worries."

During this time, the mandrill monkey (Rafiki) who presented Simba in dedication at birth also discovered Simba was still alive and went to encourage the young lion to remember who he was. Rafiki brought Simba to a body of water and told him to look down, and as Simba looked into the water he saw the reflection of his father. Then suddenly out of the clear sky, the voice of his father King Mufasa spoke to remind Simba of who he was and that he was to take his rightful place as king. And as Mufasa's presence departed and voice faded, Simba repeatedly heard the echo of the words "Remember who you are!"

Simba eventually realized who he was and the responsibility he now had, went back to the Pride Land, defeated Scar and took his rightful place as king. With the Pride Land back in the hands of the righteous leadership, the land once again flourished and prospered. Change happened when a doubting king discovered who he really was.

Many of us as believers in Christ suffer from the Simba-syndrome. Therefore, as kings in the earth (1 Pet. 2:9), we each must take our rightful place of authority in our homes, at work, in our finances, in our lives in general and in society. The world is waiting for all the kings to arise, because once true kings are in place, things are bound to change for the better. So, discover the king in you today!

Thoughts

_____
_____
_____
_____
_____
_____
_____

December 2

CHANGE IS INEVITABLE
Read: Ecc. 3:1

Living in a location that allows me to observe changing seasons has always been an interesting time, especially seeing the transition from summer to fall. Although I enjoy the flowers blooming, cool rain showers and the fresh breeze of spring, and the warmer weather of summer with the picnics and cookouts this season brings; there is just something about seeing the many changes and transitions that occur from summer to winter and then vice versa.

What really amazes me the most is to see how the color of leaves change between green, red, red-orange, yellow, and then ultimately brown before falling off the tree. So, it is generally a beautiful thing to drive down the interstate seeing trees on either side of the road in transition with the wide variety and array of colors, and in this instance one cannot stop thinking about God's creation and say THE HEAVENS declare the glory of God (Ps. 19:1).

This also signifies and highlights that within God's creation, things are bound to change. Although it is God who causes the seasons to change and other things in life to change around us, He Himself does not change (Heb. 13:8). The bottom-line here is that change is natural and is a normal part of life (Ecc. 3:1).

Just as there are natural seasons that bring about noticeable change, likewise the seasons of our lives often bring about change to us and within us. Though leaves begin to change color or may even fall from the tree, this is a natural process. It would be senseless for a tree in transition to retain dead leaves, because this would hinder the new growth waiting to spring forth.

Many times we reject what is new or unfamiliar to us because the old and recognizable is more comfortable when God is trying to do something new (Is. 48:6).

Even though the leaves may change color, wither, and even die; this does not affect the state of the tree that is planted, rooted, and grounded in the right place. We are to be trees planted by the rivers of living water, this living water being the Word of God as revealed to us through the Holy Spirit. When we are planted in the right place, even when the seasons change we continue to thrive and receive new life (Ps. 1:3).

Change is often brought about by God to get us to a new level of growth in Him (Dan. 2:20-22)! A quote by American writer Richard Bach can shed a little more light on this notion of change: "What the caterpillar calls the end of the world, the Master calls a butterfly." This simply means that we are not to fight or be afraid of transformation or change, because with change also comes a new beginning.

As our individual seasons in life change, we must allow God to begin a new work within us as we remain planted by His waters to ensure we continue to grow and flourish. "Change is inevitable. Growth is optional."

Thoughts

"Forget about what's happened; don't keep going over old history. Be alert, be present. I'm about to do something brand-new. It's bursting out! Don't you see it? There it is! I'm making a road through the desert, rivers in the badlands. Wild animals will say 'Thank you!' —the coyotes and the buzzards— Because I provided water in the desert, rivers through the sun-baked earth, Drinking water for the people I chose, the people I made especially for myself, a people custom-made to praise me" (Is. 43:16-21, The Message).

December 3
NO BLOOD, NO GLORY
Read: Heb. 9:22

There is a familiar phrase or expression frequently used to prompt or encourage individuals to succeed and press on no matter what, "No guts, no glory." In essence this means that "without taking risks one will never achieve great success; in order to be extremely successful one must be willing to fail; if one is not willing to take a chance [he or she] will never become extraordinarily successful." No matter what the situation or circumstance, when we keep proper focus, have the right mindset, and confess or say the right things; we can and will succeed even if it appears in the natural we have failed—this requires the courage to persevere.

The phrase "No guts, no glory" may be used to encourage a football team down by six points with one minute remaining in the game coming out of a huddle lining up on their own 2-yard line, with 98 yards before them. In the natural and to the average person, the opposing team would undoubtedly be the victor thus winning the game; but as the underdog team gets into position the team captain reminds the group "It's not over until it's over." With blood, sweat, determination, and an expected end in sight the team musters up the strength, courage, and fortitude to press their way down the field scoring the touchdown and field goal, winning the game by one point.

As believers in Christ, I would submit that we have an even better phrase to provide us strength, hope, and encouragement to press on in the face of apparent adversity, defeat, and failure, "No blood, no glory." Just as the above football team won the game by one, our victory for living and eternal life was achieved by one, that One was no other than Jesus Christ. Despite what He saw in the natural, He did not let the facts discourage Him from completing His mission and assignment; we are to do the same (Heb. 12:1-2).

Thoughts

_____
_____
_____
_____
_____
_____
_____

Jesus risked all while enduring ridicule, intense and horrible beating, and the pain of the cross which included shedding His very own blood. It was because He had an expected end in sight; this expected end not only brought us the promise of salvation, but the guarantee of an abundant life as well (Jn. 10:10). When Christ died, what the enemy saw as sure failure and defeat was actually the greatest victory ever won and known to man—by One we have all won.

We achieve the same victory and can overcome whatever the enemy presents to us as apparent failure or defeat when we lay aside sin, and die to our own plans and agendas to fulfill the will of the Father; His goal is that we succeed (Rom. 6:7-11, 14).

Through Christ's **propitiation** (offering of Himself to remove God's wrath) we receive **justification** (right standing) and **sanctification** (set apart to holy and righteous living); we thereby succeed because "there is no failure in God." It would be safe to say then, unless we apply the blood and die to sin we will not succeed in this life—in other words, "No blood, no glory" (Heb. 9:22)!.

December 4
IT'S MORE THAN JUST A FOUR-LETTER WORD
Read: 1 Jn. 4:8

Words are often spoken with no thought as to the power or potential they have. When words are spoken they are like seeds sown by a farmer; and when a farmer sows a seed he expects to receive a harvest. Nowadays as one flips between channels on television, just about every word imaginable can be heard. There used to be a time when certain words were not allowed on standard television channels; however, today pretty much everything goes no matter the time of day or night.

Some time ago remember sitting in the waiting room of a car dealership while having some routine maintenance performed on one of our vehicles. And as I sat there attempting to read the book I brought along, I could not believe the words on the talk show being aired at the time. At one point there were so many blank outs and bleeps to cover profane words that viewers could hardly understand what was being said or hear a complete sentence with every four-letter expletive or curse word one could think of being used. Talk about a lack of vocabulary.

It has been my experience through years of observation that when derogatory and other four-letter swearwords are used, they are generally not employed to build someone up but rather to tear them down, inflict pain, toy with emotions, or introduce some other level of discomfort.

Thoughts

With over 6800 languages in the countries of the world and billions of words being used between them all; I often wonder how many of these words are actually being used in a positive manner. Sadly, as one views a movie, goes to buy groceries, walk the hallways of school, goes to the mall, or even in a leisurely stroll through the park; many four-letter and other negative words often prevail while one important four-letter word is consistently overlooked and rarely used.

Eph. 4:29 instructs us on the type of speech that we are to have. So instead of speaking words that have the potential to bring someone down, we are to speak words that bring life. Jesus said, that His words are spirit and life (Jn. 6:63). If we are in Him and He abides in us, then we too are commissioned to speak life!

As children of the King we are to emulate and follow His example (Eph. 5:1) by speaking words that edify, build up, and bring life as well. Everything Jesus did during His time here on earth was done in, through, and out of L-O-V-E, the most important four-letter word of them all. But love is more than just a four-letter word; it goes beyond intellect, mental assent, and just mere talking or speaking—it is a command to action. Love is demonstrated, not solely by what we do to satisfy ourselves and our desires, but in what we do for others (Rom. 5:8). God did not merely demonstrate the fact that He loved us by just His words, He proved and demonstrated His love for us through action in giving His one and only unique Son for us so that we would live a full life (1 Jn. 4:8).

If we are to follow and imitate God's example as demonstrated through Jesus Christ, the finished work at Calvary, and through the Holy Spirit that now lives and abides within; we too must begin to not only use the right four-letter word, but put this word into action and practice each day. Because when love is not applied our actions are actually useless and our efforts are vain (1 Cor. 13:1-3).

Make it a purpose to sow words of love not only in speech, but also in action today; then sit back and watch God bless the harvest from the seeds that were planted.

December 5
PUT DOWN THE BOTTLE, IT'S TIME TO GROW UP
Read: John 3:16

Something that would probably seem unusual is seeing a 5-year old child sitting in a stroller drinking milk out of a baby bottle. Here is a child old enough to walk, with the ability to use the bathroom on his or her own drinking out of a bottle as if an infant.

Thoughts

_____

_____

_____

_____

_____

_____

_____

This is exactly where many of us as Christians are today; we are drinking milk from the bottle when we should be eating meat. Yes, we are to "desire the sincere milk of the word that we may grow thereby" according to 1 Pet. 2:2; however, at some point we have to put the bottle down and grow up (1 Cor. 3:1-3).

As young believers in Christ, rehearsing and reciting Jn. 3:16 or the 23rd Psalm may have been cute at the time and may have provided a spiritual foundation. But when the attacks of the enemy come, although Jn. 3:16 encourages our salvation, it does little to provide us with the armor needed to protect against devil's onslaught.

When we begin to eat the meat of the Word not only do we grow spiritually, we also begin to discover who we are, understand the promises that are ours by right, and begin to speak accordingly. Our prayers will then be less focused on what can be attained for just me and mine, but now have a more Kingdom-minded focus as we also begin to pray and intercede for the needs of others. When we make it our purpose to wean ourselves away from spiritual milk, it is then that we truly begin to focus on the meatier things (2 Pet. 1:3-8).

It's time to put the bottle down because God wants us to grow up so that we no longer just focus on self, but move to a spiritual mindset that begins to focus on others as we sacrificially give of ourselves!

December 6

WHOSE FOOL ARE YOU?
Read: 1 Cor. 3:18-23

Today, many people are looking for that next word from the LORD; something that is fresh or new. As a result, individuals travel all over the country going from conference to conference, listening to speaker after speaker, reading book after book; yet many times these individuals never receive the revelation they so desperately long for. This was as much an issue during the time of the Apostle Paul in the early church as it is for us today (1 Cor. 1:22).

However, the quest for wisdom in the early church often brought division to the congregation of God's people as individuals sought the knowledge, understanding and leading of man over the awesome wisdom God. Paul had to address this very issue in the Corinthian church where many claimed to be followers of Paul, and others of Cephas or Apollos. Not only had the church at Corinth literally "missed the boat," they had also missed the entire message as it pertained to understanding where true wisdom really came from in their feeble attempts to follow after man (1 Cor. 3:18-23).

It is often the absence of wisdom that brings about many of the problems and negative things we experience in life today. And instead of seeking the Giver of all wisdom, sadly many of us choose to base our lives, our existence and everything we do solely on the wisdom of man who is finite (limited) in both knowledge and understanding.

Thoughts

_____
_____
_____
_____
_____
_____
_____
_____

God reminds us in His Word that we are often destroyed due to a lack of knowledge (Hos. 4:6). When we place our faith and confidence only in the wisdom and knowledge of man, we become a fool of this world and thereby suffer under its influence.

Becoming a fool of this world means we are led by the dictates and the patterns of a corrupt and fallen system. However, true wisdom is bestowed upon us when we choose to be led by God's Spirit. This is when we are no longer classified as "fools," but now as God's own sons and daughters (Rom. 8:14). Man may be able to point us in the right direction in a particular situation; however, it is God who gives us wisdom and revelation through His Word by the Holy Spirit (Prov. 1:7).

Don't get me wrong, there is nothing wrong with attending conferences, reading books, or receiving counsel; however, in the end we should always remember all wisdom comes from God and God alone. True wisdom should point us to Jesus Christ and not solely to man.

So, the question I pose to you today is this: Will you be a fool for God or a fool of this world? Although the word "fool" often has negative connotations, I would much rather be a fool for God than a fool of this world any day of the week; yet this choice is entirely up to you. Whose fool are you?

"For the [LORD] gives skillful and godly Wisdom; from His mouth come knowledge and understanding" (Prov. 2:6, Amplified Bible).

December 7
SINCE YOU ARE IN SCHOOL, YOU MAY AS WELL LEARN THE LESSON
Read: Heb. 5:12

All over the United States and around the world, students sit in classrooms listening to teachers, professors, and instructors for up to seven hours a day, five times a week for the purpose of receiving an education. Many of these students sit listening intently and taking notes for review at a later time, to ensure they comprehend the material being taught. However, others only come because it is a requirement, by law, to attend school until reaching a certain age.

Thoughts

_____
_____
_____
_____
_____
_____
_____

These individuals often show up unprepared with no pencil, pen, paper, textbooks, or any other material that will help them in their learning experience. Therefore, when the time comes to demonstrate they have a grasp of the information previously taught by way of a test, many often fail miserably because they did not study and apply the learning material.

Of course we all know what happens in school when an individual fails a number of tests in a particular subject, they usually must repeat the class and then have to receive the same instruction all over again until it is passed before they are allowed to move on. Unfortunately, this is also where many of us as believers often find ourselves as we navigate through the school and course of life. God has given us instructions in His Word and through the Holy Spirit as our Teacher and Guide (Jn. 16:13).

Sadly, we often fail the tests simply because we do not take time to study or receive God's instructions (2 Tim. 2:15). It is when we make it our purpose to study God's Word on a daily basis, that we then receive the instructions of God that prepare us for the tests of life that come our way. These tests are bound to come, there is no way around it (Jn. 16:33).

Therefore, as believers we must not only hear, read, and study the Word; but put it into action through practical application to ensure that we are prepared for the tests that will come our way.

Many times in school teachers give "pop quizzes" or unannounced tests just to gauge how much instruction students have retained. Similarly, the tests of life often come unannounced and when we least expect them; it is our job to be prepared because it is our preparation that determines if we will pass or fail. In the school of life, the tests and trials we face are designed to see how much we have learned and applied from the information and instruction given; and when we don't pass the test we can rest assured that we will go through the same situation again.

These tests and trials are not designed to harm us or trip us up, but to strengthen us and build our faith (James 1:2-4). So, instead of trying to avoid the test, we should say like the psalmist David, "Teach me, O LORD, the way of Your statutes, and I will keep it to the end [steadfastly]" (Ps. 119:33).

The Holy Spirit is our Instructor who stands ready to teach us what we don't know. But we should not just learn because we have to, but because we want to have lives that are pleasing to our God.

How are you doing in your teaching sessions today? Since you are in the school of life, you may as well learn the lessons so that you can move on to better things to ensure that God gets the glory out of in and through your life.

"I [the LORD] will instruct you and teach you in the way you should go; I will counsel you with My eye upon you" (Ps. 32:8, Amplified Bible).

Thoughts

_____

_____

_____

_____

_____

_____

_____

December 8

EMPTY WORDS
Read: 1 Cor. 4:19-20

I grew up in the 70's and late 80's during a time when rap music was just beginning to develop. And since I did not grow up in a Christian home, I was able to hear many of the rap artists, attend their concerts, and purchase their albums (notice I said album and not CD, how times have changed). One of my favorite rap groups at the time was Run D.M.C. who had many familiar and popular songs, with many of these songs still being sampled or used on tracks by artist today.

Literature with a focus on poetry was one of my favorite subjects, and to me rap music was nothing more that poetry put to music. I still listen to rap music today; however, I now prefer rap/hip hop by Christian artists that proclaim the Word of God and build up others. Anyway, when I'm around certain people one Run-D.M.C. song immediately comes to mind, "You Talk Too Much."

Sound like anyone you know? Today there are many who talk and talk, but really never say anything that is productive or that adds life to a conversation. Conversations are usually self-centered with a focus on education, houses, cars, and possessions; there's nothing wrong with these things when placed in proper perspective; however, there has to be more to life and a conversation than just the accumulation of things.

Then there are others who have the "gift of gab" with eloquence of speech and can strike up a conversation with practically anyone (which is an admirable trait to have), but often never really say anything of substance. Our words will either produce one of two things: life or death" (Prov. 18:21); this is why we are to be mindful of our speech.

The Apostle Paul provided correction and instruction to the church at Corinth to individuals who had succumb to pride because of their speech (1 Cor. 4:19-20). We should all take heed to this admonition as well.

The number of words an individual speaks does not produce any additional power, especially if (he/she) is saying the wrong thing. On the contrary, deliverance can be employed and received with just two words spoken in faith, with power and life. Refuse to use empty, useless, and/or vain words; choose to speak words of life that empower others.

Thoughts

_____

_____

_____

_____

_____

_____

_____

It's not enough to talk the talk; as believers in Christ we are required to live the walk. God's kingdom is not in mere words, but in deed or action demonstrated in and with power (1 Cor. 2:4-5).

December 9
THE KEY TO REMAINING SPIRITUALLY RENEWED
Read: Ps. 16:11

In today's fast-paced society with everyone constantly on the go, rest is often an over-rated experience. Besides, resting may result in losing out on that extra overtime pay, or cause one to not be prepared for the next client even though a major and lucrative deal was just recently completed. At any rate there are not too many of us who truly understand the meaning of the word "rest."

By definition the word "rest" means "a bodily state characterized by minimal functional and metabolic activities, freedom from activity or labor, a state of motionlessness or inactivity, peace of mind or spirit, or free of anxieties." Today, this state is rarely achieved, because even when our body is still our mind is constantly on the go and on the move.

With a need to do more and get ahead in life, rest is almost foreign or an alien term for many in the world today. Besides, who can really remain still or inactive for any length of time anyway, other than those who are physically incapacitated, sleeping, or dead. However, this is precisely why many experience health issues, worry, and anxiety because we do not take the time to slow down and rest.

A lack of rest is not only an issue for those in the world, but also for many in the church as well. This simply suggest that rest and remaining connected with God are essential to any ministry we attempt to allow the LORD do in and through us. Ministry goes beyond the role of a bishop, pastor, apostle, elder, evangelist, or minister standing behind a podium/pulpit proclaiming the Word of God. Real ministry often happens outside of the church walls and in its simplest form is nothing more than meeting needs.

This ministry could be as simple as bringing a thirsty person a glass of water, cutting a neighbors grass, volunteering at a battered women's shelter, or feeding the homeless. However, God's ministry at work through us can sometimes become ineffective when we do not regularly spend time in His presence to have our strength renewed; the end result is usually physical, mental, and spiritual burnout.

One of the Ten Commandments sometimes overlooked is found in Ex. 20:8, "Remember the sabbath day, to keep it holy". "Sabbath" is another word for "rest." Therefore, when we make it a purpose to honor God's Word in this regard, we take the first step to bringing balance to our lives and finding the rest that many of us so desperately need. A sabbath does not necessarily have to be on a Friday, Saturday, Sunday or any other specific day, for that matter; it is just a time that an individual chooses to set aside and dedicate to resting and spending time with the LORD.

Thoughts

_____
_____
_____
_____
_____
_____
_____

Amid the hustle and bustle of life, oftentimes we must force ourselves to rest so we don't faint or lose heart (Gal. 6:9). Therefore, as we remain connected to our Source, God's power is made evident through the Holy Spirit which enables us to stand and not faint spiritually. When we truly learn how to rest, there is less of a chance that we will become tired or desire to merely quit or give-up because God resupplies us with the strength we need to keep pressing forward when we connect with Him in His presence. In God's presence is fullness of joy (Ps. 16:11) because "the joy of the LORD is your strength (Neh. 8:10b).

Don't run or shy away from periods of solitude, quietness, or inactivity. When we rest in God and stay connected to our Source of strength, this is when the gifts He has placed inside of us can truly begin to flow and benefit others.

Quiet time is not wasted time; the key to remaining spiritually renewed is learning how to rest in God's presence (Matt. 11:28).

December 10
GRATITUDE IN ACTION
Read: 2 Sam. 9:1

In 1 Samuel chapter 20, David the future king of Israel made a covenant with his close and very dear friend Jonathan, the son of the soon to be dethroned king Saul. It was through King Saul's disobedience that the kingdom and his reign was being removed and appointed to another, a person who had a heart for God.

The prophet Samuel was sent to deliver judgment against Saul (1 Sam. 13:13-14). David the son of Jesse was the LORD's new choice. From the moment David was not just appointed, but anointed to be king (1 Sam. 16:13), Saul despised him and sought to take his life. And over time, David's popularity eventually grew as he became a mighty warrior leading Israel in many victories, with Saul's jealousy becoming even more evident as he was provoked by what the people would say about David (1 Sam. 21:11).

Although there was friction and tension between David and King Saul; David and Jonathan (Saul's son) shared a rare bond, kindred spirit, and a relationship that would forever knit their hearts together. It was because of this relationship and love for God that David refused to touch Jonathan's father King Saul no matter how many times Saul tried to kill him. David had opportunity after opportunity to take Saul's life; however, he refused to touch God's anointed and appointed king at that particular time (1 Chron. 16:22). It was David and Jonathan's friendship that prompted a covenant between them (1 Sam. 20:13-14).

Thoughts

_____

_____

_____

_____

_____

_____

_____

438

But as David continued to flee the relentless pursuits of Saul, Jonathan was always there to provide shelter, help and protection. But one day during a battle with the Philistines, both Saul and Jonathan lost their lives. This came as terrible news to David who not only mourned the death of his best friend Jonathan, but also lamented the death of Saul, the one who pursued him out of a jealous rage.

Some years had passed after Saul and Jonathan's death, with David now sitting on the throne as king. As David sat in deep thought and pondering one day, he remembered the covenant he made with Jonathan and wanted to show grace to one of their remaining relatives (2 Sam. 9:1). David found one; it was Mephibosheth the son of Jonathan and grandson of King Saul who had been crippled and unable to walk after his nurse dropped him during the escape from the palace after receiving the news of Saul and Jonathan's death fearing an enemy invasion.

Although he was a son of royalty, Mephibosheth lived in a barren place beneath his privileges for many years; however, when he was found and brought before the king, David showed him kindness and favor because of the covenant made between his father Jonathan and David many years prior.

King David went far beyond just telling Mephibosheth 'Thank You' for the kindness that his family had showed him in the past as he demonstrated sincere gratitude (2 Sam. 9:7, 11). The king put both gratitude and love into action as he honored the covenant he previously made.

In society today there is a world filled with ungrateful people who routinely break covenant (or agreement) and fail to demonstrate gratitude or ever show thanks. However, even when we say 'thanks', just saying thank you with our words are not enough; we must go above and beyond the norm to demonstrate our 'Thank You' through our actions just as King David did (1 Thess. 5:18).

December 11
MAYBE WE NEED TO MAKE ROOM
Read: Gen. 6:14

"I' m waiting for my ship to come in, I'm waiting for my knight in shining armor, I'm waiting for the right man/woman to come into my life, I waiting for the right door to open for me". Whatever the phrase of choice maybe, many are in search of that one elusive thing or blessing that could bring the fulfillment and joy they so desperate seek after.

In the Old Testament book Genesis God was displeased with the wickedness of mankind; however, one man found favor in the sight of

Thoughts

_____
_____
_____
_____
_____
_____

the LORD, Noah. Therefore, God announced His plan to destroy man, sparing Noah and his family, to begin with a fresh start (Gen. 6:6-7). God's plan was to flood the earth destroying every living creature, but Noah received instruction to build an ark to house his family and two of every living creature (one male and one female) from the largest animal to the smallest insect that crept upon the earth.

For forty days and forty nights the rains would fall consuming and covering the entire earth with Noah's ark being the vehicle to provide safety, shelter, and the blessing needed to spare Noah, his family, and two of every living creature (Gen. 6:17-19).

However, the prerequisite of Noah's family and every creature receiving continued life and the blessing that would sustain them was that Noah had to make room; without the necessary room or space there would be no vehicle for the blessing to take place. It was Noah's obedience to God's command that ensured the blessing and deliverance would occur (Is. 1:19).

God always hears our petitions or requests, and longs to bless us, but because many of our lives are so cluttered with the things of the world, there is no place or room for the provision He has prepared for us. Therefore, just like Noah, many of us need to make room for God; however, we need to clear out every existing room or space in our life that does not allow Him to fully consume us and have complete control. God's desire is that we make Him first in our lives as we remove the idols that separate us from His favor and blessing (Ex. 20:3-5); it is then that He begins to give us our hearts desire (Ps. 37:4).

In the natural a ship can only pull into a harbor or port that has room to accommodate it; therefore, when there is no room the ship then has to anchor outside of the harbor or port. Have you made room for the LORD in your life today? Remove the clutter that keeps Him on the outside to allow Him to completely come in; with Christ resident on the inside, it is Him that opens every locked door.

"These are the words of the Holy One, the True One, He Who has the key of David, Who opens and no one shall shut, Who shuts and no one shall open" (Rev. 3:7, Amplified Bible).

Thoughts

_____
_____
_____
_____
_____
_____
_____

December 12
SAVE YOUR STRENGTH
Read: Ecc. 10:10

The neighborhood where my family and I once lived when we were last in Virginia had an abundance of trees. Each day I could literally look out any window providing a view from the back of the home and see trees and more trees as far as the eye could see. The number of trees in the community was also made quite evident each year when the season shifted from summer to autumn, with a multitude of leaves covering the lawn in both the front and back yards.

I can remember when we first purchased the home that we lived in at the time with a small unattractive tree planted in the middle of the front lawn that did little for the curb-appeal of the property. It sort of looked homely like the Christmas tree from the Peanuts classic cartoon TV special *A Charlie Brown Christmas*; you know, that scrawny tree that tipped over when only one ornament was placed on it.

So, in my finite wisdom and using the tools I had (which just happened to be the wrong tools), I decided to cut down this eyesore. With a pair of large blade hedge clippers and a hand-held sickle designed to cut grass and weeds, I embarked on a journey to completely annihilate this awkward and what was according to me, out-of-place tree.

Starting with the hedge clippers, one-by-one, I removed the smaller branches until I reached the core or base of the tree, that's when the hard work really began. At this point I began using the sickle chopping, chopping, chopping, and chopping even more with all my might, strength, and ability but making little headway.

What should have been a job that lasted forty-five minutes to an hour at the longest actually turned into a few hours of hard manual labor as I continued to struggle with this stubborn tree. And then there was a glimmer of hope.

God must have been looking down on my struggle and decided to send an angel in disguise. One of my neighbors saw me struggling with the tree as he prepared to depart home and allowed me to use a tool befitting for the task at hand, a simple ax.

With the proper tool in hand, within about thirty minutes the tree was completely cut down to include removal of the roots. All of my physical effort and toil could have been avoided had I employed the right tool from the beginning. Success in this simple task was only one tool away.

As it pertains to rebuilding our temples and the walls that surround them, as Christians we must remember that we cannot do anything in our own strength and/or ability, and sometimes outside assistance may even be required. True success in life does not come as a result of our own merit, ability, and/or strength; real success only comes from God as revealed to us through His Word by the Holy Spirit. This begins when salvation is achieved (Eph. 2:7-10).

Thoughts

With salvation comes the Word, and it is the Word of God we need to aid and assist us as we rebuild and put back together the broken pieces of our lives. When we "rightly divide" or use the Word of God, we have the ability to cut down any giant or obstacle that stands in the way of

_____
_____
_____
_____
_____
_____
_____

our success as we wield the Sword of the Spirit; it also allows us to confront the enemy that is within us (Heb. 4:12).

Human effort alone will never cause us to succeed until we begin to use and employ the right tool starting with God's Word trusting in His strength (Ecc. 10:10; Zech. 4:6)!

December 13
BROKEN BUT STILL USABLE
Read: Ps. 51:17

From the time he was a young man, David had a heart for God; and even as he carefully and lovingly watched over his father's flock of sheep, he could be found singing, worshiping, and ministering to God. This habit and lifestyle invariably carried over into his adult life. And even when he fell short of God's commands and standards, he still resolved to worship God and get it right. It was for this reason he was consistently called "a man after God's own heart."

The most memorable instance of King David giving in to temptation and sin is recorded in the book of 2 Samuel Chapter eleven. During a time when David should have been in the heat of battle leading his men, he was at home with idle time on his hands. One restless evening as David walked along the palace rooftop he saw a beautiful woman bathing; I'm sure that at this moment everything listed in 1 Jn. 2:16 went into action (lust of the flesh, lust of the eyes, and the pride of life).

It was because of his lust that he sent messengers to the woman and had her brought to the palace and I'm sure you are familiar with the rest of the story. He slept with the woman (Bathsheba) who later became pregnant, and to make matters worse she just happened to be married.

Therefore, in order to cover up both of their sin, David devised a plan to bring Bathsheba's husband Uriah home from battle hoping that he would lay with his wife and then later think that the unborn child was his. Uriah was summoned from the battle field and returned home; however, he did not take the bait that we so cleverly planned out by the king, so David had to devise yet another plan this time to completely remove Uriah from the picture.

Thoughts

_____
_____
_____
_____
_____
_____
_____

So David wrote a letter to the commander of his army, which was then hand-carried by Uriah, that provided instructions to place Uriah on the frontline of the deadliest battle, and then pull back the rest of the men leaving Uriah open, exposed, and alone. Not only did David commit adultery, but he had Uriah carry his own death sentence adding murder to his list of sins.

But just when David thought that his sins had been covered, the prophet Nathan came with a rebuke from the LORD to expose what the king had done (2 Sam. 12:1-12). David, realizing his wrong and most importantly acknowledging his sin, did what he knew to do: confess, repent, and worship God. This led to the writing of Psalm 51 (Ps. 51:1-4, 7-11, 17).

The preceding Psalm is a clear example of why David was called "a man after God's own heart." He knew how to return to right-standing with God through repentance and worship of God—David had a heart for the Word and above all else he truly loved God.

Therefore, though David may have been broken by giving in to sin, when he repented, God saw him as still being fit for Kingdom use. Likewise, there are many believers who have yielded to temptation and the power of sin who may feel as though God has written us off; however, we must not allow the enemy to trick us into wallowing and remaining in our sin and self-pity because this prevents us from contributing to the build of God's kingdom. We are simply to confess our sin and move on. Therefore, our sin is by no means ever the end; we must confess it, forsake it, and keep moving forward as we continually rebuild our lives and build God's kingdom. Though we may be broken, we are still usable by God when we have the right motives, truly desire to be transformed by the Word, and have hearts that love and continually seek after God. Your brokenness is certainly not the end of your usefulness.

December 14
PUTTING ON "ROCK"-A-WEAR
Read: Eph. 6:11

Having completed an Individual Augmentee (IA) tour in a combat zone; I know from first-hand experience the devastation and destruction war can bring, with the effects it has on those involved, and the family and friends left behind without their loved one.

Although I was on active duty in the United States Navy at the time and should have been on a ship at sea, I was actually assigned to an Army unit on shore. This experience has also given me a greater appreciation for what the ground forces and troops of each U.S. service component does or brings to the table, and the risks associated with each in combat every single day.

So, since I was and still am a Sailor, there were some things I needed to do in order to prepare me for the assignment at hand. I went through a few weeks of Army familiarization and combat training designed to give me a basic overview regulations and terminology, and also the survival skills that might be needed or employed in a hostile environment. This

Thoughts

_____

_____

_____

_____

_____

_____

_____

443

training included land navigation, how to operate and maintain the weapons assigned to me, learning the enemy's tactics, and the proper wear of my deployment gear.

Therefore, upon completion of the training not only did I have the basic skills needed to survive in a hostile combat environment, I was also given several duffle bags of combat gear and equipment designed to shield and protect me from hurt, harm, and/or danger, if and whenever the time came. But in order for this protective equipment to be effective and provide protection in accordance with the manufacturer's design, the gear and equipment had to be removed from the duffle bags, and properly worn and used.

Whether we realize the fact or not, as believers in Christ we are constantly at war and in combat with our enemy the devil; there are no neutral grounds, safe harbors or combat-free environments, and his attacks can come from any direction at any time. This is why basic training through daily study and mediation in the Word and advance training in spiritual warfare is so important. Because if we don't know what is in our spiritual duffle bag, we are less likely to pull out the right gear and keep it on when the attacks come, leaving ourselves open and vulnerable to every fiery dart that comes our way.

The above discussion has direct correlation to our lives as believers as it applies to warfare of another type; Spiritual Warfare. When we are in combat and in spiritual war with our enemy the devil, this is not a time to look cute or handsome wearing designer clothing like Nike, Adidas, Sean John, Akademiks, Rocawear, American Eagle, Enyce, Aeropostale or even Levi Jeans because these items, in this regard, are of little use or benefit; instead we should strive to put on "Rock"-a-wear to shield us from the attacks and advances of our enemy.

According to Ps. 95:1, Jesus Christ is the "Rock of our salvation" (Ps. 144:1-2). Therefore, when we properly clothe ourselves, not only do we receive protection from without, but we also receive protection from within that keeps us from yielding to sin, and also better positions us to guard our hearts (Prov. 4:23).

In order to truly guard ourselves, especially our hearts, we have to be appropriately clothed and ready for battle (Rom. 13:11-14)!

Are you properly dressed for the occasion? Are you ready for spiritual combat and/or war? Quit going into battle not prepared and improperly dressed. Put on your armor or "Rock"-a-wear, pick a side (the right side I hope), and then stand your ground (Eph. 6:13-18).

Thoughts

_____
_____
_____
_____
_____
_____
_____

December 15

THERE'S NO TIME LIKE THE PRESENT
Read: Jn. 12:1-7

Jesus had just performed one of the greatest miracles ever by raising a man from the dead, a man who had been in a tomb for over three days and had begun the early stages of decomposition. After performing this miracle it was now six days prior to the Passover, so Jesus came to the home of Lazarus who had just been raised from the dead to have dinner accompanied by His disciples.

Lazarus had two sisters, Mary and Martha who took very different approaches to making their guest feel welcomed. As Jesus sat at a table prepared with a huge feast before Him, he conversed with His disciples and Lazarus.

Martha went about serving everyone and ensuring everything was just right; making sure the table settings were in place, there was enough to eat, and that the guest had something to drink as she ran back and forth from the kitchen to the entertaining area. Mary, on the other hand, did nothing of the sort and probably did not even lift one finger to help her sister Martha. Mary instead chose to kneel before Jesus and began to anoint His feet with very expensive and costly oil (oil that was valued and almost equivalent to an entire year's wage during the time). Not only did she pour costly oil on Jesus' feet, but she went even further by wiping His feet with her hair.

Knowing the time of His death and burial was soon to come Jesus replied, "Let her alone. It was [intended] that she should keep it for the time of My preparation for burial. [She has kept it that she might have it for the time of My embalming]" (Jn. 12:7, Amplified Bible). Mary did not wait until Jesus died to anoint Him (according to the custom at the time; she chose to show her gratitude, appreciation, and worship to Him while He was yet alive.

Our work for God is important, but it is our worship that truly makes the difference. There is no time like the present to begin worshiping Him with our whole heart and entire being today!

"Seek God while he's here to be found, pray to him while he's close at hand" (Is. 55:6, The Message).

Thoughts

December 16
DON'T ALLOW YOUR PAST TO CONTROL YOUR FUTURE
Read: Phil. 3:13-14

Some time ago I was blessed to share a devotional entitled *Broken, But Still Usable* with a focus on how God was still able to use King David in His Master plan to establish the New Covenant despite of David's sinful past. Today there are many who fail to progress forward because they've been anchored in their mind with the past. Anchors are nothing more than heavy objects or weights designed to keep a mobile object from moving. And in order for this object to move in any direction, the anchor or weight first has to be lifted and then moved.

For many of us, our past seems to turn into nothing more than an anchor designed to keep us from moving forward to fulfill the plan God has already laid out for us years in advance. But it is up to us to lift the weight, present it to God, and allow Him to carry this heavy load away so that we can walk in purpose and destiny. We must release these weights to Him (1 Pet. 5:7).

We should look to the Bible and to our forefathers (the great men and women of faith) as our examples, and how they did not allow their past to determine future endeavors:

Moses was a murderer running from his past, but he eventually became the deliver sent to lead God's people out of Egyptian bondage.

Jacob was a trickster and deceiver, but when He forgot his past His name was changed to Israel and twelve nations or tribes were birth through him.

Rahab had a very colorful past filled with lust, promiscuity, and adultery; however, God used her to assist in a plan that led to the destruction of Jericho and she was also listed in the very genealogy of Jesus Christ.

Gideon saw himself as insignificant and the least person in his family, but when God reveal to him who he really was, he became a mighty man of valor.

David committed the sins of adultery, lying, and murder, but the bloodline of the Messiah was still established through Him.

Saul was a persecutor of the Church and killed many Christian, but once he had an encounter with Jesus his name was changed to Paul and he then became one of the biggest advocates of the Gospel message being credited with writing the majority of the New Testament.

Thoughts

_____

_____

_____

_____

_____

_____

_____

Though our past is often used to shape us into who God desires us to be, we can't allow the negatives of our past ruin our future. So, instead of reminding God about your past, allow Him to reveal your purpose and speak into the days that are in front of you. Forget your past and start reaching for what is ahead, speaking in faith and seeing yourself the way God sees you, as you SHALL BE. Leave the old things behind, and above all else don't allow your past to control your future and destiny!

"I'm not saying that I have this all together, that I have it made. But I am well on my way, reaching out for Christ, who has so wondrously reached out for me. Friends, don't get me wrong: By no means do I count myself an expert in all of this, but I've got my eye on the goal, where God is beckoning us onward—to Jesus. I'm off and running, and I'm not turning back" (Phil. 3:13-14, The Message).

December 17
MILK REALLY DOES THE BODY GOOD
Read: 1 Pet. 2:2

During the early 90's there were a series of television commercials, ads, and billboards used by the National Dairy Council designed to encourage Americans to recognize the benefits associated with drinking milk. The primary and most recognizable benefits often highlighted and promoted by this campaign was that that milk encouraged strong teeth and healthy bones.

Within the human body there are over 206 bones that comprise our skeletal system, which all play not only major but in many cases vital functions. Our bones are designed to provide us with support, protection, assistance in movement, and even have the ability to produce blood cells.

A human being without a skeletal system would be nothing more than a pile of flesh, muscle, and tissue with no protection and unable to move. But, with a strong skeletal system and the proper nutrients being received by way of regular milk (calcium) intake, we receive the support and protection we need, and are also able to move forward freely.

This is where God's Word comes into play since many believers often suffer from spiritual calcium deficiency because we refuse to receive the daily dose of milk we need to sustain us (1 Pet. 2:1-3). The milk described in the preceding Scripture is the spiritual milk of God's Holy Word.

The Word of God contains the daily nutrients we need to sustain us in every way. According to John 1:1, 14 Jesus Christ is the Living Word. In other words, it is Jesus we really need to sustain us in this day and age, because in Him we find Truth. Not only does the Living Word provide us with nutrients, He also provides other basic necessities:

Thoughts

_____
_____
_____
_____
_____
_____
_____
_____

First, in the Word we find support and protection (Ps. 91:1-4). Secondly, through the Word we are able to move freely (Acts 17:24); and it also provides direction (Ps. 119:105). Truth encourages us to not continually look back at what we may have said or done, but allows us to constantly move forward! Thirdly, when we keep the milk of God's Word in our mouths, it brings us success, causes us to prosper, and keeps us on track (Josh. 1:7-9). And lastly, the Word produces life. Just as life-giving red blood cells are produced in the marrow of the larger bones in the body; the blood of the Living Word of God produces life within us because without the shedding of blood by the spotless, unblemished Word of God (Jesus Christ Himself), there is no remission of sins or any prospect of a new spiritual life. There is life in the Word!

The Word of God and the Truth therein is what we need to sustain and keep us from day-to-day, no matter where we may be in life or what we may be going through. If natural milk does the physical body good, then the spiritual milk of the Word brings us even greater support, protection, and gives us better mobility to carry the Truth of the Gospel into the world.

So, ensure that you not only receive the milk, but also the meat of God's Word on a regular basis to be certain that you obtain your recommended daily dosage of spiritual nutrients. "Got milk?" Or better yet Got Truth? Truth does the body good!

"Every word of God is tried and purified; He is a shield to those who trust and take refuge in Him" (Prov. 30:5, Amplified Bible).

December 18
NOTHING LEFT TO SAY
Read: Matt. 22:15-22

Throughout the New Testament the religious leaders, primarily the Sadducees and Pharisees, were constantly looking for ways to ensnare Jesus with His own words or attempted to get Him to say something contrary to the Roman authorities in power at the time. Their ultimate goal was to manipulate and persuade Him to speak out against the Roman Empire so He would be brought up on charges and receive the requisite punishment for an act of this nature.

Thoughts

_____
_____
_____
_____
_____
_____
_____

Here was the Holy One that Scriptures foretold of His coming, One who literally had no sin within Him, One who had done no wrong, and One who routinely did nothing more than spoke words of peace and words that brought deliverance to those who were held captive to all manner of bondage, sickness, and disease (Acts 10:37-38). Yet no matter how much good Jesus did, there were always those attempting to find fault in whatever He did.

One day the Pharisees devised a scheme by posing a question and asking Jesus about Jews paying taxes to Rome. In His response Jesus simply said render unto Caesar what was his and give God what was His. As a result the Pharisees were left speechless (Matt. 22:15-22).

Jesus was able to use wisdom in dealing with the devious plot of the religious leaders because He was literally filled with truth, He was the Truth (Jn. 14:6) and God was with Him; therefore, the Pharisees were literally left speechless with nothing else to say.

Since Jesus lived an upright lifestyle that was filled with love, compassion, giving and He dealt with every situation based on truth; the accusations of those seeking His demise had no legs to stand on which caused them to routinely walk away baffled with no retort to the truth He spoke (Prov. 16:22).

In life we will encounter individuals who, for whatever reason, do not like us or seek to discredit the God we serve in an attempt to hold us back and prevent us from moving forward in life. In this instance we do not have to get belligerent, defiant, or defensive because the battle is not ours anyway, the battle belongs to LORD (1 Sam. 17:47) and He will fight on our behalf; on these occasions we must learn how to just be still (Ex. 14:13). What the LORD simply requires of us is to live a Spirit-filled life that is pleasing in His sight while honoring Him in everything that we do, because in the end truth will be revealed (Col. 1:5-7,9-12).

When false accusations come against us God will make our enemies our footstool as we continue to put our complete confidence, trust, and faith in Him (Ps. 110:1, King James Version). So, when the "haters" come your way, don't fret or be dismayed; instead keep on living for Christ (the Truth), then they too will be left standing like the Pharisees and Sadducees with NOTHING LEFT TO SAY!

"The LORD is my light and my salvation—so why should I be afraid? The LORD is my fortress, protecting me from danger, so why should I tremble? When evil people come to devour me, when my enemies and foes attack me, they will stumble and fall. Though a mighty army surrounds me, my heart will not be afraid. Even if I am attacked, I will remain confident...For he will conceal me there when troubles come; he will hide me in his sanctuary. He will place me out of reach on a high rock" (Ps. 27:1-3, 5, New Living Translation).

Thoughts

_____
_____
_____
_____
_____
_____
_____

December 19

LOSING SIGHT WHILE GAINING VISION
Read: Prov. 29:18

Having sight is a wonderful gift to have, especially when an individual is able to look around and enjoy the wonder and amazement of God's creation: how clouds remain in the sky, how birds are capable of flying through the air, seeing how specific warm-blooded mammals have the able to live and survive both in water and on dry land, and how the universe is strategically set in place.

On the other hand, there are those who may have been born without the benefit of having sight or may have slowly lost their sight due to some degenerative eye condition, but are now able to experience the beauty of creation in other unique ways.When I was required to wear eyeglasses at a young age, there were a few phrases commonly used to describe a person who was not be able to see without the aid of glasses, "four eyes" and "you are blind as a bat" immediately come to mind. I will focus on the latter phrase.

The phrase "blind as a bat" is of course a reference to the small flying mammal the bat, which does not have the ability to see as humans do and is actually blind by our definition of the word. Instead of seeing the way humans are designed to, based on the degree of light perception received through the eyes, bats use the echo from sound waves to navigate around obstacles and to identify their prey. In simplistic terms, bats are guided by sound.

According to Jn. 10:27-28 Jesus said my sheep know my voice. Therefore, through salvation in Christ and submission to His Lordship and authority now gives us the faith we need to overcome every obstacle in this life and live according to His plan; that is when we position ourselves to clearly HEAR Him.

Just as bats are able to navigate based on an echo, which is nothing more than sound that is returned to its originated source; our faith as believers, and our relationships are strengthened and fortified the right way when we begin to echo the voice of the Good Shepherd Jesus Christ as it is given to us through His Word. "So then faith comes by hearing, by the Word of God" (Rom. 10:17). This means we must hear God's Word and then begin to speak it and live it as we allow His echo (The Holy Spirit) to guide and direct us.

Thoughts

_____

_____

_____

_____

_____

_____

_____

As believers we are not to live solely by what we see, but by what we hear, speak, and live according to God's Holy Word walking by faith (2 Cor. 5:7). Going beyond sight and what we can see allows us to have vision for what God has already planned and the right relationships that He Himself has already established (Jer. 29:11).

An individual may be able to survive and get by without the benefit sight in the natural; however, in a spiritual sense when we have no vision, as we allow people and things to get in front of us and in our periphery, this blocks our view of the standards in God's Word needed to safely guide us. This is when we begin to die a slow spiritual death as our spiritual sight over time continues to diminish. Where there is no vision, death is the end result (Prov. 29:18). It is faith that gives us the vision we need to sustain, lead, guide, and direct us from day-to-day, specifically in our relationships.

Are you struggling to walk according to the Master's purpose and plan for your life, particularly as it pertains to the relationships that have been or plan to be established in your life? Are you struggling in the area of exercising faith so that God can keep you from making the wrong choices? Then quit living by natural sight allowing emotions and feelings to dictate your actions, but instead begin to use vision that is coupled with faith that comes from hearing the sound of the right voice. Choose to be led by Him!

December 20
AN EXPRESSION OF LOVE
Read: 1 Jn. 4:10

There is often talk with regards to or questions related to why God created man, for instance: was He bored, was He lonely, or did He just simply have nothing else better to do? However, for answers to these type of questions all one has to do is turn to the book of Genesis in the Old Testament of the Bible.

God created man to be like Him (Gen. 1:27) and part of this creation package deal was for man to exercise God-given authority here in the earth (Gen. 1:28). So, to believe that God was just bored, lonely or simply didn't have anything better to do would be a naïve assumption, because Scripture also clearly indicates that He was definitely not alone when the worlds were created.

Gen. 1:1 describes God "the Spirit" hovering over the waters, and in Gen. 1:26 God is recorded as saying "Let US make man in our image, after OUR likeness." Not to insult anyone's intelligence but just in case you didn't know it in the English language the words "us" and "our" denote more than one. Therefore, this clearly indicates the presence of all three persons of the Godhead and their involvement in creation (God the Father, God the Son, and God the Holy Spirit) who are all one (1 Jn. 5:7).

Thoughts

Based on these facts, it would then be safe to say that God was never lonely and/or alone, instead God created man as an expression of the very essence of who He was and still is today, "God is love" (1 Jn. 4:8). Notice that Scripture does not say God gives love or God has love but that love "IS" who God actually is. This is why, out of all other created animals and beings, man is the only one created in the image and likeness of God. And after He created us, He was so pleased with the handiwork of His most prized creation that He said it was "very good" (Gen. 1:31).

Man was created to share in exercising God's authority here in the earth, and to commune and have unbroken fellowship with the Father. Therefore, in response to man's separation from God through Adam's sin in the Garden of Eden, He gave us sixty-six books (a.k.a. the Bible) as a record of His plan to restore the fellowship we were originally intended to have. And no matter how many times man fell and even when God occasionally articulated His displeasure in man's action; He consistently demonstrated His unfailing love.

God loved man so much that He sent that which was most precious and dear to Him, He sent His only begotten or "One Unique" son to become a sacrifice to bridge the gap between He and man—-He sent His son Jesus (Gal. 4:4-6).

Jesus was the only one uniquely fashioned and qualified to accomplish God's redemptive plan for man; God did this all because of who He is: LOVE. And the amazing thing about all of this is that Jesus, God's Kingdom, and this same love now lives inside of you (Lk. 17:20-21). Therefore, if the Kingdom of God is in you, then so is LOVE.

So, contrary to popular belief, man did not come from the "primeval ooze," evolve from a monkey, or some other primate; you were and are still God's greatest expression of love (James 1:18). Not only are you God's greatest expression of love, but you have been commissioned to reciprocate and also share this love with others.

Therefore, it does not matter how you came into being (whether legitimately or not), or how you may feel about or view your value and/or self-worth. Know today that you are an expression of God's great love and this love now lives inside of you (1 Jn. 4:10).

December 21
HAND-ME-DOWN GENES
Read: Prov. 13:22

Thoughts

_____

_____

_____

_____

_____

_____

_____

When our four daughters were much younger, and since they were fairly close in age; in order to save money, when one child outgrew their clothing and as long as the fabric or material was still in good condition, it would get passed down from one child to the next. Shirts, dresses, shoes, jeans, etc.; hand-me-down clothing was the way to go until they came of age and understood that although the clothing may have been new to them, in actuality it was not new at all; instead it was just something used that one of their other sisters could no longer wear or no longer needed.

But when our daughters got older, the idea of receiving hand-me-down clothing didn't go over too well because now they wanted something new. As I was driving one day and listening to a preached message on my iPod (listening to it through the vehicle's stereo system and not with headphones of course--safety first), the man of God briefly discussed how genetics work and that through genes parents often pass on various physical traits, such as eye color, skin tone, hair texture, dimples, cleft chins, etc., on to their children.

It has been documented that genetics also contribute to the mannerisms and behavior of individuals from one generation to the next, as certain traits are passed down from individual-to-individual over the years. For instance, there is a debate over whether or not alcoholism is inherited. Statistics from one organization concluded that "a person's risk of developing alcoholism is 60% determined by his or her genetics and 40% caused by his or her environment." In other words, genetics may play a role, but a child exposed to alcohol on a routine basis is also more likely to adapt to this manner of lifestyle and behavior as well.

O.K., I can hear someone saying what's the big deal about a little alcoholic beverage every now and then; even Jesus turned water into wine (Jn. 4:46), and Timothy said to take a little wine for the stomach's sake to ease infirmity (1 Tim. 5:23). Although these are two valid points, I would submit to you that there are actually more Scriptures that talk about the negative side effects of alcohol and drunkenness than the two Scriptures most immediately run to for justification of their desire to consume alcohol. Don't get me wrong, I'm not condemning anyone who chooses to use and drink alcoholic beverages, but just wanted to highlight the negative impact and the consequences this may bring to the individual as well as to the future lives of others.

There is nothing in the Bible stating that drinking alcohol is a sin; however, being in a state of intoxication or drunkenness is (1 Cor. 6:9-10).

Though an individual may be able to handle their alcohol and not get drunk, a child that has observed this lifestyle over a period of time is more likely to adopt the same habit, but may not be able to handle it in the same way, and end up going down a path of alcohol abuse and self-destruction (1 Cor. 10:23).

In the preceding Scripture, Paul was saying that although certain things were legal and within his rights to do, he chose not to do them to ensure he would not be a stumbling block to someone else who might not be as strong. What genes are you handing down to the next generation? What legacy are you leaving for your children and your children's children? Make it a purpose to leave a lasting legacy that

Thoughts

_____
_____
_____
_____
_____
_____
_____

will bring prosperity and hope for generations to come; because old hand-me-down "genes" just may not work (Prov. 13:22).

December 22
HE'S REALLY BIGGER THAN YOU ALLOW HIM TO BE
Read: Ps. 34:3

When I was in high school and early on in college years, biology was one of my favorite subjects. Learning about nature, the origin of things and how they work has always fascinated me; therefore, this was something I came to enjoy. Therefore, shows on the Discovery or National Geographic channel often provided me with information on various organisms and animal species detailing their genetic make-up, their natural habitat, and how they interacted with other animals and with the environment in general. This fondness of biology is probably why I later developed an affinity for television shows like "C.S.I.," seeing how an entire case or mystery could be solved with the eventual conviction of a felon solely being determined by seemingly small bits of biological evidence or information.

During many of the episodes, with the aid of sophisticated technology and high-powered microscopes, the C.S.I. lab analysts were able to see the smallest and most minute particle to determine its composition and make-up to assist investigators in putting the crime scene puzzle together, one piece at a time. And since the majority of the items at the scene were generally small in nature, magnification of these articles was extremely important in determining a motive and providing leads to a suspect. The smaller the evidence, the more magnification was required; therefore, the right magnification was extremely essential.

According to one dictionary definition, to "magnify" simply means "to cause to be held in greater esteem or respect, to increase in significance, or to enlarge in fact or in appearance."

Well, many times as Christians we tend to place our focus on and magnify the wrong things even though the Bible clearly declares that while we are in this world we will experience hardships and tribulation, but we can still have cheer in the midst of our trials because Jesus has already overcome the world (Jn. 16:33). He did so by demonstrating His awesome love for us by freely and willingly sacrificing His life on the cross so that many would live.

Thoughts

_____

_____

_____

_____

_____

_____

_____

Occasionally as we go through our trials and tribulations, we often focus on the small distractions that are placed before us instead of seeing the bigger picture of God's unfailing love

454

for us and how He uses tests and trials for His greater plan, to prepare us for our destiny, to encourage a greater trust in Him, and to allow what He has placed in us to be used for His glory. Sadly, instead of magnifying or increasing God's ability to fix our problems, we as Christians often begin to increase and make the situations and issues we face larger than they need to be when the opposite should be the correct course of action.

In Ps. 34:3 the psalmist simply said "Oh, magnify the LORD with me". In other words, what David was basically saying here is that in the face of adversity and challenge he resolved to make God bigger that anything he faced and he made the choice to lift God higher than any situation or circumstance thereby demonstrating a unique trust in Him. Well, I'm here to tell you today that we serve a big God who is more than capable of doing great and mighty things. He does this simply because He loves us, but we must be willing to trust Him and allow Him to do His job while looking beyond what we can see in the natural.

Our Heavenly Father has provided us with the proof and evidence of His faithfulness from generation to generation throughout His Word. So, instead of enlarging the facts about your problem, you need to enlarge your All-Powerful and Almighty God. Adjust your lenses to get a better view; God is really bigger than you allow Him to be (Ps. 69:30).

December 23
FOLLOWING THE RIGHT STAR
Read: Matt. 2:9

Change is something that is always constant and evolving; because the one constant in change is that change is always being constant. Over the centuries there have been significant cultural changes in both the eastern and western hemispheres of the world that have reshaped mindsets and many of the standards that where once very near and dear to all.

We now see and encounter stars (or entertainers) of varying type via television, movie, print media and the like; including individuals in professional sports, actors/ actresses, dancers, authors, movie producers, and political leaders who, for the most part, command the attention of many adoring fans. With charisma, skill, flare or with their particular and/or unique style, they easily attract a large following. But, when one of these stars just so happens to fall into an area of sin or succumbs to temptation, the once adoring fan becomes discouraged and/or disheartened.

Thoughts

Many individuals pattern their very lives after these stars by attempting to dress like them, act like them, and in some instances even become them; but when these star fall from the popular scene, out of public graces or have their reputation tarnished; the once faithful and adoring fans often become depressed and despondent. Why? It's simple; they were attempting to pattern their lives after and follow the wrong star. God-like attributes are often ascribed to many famous people (or stars), when in actuality these individuals are only human and are subject to the same temptations that we each face on a daily basis (1 Pet. 5:9). This is why our goal should be to pattern our lives after the correct influence and follow the right star.

In the story that leads to the birth of Jesus, we are told of a group of wise men hearing of a prophecy that foretold the coming of a new Messiah. And in eager anticipation of the birth of this new Messiah, they made haste to travel to the place where this newborn King would come into the world (Matt. 2:9).

Their journey was obviously not a short trip with these men just walking around the corner or a few blocks down the dirt road to reach their destination. Instead, they packed and loaded their camels with essential items needed for travel and gifts to present, with each of the wise men traveling a considerable distance being guided only by a light that shone brightly in the distant sky.

The wise men eventually located the babe lying in a manger (which was nothing more than a trough used to hold food for animals in a stable). They were able to locate the Messiah, the Anointed One and King of Kings simply by hearkening (or listening) to the voice of God and following a star. Not only did they follow the right star, they found the True Star and the One who would bring light and salvation to the world; that Star was the baby Jesus. And once they found Him, they demonstrated reverence by bowing before Him and presenting gifts (Matt. 2:11). Not only is Jesus "the light of the world" (Jn. 9:5), according to Rev. 22:16, He is also "the bright and morning star." Just like the wise men, we must make it our purpose to reverence Him (Jesus Christ) and present our gifts (talents, etc.) back to Him through true and authentic worship.

True life and success only comes as we have the proper focus, are under the correct influence, and are actually following the right Star. Don't allow the wrong influence to rob you of the joy and peace that are rightfully yours, because real life only begins under and through the influence of Christ! As it has commonly been said, "Wise men still seek Jesus" (Jn. 8:12)!

Thoughts

_____
_____
_____
_____
_____
_____
_____

December 24
SOME ASSEMBLY REQUIRED
Read: 1 Cor. 3:9-11

It is Christmas Eve and there are several unwrapped gifts remaining for the kids in extremely large boxes with the all too familiar words boldly written on the side, "Some Assembly Required." So being the skilled person that you think you are, you immediately begin to assemble the items without the aid of or the slightest thought of looking at the instructions because you don't even remove the small booklet from its protective plastic covering. You know those instructions that were so kindly included by the manufacturer who designed the product.

But because of hastiness, a little overconfidence, and a pinch of pride you now have unconnected parts spread out all over the floor. And now a job that should have taken maybe an hour or two tops goes past midnight into early Christmas morning. However, this entire episode could have been avoided if only the instructions provided for assembly were used at the beginning.

This is also a pattern that is experienced by many of us in life today. We suffer needlessly and constantly struggle by doing things our own way and through human effort simply because we choose not to follow the instructions that have been established and provided.

Whenever established instructions, laws, or principles are not followed or adhered to, heartache and suffering are generally the end result. Sadly, many of us try to build or govern our lives without following the instructions that have so freely been given to us by our Heavenly Manufacturer, the One who designed and created us (Ps. 139:14). And as a result, we often delay or miss out on the blessings God already has in store for us and are ready for us to receive simply because we attempt to do things our own way, in our own strength and ability, and with little regard for the instructions that He has given.

Each one of us have been intricately designed by God, we are His building, and the instruction manual so graciously given to us is the Bible [B-Basic I-Instructions B-Before L-Leaving E-Earth] or His Holy Word. So whenever there is a malfunction in our life where health, peace, joy, forgiveness, or even love may be needed; we should dare not attempt to figure out the answers to these concerns on our own, but instead we are to directly refer to the Manual and the Manufacturer for His guidance and instruction.

We must stop wasting time trying to make it through life based on our knowledge, strength or intellect, especially when there are established instructions and principles in place to get our lives where they need to be. Are you frustrated with the unassembled parts of your life laid out all around you not knowing what to connect next? If so, then allow God's Word with the instructions and principles contained therein to be your blueprint as you allow Him to put the pieces of your life back together. Even though some assembly is required, follow the instructions as given because His Manual actually works!

Thoughts

_____

_____

_____

_____

"...You are God's house. Using the gift God gave me as a good architect, I designed blueprints... Let each carpenter who comes on the job take

_____

_____

care to build on the foundation! Remember, there is only one foundation, the one already laid: Jesus Christ. Take particular care in picking out your building materials. Eventually there is going to be an inspection" (1 Cor. 3:9-11, The Message).

December 25
HAVE YOU MADE ROOM?
Read: Luke 2:7

During the weeks leading up to the day many celebrate as Christmas or the day Christ the Savior was born, homes are often decorated with lights, garland, wreaths, and model depictions of what is commonly called "The Nativity" commemorating the birth of Christ as he laid in a manger. Yet in the midst of the hustle and bustle and all the worldly hype associated with the season, few actually pause to think about what this really means.

Joseph with his espoused wife (or fiancée in modern terms) Mary, who was also pregnant with child, traveled a considerable distance to honor the laws of the land to pay their taxes as required by Roman law at the time. No matter where individuals lived at any given moment or what city they were affiliated with, they were still required to return to their hometowns so taxes could be paid.

So, after a long and tedious journey as Mary carried the unborn child conceived by the Holy Spirit who was almost ready to be delivered; the couple diligently looked throughout the city of Bethlehem for a place to stay, but unfortunately there were no accommodations to be found. They went from house to house and Inn to Inn, yet there was no room for them anywhere. Then in what must have been the Spirit of God moving upon his heart, one particular Innkeeper having just rented his last room suddenly remembered there was a small space available in the corner of his stable filled with an assortment of animals.

The couple found a secluded spot among the animals, and it was in this humble setting the Messiah, Emmanuel (God with us), the King of Kings was born into the world. He was born in a stable and laid in a feeding trough simply because there were no vacancies to be found anywhere throughout all the city (Lk. 2:7).

Thoughts

_____
_____
_____
_____
_____
_____
_____

The word "inn" in the preceding verse is literally translated as "kataluma" which means "guest room" or "resting place" in the Greek. In other words, this would indicate that no one in the entire city could even spare a simple guest room or make accommodations for the birth of Israel's future King. Unfortunately this same issue still persists today. Because even with the luxuries so many of us enjoy with large homes, or spacious apartments, townhomes and condominiums, both non-believers and believers alike still find it difficult to make room for Jesus the Savior in our lives.

Just in case you did not know it, we each have been designed to be the very temple and building for the Spirit of God, a place where His Spirit can abide and dwell (1 Cor. 6:19-20).

Jesus the Savior, through the person of the Holy Spirit, still seeks to take up residence in the hearts of His people, yet too often we have no room for Him because other things have taken priority, have taken up the space that He longs to inhabit, and have in essence become idols in our lives and our gods.

Is your spiritual house so full that you have no room for the Savior? We must choose to evict the enemy and anything that separates us from the abiding presence of God so that He may occupy permanent residence within us. There should never be a point in time when we have no room for the One who gave His all for us. Do you have any vacancy? Do you have any room for the King of Kings in your life today (Jn. 15:4)?

December 26
REMOVING THE "X"
Read: Is. 9:6-7

During the Civil Rights Movement of the 1960's in the United States, a young red-headed African American named Malcolm Little rose to prominence and fame. However, during his early and formative years, he associated himself with the wrong crowd, did the wrong things, and ended up in prison. While in prison he became a Muslim and joined the Nation of Islam, a group that originally set out to improve the social, economic, and spiritual status of African Americans in the U.S., however, over time this group began to promote hatred towards other races.

So, during a time of racial inequality and injustice Malcolm devoted himself to study and training of the Muslim way, and he eventually became a minister and the primary mouthpiece for the Nation of Islam, as he advocated equality for the African American, but disdain and hatred for anyone who was white. This hatred also led Malcolm to change his last name, which was considered the white slavemaster's name given to his ancestors, from "Little" to "X." The "X" here represented the fact that he did not know his true African family name; therefore, he had no true identity. In essence Malcolm X was attempting to disassociate himself from his birth-given surname to something that was unknown.

Thoughts

_____

_____

_____

_____

_____

_____

_____

A very similar occurrence generally happens at least once a year during the holiday season celebrate as Christmas, but in a more subtle way. Each year many choose to abbreviate the word Christmas with the shorter version "X-mas," which completely changes the identity, meaning and etymology of the word. When the word "Christmas" is broken down we get "Christ" (the Anointed One) and "mas" which means "a gathering." When the two components of the word are put together, Christmas actually means "a gathering for Christ (the Anointed One). But when Christ is removed from Christmas, who or what are we actually gathering for? Whenever Christ is removed we are just left with "mas," a gathering that serves no purpose.

The world would say that Christians over-react because of the usage of the term "X-mas" every year since the "X" is often said to have been derived from a Greek letter that actually means Christ. However, I would submit that a large majority of Americans are probably unaware of this fact and that this is nothing more than a subtle tactic of the enemy, the devil, to dilute and attempt to blot out the true meaning and purpose of this holiday and significant event.

The word Christ is made up of six letters, and the number six in the Bible represents "the number of man." When individuals choose to replace "Christ" with "X" in Christmas, this is symbolic of man's attempt to remove Christ from the equation and replace Him with some other focus that draws everyone's attention away to something else, something that is less authentic.

Without Christ there can be no true Christmas, Jesus is truly "the reason for the season;" He is Emmanuel, God with us. Christ came to give the greatest gift of all-time; He gave Himself so that many could live. He was born to die so that we all might live abundantly (Jn. 10:10).

Don't allow the world to rob you of the joy and true life that Christmas brings as we not only give gifts and presents, but learn to give of ourselves and recognize His presence. Without Christ there can be no "Christ"mas, because He is the true reason for the season. Remove the "X" and allow Christ to stand in His proper place as the Head, then Have Yourself a true Merry Christmas!

Thoughts

_____
_____
_____
_____
_____
_____

December 27
CROSS YOUR HEART AND LIVE
Read: Jn. 10:17-18

Just the other day I was reminded of some of the childhood phrases that many of us used in ignorance; phrases that may have been popular to say at the time that really had no meaning or substance. For example, "If you step on a crack, you break your momma's back," "Don't count your chickens before they've hatched," "Liar, Liar pants on fire," "Take a chill pill," "Na, Na, Na, Na, Boooo, Boooo," and "Cross my heart and hope to die;" of course this list could go on and on.

These phrases were said at various times and in various situations, but really brought nothing of substance or significance to the conversation or to either party. Take the phrase "Cross my heart and hope to die;" this was often said when an individual made some type of commitment or promise to another. This was to signify that the person using the phrase would follow-up or fulfill his or her promise even to the point of death. But, how many children or adolescents using this phrase do you think were actually willing to die if they did not keep their promise or commitment? Probably not too many at all.

This just goes to show that words are often used without any thought to the future ramifications they may have; therefore, we must be careful in our word choice because our words produce either life or death (Prov. 18:21; Matt. 12:36-37). Well, Jesus made a promise to us over two thousand years ago and He has proven He can back-up and keep His Word (Gal. 3:14).

But instead of crossing His heart, He chose to willingly die on a wooden cross to redeem a sinful man (Jn. 10:17-18) and because of this promise our hearts can now be forever changed.

Refuse to use idle words that are unfruitful and meaningless. And instead of crossing your heart and hoping to die, receive life through a true confession and profession of faith, apply the cross to your heart and live.

"This is the agreement (testament, covenant) that I will set up and conclude with them after those days, says the Lord: I will imprint My laws upon their hearts, and I will inscribe them on their minds (on their inmost thoughts and understanding)" (Heb. 10:16, Amplified Bible).

December 28
BREAKING THE ICE
Read: Matt. 5:13

When winter is upon us, the many changes in weather and weather patterns across the United States (U.S.) not only keep meteorologists or weather guessers on their toes, but everyone else (especially commuters) as well. From the Midwest to the northeastern portions of the U.S., cold fronts can bring a deadly mixture of snow, sleet, and ice that often turn highways

Thoughts

_____
_____
_____
_____
_____
_____
_____

and roads into what appears to be combat zones as patches of "black ice" cover roadways causing multiple accidents and pile ups.

So during this season, not only are meteorologists required to put in extended hours, but members of the Department of Transportation (DOT) for specific regions are also required to put in overtime as well.

As snow, sleet, and ice cover many of the main thoroughfares and traffic routes, transportation specialist crank up the snow plows and go into action. These specialized trucks are not only fitted with large shovel-like devices attached to the front to plow through piles of snow and ice on the road, but they also have spreaders connected to distribute salt along the path as well.

Scientifically, "Salt lowers the freezing/melting point of water...If you ever watch salt melting ice, you can see the dissolving process happen -- the ice immediately around the grain of salt melts, and the melting spreads out from that point." Therefore, based on its superb chemical make-up and properties, salt is the primary agent used to break through the ice.

In our society today, there seems to be more focus on individual achievement with many attempting to climb the ladder of success, oftentimes at the expense of others. As a result, for the most part especially in western society, the average person nowadays is out for himself or herself with catchphrases and mottos like "Get all you can and can all you can get" being used. Because of this need to succeed, we have turned into a society filled with pride, selfish motives, and hearts that have grown cold. This is where we as believers and followers of Christ are to come in with a different perspective.

The Apostle Paul reminds us in Phil. 2:4 to "Let each of you esteem and look upon and be concerned for not [merely] his own interests, but also each for the interests of others" (Amplified Bible). The coldness and callousness in our society today is really an issue of the heart and of love, because it is the love of God that compels us to go above and beyond to extend a helping hand to someone else in need. Therefore, when we esteem others over and above ourselves, this does not mean we are to think less of ourselves but instead we are to think about ourselves less. This is why believers have been commissioned to be salt and light in this present world (Matt. 5:13).

Therefore, as we let our lights shine and begin to pour out a little salt, we have the power and fire of the Holy Spirit who resides within us to start breaking the coldness and ice of the hardened heart. Just as the chemical properties of salt melts the ice on highways and as the heat from light melts the hard winter surfaces, we as bearers of the Light can be the change-agents used to break up the cold, stony hearts of apathy and indifference in a world where many seek their own and forget about the needs of others. So, let's make it a purpose to turn on our light

Thoughts

_____
_____
_____
_____
_____
_____
_____

and pour a little salt as God uses us to begin breaking the ice of the stony hearts of those around us wherever we may be.

In this season of giving, let us not only apply a little salt to our own hearts, but be the agents of change used to encourage others to do the same. A pliable heart often responds and then begins to operate in a spirit of love (Hos. 10:12).

December 29
DON'T FEAR THE LIGHT
Read: Lk. 2:8-20

Imagine driving along a highway or interstate as you made your way to visit family and friends for the holidays, then all of a sudden in the darkness behind you look in the rear-view mirror to see flashing lights rapidly approaching. Immediately you begin to panic wondering what you have done wrong: Was my lane change improper? Did I cut someone off? Was I speeding?

So, with a myriad of thoughts going through your head, you instinctively let your foot up from the gas pedal as if you already know you are guilty of some infraction. Meanwhile the lights from behind are getting closer and closer with the high-pitched scream of the siren getting even louder. Not wanting to add further insult to misery, you do what a good citizen and someone with a desire to obey the law would do, you pull over to find out what you did wrong and prepare to receive your fine so that you can proceed on.

But as you pull over, to your surprise the vehicle with the flashing lights races by as if you were not even there. After regaining your composure, you get back on the road and continue down the highway eventually coming upon an accident involving a small car and a very large tractor trailer with slightly injured motorists in each vehicle.

It turns out the flashing lights that prompted you to pause and let fear grip your heart were actually rescue workers coming to render help, assistance, and treat the wounded. Well, a similar scene played out the night Jesus came into the world. On the night Jesus was born shepherds were in the field tending and caring for their flocks; and then suddenly in the midst of the darkness a bright light shone bring fear upon all who were in the field. Can you imagine the multitude of emotions the shepherds must have experienced?

There was undoubtedly fear, confusion, and panic concerning the impending doom that was certain to come. But as the light shone over and around them, instead an angel sent from God delivered a very important message as the

Thoughts

_____
_____
_____
_____
_____
_____
_____

messenger first immediately consoled them by saying "Fear not" (Lk. 2:10). This angel had not come to bring judgment or condemnation upon the shepherds, but to deliver the Good News about the birth of the Savior Jesus Christ, the Light of the World who came to redeem or purchase man out of darkness; the Light came to bring us life (Jn. 8:12, Amplified Bible. The shepherds were fearful and running away from a representation of that which was designed to bring salvation and life to the world.

Unfortunately many today still choose to fear and run away from light, sometimes out of ignorance and not truly understanding what the Light represents or because their deeds are dark and they do not want the Light to expose their sins.

However, if we truly expect to receive the life that has been promised to us by Jesus in the Word (Jn. 10:10), then instead of running away from the Light, we should allow the Light to shine on us in order to dispel and disperse the darkness from our lives.

Remember, without Jesus Christ who is the Light that brings life, we would not be able to celebrate this holiday season because without CHRIST there would be no CHRISTmas. So, just as the rescue workers described above rendered assistance to the accident victims, the light that shone on the night of Jesus' birth came to prepare the way for the healing and deliverance He would bring. So let us all make it a purpose to run to the Light while light is yet available and remember all the CHRISTmas truly brings.

December 30

REFUSE TO TAP OUT
Read: Eph 6:12

Over the years, television sporting events have gradually earned higher viewer ratings than many of the most popular talk shows, documentaries, dramas and even soap operas. Viewers intensely sit before television screens to see opposing teams go head to head anticipating the final outcome and to see who will emerge victorious.

One sport that has gained popularity, a large following and much notoriety in recent years is that of professional wrestling. I can remember growing up as a young man watching wrestling matches on television and even being able to see live matches in action whenever these wrestling personalities came to town. Back then wrestling had less talk and drama and was a little more physical, disciplined and methodical with skilled wrestlers like Tony Atlas, Andre the Giant, Randy "Macho Man" Savage, Jake "The Snake" Roberts, The Ultimate Warrior, The Junkyard Dog, The Road Warriors, Dusty Rhodes, and the list could go on; I know, I'm showing my age again.

Thoughts

_____

_____

_____

_____

_____

_____

Whether or not all of the wrestling combinations and moves were actually genuine back then I couldn't tell you, but at least the matches and match-ups had the appearance of reality and were not just flamboyant shows. Over time this sport seems to have transformed from the true art of wrestling to that of just being sports-entertainment, or what I like to call a "Sports Soap Opera" with scripted commentaries, scripted storylines, choreographed wrestling moves and predetermined winners. What this means is that no matter what submission hold is applied or whatever pain is inflicted to cause the modern-day wrestling star to conceded or give up; the script has already been determined to ensure that he or she wins. So the primary goal of the wrestler is simply to remain in the fight and refuse to "tap out."

You may be wondering what all of this has to do with my spiritual growth and development as a believer in Christ. Well, if your spiritual ears are open, the above dialogue provides some very practical advice for those of us who continue in the struggle of the spiritual fight as the year closes out. Even though the year is almost over and it may appear that goals were not achieved, debt was not paid off, numerous spiritual attacks came and the enemy may even seem to have us pinned to the canvas now, remember there is hope because a new year is coming.

Until Jesus returns, there will always be a constant struggle between good and evil, the people of God and the forces of darkness; and whether a we realize it or choose to believe it or not, we are at continuous war with our enemy the devil and his forces, and are in a constant spiritual wrestling match to overcome his powers (Eph. 6:12-13).

However, even in the midst of unrelenting spiritual attacks the ultimate goal is to stand firm in faith and continue to do what is right in order to receive the life that has been promised to us in God's Word (Jn. 10:10). So, with the end of the current year upon us, remain in the fight and refuse to tap out because a New Year is approaching and we have another opportunity to succeed and to be victorious. Remember, the fight has already been fixed and the predetermined Script (the Bible) already informs us that we outcome and WE WIN (1 Jn. 5:4; 1 Cor. 15:57).

December 31
DOUBLE FOR YOUR TROUBLE
Read: Job 42:12

Thoughts

In the Old Testament book of Job, the main character Job endured a series of hardships and trials that involved many unexplained and very unusual occurrences, especially at the rate of rapid succession that each trial came about. With back-to-back and in some instances simultaneous adversities coming his way, Job suffered the lost of land, cattle, possessions, and even his closest family members in a very short span of time without having an opportunity to even prepare for the calamity that came his way (Job 1:13-22).

Therefore, in this story of unlikely events we find Job who is a righteous man; one who undoubtedly paid his tithes, loved his wife and family deeply ensuring that their needs were provided for, and faithfully served the LORD and was surely one of the most upright men within his community. But even though Job had many positive attributes, calamity still came his way.

Yet even with his world and life seeming to crumble around him, unlike many of us today when we begin to feel the pressures and tumultuous waves of life crashing down upon us, Job refused to turn his back on God in the midst of his difficulty. Instead of cursing God like many of those who were very close to him suggested, he continued to bless the LORD God his Creator placing complete trust in Him (Job 13:15).

And even after all of his possessions and his children had been lost, leaving him with nothing more than his wife and the clothing on his body and repeatedly being encouraged to just curse God and die, Job chose to hold fast to his faith in a Sovereign, All-Powerful God (Job 19:25). Job was confident that no matter what circumstance came his way and no matter how things may have appeared in the natural, God was faithful to deliver him (Ps. 34:19).

The story of Job should be an example and a constant source of encouragement to us in the midst of our calamity and what we often perceive as affliction. Because no matter what circumstance may come our way, when we remain in covenant with God and obey His Word, we come out on top every time.

I've heard it said that "Quitters never win and winners never quit." In other words we must take a stand like Job knowing that our Redeemer lives, and that He is ready, willing, and able to save and deliver us from our current circumstances. Our job is to simply holdfast and refuse to quit, because there is blessing and restoration just on the other side.

You see, many times we suffer and go through temptation, trials, and testing not because we've done wrong but because God wants to use our right response in and through the test to display His glory while developing our faith and building character. Therefore, as we look back over past year many of us should all thank God for the light affliction and suffering in our lives that was preparing us for the year that is to come. Know that in and through every test, trial, or tribulation experienced in the closing year that your God has been faithful and had your back the entire time (1 Cor. 10:13). And even though where you stand today may look like rubble and/or a pile of ashes, do not be dismayed but instead activate your faith as you remain connected to your true Source (God) in the New Year and just as He did for Job, when you remain faithful He will give you DOUBLE FOR YOUR TROUBLE (Job 42:12)!

Thoughts

_____
_____
_____
_____
_____
_____
_____

Quotes by Sheldon Malone

Faith

"Evidence is the result of expectation, expectation comes through faith, and faith only comes by the Word. Begin to speak the Word in faith to bring evidence to your expectation today. You have not because you ask not – ask for the right things."

"Seeing does not always result in believing. A blind person cannot see, yet still believes. Faith goes beyond what the natural eye can see."

"Don't be near-sighted in your faith today. Adjust your vision, and look to the things that are not seen for they are eternal. See yourself in the future."

"Dreams become reality when YOU remove the limitations from yourself, and quit limiting God. All things are possible to the one who just believes. Believe in yourself and who you are."

"Inspiration without application leads to frustration. Until we begin to truly apply God's Word to our lives without becoming a doer, we will live a defeated life. Faith without works is dead."

"Sometimes we become enablers to another's dependency as they never learn how to stand in faith. Though we are to help and assist others, sometimes by saying "no" we actually do them a favor as they learn how to depend on God."

"To receive the blessings associated with open doors in our lives, regular maintenance is required. We must oil the hinges with prayer, and then apply faith."

"Impossibilities become realities when we look through eyes of faith and refuse to doubt."

"A delay does not necessarily constitute a denial of a request or promise; it just means "Not Yet." The process of waiting involves faith (looking to the things that are not seen), trust (complete confidence in the Sovereignty of God and taking Him at His Word), and obedience (allowing our faith and trust to be demonstrated through our actions and manifested in our speech)."

Words

"Your confession is not designed to line up with reality; reality must align itself based on your confession. Use words of faith to shape your future by saying the right thing!"

"There is tremendous power in the spoken Word. The only powerless word is a word not spoken in faith. Say, believe, then you receive."

"Though the state of the economy may have many believers speaking fear, doubt, and lack. We are under a different system; in God's Kingdom, the Covenant has our back. Speak and declare increase!"

"The Word of God is not designed just to make individuals smart. But when one meditates on it and it is properly applied, the result is a transformation of the heart."

"The mouth only speaks based on what's already inside. If you don't like the product, then check the source. Guard your heart, for out of it the mouth speaks."

"Though seasons in our lives may vary, our words are often the catalyst that bring about the change."

"Locked doors easily open when you use the right key; God's Word is the Master Key to the locked doors of your blessing."

"Action without commitment is better than making a commitment but doing nothing. True commitment is not achieved until we follow through. Actions really do speak louder than words."

"Don't let God's Word just be a source of information and inspiration; but let it be the seed for transformation in your life today."

"Words have unbelievable power. So, use them to build others up instead of tearing them down. Then sit back and watch the positive results."

"We must learn to think before we speak. Once a word is spoken, it cannot be taken back. And once damage is done, it is often difficult to mend that which has been broken."

"No matter what you say, whether a lie or be it true; it's your actions not your words that expose the real you."

"What we hear we often receive, and what we receive we begin to believe. Learn to speak, hear, and receive the right things by faith allowing the right seeds to be sown and then watch God transform your very life. Never underestimate the power of the tongue or your words."

"It's not enough to just talk the talk, we must also learn to live the walk. Words mean nothing without action."

Love

"Time is the one thing that once lost you can never regain back. Use your time wisely to make a difference in the lives of those you encounter each day, especially those who are near and dear to you. You are able to express and reciprocate love because God first loved you. Redeem the time today."

"Though many refuse to admit it while rejecting the things from above. When the root of the matter is addressed, what we really seek is love. Love provides hope and true love never fails."

"As the saying goes, 'People don't care how much you know, until they know how much you care.' Love is not just demonstrated in word, but in deed. Love must be expressed with corresponding actions."

"Before you can truly love others, you must first learn to love yourself and find the source of true love. You cannot give what you don't have."

"Doing good for others does not take a sign from heaven above; all it takes is a heart of mercy and compassion, demonstrating the Father's love. Love requires action."

"Real love is not always telling a person what he or she wants to hear; it involves speaking the truth even when the truth hurts. However, make every effort to speak the truth in love."

"Before you can show love to others, you must first receive love and then learn how to love yourself. It is hard to give what you do not have."

"There a many four-letter words used today that are profane, demeaning, and vulgar; and add no benefit to the hearer. However, there is one four-letter word that has the power to change darkness into light, and make even our saddest days seem bright: L-O-V-E. Just try using it."

"As lights in a dark world, believers have the power to illuminate dark areas, ignite fires, and initiate transformation with focused action through love. The greater the concentration (or focus), the greater the light."

Life

"When life throws you lemons, don't become bitter; just add sugar to make your lemonade sweeter. Your attitude in bad situations and circumstances is just like the sugar added to the lemonade; you control how sweet the end product will be. It's all about your response and attitude."

"When you find yourself in a dark place, maybe your light is needed there. No one controls the on/off switch but you. So, refuse to complain about the place and instead allow your light to shine. Light is only needed in dark places."

"Some of the best lessons in life come by way of mistakes; but making a mistake is not the end. The tragedy comes when one does not learn from his or her mistake--this is often the difference between future success or failure. Learn, grow, and move on!"

"Contrary to popular belief, life is not "a box of chocolates." Although life may be filled with variety to include struggle, twists, and turns; we don't have to just settle for what we get. We can change our destiny by changing the way we think and speak—the power of life and death is in the tongue."

"Begin to live life with PURPOSE, on PURPOSE. We were all created to walk in authority and have dominion in the earth. Too many settlle for crumbs, while a feast is readily available at the Father's table. We were created to rule and reign!"

"Meekness should never be confused with weakness. On the contrary, meekness for the believer is not a sign of weakness at all, but is strength in reserve and under control. The meek will inherit the earth!"

"The twists and turns in life often cause many to break. In hindsight when the truth be told, calamity results from the choices we make. Make choices not just in the heat of the moment, but in light of eternity."

"True courage in the face of challenge and adversity is not only the ability to move forward boldly, but being able to move forward even though you are afraid. Do it afraid, then let faith do the rest. Faith without works it dead."

"There is a distinct difference between happiness and joy. Happiness is based on external factors, but true joy comes from within. No one can take your joy unless you allow it."

"Integrity requires more than great intentions, but must be solidified by corresponding actions whether in public or when no one else is around. Integrity speaks to the heart of individual character."

"When the enemy attempts to distract you while putting you to the test. Just remain focused and sternly remind him; you are too blessed to be stressed.""It's difficult to see what's ahead when you are constantly looking in the rear-view mirror."

"Peace is not always the absence of conflict or chaos; but is often an abiding, reassuring presence in the midst of the storm."

"A gift is not truly a gift until it has been received. God freely gives the gift of life each day; it's up to us to receive it."

"Just as it is virtually impossible to pick-up a coin from the ground with closed hands; it's impossible to receive love with a closed heart. You must open both your hands and heart if you truly expect the blessings of God to flow."

"When your past attempts to weigh you down, and your life seems to be off track. Instead of getting discouraged, keep pressing forward and refuse to look back. Yesterday is gone and better days are ahead of you."

"Many times setbacks are setups for future success. Obstacles are often used to prepare us for the next level; therefore, we must learn to endure and overcome the obstacle, because the blessing is usually just on the other side."

"We begin to experience true enjoyment and fulfillment when we transition from just making a living to making a life."

"When the fiery trials of life come your way, refuse to give in. Know that although you may be in the fire, you will not be consumed."

"We must learn to remove self out of the way. "I" is at the center of the word pr"I"de; when "I" is removed there is no pride (prde) and "I" is no longer at the center."

"When your circumstances create the illusion that your days just never seem to end. Instead of counting your days; begin to make every day count."

"Allow God's Word to be your blueprint. It is much easier to design the plans of your life when you follow the instructions."

"For every action there is a consequence; whether good or bad. Ensure that your actions bring you the right results."

"True peace is not just the absence of conflict; but being able to rest in God's presence in the midst of chaos."

"Many fail to realize that God's timing is not our timing. If He has promised it, then He will bring it to pass in His time. Our job is simply to be patient and learn how to wait."

"True change does not begin without, but from within. Change only from the outside tends not to last for long; it is change on the inside that makes the difference."

"Although we may not be able to alter our past; we can bring our past to the altar."

"Life is too valuable, and time waits for no one. Therefore, we must stop majoring on minor things and truly focus on what really matters."

"We only have 'One Life to Live,' so we must ensure that we follow 'The Guiding Light' to the bright and 'Morning Star;' He is the only true 'Light of the World.' The way to get there is on a highway called 'Holiness' through 'Route 66' (39 O.T. + 27 N.T.) of the Bible. Are you up for the journey?"

"Slow progress is better than no progress at all. It's not about how fast we mature in God; but about enduring until the end. Keep moving forward." "Our relationship with God is not just a one-night stand, but a life-long commitment."

"As believers we are called to be lights in this world. So, when darkness surrounds, we just turn up our light. The darker our environment, the brighter we should shine." "It is hard to receive with a clenched fist. Open hands make it easier both to give and to receive."

"Refuse to be classified by popular opinion, society, or the opinion of man; dare to be different, aspire to greatness, and purpose to make a difference."

"Though it may seem as if your blessing is being blocked while you are in the process of waiting for your miracle to happen; make sure that you exercise faith, check your attitude, and most importantly continue to demonstrate gratitude. The last obstacle to your promised blessing may very well be YOU."

"When faced with telling the truth or compromising by telling a lie, remember that it is TRUTH that makes us free."

"When your "Cheer" doesn't do the job; you've attempted to change the "Tide" but still can't "Wisk" it away; you have given your "All;" and you can't even "Shout" it out; put it under the blood of Jesus and watch the stains of sin fade away. Don't allow sin to make you feel worthless, unusable, and of no value."

"Spiritual seasons often come to bring about a change in us. And though our seasons may change we can be confident in one important fact; our God remains the same and continues His faithfulness towards us regardless of our season."

"Vision without purpose can cause you to travel in circles not knowing your end from the beginning."

"We were created by God for fellowship, relationship, and worship. Our worship is not a one-time act to be performed only when we enter the sanctuary of God's house, but every single day. WORSHIP IS A LIFESTYLE!"

"When we try to be like others we deny the very essence of who God created us to be; unique in every way."

"Instead of worshipping created things, we have been designed to worship the Creator."

"It's hard to be the church while remaining inside. True ministry must go beyond the proverbial "Four walls."

"Yesterday is a memory, today is reality; but only God knows what tomorrow holds! Live each day with anticipation and hope for a brighter tomorrow."

"True beauty is not just a matter of opinion, but rather a state of being and knowing who you are. External beauty is only temporary; it is beauty from within that lasts a lifetime."

"Although truth may not always come in pretty, nicely wrapped packages; it is still our responsibility to deliver it."

"A one-way ticket to heaven through Jesus Christ: GUARANTEED; walking in the authority of the Word: GOD'S WILL; living out the blessing through obedience, truth, and wisdom: PRICELESS!"

"The first and most important step to receiving healing is learning how to identify the wound. Once identified it often must be uncovered to allow the healing process to take place."

"Everyone experiences face similar tests, trials, and temptations; the only difference in outcome is how we choose to respond—either in fear or faith."

"Success is often wrapped in a package marked failure. Many of the most successful people in life failed miserably before achieving greatest. Refuse to let one failure stop forward progress in attaining your goals and don't give up, instead just try again."

"The tests of life often come unannounced and when we least expect them; it is our job to prepare because it is our preparation that determines if we pass or fail. We must study to show ourselves approved."

"Although life offers and is filled with so many choices, eternity on the other hand only presents us with two: Heaven or Hell. It is up to us to choose."

"Instead of enlarging the facts of a particular problem, we must learn how to enlarge our God and then adjust our lenses to get a better view; God is really bigger than we allow Him to be."

"Setbacks are often staging grounds for steps upward into what God has already prepared for us in advance. Failure in one area may just be the catapult needed to propel us to the next level."

"True wisdom goes far beyond head knowledge, mere facts, or random statistics. Wisdom involves being able to correctly apply what we have learned to everyday life."

"Although God can do, create, and make anything; He will never make you someone else. Find identity in the unique YOU and be content with who YOU are—there can only be one YOU."

"God does not open doors that were never intended for us to enter. Every closed door should be an indication that the blessing is designed to come through an alternate way. Be patient and allow Him to open the right door."

"We can never make any lasting progress as long as we continue to drag the negative effects of the past behind us. We must learn how to release it and let it go."

"Seeds of discouragement and bitterness cannot take root in a heart filled with gratefulness and gratitude. Learn to praise and give thanks in the midst of adversity, and then watch things begin to turn around for good."

"Too much focus on the external may be an indicator that one has not reconciled within themselves who they are on the internal. Until we are confident with who we are on the inside, we will continue to place more focus and unnecessary attention on things outside that do not really last."

Holidays

JAN 1 - NEW YEAR'S DAY

JAN 17 - MARTIN LUTHER KING DAY

FEB 14 - VALENTINE'S DAY

APR 22 - GOOD FRIDAY

APR 24 – RESURRECTION DAY (EASTER)

MAY 8 - MOTHER'S DAY

MAY 30 - MEMORIAL DAY

JUN 19 - FATHER'S DAY

JUL 4 - INDEPENDENCE DAY

SEP 5 - LABOR DAY

SEP 11 - PATRIOT'S DAY

OCT 31 – HARVEST

NOV 11 - VETERAN'S DAY

NOV 24 - THANKSGIVING DAY

DEC 24 - CHRISTMAS EVE

DEC 25 - CHRISTMAS DAY

DEC 31 - NEW YEAR'S EVE

Bible Translations

AMP – Amplified Bible

CEV – Contemporary English Version

GWT - GOD'S Word Translation

KJV – King James Version

LB – Living Bible

MSG – The Message

NCV – New Century Version

NKJV – New King James Version

NLT – New Living Translation

CPSIA information can be obtained
at www.ICGtesting.com
Printed in the USA
LVOW03s0324230717

542196LV00001B/4/P